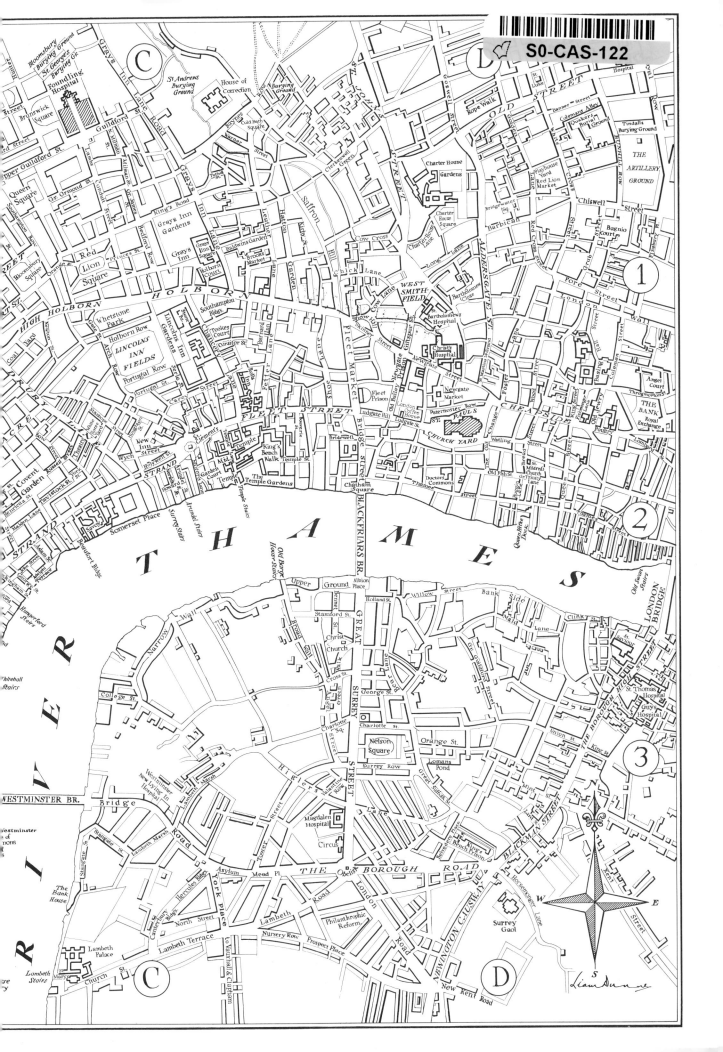

WILLIAM SHELLEY

An oil portrait by Amelia Curran of the Shelleys' son, 1819

Shelley and his Circle

being an edition of the manuscripts of

PERCY BYSSHE SHELLEY

MARY WOLLSTONECRAFT SHELLEY

CLAIRE CLAIRMONT

LORD BYRON

WILLIAM GODWIN

MARY WOLLSTONECRAFT

LEIGH HUNT

JOHN KEATS

THOMAS LOVE PEACOCK

THOMAS JEFFERSON HOGG

EDWARD JOHN TRELAWNY

EDWARD E. WILLIAMS

AND OTHERS

between 1773 and 1822

in

The Carl H. Pforzheimer Library

COORDINATING EDITOR · VOLUMES V–VI

DOUCET DEVIN FISCHER

CONTRIBUTING EDITORS · VOLUMES V–VI

Manuscripts of Lord Byron

DAVID V. ERDMAN

E. J. Trelawny (Life and Works) and Trelawny and Augusta White

R. GLYNN GRYLLS

The T. J. Hogg-T. L. Peacock Correspondence and Peacock in Leadenhall Street

SYLVA NORMAN

The Journal of Claire Clairmont, 1818

MARION KINGSTON STOCKING

THE CARL H. PFORZHEIMER LIBRARY

Shelley and his Circle
1773–1822

EDITED BY

DONALD H. REIMAN

VOLUME VI

HARVARD UNIVERSITY PRESS

Cambridge, Massachusetts

1973

Copyright © 1973 by
The Carl and Lily Pforzheimer Foundation, Inc.
New York, N.Y.

This is the sixth volume of a complete edition of the manuscripts
in the Shelley and his Circle Collection (1773–1822) of The
Carl H. Pforzheimer Library, New York, N.Y.

DESIGNED BY BRUCE ROGERS

Supplemental typography and binding design by Burton L. Stratton
Composed under the supervision of James Cosgrove in Monotype Caslon
Maps drawn by Liam Dunne

Printed photolithographically, text and endpaper maps by Halliday Litho-
graph Corporation, West Hanover, Massachusetts, illustrations by Meriden
Gravure Company, Meriden, Connecticut. Typesetting, reproduction proof-
ing, text negatives by the Plimpton Press, Norwood, Massachusetts. Binding
by Robert Burlen & Son, Inc., Hingham, Massachusetts

Library of Congress Catalog Card Number 60–5393
SBN–674–80612–3
PRINTED IN THE UNITED STATES OF AMERICA

To the memory of

CARL H. PFORZHEIMER

January 29, 1879

April 4, 1957

Contents

VOLUME VI

List of Manuscripts and Essays   ix

List of Illustrations and Maps   xiv

MANUSCRIPTS AND ESSAYS, 1818–1819   517

APPENDIX: BYRON MANUSCRIPTS, 1807–1815   1111

Works of Reference, Abridged Title List   1141

Index of Names   1153

List of Manuscripts and Essays

VOLUME VI

1818

SC 467	J. A. Hessey to John Taylor (*ALs*), March 17	517
SC 468	T. L. Peacock to T. J. Hogg (*ALs*), March 20	518
SC 469	P. B. and M. W. Shelley to Leigh and Marianne Hunt (*2 ALs*), March 22	523
SC 470	John Taylor to Leigh Hunt (*AL, draft*), March 23	530
SC 471	William Godwin to ?Amelia Curran (*ALs*), March 27	539
SC 472	P. B. Shelley to Lord Byron (*ALs*), April 13	542
SC 473	T. L. Peacock to T. J. Hogg (*ALs*), ?April 15–27	548
SC 474	Leigh Hunt to M. W. and P. B. Shelley (*AL*), April 21–24	553
SC 475	P. B. Shelley to Lord Byron (*ALs*), April 22	563
SC 476	J. F. Newton to T. J. Hogg (*ALs*), April 25	569
SC 477	P. B. Shelley to Lord Byron (*ALs*), April 28	574
SC 478	E. J. Trelawny to Augusta White (*ALs*), April 29	580
SC 479	P. B. Shelley to T. J. Hogg (*ALs*), April 30	582
SC 480	Edward DuBois to T. L. Peacock (*ALs*), May 15	592
SC 481	Edward DuBois to T. L. Peacock (*ALs*), May 26	593
SC 482	M. W. Shelley to Maria Gisborne (*ALs*), June 5	597
SC 483	Leigh Hunt to T. J. Hogg (*ALs*), June 7, 14, or 28	600
SC 484	T. L. Peacock to T. J. Hogg (*ALs*), June 12	601
SC 485	T. L. Peacock to Charles Ollier (*ALs*), June 29	603
SC 486	Leigh and Marianne Hunt to P. B. and M. W. Shelley (*2 ALs*), *ca.* July 14–August 4	605
SC 487	P. B. Shelley, Annotations in a Copy of *Herodotus* (*Hol. Notes*), ?July 16–August 2	618
SC 488	P. B. Shelley, "On Love" (*Ms., transcript*), July 20–25	633
SC 489	Lord Chancellor's Orders (*Document, transcript*), July 25	647
SC 490	P. B. Shelley to Brooks, Son & Dixon (*ALs*), July 31	653

List of Manuscripts and Essays

SC 491	P. B. Shelley to T. L. Peacock (*ALs*), August 16	656
SC 492	P. B. Shelley to Charles Ollier (*ALs*), August 16	664
SC 492A	P. B. Shelley to Brooks, Son & Dixon (*Autograph Check*), August 16	668
SC 493	E. J. Trelawny to Augusta White (*ALs*), August 18–20	669
SC 494	P. B. Shelley to M. W. Shelley (*L, copy*), August 23–24	672
SC 495	William Godwin to James Broughton (*ALs*), September 1	681
SC 496	T. L. Peacock to T. J. Hogg (*ALs*), September 7	684
SC 497	P. B. Shelley to Lord Byron (*ALs*), September 13	689
SC 498	P. B. Shelley to Claire Clairmont (*ALs*), September 25	692
SC 499	Thomas Hume to Brooks, Son & Dixon (*Autograph Check*), October 12	695
SC 500	Leigh Hunt to T. J. Hogg (*ALs*), October 13	696
SC 501	William Godwin to David Booth (*ALs*), October 14	703
SC 502	P. B. Shelley to Lord Byron (*ALs*), October 17	706

PEACOCK IN LEADENHALL STREET 709

SC 503	T. L. Peacock, Ryotwar & Zemindarry Settlements (*Hol. Ms.*), November 2	724
SC 504	Leigh Hunt to P. B. and M. W. Shelley (*ALs*), November 12	739
SC 505	William Godwin to Joseph V. Bevan (*ALs*), November 13	745
SC 506	Lord Byron, Codicil to Will (*Document signed*), November 17	747
SC 507	Edward DuBois to T. L. Peacock (*ALs*), November 18	754
SC 508	Lady Byron to Reverend Richard Wallis (*ALs*), November 27	757
SC 509	T. L. Peacock to T. J. Hogg (*ALs*), December 15	761
SC 510	P. B. Shelley to T. J. Hogg (*ALs*), December 21	763

1819

SC 511	William Godwin to John Payne Collier (*ALs*), February 6	769
SC 512	?R. W. Hayward to William Godwin, Legal Opinion (*Document unsigned*), ca. February 17	772
SC 513	William Godwin to Constable & Co. (*Copy of AL*), February 18	773

List of Manuscripts and Essays

sc 514   William Godwin to Archibald Constable (*Copy of AL*),
February 18   774

sc 515   P. B. Shelley to Charles Ollier (*ALs*), February 27   781

sc 516   P. B. Shelley, Translation of Plato's *Republic* (*Hol. Ms.,
fragment*), March 1819–March 1821   784

sc 517   Leigh Hunt to M. W. Shelley (*ALs*), March 9   790

sc 518   John Keats, "Isabella; or, The Pot of Basil" (*Hol. Ms.,
fragment*), April   798

sc 519   P. B. Shelley to Brooks, Son & Dixon (*ALs*), April 4   800

sc 520   T. J. Hogg to T. L. Peacock (*ALs*), April 29   801

sc 521   Leigh Hunt to J. H. Reynolds (*ALs*), April 30   805

sc 522   William Godwin to Archibald Constable (*AL, draft*), May 5   809

sc 523   William Godwin to Archibald Constable (*L, draft*), May 5–6   810

sc 524   Lord Byron to Teresa Guiccioli (*ALs*), May 15   811

sc 525   Edward Ellerker Williams, Private Journal (*Hol. Ms.*),
May 28–June 2   816

sc 526   William Godwin to John Taylor (*AN*), June 10   833

sc 527   William Godwin to John Taylor (*ALs*), June 14   833

sc 528   Leigh Hunt to T. J. Hogg (*ALs*), June 30   836

sc 529   Leigh Hunt to P. B. Shelley (*ALs*), July [8]   839

sc 530   Leigh Hunt to M. W. Shelley (*ALs*), July [25–27]   845

sc 531   P. B. Shelley to Leigh Hunt (*AL*), August 15   850

sc 532   P. B. Shelley, Dedication of *The Cenci* to Leigh Hunt
(*Hol. Ms.*), August [16–19]   865

sc 533   P. B. Shelley to Charles Ollier (*ALs*), August [17–19]   874

sc 534   Leigh Hunt to P. B. and M. W. Shelley (*ALs*), August [23]   879

sc 535   Leigh Hunt to P. B. and M. W. Shelley (*ALs*), September 6   886

sc 536   P. B. Shelley, *The Mask of Anarchy*, Stanza (*Hol. Ms., draft*),
September 6–23   892

sc 537   P. B. Shelley to T. L. Peacock (*ALs*), September 9   895

sc 538   William Godwin to ?John Richardson (*ALs*), September 11   902

sc 539   Leigh Hunt to M. W. Shelley (*ALs*), September 12   904

List of Manuscripts and Essays

sc 540   Leigh Hunt to P. B. and M. W. Shelley (*ALs*), September 20   910

sc 541   T. J. Hogg to T. L. Peacock (*ALs, draft*), September 26   916

sc 542   T. L. Peacock to T. J. Hogg (*ALs*), October 2   922

sc 543   P. B. Shelley to Charles Ollier (*ALs*), October 15   926

sc 544   Leigh Hunt to T. J. Hogg (*ALs*), October 26   935

sc 545   P. B. Shelley to Brooks, Son & Dixon (*ALs*), October 30   937

SHELLEY'S TREATISE ON POLITICAL ECONOMY   945

sc 546   P. B. Shelley, *A Philosophical View of Reform*
         (*Hol. Ms.*), November −?1820   961

sc 547   P. B. Shelley, Note on *Ode to the West Wind* (*Hol. Ms.*),
         ?November–December   1066

sc 548   P. B. Shelley, *Prometheus Unbound*, II.iii.82–89 (*Hol. Ms.,
         fragment*), ?November–December   1069

sc 549   P. B. Shelley, *Prometheus Unbound*, IV.319–322, 376–377,
         397–399 (*Hol. Ms., fragment*), ?November–December   1071

sc 550   Leigh Hunt, *Angling* (*Hol. Ms.*), November 15 or 16   1075

sc 551   P. B. Shelley to Leigh Hunt (*ALs*), November [16]   1080

sc 552   Leigh Hunt to P. B. Shelley (*ALs*), December 2   1088

sc 553   P. B. Shelley to Maria and John Gisborne (*ALs*), December 14   1094

sc 554   P. B. Shelley to Charles Ollier (*ALs*), December 23   1096

sc 555   P. B. Shelley to Leigh Hunt (*ALs*), December 23   1106

APPENDIX: BYRON MANUSCRIPTS, 1807–1815   1111

sc 556   Lord Byron, "To E. N. Long" (*Ms., signed*), April 19, 1807   1113

sc 557   Lord Byron to John "Gentleman" Jackson (*ALs*),
         March 27, 1808   1118

sc 558   Lord Byron to John Hanson (*ALs*), June 21, 1809   1122

sc 559   Lord Byron to Doctor [   ] (*ALs*), June 20, 1810   1123

sc 560   Lord Byron, "On Parting" (*Hol. Ms.*), ?March 1811   1124

sc 561   Lord Byron to Louis Fauvel (*Ms., signed*), March 10, 1811   1126

sc 562   Lord Byron to Francis Hodgson (*ALs*), November 4, 1811   1128

List of Manuscripts and Essays

sc 563 Lord Byron to Samuel Rogers (*ALs*), March 27, 1813   1130

sc 564 Lord Byron to John Murray (*ALs*), June 19, 1813   1131

sc 565 Lord Byron, *The Bride of Abydos* (*Hol. Emendation*),
        December 2, 1813   1132

sc 566 Lord Byron to John H. Merivale (*AL*), January 1814   1134

sc 567 Lord Byron to Thomas Claughton (*ALs*), September 4, 1814   1136

sc 568 Lord Byron to ?[Matthew G.] Lewis (*ALs*),
        ?Spring–Summer 1815   1139

List of Illustrations and Maps

VOLUME VI

New Plan of the Cities of London and Westminster   *endpapers*

William Shelley, portrait by Amelia Curran   *frontispiece*

Map of the Shelleys' Wanderings in Italy during the Years 1818–1819   544

Leigh Hunt to P. B. and M. W. Shelley, April 21–24, 1818, address leaf
     with notations by P. B. Shelley   559

Page from Leigh and Marianne Hunt to P. B. and M. W. Shelley,
     ca. July 14–August 4, 1818   607

Map of Venice, Ferrara, Ravenna, and Environs   677

William Godwin to James Broughton, September 1, 1818   683

T. L. Peacock, pages from "Ryotwar and Zemindarry Settlements,"
     November 2, 1818   725

Watermarks and seals   752

Lord Byron to Teresa Guiccioli, May 15, 1819   813

Pages from Edward Williams' Journal, May 28–June 2, 1819   819

Map of the Scene of Shelley's Last Years   855

Two of Shelley's houses: Villa Valsovano outside Leghorn
     and Albion House in Marlow   856

P. B. Shelley, manuscript containing fragment from *Prometheus Unbound*,
     ?November–December 1819, his "Dedication" to *The Cenci*, August
     [16–19], 1819, and a draft stanza from *The Mask of Anarchy*, September
     6–23, 1819   867

P. B. Shelley to Charles Ollier, August [17–19], 1819   875

P. B. Shelley, silhouette portrait and lock of his hair   889

P. B. Shelley, *A Philosophical View of Reform*, November 1819–?1820,
     pages from notebook   1005

P. B. Shelley, fragments from *Prometheus Unbound*,
     ?November–December 1819, from notebook   1073

P. B. Shelley to Charles Ollier, December 23, 1819   1097

Shelley and his Circle

Manuscripts and Essays

1818–1819

Hessey to Taylor   *March 17, 1818*

SC 467   J. A. HESSEY TO JOHN TAYLOR, MARCH 17, 1818

AL signed *J A H*, with excerpt of letter from P. B. Shelley to Leigh Hunt, 1½
pages. Double sheet, 4ᵗᵒ (9 x 7.3 inches).
Wove paper. Watermark: GATER| 1815|.
Seal (trace): wafer, red.
Addition: paper badly stained.

PROVENANCE: Taylor and Hessey; Walter T. Spencer, 1922.

My dear John
    *Mr Hunt has sent the Twenty Guineas & Interest thereupon for which
I have given a Receipt — Miss Kent came with it, and she says Mr Shelley
never told Hunt that the Money was to be paid for immediately, but that*
5 *we were to hold the Rimini & their produce as a sort of Security —   I
will tell you more about it when I see you*

                                    Yrs very truly   J A H

    Mar. 17. 1818

    Annexed is a Copy of part of Mr Shelley's
10   *Letter to Hunt just recᵈ —*

        *"With respect to Tailor & Hessey I am ready to certify if nec-
essary in a Court of Justice that ~~they~~ one of them said he would give up
his copyright for the 20£ and that in lieu of that he would accept the
Profits of Rimini until it was paid"*

15   *Yrs very Affectionately
                                     signed   P B Shelley"*

                    copy   J A H

[Address, page 4]
Mr Taylor

line 3. *says: s* written through indecipherable   line 11. *Tailor* (sic).
letter.

THE PARAGRAPH transcribed by James Augustus Hessey in this letter
to his partner was the second and last in Shelley's letter dated
Calais, March 13, 1818.[1] Shelley and Hunt had probably discussed the

1. Shelley, *Letters*, II, 1.

SC 467 dispute with Taylor and Hessey (see sc 402) during their last days together in England, and Shelley, besides probably furnishing the twenty
guineas and interest to pay Hunt's debt, must have agreed to write a
statement in support of Hunt's position so that the publishers would not
dare pursue the matter in the courts. That Elizabeth Kent immediately
showed the letter to Hessey argues that there was some agreement between Hunt and Shelley to this effect; Shelley did not customarily defend his testimony by promising "to certify if necessary in a Court of
Justice."

    Shelley's statement may have saved Hunt from a legal action, though
from our perspective it is hard to imagine Taylor and Hessey resorting
to the courts once Hunt had paid his debt with interest. But the incident
certainly caused Taylor and Hessey to have ill feelings toward both
Hunt and Shelley (see sc 470), and their judgment was probably transmitted to members of their circle, including Keats. It is significant that
Charles Brown, in later years Hunt's best friend among the Keats circle,
was also Taylor's enemy.[2]

2. Brown, *Letters*, pp. 85–86, 106–107.

SC 468 T. L. PEACOCK TO T. J. HOGG, MARCH 20, 1818

AL signed *T. L. Peacock.*, 2¾ pages. Double sheet, 4to (9.5 x 7.4 inches).
Wove paper. Impressed stamp: [crown]| BATH|.
Seal: wax, red*:* [peacock]|.
Postal fees: 1. 7; 2. 1/1.
Postmarks: 1. (mileage stamp)*:* MARLOW| 33|; 2. (morning duty stamp, Lon-
don)*:* c| 23 [MR] 23| 1818|.

PROVENANCE: Thomas Jefferson Hogg; Prudentia Hogg Lonsdale; John Ewer
Jefferson Hogg; Major R. J. Jefferson Hogg (Sotheby, June 30, 1948, lot 99).

Marlow, March 20, 1818.

My dear Hogg,

    *I have been here since Monday, as lonely as a cloud, and as melancholy
as a gib cat. Your letter was most welcome to my eremitical perceptions.*
5 *Shelley left town on Wednesday, the 11th, at 5 in the morning. We had a*

SC 468 *farewell supper in Russell Street, with M^r & Mrs Hunt, on Tuesday night*
after the opera. I stayed three or four days in pure dread of facing the
associations of this scenery, and did not venture abroad for two or three
days more after my return. However I have been forth into the woods and
10   *broken the spell in some measure, and now think of passing the summer*
where I am. But of this I am still deliberating and shall be able to speak
with more certainty when I next write to you. Your septuagint is very orthodox
with its four pip< > of port Vinum Opimianum Octo. *I am sorr<   >*
have so heretical a taste on this subject, and see through a glass darkly. –
15   *This is a divine day: a western wind and a cloudless sky. Sunshine and*
flowers are something still. I have been gathering primroses under the fisher-
man's cliff. My geraniums and auriculas are putting forth their flower-buds
and some of the buds of the Camellia have stood the winter and are on the
point of opening. I have filled my shelves with a portion of Shelley's books. I
20   *intend to pass the interval between Easter & Christmas   – longum inter-*
vallum – in writing a novel of which the scene will be in London. If you
pick up a quiz in your travels, pray sketch off his outline, and send it to
me to fill up. When I have finished the novel I shall write another Pagan
poem. If I remain here all the summer I shall be very social with the Greek
25   *poets & shall pass a day occasionally with Plato and Plutarch. You have*
promised me a week in June,<   > I hope you will have your hands in
good order <   > the towing line, your feet for Virginia & Pangbourn, &
your ears for that conceited clerke Homere. The piano is in the parlour, a
melancholy object in its soundlessness though you will not join with me in
30   *saying: "Here's the harp she used to touch – Oh! how that touch enchanted!"*
But Mon dieu! as Voltaire said of D'Alembert les hommes sont bien fous à
commencer par les sages. I do not pretend to be σοφος *but only* φιλο σοφος
and Διονυσος *and* Αφροδιτη *run away with too large a portion of the* φιλια
which Σοφια *claims more exclusively in some better ordered intellects   I*
35   *see I am becoming very absurd and rhapsodical and shall therefore hasten*
to conclude, with wishing you well through your share of the briefs and the
port wine, and with an earnest wish to hear from you again very soon.

Most sincerely yours,

T. L. Peacock.

Peacock to Hogg   *March 20, 1818*

SC 468   [Address, page 4]
         T. J. Hogg Esqre
                  Norton, near
                       Stockton-upon-Tees.

line 5. *11th,*: written in large block characters through smudged-out *?12.*

line 13. *pip<es>*: corner of page torn away.

   sorr<y ?to>: corner of page missing; the tail of the *y* is visible curving back under the two *r*'s of *sorry*.

line 26. *<?when>*: corner of page torn away; possible reading.

line 27. *<?for>*: corner of page torn away; possible reading.

   Pangbourn (sic): for *Pangbourne*.

line 31. *Mon*: *M* written through *m*.

line 33. *away*: written through *?onl*.

line 34. *intellects*: final five letters written on fragment of paper adhering to seal.

line 35. *rhapsodical*: final six letters written on fragment of paper adhering to seal.

line 36. *your*: *y* written through *?t*.

THOSE WHO persistently misread Peacock as a cold, unfeeling scholar can be given no better refutation of their views than this sad, nostalgic letter. Peacock had parted from Shelley ten days previously; perhaps he had some shadowy apprehension that the parting was indeed conclusive and that, although a spate of fine descriptive letters would pour from the exile over the next four years, he would never see his friend again in the flesh. It is true that T.L.P. was undemonstrative, that he would not have considered writing such a eulogy as that of the newly enlightened William Thomas Baxter; but neither would he have shifted in two months from enthusiasm to disillusionment. He was to mock at Shelley-Scythrop in a lighthearted satire that the poet relished, for their senses of humor mingled in responsive chimes. Peacock loved his Marlow meadows without kissing the soil of them; so too he loved Shelley, deeply and silently. For the past year the beauty of Shelley and the beauty of his river-home had been as one to him, and now he could hardly bear to return to the landscape that cried out, in its loneliness — *his* loneliness — for Shelley's presence. No Wordsworthian daffodils, though indeed they "take the winds of March with beauty,"[1] could enrapture his cloudlike wanderings. To curb his sentiment he would be melancholy only as a

1. Shakespeare, *The Winter's Tale*, IV.iv. Wordsworth's "I Wandered Lonely as a Cloud" had been published eleven years earlier in *Poems in Two Volumes*, 1807.

Peacock to Hogg   *March 20, 1818*

SC 468   gib cat[2] — or at least when writing to the more jocular Hogg, whose letter had made a salutary break in his meditations.

Simply and quietly Peacock gives Hogg the cause of it all: Shelley had left town on the eleventh. Not only town but England. The farewell party on the tenth proved unforgettable. More than forty years later, writing his Memoirs of Shelley for *Fraser's Magazine*, he recalled it with exactitude:

> I saw him for the last time on Tuesday the 10th of March. The evening was a remarkable one, as being that of the first performance of an opera of Rossini in England, and of the first appearance here of Malibran's father, Garcia. He performed Count Almaviva in the *Barbiere di Siviglia*.[3] Fodor was Rosina; Naldi, Figaro; Ambrogetti, Bartolo; and Angrisani, Basilio. I supped with Shelley and his travelling companions after the opera. They departed early the next morning.

Having to some degree "broken the spell" that prevented his enjoying sunshine and flowers divorced from Shelley, Peacock scrapes up a few classical jokes suitable for Hogg. His *Vinum Opimianum Octo* has its origin in Opimian, a celebrated Roman wine[4] that Peacock was to bear in mind as late as 1860 when in *Gryll Grange* he named one of the characters (whose cellar was kept stocked with "the best vintages") the Reverend Doctor Opimian. But Shelley still dominates in absence; on leaving Albion House he had turned over some of his possessions to Peacock's care. The books could be shelved — and read too, when it pleased him; but the piano had become a silent mockery, since neither Peacock nor his mother could play on it. Quoting one of Tom Moore's ballads, Peacock again whimsically expressed his desolation.[5]

2. Peacock had previously characterized Mr. Hippy in *Melincourt* (1817) as occasionally being "as melancholy as a gib cat," and David Garnett (Peacock, *Complete Novels*, I, 115) identifies the source of the remark as Shakespeare's *I Henry IV*, I.ii, in which Falstaff tells Hal, "I am as Melancholly as a Gyb-Cat, or a lugg'd Beare." The expression also figures in Lamb's essay "The South-Sea House" (1820), in which the cashier appears "as melancholy as a gib-cat over his counter all the forenoon."

3. The opera was first produced in Rome at the Teatro Argentina in 1816 and, contrary to expectation, proved an immediate success.

4. "Of the vintage of the year A. U. C. 633 (c. 121 B.C.) when Opimius was Consul." (Peacock, *Complete Novels*, II, 775.)

5. The quotation is from "Here's the Bower" (*The Poetical Works of Thomas Moore*, ed. A. D. Godley, Oxford University Press, 1910, p. 312):

> Here's the bower she loved so much,
> And the tree she planted:
> Here's the harp she used to touch —
> Oh how that touch enchanted.

SC 468   Through the help of Hunt and Vincent Novello, Shelley had acquired the piano in April 1817 from Joseph Kirkman, undertaking to pay seventy-five guineas for it within three years; it had been used largely by Claire Clairmont and his musically trained visitors. The question of payment was to worry Shelley long after the three years were up: on April 5, 1820, when the bill was due, he asked Hunt to solicit a renewal as he had not the money to pay at once. To Peacock, on November 8, 1820, he wrote, "A person will call on you with an order from me to deliver him the piano. — If it is at Marlow you can put him in the requisite train for getting it." This would seem to imply that the piano was being returned. Peacock, who had by that time been in London for two years, answered on December 4 from the India House, "I have had the piano with me in London from the first, and have kept it regularly tuned. I will deliver it as you desire. The person has not yet called."[6] Evidently the person either did not call or went away without the piano, for on January 20, 1821, Shelley asked Vincent Novello to thank Mr. Kirkman for his forbearance which had been procured on Novello's "interference." That is to say, Novello had paid a proportion of the debt, and Shelley next asked that Kirkman allow him "a year from this date for the payment of the remainder."[7] The piano later appears in Hunt's possession, for Peacock wrote to Shelley on June 3, 1821, that "Hunt has your piano . . . according to your desire."[8]

Peacock ends his letter with another attempt at irrelevant gaiety. "Men are pretty mad, beginning with the wiseacres" (lines 31–32) — as Voltaire said of d'Alembert. It would appear to be something of a leg-pull.[9] For himself, whether mad or sane, "I do not pretend to be *wise* (lines 32–34) but only *a lover of wisdom* [or a *philosopher*] and *Dionysius* and *Aphrodite* run away with too large a portion of the *love* which *wisdom* claims . . . in some better ordered intellects." So ends this bravely sad epistolary effort, with a confession that he has sunk to the absurd. It throws a pleasing half-light on the reticent Peacock.

6. Peacock, *Works*, VIII, 218.

7. Manuscript in The Carl H. Pforzheimer Library.

8. Peacock, *Works*, VIII, 222.

9. Voltaire's editor Theodore Bestermann comments, "the quotation is so general as to be unidentifiable." He doubts that Voltaire really wrote this.

SC 469 P. B. AND M. W. SHELLEY TO LEIGH AND MARIANNE HUNT,
MARCH 22, 1818

> AL signed *PBS*. and *MWS*, 6¼ pages, crosswritten on pages 1–3. Double sheet,
> 4ᵗᵒ (9.2 x 7.2 inches).
> Laid paper. Watermark: [circle, with design obscured by mending tape]|.
> Seal (trace): wax, red.
> Postal fee: 1/2.
> Postmarks: 1. P[   ]| LYON|; 2. (trace); 3. (Foreign Post Office stamp, Lon-
> don): FPO| MR 30| 1818|; 4. (Penny Post delivery stamp, London): 12 o'Clock|
> MR 30| 1818 Nⁿ|; 5. (Penny Post delivery stamp, London): 4 o'Clock| 30 MR|
> 1818 EV.|.
> Notation, page 4, in blue ink: *Frederick Locker*|.
> Additions, page 4: 1. seal tear mended with tape; 2. left and right edges rein-
> forced with tape—perhaps letter was once mounted in an album.

> PROVENANCE: Frederick Locker-Lampson (*The Rowfant Library: A Catalogue of
> the Printed Books, Manuscripts, Autograph Letters, Drawings and Pictures, Col-
> lected by Frederick Locker-Lampson*, London, 1886, p. 214); Harry B[ache] Smith
> (American Art Association, April 9, 1936, lot 740). *De Ricci 372* (p. 149).

Lyons, March 22   1818.———

My dear friend

> *Why did you not wake me the night before we left England,
> you & Marianne   I take this as rather an unkind piece of kindness in*
5   *you, but which in consideration of the 600 miles between us I forgive. —*

> *We have journeyed towards the spring that has been hastening to meet
> us from the South— & though our weather was at first abominable, we have
> wa now warm sunny days & soft winds & a sky of deep azure, the most
> serene I ever saw.   The heat in this city to day is like that of London in*
10   *th middle of summer—   My spirits & health sympathise in the change.
> Indeed before I left London my spirits were as feeble as my health – and
> I had demands upon them which I found difficult to supply.*

> *I have read Foliage—— With most of the poems I was already familiar.
> What a delightful poem the Nymphs is, & especially the second part. It*
15   *is truly poetical in the intense & emphatic sense of the word. If 600 miles
> were not between us I should say what pity that glib is not omitted & that
> the poem is not as faultless as it is beautiful! But for fear I should spoil*

[523]

SC 469　*your next poem I will not let slip a word on the subject———— I Give my love*
to Marianne & her sister & tell Marianne that she defrauded me of a kiss
20　*by not waking me when she went away, & that as I have no better mode of*
conveying it I must take the best, & ask you to pay the debt.　When shall
I see you all again ?　O that it might b< > in Italy.　I confess that the
thought of how long we may be divided make< > me very melancholy:–
Adieu –my d<　> friends——　write soon– ever most affectionately Yours

PBS.

25

　　Now, my dear Hunt & my dear Marianne, we see Jura & Mont Blanc
again from the windows of our hotel and the Rhone rushes by our window– we
are The sun shines bright and it is a kind of Paradise which we have arrived
at through the valley of the shadow of death– for certainly the greater part of
30　*our journey here was not the most pleasant thing in the world– I think if*
Peacock had been with us he he would hav have taken fright and returned.
The first night after quitting Calais we slept at St. Omers–we arrived after
the shutting the gates– The postillions craked their whips to give signs of
our approach and a female voice was heard from the battlements　demanding
35　*the name and number of the invaders　　she was told that it was some English*
ladies with their children and she departed to carry the intelligence to the
Governor who lived half a mile off—　In about half an hour she retu the
gates were thrown open and about a dozen soldiers came out headed by this
female who demanded our passport—　she received it and began to read it
40　*when recollecting herself she said—Mais Medames you will remember the*
guard. We told her that we certainly would　　Ah then– said she– you may
enter directly—So we passed through the various windings of the fortifica-
tions and through three immense gates with which were successively closed
after us with a clanking sound. But these are the frontier towns and when
45　*we came to the middle of France we found nothing of this. The largest towns*
here are not fortified—— but these kind of things appear to spring up up
in the north of France– that is that part of it that borders Flanders　　like
mushrooms or toadstools great large round things with a ditch & wall round
them swarming with people—There is Douai—with I do not know how
50　*many thousand inhabitants– who ever heard of Douai? Why to be born in*
such a town is like living out of the circle of human things– an ambitious

Shelleys to Hunts   **March 22, 1818**

SC 469   *individual of Douai would almost like Erostratus wish to burn down a fine*
building or two to let his fellow men know that there was such a place in
the world. Now Lyons is a pleasant city and very republican—The people
55   *have suffered dreadfully— You know the horrors they went though in the*
revolution and about six months ago they were not much better off. If it
had not been for Napoleon said one man to us, my head would not have
been where it is   he brought peace to us— and I say nothing but there are
people who wish him back— When the Angouleme party had the lead dread-
60   *ful atrocities were committed here mais ce Monsieur q'on appelle Louis*
XVIII is a better man and restrained them.

This same man told us some horrible ~~st~~ *facts which* ~~n~~ *could never have*
been committed if there was liberty of the press and such things could have
been published. I do not relate them for you ~~are~~ *do not like to hear of in-*
65   *humanties*

Such is our little history at present— Is yours a pleasant one— You
have promised to write often— and I am sure that here your kindness would
stand instead of promise or any thing̶s else— it would bind you to us exiles
who love you very sincerely and wish to hear every good news concerning you.
70   *Shelley's health is infinitely improved and I hope the fine climate we now*
enjoy and are proceeding to will ~~t~~ *quite restore him— The children bear the*
journey exceedingly well and thus far we are fortunate and in good spirits.
La prima donna desires her love to you and Bessy

Adieu— We will write again soon and hope to find a letter waiting for
75   *us from you at Milan*

Most affectionately yours, my dear friends— <u>*MWS*</u>

[Address, page 4]
Mr *Leigh Hunt*
13 Lisson Grove North
Paddington
80   <u>*London*</u>
Angleterre

---

line 3. *the*: altered from *that*.   line 22. *b<e>*: letter obliterated by trace of
line 4. *kindness*: probable reading; word is   seal. Fragments of seal also affect *make<s>* and
blotted and cramped downward into the margin.   *d<ear>* (lines 23, 24).
line 10. *th* (sic): for *the*.

SC 469   line 26. Lines 26–81 (*Now . . . Angleterre*) cross-written in Mary Shelley's hand. See Bibliographical Description.

line 33. *craked* (sic).

line 35. *she*: first word of a new line. The edge of the manuscript thus provides a break, though punctuation is missing.

line 40. *Medames* (sic).

line 49. *swarming with*: *g with* disfigured by a large inkblot.

line 55. *though* (sic).

line 60. *q'on* (sic).

line 64. *inhumanties* (sic).

WRITING NOTES on Shelley's poems of 1820 for the collected edition of his *Poetical Works* (1839), Mary Shelley stated that, had not she and Shelley feared for the health of their last surviving child, "I believe we should have wandered over the world, both being passionately fond of travelling."[1] In this double letter one sees the beginnings of the stimulation that the Shelleys felt as they journeyed toward Italy. Shelley's spirits and health warm with the weather and Mary's revive as they enter the land of familiar sights — the Jura, Mont Blanc and the Rhone.

But although the Shelleys enjoyed the idea of travel and responded both to new scenes and to familiar scenes revisited, the physical act of traveling was often painful to Mary, who was strongly susceptible to motion-sickness. Years later, she recalled this journey: "I had been a bad traveller; and, even in a comfortable English travelling chariot, suffered great fatigue, and even illness."[2] The Shelleys' dissatisfaction with the first part of this journey can be attributed to Mary's characteristic illness and some other factors: the season, the weather, their route (which included some very bad roads), and the heavy responsibilities that fell upon Shelley in managing a party comprising, besides himself, four women and three children in two vehicles (Shelley's chariot and the calèche bought at Calais).[3]

Shelley, Mary, and Claire had traveled through France three times previously — on the elopement trip in July 1814, on their way to Geneva in May 1816, and on their return from Switzerland in August of that same year.[4] The beauty of the countryside during those summer journeys

1. Shelley, *Poetical Works* (1839), IV, 54. See also Mary Shelley's *Rambles in Germany and Italy in 1840, 1842 and 1843* (London, 1844), I, 160.

2. *Rambles in Germany and Italy*, I, 7.

3. See "Shelley's 'Chariot,'" *Shelley and his Circle*, III, 170-171.

4. For accounts of these trips, see *Mary Shelley's Journal*, pp. 4–10; Claire Clairmont, *Journals*, pp. 23–26; sc 264 and Commentary (III); "Shelley's Journeys," *Shelley and his Circle*, IV, 690-702.

SC 469 must have contrasted sharply with the scenes of this March, plagued by cold or "abominable" weather (line 7). Moreover, the Shelleys — perhaps desiring to see a different part of France — took a new route, to the north and east of Paris. On Friday, March 13, they left Calais and traveled to Saint Omer. The next day they continued "thro a dismal country"[5] (and the fortified towns of Aire and Bethune) to Douai. Mary's letter expresses her contempt for fortified cities, Douai in particular, and suggests her twenty-year-old, dissenter/skeptic-educated ignorance of the history of this city, a center of English Catholic learning from 1562 through 1793.[6]

Sunday, March 15, saw the Shelleys proceeding south to La Fère, a journey that took them through the cathedral city of Cambrai, which should have been meaningful to them because of Fénelon and Godwin's famous illustration of "justice" in *Political Justice* (1793).[7] On the sixteenth, they breakfasted in the fortified city of Laon (perhaps of interest to Shelley at this date on account of its name) and spent the night at Rheims. Claire's journal speaks of the inn and cathedral at Laon, but Mary records nothing of the journey for this day except that Shelley read Schlegel aloud[8] — perhaps to take her mind from her illness. Shelley continued to read aloud from Schlegel during the "hard days journey" of March 17: this carried them into the Marne Valley, through Châlons-

5. That the entries for Saturday and Sunday in Mary's Journal are in Shelley's hand may perhaps indicate that Mary was unwell.

6. Erostratus (or Herostratus or Eratostratus), to whom she alludes in line 52, was the Ephesian who burned down the famous temple of Artemis in that city — one of the Seven Wonders of the ancient world — to make his own name memorable. This supposedly happened on the night that Alexander the Great was born.

7. Godwin viewed as "just" a man's sacrifice of himself, friend, or relative for the life of one whose existence is more beneficial to mankind. He exemplifies this by insisting that it would be a "breach of justice" for a chambermaid to refuse to surrender her life for that of the Archbishop of Cambrai, François de Salignac de la Mothe-Fénelon (1651–1715), author of *Telemachus*. See *Political Justice*, Book II, chapter 2 (London, 1793; I, 82–83).

8. August Wilhelm von Schlegel's *Über dramatische Kunst und Litteratur* (1809–1811). Shelley must have been using John Black's translation, *Lectures on Dramatic [Art and] Literature* (1815). Neither Mary nor Claire knew German in 1818 (Claire only began to study the language in October 1820; see her *Journals*, p. 180), and Shelley would have found translation with the aid of a dictionary (which he would have required) awkward in a moving carriage. Claire's record of reading Schlegel in Rome in 1819 (*Journals*, pp. 101, 103–104) provides additional evidence, because she would probably have used the same two volumes Shelley brought with him.

SC 469   sur-Marne and Vitry-le-François to Saint Dizier, where they spent the night.

The entries in Mary's Journal beginning with that for March 18 have a more cheerful tone: "We arrive at more pleasant country — hills covered with vines while the road winds with the river Marne through the valley — we sleep at Langres. Shelley reads Schlegel aloud."[9] The road from Chaumont to Langres was one that the Shelleys had followed in July 1814 (see The Elopement Trip of Shelley and Mary, III, 359), and the following night they slept at Le Chapeau Rouge (Claire's Journal) in Dijon, through which they had passed in both May and August 1816 — then traveling on the east-west road rather than the north-south route. On the way from Langres to Dijon Mary records that they traveled "in a pleasant country among nice people," and, finally, in her entry for March 20 (omitted from printed versions of the Journal), Mary writes: "(A) pleasant days ride — S. reads Schlegel to us. We sleep at [?Thounu(s) or ?Thomirey]."[10]

On March 21, the Shelleys reached Lyon, though they were delayed three hours at Mâcon by a broken spring in the calèche. The Shelleys remained three days at Lyon, staying at "l'hôtel de l'Europe." On the first day (Easter Sunday, March 22) they reached an agreement with a *voiturier* to conduct them to Milan.[11] Throughout France they had followed the post roads, hiring horses and postilions at the regular prescribed intervals (between five and five-and-a-half English miles).[12] But to cross national boundaries — from France, through the Kingdom of Sardinia, into Austrian-occupied Lombardy — they preferred to be under

9. The separate Journal entries for March 16–21 were telescoped (and one omitted) in the version given in *Shelley and Mary* (and hence in Jones's edition).

10. The difficulty of deciphering this name may have led the editors of *Shelley and Mary* to omit this entry. Tournus, about halfway between Dijon and Lyon, would have been a logical stopping point; Mary may have simply misspelled it. Thorey and Thomirey, other possibilities, were small villages near Beaune. Occasionally the Shelleys spent the night in a small village if there was a suitable inn. Inasmuch as Thorey and Thomirey are not on most contemporary maps (though they appear in contemporary gazetteers), Mary had a good excuse for misspelling the name, if she attempted to write one of these.

11. Claire records that they hired two *voituriers*, but one could have arranged for a second driver (*Journals*, p. 87).

12. The various methods of travel are described in detail in *Galignani's Traveller's Guide through France* (2nd edition, Paris, 1819), and, again, in William Brockedon's *Road-Book from London to Naples* (London: John Murray, 1835).

Shelley and his Circle : Manuscripts

SC 469   the direction of a single guide and business manager who furnished horses
and arranged for food and lodgings for a sum agreed to in advance.
Customarily the *voiturier* also provided a carriage, and it is possible —
even likely — that the Shelleys disposed of the calèche at Lyon, proceeding to Milan with their chariot and a second carriage belonging to
the *voiturier* (who would, of course, wish to engage other travelers for
the return trip from Milan to France).

On their second day in Lyon, the Shelleys went to the Isle de Barbe
where they witnessed a festival,[13] and in the evening they attended a
"very amusing" comedy (which, Claire writes, was entitled "L'homme
Gris et le Physiognomiste").

It is noteworthy, in view of the widespread conception that Mary
always loved society and Shelley preferred solitude, that in this letter
Shelley looks back to the pleasures of the Hunts' society in England (and
hopes for a reunion in Italy), while Mary describes more objectively the
vicissitudes and pleasures of their journey and the political situation in
Lyon.[14] In closing, she mentions the good health and spirits of Shelley
and the children and sends them the greetings of Claire, the "prima
donna."

Shelley's praise of Hunt's "The Nymphs" is measured and contains
some cautionary hints against introducing low diction into an idealized
poem.[15] "The Nymphs," however unappealing it may seem to modern

13. "The traveller must not quit this town without visiting the Isle Barbe, where all the inhabitants
go, at the feasts of Easter and Pentecost." (*Galignani's Traveller's Guide through France*, p. 141.)

14. The Angoulême party was the ultra-royalist émigré party lead by the Compte d'Artois (later
Charles X), his son the Duc d'Angoulême, and the Duchesse d'Angoulême. In 1816, Louis XVIII
had suppressed this unpopular group. The persecutions of "about six months ago" probably grew
out of the discovery in June 1817 of a seditious conspiracy centered in Lyon. (The *Examiner* had
reported on the trials of those implicated; see issues of June 29, 1817, #496; July 6, 1817, #497;
August 10, 1817, #502; September 21, 1817, #508.)

15. "The Nymphs" is the longest work in "Greenwoods, or Original Poems," the first part of
Foliage; or Poems Original and Translated (London: C. and J. Ollier, 1818). The Pforzheimer Library
presently has four copies of the first edition, three of which Hunt inscribed on their title pages:
(1) "To Francis Jeffrey Esqre with the Author's best compliments."; (2) "To T. L. Peacock, with
the author's regards. —"; (3) "To Horatio Smith with the Author's best regards." The Peacock
copy includes the following textual corrections in Hunt's hand: in "The Nymphs" (p. xxxii), line 9,
"freshness" is changed to "fierceness"; in "Fancy's Party" (p. xlii), line 1, "moon" is changed to
"morn." To the Smith copy Hunt added the following list of corrections:

> Page 2. (Preface) insert *as* after *ancient*.   xxxii. For *freshness* read *fierceness*.
>   cv. For *Procustes-* read *Procrustes*.   xlii. For *moon* read *morn*.

SC 469 tastes, probably taught Shelley something, for it is in the mythmaking mode that he was to use with great effect in such poems as *Prometheus Unbound* and "The Witch of Atlas." The tone and pace of some of Shelley's lyrics have, in fact, more in common with "The Nymphs" than with such earlier, more overtly philosophical poems as "Hymn to Intellectual Beauty" and "Mont Blanc." In Part I of "The Nymphs" Hunt imaginatively characterizes and describes the different varieties of nymphs — Dryads, Hamadryads, Napeads, Limniads, Oreads, Ephydriads, Naiads, and Nereids (nymphs of the forest, individual trees, [?] soil, lakes, mountains, fountains, streams, and seas respectively). Part II is devoted entirely to Nepheliads (cloud nymphs) and contains a song by these creatures (lines 135–204) that may be the most direct inspiration for Shelley's "The Cloud." Passages of Hunt's poem are "poetical" by almost any definition, but other lines are seriously marred by unfortunate diction. The poem, moreover, has no development or structure in the accepted sense, and Hunt was probably wise, in preparing his volume of collected poems published in 1832, to republish only selected passages.[16] He also remembered Shelley's advice and replaced "glib" with "fast" (I, 168) and "smooth" (I, 222) where it appeared in those passages he reprinted.[17]

The first emendation on the list, however, seems to belong not to the Preface, but to the Dedication, which would read, "ancient [as] well as modern."

16. I, 47–86, as "The Dryads"; I, 162–184, as "The Ephydriads, or Nymphs of the Fountains. — A Sketch"; I, 205–229 as "A Picture of Naiads"; and II, 1–24 as "The Cloud. A Fragment." He did not reprint the song of the Nepheliads (II, 135–204), perhaps because Shelley had excelled him in his own conception in "The Cloud."

17. In "The Nymphs," "glib" had also appeared at I, 256, in a passage not reprinted.

SC 470 JOHN TAYLOR TO LEIGH HUNT, MARCH 23, 1818

AL (draft) unsigned, 4 pages. Double sheet, 4to (9 x 7.4 inches).
Wove paper.
Addition: manuscript is badly stained, with small sections worn away.
PROVENANCE: Taylor and Hessey; Walter T. Spencer, 1922.

SC 470   *91 New Bond St.   23 March*
                                        1818

Sir

   I was not in Fleet Street at the time you sent

                                        but
5 *Mr Shelley's Letter for my Perusal, Mr Hessey* ~~*therefore*~~

               for me
   copied ~~*from it*~~ *that part which related to the Subject*

                              viz
10 *on which we differ,* ~~*as follows*~~ *"With respect to Taylor &*
   Hessey I am ready to certify if necessary in a Court of Jus-
   tice that one of them said he would give up his Copyright
   for the 20 £, and that in lieu of that he would accept the

                                   I affirm on the other
15 *profits of Rimini, until it was paid."* ~~*My Statement is,*~~
   hand
   ∧ that at the Conversation alluded to Mr Shelley requested,
   as a very great kindness to be conferred on you
   ~~*for you*~~ *that we would relinquish the Copyright of your Poems*
20 *(not the Publication of them,*
                  and   *in addition to what had been paid*
   Stating that∧whatever we might ask∧as a Compensation for the
                  glad   gladly given   *not*
   Loss would be∧ ~~*cheerfully.*~~ *— I replied that we had∧sought our*
25 *own Advantage in this Transaction from the Beginning, —*
          you named the Price of the work   *w< >h you* ~~*asked*~~ *named*
   that we ~~*did not*~~ *had advanced the Money <   > required*
                                   own
               own particular   not by our∧desire
30 *for the Work, at your∧Solicitation∧* ~~*and*~~ *therefore that now*
   if it would be doing you a Favour to relinquish the
                           at what we gave for it 20 Gs not 20£
                           so, on the original Terms
   Property, we were willing to do∧provided the ~~*Money*~~
                  even without   in the way of Premium
35 *20Gs not 20£, as he States it   && that so far from taking any advantage∧of you we would not*
   ∧were repaid instantly—∧ ~~*nor would we charging any Interest*~~
   even charge ~~*the*~~ *Interest   Purchase Money*
   for the 6 Months that you had been in possession of the
                  offered
40 *when these conditions were* ~~*named*~~ *by me, Mr Shelley spoke in strong Terms of our*
   ~~*The Terms of foregoing were named by me, not by M^r*~~

SC 470   Liberality; so that the Alternative ~~of a~~ Proposition from you that <————>
                be paid   on
   45   ~~Shelley, and Rimini~~ the Profits ~~to accrue from~~ <   >ni
                                    opportunity or Need ~~for~~
           not only   but there was no ~~opportunity of~~ proposing it; nor
           was ∧ never mentioned. ∧ — ~~Mr Shelley & I therefore~~
                                                                        <————————>
   50   ~~are at Variance— we~~ Should I have heard ~~it named~~ with common Patience, so
           unreasonable and absurd ~~an Expectation stated~~ ~~Proposal made~~ an Expectation stated
           ~~cannot both be right; and~~ If this affair had been carried
                                either Mr S. or I   have ~~been sworn~~
           before a Court of Justice, ~~one of us~~ must ~~be proved to~~
   55   ~~to a Falsehood~~   been forsworn
           ~~be in the wrong.~~ — I am glad, ~~though not on my own acct~~
                    so   an
           that ~~this~~ public ∧ Exposure ~~did not take~~ is not necessary
                                            sake
   60   though not for my own ~~acct~~ as you will see from
                                ~~I have had the good Fortune~~ to meet with
                                                                it to you th
           the following ~~Copy of a~~ letter which ∧ I wrote ~~to you a few~~
           on the 2nd of April 1817 only
   65   my   with Mr Shelley
           weeks only after ~~that~~ Conversation ~~& offer had taken place~~
                                had
           ~~and which I have the good fortune to meet with & of which~~
           I have had the good fortune to find a Copy of it. ~~as follows~~
   70   2. April 1817– To Mr Leigh Hunt– Esqe
               Dear Sir, we have not heard from you since we
           consented to annul the Bargain for your poems on
           Condition of being repaid the Sum for which we had
           bought them. We mention the Circumstance for fear
   75   there should be some Mistake, as Mr Shelley assured
           us the Money would be returned immediately.– If we
           are still to consider the Copyright ours, we shall be
           glad to receive the MS as soon as possible that
           we may publish without Delay"—~~Can anything be plainer~~
   80   after waiting more than 2 Months
           ~~Two Months~~   ~~on June 10~~ afterwards
                        Two   (June 10)   Your
           ~~Three Months after this~~ ∧ we received ~~an~~ Answer
           Albion House Marlow using ~~Mr Shelley's at Marlow~~ when at which Time it ~~seems~~
   85   ~~from you,~~ dated ∧ ~~from Mr Shelley's~~ where the above

Taylor to Hunt   **March 23, 1818**

SC 470

                          Mr Shelley

would seem that neither You nor ~~he~~ had any thoughts of ~~contradicting me~~

      <   >ing me to the ~~existing~~ Profits on Rimini ⟨————⟩ ~~attempted to be~~

Statement <   > ~~not attempted to be contradicted; but~~

90

                      a

       on the contrary ∧ further Indulgence of a few weeks is

~~Time was~~ requested, and in the meanwhile (it is then

                     you have ordered

for the first time stated) ~~that having~~ our Names to be

95

                               trust

put in the Title page of Rimini which you ~~hope~~ will

                         (as you express it) ~~of which I have been guilty"~~

make us, ~~as you express it~~   #I quote your own words

~~us some~~ " Amends for the Delay;

100

                              then

~~in the~~ They Shewn the Light in which Rimini was considered; ~~that it was~~

                     ~~accidental not essential to the Transaction and these~~

~~as Recompense for the Delay & nothing can~~

and completely disprove the assertion that ~~it formed part of the~~

105

~~arrangement between which whose has been made respecting it~~

of yourself and Mr Shelley   Further: when M^r

Shelley called to offer us his Poem, I mentioned that we

                Negociation   by you

had never had that ~~Transaction~~ completed ∧ which began

110

in the Conference I had formerly had with him — He

                           remind you of it

expressed his Surprise, & said he would ~~mention it to~~

~~you;~~ but not a word was said of Rimini — though ac-

                      we were then getting

115

cording to his present Declaration ~~I had no Right to~~

         even then in train   to have

~~claim any other Return that what~~ our Debt liquidated

           Agreement   that work

according to our ~~own~~ Wishes by the Profits in ~~Rimini~~

120

    But further   which   & you   as

— and what were those Profits ~~that~~ he ∧ speaks of, ~~for~~

and in what manner have they been

~~and which were~~

~~if he says Truth, some Profits~~ never were never to

125

    ing   by

accrueng to us from the publishing of Rimini?– all I

                   of anything of that kind coming to us

can says is that we never knew ∧ it before you men

SC 470 tioned it a few Days since, and that Mr Triphook

from whom we received those Copies which we have

had, is ignorant of it, for he charges the Books to

we sell our Publications for ~~all to~~

us at the same price that ^other Booksellers ~~pay~~, &

he requested us from the Beginning to consider ourselves

135 indebted to him & not to you for the Amount

that

~~I told you before~~ ^this was a ~~bad Business.~~ ~~Mr Shelley's Declaration makes~~

much   its

~~it worse~~ The only thing that can add to ~~the~~ Blackness ~~of~~

140   this affair

~~this affair~~ is, that it seems to have had a character

of Insincerity from the Beginning.– You ask us if we

it possible   any original ~~unpublished~~

think ^that you meant to sell ~~the~~ Poems ~~in question~~

145 ~~original as well as reprinted~~

for so small a Sum as Twenty Guineas.– We say that

—we did not fix it, nor desire it;

you named that Price yourself ^& we have a Letter of

the ~~what~~ original Poems which

150   propose

yours which mentions ~~the Poems~~ you ~~sell~~ adds to those

to make ~~it worth our~~

which had been printed before, ~~in the Examiner News-~~

155   even

it ~~the while~~ worth our while to give ^that Sum, for ~~the~~

~~paper which latter~~, in fact, any person may republish

the latter   Again

^without paying a Farthing for the Copyright.— ^You

say that Mr Shelley expressed his Surprise at the

160   ⟨—⟩when ☐he heard of it   indeed may be a good R<   >

~~Nature of the Bargain~~ ^but that ^rather ~~confirms~~

your   and

for ~~his~~ wishing to get it annulled, ~~would~~ for his calling

us

165 on ~~me~~ and ~~stating~~ requesting that we would consent

does it not   also

to relinquish our Claim — but ~~it does not~~ prove,

a

that ~~at first~~ we had ~~no~~ right to expect the Ful-

170 filment of your Engagement, & that the Poems we

[534]

Taylor to Hunt   **March 23, 1818**

SC 470

                  not   alone

had purchased were ^those ^to which no Copyright

         Lastly

175   attached.— ^You speak in your first letter as if you

were glad of the prospect of fixing with us as your

           & in your latest you continue to

Publishers,— ~~you~~ profess yourself ~~to~~ be under obligation

    to us, ~~whatever you felt on that account,~~ ~~our Forbearance was not~~

      the sense of which was not likely

180   ~~to us~~ ~~in your last~~ yet as soon as an opportunity

    likely to diminish by the continuance of its cause   but

offers you ~~offend against common Justice by~~, pub

    not only forget all these professions

               those very   to

185   lishing at another House, ~~the~~ Poems which were

~~had reason to which we went lawfully by Right~~

    still

ours by Purchase.—

                    our

        As we are now ~~quite~~ repaid ~~the~~ Twenty Guin[s]

with the Interest, and all Transactions are at an End

between us we must be allowed to say that we feel

    nor Mortification not

195   no Regret ^at ~~your~~ having published the Work ~~at~~

~~another House~~ place in proof of which as refer to

    the Circumstance of you ~~(being~~ having made

~~the Original Proposals made by you,~~— to the ~~Freedom~~

    willingness we expressed to relinquish the Copyright

200   —and to the

        I am very sorry that any Circumstances

                  in such a Manner

should have induced you to act ^towards us, ~~as I~~

in a Way which I have so much Reason to ~~complain~~

205   and you to be ashamed of

complain ~~of and which your own Heart must~~

    I told you before what I thought   that it was altogether

    ~~You know my opinion~~ of this Transaction, ~~if anything could~~

~~make it worse it is this Declaration of Mr Shelleys~~ bad, but the ~~latter~~

210   what

End *You know ~~that~~ I thought ~~of~~ this ^Transaction before Mr Shelley's

[535]

Taylor to Hunt   **March 23, 1818**

SC 470

        was rec^d
answer came, You will judge now what my opinion must be now
               ^x*I am sick*

[Written reverso, bottom of page 4]

215
                       91 New Bond Street
                          19 March 1818

    Sir,

      As I was not in Fleet Street at the Time
you sent Mr Shelley's letter for my Inspection, M^r

220
             copied
Hessey extracted from it the

A major portion of the uncanceled text of SC 470 may be consulted in the Commentary, below.

line 6. *Perusal,*: *rus* written through another *rus* which had an additional loop.

line 8. *related*: *d* is formed like an upper-case *D* and is written through an indecipherable letter.

line 22. *Stating*: squeezed into the right margin after the rest of the line was written.

    Compensation: Taylor's *m*'s frequently resemble *n*'s.

line 26. *w<hic>h*: paper is worn away along the center fold.

line 27. *<you>*: probable reading; paper worn away along center fold.

line 39. *the*: second *the* written through *them*.

line 41. *these*: written through *those* or vice versa.

line 42. *not by*: probable reading.

line 43. ⟨———⟩: paper worn away along the edge.

line 45. *<Rimi>ni*: paper worn away along the edge.

line 49. ⟨———⟩: canceled word illegible.

line 68. *have*: written through *had*.

line 69. *I . . . follows*: occupies four short cramped lines on page 2 to the right of line 70, along the margin.

line 79. *may publish*: *may* was originally written *maybe*, and the *p* of *published* was converted from *be*.

line 83. There are three levels of interlineations to this line. Taylor first inserted *Two* and

June 10, then abandoned these changes for new phrases.

line 87. *me*: *e* written through *y*.

line 88. *<   >ing*: paper worn away.
    ⟨———⟩: heavily canceled words illegible.

line 89. *<   >*: paper worn away.

line 92. *then*: *en* written through indecipherable letters.

line 101. *in the . . . Transaction*: originally one line in manuscript. This line, with its interlineations, was originally cramped in above line 107 (*Shelley . . . we*) and preceded by a caret. Lines 104–106 (*and . . . Shelley*) were written in the left margin of page 2, perpendicular to the rest of the text, and an elaborate series of markings indicated the place where the insert belonged. *Further: when M^r* (line 106) originally followed *Delay;* (line 99), but we have changed its position to conform to Taylor's markings and have moved line 103 (*as . . . can*) above the long marginal insertion for clarity.

             ing
line 126. *accrueng*: when this word was altered, the full line above it was canceled completely and line 123 was inserted at the bottom of the previous manuscript page (page 2).

line 128. *says* (sic).

line 135. *indebted*: possibly *endebted*.

line 139. *it worse*: added in space left for paragraph indention.

line 156. *person*: *per* written through indecipherable letters.

Taylor to Hunt **March 23, 1818**

SC 470   line 160. ⟨——⟩: canceled letters indecipherable.
⟨R⟨*eason*⟩: probable reading; paper worn away.

line 167. *prove,*: comma written through *s*.

line 170. *&*: written through *or*.

line 171. ⟨———⟩: the word was probably first written *only*, but altered to *alone*; then the word was canceled and inserted on the line below.

line 177. *latest*: *est* written through indecipherable letters.

line 180. *likely*: Taylor repeated the word (line 182) accidentally.

line 183. ~~*Justice*~~: ~~*us*~~ written through indecipherable letters.

line 198. ~~*Proposals*~~: *s* written through comma.

line 203. *you*: *y* written through *?to*.

line 210. ⟨*?very bad*⟩: possible reading.

line 211. *You*: *Y* written through *y*.

line 214. ˣ*I am sick*: written at the bottom of page 4.

THIS DRAFT, written in anger, contains several statements of interest that Taylor omitted from the letter that he finally sent to Hunt (transcribed below). The most significant (lines 106–107) tells that "Mʳ Shelley called to offer us his Poem"; this would have been in late September or early October 1817, when Shelley went to London immediately after completing *Laon and Cythna* and remained "in town much teazed."[1] From the draft we also learn that Hunt had not really arranged with Triphook for Taylor and Hessey to become joint publishers of the second edition of *Rimini*, in spite of their precedence on the title page. A third point is Taylor's charge that Hunt — and Shelley — dealt insincerely "from the Beginning" (line 142).

Certainly neither Hunt nor Shelley emerges unscathed from this correspondence. The kindest judgment that can be made is, perhaps, the one suggested by Taylor in this draft, that "circumstances" drove Hunt to act in a way that he later regretted and — as his sending Elizabeth Kent to make the final settlement indicates — was ultimately ashamed of (see SC 467). Shelley could plead his deep concern for Hunt's immediate material welfare. But in the long run, the alienation of Taylor and Hessey doubtless hurt Hunt, who might otherwise have become a contributor to the *London Magazine*, and Shelley himself, who might have had an alternative to Charles Ollier as publisher of his poems.

Taylor obviously did not send the letter as he drafted it. A fair copy, presumably of the letter finally dispatched to Hunt, reads as follows:[2]

1. Mary Shelley, Journal. On October 6 Shelley asked Mary to tell Claire "that I have offered her book to Lackingtons & to Taylor & Hessey & that they have both declined." (Shelley, *Letters*, I, 561.)

2. Manuscript in The Carl H. Pforzheimer Library.

Taylor to Hunt   **March 23, 1818**

SC 470   Sir

I was not in Fleet Street at the time you sent Mr Shelley's Letter for my perusal, but Mr Hessey copied for me that part which related to the subject on which we differ viz. "With respect to Taylor & Hessey I am ready to certify if necessary in a Court of Justice that one of them said he would give up his Copyright for the 20£ and that in lieu of that he would accept the Profits of Rimini, until it was paid." I affirm, on the other hand, that at the Conversation alluded to, Mr Shelley requested as a very great kindness to be conferred on you, that we would relinquish this Copyright of your poems, and whatever we might ask as a Compensation for the loss would be gladly given. I replied, that we had not sought our own advantage in this Transaction from the beginning — that we had advanced the money which you named for the work at your own particular solicitation, not by our Desire — that now therefore, if it would be doing you a Favour to relinquish the Property we were willing to do so at what we gave for it, provided the Twenty Guineas (not £20 as he states) were repaid instantly, — & that so far from taking any advantage in the way of premium, we would not even charge Interest for the six months that you had been in possession of the purchase money — when these conditions were offered by me, Mr Shelley spoke in strong terms of our liberality — so that the alternative proposition from you that we should be paid out of the Profits$_\wedge$of Rimini, was not only never mentioned, but there was no opportunity or need for proposing it — nor should I have heard with common patience so unreasonable & absurd an expectation stated —

If this affair had been carried before a Court of Justice, either Mr Shelley or I must have been forsworn, I <   > that so public an exposure is not necessary, though <   > for my own sake, as you will see by the Letter which I wrote to you on the 2nd of April 1817, only a few weeks after my Conversation with Mr Shelley — I have had the good fortune to find a copy of it —

"Dear Sir,   We have not heard from you since we consented to annull the Bargain for your poem *on Condition of being repaid the sum for which we had bought*. We mention the Circumstance for fear there should be some mistake, as Mr Shelley assured us the money would be returned *immediately*. If we are still to consider the *Copyright* ours — we shall be glad to receive the M. S. as soon as possible that we may publish without delay."

After waiting more than two months, we received your answer, dated "Albion House Marlow 9 June 1817" at which time it would seem neither you nor Mr Shelley had any thoughts of referring to these Profits of Rimini: on the Contrary, a further Indulgence of a few weeks is requested, and in the meanwhile (*it is then for the first time stated*) you have ordered our *names to be put on the title page of Rimini*, which you trust will make us "Amends for the *Delay*. I

Godwin to ?Curran   **March 27, 1818**

SC 470   quote your own words: They show in what light Rimini was then considered,
and completely disprove the assertion of yourself & Mr Shelley —
    You know what I thought of this transaction before Mr Shelley's answer
was received, you will judge what my opinion must be now —
I am, Sir
Your Humble Servt.

SC 471   WILLIAM GODWIN TO ?AMELIA CURRAN, MARCH 27, 1818

AL signed *William Godwin*, 1 page. Single sheet, 8vo (7.4 x 4.6 inches).
Laid paper. Watermark: [posthorn in crowned shield (upper quadrant)]||.

PROVENANCE: Emily Driscoll, October 1949.

Skinner Street,
Mar. 27, 1818.

Dear Madam
        I did myself the pleasure of sending you on Sunday last a double
5   *general-ticket of admission to Mr Hazlit's Lectures at the Crown & Anchor.*
I confess myself a little mortified that I had neither the pleasure of meeting
you there on Monday evening, as I had hoped; & that you have not returned
me the ticket, nor even acknowledged the receipt of it. If you have no use
for it, do me the favour to deliver it to the bearer.
10   *very truly yours*
William Godwin

line 5. *Hazlit's*: the single final *t* follows Godwin's rule that final consonants not be doubled.

WILLIAM HAZLITT gave the first of his *Lectures on the English Poets*
at the Surrey Institution on Tuesday, January 13, 1818. These
eight lectures occupied successive Tuesdays, concluding on March 3. Of
their success Catherine Maclean writes: "Hazlitt's audience had been
steadily increasing throughout the series of lectures. . . . At the last lecture, on The Living Poets . . . the Hall was 'crowded to the very ceiling.'"[1]

1. Maclean, *Born Under Saturn* (New York, 1944), p. 377. See also Hazlitt, *Memoirs*, I, 235-239;
Howe, *Hazlitt*, pp. 219-224; Herschel Baker, *William Hazlitt* (Harvard University Press, 1962),
pp. 252-254.

[539]

Godwin to ?Curran   March 27, 1818

SC 471   Among those who attended the lecture "On the Living Poets" on March 3 were William and Mary Jane Godwin. Godwin had not attended the earlier sessions, perhaps because during January and February he had been so involved with the Shelleys and in trying to stabilize his own financial situation and partly, no doubt, because it was inconvenient for him to travel at night to the Surrey Institution (at the south end of the Blackfriars Bridge).

Hazlitt's biographers mention the repetition of his lectures on the English poets at the Crown and Anchor Tavern, but they fail to specify what nights these were given or who attended. Godwin's Journal yields new information on both these points. The lectures at the Crown and Anchor (which was in the Strand, west of Temple Bar) were given on Monday and Friday evenings, commencing on Monday, March 23 (the day after Easter), and apparently concluding on Friday, April 17. Godwin attended six of these; he did not go to the fifth lecture ("On Thomson and Cowper," April 6) or to the final one, which he had already heard at the Surrey Institution.

Godwin's Journal references and the present letter indicate that Hazlitt asked Godwin to help promote his series of lectures.[2] Hazlitt called on Godwin on Easter Sunday, March 22, the day before the series began. He dined at Godwin's the following Sunday, called on him on Saturday, April 4, called again on April 7 (the day after Godwin had skipped the fifth lecture), and supped with Godwin on April 14.

Although one cannot positively identify the lady to whom this curt note was sent, circumstantial evidence points to Amelia Curran as a possible recipient. Hazlitt must have given Godwin tickets of admission when he called on Easter, and Godwin says in SC 471 that he sent the ticket to his correspondent the same day. Godwin's Journal for the day records that Hazlitt and Amelia Curran had been invited for the evening of Easter Sunday but neither was able to come. Godwin could well have sent Miss Curran the tickets with the messenger who brought her regrets. As we have seen (SC 461), Godwin took an interest in Amelia's affairs during her stay in London following John Philpot Curran's death,

---

2. They were not mentioned in the *Examiner* until Sunday, March 29 (#535, p. 201), when the reviewer suggests that the later lectures are more interesting for a live presentation (the earlier being better for private reading).

Shelley and his Circle : Manuscripts

SC 471   and providing her with a ticket to the lectures of a good friend of her late father would be further evidence of his concern.

This note was sent on Friday, March 27, the day of the second lecture, Godwin undoubtedly wishing to recover the ticket in time to give it to someone else, if his correspondent did not intend to use it. His note to her of February 24 was addressed to "Dear Amelia," in contrast to the "Dear Madam" of this one. But inasmuch as the present note was written in a spirit of irritation, if not anger, the altered tone of the salutation would not be unnatural. Godwin's Journal mentions Amelia Curran's attendance at only one of the lectures, on March 30, the night after she dined at Godwin's with Hazlitt and "E Collins." Perhaps, embarrassed by Godwin's note, she sent him an explanation or apology, and he again invited her and Hazlitt to dine.

Among the others whom Godwin records as attending one or more of Hazlitt's lectures at the Crown and Anchor were the "Aldises" — presumably Charles Aldis (?1775–1863), surgeon and antiquary, with his wife;[3] Thomas Massa Alsager;[4] Charles Kemble, the actor; Martin Burney, brother of Fanny Burney and a racquets-playing crony of Hazlitt;[5] the Basil Montagus; "Hill" — presumably Thomas Hill (1760–1840); "Reid" — probably Dr. John Reid (1776–1822), who like Hazlitt had attended the nonconformist academy at Hackney;[6] Henry Blanch Rosser, the young Cambridge student whom Godwin befriended;[7] William Hone, the radical publisher; "J Taylor" — either Godwin's friend John Taylor of the *Sun* or Keats's publisher, John Taylor of Taylor and Hessey; Thomas Moore, who attended the seventh lecture on April 13, just before

---

3. The catalogue of Chauncey Brewster Tinker's collection (*The Tinker Library*, New Haven, 1959, p. 211) lists a copy of Godwin's *Memoirs of the Author of A Vindication of the Rights of Woman* bound together with a work by Sir Charles Aldis: *A Defence of the Character and Conduct of the Late Mary Wollstonecraft Godwin, Founded on Principles of Nature and Reason, as Applied to the Peculiar Circumstances of Her Case; in a Series of Letters to a Lady* (London: Printed for John Wallis . . . by Slatter and Munday, Oxford, 1803).

4. On Alsager, see SC 412 and Commentary.

5. See *Bryan Waller Procter (Barry Cornwall): an Autobiographical Fragment and Biographical Notes* . . . ed. Coventry Patmore (London, 1877), p. 179.

6. Henry Crabb Robinson records attending Hazlitt's lecture of January 28, 1812, with "Dr. Reid." (*On Books*, I, 62.)

7. Kegan Paul says that Godwin first met Rosser in 1819, but Rosser's name appears in Godwin's Journal at least as early as July 11, 1817. Shelley and Rosser supped together at Godwin's on November 19, 1817.

SC 471   the one on contemporary poets; and Charles and Mary Lamb, who attended the fourth lecture on April 3, devoted to Dryden and Pope.[8]

Godwin undoubtedly made no attempt to list all of his acquaintances. (The lecture hall at the Crown and Anchor was "capable of seating upwards of two thousand persons."[9]) His brief notes in the Journal may be assumed to represent only a cross-section of his friends present on each evening. If Godwin's list is, however, at all representative of the Crown and Anchor audience, they were more likely to have responded favorably to Hazlitt's iconoclastic political and literary opinions than did the bourgeois audience that Thomas Noon Talfourd describes as attending the series at the Surrey Institution.[10]

8. Lamb's biographers have declared — on the basis of his letter to Mrs. Wordsworth, February 18, 1818 — that Lamb attended none of Hazlitt's *Lectures on the English Poets*.

9. Henry C. Shelley, *Inns and Taverns of Old London* (Boston, 1909), p. 105. The Crown and Anchor had been the scene on January 24, 1798, of Fox's birthday celebration at which the eleventh Duke of Norfolk (patron of Sir Bysshe Shelley) had capped a series of radical toasts with, "our sovereign's health: 'The majesty of the people.'" Shelley's *Proposal for Putting Reform to the Vote* (1817) had urged that a meeting of reform leaders be held at the Crown and Anchor.

10. See Hazlitt, *Memoirs*, I, 236–238. On March 25 Haydon wrote to Keats (then in Devon): "Haslitt is going to lecture at Crown & Anchor. I am sorry for it, tho' he will get money, it is letting his talents down a little." (Keats, *Letters*, I, 259.) Set in its context in the letter, Haydon's remark reflects his political prejudice against the Crown and Anchor — perhaps reinforced by some jealousy of Hazlitt's success.

SC 472   P. B. SHELLEY TO LORD BYRON, APRIL 13, 1818

AL signed *P B Shelley*, 2 pages. Double sheet, 4to (9.6 x 7.3 inches). Laid paper. Watermark: ALMASSO [letters written on banner held aloft by cherub]|; countermark: GM|.
Seal: wax, red.
Postal fee: 7.
Postmark: VENEZIA| 17 A[ ]|.

PROVENANCE: Lord Byron; Lord Broughton (John Cam Hobhouse); Lady Dorchester; Sir John Murray; A. S. W. Rosenbach. *De Ricci 375* (p. 33).

Milan, April 13. 1818

My dear Lord Byron

    I write chiefly to inquire whether you have recieved a letter from me dated Lyons; & to inform you that your little girl has arrived
5   *here in excellent health & spirits with eyes as blue as the sky over our heads.*

SC 472   *Mary & I have just returned from the Lake of Como where we have
been seeking a house for the summer. If you have not visited this sublime &
lovely scene I think it would repay your toil. Will you spend a few weeks
with us this summer ?   Our mode of life is uniform & such as you re-*
10   *member it at Geneva, & the situation which I imagine we have chosen (the
Villa Pliniana) is solitary, & surrounded by scenery of astonishing grandeur; with the lake at our feet—   If you would visit us— and I don't
know where you could find a heartier welcome—   little Allegra might return
with you—*

15   *Mary unites with me in best regards & Clare bids me ask if you have
recieved a lock of Allegra's hair which she sent in the winter*

Most sincerely Yours

P B Shelley

PS.

20   *I have got some books for you packed up at the bottom of a large box of
my own—*

Shall I send them to Venise? —

[Address, page 4]

Au Milord Byron

chez Messrs Siri

25   *& Wilhelm*

Banquiers.   *Venice*

---

line 3. *recieved* (sic).   line 22. *Venise*: French spelling.
line 7. *house*: possibly *home*.   line 24. *chez . . . Banquiers.*: written by Shelley
line 16. *recieved* (sic).   later and in a smaller hand.

SHELLEY'S PARTY left Lyon on March 25; that night they slept at
Tour-du-Pin. The long entry in Mary's Journal for March 26 is in
Shelley's hand; perhaps Mary did not feel well after the ascent from
France into Savoy. The group spent that night and the next day and
night at Chambery, where relatives of Elise, their Swiss servant, visited
her[1] and where Shelley was helped in getting his books through the

1. Mary refers to these visitors as "Elise's Mother, Father-in-law and little girl"; Claire writes
simply: "Monsieur et madame Romieux et la petite Aimèe." Mary was probably using "father-in-

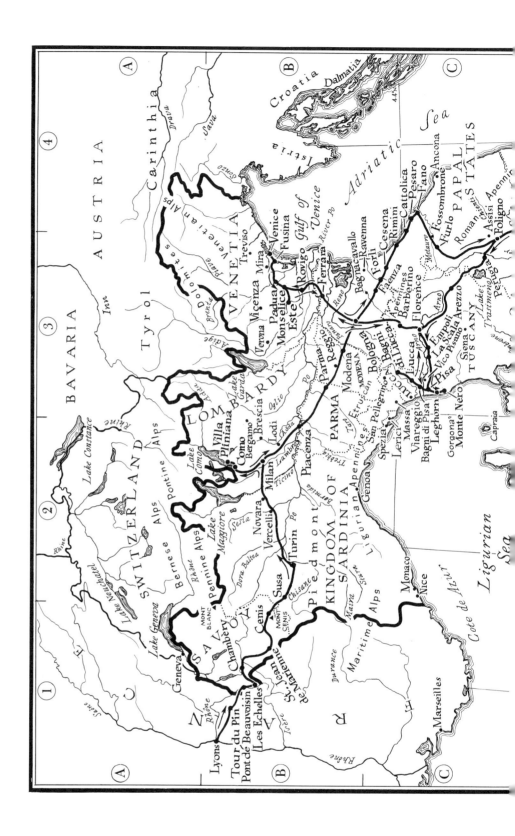

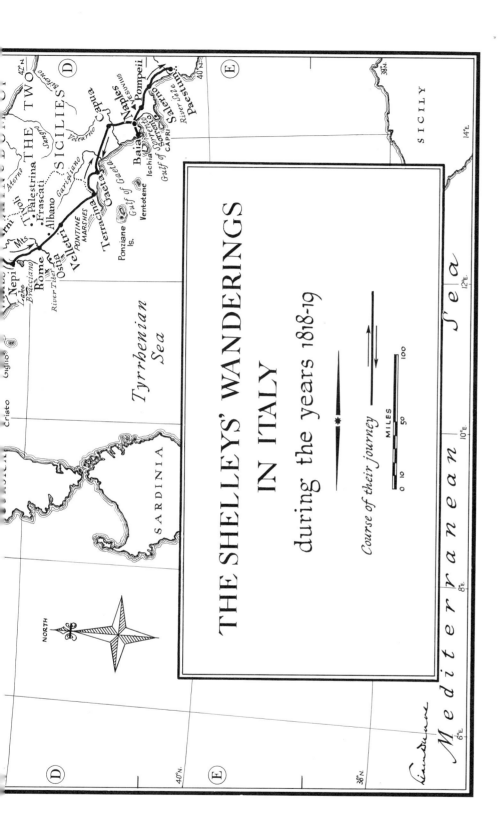

THE SHELLEYS' WANDERINGS
IN ITALY

during the years 1818-19

Course of their journey

MILES

SICILY

Tyrrhenian Sea

SARDINIA

Mediterranean Sea

Cristo

Giglio

NORTH

SC 472 censor's office by a canon who had met Shelley's father at the Duke of Norfolk's house.[2]

The remainder of the journey to Milan (which they reached Saturday evening, April 4) is described in Claire's long journal entry for April 8 (in which she records the highlights of the trip across France and the Alps to Milan) and in Mary's Journal for the appropriate dates. Shelley related his early impressions of Italy to Peacock in letters written on April 6 and April 20 and to Hogg in one dated April 30 (SC 479).

The three letters that Shelley wrote to Byron from Milan (the above letter and SC 475 and SC 477) deal chiefly with the question of Allegra's future. Though this correspondence lacks the literary interest of Shelley's finest travel letters to Peacock, it shows Shelley's tact in mediating between Claire and Byron in the best interest of all parties, including their young daughter.

Shelley had written to Byron from Lyon on March 22, but the letter apparently miscarried. Had Shelley discussed politics, the letter could have been confiscated by the French, Savoyard, or Austrian censors, or stolen, or lost in transit, or simply discarded in Lyon for the postage.[3] There is certainly no suggestion in Byron's published letters that he knew of Allegra's journey to Italy with the Shelleys until after he had received this letter (postmarked in Venice on April 17).

Shelley's idea was, apparently, to revive the spirit of his literary summer of 1816 with Byron at Geneva. The setting on Lake Como may have brought back pleasant memories of those weeks, or the Shelleys may have consciously sought surroundings that resembled Lake Geneva.

law" (as Shelley uses "mother-in-law" in the Preface to *The Cenci*) in the sense of "stepfather" (see *OED*). Thus Monsieur Romieux would be the second husband of Elise's mother; it is possible that Elise had assumed her stepfather's name, but if not, we still have no surname for her until she marries Paolo Foggi. It remains a moot question whether Aimèe was Elise's daughter (as has been assumed by many Shelley scholars) or the young daughter of Elise's mother and stepfather and, hence, a much younger half-sister of Elise. If Mary was using "father-in-law" to mean "stepfather," there would be no reason to assume that Elise had been married and had a daughter; there is no record of any complication when Elise married Paolo (see Shelley to Peacock, January 23–24, 1819, Shelley, *Letters*, II, 76), and the supposition that she had not been married accords with R. B. Hoppner's later statement that Elise was "a young Swiss girl, who . . . had no kind of experience as to caring of children" (Iris Origo, *Allegra*, London, 1935, p. 39 fn.).

2. Claire Clairmont, *Journals*, p. 88.

3. That is, the messenger to whom Shelley had given the letter and money for the postage may simply have thrown away the letter and pocketed the money.

Shelley and his Circle : Manuscripts

SC 472 In any case, they were much impressed with the shores of Lake Como; Shelley introduced it as the setting for the beginning and end of *Rosalind and Helen*, which he had begun writing in England and completed at Bagni di Lucca in August 1818.[4]

The Villa Pliniana, which Shelley mentions in several letters as the house he hoped to rent for the summer ("I imagine we have chosen"), is a famous landmark that has been treated by guidebooks to the Como area from Shelley's time to our own.[5] Richard Bagot, who devotes almost an entire chapter to the villa in *The Italian Lakes*, writes: "With the single exception of the Palazzo Gallio at Gravedona, it is unequalled for the solitary grandeur of its situation, nor is there any villa or palace on the other Lombard lakes which can at all compare with it in point of natural and historical interest."[6] Part of this interest is provided by a famous intermittent spring described at length by Pliny the Younger in a letter to Licinius Sura.[7] In 1570 Count Giovanni Anguisola built the present villa on this site, enclosing the pool described by Pliny within a graceful double loggia. "Terraced gardens, steep rock-cut steps, and paths lead through the silent woods and up towards the great crags which tower behind the villa."[8]

Shelley was very impressed with this setting, though he describes the house itself to Peacock (April 20), as one "which was once a magnificent palace, & is now half in ruins," with apartments "immensely large, but ill furnished & antique."[9] Mary was not as enthusiastic about the Pliniana; of the houses they had looked at earlier she noted that the Villa Lanzi was "a very nice house but out of repair with an excellent garden but full of serpents" (Journal, April 10). The Shelleys then pro-

---

4. Bodleian Ms. Shelley adds. e. 16 contains drafts for lines 40–206 and 219–349 of *Rosalind and Helen*. In this early version (in which Helen is called Isabel) there appear to be no allusions to Lake Como.

5. See, for example, W. A. Cadell, *A Journey in Carniola, Italy, and France in the Years 1817, 1818* (Edinburgh, 1820), II, 137–141; "G.V.," *Itinerario Italiano, o sia Descrizione dei Viaggi ... alle Principali Città d'Italia* (Milano, 1820), p. 37; Lady Morgan, *Italy* (London, 1821), I, 178–183; Karl Baedeker, *Northern Italy* (Leipzig, 1899), p. 145; *The Blue Guide, Northern Italy*, ed. L. R. Muirhead (London, 1960), p. 103.

6. Richard Bagot, *The Italian Lakes* (London, 1905), p. 119.

7. Pliny, *Letters*, Book IV, xxx.

8. Bagot, *The Italian Lakes*, p. 124.

9. Shelley, *Letters*, II, 7.

SC 472 ceeded to the Tremezzina (the area at the foot of Monte di Tremezzo on the west side of the lake, opposite Bellagio), and after staying at an inn in an unspecified location, they looked at one house "beautifully situated but too small" and, across the lake, at a "magnificent one which we shall be very happy if we obtain." After this they returned down the lake to Como, visiting "a very fine waterfall and the Pliniana" on the way. It would appear that either the "magnificent" house was, indeed, unobtainable or else that the Villa Pliniana (with its famed spring and leaping waterfall) captured Shelley's imagination and — as when he selected his last residence on the Gulf of Spezia — he was attracted to a house for its beautiful setting in spite of its practical inconveniences.

When Shelley wrote to Peacock, he was "waiting the issue of our negotiation about a house" and on April 22 he was still urging Byron to visit him on Lake Como (SC 475). But in his letter to Byron of April 28, Shelley explains that they are leaving Milan for Pisa in part because "we have been dissappointed in our house at Como" (SC 477). Contemporary guidebooks and travel books disclose the probable reason for Shelley's failure to rent a suitable villa on Lake Como for the summer. The *Itinerario Italiano* says of Lake Como: "È circondato da molte case di piacere, soggiorno dei Milanesi nella stagione estiva."[10] W. A. Cadell writes that the Pliniana "is handsome, and is frequented by the proprietors in the hot weather, when it is a most agreeable retreat, being exposed to the west, and cooled by the water-fall and the shade of trees, which cover the abrupt side of the hill above the house."[11]

10. "It is surrounded by many pleasure houses, in which the Milanese stay in the summer season" (p. 37).

11. Cadell, *Journey in Carniola*, II, 139–140.

SC 473 T. L. PEACOCK TO T. J. HOGG, ?APRIL 15–27, 1818

AL signed *T. L. Peacock.*, 2½ pages. Double sheet, 4to (8.8 x 7.3 inches). Wove paper. Watermark: VALLEYFIELD| 1816|. Impressed stamp, London: [crown]| BATH|.

Seal: wax, red: [peacock]|.

Postal fee: 7.

Postmarks: 1. (mileage stamp): MARLOW| 33|; 2. (morning duty stamp, London): c| 28 AP 28| 1818|.

Peacock to Hogg ***?April 15–27, 1818***

SC 473 PROVENANCE: Thomas Jefferson Hogg; Prudentia Hogg Lonsdale; John Ewer Jefferson Hogg; Major R. J. Jefferson Hogg (Sotheby, June 30, 1948, lot 100).

My dear Hogg

I shall be very glad to see you at Whitsuntide: I suppose you will come down Saturday. We shall have plenty of water for navigation as at present the whole country is inundated. – I do not feel that the act
5 *of termination is melancholy. That which is pleasing I miss when it is gone: but while it is going it is still present, and while its absence is only a matter of prospective knowledge and not of actual feeling it does not oppress me with any intolerable weight. In literary pursuits I always feel glad to finish anything whether in reading or writing & to begin something new.*
10 *Shelley has left behind him some volumes of Plato but he has taken with him the 1st and 10th & the Symposium is in the latter. – I have not heard a word of Shelley since his departure. – Have you seen Il Barbiere di Seviglia? It did not please every one. To me it was delightful. I never heard music speak so intelligibly and with so much of the vis comica. – I have*
15 *been considering the question of marriage and divorce and have read everything I can get on the subject including that strange tissue of chimæras the Empire of the Nairs. I rather incline still to the orthodox side: but I shall*

write when I have leisure a dialogue on the subject ~~when I shall~~ ᵗᵒ *get a clearer*
20 *view of my own notions. My London novel I postpone till next winter when*
I shall take sketches on the spot. At present I am ᵂʳⁱᵗⁱⁿᵍ *a comic romance with the title of Nightmare Abbey and amusing myself with the darkness and misanthropy of modern literature from the lantern jaws of which* ~~death's head~~
25 *I shall endeavour to elicit a laugh.*

I had written thus far almost immediately after receiving your letter and postponed concluding from day to day in the hope of being able to give you some intelligence of Shelley from whom at length I have received a letter dated Milan. He seems in excellent health and spirits and is full of sanguine
30 *expectations of finding paradise on the banks of the Lake of Como. Write soon. and believe me to remain   most sincerely yours*

T. L. Peacock.

The Carl H. Pforzheimer Library

Peacock to Hogg   **_?April 15–27, 1818_**

Hor: Sat. 1.2. 31. sqq.

[Address, page 4]

T.J. Hogg Esqre

35   *1 Garden Court*

Temple

London

THIS LETTER, written at two different times many days apart, was
mailed at Marlow (the London morning duty postmark reveals)
on April 27 — in plenty of time to invite Hogg for the four-day Whitsuntide holiday (May 10–13 in 1818). When it was begun we are unable
to determine. It responds to Hogg's answer to Peacock's letter of
March 20 (sc 468) and therefore could, theoretically, date from the end
of March, but Peacock's expression of concern that he has not heard
from Shelley (line 11) would suggest a date of about mid-April. Shelley's
first letter to Peacock, written at Milan on April 6, was stamped at
London on April 23 and presumably reached Marlow the next day (a
Friday). Peacock completed his letter sometime between Friday and
post-time on Monday.

Apart from a watery welcome to his flooded countryside, Peacock
at once gets down to what looks like a *volte face* for the perverse pleasure
of argument. Hogg's answer to the plaintive pipings of March 20 (sc 468)
is not available; we may guess at an attempt — more or less clumsy, in
the Hoggian style — to sympathize with Peacock's awareness of an
ended era. By now the satirist is not anxious to be reminded that he had
pinned his heart on his sleeve a few weeks past. He becomes contrary
and takes refuge in a shifted argument about feeling no oppression while
the departing object is still present — an argument that is no doubt
beside the mark. Truth will out: his thoughts are almost immediately
back on Shelley, of whom he has heard nothing since his departure; that
is, since the brilliant evening they spent together at the opera. Hence
the apparent leap, which is *no* leap, to ask if Hogg has been to *Il Barbiere*;
Peacock's mind still runs on those delights. There is even a chance (but
this is speculative) that one of the questions he and Shelley discussed
at supper had been marriage and divorce (line 15); *The Empire of the*

Shelley and his Circle : Manuscripts

Peacock to Hogg   *?April 15–27, 1818*

SC 473   *Nairs*[1] was out of the line of Peacock's usual reading, and Shelley may have recommended it, though his own passionate involvement of six years ago had cooled to a disinterested appraisal.

On August 17, 1812, Shelley had written to its author, J. H. Lawrence, that the book, which he had read that spring, "succeeded in making me a perfect convert to its doctrines." Not that, as a follower of Mrs. Wollstonecraft, he had any doubts of the evils of marriage, but he "had been dull enough not to perceive the greatest argument against it, until developed in the 'Nairs,' viz., prostitution both *legal* and *illegal*."[2] He went on to explain — with that voluble ardor typical of the youthful poet — that he had put Love in chains despite his conviction, through the need to protect his loved one from a misjudging world. The phrase would now be old history to Shelley, who had since put Love in chains a second time. Nor is it surprising that Peacock found the book a strange tissue of chimæras, worthy perhaps of discussion in a dialogue; more worthy, it might be said, of his satirical conversations. There would be enough on the matter of love and partnership in general, and on Shelley's entanglements in particular, to amuse him in the writing of *Nightmare Abbey*.

Shelley already knew of this work in progress. In his letter of April 20 from Milan, he deplores the sense that a spot (such as Marlow) being known can never be *unknown*, remaining in the mind while Time flows on and friends are gone. He ends, "See, I have sent you a study for *Night Mare Abbey*."[3] The postponed London novel was left unwritten. By "next winter" Peacock, although on the spot, would be busy studying Indian finance and revenue collection in preparation for his appointment

---

1. *The Empire of the Nairs; or the Rights of Women. An Utopian Romance, in Twelve Books* by James Henry Lawrence (1773–1840) was published in four volumes by Thomas Hookham and E. T. Hookham (1811). The Nairs were a matriarchal caste in Malabar, for whom marriage did not exist and in which fathers had no responsibilities to their children. Lawrence's ideas (some of which derived from Mary Wollstonecraft) influenced Shelley's attack on marriage in *Queen Mab* (V.189 ff. and note).

2. Shelley, *Letters*, I, 322–323. The first (unrecorded) printing of this letter was in Cyrus Redding's "Memoir of Percy Bysshe Shelley" in the Galignani edition of *The Poetical Works of Coleridge, Shelley, and Keats* (Paris, 1829), page vi of the Shelley section. Despite Jones's assertion (Shelley, *Letters*, I, 323 fn.), there is no evidence that Shelley knew James Henry Lawrence personally. The "Lawrence" cited in Hogg's *Life* probably refers to Dr. William Lawrence, Shelley's physician.

3. Shelley, *Letters*, II, 6.

SC 473   with the East India Company. The study absorbed both time and interest, leaving him little of either for novel-writing.[4]

When Shelley departed for Italy he left many of his books with Peacock, among them several volumes of Plato. Hogg apparently asked to borrow the *Symposium,* but Peacock explains that Shelley took volumes I and X. Shelley must have taken another volume also, because he mentions to Hogg in a letter dated October 22, 1821, that he has three volumes of his own edition with him.[5] It has been established that Shelley was using the Bipont edition of Plato, volume I of which contains *Euthyphro, Apology, Crito, Phaedo,* Diogenes Laertius' *Life of Plato,* and Fabricius' notes on Plato. The tenth volume includes Timaeus of Locri's *De anima mundi,* the *Critias, Parmenides, Symposium,* and *Phaedrus.*[6] We are unable to identify the third volume that Shelley took to Italy.

Peacock concludes his letter with the expected word from Shelley and its too-optimistic hope of residence on Lake Como.[7] The laconic citation of Horace's *Satires* (line 33) contains more human interest than its dry scholarly form suggests. The passage cited (beginning "*quidam notus homo cum exiret fornice*") concerns Cato's favorable judgment on an acquaintance he saw leaving a brothel. "A blessing on thy well-doing, for when shameful passion has swelled the veins, 'tis well that young men come down hither, rather than tamper with other men's wives."[8] Horace's main targets in the Second Satire of the First Book are the foolish extremes to which lust can drive men — adulterous affairs and the snares of prostitutes. His solution, set forth as an ideal at the end of the poem, is a continuing union with a virtuous woman. It is not clear how many lines of the poem are to be included by the "sqq."; the immediate reference is to Cato's praise of brothels, but in its larger context, the citation represents part of Peacock's reading on "the question of marriage and divorce" and tends to support the orthodox side.

---

4. See "Peacock in Leadenhall Street," below, pp. 709–723.

5. Shelley, *Letters,* II, 361.

6. See Notopoulos, *Platonism,* pp. 41–42n., 55.

7. Shelley wrote from Milan on April 6, "we design to spend the summer on the shore of the Lake of Como." See Shelley, *Letters,* II, 3. See also sc 472, sc 475, sc 477 and Commentaries.

8. *Horace: Satires, Epistles and Ars Poetica,* trans. H. Rushton Fairclough (Loeb Classical Library edition), pp. 20–21.

SC 474 LEIGH HUNT TO M. W. AND P. B. SHELLEY, APRIL 21–24, 1818

AL unsigned, 3 pages. Double sheet, folio (12.5 x 8 inches).
Laid paper. Watermark: [Britannia in crowned oval]|; countermark: B TURNER|
1809|.
Seal: wax, red: [angel with olive branch, following serpent]|.
Postal fees: 1. 1/ 11; 2. 13.
Postmarks: 1. (Foreign Post Office stamp, London): F 18| 2|; 2. (transit stamp):
ANGLETERRE|; 3. MIL[ANO]| 8|; 4. (?see Notatation 1, below).
Notations, page 4: 1. (sideways on address section): *79.17.1*|; 2. (in Shelley's hand): [sketch]|?*considarodi*|; 3. (in Shelley's hand): *Au Mademoiselle*|;
4. (in Shelley's hand): *Isthmus of Consentia*|.

PROVENANCE: Colonel Charles Shelley Leigh Hunt; Mrs. Beryl Dodgson (Sotheby,
April 8, 1935, lot 205); see SC 414, Commentary.

Lisson Grove North
24 April 1818.

    Well, dear & illustrious vagabonds, and how do you find yourselves?
We are all well here, and as musical & flowery as ever, notwithstanding
5 *Marianne's school two hours of a morning, which makes us all good boys*
& girls, & gets me up, & keeps all sorts of peevishness & noises down.
We rejoiced at having your letters from Calais & Lyons, albeit Shelley
found out the weak side of my friendliness in not waking him,– which is
very savage & "young-eyed" of him. "On which– <u>Shelley</u> looked meek, &
10 *taking forth a-<u>pen</u>" &c. We thought you would have a roughish passage.*
Just as your first letter came, some one had horrified us by telling us of a
carriage which was met in the sea by a person coming over. It ~~is~~ was not
a present to Amphitrite, was it,– to make interest at court? It is delightful
to hear of Shelley's improving health. The nearer he gets to the sun, the
15 *better he will be, I doubt not; but don't let him be too much out in it & burn*
his wings. It was very good of Marina to write such a circumstantial letter
from Lyons, & almost as good of Shelley (there's modesty for you) to think
so much of the Nymphs. I hope to hear a thousand things of Italy.– of the
Alps, of Milano la Grande, Firenze la Bella, & Napoli la Gentile,– of the
20 *ladies, the country, the books, the operas, and of Raphael & Julio Romano,*
which reminds me that there is a place also called Rome. I mention Julio

SC 474   *Romano rather than Michel Angelo, because in the prints I have seen from him there is a poetical something more to my taste than in the heavy-built dreams, neither natural nor supernatural, of Michael,– of whom, remem-*

25   *ber nevertheless, I have seen nothing but in the same kind of translation, & who, I dare say, must have done great things to get so great a reputation. ~~When~~ If you go to Venice also, you must give me your impressions very particularly, as I am writing a comedy, mixed with quieter matter, the scene of which is laid there. I am in the second act, & am introducing the most*

30   *beautiful of the Venetian airs. A gentleman has lent me a number of books about Venice, among which is a large one consisting of all the chief buildings & views in it, designed & engraved by Luca Carlevariis. I mention it in order that you may see I shall have some true ideas of the look of the place, & that in case you meet with the book, I may have the pleasure of your*

35   *pointing out to me some of the spots in it, & so enjoy them in a manner along with you in spite of distance. When you get at all settled, pray tell us how you ɤ live,— how you spend your days, generally speaking, one with an- other. Ecce signum. We are more orderly again than we used to be, as before mentioned. We also go oftener to the theatre, & I am making my critical*

40   *sensation again. Marian & Bess are so bold, that on Friday evenings, when I am writing my theatrical, they sometimes go to the play together, & come home full of what they have seen, & make the best company in the world. We go to plays, to operas, & even to concerts, not forgetting a sort of conver- sazione at Lamb's, with whom & Alsager I have renewed the intercourse,*

45   *with infinite delight, which sickness interrupted. One of the best consequences of this is, that Lamb's writings are being collected for publication by Ollier, & are now indeed going through the press. So we have still proof sheets fluttering about us. As to myself in particular, I walk out quite a buck again, with my blue frock coat, & new hat, waving my (orange-) lily hands.*

50   *I also go to the office on Saturdays. At present, I have made myself a nook to write in of a morning in the corner of the room where Raphael stood.– as*

                           under the print of Shakspeare

  thus:– I have taken his place, in a chair with a table ⟨——————⟩ before me, put his bust on it with a rose-tree at the side towards the door, & filled

                                         heartsease

55   *the outside of the window with geraniums, myrtle, daisies, & a vase full of*

Hunt to Shelleys   *April 21–24, 1818*

SC 474

_{my books on the right,}

gay flowers; so that with the new spring green in the garden,ˌthe picture of
Jaques & the stag under Milton, & two plaister-cast vases, which Hogg

60   has just sent us, on each side of the Mercury on the piano, I have nothing
but sights of beauty, genius, & morality all about me. (Here Shelley says,
with lit-up eyes & a smile, "Oh Hunt! – Clare rubs her hands & twinkles
her head, – and Marina looks placid & sly.) Hogg admired my bower the
other evening, & shrieked at the sight of the heartsease. ⟨———⟩ I overtook

65   him the other day walking through the flowery part of Covent Garden market,
& peering with infinite complacency on each side of him. He has been to
tea here several times, & the other night met Lamb & his sister. He tells me
to say, that he is alive & has as many prejudices as usual. He means to
write. Peacock went with us to the play just after you left us, & we also met

70   him a few nights afterwards ~~t~~ ^{at} the opera; but he has since been at Marlow,
& we have neither seen nor heard of him. Mʳ Godwin, I hear, is well. I am
going to send him Drake's books about Shakspeare, which Lamb tells me he
wishes to see. Adieu. I leave the rest of the paper for Marianne.   "What

75   do you say to Mʳ Shelley, Thornton"? – "My love, & I shall be glad if he's
happy." – Thornton is now reading almost all day, nestled up in an arm
chair. "What shall I say for you, John?" —— Why– – Why– – his love;–
–na–don't say his love;– say, my love, & I shall be glad if he has got a
great stone in his hand." (Here he & Thornton & Mary burst into a loud

80   fit of laughter.) "What shall I say for you, Mary?"–"Say" (hardly able
to speak for laughter) that I shall be glad if he's love." Here, in comes
Molbincha just apropos, with little Percy in her arms, who is looking as
grave & intent as if had all the ideas of his namesake in his head. But I

^{& from all;}

85   must have done. Love to all,ˌ& God bless you. What a nice good kind-tempered

^{When}

girl Marina was during the bustle of going away! ~~If~~ you write to Lord
Byron, pray remember me particularly to him. Oh for some of your Italian
sunshine, & even some of our old clouds, to make a proper April with, for

90   we have had nothing hitherto but dust & earth   the Nepheliads have
treated me with too distant a respect. What are you writing, Shelley!—and
what Marina? Tell us every thing;—but again; –again– I must have done.

SC 474   *Horace Smith is married, & sent me a very nice letter on the occasion. We are going to have a house-warming with him in a day or two at his Fulham*

95   *villa. (We'll take care of the books & other matters.) Shelley's books is going off; & Frankenstein is in request as usual.*

24. April

Marianne after all says she will write a letter by herself,— theres an epistolary resolution for you;— so I sit down to have a little more chat. And

100   *now I must thank you for your letter from Milan, which saluted us last night on our return from the play; & I must inform you also, that though somewhat smitten at finding you arrived so soon, & though my letter (above)*
           by mistake
is dated₍₎24, my conscience was saved in other respects, for it was really

105   *written on Tuesday, the 21ˢᵗ It is exceedingly pleasant to hear so good an account of Italy, especially when on the same day I received a book from*
       well-meaning
a ⟨——⟩ though not a very knowing sort of person, who gives a very different one. You shall hear all about the plays & operas, in a little bundle

110   *of slips from the Examiner which I mean to poke in a corner of Peacock's packet, when ~~he~~ I hear it is ready; & there shall also be a selection of such politicals, as I think have any thing in them. You tell me, Marina, to write long letters? Have I not begun like a good boy? Be a good girl in return, &*
           even

115   *write me as long ones,₍₎if Shelley takes too long siestas to halve them for you. God bless him, & bless you all. Tell Clare I have just had a how-d'ye-do visit from Hobhouse.*

[Address, page 4]

Pisa   *Single Sheet*

A Mons. Monsieur Shelley,

120   *Messʳˢ Marietti*
        Banquiers,
         Milan,

Milano   *Italie.*

    Italia.

SC 474   line 52. *Shakspeare*: contemporary spelling; see also line 73.

line 53. ⟨——————⟩: canceled word is illegible.

line 59. *plaister*: obsolete spelling.

line 64. ⟨———⟩: canceled word is illegible.

line 83. *as if had* (sic).

line 90. *earth*: *h* written on fragment adhering to seal, as is *what* (line 92) and *a* (line 93).

line 93. *Horace . . . usual.* (line 96): added after the rest of page 3 was filled. This segment, written in a very fine hand to the left of *24. April* (line 97), takes up six lines which occupy a space .8 x 2.5 inches along the left margin.

line 108. ⟨*good*⟩: probable reading.

line 118. *Pisa*: this is a forwarding address, possibly added by "Messrs Marietti."

W HEN THE Shelleys left England, they felt closer to the Hunts than to any other friends. In the early stages of the journey into Italy Shelley and Mary wrote regularly to them and hoped that the Hunts would provide them with news of England and their acquaintances there. Hunt tried to do so, but circumstances and his own indolence interfered, and it was not until after the death of William Shelley in June 1819 that the Hunts' letters reached the Shelleys frequently. Shelley and Mary then renewed their side of the correspondence on a regular basis until the Hunts again defaulted.

The extant correspondence from March 1818 through the end of 1819 consists of nineteen letters from Shelley and Mary to the Hunts and twelve letters from Leigh and Marianne Hunt to the Shelleys. Of these, all twelve of the Hunts' and four of the Shelleys' letters — besides Shelley's original draft of the dedication of *The Cenci* to Hunt — appear in these volumes.

Hunt got off to a bad start by failing to mail this, his first letter, until after the arrival of the Shelleys' third — Mary's letter written from Milan early in April.[1] By the time Hunt's letter reached Milan (a trip that at this season required about two weeks), the Shelleys had left that city (May 1) to travel to Pisa (which they reached on May 7). On May 9, they went on to Leghorn, where they remained until June 11. Hunt's letter had not caught up with them by May 13, when Mary wrote a fourth time to the Hunts,[2] but probably reached the Shelleys before they left Leghorn for the Bagni di Lucca. Mary's Journal records that the Shelleys wrote twice to the Hunts from Bagni di Lucca. She later men-

---

1. Mary Shelley, *Letters*, I, 47–49.   2. Mary Shelley, *Letters*, I, 50.

SC 474   tioned writing from Venice (this letter was, with others, destroyed by the hotel keeper so that he could keep the postage), and Naples (perhaps Shelley's letter of December 20–22, 1818, to which she added a postscript).[3] Hunt's letter of *ca.* July 14–August 4, 1818 (SC 486), contains allusions to a lost letter from the Shelleys, probably written from Lucca or the Bagni in reply to SC 474.

The present letter shows Hunt in good spirits, trying to amuse his friends. It sheds considerable light on the way of life of the Hunt family and on Hunt's relations with various acquaintances. The most important literary information is that Ollier's publication of Charles Lamb's *Works* (two volumes, 1818) resulted from Hunt's mediation (lines 44–47). E. V. Lucas has noted that "Lamb had the book in mind as early as 1816, and John Murray was approached, but did not care for it."[4] Thus Hunt continued to play midwife for the brainchildren of his friends, as well as to greet them enthusiastically once they saw daylight.

Just three days before writing of his renewed friendship with Lamb, Hunt had attended a social evening at Lamb's, a party described by Crabb Robinson, who found Marianne Hunt "a very disgusting woman" but wrote of Hunt in a more positive vein:

> ... he, though a man I very much dislike, did not displease me this evening. He has improved in manliness and healthfulness since I saw him last, some years ago. There was a glee about him which evinced high spirits, if not perfect health, and I envied his vivacity. ... Talfourd was there, and injudiciously loquacious. ... Hunt, who did not sympathize with Talfourd, opposed him playfully, and that I liked him for.[5]

This testimony about Hunt's manner is especially valuable because Crabb Robinson was struck by the contrast between the mild-mannered, vivacious Hunt of 1818 and the Hunt of 1812, when they had formerly met at the homes of Lamb and Barron Field.[6] Cyrus Redding also noticed

---

3. See Mary to Marianne Hunt, March 12, 1819, Mary Shelley, *Letters*, I, 63.

4. Lamb, *Letters*, II, 229.

5. Robinson, *On Books*, I, 221.

6. Barron Field (1786–1846) was a lawyer and miscellaneous writer. "Through his father's intimate connection with Christ's Hospital, and through the fact that his brother Francis John Field was a clerk in the India Office, he became acquainted with Charles Lamb, had a large share in his affections, and was admitted a member of that distinguished cluster of literary men which included Coleridge, Wordsworth, Hazlitt, and Leigh Hunt." While in legal training at the Inner Temple (1809–1814),

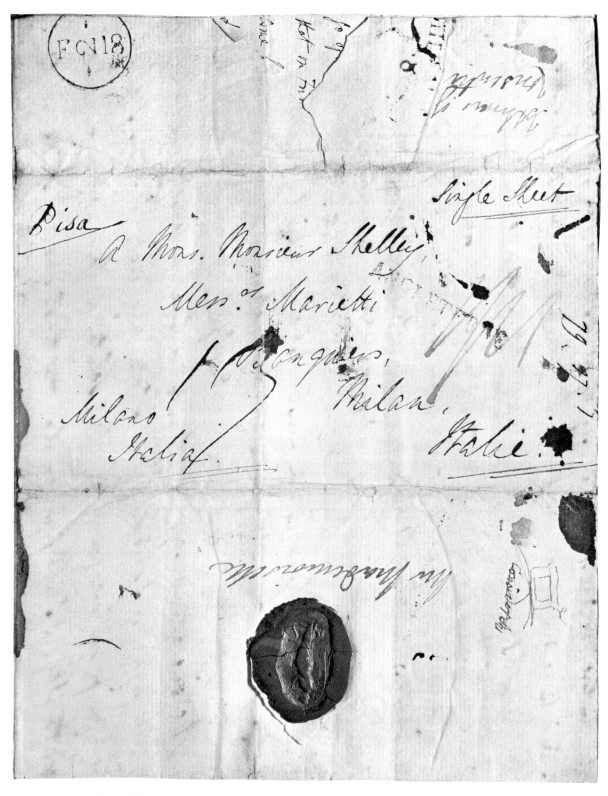

Leigh Hunt to P. B. and M. W. Shelley, April 21–24, 1818 (SC 474),
address leaf, with notations and sketch by P. B. Shelley

The Carl H. Pforzheimer Library

SC 474   a change in Hunt's manner and his style of writing between those dates, but he did not view the change so favorably. Redding, who never lost his own vigorously partisan tone, felt that as Hunt's interests shifted from politics and reform to *belle lettres*, his writing style lost force and clarity and his character the firmness and sturdy independence that marked his brother John Hunt, Redding's special friend.[7]

Most of Hunt's letter concerns domestic trivia or chitchat about acquaintances of the Shelleys, but a few allusions require comment. The Venetian comedy that Hunt was engaged in writing at this time (lines 27–29) was soon laid aside in favor of a serious play on the story of the Cid (see SC 486). Although Hunt never completed the comedy, he eventually published a portion of it with a plot summary as "Scenes from an Unfinished Drama" in the *Indicator* for March 1, 1820.[8] In calling Shelley "young-eyed" (line 9), Hunt was probably continuing a game of coining or applying Homeric epithets that the friends had indulged in.[9] Hunt's allusions to Icarus (lines 14–16) and to Amphitrite, queen of the ocean, are playful in this context, but the latter may be significant for Shelley, who, after receiving this letter, wrote of the past, present, and future of Venice in these words:

> Underneath Day's azure eyes
> Ocean's nursling, Venice lies,
> A peopled labyrinth of walls,
> Amphitrite's destined halls . . .[10]

We do not know how long Marianne pursued her resolution to hold a school for her young family — probably until she persuaded Hunt to

---

he supported himself by his writing, contributing several essays to Hunt's *Reflector* in 1811. (*DNB*.) From August 1816 through June 1824 Field served as judge of the supreme court of New South Wales. A copy of Shelley's *Revolt of Islam* with his bookplate was offered for sale by Ximenes: Rare Books in December 1970 (Occasional List #18, item 108).

7. Cyrus Redding, *Personal Reminiscences of Eminent Men* (London, 1867), II, 184–229. Before Leigh Hunt's death, Redding had not been so candid; compare his *Fifty Years' Recollections, Literary and Personal* (London, 1858), I, 274–278.

8. See the *Indicator* (London, 1820), I, 161–168.

9. In her letter from Milan, Mary described the white oxen of northern Italy, adding that their eyes "justify the Homeric epithet, ox-eyed Juno." (Mary Shelley, *Letters*, I, 48.)

10. "Lines written among the Euganean Hills," lines 94–97. See Donald H. Reiman, "Structure, Symbol, and Theme in 'Lines written among the Euganean Hills,'" *PMLA*, LXXVII (September 1962), 404–413.

SC 474   move into a larger house (see sc 486). That move — like Hunt's buckish blue frock coat, new hat, and orange gloves — was made possible by Hunt's relative prosperity following Shelley's £1,400 gift to him.[11] One can detect a reversion to old habits that had brought Hunt to financial jeopardy in the first place. Ten years later he was to reflect:

> the writer of this memoir . . . is proud to relate, that Mr. Shelley once made him a present of fourteen hundred pounds, to extricate him from debt. I was not extricated, for I had not yet learnt to be careful: but the shame of not being so, after such generosity, and the pain which my friend afterwards underwent, when I was in trouble and he was helpless, were the first causes of my thinking of money-matters to any purpose.[12]

However, Hunt obviously felt no shame for the small extravagances recorded in sc 474; he merely enjoyed the vivacity and good spirits attendant on his temporary release from financial worries. His *joie de vivre* shows in his descriptions of his study "nook" (lines 50–61), the social life enjoyed by the entire family, and the playgoing of Marianne and Bessy Kent (lines 40–42), as well as in the lighthearted record of his children's banter. It is not hard to see why he was the delight and the despair of his friends.

Thomas Jefferson Hogg, as we have seen (sc 452 and Commentary), fell under Hunt's spell during 1818 and saw him fairly frequently. Hunt often invited him to tea and introduced him to Charles and Mary Lamb; Hogg responded to Hunt's friendship by presenting him with the vases mentioned in line 59. Peacock and Hunt, on the other hand, seem to have made no effort to keep in touch with one another.[13] Peacock at Marlow led a quiet life of walking, boating, reading, writing *Nightmare Abbey* and — far more faithfully than Hunt during this period — corresponding with the Shelleys and carrying out their small commissions.[14]

11. See sc 454, Commentary.

12. Hunt, *Lord Byron and Some of His Contemporaries*, p. 192.

13. In 1859 Hunt's later resentment toward Peacock burst forth in his "Occasional," no. XV, "A Word or Two Respecting the *Shelley Memorials*" in the *Spectator*, August 13, 1859, pp. 834–835. There, after denying that Shelley had been the victim of a hallucination in thinking himself attacked at Tanyrallt, Hunt added: "In answer to these and other insinuations of his want of veracity, made apparently in a very spirit of fondness by those who would willingly find him as truthless as themselves, I have this to say: — that during all the years in which I knew him, I never once observed in his conversation the smallest departure from matter of fact."

14. See Peacock's letters to the Shelleys (Peacock, *Works*, VIII, 192 ff.).

SC 474 Relations between Godwin and Hunt, which had never been close, remained at least correct, with Hunt planning to send Godwin Nathan Drake's *Shakspeare and His Times*.[15]

Horace Smith's marriage on March 17, 1818 (his second), was to Miss Ford of Devonshire, one of four sisters famed for their beauty. At this time he moved from 3 Knightsbridge Terrace, Kensington Road, to Elysium Row, Fulham (a village in Middlesex, four miles southwest of London). Here the couple lived until 1821, when they left England to join the Shelleys at Pisa — a journey that ended in Paris. Although few letters between Shelley and Smith survive (and these all of 1820–1822), they corresponded regularly from the time the Shelleys went to Italy. Mary Shelley wrote to Maria Gisborne on July 2, 1818: "A friend in England asks us if a family of 3 persons can live at Pisa with 4 servants — an excellent storehouse furnished, a horse & chaise — a garden of 2 acres — denying themselves no comforts required by a respectable family — for less than £500 per annumm — I say no — what do you say?"[16] This friend was almost certainly Horace Smith, to whom Shelley wrote on April 30 (Mary Shelley, *Journal*), perhaps a letter of congratulation upon receiving from Smith himself news of his marriage. (Smith had a daughter, Eliza, by his first marriage in 1810, who would have been the third in this family of three.)[17]

Hunt's remark to "tell Clare" that Hobhouse called is rather cryptic. John Cam Hobhouse was one of Byron's friends who knew that Claire was the mother of Byron's natural daughter (about whom he wrote quite freely, but usually without identifying the mother).[18] Does Hunt think that the visit would be of interest to Claire simply because Hobhouse was Byron's close friend? Or did Claire have some hope or fear that Hobhouse was likely to influence Byron in her favor or against

15. Two vols., 1817. For Drake, see *DNB*.

16. Mary Shelley, *Letters*, I, 55.

17. Smith's son by this marriage, Horatio Shakespeare Smith, "died when a school-boy at Boulogne-sur-Mer" (Beaven, *James and Horace Smith*, pp. 123–124).

18. Byron wrote to Douglas Kinnaird all about his affair with Claire and the impending birth of a child on January 20, 1817 (quoted in Marchand, *Byron*, II, 681); Hobhouse knew at least by April 1818 that the child was being brought to Italy by Shelley (Byron, *Correspondence*, II, 79) and presumably knew about Claire herself.

SC 474 her, so that knowing that he was still in England (rather than with Byron at Venice) might be of more substantial interest?

Hobhouse's visit to Hunt may have been made to mend fences for his own literary or political career. In April 1818 his *Notes and Illustrations to the Fourth Canto of "Childe Harold's Pilgrimage"* appeared. By April he may already have been campaigning for Douglas Kinnaird's election and Sir Francis Burdett's reelection to Parliament from Westminster.[19] In the fall of 1818 Hobhouse himself was nominated for the parliamentary seat from Westminster, left vacant by the suicide of Sir Samuel Romilly on November 2, 1818, but lost this election. By his visit to Hunt, Hobhouse may have hoped to gain the *Examiner*'s support for his political and literary interests.

Shelley's notations on Hunt's letter are mildly puzzling. "Au Mademoiselle" probably indicates that Claire was not present when Shelley and Mary read the letter and that Shelley sent Elise or another servant to carry it to her. (The nearby sketch may be a rough map to guide the servant to Claire — perhaps visiting at another house in Leghorn.) The phrase "Isthmus of Consentia" may refer to something in Shelley's reading. Consentia (the modern Cosenza) was an important city of Magna Graecia and the chief town of the Bruttii. There Alaric, king of the Goths, died A.D. 410. As the central town of the "toe" of Italy, it may have given its name to that entire subpeninsula, which (according to Virgil, Ovid, Statius, and other writers) had once been an isthmus connecting Sicily to the mainland.

19. The *Examiner* for the months of April through July 1818 makes no particular mention of Hobhouse's *Notes and Illustrations*. Beginning with the issue of June 7, the magazine gives a running account of the Westminster parliamentary election, including two editorials addressed to the electors of the district, the first counseling them to vote for Burdett and Kinnaird, the second congratulating them on their good sense in electing Burdett. The *Examiner* would probably have supported Burdett with no urging from Hobhouse, but his visit may have convinced Hunt that Douglas Kinnaird also deserved the help of the *Examiner*.

SC 475 P. B. SHELLEY TO LORD BYRON, APRIL 22, 1818

AL signed *P.B.Shelley.*, 5 pages. 1 double sheet, 1 single sheet, 4to (9.5 x 7.4 inches).
Laid paper. Watermark, double sheet: ALMASSO [letters written on banner held aloft by cherub]|; countermark: GM|; watermark, single sheet: ALMASSO [letters written on banner held aloft by cherub]|.

The Carl H. Pforzheimer Library

SC 475   Seal: wax, red.
Postal fee: 8.
Postmark: VENEZIA| 23 APR|.
Docket, page 6: *Shelley*|.
Addition: seal tear has been crudely mended.

PROVENANCE: Lord Byron; Lord Broughton (John Cam Hobhouse); Lady Dorchester; Sir John Murray; A. S. W. Rosenbach. *De Ricci 377* (p. 33).

I cannot concieve how my letter from Lyons should have failed.

Milan, April 22, 1818.

My dear Lord Byron

    Clara will write to you herself a detail of her motives &
5 *feelings relating to Allegra's being sent as you desire. Her interference as*
the mother of course supersedes <u>mine</u> which was never undertaken but from
the deep interest I have ever felt for all the parties concerned. Here my letter
might well close, but that I would not the affair should finish so.

    You write, as if from the instant of its departure all future intercourse
10 *were to cease between Clare & her child. This I cannot think you ought to*
have expected or even to have desired. Let us estimate our own sensations
& consider, if those of a father be acute what must be those of a mother.
What should we think of a woman who would resign her infant child with
no prospect of ever seeing it again, even to a father in whose tenderness she
                                    forces
15 *entirely confided? If she ~~brings~~ herself to such a sacrifize for the sake of*
her childs welfare, there is something heroically great in thus trampling upon
the strongest affections & even the most unappeasable instincts of our nature.
But the world will not judge so: she will be despised as an unnatural mother
20 *even by those who might see little to condemn in her becoming a mother with-*
out the formalities of marriage. She would thus resign her only good, &
take to herself, in its' stead, contempt on every hand. Besides she might say,
"What assurance have I of the tenderness of the father for his child, if he
treats the feelings of the mother with so little consideration?" Not to mention,
25 *that the child itself would on this supposition grow up either in ignorance*
or in contempt of one of its parents; a state of things full of danger. — I

SC 475 *know the arguments present in your mind on this subject; but surely rank*
& reputation & prudence are as nothing in comparison to a mother's claims.
If it should be recorded that you had sought to violate these, the opinion of
30   *the world might indeed be fixed on you with such blame as your friends could*
not justify; & wholly unlike those ridiculous & unfounded tales which are
          your friends
told of every person of eminent powers & which made us so merry in England
at the the expense of those who fabricated them. I assure you, my dear Lord
35   *Byron, I speak earnestly & sincerely.— It is not that I wish to make out*
a case for Clare: my interest as you must be aware is entirely on the opposite
side. Nor have I in any manner influenced her: I have esteemed it a duty to
leave her to the impulse of her own feelings in a case where if she has no
feeling she has no claim. But in truth, if she is to be brought to part with her
40   *child, she requires reassurance & tenderness. A tie so near the heart should*
not be rudely snapt. It was in this persuasion that I hoped (I had a thousand
other reasons for wishing to see you) that you would have accepted our invi-
tation to the Pliniana.– Clare's pain would then have been mitigated by the
prospect of seeing her child with you.– Are you not to & she would have
45   *been reassured of the fears which your letter has just confirmed, by the idea*
of a repitition of the visit. Your conduct must at present wear the aspect of
great cruelty however you justify it to yourself. Surely it is better if we err,
to err on the side of kindness than of rigor. You can stop when you please,
& you are not so infirm of purpose that soothing words & gentle conduct
50   *need betray you in essential matters further than you mean to go.*

I am a third person in this painful controversy, who, in the invidious
office of mediation, can have no interest but in the interest of those concerned.
I am now deprived of the power to act, but I would willingly persuade.

Let me You know my motives, & therefore I do not fear to ask you
55   *again to come to see us at Como, & for the sake of your child's welfare to*
          As I understand
soothe Clare's wounded feelings by some reassurances in the meanwhile. You
her, with these assurances she would send the child.
are afraid perhaps that she might be inclined to teize you, but her first
60   *impression on seeing your letter (which by the bye I did not mean her to see)*
was that if your coming to see us depended upon her absence she would

SC 475 *willingly place herself in pension in the city during that period. But in fact, so far as gossip is concerned if you have any motive for caring about it, they cannot say more at Como than they do at Venice. You have no idea*

65 *of the absurd stories which the multitude believe of you, but which every person of sense, & indeed every enlightened circle of our own countrymen laugh at. This is the common lot of all who have distinguished themselves among men. When Dante walked thro' the streets, the old women pointed at him & said– "That is the man who went to Hell with Virgil: see how his*

70 *beard is singed." Stories unlike this, but to the full as improbable & monstrous are propagated of you at Venice.– but I know not wherefore you should regard them. With us you would find a sincere & frank welcome, & as we should be all unknown, or might be, I can see no loophole for calumny.*

If your messenger arrives before Clare & you have come to an under-
75 *standing on this subject, I shall detain him until further orders, unless your instructions are explicit <   >at he shall not stay. — Allegra has an English nurse, a very clean & good tempered young woman, whom in case of a termination of these melancholy differences I can safely recommend to you.*

The expenses of which you speak have been in our family so extremly
80 *trifling, that I know not how to name any sum that will not leave me, what I cannot accept, a pecuniary profit. Perhaps you will be kind enough not to place me in so degrading a situation as to estimate a matter of this kind. —*

I feel confident that you will attribute to its right motive the earnestness with which I have written on this painful subject & believe me my dear
85 *Lord B. Most sincerely attached to your interest & honor.*

P.B.Shelley.

Allegra is daily improving in beauty, but she is suffering just now from cutting her teeth.

[Address, page 6]
Right Hon.
90   *Lord Byron*
aux soins de Messrs Siri & Wilhelm
            Banquiers
            Venice

Shelley to Byron
April 22, 1818

SC 475   line 1. *concieve* (sic).

line 5. *Allegra's*: followed by random marks, perhaps of later date.

line 13. *would*: written through *should*.

line 16. *sacrifize* (sic).

line 19. *will*: second *will* written through *would* or vice versa.

line 27. *mind on*: between these words is a stray ink mark resembling a period.

line 33. *made*: *d* written through *k*.

line 34. *the the* (sic).

line 40. *A*: written through *To*.

line 46. *repitition* (sic).

line 59. *teize*: the usual form of the obsolete spelling was *teise*.

line 71. *propagated*: second *a* may be an *o*.

Venice: two periods follow *Venice*, the second apparently because the first was too high.

line 72. *frank*: *k* written through *?o*.

line 76. *explicit*: *licit* practically illegible because the portion torn off when the seal was broken has been pasted back very unevenly.

<th>at: obscured by seal.

line 79. *extremly* (sic).

line 85. *interest & honor.*: written at the bottom of page 5 in the middle of the line, next to signature.

line 87. *Allegra . . . teeth.*: the postscript is written on the top flap of the address page.

daily: *dai* written through *eve*.

S HELLEY's letter written at Milan on April 13 was stamped as received in Venice on April 17, and Byron's reply, written on April 17, reached Shelley on April 21. The general tone of Byron's lost letter can be inferred from the above reply by Shelley and from Claire's answer, which is in the Murray archives and has been published in part in *"To Lord Byron."*[1]

Byron would not come to Como to visit the Shelleys, fearing that any new association with Claire might be misconstrued by her and lead her to renew her unwelcome pursuit of him.[2] Byron may have declared — as he did to Hobhouse, to whom he also wrote on April 17 on another matter — that he would not "stir from Venice — by anything but absolute force."[3] He seems also to have hinted strongly that he himself did not wish to see Claire again, a sentiment which appeared to threaten Claire's chances of seeing Allegra in the future.

Shelley probably took too personally Byron's refusal to visit him at Como. Byron was already irritated with Hanson, his London attorney,

1. George Paston and Peter Quennell, *"To Lord Byron": Feminine Profiles* (London, 1939), pp. 234–235.

2. The tone and substance of Byron's letters from Venice to his English correspondents show that he was overcoming any shame he may have once felt about his amours being the staple of English gossip — though he used his irritation at such gossip as an excuse to avoid unwelcome acquaintance. See Marchand, *Byron*, II, 739, 740, 747, 752–753, 767–768.

3. Byron, *Correspondence*, II, 77; see also II, 78, 80.

The Carl H. Pforzheimer Library

SC 475   for wanting him to travel all the way to Geneva to sign some legal documents,[4] and he could hardly have expressed himself to Shelley in a tone
more flippant and emphatic than that in which he addressed his friends
Hobhouse and Kinnaird in England. Shelley, suspecting that his letter
to Byron from Lyon might not have really miscarried (see line 1) and
remembering Byron's long period of silence following Allegra's birth,
probably felt not only that Byron's outright rejection of Claire was cruel
in itself but that it might be a sign of indifference toward himself or
hostility toward the child. Then, too, Shelley had heard stories of Byron's
licentious life in Venice (lines 62–67 and 70–71),[5] which did nothing to
reassure him or Claire.

In this letter Shelley assumes the role of a concerned mediator who
has too great respect for Byron to allow him to trample on the feelings
of the mother or disregard the welfare of the child. His sincerity in this
stance is beyond question. The depth of his feelings for Allegra appears
most clearly, perhaps, in his idealized portrait of the child, with his
hopeful projection of her future, in *Julian and Maddalo*.[6] Shelley reiterates his position by refusing to set a price on his services to Allegra — the
full cost of the child's birth and care until fifteen months old — and by
emphasizing that it is Byron and Claire who must "come to an understanding" on the question of Allegra's future (lines 74–75).[7]

Shelley's fullest argument against Claire's complete surrender of her
child is based on two questions of *appearances*. First, even were Claire
to give up Allegra from the best of motives — the ultimate welfare of
her child — she would *appear* to the world to be heartless. Here Shelley
may have had in mind the negative example of Rousseau, who left each
of his children on the doorstep of a foundling home and then duly recorded his actions and motives in his *Confessions*. (Critics naturally
seized upon this confession to discredit all doctrines of justice and philan-

---

4. Some of these documents were apparently related to the sale of Byron's property at Newstead.
One of them may have been a codicil to Byron's will making a bequest to Allegra. See SC 506. For
details on Byron's irritation at Hanson's request and his determination to remain in Venice, see
letters to Kinnaird and Hobhouse in Byron, *Correspondence*, II, 65, 77–80, 82, 85, 90.

5. Dowden, *Shelley*, II, 198–199.

6. See *Julian and Maddalo*, lines 142–157, 583–595.

7. Byron had not been communicating with Claire directly for some time (see SC 472, SC 477 and
Commentaries).

SC 475   thropy emanating from a philosopher whose circle of responsibility did not extend even to his own offspring.) Shelley's second point is that, in forcing Claire to relinquish all intercourse with her child, Byron would himself appear to be callous and cruel to a mother's natural feelings. Shelley's letter is a very skillfully pointed rhetorical appeal aimed at Byron's self-interest and self-respect.

Shelley must have written this letter on the morning of April 22, for both Mary and Claire record on that day a call by Mr. Merryweather, Byron's messenger, whom Shelley had not seen when he wrote this (lines 74–76).[8] Allegra's English nurse, to whom Shelley refers in this letter, was Amelia ("Milly") Shields, whose aunt lived at Little Marlow. As we shall see (SC 477), she remained with the Shelleys, while Elise, the Swiss nurse, went to Venice with Allegra and Francis Merryweather.

8. On Francis Merryweather, see Marchand, *Byron*, II, 732–733 and note. The original documents and a copy of the pamphlet by Leonardo Olschki describing them, to which Marchand refers in his note, are now in The Carl H. Pforzheimer Library.

SC 476   J. F. NEWTON TO T. J. HOGG, APRIL 25, 1818

AL signed *John Frank Newton*, 3 pages. Double sheet, 4to (9 x 7.4 inches).
Wove paper. Watermark: 1812|.
Seal: wax, red: [head of a Renaissance man]|.
Postal fee: 10.
Postmarks: 1. (dated mileage stamp): WEYMOUTH| 25 AP 25| 181[8]| 131|; 2. (dated mileage stamp): WEYMOUTH| 26 AP 26| 181[8]| 131|; 3. (morning duty stamp, London): G| 27 AP 27| 1818|.

PROVENANCE: Thomas Jefferson Hogg; Prudentia Hogg Lonsdale; John Ewer Jefferson Hogg; Major R. J. Jefferson Hogg (Sotheby, July 26, 1948, lot 275).

My dear Sir

    We are no longer inhabitants of the wilderness. Among the gayest buildings of a watering place I have taken a house under the immediate influence of one of the great principles of nature who roars day and
5 *night against the gravel walk which almost touches our walls. This change from the tranquillity of Burgate is not a little welcome to the children, & we*

SC 476   *all hope it will not be very long before your physician (no, I will not be*
careless enough to say that) but rather your inclination may urge you to the
sea-side. Near us is Portland Island & also some other places that deserve
10   *to be visited. Hitherto the weather has scarcely permitted these pleasures. I*
thank you and the Author heartily for the perusal of Rhododaphne. Ere now
probably you want your book again. If so, I will send it up immediately.
Were I a critic, I should indeed have much to say in favour of this elegant
poem. Is Nightmare Abbey out yet? Our young Baronet is I conclude already
15   *on the confines of "il bel paes che l'apennin parte." At his time of life (well*
do I recollect it) the thirst for travelling is not easily controllable, and one
cannot perhaps do better, if otherwise disengaged, than give way to it. From
these delights and fatigues you, my very good friend, are at present debarred
or exempted by your professional labours, and you have my ardent wishes
20   *that you may soon bring together a considerable fortune. How were you*
satisfied with the northern circuit? Will the Dorchester Assizes be likely ever
to draw you in the direction of Weymouth? That county town is eight miles
from us. My children have already got a french and a music master. As
to all instruction we are well provided here. Coals are at a reasonable pli
25   *price, vegetables abundant, the air delightful, the bathing perhaps the best*
in England. All this talkative little circle desire to be kindly remembered
to Mʳ Jefferson, who will have the goodness to present my best wishes to
my old acquaintances who are good enough sometimes to speak of me, and
not fail to believe that I ever am most sincerely his

30   *John Frank Newton*

Weymouth
      April 25—
           1818——

[Address, page 4]
Thomas Jefferson Hogg Esqʳ
35   *Nº1 Garden Court*
           Temple
              London

line 15. "*il bel paes . . . parte.*": the phrase may be translated: "the beautiful country which the Apennines divide." See Commentary, below.

Shelley and his Circle : Manuscripts

SC 476   JOHN FRANK NEWTON, whose sociability has already been evidenced in
these volumes, took up Hogg's remark that "no ~~error~~ mistake is so great
as that of living in the wilderness."[1] He did not, however, move his five
motherless children back to London, but to the south coast resort of
Weymouth, Dorset.[2] From Newton's description, his family must have
lived on or very near the Esplanade, a fashionable street separated from
the sea — "one of the great principles of nature" — only by a street and
a walk. The presence at Weymouth of a theater, regular public dances,
and libraries, assured the Newton children the cultural advantages so
important to their formative years in the English social context, and the
clientele of such a resort increased Newton's own chances of enjoying the
sort of intellectual discussion on which his "talkative little circle" obviously throve. Another recommendation advanced by Newton — the
cheapness of provisions — is verified (for the earlier, war years, at least)
by Feltham's *Guide*. Finally, Newton — who had suffered from ill-health
most of his life — may have been attracted to Weymouth by its salt-
water baths and the medicinal mineral springs at nearby Nottington.

In *Alumni Oxonienses* the entry for Augustus Newton describes his
father, John Frank, as living in Begbrooke, Oxfordshire, and his profession as "army." The "John Newton" appearing in the *Army Lists*,
at least for the years from 1803 through 1830, as a half-pay lieutenant
in the 15th Dragoons was probably John Frank Newton. Although the
family moved to Weymouth in 1818 and was living there when Newton's
Three Enigmas Attempted to be Explained was published in 1821, they must
have moved to Begbrooke (a village between Oxford and Woodstock)
about the time Augustus matriculated in 1822. They later returned to
Weymouth, for Newton inscribed a copy of his *Return to Nature* to Fanny
Burney at "Weymouth, 25 August 1827"; and he died there in 1837.[3]

1. See sc 462.

2. For an account of Weymouth and its rise to prominence as a bathing resort, see John Feltham's
Guide to . . . Watering and Sea-Bathing Places (London: Richard Phillips, 1804), pp. 429–441. Henry
Fielding's friend Ralph Allen of Bath had introduced bathing machines at Weymouth about 1760,
and visits by members of the royal family beginning in 1789 had made it by 1804 "one of the most
fashionable of all the sea-bathing places." Portland Island (line 9) was a tourist attraction near
Weymouth famous for a castle dating from the reign of Henry VIII and for its honest and fun-
loving peasantry.

3. Cameron, *The Young Shelley*, p. 371.

The Carl H. Pforzheimer Library

sc 476   Nowhere in his draft letter to Newton of February 25 does Hogg mention *Nightmare Abbey*; he may have added a reference to it in the final version of the letter he sent, but Peacock's letter to Hogg postmarked April 28, 1818 (sc 473) indicates that Peacock had not previously told Hogg about that "comic romance." Thus Newton seems to have known about *Nightmare Abbey* before Hogg did, and the obvious explanation is that Peacock wrote directly to Newton in the interval, mentioning his plans for the novel.

Peacock described *Nightmare Abbey* to Shelley early in its composition.[4] He felt, no doubt, that before the book appeared he must declare his general purpose to those friends who might find their partial likenesses in the novel, so that they would not become hurt or angry. It has become a commonplace to say that in *Nightmare Abbey* Peacock caricatured John Frank Newton in the character of Mr. Toobad, "the Manichæan Millenarian," whose gloomy refrain throughout the novel is: "Woe to the inhabiters of the earth and of the sea! for the devil is come among you, having great wrath . . ."[5] Newton expressed in his conversation and writings ideas that are put into the mouth of Mr. Toobad, but neither the anecdotes about his way of life that appear in Shelley biographies, nor his published writings, nor his letters in these volumes (sc 383 and sc 476) suggest a gloomy disposition or any constitutional resemblance to Mr. Toobad. In the preface to the 1856 edition of *Melincourt*, Peacock declared that, though he had treated the "opinions and public characters" of the disputants "shadowed in some of the persons of the story," he "never trespassed on private life."[6] It is, perhaps, worth the effort of recovering some sense of the personality of John Frank Newton, if only to corroborate, in this particular instance, Peacock's description of his fictional method.

Peacock may have told Newton that Shelley had arrived in Italy early in April. Petrarch was a favorite poet of the Boinville circle at Bracknell, and it is not surprising that Newton here defines Italy in a

---

4. Peacock, *Memoirs*, pp. 193, 195, 198, 202, 204. See Shelley to Peacock, April 20, 1818, Shelley, *Letters*, II, 6.

5. Peacock, *Complete Novels*, I, 361.

6. Peacock, *Complete Novels*, I, 102.

SC 476   phrase (slightly misquoted) from Petrarch's Sonnet cxlvi ("O d'ardente vertute . . ."), which ends:

> Poi che portar no 'l posso in tutte e quattro
> Parti del mondo, udrallo il bel paese
> Ch' Appennin parte e 'l mar circonda e l'Alpe.[7]

In speaking of Shelley's travels, Newton alludes to his own earlier wanderlust. Most of our knowledge of Newton's life before he met Shelley comes from his own writings. From his *Early Days of . . . George Canning . . . and of Some of His Contemporaries* (London, 1828) we learn that Newton graduated from Harrow, returned for a time to his childhood home on St. Christopher's (St. Kitts) Island in the West Indies, and attended Christ Church, Oxford (matriculated July 8, 1786), where he was a leading member of a secret debating society that included (Sir) William Drummond, George Canning, Robert Banks Jenkinson (later Lord Liverpool), Lord Henry Spencer, and Charles Goddard (private secretary to Lord Grenville and later Archdeacon of Lincoln). Newton then perhaps for reasons of health returned to St. Kitts, where Canning wrote him a long letter dated September 1, 1788. At that time Newton was contemplating a trip to the Continent. According to comments in *The Return to Nature* (London, 1811), Newton traveled in both Spain and Italy, having been at Rome in 1794. By 1809 he and his family were living at Chester Street, Grosvenor Place, London, where they still resided when Shelley met them on November 5, 1812.[8]

The most important implication of Newton's early friendships was that he may have reinforced Shelley's interest in the works of Sir William Drummond, whose *Academical Questions* Shelley first mentioned (somewhat critically) in the note to *Queen Mab*, VII.13 ("There is no God"), but afterward spoke of with highest praise.[9]

7. Francesco Petrarca, *Le Rime*, ed. Giosuè Carducci and Severino Ferrari, revised by Gianfranco Contini (Florence: Sansoni, 1960), p. 233.

8. See Dowden, *Shelley*, I, 306–307.

9. See C. E. Pulos, *The Deep Truth: A Study of Shelley's Scepticism* (University of Nebraska Press, 1954).

The Carl H. Pforzheimer Library

SC 477 P. B. SHELLEY TO LORD BYRON, APRIL 28, 1818

AL signed *P. B. Shelley.*, 3¼ pages. 1 single sheet, 1 double sheet, 4ᵗᵒ (9.7 x 7.6 inches).
Wove paper.
Seal: wax, red: [Judgment of Paris]|.

PROVENANCE: Lord Byron; Lord Broughton (John Cam Hobhouse); Lady Dorchester; Sir John Murray; A. S. W. Rosenbach. *De Ricci 378* (p. 33).

Milan, April 28. 1818.

My dear Lord Byron

It certainly gave me much pleasure to be able to bring your little girl to Italy, as indeed I was puzzled to find a person to trust
5 *her with: but the purpose of my journey was, I lament to say, in no manner connected with it. My health which has always been declining had assumed such symptoms that the physicians advised me to proceed without delay to a warmer climate.*

Allow me also to repeat my assertion that Clare's late conduct with
10   *& uninfluenced by*
respect to the child was wholly unconnected with ₍ₐ₎*me. Her conduct was nothing—The correspondence from which these misinterpretations have arisen was undertaken on my part solely because you refused to correspond with Clare. My conduct in the affair has been simple & intelligible.   I am sorry*
15   *both*
that I misunderstood your letter, & I hope that on all sides there is here an end of misunderstandings.

You will find your little Allegra quite well. I think she is the most lovely & engaging child I ever beheld, tell us what you think of her, & whether or
20 *no she equals your expectation. Her attendant is not the servant whom I alluded to in my last letter, but a Swiss, who has attended my own children, in whom Mʳˢ S. intirely confides, & who even quits us somewhat unwillingly; —Mary & whom Mary parts with solely that Clare & yourself may be assured that Allegra will be attended almost with a Mothers' care.— Her*
25 *wages are 18 louis a year*
Clare as you may imagine is dreadfully unhappy. As you have not

[574]

Shelley to Byron   *April 28, 1818*

SC 477   *written to her it has been a kind of custom that she should see your letters,*
& I dare say you know that you have sometimes said things which I do I
do not think you would have addressed to her. It could not in any way com-
30   *promise you to be cautious in this respect, as unless you write to her, I*
cannot well refuse to let her see your letters. I have not seen any of those
which she has written to you, nor even have I often known when they were
sent.

　　You will recieve your packets of books. Hunt sends you one he has
35   *lately published , & I am commissioned by an old friend of yours to convey*
of the author

Frankenstein to you, & to request that if you conjecture the name that you
will regard it as a secret. In fact it is M^rs S's.   It has met with considerable
success in England, but she bids me say "that she will re^c would regard
40   *your approbation as a more flattering testimony of its' merit"*

　　Address your next letter "Poste Restante Pisa." As we leave Milan for
that city tomorrow.— We have been dissappointed in our house at Como;
& indeed I shall attempt to divert Clare's melancholy by availing myself of
some introductions at Pisa. Clare is wretchedly disconsolate & I know not
45   *how I shall calm her until the return of Post. I ought to say that we shall be*
at Pisa long before the return of Post.——— when we expect (pray dont
dissappoint us) a letter 　　　　*My dear Lord Byron*
from you to assure us of 　　　　　*Yours always sincerely*
　　P S
the safe arrival of our little 　　　　　　*P. B. Shelley.*
50   *favourite. Ni M^rs S Mary begs to unite with me in best regards & to express*
her affection & anxiety about little Allegra, whom she has been accustomed
to regard almost as one of her own children.—

　　I ought to say that by an unfortunate mistake I left behind me the
2^d part of the voyage to Corea & a Poem called Beppo which Murray had
55   *sent to me for you. Peacock has a parcel for me which I expect at Midsummer*
in which these will be included. Elise's wages with us were 20 louis

[Address, page 6]
To the Right Honble
　　Lord Byron

The Carl H. Pforzheimer Library

Shelley to Byron

April 28, 1818

line 12. *nothing*: probable reading.

line 22. *in*: *i* written through *a*.
    intirely (sic).

line 25. *year*: written through another canceled word.

line 27. *her*: *h* written through *y*.

line 34. *recieve* (sic).

line 35. *published* ,: Shelley seems to have started a new word with *?s*; he then canceled the letter, changing it into a comma.

line 37. *conjecture*: Shelley seems to have omitted the final *e*.

line 42. *dissappointed* (sic).

line 45. *her*: the word was first written lightly and then written over for clarity.

line 46. *when we*: the text from *when* to the end (line 56) was added after Shelley had originally closed and signed the letter.

line 47. *dissappoint* (sic).

line 56. *Elise's . . . louis*: written in Mary Shelley's hand.

line 57. The address is in Mary Shelley's hand.

SHELLEY'S LETTER to Byron written the morning of April 22 must have gone almost immediately into a mail bag bound for Venice, for it was stamped received in that city on April 23. Byron's half-irritated, half-humorous reaction is recorded in his letter to Hobhouse of April 24:

> Shelley has got to Milan with the bastard, and its mother; but won't send the shild, unless I will go and see the mother. I have sent a messenger for the shild, but I can't leave my quarters, and have "sworn an oath." Between attorneys, clerks, and wives, and children, and friends, my life is made a burthen . . . .[1]

To settle the matter without further trouble, Byron replied promptly in a conciliatory letter (now lost) that reached Shelley on April 27.[2] Byron must have denied any intention of cutting off Claire completely from her daughter, for Shelley apologizes for misunderstanding Byron's previous letter. Byron, it seems, also thanked Shelley for the trouble to which he had gone in bringing Allegra to Italy, to which Shelley graciously replies that he would have undertaken that trip in any case because of his health. In response to what must have been complaints about Claire's behavior, Shelley dissociates himself from her conduct — though he does not intimate that he thought her unreasonable (lines 9–17).

Byron obviously suspected that the invitation to Como had been intended to draw him and Claire together again. Whether because he was contented with his life (and sex-life) in Venice or because he did not wish to hurt Claire any more emotionally, or simply because he heartily disliked her, Byron preferred to keep his distance from her. That he was

1. Byron, *Correspondence*, II, 79.
2. Mary Shelley, *Journal*.

Shelley and his Circle : Manuscripts

SC 477   correct in his estimate of Claire's emotional involvement seems clear not only from the portions of her letters of 1817–1818 published in "*To Lord Byron*," but also from her later reflections. In a manuscript obviously written after Byron's death, beginning "Silly thoughtless Teresa!," Claire demonstrated that her jealousy of Byron's other loves remained even after her affection for him had turned to bitterness or even hatred. She writes:

> Albè was familiar from his earliest years with every form of vice — hypocritical envious, mean suspicious and to an unparalelled degree revengeful . . . a man who delighted in mystery in secrets, in intrigue. . . . It was to gratify this . . . craving for intrigue that he never plunged into one attachment that demanded no plotting no planning; . . . a man with a straight forward honest mind, placed in his situation, rejected by his wife would have attached himself to a young unmarried girl and established her in his house as if she were his wife and would have lived with a certain [?] sort of respectability with her.[3]

If Claire believed, even after Byron's death, that he should have contracted a permanent alliance (such as Mary and Shelley had done), clearly she hoped and intended, between 1816 and 1818, to become that "young unmarried girl." When Byron had made plain that he intended to assume responsibility for Allegra without resuming his relationship with Claire, Claire was persuaded — perhaps by Mary[4] — to send the child to Venice with Francis Merryweather.

The Shelleys' decision to send Elise rather than Milly Shields with Allegra is curious. Shelley's explanation here sounds reasonable enough, but were there reasons of greater significance behind the choice? Several possibilities suggest themselves: First, Elise could read and write, whereas

---

3. Manuscript in The Carl H. Pforzheimer Library.

4. Some scholars believe on the basis of Shelley's statement to Claire in a letter of March 1822, that Shelley advised her against sending Allegra to Byron (Shelley, *Letters*, II, 400). But the rather confused words of Shelley — especially if one follows Jones's text rather than Dowden's (*Shelley*, II, 199–200) or Prothero's (Byron, *Letters and Journals*, V, 501–502) — give little scope for such a judgment. In their context, Shelley's statements simply mean that he once told Claire that the sending of Allegra to Byron in 1818 was irrevocable. As he puts it most forcefully, "let the *past* be *the* past. —" In April 1818 Shelley probably warned Claire against her perpetual hope that through Allegra she could win Byron's love; he may have told her not to send Allegra to Byron if *this* was her expectation, and he may have given some conditional warnings about Byron's character. But the main force of his argument in the letter of March 1822 is to persuade Claire not to compound his and her problems by provoking Byron's further wrath. To get her to accept the past, he emphasizes that the decision to send Allegra to Byron was primarily hers in the first place.

SC 477   there is no evidence that Milly Shields could.[5] Was Elise sent simply so that she could write Claire direct reports about Allegra (and, perhaps, about Byron)? Or, a second possibility: Did Milly Shields — who was probably homesick for England[6] — refuse to exchange life with the Shelleys for the unknown mercies of Byron's household? Or did Elise prefer staying in Venice (relatively close to her Swiss home) to traveling south into Italy with the Shelleys?

Any one or a combination of the above possibilities might have figured in the decision to send Elise to Venice with Allegra. But looming in the distance one sees the so-called "Hoppner scandal" — the mystery of "Shelley's Neapolitan child." Elena Adelaide Shelley was born, according to the records, on December 27, 1818.[7] If we count back the "normal" gestation period of 270 days to April 1 and allow for the possibility that the child could have been born anywhere from two months early[8] to two weeks late, we find that Elena Adelaide was conceived sometime between March 15 and June 1, 1818, with a high probability that the date fell between April 1 and April 15. The exchange of duties between Elise and Milly may be in some way related to the "Hoppner scandal," and in the full examination of that problem in later volumes, we shall explore such possibilities and their implications.[9]

Shelley had written to Murray before he left London, offering to carry books to Byron,[10] and this letter confirms Murray's acceptance of the offer. Though he failed to deliver *Beppo* and either John McLeod's *Narrative of a Voyage in His Majesty's late Ship Alceste to the Yellow Sea,*

---

5. Claire or the Shelleys received letters from Elise on May 8, August 14, and August 16, 1818. Claire wrote to Elise on July 10–11, 1818. Two of Elise's letters of 1822 are printed in *Shelley and Mary*, pp. 786–787. On Milly's lack of communication with her family, see Shelley to Peacock, November 6, 1818, Shelley, *Letters*, II, 48, and Peacock's reply of November 29, 1818, Peacock, *Works*, VIII, 209.

6. See Mary Shelley, *Letters*, I, 64, on Milly's homesickness.

7. For the documents on the birth, baptism, and death of Elena Adelaide Shelley, see White, *Shelley*, II, 546–550.

8. Elena's birth was registered on February 27, 1819, and the declared date of her birth (December 27) may not be correct. She could, conceivably, have been born at some date between December 27 and February 27.

9. For two accounts of the "Hoppner scandal," see White, *Shelley*, II, 306–315, and Ursula Orange, "Elise, Nursemaid to the Shelleys," *Keats-Shelley Memorial Bulletin*, VI (1955), 24–34.

10. Shelley, *Letters*, I, 598.

Shelley and his Circle : Manuscripts

SC 477   *along the Coast of Corea* or Basil Hall's *Account of a Voyage of Discovery to the West Coast of Corea*, he did send Hunt's *Foliage*, Mary Shelley's *Frankenstein*, and probably Godwin's *Mandeville* and his own *Revolt of Islam*.[11]

The "introductions at Pisa" that Shelley mentions (line 44) probably refer simply to those that Godwin had written for Mary to Margaret King Moore, Countess of Mount Cashell, who lived at Pisa, and to Maria Gisborne, who lived at Leghorn (see sc 465 and Commentary). The proximity of Pisa to Leghorn may have induced Shelley to lump together letters of introduction to people in both places. Lady Mount Cashell, as a girl of fourteen to fifteen years, had been a pupil of Mary Wollstonecraft for a year. In the summer of 1800, Godwin visited Dublin and met her several times.[12] In 1805 she had left her husband to live with George William Tighe as "Mr. and Mrs. Mason."[13] In 1807 she visited the Godwins in London, and in 1814–1815 Mary Jane Godwin wrote several times to her at Leghorn when the Godwins feared that Shelley and Mary were on their way to Italy (with Claire) following their elopement.[14] The Godwins had then warned the "Masons" against Shelley, and this is probably why Mary insisted that Godwin write her a letter of introduction to Lady Mount Cashell under the changed circumstances of 1818.[15]

We know of no one else in Italy to whom the Shelleys carried letters besides Mrs. Gisborne and Lady Mount Cashell. From Mary's letter of May 13 to the Hunts, it seems clear that Mrs. Partridge of Leghorn, an aunt of Robert Benjamin Haydon whom they visited on June 5, was

11. The books by McLeod and Hall — published by Murray in 1817 and 1818 respectively — were both one-volume works; since one was quarto and the other octavo, it is unclear how Shelley could have thought that one (presumably Hall's more recently published *Account*) was the second part of the other. On some of the books Shelley did send, see sc 437 and Commentary. Byron first mentions *The Revolt of Islam* in his letter to Murray of November 24, 1818 (*Letters and Journals*, IV, 273).

12. Godwin describes her in a letter to Marshal dated by Kegan Paul August 2, 1800 (*Godwin*, I, 369–370).

13. For the story of Lady Mount Cashell's life, see McAleer, *The Sensitive Plant*.

14. For a detailed description of this correspondence and a critique of its factualness, see Dowden, *Shelley*, II, 541–551.

15. Godwin's strange letter of introduction is in the Abinger Manuscripts, Pforzheimer Microfilm, reel V, file 7. It is possible, McAleer argues, that Shelley met Lady Mount Cashell as early as 1812 at Godwin's (*The Sensitive Plant*, p. 123).

SC 477 introduced to them by the Gisbornes rather than through a letter from England.

For some reason the Shelleys did not meet Lady Mount Cashell during their first visit to Pisa. They set out from Milan on May 1, 1818, and arrived at Pisa on May 7, 1818. After receiving a letter from Elise the following day, they left Pisa for Leghorn on May 9. Mary's Journal records no calls during their brief stay in Pisa. It is possible that the "Masons" had retired for the summer to one of the resorts in the cooler mountains or to the Baths of San Giuliano, where the Shelleys summered in 1820 and later.[16]

16. Mary Shelley, *Letters*, I, 52.

SC 478 E. J. TRELAWNY TO AUGUSTA WHITE, APRIL 29, [1818]

AL signed *Trelawny*, 3 pages. Double sheet, 4to (8.8 x 7.3 inches).
Wove paper. Watermark: BASTED MILL| 1816|.
Seal (traces): wax, red.
Notations in pencil: 1. (page 1, upper right corner): *1818* [second *8* written through *9*]; 2. (page 4): *April 28th| 1818|.

PROVENANCE: Augusta White Draper; Misses Kathleen and Molly Draper of Montreal; Gannon, May 1943.

April 29th
The multiplicity of business during my transitory sojourn in Town,
precluded the pleasure of seeing you as much as I could have wished, and a
                                                    away
5   *sudden thought took me from Town sooner than I had intended,*

Fatigu'd at last, a calm retreat I chose,
And sooth'd my haras'd mind with sweet repose,
Tis not that rural sports alone invite,
But all the grateful country breathes delight;

10   *In sooth my mind & body requier reteirement, I begin to feel the effects,*
of my long smothered passions, and fear me their long rooted residance in
my bosom, has gradually undermined my health, for off late I have had
frequent billious attack's,   Let me hear how your Mother goes on, I am

Trelawny to White   *April 29, [1818]*

SC 478 *very busy putting Trelawny's Villa in fit state to receive its illustrious owner,*
I need not say, as you have heard a catalogue of its state, how important
the task is, it in deed requieres all my well known activity, & ingenuity, to
do justice to the internal splendours and external magnificence of this princly
habitation, am happy to report that all things are going on as well, and
with as much expedition as the extent of the undertaking will allow!

20   *A very short time will again call me to Town, tell me how Turner*
    is   my best condolence with him!

                    Tell Mrs Tolson I cannot reenter Town till she is bound in sureties
    to keep the peace, for she parted in such heat, & fiery fury as betoken's,
                                                                    acts
25 *deeds of dreadful note! and Sarah's discription of the dire ~~deeds~~, done in*
    those lapses from reason, scribed so forcibly on my mind, as with the little
    strenth fear had left me I hastened to find safty in ignoble flight, for valour
    I have heard say will come, and, go, and now I find ti's so! for mine was
    not proof against her <   >dy looks, and saucee glaring eyes,

30   *My fair & amiable nurse is the post of my conveyance–*
                    Say When the Jhonstons will be in Town! In good faith
                                                    thy
                                                    Trelawny
                                                    Cannon. Farm
35   *near Pinner*
                                                    Middx.

[Address, page 4]
                    Miss Crust White
                    118– Long Acre
                    Covent Garden

In this volume, as in Volume V, we omit nearly all references to Trelawny's misspellings and miswritings. See SC 379, Commentary.

line 1. *29th*: *9* written through *8*.

line 12. *off*: possibly *oft*.

line 13. *Mother*: written at the bottom of page 1 as a catchword but not repeated; the same is true of *discription* (line 25).

line 31. *Jhonstons*: for *Johnsons*.

A FTER A GAP of five months in the correspondence of Trelawny with Augusta, we find Augusta in London — presumably staying with her mother at Mrs. Tolson's home on Longacre Street, Covent Garden

The Carl H. Pforzheimer Library

Shelley to Hogg   *April 30, 1818*

SC 478 (SC 460, Commentary). Sarah (line 25) seems to be Mrs. Tolson's daughter (compare SC 415 and SC 417, Commentary). During the interim, it seems, Trelawny escorted Augusta from Bath to London. Now he has retreated from London, perhaps for his health and perhaps also, as his comments on his "long smothered passions" suggest, because of the danger in his proximity to Augusta.

Trelawny's movements, seen in the light of the course of his earlier letters to Augusta, take on the character of a strategic withdrawal from the obligation to give substance to the sky-castles he and Augusta together had created. We may imagine her urging him to elope with her (what had she to lose?), while he expatiated on his fraternal feelings for her, his duty to her mother and sisters, and his unwillingness to surrender to ignoble, lower passions. Perhaps — but this is pure speculation — Mrs. Tolson's quarrel with Trelawny (lines 22–29) stemmed from his ambiguous treatment of Augusta.

Pinner, Middlesex, the address of Trelawny's cottage (a very humble one, to judge from his banter about his "princely habitation"), was a hamlet fourteen miles from London and only three miles northwest of Harrow-on-the-Hill, site of Byron's school. Trelawny closes the letter much more formally than those written across the safe distance from London to Bath.

In line 30 Trelawny tells us how he has sent the letter to London. Who, one wonders, was his "fair & amiable nurse" and what ministrations had been prescribed for one ill from "long smothered passions"?

SC 479 P. B. SHELLEY TO T. J. HOGG, APRIL 30, 1818

AL signed *P. B Shelley*, 3 pages. Double sheet, 4to (9.7 x 7.7 inches).
Wove paper.
Seal (trace): wax, red.
Postal fee: 1/ 11.
Postmark: [trace, red]|.
Additions: 1. seal tear and fold tears mended; 2. (page 4): address canceled so heavily that ink stains affect clarity of some words on pages 1–3.

PROVENANCE: George Manners (Sotheby, June 14, 1870, lot 768); Alfred Morrison (by 1884; Sotheby, December 9, 1918, III, lot 2567). *De Ricci 379* (p. 134).

Shelley and his Circle : Manuscripts

SC 479   *Milan, April 30. 1818.*

My dear friend

     I recieved your note a few hours before I left England: &
have designed to write to you from every town on the route, but the difficulty
5 *not so much of knowing what to say as how to say it prevented me till this*
moment. I was sorry that I did not see you again before my departure. On
my return which will not perhaps take place so soon as I at first expected
we shall meet again; meanwhile my letters to Hunt & Peacock are as it
were common property, of which if you feel any curiosity about me which
10 *I neglect to satisfy myself, your are at liberty to avail yourself of. — To-*
morrow we leave this city for Pisa, where or in its neighbourhood we shall
remain during the summer.

     The Italians— at least those whom I have seen—are a very different
people from the French. They have less character; & the women especially
15 *seem a very inferior race of beings. Thier manners so far as I can judge*
from their mein & phisiognomy are at once prudish & coquettish, their
features bony, their figures thin, & those who have any claims to beauty,
have a beauty superficial, & of a cold & unfeeling character. Their voices
have none of that winning persuasiveness of those of France, but are hard,
20 *& without inflexion or variety of tone. But this holds good as I know only*
to Milan, as my experience extends no further. The Architecture of the
Cathedral of this city exceeds any thing I ever saw in the Gothic style, it is
far superior to York Minster or Westminster Abbey. The Opera is very good
& the house larger, or at least as large as that of London. They have Mad.
25 *Camporesi here as the prima donna – a cold & unfeeling singer & a bad*
actress. The best singer is a man called David. Their ballets, which are a
kind of pantomimic dance illustrative of some story are much superior to
any thing of the kind in England. Indeed they are wholly unlike any thing
*   a*
30 *represented on our stage; being combination of a great number of figures*
grouped with the most picturesque & even poetical effect & perpetually
changing with motions the most harmoniously interwoven & contrasted with
great effect. Othello is represented in one of these ballets & the story is so
well told in action as to leave upon the mind an ap impression as of a real
35 *tragedy.—*

SC 479   *We have been to the Lake of Como, & indeed had some thoughts of taking our residence there for the summer. The scenery is very beautiful, abounding among other things with those green banks for the sake of which, you represented me as wondering over the world. You are more interested*

40   *in the human part of the experience of travelling; a thing of which I see little, & understand less, & which if I saw & understood more I fear I should be little able to describe. I am just reading a Novel of Wielands called Aristippus which I think you would like. It is very greek, tho perhaps not religious enough for a true Pagan. If you can get it otherwise do not*

45   *read it in the French translation, as the impudent translator has omitted much of the original, to accommodate it as he says to the "fastidious taste & powerful understanding of his country men"!–*

three

I have read some greek but not much on my Journey– two or few plays

50   *of Euripides— & among them the Ion which you praised & which <   > is exquisitely beautiful— But I have also made some Italian book my companion from my desire to learn the language so as to speak it. I have been studying the history of Tasso's life with some idea of making a drama of his adventures & misfortunes. How far such a subject would suit English poetry*

55   *I cannot tell. — Address Poste Restante Pisa –*

> *Most sincerely yours*
> *P. B Shelley*

If you see Miss Lamb present my Complts & tell her that I did not pass thro Paris, but that I put her letter in the nearest post— remember me

60   *also to the D^r————*

[Address, page 4]
~~T. Jefferson Hogg~~
      ~~1. <————————>~~
            ~~Temple~~
            London

65   *Angleterre*

Angleterre

line 3. *recieved* (sic).   line 15. *Thier* (sic).
line 10. *yourself of.*: *of* smudged and perhaps can-   line 16. *mein* (sic).
celed.   *phisiognomy* (sic).

Shelley to Hogg   *April 30, 1818*

SC 479

line 19. *winning*: written through *winny*.

line 30. *a*: there is an extra stroke on the *a* indicating that Shelley may have intended to write a longer word.

line 39. *wondering* (sic).

line 47. *men"!*: exclamation point almost obscured by heavy canceling on address page; see Bibliographical Description.

line 49. *two or few*: *two* written through *a*; *few* is a probable reading.

line 50. <   >: seal tear has been mended.

line 54. *far*: probable reading.

line 62. ⟨————————⟩: line has been heavily and repeatedly canceled through, as have lines 61 and 63.

line 66. *Angleterre*: written perpendicular to and to the left of the address.

THE EMOTIONAL distance between Shelley and Hogg can be gauged in part by the fact that Dowden, who first published this letter from the manuscript, thought that it was written to Horace Smith.[1] There are, of course, a few personal touches, but in tone it is certainly unlike those earlier letters that were familiar to Dowden from Hogg's *Shelley*.

The remarks which particularize this letter in terms of Shelley's relations with Hogg in 1818 can be quickly enumerated. In the postscript, Shelley sends a message to Dr. William Lambe and his daughter Mary. Inasmuch as Lambe was a leading vegetarian — the mentor and friend of John Frank Newton[2] — both Shelley's and Hogg's acquaintance with him undoubtedly came through Newton. According to Mary's and Claire's journals, Mary Lambe called on the Shelleys on Tuesday, March 10, the day before they left London. She obviously asked Shelley to mail a letter destined for Paris, and perhaps she also delivered Hogg's

1. Dowden, *Shelley*, II, 200–202. Dowden said that "the address has unfortunately been lost," but Ingpen is more accurate: "Most of the address of this letter is carefully scored through, but some words can still be deciphered" (Shelley, *Complete Works*, IX, 307 n.). The letter is addressed to Hogg, and it is uncertain both how this letter came into George Manners' collection before 1870 (see Provenance) and why the address was scored through.

2. Dr. William Lambe appeared earlier in these volumes as Harriet Shelley's candidate for guardian of Charles Shelley in March 1816 (see sc 327, Appendix, IV). Apparently Lambe's role — passive or active — on Harriet's behalf had not caused a permanent breach between him and Shelley, and this may well have been due to Hogg's good offices. However much Hogg may have ridiculed the enthusiasms of the Newton-Boinville circle (see sc 251, Commentary, III), he clearly developed lasting friendships with two of the chief enthusiasts — John Frank Newton himself and Dr. Lambe. During his Continental tour of 1825–1826, Hogg called on Walter Savage Landor in Florence armed with a letter of introduction from Dr. Lambe, who had been a great friend of Samuel Parr and Landor in Warwick, where he had taken over the practice of Landor's father in 1794. (R[obert] H. Super, *Walter Savage Landor*, New York University Press, 1954, pp. 186, 522–523.) See also H. Saxe Wyndham, *William Lambe, M.D.* (London: London Vegetarian Society, 1940).

SC 479   farewell note, which Shelley received "a few hours" before he left London
(line 3). Shelley's mention of his readings in Greek (and his half-apology
for reading Italian as well), combined with his recommendation of
Christoph Martin Wieland's *Aristippus*[3] as being "very greek, tho perhaps not religious enough for a true Pagan" are characteristic allusions
for a letter directed to Hogg, the would-be "Athenian."

By inviting Hogg to read his letters to Peacock and Hunt, Shelley
shows that he has no objection to Hogg's seeing his political comments
and his personal reactions to travel, but he confines this letter — delayed
not for want of something to say, but on account of uncertainty as to
what tone to adopt (lines 4–6) — to those subjects on which there was
little likelihood of radical controversy.

Shelley's judgments on Italian women show more than anything
else, perhaps, his slight, tourist's acquaintance with the populace. On
April 6, Shelley had written to Peacock that "a ruined arch of magnificent proportions in the Greek taste . . . & a *blonde* woman of light &
graceful manners, something in the style of Fuseli's Eve were the first
things we met in Italy." In July he wrote to Godwin from Bagni di
Lucca: "The modern Italians seem a miserable people — without sensibility or imagination or understanding . . . The women are particularly
empty: and though possessed of the same kind of superficial grace, are
devoid of any cultivation and refinement." In December, after having
spent time with Byron at Venice, Shelley wrote to Peacock: "the Italian
women are perhaps the most contemptible of all who exist under the
moon; the most ignorant the most disgusting, the most bigotted, the
most filthy. Countesses smell so of garlick that an ordinary Englishman
cannot approach them."[4] Not until Shelley reached Rome in the spring
of 1819, where he had more opportunities to mix with upper-class Italians,
did his opinion of Italian women change markedly for the better.[5] Many
years later, Mary Shelley attributed some of Shelley's negative opinions
of Italians to general English prejudices transmitted by travelers and

3. Shelley could have read the work in the German original but Mary and Claire certainly read it
in the French translation that he warns Hogg against. See SC 448, Appendix.

4. Shelley, *Letters*, II, 4, 22, 58. See also Shelley's letters to Hunt, December [?20], 1818 (*Letters*,
II, 67), and to Hogg, December 21, 1818 (SC 510).

5. See Shelley to Peacock, April 6, 1819, Shelley, *Letters*, II, 92–93.

SC 479   travel guides alike.[6] For an estimate of the women, one may compare the opinion of another writer of the period, who cannot be considered overfastidious. William Hazlitt wrote:

> The women in Italy (so far as I have seen hitherto) are detestably ugly. They are not even dark and swarthy, but a mixture of brown and red, coarse, marked with the small pox, with pug-features, awkward, ill-made, fierce, dirty, lazy, neither attempting nor hoping to please. Italian beauty (if there is, as I am credibly informed, such a thing) is retired, conventual, denied to the common gaze. It was and it remains a dream to me, a vision of the brain![7]

Shelley's praise of the cathedral of Milan as the finest Gothic building he had ever seen requires scrutiny. Was this preference a considered one, based on an appreciation of the purposes and effects of its architectural distinctiveness? Or was he simply reflecting the tourists' taste of the time? One must keep in mind that the façade of the Milan cathedral had been completed under the sponsorship of the Napoleonic regime between 1806 and 1813, and that in 1818 the church presented the newest front of any major cathedral in Europe.[8] Claire, praising the edifice in her journal entry of April 9, credits Napoleon with both the façade ("carved pinnacles whiter than snow rise into the clouds") and the marble staircase leading to the roof. Seeing the front of a Gothic structure before time and age had weathered and darkened its surface must have been impressive in itself. In his April 20 letter to Peacock, Shelley had given his opinions of the cathedral at greater length, and there he states that he is more impressed by the exterior, "piercing the solid blue with those groupes of dazzling spires" than by the interior "overloaded with antique figures" — though he had there found a "solitary spot" behind the altar in which to read Dante.[9]

The style of the Milan cathedral is not, of course, pure Gothic. Begun in 1386, when the Gothic impulse was beginning to wane north of the Alps, and built in a country that revered the Greek and Roman architectural orders, it exhibits some peculiarities that distinguish it from the best French, German, and English Gothic. Most of these distinguish-

6. See *Rambles in Germany and Italy in 1840, 1842 and 1843* (London, 1844), I, ix–x, and II, 106–107.

7. *Notes of a Journey through France and Italy* (London, 1826), p. 210.

8. See Carroll L. V. Meeks, *Italian Architecture, 1750–1914* (Yale University Press, 1966), p. 106.

9. Shelley, *Letters*, II, 7–8.

SC 479 ing features move in the direction of simplicity, unity, and symmetry in larger structural design, with superficial elaboration achieved through numerous turrets and pinnacles and the 4,440 statues built into niches throughout the façade and interior and rising from the roof. John Chetwode Eustace, an English Catholic, whose so-called "Classical Tour" of Italy was the most popular travel guide available in Shelley's time, described some of these effects and justified the departures from the Gothic norm:

> The admirer of English Gothic will observe one peculiarity, which is, that in the cathedral of *Milan*, there is no screen, and that the chancel is entirely open, and separated from the nave only by its elevation.
> . . . there are no chapels properly so called, because the Ambrosian rite, which long retained the ancient custom of allowing one altar only, and one service in each church, not having conformed to the modern mode when the cathedral was commenced, no provision was made in the plan for private masses and oratories. This omission contributes much to the simplicity and unity of the edifice.[10]

The great façade of the cathedral had been begun on a baroque plan, incorporating portals and windows designed by Pellegrino Pellegrini in 1567. These merged in the symmetrically proportioned façade, about a fourth again as wide as it is high.

Shelley had previously seen not only York Minster, Westminster Abbey, the Oxford colleges and churches, and other Gothic churches in England, but at least the cathedrals of Notre Dame de Paris ("the interior of which much dissapointed our expectations"), Troyes, Cambrai, Rheims, and Laon, probably Lyon, and possibly Cologne (a glimpse, at most, one would guess from *History of a Six Weeks' Tour*).[11]

There was, perhaps, ample justification for Shelley's enthusiasm for Milan cathedral, which remains the largest church in Europe after St. Peter's (which he had not yet seen) and the cathedral at Seville. That admiration was, moreover, consonant with his aesthetic principles. In another publication, I have shown how Shelley contrasted the classical buildings and monuments of Rome with the baroque, to the disadvantage

10. Eustace, *A Tour through Italy, exhibiting a View of Its Scenery, Its Antiquities, and Its Monuments; particularly as They are Objects of Classical Interest and Elucidation* . . . (London, 1813), II, 341.

11. On Notre Dame, see Mary Shelley, Journal, August 5, 1814; on Cambrai, Rheims, and Laon, see Claire Clairmont, *Journals*, p. 87; on Troyes and Cologne, see *History of a Six Weeks' Tour*.

SC 479   of the latter.[12] Here, in Shelley's admiration of Milan cathedral, one sees his preference for classical architecture over Gothic. This preference was an element both of the taste of Shelley's time and of his own individual aesthetic. Although his poetry has occasionally been termed "baroque" and compared with that of Crashaw, Shelley himself followed classical canons of taste and classical structural patterns, emphasizing unity and symmetry. Most of his mature poems exhibit such a classical simplicity of structure,[13] and when he did not achieve this symmetry, he characteristically apologized either to his friends or publicly in a preface or note.[14] Shelley's praise of the Milan cathedral as the best of Gothic architecture comes, then, from a man whose aesthetic principles contrast sharply with the ideals that Ruskin and later critics were to point out as central to the Gothic.[15]

Shelley attended the opera at Turin once and La Scala at Milan at least four times.[16] Sitting in a loge at Turin, the Shelleys were prevented from hearing most of the opera by the "perpetual talking of the audience." In their first visit to La Scala, they tried the "pit" which satisfied them,[17] but on her return to Milan over twenty years later, Mary Shelley noted (as a matter of common knowledge) that "the theatre of

12. Donald H. Reiman, "Roman Scenes in *Prometheus Unbound*, III, iv," *Philological Quarterly*, XLVI (January 1967), 69–78.

13. On the symmetrical structure of such poems as *Queen Mab, The Revolt of Islam,* "Lines written among the Euganean Hills," *Prometheus Unbound, The Cenci, Adonais,* and *Hellas,* see Donald H. Reiman, *Percy Bysshe Shelley* (New York: Twayne's English Authors Series, 1969).

14. See, for example, his description of "Mont Blanc" as "an undisciplined overflowing of the soul" (Preface to *History of a Six Weeks' Tour*) and his remark that *Rosalind and Helen* "only pretends to be regular inasmuch as it corresponds with, and expresses, the irregularity of the imaginations which inspired it." (Advertisement to *Rosalind and Helen.*)

15. On first seeing the cathedral at Milan, Ruskin like Shelley was impressed by its "vastness of scale." He noted that "the duomo impressed me to the full at once: and not having yet the taste to discern good Gothic from bad, the mere richness and fineness of lace-like tracery against the sky was a consummate rapture to me." His later reactions to the cathedral were much altered. He wrote, "The duomo of Milan is of entirely bad and barbarous Gothic." Ruskin did not believe the Milan cathedral to be characteristic of Gothic architecture; in the autumn of 1849, after again visiting the cathedral, he entered these observations in his diary: "Throughout the cathedral there are mixtures of stealing from every style in the world; and every style spoiled. . . ." (*The Works of John Ruskin,* ed. E. T. Cook and Alexander Wedderburn, London, 1903, XXXV, 117; XXIII, 22; IX, 469 n.)

16. The dates, from Mary's and Claire's journals, are April 1 (Turin) and April 5, 20, 21, and 29 at Milan.

17. Mary to the Hunts, April [6–8], 1818, Mary Shelley, *Letters,* I, 48.

The Carl H. Pforzheimer Library

SC 479 La Scala serves, not only as the universal drawing-room for all the society of Milan, but every sort of trading transaction, from horse-dealing to stock-jobbing, is carried on in the pit."[18]

The ballet of *Othello* that so impressed Shelley remained forcefully in Mary's recollection throughout that period: "In this theatre I had seen Othello acted in *ballet*, with such mastery of pantomine, that words seemed superfluous for the expression of passion or incident; but no such good actors as were celebrated then, exist now."[19] Shelley's enthusiasm for music — especially vocal music, for the dance, and for painting and sculpture must be kept in mind when one turns to his *Defence of Poetry*. His high estimate of literature there was certainly not based on a prejudice against other creative arts. His appreciation of painting, sculpture, and the performing arts, having been stimulated by the Hunts and Peacock during his last year and a half in England, blossomed in Italy. Mary Shelley later expressed the cultural impact of that land on all travelers: "When we visit Italy, we become what the Italians were censured for being, — enjoyers of the beauties of nature, the elegance of art, the delights of climate, the recollections of the past, and the pleasures of society, without a thought beyond."[20] Shelley's personal appreciation of these delights is apparent from sc 479, but at this time the household did lack "the pleasures of society."

When Shelley writes that Hogg is more concerned with "the human part of the experience of travelling," he means that Hogg paid a great deal of attention to such matters as his mode of transportation, the quality of his meals, and the comfort of his beds, as well as the idiosyncrasies of his traveling companions. Hogg's published record of his first trip to the Continent yields one epitomizing example from a description of the region of the Italian lakes: "The sofas in this district are lofty, extensive, and luxurious."[21]

Shelley's reading in Greek, German, and Italian authors shows the range of his interests. He read at least two lives of Tasso, and perhaps

18. Mary Shelley, *Rambles*, I, 111.

19. Mary Shelley, *Rambles*, I, 112. See also sc 448, Commentary.

20. Mary Shelley, *Rambles*, I, xvi.

21. *Two Hundred and Nine Days; or, The Journal of a Traveller on the Continent* (London, 1827), I, 248.

SC 479　more, during his early days in Italy. Claire mentions reading "The Life of Tasso" in her Journals for April 10 and April 11, while Shelley and Mary were away at Como, but Mary also notes on April 11 that "Shelley has finished the life of Tasso and reads Dante —." Claire was again reading the "Life of Tasso" on April 15 and 18. On April 20, she writes: "Read the Life of Tasso by Marcantonio Serassi." On May 11, Mary mentions that "Shelley reads Manso's life of Tasso." It seems reasonably certain that his April reading of Tasso's life included at least Pierantonio Serassi's *La Vita di Torquato Tasso* and perhaps John Black's *Life of Torquato Tasso with an Historical and Critical Account of His Writings* (Edinburgh, 1810).

Shelley's interest in Tasso was very likely stimulated by Byron's *Lament of Tasso*, parts of which he admired, but which — it is clear from his remarks to Byron[22] — he did not feel had exhausted its subject. It is likely that he acquired the biography by Black before leaving England and in Italy picked up Serassi's *Vita*, upon which Black had commented at length.[23] One may suppose that *La Vita di Torquato Tasso* by Tasso's friend Giovanni Battista Manso (Venice, 1621) was not as readily available and Shelley may have bought or borrowed it a few weeks later at Pisa or Leghorn, shortly before Mary's May 11 reference to it.[24]

Shelley seems to have given up his attempt to write a drama on Tasso's life sometime before his visit with Byron at Venice in August 1818.[25] One reason that he did not renew this attempt when his poetic

22. See sc 419.

23. See C. P. Brand, *Torquato Tasso: a Study of the Poet and of His Contribution to English Literature* (Cambridge, 1965), pp. 212–216. Leigh Hunt in the Preface to his translation of Tasso's *Amyntas* (London, 1820) calls Black "an impartial and accurate biographer" (p. xx). Hunt used both Black and Serassi — apparently the biographies of Tasso in general use by English readers for a considerable period — in his *Stories from the Italian Poets* (London, 1846), II, 289.

24. In "Shelley's Library Catalogue" published by Jean de Palacio (*Revue de Littérature Comparée*, XXXVI, 1962, 270–276), Mary Shelley lists both "Vita di Tasso — 2 vols" and "Vita di Tasso di Manso." If the first title is Serassi's biography, it cannot have been the Rome edition of 1785 (which was in one volume), but it may have been the Bergamo edition of 1790 and/or 1791 (two volumes) or a later reprint. The presence on the list of Keats's *Endymion* and Ollier's *Altham and His Wife*, which Shelley received in August 1819 (Shelley, *Letters*, II, 110), shows that the list postdates that time.

25. G. M. Matthews follows White in dating the extant fragments of the drama "either between May 10 and June 10 at Leghorn . . . or (more likely) between June 12 and July 8 at the Bagni di Lucca." ("A New Text of Shelley's Scene for *Tasso*," *Keats-Shelley Memorial Bulletin*, XI, 1960, 46.)

SC 479 inspiration returned in the fall of 1818·was undoubtedly that, having in the meantime read Byron's second treatment of Tasso in *Childe Harold*, IV (stanzas xxxv–xxxix), and Hobhouse's extended commentary in the Notes to that poem and in *Historical Illustrations of the Fourth Canto of Childe Harold*, Shelley realized that the subject had been preempted by his more famous contemporary and that his own treatment would inevitably seem derivative.[26]

26. Though Shelley had heard rumors of the fourth canto since at least as early as September 24, 1817 (see sc 419, sc 437, and sc 442), he had not seen it before seeing Byron at Venice in August 1818, when Byron recited some stanzas of it to him (see sc 494). The official publication date in London for both the fourth canto and Hobhouse's Commentary was April 28, 1818.

SC 480 EDWARD DUBOIS TO T. L. PEACOCK, MAY 15, 1818

AL signed *Edw. DuBois.*, 1½ pages. Double sheet, 4^(to) (9.8 x 7.9 inches). Laid paper. Watermark: [fleur-de-lis]|. Seal: wax, red.

PROVENANCE: Thomas Love Peacock; Edith Nicolls Clarke; Mrs. K. Hall Thorpe (Sotheby, November 15, 1949, lot 499).

Temple, Brick Court.
May 15. 1818.

Dear Sir,

    There are two perhapses—Perhaps you may remember that we met some-
5 *time ago at Horace Smith's; but as you then took your Nap, perhaps you went to sleep and forgot it. Be this as it may, you are entitled to my thanks for a present I have just received from Mr Hookham—your Rhododaphne—which it is true, like most <u>poetical laurels</u>, is κακον δρισον but I found it a very pleasant light repast.*

10   *My further traffic with you relates to your motto, which of course you understand. What is <u>plus sciæ</u>? I dont require at your hands any of the dim rays of light shed by the Commentators, which are, as I think, only calculated to prevent the bewildered from finding the right path. You give the text as you found it, which, as the act implies approbation of it, at least*
15 *as to some sense suitable to your purpose, I should be glad to know how you construe it.*

DuBois to Peacock   *May 26, 1818*

SC 480   *I have very little doubt about what the reading should be, but am curious*
to learn how you have satisfied yourself with it in its present shape.

                                                    Yours truly
20   *Edw. DuBois.*

[Address, page 4]
T   Peacock Esqre

SC 481 EDWARD DUBOIS TO T. L. PEACOCK, MAY 26, 1818

AL signed *Edw. DuBois.*, 2½ pages. Double sheet, 4to (9.8 x 7.8 inches).
Laid paper. Watermark: W T| 1816|.
Seal: wax, red.
Postal fee: 7.
Postmark: (evening duty stamp, London)*:* B| MY| 28|·818.

PROVENANCE: Thomas Love Peacock; Edith Nicolls Clarke; Mrs. K. Hall
Thorpe (Sotheby, November 15, 1949, lot 499).

                                              Temple. May 26. 1818.

   Dear Sir,
      I received your letter today, and I thank you for it; but you give me
nothing that Scheffer and others have not supplied. As to the sense, it is all
5 *guess work, for, according to the interpretation surmised, you have not, fail-*
ing in every other support, even use to bear you out—"Consuetudo omnium
domina rerum, tum maxime verborum." It is but honest to suppose it means
something, and, as there is such a word as Scius ("scius omni artificio.
Hyginus"—Lat. Diction^{y}) plus sciæ (at a venture) is "more knowing than
10 *other women"! Can you be content with this? "More knowing" is I admit*
a sort of English, but tho' you turn plus sciæ into more knowing, would
you, speaking of some bluestockings, consider the turn so good as to deserve
another, and for "more knowing" say plus sciæ? Really, really this is too
much—you would not have helped an Englishman in this way. As to πλειονα
15 *ειδως, to which you conceive it has "an allusion"—it certainly has, after*
your translation, but the phrases had previously nothing in common.
      Now you shall hear what Davus has to say, touching this riddle. I

DuBois to Peacock   **May 26, 1818**

SC 48 I   *should think that no one, considering the matter well, can doubt that the*
          passage is corrupt, and I have as little, that plus sciæ is an abbreviation, in
20   *which the c was written t, for which it might easily have been mistaken, and*
          perhaps designedly for the purpose of giving something like a latin word.
          Then I read plus stiæ thus, PaLUdiS STygIÆ.   Styæ à στυγεω, adio
          prosequor, will suit these Ladies very well, and it travels on all fours with
          "Nocturnæ &ᵉᶜ"—sunt is repeated, observe and why.

25   *I beg pardon for compelling you "Stygiamque innane paludem" (Hr,*
          VI. v.369) but you are a poet, and if your great Ancestor, Orpheus sought
          his wife in Hell (knowing it seems exactly where to find her) you cannot
          reasonably object to a trip to the same place, in search of what is so likely
          to be found where she is—words.

30   *Yours truly*
                                                          Edw. DuBois.

          PS. I don't like to let all this paper go waste (tho' you'll perhaps think
          I've hit on a mighty bad remedy) therefore I'll ask you whether you ever
          met with some spanish lines on the subject of Orpheus? You'll esteem his
35   *infernal Majesty more and more, when you see how he administers justice*
          in mercy:

                    Y aunque su mujer le diò
                      Por pena de su pecado,
                        Por premio &ᵉᶜ
40   *and*
                    *But the God at his visit was wrath*ₐ*yet he,*
                    As the man was her Husband, thus shaped his decree:–
                        "I'll tell you, said he, what I'll do, Sir,—
                        "Take your wife, 'tis a punishment due for the wrong;
45   *"But, as a reward for your excellent song,*
                            "I'll take care you quickly shall lose her."

          Pray mind these verses, and be grateful that I gave you no more.

          [Address, page 4]
          T. L. Peacock Esqʳᵉ
              Marlow

DuBois to Peacock   May 26, 1818

SC 481   line 22. στυγεω: στ is a digraph in the manuscript.   line 47. *these*: emended from *the* by squeezing
line 24. —*sunt . . . why.*: the phrase was added   in *se*.
later in a smaller hand and darker ink between
the paragraphs.

DUBOIS, wrote Leigh Hunt, "was one of those wits who . . . have no faculty of gravity." "His handsome hawk's-eyes looked blank at a speculation; but set a joke or a piece of raillery in motion, and they sparkled with wit and malice. . . . his quips and cranks were infinite. He was also an excellent scholar."[1] Edward DuBois (1774–1850), though a lawyer (admitted to the Inner Temple in 1809), spent most of his time as a periodical editor and miscellaneous writer. Among his productions was a parody of Godwin's *St. Leon* entitled *St. Godwin: A Tale of the Sixteenth, Seventeenth, and Eighteenth Century, by Count Reginald St. Leon* (London, 1800), which included a satire of *Political Justice* in the final chapter.[2] Hunt describes DuBois as one of the circle of literary men and wits invited to Thomas Hill's house at Sydenham, a circle that included Thomas Campbell, Horace Smith and his brother James, Theodore Hook, and Charles Mathews, the comedian. Horace Smith later described his first encounter with DuBois, whom he knew only from *The Wreath*, published in 1799:

The Wreath . . . displayed great erudition and research, involving a critical knowledge of the Greek, Latin, and Hebrew languages. I fully expected when appraised that I was to meet the author at Hill's cottage at Sydenham, to encounter an elderly Scholastious . . . gravely loud and dogmatical in the display of his lore . . . Guess my surprise when I beheld a young, gay-looking, soft-spoken wag, whose ever-ready and ever-pungent wit supplied constant amusement to the party, while his quiet chuckle showed that he had a quick appreciation of the same quality in others.[3]

1. *Lord Byron and Some of His Contemporaries*, pp. 273–274. Hunt, the *DNB*, and earlier volumes of *Shelley and his Circle* have spelled this man's name "Dubois," but his signatures on these two letters and sc 507 show that he preferred "DuBois."

2. For further information about *St. Leon* and *St. Godwin* see sc 25 and Commentary (I).

3. "A Greybeard's Gossip about His Literary Acquaintance, No. VII," *New Monthly Magazine*, LXXXI (1847), 83. The full title of the DuBois work is *The Wreath: Composed of Selections from Sappho, Theocritus, Bion, and Moschus. Accompanied by a Prose Translation, with Notes To Which are added Remarks on Shakespere, &c.*

The Carl H. Pforzheimer Library

SC 481   In 1817 Keats dined at Horace Smith's with a party that included Hill and DuBois, and found their wit cold and inhumane: "They talked of Kean & his low company — Would I were with that company instead of yours said I to myself!"[4]

The two letters above and sc 507 below show DuBois' somewhat forced facetiousness, his penchant for raillery, and his interest in classical scholarship — or pedantry. Superficially Thomas Love Peacock must have seemed a younger soul-mate of this self-educated wit. That there was a mutuality of interests is demonstrated by Peacock's gifts of copies of *Rhododaphne* and *Nightmare Abbey* and by DuBois' response in these letters.

The target of DuBois' inquiry is the epigraph or motto from Petronius that appears on the fly-title of *Rhododaphne*: "Rogo vos, oportet, credatis, sunt mulieres plus sciæ, sunt nocturnæ, et quod sursum est deorsum faciunt." Whether either Peacock or DuBois construed this sentence successfully or whether both were stymied by textual difficulties is a question for the Petronius scholars.

For students of Peacock the significance of this DuBois correspondence is twofold. First, it shows how potentially important to Peacock was his association with Shelley during his Marlow and London residences of 1817–1818. Through Hunt, Shelley met Horace Smith and through Shelley Peacock was introduced into Hunt's and Smith's circles, thereby broadening his acquaintance among London literary men. Clearly such introductions were of primary importance to him if he were to break out of his isolation at Marlow and pursue a successful literary career.

Second, *Rhododaphne*, on which Peacock had obviously rested his hopes of achieving literary recognition,[5] had not proved very useful to him. He had obviously instructed Hookham to send a copy of the poem to DuBois with the hope that if DuBois were impressed by it, he might help Peacock find employment or at least praise his literary powers in certain London circles. Instead, DuBois damns it with very faint praise (in Greek it is a "bad sacrifice" and in English only a "pleasant light

4. To George and Tom Keats, December 21, 27(?), 1817, Keats, *Letters*, I, 193. For the fullest account of DuBois, see David Bonnell Green, "Studies in Keats with Biographical Sketches of His Acquaintances Thomas Hill and Edward DuBois" (unpublished dissertation, Harvard University, 1953). In Green's dissertation, however, DuBois is never mentioned in connection with Peacock.

5. See sc 424 and Commentary.

SC 481   repast") before proceeding to quibble about the motto. And if Peacock displayed his erudition in his answer to sc 480, DuBois merely out-pedants him. (Johann Scheffer, to whom DuBois alludes in sc 481, line 4, was a seventeenth-century textual critic at Upsala who edited Petronius, among others.[6]) This exchange should be taken into account when reading the resigned remark in Peacock's May 30 letter to Shelley: "I have no idea and no wish remaining to leave Marlow at all, and when you return to England you will find me still here, though perhaps not in the same house."[7]

DuBois' response to *Rhododaphne*, coupled with the general lack of enthusiasm in the reviews,[8] must have wounded Peacock's pride and stifled his hopes of achieving poetic popularity. These wounded feelings may, in turn, account in part for the change of tone from *Melincourt* to *Nightmare Abbey*, Peacock's attack on what he described as a "systematical 'poisoning' of the 'mind' of the 'reading public'" — a public that thought more highly of the Fourth Canto of *Childe Harold's Pilgrimage* than it did of *Rhododaphne*.[9] In the longer view, Peacock's failure as a poet coupled with reactions like DuBois' condescension toward "*poetical laurels*" certainly underlies his *Four Ages of Poetry*.[10]

6. See John E. Sandys, *A History of Classical Scholarship* (New York, 1967), II, 368 and III, 341. "Davus" (line 17) is, of course, not a learned commentator, but the humble yet clever slave of Roman comedy — i.e., DuBois himself. Cf. Terence, *Andria*, I.2.23: "*Davus sum, non Oedipus.*" See also Horace, *Satires*, II.vii.

7. Peacock, *Works*, VIII, 193.

8. A total of six reviews of *Rhododaphne* have now been identified: *Literary Gazette*, No. 57 (February 21, 1818), pp. 114–115; *La Belle Assemblée*, n.s. XVII (March 1818), 128–131; *Monthly Magazine*, XLV (April 1818), 250; *Literary Panorama*, n.s. VIII (May 1818), 212–216; *Monthly Review*, LXXXVIII (February 1819), 178–182; *Fireside Magazine; or, Monthly Entertainer*, I (April 1819), 151.

9. To Shelley, May 30, 1818, Peacock, *Works*, VIII, 193.

10. Some of Peacock's contemporaries recognized this correlation between his failure as a poet and his attacks on the poets of his age. See Hazlitt's dialogue "The New School of Reform" in *The Plain Speaker* (Hazlitt, *Works*, XII, 179–195, especially 186–187).

SC 482   M. W. SHELLEY TO MARIA GISBORNE, JUNE 5, 1818

AL signed *Mary W. Shelley.*, 1 page. Single sheet, 8ᵛᵒ (7.3 x 4.7 inches). Wove paper.
Notation, upper right corner of page 1, in John Gisborne's hand: *C. di Malta| June 1818|*.

Shelley to Gisborne   **June 5, 1818**

SC 482 Addition: mounted on heavy paper backing (watermark, 1826), containing notation in John Gisborne's hand: *Note from Mrs Shelley to Mrs Gisborne|.*

PROVENANCE: Maggs, December 1941.

Dear Madam
        The physician will be with us at 7 this evening– Shall we come this
                                                                            the
evening earlier for our walk and then you can return with us at ̮right hour?
5   *I send you somthing that will amuse you*
                                        Most truly yours
                                        Mary W. Shelley.

Livorno
Friday morning.

10 *Compts to Mr G. and Il Re*
    della Macchina

line 5. *somthing* (sic).

T HE SHELLEYS left Milan on the first of May and traveled the route of the Roman Via Aemilia, sleeping on the first three nights at Piacenza, Parma, and Modena. Dining at Bologna on May 4, they pushed on into the mountains and spent that night "in a solitary inn among them."[1] The next night they slept at Barberino; on Wednesday, May 6, they entered the Arno valley west of Florence — bypassing the Tuscan capital[2] — and slept at La Scala. They reached Pisa on May 7, but stayed there only long enough to receive a letter from Elise announcing her safe arrival with Allegra at Venice. On Saturday, May 9, the Shelleys and Claire went on to Leghorn (Livorno).

1. Mary Shelley, Journal; see also Claire's journal (SC 448).

2. Originally the Shelleys must have intended to stop in Florence because Godwin's letter of June 8, 1818, was addressed to "Monsieur Percy Bysshe Shelley/ Ferma in Posta/ Firenze/ Italia"; postmarks indicate that it was forwarded first to Leghorn (probably in response to a written request from Shelley to the Florentine postmaster), where it was readdressed to "Casa Bertini/ Bagni di Lucca." Godwin's letter of July 7, the next surviving letter to the Shelleys that went through the post, was addressed to Mary in care of the Gisbornes in Leghorn and forwarded to Bagni di Lucca from there (Abinger Manuscripts, Pforzheimer Microfilm, reel V, file 7).

Shelley and his Circle : Manuscripts

SC 482   Although the Shelleys considered the cosmopolitan commercial port of 50,000 people "a stupid town," they remained there for about a month, initially at an inn identified by Claire as L'Aquila Nera, but later at one called La Croce di Malta.³ The only compensation proved to be the companionship of Maria Gisborne, her husband John, and Henry Reveley, her son by a previous marriage.⁴

This note is the original of one of the twenty-seven letters from Mary to Maria Gisborne that Frederick L. Jones published in 1955 from John Gisborne's transcripts in Lord Abinger's collection.⁵ The "physician" mentioned here may be the individual referred to by Jones as "Mr. Beilby," but the identification is complicated by the alteration of his name in the published version of *Mary Shelley's Journal* and in Shelley, *Letters*. In Mary's Journal entry for May 13, omitted from the printed versions, she wrote: "Mr. & Mrs. Gisborne call in the evening with Mr. Bilby–." The name also appears as "Bilby" in the manuscript Journal entries for May 17 and June 5; the transcriber for *Shelley and Mary* altered Mary's spelling and Jones followed him both in the *Journal* and in Shelley's letter to the Gisbornes of October 14, 1819.⁶

Maria Gisborne wrote to Mary Shelley on June 21, 1818, and (according to the text in *Shelley and Mary*) said in her final paragraph:

Beilby had read "Mandeville." He complains of the hard words, and the frequent quotations of Scripture. He says, however, that he has discovered an anachronism in the allusion to the tea-tables of Petersfield. We would not give him "Frankenstein"; as he is a solitary man, we were fearful of the effect it might produce on his imagination!⁷

3. This and La Croce d'Oro were the two inns at Leghorn named as suitable in both *Guide des Voyageurs en Italie* (Florence, 1817) and *Itinerario Italiano* (Milan, 1820).

4. See SC 465, Godwin to Maria Gisborne, March 10, 1818. In alluding to Mrs. Gisborne's son Henry Reveley as "The King of the Machine," Mary reflects the visit that she and Shelley made to see Reveley's steam engine on Thursday, May 28 (Mary Shelley, Journal).

5. "Mary Shelley to Maria Gisborne: New Letters, 1818–1822," *Studies in Philology*, LII (January 1955), 39–74.

6. Shelley, *Letters*, II, 124. In another of the many entries of 1818 omitted from the printed versions of her Journal, Mary wrote for Sunday, June 7: "in the evening walk with S. Clare Mr. & Mrs. G— with Sig^or Balbi a greek." It is not certain whether there is any connection between the names "Mr. Bilby" and "Signor Balbi"—perhaps a Greek, or as his name suggests, an Italian.

7. *Shelley and Mary*, I, 290.

Hunt to Hogg   *June 7, 14, or 28, 1818*

SC 482 Mrs. Gisborne's spelling of the name (if indeed the compilers of *Shelley and Mary* were not altering *her* spelling as well as Mary Shelley's) is likely to be correct, although *Alumni Cantabrigienses* lists ten Cambridge students of the fifteenth through the seventeenth centuries who, among them, used the following variant spellings of this name: Bealby, Beilby, Beylby, Bielby, Bilbe, Bilby, and Bilbye. *Shelley and Mary* omits one other reference to the man in Mary's letter to Maria Gisborne of August 17, 1818: "Shelley translated the Symposium in ten days (an anecdote for Mr. Bielby)."[8]

John Gisborne's notation, placing the letter in June 1818, limits the date to June 5, the only Friday in June during the Shelleys' visit.

8. Mary Shelley, *Letters*, I, 56.

SC 483 LEIGH HUNT TO T. J. HOGG, JUNE 7, 14, OR 28, 1818

AL signed *Leigh Hunt.*, 1 page. Single sheet (3.4 x 7.7 inches). Laid paper.

PROVENANCE: Thomas Jefferson Hogg; Prudentia Hogg Lonsdale; John Ewer Jefferson Hogg; Major R. J. Jefferson Hogg (Sotheby, June 26, 1948, lot 276).

Lisson Grove —Sunday June 1818.

My dear Hogg,

Though I tell you that your notes are unnecessary to usher in the pleasure of your visit, I do not mean to deprive myself of them in future,
5 *whenever you are in the humour for writing one; & indeed they may in one respect be as well for you, as they ascertain whether I shall be at home or not. I shall be so this evening; I am almost invariably so on Sundays as well as every other day when there is no call on me at the theatre; & I need not repeat I shall always be happy to be favoured with your society. I re-*
10 *member the pensive hedge hog; but I deny the attempt to prove that Pope's versification was "jarring & discordant." Did I ever say that to be sickened with honey was to be torn asunder with horses? Answer me that, you rogue.– Will you be with us at 5, & take a walk into the dulcia arva?*

Ever your's   Leigh Hunt.

[600]

Peacock to Hogg
June 12, 1818

SC 483   [Address, verso]
To T. J. Hogg Esqre
Garden Court, Temple.

line 13. *dulcia . . . Hunt.*: occupies one line in the manuscript.

IT IS DIFFICULT to determine on which of three June Sundays in 1818 Hunt sent this note to Hogg. Sunday, June 21, is unlikely, for Peacock wrote to Shelley on June 14 that Hogg finally was coming to Marlow on Wednesday, June 17, for their excursion up the Thames, and it is improbable that Hogg returned to London and solicited this invitation from Hunt for a long walk the following Sunday. Until further evidence is forthcoming, this letter can be assigned to June 7, June 14, or June 28, 1818.

Aside from Hunt's expressed enjoyment of Hogg's note to him and the good relations evident between the men at this date,[1] the point of greatest interest concerns Hunt's attitude toward the versification of Alexander Pope. Hogg has twitted him for calling Pope's verse "jarring & discordant," but Hunt denies that he ever said this.[2] Pope's couplets, Hunt suggests, sicken with the honey of uniform smoothness, an image which the modern critic would apply with far more justice to the verse of Hunt and his followers — even the early Keats — than to Pope. The invitation to Hogg to join Hunt at five for a walk into the "sweet fields" suggests Hunt's characteristically sentimental attitude toward nature, but the Latin phrase mutes the sentiment.

1. On the long-term relations between Hunt and Hogg, see SC 452, Commentary.

2. The "pensive hedge hog," if not literally such an animal observed on a previous walk, was probably Hogg, on whose name all punned. Perhaps the occasion of the alleged judgment on Pope was an earlier walk along the hedges of a country lane.

SC 484   T. L. PEACOCK TO T. J. HOGG, JUNE 12, 1818

AL signed *T.L.Peacock*, 1 page. Double sheet, 4to (8.7 x 7.3 inches). Wove paper. Watermark: VALLEYFIELD| 1816|. Impressed stamp: [crown]| BATH|.
Seal: wax, red: [peacock]|.
Postal fee: 7.
Postmarks: 1. (mileage stamp): MARLOW| 33|; 2. (morning duty stamp, London): C| 13 JU 13| 1818|.

The Carl H. Pforzheimer Library

Peacock to Hogg   **June 12, 1818**

My dear Hogg

I have just learned that Hampton Races are next week which will mar all accommodation from Chertsey to Twickenham. And London is not very inviting in this intensely hot weather. Therefore suppose we change

5 *our schemes and that you come down ~~as~~ here as soon as possible, and go ~~off~~ up the river to Oxford with me next week. If you could get down tomorrow*
                              come as soon as you can
night I should be glad but ~~I fear this time is too short~~: and bring with you the Cobbetts from N° 19 and if you could by any means lay your hands on a

10 *map of Oxfordshire it would be a great acquisition*

Yours most sincerely

T.L.Peacock

June 12. 1818

[Address, page 4]

T.J. Hogg Esq.

15 *1 Garden Court*

Temple

London.

line 6. ~~off~~: may possibly be *up* miswritten and then canceled.

line 8. *this*: probable reading of this word in the heavily canceled passage.

HAMPTON, Chertsey, and Twickenham — Thames-side resorts between Marlow and London — would all be popular gathering-points for spectators during the week of the river-races. Peacock proposes to avoid the crowds by going up-river instead of down, and so into Oxfordshire. In fact, according to Peacock's letter to Shelley of July 1818: "Hogg has passed a week with me, and we had some long walks — one to Virginia Water; one to Cromwell's House and *Velvet lawn*, which Hogg said must be one of the folds of Parnassus transplanted to Buckinghamshire."[1]

1. Peacock, *Works*, VIII, 199. Peacock's reference to Cromwell's house is to Chequers, which he also mentions to Shelley on June 14 as "the seat of Cromwell" (Peacock, *Works*, VIII, 195). Although Cromwell never lived in this house, it was associated with him through his heirs.

SC 485   T. L. PEACOCK TO CHARLES OLLIER, JUNE 29, 1818

AL signed *T. L. Peacock*, 1¾ pages. Double sheet, 4ᵗᵒ (8.7 x 7.3 inches).
Wove paper. Watermark: VALLEYFIELD| 1816|. Impressed stamp: [crown]|
BATH|.
Seal (trace): wax, red.
Postal fee: 7.
Postmarks: 1. (mileage stamp)*:* [trace]; 2. (morning duty stamp, London)*:*
c| [30 JU] 30| 1818|.
Notation, page 4, probably in the hand of Charles Ollier (see SC 442 and SC 453):
Entick's Dicty| Murray's Abridgment| 1 Qu Bath Paper| ¼ [   ] *Pens|*.
Additions: 1. spindle hole; 2. extensive wear along folds.
PROVENANCE: Wilfred Meynell–Mrs. Murray Sowerby (Sotheby, October 26,
1959, lot 312).

Dear Sir

    I have ɟ not at present anything to send Mʳ Shelley having just for-
warded a small box by another opportunity: but if you send again I shall be
obliged by your informing me, when I may perhaps trouble you with an
5   *enclosure. Messieurs R. & H. Richardson Nᵒ 3 George Yard Lombard Street*
will take charge of a box of any size for Leghorn.
    Mʳ Shelley wishes the Examiner to be sent to him by the post which
you will oblige him and me by doing as it can only be done through the
medium of the London Post-Office. The person to apply to is Mʳ Thornhill
10   *at Mʳ Freeling's office in Sherborn Lane adjoining the General Post-Office.*
    Mʳˢ Shelley has requested me to send her a tortoise shell comb, 3 inches
across and teeth 2 inches: and a nail brush like Mʳˢ Hunt's. As I cannot
obtain the former here and have not convenient access to the model of the
latter perhaps you will have the goodness to include these things in your
15   *package: and also to send his linen – all except the cotton sheets. He says*
it will be found at Mʳˢ Hunt's or if not there at the lodgings he last occupied
in London. I shall be glad to hear from you on these points. I was in town
for a day or two last week but time did not admit of my executing half my
intentions one of which was to have called on you.
20   *I am Dear Sir*
                                  Your most obedient sevᵗ
                                     T. L. Peacock

The Carl H. Pforzheimer Library

Peacock to Ollier   *June 29, 1818*

SC 485   *Marlow June 29 – 1818*

[Address, page 3]

Mʳ C. Ollier

25   *Vere Street*

Bond Street

London.

line 10. *Sherborn* (sic): for Sherborne.
line 11. *Mʳˢ Shelley*: Peacock began the new paragraph with a fine pen; the previous two paragraphs were written in a heavy, somewhat blotted script.

SHELLEY's and Mary's requests listed in this letter are well documented. In his letter to Peacock from Milan, April 20, 1818, Shelley added in a postscript: "Mary requests you to send with your midsummer parcel several papers of pins a few sticks of sealing wax a nail brush like Mrs. Hunt's & a tortoise shell comb 3 inches across & teeth 2 inches." On June 5 he wrote from Leghorn: "And I have determined to take the Examiner here; you would therefore oblige me by sending it weekly after having read it yourself, addressed to the same direction & so clipped as to make as little weight as possible. — Also to send our linen which you will find at Mrs Hunts & of which we have very great need. Send *all* except the cotton sheets. If the sheets are not at Mrs Hunts they are at the lodgings which we occupied in London last."[1]

Peacock here passes on these requests to Ollier — who is thus called in on matters more domestic than literary. On July 5 Peacock wrote to Shelley from Marlow: "The tortoise-shell comb I could not procure here, nor the nailbrush like Mrs Hunt's, from want of access to the model; but as I heard from Ollier that he was going to send you a package, I requested him to send them." He then repeated to Shelley the information he had given Ollier about sending the *Examiner* through the London Post Office.[2]

1. Shelley, *Letters*, II, 18.

2. Peacock, *Works*, VIII, 196–197. Although officials of the Post Office had been under attack for years for the graft evolving from their monopoly on the franking of newspapers sent abroad, Parliament continued to retain this lucrative sideline because censorship was so strict in some countries that English newspapers could not have entered except under the aegis of the British government. See Herbert Joyce, *History of the Post Office* (London, 1893), pp. 402–404.

SC 485   Mary had a way of asking Peacock for small domestic commodities in postscripts to Shelley's letters; in November and December 1818 she requests "a pair of pointed scissars & a penknife," then "2 hairbrushes & a small tooth comb." This did not improve Peacock's image of the *bel paese:*[3] on January 13, 1819, he commented to Shelley, "What an idea does it give one of Italy, being obliged to send for such things from Rome and Naples!"[4] Another of Mary's postscripts follows a request from Shelley for gems and seals on March 21, 1821. Mary adds, "Also, if you will be so kind. 4 skeins of white netting silk. 2 green & 2 crimson — all of a size fit for purses."

3. For *bel paese*, see sc 476 and Commentary.
4. Peacock, *Works*, VIII, 216.

SC 486   LEIGH AND MARIANNE HUNT TO P. B. AND M. W. SHELLEY, CA. JULY 14–AUGUST 4, 1818

2 AL signed *M.A. Hunt.* and *Leigh Hunt*, 7½ pages. 2 double sheets, 4to (9.9 x 7.3 inches and 9.1 x 7.3 inches).
Laid paper (first double sheet). Watermark: [fleur-de-lis]|.
Wove paper (second double sheet). Watermark: J HALL| 1816|.
Seal: wax, red: [impressed oval containing olive branch and inscription]| E SOLO LIBERO|.

PROVENANCE: Colonel Charles Shelley Leigh Hunt; Mrs. Beryl Dodgson (Sotheby, April 8, 1935, lot 205). See sc 414, Commentary.

> *August 4*^th   *My dear Mr Shelley   many happy returns of the day – may you be happier next year than last*
>   (*M H*)
>
> *My dear Mary*
>
> 5   *I sit down to write to you with every intention of saying a great deal, if my wits will bear me out— In the first place you know mine are to be mere letters of chit, chat: more I cannot even <u>aim</u> at.—— How are you all   Is M*^r *Shelley better? I am sorry to hear no better accounts of*
>   *make*
> 10   *him:- better health for him, seemed the only thing to*ᴧ*your absence for so long a time and at such a <s>distant</s> at all comfortable —we miss you much;*
>   *distance*

SC 486 *and often, as you may suppose, talk of you all.— The summer is a re-*
markably fine one, extremely warm, and vegetation in high luxuriance. We
15 *have moved into a new house which Mr Hunt has taken for seven years with*
the power of leaving it at the end of the fourth year by paying £20; but we
all, I think, know his dislike to change (which bye the bye does not extend
to houses); nevertheless if we stay 4, the probability is we shall stray seven,
                                                                    in it;
20 *and spend many a day together — – it is a nice roomy house, just gone*
through a thorough repair, fresh painted and papered through out, 3 rooms
on a floor with windows to the floor, and folding doors in the drawing room
which you may perhaps remember I am no friend to:- it is in the new road
between Baker street and Gloucester place paralell with Portram Square
25 *(8. York buildings)   Mr Hunt has had his portrait taken in chalk as*
large a life half lenghth by Mr Wildman, Thorntons drawing Master; it is
one of the most astonishing likenesses that ever was seen; you would almost
think it was going to speak to you. and the execution as a drawing, equals
the likeness.— You will like to hear Thornton proceeds with every rapidity
30 *possible under his tuition; indeed he promises to be a most eminent artist—he*
has certainly every advantage in beginning so very early. How bitterly to
do I regret the same care was not bestowed upon me! I might have been
worth something by this time, if it had. Another change has taken place:
my sister has left us and gone to live with my Brother who has begun practice
35 *as a Surgeon &c Cupper about a fortnight since ——— ——— We are*
all tolerably well:- my little Percy has got six teeth and is one of the nicest
little fellows you ever saw; such a lively good tempered little creature!———
Do you see Alba? How far distant is she?——send us word how Willy, and
Clara dgo on, if they grow &c——We have seen Mr Hogg very often who is
40 *as severe as ever:- you will hardly know him, he is grown such a beau. I*
suppose it was in mercy to you he dressed so badly before, for I assure you
he looks quite handsome now.—— Mr Peacock ⟨ ⟩ we have not seen since
Mr Hunt wrote (I think); he was in town a couple of days, but he did not
honor us with a visit.—— He sends Mr Ollier word you want the linen
45 *I have got of yours. I think there must be some mistake about it; for I*
have only a pair of callico sheets and a table cloth, 2 little blankets and a

does not ninitar indeed you write very shabby letters I am
sure I have set you a very good example as to length
tell us a little more of yourselves — Did you pay
Lockes' bill (the dyer) he has sent me in a bill of nearly £ but
as he had your address when you were in London I did
not choose to pay it without asking you. I will leave
Mr Hunt a little room. Yours affectionately M. A. Hunt

14th July 1818

*Leigh and Marianne Hunt to P. B. and M. W. Shelley,
ca. July 14–August 4, 1818 (SC 486), page 4, showing
the difference between the hands of the two Hunts*

The Carl H. Pforzheimer Library

Hunts to Shelleys   *ca. July* 14–*August* 4, 1818

SC 486   *pillow case, which came in an unlocked box with a cannister of coffee, a*
coffee pot, and mill, and a few loose books.——— ——— Have you seen
the life of Curran? there is a curious anecdote or two of Mr Godwin. bye
50 *the bye I wish you would commission Mr Wildman to take his portrait*
    Mr Godwins I mean
    ∧*his terms are ten guineaus   I am quite sure you would like it and it would*
        Mr G being a public man
help him∧*: for he has strugled through a great deal of misery, and almost*
55 *starvation: with a ƒ wife and four children,* ~~wh~~ *with great talents for drawing*
but no connexion: however we are in hopes this likeness of Mͬ *Hunts will*
be of service to him; indeed it was with that veiw he asked Mͬ *Hunt to sit*
to him. I dont know that I have much to tell you about any body you know.
Mͬ *Coulson we have not seen some time. M*ͬ *Keats is gone to Scotland. You*
60   *be*
will sorry to hear poor Miss Lamb is ill again:– what a sad thing it is for
such an admirable woman. I dont know how it is but those thing seem to
fall on the most deligtful and amiable of mankind I dont mean her particular
complaint but distress and uneasiness in general. ——— ——— If you
65 *send any parcel over will you send some Italian chalk for drawing black and*
white: Thornton would be so much obliged to you; for it is so very difficult
to get good here—— How is it Mͬ *Shelley does not write   indeed* you
write very shabby letters I am sure I have set you a very good example as
to length   tell us a little more of yourselves — ~~in the~~ *Did you pay Lockes'*
70 *bill (the dyer)? he has sent me in a bill of nearly £3 but as he had your*
address when you were in London I did not choose to pay it without asking
you. I will leave Mͬ *Hunt a little room. yours affectionately* M.A. Hunt.
*14*ᵗʰ *July 1818*

Very well, Madam; a little room! But I shall turn it into a large one, by
75 *making my letters little; as all the devils got into Pandæmonium by shrinking*
themselves. And first, to tell you, my dear friends, why Marianne's letter
has been so long delayed after the date. You must know, first of all, that it
waited for a parcel of Mͬ *Ollier's; then it struck us that M*ͬ *Wildman might*
as well make a copy of my head, *which accordingly comes to ask you how*

SC 486 *you do; then Mr Ollier waited for us; then I believe he sent off his letter before his parcel; then we all think we are waiting for each other, & then we all feel wonder & remorse, & Shelley spares his dilatory friend in behalf of his late good epistolary behaviour, not to mention his present (in two senses). Can you manage to carry the head about with you, like the pot of*

85 *basil in Boccaccio? It is as large as life, you see, though the picture itself is not so large as the original, which includes part of the body. It is also very spiritedly done, & reckoned a great likeness, though I must tell~you~in greater justice to the artist, that it is not so finely wrought up as the original,*

90 *albeit he himself thinks the contrary. (Should ~~this~~ the box still come after the letter, you will conclude that the ~~head~~ picture is travelling in it. I am sorry I find there is nothing miraculous in my head, or it would ~~have~~ naturally have saved us the trouble of packing, & gone to the land of Loretto the shortest*

95 *way.) And now, who will sent us a head~or heads~in return, drawn by some Italian? Pray think of that, & shew for once you have some respect for the Mosaic institution, which enjoins the payment of limb for limb. I wonder people never send portraits of hands to each other as well as heads. The thought has*

100 *just struck me. It is a very cordial member; and if any one sets me the example, I'll follow it. Think of that also. And now, thank ye heartily Marina, for your last letter; & thank ye, Shelley, for yours; & thank ye, Clare, for your Venetian music, which I think very natural & dansatory indeed. Little Mary fell into the measure of it directly, & twirled herself*

105 *about the room with all sorts of clappings of hands & sidelong nods. You must know they say she grows handsomer & finelier shaped every day,– which I hear of course with the old paternal scepticism. ⟨   ⟩Tell (hallo, I'm out of Pandæmonium) tell us all about ~~all~~ the little ones, & more than all about the large ones. Shelley indeed (by the way, do you know he has deviated*

110 *into three of these "feminine" letter-marks himself?) has given a very nice full account of the way in which you spend your time. So he won't tell me about the mountains,– & talks of my microscopic eyes! Well,–tell him I think him great nevertheless. I envy you your vines & fire-flies certainly; but with regard to climate & summer, Marianne has told you we have had*

[609]

The Carl H. Pforzheimer Library

Hunts to Shelleys   *ca. July* 14–*August* 4, 1818

sc 486   *a reasonable season, & it remains so still. It is said there has not been such a one for 40 years. I certainly remember nothing like it myself, for con- tinuance,– real, uninterrupted southern continuance. Day after day, day after day, there is nothing but sunshine & blue sky, with once & away a good large drenching rain that seems to come purely to lay the dust & water*

120   *the vegetation. Never was a finer time for the theories of your humble servant the Bee. I long to hear of Rome, & Naples, & the paintings, &c. &c., particularly of the ladies & the out-of-door amusements. Shelley will become a connoisseur in the best part of paintings,– the sentiment & imagination. Pray tell me, in special, of ~~the~~ Rafael's pictures of Cupid & Psyche at the*

125   *of his ~~Gatea~~ Galatea,*
Chigi palace, of his Poetry & Parnassus,‸of the picture where the officiating deacon ~~is~~ (a sceptic) is blushing at the sight of a miraculous cross on the host, of the School of Athens with all the philosophers & Shelleyites of old in it,– of the sculpture,– & of what you see of Julio Romano's. Ariosto, I

130   *must own, though reluctantly, does not answer the expectations formed of him by a reader accustomed to Shakspeare's inexhaustible thinking & Spenser's imagination. He seems wordy & superficial in the comparison. But ~~his~~ he has a vein of fine natural poetry in him nevertheless, & delightful spirits; & I have no doubt, the idiomatic charm they speak of is ~~much~~*

135   *very great*
~~greater~~ to ~~the~~ his countrymen, as foreigners can even relish it. Ariosto always seems to me one of nature's gentlemen,– if you understand that mixture of the aboriginal & sophisticated.   But I must own that I prefer his prede-

         general
140   *cessor Boyardo for‸entertainment, & Pulci for perfect freedom & a greater flesh-&-blood variety in his knights; & I think by the way, that an ac- quaintance with these two poets diminishes still further one's special admira- tion of Ariosto, who has succeeded so much perhaps with his countrymen because he has hit a more universal intelligibility of style & <u>address</u>,– a*

145   *and not*
great thing certainly,– but then it is the means ~~rather than~~ the end. I think you would like Ariosto's minor poems & satires. But Petrarch, Boccaccio, &

         Dante,
Dante, are the morning, noon, & night of the great Italian day,– or rather‸
150   *Petrarch, & Boccaccio are the*
night, morning, & noon. "And the evening & the morning were the first

SC 486 *day." Shelley told me once he would read Boccaccio. Pray make him do so*

now, espècially the tales of the Falcon, of the Pot of Basil, of the King who

came to kiss the young girl that was sick for love of him, & of the lover who

155 *returned & found his mistress married on account of false reports of him,*

& who ~~lay~~ coming in upon her at night-time & begging her to let him lie

down a little by her side without disturbing her husband, quietly broke his

heart there. I have not gone on with my Coventry story yet, though I most

assuredly mean to do so; but it must wait for this drama of mine; & this

160 *drama, you must know, in a grave Shelleian fit, I have turned from a comedy*

to a tragedy or rather serious play, and made the famous Cid the subject

of it, being moved thereto, not by any sympathies or emulations with Master

Corneille, but by an account of his Spanish original ~~by~~ Don Guillen de

                       Lives

165 *Castro in Lord Holland's ~~Life~~ of him & Lope. The Cid, you know, revenges*

a blow given to his old father. I mean to make him punish the giver of it, &

yet be above the feeling of the revenge, as revenge:– Now will Shelley say,

"That's admirable!"– Marina. "It is; but will it succeed, Hunt?–" First

Lady. Succeed! It ought & must; & if it don't, I hope Hunt will give all

170 *the actors & managers a good cutting up;– but lord! I'm sorry it isn't the*

comedy. I'd have got him to mention Florence ~~phials~~ vials in it." Shelley.

"Oh, how very ridiculous!" First Lady. "Well, you may laugh, Shelley,"

but I would. Why the scene lies in Italy you know at Venice,–& why mayn't

one speak of Florence vials at Venice as well   *tea-cups in Lon-*

175 *don? I'm serious now." Marina. Yes, now you are, Clare, or pretend to*

be. If you were really so, you'd laugh again." ~~Clare~~ First Lady. (giggling.)

"Well."— I am delighted to hear that Shelley is on the subject he men-

tions; it completely suits him, being at once logical, philosophical, poetical,

           &

180 *mysteri< >s I shall hail his Homer's Hymns too, to begin the year with.*

I can tell him that his name gets more known & respected every day, in

spite of the Quarterly Reviewers, who have attacked him, & me, & Hazlitt,

                              false,

(though not Shelley by name) in their old ^ furious, & recoiling way. The

185 *candid part of their friends are, I believe, really ashamed of them,– one or*

two, I know, are. They surely never felt any real dignity or contempt for

The Carl H. Pforzheimer Library

Hunts to Shelleys   *ca. July* 14–*August* 4, 1818

SC 486   *meanness themselves; or they would avoid extravagances which enable one*
to despise them. Hazlitt has written a masterly character of Gifford, much
more coolly done than these things of his in general; & this single circum-
190   *stance shews what sort of feelings the poor creature generates. I have noticed*
him only in passing, truly & unaffectedly feeling too much scorn, as you
may imagine; but I think I shall say something further after all, as far as
others are concerned, whose contempt perhaps is not close at hand enough
to be so effective. There is the allusion that Shelley expected to the book at
195   *the Chartreuse, but they only quote the word* αθεος. Φιλανθρωπος *they chose*
to let alone.– But perhaps you have seen or heard of all this. Marianne has
told you of our new house. It is very comfortable with the single exception of
it's looking out upon houses back & front; but I have a study to myself, &
fill the window with hydrangeas, in the freshness of which I am now writing
200   *this letter on Shelley's birthday, which God grant may return many & many*
a time, with all the blessings for him & his, that can be wished them by their
most affectionate friend

Leigh Hunt.

(A little bit more chit-chat. Coulson has come back from a peregrination
205   *among the microscopics in the Lakes. Hogg is gone to Durham. Miss Lamb*

& sometimes Alsager.

is getting better, & her brother of course. We see him frequently,ᴧ–Thornton's
"love", & "he shall be happy to know where you are, & that you enjoy
yourselves very much." All the others send their loves with equal gravity this
210   *time, including little Willy. You shall hear of the details of our new house,*
when we are settled.)

Mr Novello begs his particular respect & remembrances.

Many happy returns—

     EK

SC 486   *Bessy's very well & comfortable:*

Coulson begs remembrances.

[Address, page 8]

      Signor Shelley

To

      Percy B. Shelley Esqre

220   *Alla cura*

          del Signor Giovanni Gisborne

           Livorno

For Leghorn.

              Italia.

line 8. *you all*: wear along the margin of the page may have destroyed a question mark.

line 18. *stray* (sic).

line 21. *through*: second *through* written through *thorough*.

line 24. *paralell* (sic).

    Portram: should be *Portman*.

line 25. (*8. York buildings*): final punctuation omitted because page 1 ends.

line 26. *large a life* (sic).

    lenghth (sic).

line 38. *How*: altered from *how*.

line 40. *severe*: may be *serene*.

line 42. ⟨ ⟩ *we*: two illegible letters canceled by smearing wet ink.

line 54. *strugled* (sic).

line 57. *veiw* (sic).

line 61. *thing*: *g* written through *k*.

line 62. *thing* (sic).

line 63. *deligtful* (sic).

    mankind: probable reading; word crowded at edge of page.

line 67. *write*: probable reading.

line 101. *heartily*: no comma follows this word, probably because it ends a line.

line 103. *which*: probable reading.

    dansatory: a playful coinage.

line 107. ⟨ ⟩*Tell*: the illegible marks may possibly be *4£*, smeared while the ink was wet.

line 127. *is*: canceled by the parenthesis.

line 131. *Shakspeare's*: contemporary spelling.

line 137. *you*: written through *one*.

line 140. *Boyardo*: contemporary spelling.

line 156. *lay*: questionable reading.

line 168. *Marina.*: preceded by canceled quotation marks.

line 170. *but lord! . . . comedy.*: quotation marks before and after this passage are canceled.

line 174. *well*: this word ends a line; Hunt left a large space at the beginning of the next line.

line 180. *mysteri<ou>s*: damaged by seal tear, with *s* adhering to seal (right-hand margin of page).

line 181. *him*: *h* split by seal tear.

line 182. *Quarterly*: *Q* split by seal tear.

line 191. *feeling*: this word begins page 8 of the letter, but Hunt left about an inch of margin at the top of the page in which he later wrote his first postscript (lines 204–211).

line 209. *All*: may be canceled.

line 210. *new . . . settled.*): written between the top two lines of manuscript page 8.

The Carl H. Pforzheimer Library

SC 486   line 212. The four final postscripts are written sideways in the right margin of the address flap. Lines 213–214 in the hand of Elizabeth Kent, are written next to line 212, which occupies two lines in the manuscript; line 215 is written in between Hunt's and Bessy's remarks. Hunt wrote the very last postscript in a fine hand about an inch beneath the other three.

DURING THE EARLY months of the Shelleys' stay abroad, the Hunts wrote long letters, but they wrote few and delayed mailing them (see sc 474, Commentary). This double letter by Marianne and Leigh Hunt provides a classic example. Marianne began it sometime in July, finishing and dating her part on July 14. After a delay of about three weeks, Hunt took up his writing. The letter was completed (including postscript greetings from Marianne and Elizabeth Kent) on Shelley's birthday, August 4, 1818. It did not reach Shelley until mid-August 1819 and thus was already something of a historical artifact when the Shelleys finally read it because Hunt sent it, along with his portrait by Wildman, in Ollier's parcel — probably to save postage.[1]

Thornton Hunt's drawing master (line 26) was probably John R. Wildman, who between 1823 and 1839 exhibited a total of twenty-one pictures — principally "figures" — at the Royal Academy, the British Institution, and the Suffolk Street Gallery (of the Society of British Artists).[2] Being very poor and having "no connexion," it is unlikely that he was related to Colonel Thomas Wildman (1787–1859), Byron's schoolfellow at Harrow who purchased Newstead Abbey in 1817.[3]

Exactly when the Hunts moved into their new and more spacious house is not clear. Marianne's description of it in this letter is the earliest dated record of their move that we have been able to discover, and inasmuch as she would probably not have had time to write until at least a week or two after the move, we conjecture that about the beginning of July 1818 the Hunts moved the few blocks from Lisson Grove North to York Buildings, New Road (Plan of London, Al, Front End-

1. See sc 533 and Commentary.

2. See Algernon Graves, *A Dictionary Of Artists Who Have Exhibited Works In The Principal London Exhibitions From 1760 To 1893* (3rd edition, 1901; reprinted, Bath, 1969), p. 302. John rather than the alternative Edmund Wildman was befriended by Hunt, as is evidenced by Hunt's *Literary Pocket-Book* for 1820, which lists among "Eminent Living Artists" not only "Blake, W. poetical subjects," but also "Wildman, J. crayons and miniature" (pp. 169, 172).

3. See Byron, *Letters and Journals*, IV, 186–187 n. Most contemporary references to "Wildman" that we have been able to locate seem to refer to members of the family of Colonel Wildman.

Shelley and his Circle : Manuscripts

Hunts to Shelleys   *ca. July* 14–*August* 4, 1818

SC 486 papers). SC 474, Commentary, suggests what this move portended for the Hunts' temporary economy drive.

Marianne announces another change in their household that should have struck a sympathetic response from Mary Shelley; Bessy Kent has left the Hunt household to live with her younger brother Thomas Kent, who was beginning what was to prove to be an unsuccessful medical career (lines 34–35). According to Thornton Hunt's later account, the "younger brother-in-law" was a "somewhat 'fast' medical student, — a skillful manipulator and sharp-sighted observer who could not stick to his own profession, and wandered dubiously through life, now among uncongenial proprieties, then among utterly unintelligible aesthetics, until at last he found a nest of his own, apart."[4] Marianne goes on to give (lack of) news of Keats and Coulson and to mention Mary Lamb's latest attack of recurrent insanity. This last report is significant because it is the only record that Lamb's biographers have of Mary's illness in 1818.[5] Marianne's reference to a life of John Philpot Curran (lines 48–49) is to one of three memoirs published by 1818 — by William O'Regan, Alexander Stephens, and Charles Phillips — but it is not clear which specific one she has seen.

Between the time Marianne finished her part of the letter and Hunt began to progress with his, at least two letters from the travelers reached the Hunts (lines 101–102). These are not extant, though Mary's Journal provides dates: on June 15 and July 2 the Shelleys wrote to the Hunts from Bagni di Lucca. One important aspect of Hunt's chatter is, then, that it provides information about the contents of lost letters from Shelley. We learn that Claire had sent Hunt the melody of some Venetian air (lines 102–103)[6] and that Shelley had been reading Ariosto (lines 129–147) and translating some of Homer's Hymns (line 180). He also sent an account of his daily life in Italy and some account of the sights, including vines and fireflies (line 113). Hunt characterizes Shelley's lapse into such commonplace epistolary topics as "'feminine' letter-marks" (line 110), likening Shelley's observations on small details to his own

---

4. Blunden, *Leigh Hunt*, pp. 359–360.

5. See E. V. Lucas, *The Life of Charles Lamb* (London, 1905), II, 7.

6. Mary Shelley, in a postscript to Shelley's April 30 letter to Peacock, had announced her intention of buying Hunt "some airs ... from an opera we saw here" (Shelley, *Letters*, II, 16).

The Carl H. Pforzheimer Library

Hunts to Shelleys   *ca. July* 14–*August* 4, 1818

SC 486   "microscopic eyes" (line 112). Later, in his first postscript, Hunt mentions Walter Coulson's travels "among the microscopics in the Lakes," thus tying his own delight in homely details and Shelley's new interest in them with the characteristic mode of the "Lake Poets" — particularly Wordsworth. Hunt's remark about Shelley's change in perspective seems from our distance a shrewd intimation of a new vein that was to emerge in several of Shelley's later poems — most notably, perhaps, in *Julian and Maddalo* and "Letter to Maria Gisborne."

Hunt's enthusiasm for things Italian — language, literature, music, art, and history — was great but indiscriminate. Here he praises Venetian music, Boccaccio's tales (including the Pot of Basil, which Keats was to use the following spring as the basis of his "Isabella"), the paintings of Raphael and his pupil Giulio Romano (?1492–1546), and several great Italian writers. In response to what must have been Shelley's expressed disappointment with Ariosto,[7] Hunt launches into half a defense of his poetry, but ends by comparing him unfavorably to Boiardo and Pulci, as well as to Petrarch, Dante, and Boccaccio.[8] Hunt's interest doubtless stimulated Shelley to devote more attention to Italian art and letters than he might otherwise have done, had he received no such encouragements. The letters of Peacock and Godwin were filled with English political news and personal affairs. Only Hunt, among Shelley's English friends, really envied the Shelleys their sojourn in what seemed to him the paradise of the arts.[9]

We earlier observed Hunt's strong reaction to Lord Holland's *Life of Guillen de Castro* and quoted the somewhat romanticized account in Hunt's *Autobiography* of how Hunt came to write his drama on the Cid (sc 387 and Commentary). In the present letter Hunt gives Shelley an account of the genesis of his tragedy which is basically the same as the

---

7. For Shelley's opinion, see his letter to the Gisbornes, July 10, 1818, Shelley, *Letters*, II, 20.

8. Luigi Pulci (1432–1484), whose *Morgante Maggiore* inspired Byron's *Don Juan*, is the one writer among these not identified in college desk dictionaries.

9. Hunt's interest in Italian literature extended to several of his later publications. Some of these which provide translations and/or selections of Italian writers include: *Amyntas: A Tale of the Woods; from the Italian of Torquato Tasso* (London: T. and J. Allman, 1820); *Bacchus in Tuscany, a Dithyrambic Poem, From the Italian of Francesco Redi* (London: John and H. L. Hunt, 1825); and *Stories from the Italian Poets: with Lives of the Writers* (London: Chapman and Hall, 1846). For further illustration of Hunt's great interest in Italian literature, see W. J. Burke, "Leigh Hunt's Marginalia," *Bulletin of the New York Public Library*, XXXVII (February 1933), 87–107.

SC 486   one later published in his *Autobiography*. Hunt worked on *The Cid* throughout 1818 and wrote of his progress to the Shelleys; by the time *The Literary Pocket-Book* appeared in late 1818,[10] Hunt reported to Charles Cowden Clarke that he had written "two acts of a tragedy."[11] This play was completed in February 1819, but it was never acted and was finally published in part in the *Companion* for May 28 and June 4, 1828, only because Hunt was ill and could not write his regular essays (sc 504, sc 517, sc 529, and Commentaries). The "Coventry story" that Hunt abandoned in favor of *The Cid* must have been a novel or poem about Lady Godiva. Reflections of his interest in that legend may be found in "Godiva" in the *Indicator*, I (October 27, 1819), 17–19, and his poem "Godiva" in the *New Monthly Magazine*, LXXXVIII (March 1850), 285–286.

      Hunt's mention of the *Quarterly Review*'s attacks on himself, Shelley, and Hazlitt refers to the January 1818 issue;[12] there Hunt's *Foliage* was reviewed unfavorably, probably by Shelley's Eton classmate John Taylor Coleridge,[13] and the review contains a passage attacking Shelley (pages 328–329), though not by name.[14] The issue also contains a vicious attack on Hazlitt's *Characters of Shakespear's Plays* (pages 458–466). Hunt, obviously stung by these articles, fails to mention in this letter that the same issue of the *Quarterly* contains a not entirely unfavorable review of *Frankenstein*.[15] On Hazlitt's *Letter to William Gifford, Esq.*, which first appeared in the *Examiner* for June 15, 1818, see sc 517 and Commentary.

10. *The Literary Pocket-Book* for 1819, like all pocket diaries, would necessarily have appeared sometime in late 1818 prior to the start of the new calendar year. For a complete description of this publication and a table of contents see T. J. Wise, *Catalogue of the Ashley Library*, ([London], Privately Printed, 1922), II, 196–197.

11. Clarke, *Recollections of Writers*, p. 200.

12. Vol. XVIII, no. xxxvi. Hill and Helen Chadwick Shine, *The Quarterly Review Under Gifford* (Chapel Hill, 1949), p. 59, give the date of publication of this number as June 1818. More specifically, Godwin mentions that "'Frankenstein' would be reviewed in the next Quarterly Review to be published June 12" (*Shelley and Mary*, I, 290 A).

13. See Shine, *The Quarterly Review*, p. 59.

14. Reprinted by White, *Unextinguished Hearth*, p. 125.

15. Note pp. 379–385. Hunt mentions this review in sc 504. Interestingly enough, Godwin, who is attacked in the review of *Frankenstein*, found it "very innocent" (*Shelley and Mary*, I, 290 A), whereas Peacock describes it as "in no very friendly style" (*Works*, VIII, 194).

Shelley, Notes on Herodotus   **?July 16–August 2, 1818**

SC 486   There is a final irony in Hunt's praise of the exceptionally hot English summer of 1818. One of the Shelleys' reasons for leaving Marlow — and England — was the discomfort and ill-health they experienced during the cold, damp summer and fall at Albion House. The period from 1812 through 1817 was exceptionally cold throughout the northern hemisphere, the worst year being 1816;[16] this change in climate doubtless drove many upper-class Englishmen besides the Shelleys — starved for foreign scenes by the long French wars — to flock to France and Italy.

16. See Patrick Hughes, "Eighteen Hundred and Froze-to-Death," *ESSA: The Magazine of the Environmental Science Services Administration* (July 1970), pp. 32–35.

SC 487   P. B. SHELLEY (AND WILLIAM GODWIN) HOLOGRAPH NOTES IN A COPY OF *HERODOTUS*, ?JULY 16–AUGUST 2, 1818

HOLOGRAPH NOTES, CORRECTIONS OF THE TEXT, AND MARGINAL SCORINGS in a bilingual (Greek and Latin) edition of Herodotus (7 vols. 8ᵛᵒ; Edinburgh, 1806).*

PROVENANCE: Percy Bysshe Shelley; sale of Shelley's books, Rownhams, near Southampton, England, February 1920; George Winter, Esq., London (Peck, *Shelley*, II, 351); Stonehill of New Haven, February 1966.

*HERODOTUS| GRÆCE & LATINE.| ACCEDUNT ANNOTATIONES SELECTÆ| NECNON| INDEX LATINUS,| EX EDITIONIBUS| WESSELINGII ET REIZII.| TOM. I. [II–VII]| [swell rule]| EDINBURGI:| 𝕰 𝔓𝔯𝔢𝔩𝔬 𝔄𝔠𝔞𝔡𝔢𝔪𝔦𝔠𝔬,| IMPENSIS GULIELMI LAING.| [short rule]| MDCCCVI.|

COLLATION: Vol. I: [ ]¹, [A]⁵, B–T⁸, U³. Vol. II: [ ]¹, A–R⁸, S⁷. Vol. III: [ ]¹, A–S⁸ [R3 unsigned], T⁵. Vol. IV: [ ]¹, A–R⁸ [B3 unsigned], S⁴. Vol. V: [ ]¹, A–U⁸ [A4 missigned A3; C3 and Q4 unsigned], X¹. Vol. VI: [ ]¹, A–S⁸, T⁷. Vol. VII: [ ]¹, A–L⁸, a–f⁸ [f3 missigned f2; f4 unsigned].

CONTENTS: Vol. I: Title (verso, blank); Dedication leaf to Richard Porson (verso, blank), pp. [?1–2]; *Notitia Literaria de Herodoto*, pp. [9]–16; *Clio*, pp. [17]–299; blank, p. 300; *Notæ in Librum I*, pp. [301]–310.

     Vol. II: Title (verso, blank); fly-title to *Euterpe* (verso, blank), pp. [1–2]; *Euterpe*, pp. [3]–237; blank, p. [238]; fly-title to *Thalia* (verso, blank), pp. [239–240]; *Thalia*, pp. [241]–278; *Notæ in Librum II*, pp. [279]–286.

     Vol. III: Title (verso, blank); fly-title to *Thalia* (verso, blank), pp. [1–2]; *Thalia* (continued from Vol. II), pp. [3]–174; fly-title to *Melpomene* (verso, blank), pp. [175–176]; *Melpomene*, pp. [177]–283; blank, p. 284; *Notæ in Librum III* (and *Librum IV* after p. 293), pp. [285]–289 [i.e., 297]; blank, p. [298].

Shelley, Notes on Herodotus   *?July 16–August 2,* **1818**

SC 487
Vol. IV: Title (verso, blank); fly-title to *Melpomene* (verso, blank), pp. [1–2]; *Melpomene* (continued from Vol. III), pp. [3]–114; fly-title to *Terpsichore* (verso, blank), pp. [115–116]; *Terpsichore*, pp. [117]–267; blank, p. [268]; *Notæ in Librum IV* (and *Librum V* after p. 273), pp. [269]–279; blank, p. [280].

Vol. V: Title (verso, blank); fly-title to *Erato* (verso, blank), pp. [1–2]; *Erato*, pp. [3]–159; blank, p. [160]; fly-title to *Polymnia* (verso, blank), pp. [161–162]; *Polymnia*, pp. [163]–311; blank, p. [312]; *Notæ in Librum VI* (and *Librum VII* after p. 320), pp. [313]–322.

Vol. VI: Title (verso, blank); fly-title to *Polymnia* (verso, blank), pp. [1–2]; *Polymnia* (continued from Vol. V), pp. [3]–125; blank, p. [126]; fly-title to *Urania* (verso, blank), pp. [127–128]; *Urania*, pp. [129]–292: *Notæ in Librum VII* (and *Librum VIII* after p. 297), pp. [293]–301; blank, p. [302].

Vol. VII: Title (verso, blank) fly-title to *Calliope* (verso, blank), pp. [1–2]; *Calliope*, pp. [3]–152; fly-title to Περι ῾Ομηρου (verso, blank), pp. [153–154]; Περι ῾Ομηρου, pp. [155]–175; blank, p. [176]; Index, pp. [1]–93; blank, p. [94]; Publisher's Advertisement, pp. [95–96].

Bound in contemporary calf, with panels of blind-stamped double fillets on covers with gold-tooled ornaments in the four corners. Spines in compartments between raised bands, with blind- and gold-tooled decoration and title, HERODOTUS| TOM. I (etc.). Set has been repaired, some corners renewed, and gray endpapers added. Sprinkled edges. All volumes neatly rebacked, with original backstrip of volumes II–VI laid down and spines newly decorated for volumes I and VII.

The text of SC 487 is presented differently from other units in these volumes because of the nature of the annotations and markings. We have arranged the material in three columns: The first column contains the page location; references to the Greek text (which is in a single column and occupies roughly the upper two thirds of each page) are to line only; those to the Latin text (in double columns at the bottom of each page) are to column and line. The second column lists Shelley's annotations themselves (or Godwin's, where so indicated), printed in italic type, with descriptions of miscellaneous markings in roman type. The third column gives the standard book and chapter references to Herodotus (the numerals in square brackets indicate the limits of the full context). Annotations and markings are in pencil unless otherwise noted and material within wide-angle brackets is conjectural.

The Carl H. Pforzheimer Library

SC 487

LOCATION	ANNOTATION	BOOK AND CHAPTER
	Volume I	
First binding leaf, recto	*Solon & Cræsus–* 50	I.30 [29–33]
	βαλανηφαγοι ανδρες 96	I.66
	Cræsus & his Son—128	I.85
	Deioces the Institutor of Royal government among the Medes *interesting. 150*	I.98
	The subjugation of Lydia ⟨222⟩ *to effeminacy*	I.156 [155–157]
	An instance contrary to the received opinion of the ⟨223⟩ *Power of legislating to* ⟨the manners of an⟩ *extensive nation*	I.157
	The same customs as the Nairs were practised by the 243 Lycians	I.173
Page 38, line 12	*x* written in left margin; "συνηνείχθη" underlined	I.19
Page 48, column 2, lines 3–5	slight ink smear	I.27–28
Page 50, lines 8–12	ink blotting in left margin	I.30
Page 64, line 13	*x* in pencil and ink following φράζειν	I.39
Pages 66–67	ink smears and blots on both pages; perhaps some attempt to change text at page 67, line 13	I.42–43

[620]

Shelley, Notes on Herodotus   *?July 16–August 2, 1818*

SC 487	Page 73, line 16	*x* in ink in right margin	I. 49
	Page 91	ink blottings on lower half of page	I.62
	Page 104, line 8	*x* in ink preceding αὐτοὶ	I.70
	Page 289, line 2	Περισηῶν corrected to Περοσηων	I.207
	Page 295, column 1, line 9	"Sparagapises" corrected in ink	I.213

Volume II

Front end-paper, verso	written in ink:	
	Pyramids– *13*	II.8
	There were elder	II.23
	Poets than Homer	
	30	
	written in pencil:	
	Might not the discovery	II.106
	of the characters in which	
	Herodotus has here translated	
	into Greek, lead to the key of	
	the Egyptian Hiero	
	glyphics?— 129	
	Curious reasoning about	II.120
	Homers Story of Helen	
	148	
	Story of the Architect	II.121
	who stole the Treasures of	
	Rampsinitus 150	
	Page 24, lower margin	*huic alveo aquae*	II.17

SC 487

LOCATION	ANNOTATION	BOOK AND CHAPTER
Page 31, line 14	o/ in left margin correcting ἐόντες to ἐόντος	II.25
Page 127, line 1	*The Jews* written in right margin above this line; Σύροι οἱ ἐν τῇ Παλαιστίνη underlined in pencil; vertical line drawn to the right of lines 1–2	II.104
Page 129, lines 9–10	vertical line in right margin marking inscription on the statue of Sesostris	II.106
Page 171, line 1	*?* written in right margin	II.132
Page 177, column 2, line 7	short slant stroke in right margin	II.136
Page 181, line 13	τ in right margin correcting Ποὺς to τοὺς	II.139
Page 206, line 6	γ in left margin correcting λυπτίων to γυπτίων	II.156
Back free endpaper, recto	*Rhodopis the courtezan Charaxus Sappho Esop. 175.*	II.135

Volume III

Front free endpaper, verso	*Characteristic anecdote of Sparta 161*	III.148
	The Devotion of Zopyrus 164	III.153
	written in ink:	
	Horrible vaticination in Scythia 248	IV.69
	Zalmoxis, the Thracian God 280	IV.95 [94–96]

Shelley, Notes on Herodotus   **?July 16–August 2, 1818**

SC 487	Front binding leaf, recto	*New instance of the power of Custom* *A speech of Darius 19–20*	III.38
		Story of Lycophron Son of Periander Tyrant of Corinth 32	III.48 [should be 50–53, pp. 33–40]
		Heroism in Prexaspes 72	III. 75–76
		Otanes the Persian democrat 84	III.83 [80–84]
		9540 Euboic talents of Silver *4680 of gold, the annual tribute of the Empire of Darius* ⟨ ⟩ *of India 102*	III.89–100
	Page 15, lower right margin	*Croesus/ has/ every/ ap/ pearance/ of being/ a fictitious/ charac/ ter*	III.36
	Page 72, lines 2–4	vertical line in left margin	III.75 (end)
	Page 84, lines 4–8	vertical line in left margin	III.83
	Page 88, lines 5–8	vertical line in left margin next to lines 5–6, with the following: *How did/ D's groom/ manage/ this/.*	III.86
	Page 102, line 8	comma after οὐδὲν deleted in ink	III.100
	Page 122, lines 13–16	vertical line in left margin with the following: *The reasoning/ of ⟨Iphigenia⟩*	III.119

The Carl H. Pforzheimer Library

Shelley, Notes on Herodotus　　　　　　　*?July 16–August 2, 1818*

SC 487

LOCATION	ANNOTATION	BOOK AND CHAPTER
	Volume IV	
Front binding leaf, recto	*The wisdom of a child　175*	V.51
	The preferableness of republicanism to monarchy 206	V.78
	Speech in favour of liberty by Sosicles of Corinth　　223	V.92
Page 35	dirt or charcoal smear in lower margin	IV.131
Page 175, lines 6–11	vertical line in right margin	V.51
Page 185, line 6	horizontal stroke in right margin	V.62
Page 206, lines 10–16	vertical line in left margin	V.78
	Volume V	
Front binding leaf, recto	*Casts in Sparta as in India & antient Egypt 64*	VI.60
	A mysterious conception　75	VI.69
	Instances of three particular providences driving a man mad 83	VI.75
	Battle of Marathon　　111	VI.100 [–117]
	Self sacrifize of two Spartans　　306	VII.134–135
Page 27, line 10	μο in ink in left margin correcting ύνοισι to μούνοισι.	VI.25
Page 83, lines 6–11	vertical line in right margin	VI.75 (end)

[624]

SC 487	Page 139, line 5	ή in ink in right margin correcting ψύγματος to ψήγματος	VI.125
	Page [161]	pressed flower before fly-title of Polymnia	
	Page 183, column 1, line 11	*t/* in ink in left margin correcting *superavi* to *superavit*	VII.10
	Page 189, line 13	Ξ in ink correcting Πέρξης to Ξέρξης	VII.12
	Page 271, line 15	κ in ink correcting ἔσαστον to ἔκαστον	VII.100
	Page 276, column 1	first line of Latin translation canceled and inserted in ink in Godwin's hand after final line in column 2	VII.103

Volume VI

	Front binding leaf, recto	*Leonidas & the battle of Thermopylæ 86*	VII.204–205
	Page 25, line 9	θ in ink correcting δεῶν to θεῶν	VII.153
	Page 60, line 11	τ in ink correcting πούτῳ to τούτῳ	VII.180
	Page 164, line 2	*x* written faintly in left margin	VIII.36
	Page 164, line 4	ink spot in left margin	VIII.36
	Page 202, line 3	παρ of παροιχώηεε underlined	VIII.72
	Page 214, line 12	κρούεσθε of ἀνακρούεσθε underlined.	VIII.84

The Carl H. Pforzheimer Library

SC 487

LOCATION	ANNOTATION	BOOK AND CHAPTER
Page 262, line 16	ων/ in ink in left margin correcting θέλον to θέλων	VIII.124
Page 277, line 16	ink slash in right margin	VIII.136
Page 277, column 2, lines 1–3	ink smudge	VIII.136

Volume VII

Second binding leaf, recto	written in ink:	
	Wonderful escape of Hegesistratus 52	IX.37
	Horrible revenge of Amestris *143*	IX.113 [112]
Page 7, column 2, line 8	"hominesque" canceled in ink	IX.5
Page 14, line 14	ε/ in ink in right margin correcting ἐπελθόντος to ἐπελθόντες	IX.11
Page 141, column 2	final line of Latin text canceled in ink and rewritten in Godwin's hand on page 142 beneath last line of column 2: *hil audisset Masistes, metuens.*	IX.111–113

It is always difficult to determine exactly when Shelley read and annotated a classical author like Herodotus. Though this 1806 edition[1] was available from Shelley's schooldays on, the probability is that Shelley wrote his annotations when he read Herodotus daily at Bagni di Lucca from July 16 through August 2, 1818.

1. Lowndes (II, 1052–1053) describes it as "a neat and correct edition," and gives the price as £2.2.0.

Shelley, Notes on Herodotus   *?July 16–August 2, 1818*

SC 487   Shelley's first recorded mention of Herodotus occurs in a want-list of books sent to Thomas Hookham from Tanyrallt on December 17, 1812. There, apparently responding to Godwin's early exhortations that he should study history, Shelley asked for several modern histories and for works of Herodotus, Thucydides, Xenophon, and Plutarch "with Latin or English subjoined." Hookham's markings on the list seem to indicate that he supplied the first three, but not Plutarch.[2] Herodotus is mentioned in the reading list in Mary's Journal for 1815, but the only period during which there is a record of Shelley's reading Herodotus day after day is in July and August 1818. From the time the Shelleys reached Bagni di Lucca on Thursday, June 11, Shelley read classical accounts of Greek life during the fifth century B.C. From June 12 through June 16 he read Xenophon's apologetic *Memorabilia Socrates*;[3] and then, perhaps to get another point of view, he read the works of Socrates' enemy Aristophanes, beginning with *The Clouds* (June 17–July 6). At the same time Shelley (and Mary, occasionally) read "Anacharsis," not the spurious Greek letters published as those of the Scythian prince,[4] but the novel by the great French classicist the Abbé Jean Jacques Barthélemy entitled *Voyage du jeune Anacharsis en Grèce, dans le milieu du quatrième siècle avant l'ère vulgaire*.[5] Then on July 7 Shelley began to read and translate Plato's *Symposium*, completing a draft of that translation on July 17.

        Mary's Journal entries show that Shelley began reading Herodotus on July 16, the day before he finished his translation of *The Symposium*, and Shelley himself mentions this reading in his July 25 letter to Peacock as part of his daily routine.[6] He read the Greek historian faithfully every

2. Shelley, *Letters*, I, 342. SC 487 was in Godwin's possession at one time — or was at least read by him — for corrections of the Latin text in volume V, page 276, and volume VII, pages 141–142, are clearly in his hand. That Shelley corrected the Greek text and Godwin the Latin shows in which language each read Herodotus.

3. At least three volumes of Shelley's copy of Xenophon's works survive; see Peck, *Shelley*, II, 348–351.

4. See Sir William Smith, *A Classical Dictionary of Greek and Roman Biography, Mythology and Geography*, revised by G. E. Marindin (4th edition, London, 1894), pp. 65–66, and the British Museum catalogue under Anacharsis.

5. See SC 448, Appendix.

6. Shelley, *Letters*, II, 26.

SC 487   day[7] until on August 2 Mary noted: "S. finishes Herodotus." The next day Shelley read *The Persians* by Aeschylus.

One reference that throws the dating of the annotations in the present volumes into some doubt appears in Shelley's letter to Peacock, September 21, 1819. There he writes that when John Gisborne goes to England he will deliver to Peacock the manuscript of *Prometheus Unbound*, as well as "some volumes of Spenser the two last of Herodotus & Paradise lost — which may be put with the others."[8] The "two last" volumes of Herodotus sound very much like the sixth and seventh volumes of the present edition; the possibility exists, therefore, that Shelley never took the first five volumes of this edition to Italy (as he is known to have taken only selected volumes from his Bipont Plato[9]). But it is equally possible that Shelley had sent the first five volumes of Herodotus back to England sometime between August 1818 and September 1819 — perhaps from Venice in the autumn of 1818 via carriers engaged on behalf of Byron or perhaps packed with the 250 copies of *The Cenci* that Shelley prepared for shipment from Leghorn early in September 1819.[10]

Whether or not all of Shelley's annotations in these volumes of Herodotus date from the summer of 1818, they exhibit Shelley's interest in a work he studied carefully at this time. Mary's Journal records Shelley as later reading Herodotus only on October 1, 1820, and — with Mary, probably to help her learn Greek — in December 1821.[11]

Though Shelley was almost always reading one or another Greek writer, it would seem logical to suppose that his reading of Herodotus in July and August of 1818 would be reflected in his "Discourse on the Manners of the Antient Greeks Relative to the Subject of Love," the

---

7. Jones's edition of *Mary Shelley's Journal* omits the final sentence in the Ms. Journal entry for July 19 — "S. corrects the Symposium & reads Herodotus — Ride out in the evening" and omits the entire entry for July 23: "Read Livy — Anacharsis & Horace   Transcribe the Symposium — ride out in the evening — S. reads Herodotus and Hume's England aloud in the evening."

8. Shelley, *Letters*, II, 120.

9. See SC 473 and Shelley to Hogg, October 22, 1821, Shelley, *Letters*, II, 361.

10. See SC 537 and Commentary.

11. After Shelley sent his seven-volume edition of Herodotus back to England, he may have used the collective edition of "Greek Historians 8 vols" recorded by Mary among the books belonging to Shelley in the possession of the Gisbornes, January 1820. See Jean de Palacio, "Shelley's Library Catalogue," *Revue de Littérature Comparée*, XXXVI (1962), 273.

SC 487 fragmentary essay intended as an introduction to Shelley's translation of Plato's *Symposium*.[12] For that essay contains generalized comparisons of ancient Greece and post-Renaissance Europe. But a reading of the "Discourse" reveals that he was drawing his conception of Greek character primarily from other sources. In speaking of the beauty of lost Greek painting, he cites Pliny and Pausanias.[13] When discussing heroic Greeks, he names Phocion (402–317 B.C.), Epaminondas (d. 362 B.C.), and Timoleon (d. 337 B.C.) — none of whom falls within the scope or dates of the history of Herodotus.[14] But perhaps the most telling evidence that Shelley relied on the moralistic biographers like Plutarch and Diodorus, rather than on the histories of Herodotus and Thucydides, is this excerpt from the "Discourse": "The study of modern history is the study of kings, financiers, statesmen, and priests. The history of antient Greece is the study of legislators, philosophers, and poets; it is the history of men, compared with the history of titles."[15]

In Shelley's fragment of a letter to an unidentified lady on the study of foreign languages, he remarks that an English translation of Tacitus, Livy, or Herodotus is as "undelightful and uninstructive in translation" as a French translation of *Paradise Lost* or *King Lear*.[16] More pointedly, Shelley writes in his *Defence of Poetry*:

The parts of a composition may be poetical, without the composition as a whole being a poem. . . . And thus all the great historians, Herodotus, Plutarch, Livy, were poets; and although the plan of these writers, especially that of Livy, restrained them from developing this faculty in its highest degree, they make copious and ample amends for their subjection, by filling all the interstices of their subjects with living images.[17]

12. The only readily available complete text of the "Discourse" is found in Notopoulos, *Platonism*, pp. 404–413, although there was a private printing of one hundred copies of *Plato's Banquet* and the "Discourse" edited by Roger Ingpen and printed at the Curwen Press in 1931.

13. Notopoulos, *Platonism*, p. 404.

14. Shelley's sources of information on these men were probably Plutarch, Diodorus Siculus, and Cornelius Nepos.

15. Notopoulos, *Platonism*, pp. 406–407.

16. Shelley, *Letters*, II, 278.

17. Shelley, *Complete Works*, VII, 115–116. Shelley's comment was, presumably, in response to Peacock's remarks in *The Four Ages of Poetry*: "The transition from Homer to Herodotus is scarcely more remarkable than that from Herodotus to Thucydides: in the gradual dereliction of fabulous incident and ornamented language, Herodotus is as much a poet in relation to Thucydides as Homer is in relation to Herodotus. The history of Herodotus is half a poem: it was written while the whole

The Carl H. Pforzheimer Library

Shelley, *Notes on Herodotus*   **?*July* 16–August 2, 1818**

SC 487   These remarks show that Shelley valued the history of Herodotus as much for its intrinsic literary qualities as for the information it gave him about men and manners of classical time, though his annotations in the 1806 edition provide little or no evidence of this aesthetic interest. Perhaps one value of comparing Shelley's dry, factual, and linguistic markings in Herodotus with his other comments on the work is to remind ourselves that the records of Shelley's day-to-day activities — his letters, accounts of his visits and his reading, and so on — give at best a very superficial and fundamentally unreliable indication of what was going on within his mind and imagination.

When the Shelley notebooks in the Bodleian and Huntington libraries have been systematically indexed and the sources of their references and allusions traced, Shelley's annotations in the Pforzheimer copy of Herodotus can be combined with whatever relevant references or quotations there may be in those notebooks[18] to establish more clearly Shelley's interest in the first Western historian and the possible impact of this reading in 1818 on Shelley's later poetry — especially *Hellas*. In the meantime, we can make a few observations on the annotations before us. Herodotus appealed to several of Shelley's keen interests. At the lowest level, his accounts of the marvelous and horrible revived a curiosity that Shelley exhibited in his early Gothic fiction and poetry (and even in the torture scenes of *Laon and Cythna*). To this category we may assign the story from Herodotus, II.121,[19] that relates how an architect and his sons ingeniously stole treasures from the Egyptian king Rhampsinitus; the account in Herodotus, IV.68–69, of the cruel customs of the Scythians both in having soothsayers denounce innocent men and in burning "false prophets" and destroying their male children; and the tale recounted in IX.112–113 of the "horrible revenge" of Xerxes' wife, Amestris, upon her supposed rival, the wife of Xerxes' brother Masistes.

Sometimes, as in the customs of the Scythians, the cruelties that

---

field of literature yet belonged to the Muses, and the nine books of which it was composed were therefore of right, as well as courtesy, superinscribed with their nine names." (Peacock, *Works*, VIII, 9–10.)

18. For example, page 11 of Bodleian Ms. Shelley adds. e. 11 contains Shelley's notes, certainly dating from 1818, on Herodotus, Book I, chapters 7–14.

19. In the Commentary, unless the reference is specified as by volume and page, the roman and arabic numerals will designate books and chapters in the standard subdivisions of Herodotus.

Shelley and his Circle : Manuscripts

Shelley, Notes on Herodotus   **?July 16–August 2, 1818**

SC 487 are dwelt upon lend themselves to moral analysis as evidence of the evils of religious superstition. Notable here is the story of Zalmoxis, the Thracian god (IV.94–96), whose worship could be read by Shelley as a grim parody of certain features of Christianity. Besides, Shelley undoubtedly appreciated the dryly urbane commentary of Herodotus, who after he had described the religious custom of impaling men alive to send them as messengers to Zalmoxis, said of the Thracians (IV.96): "These people, then, who observe such a custom, when they were subdued by the Persians, followed the rest of the army." For in Shelley's experience, the most extreme religious orthodoxy did not affect the behavior of the English aristocracy enough to distinguish them from their cynical contemporaries. Shelley also marked an instance of a "mysterious conception" paralleling the Virgin Birth (VI.69) and one where divine punishment was attributed to three separate crimes (VI.75). Shelley appreciated the comparative anthropology in Herodotus, who was quite aware of the power of arbitrary custom leading men of different nations to opposite superstitions (see III.38), and he notes that the Lycians had a matriarchal system (I.173) similar to that attributed to the Nairs of Malabar by James Lawrence.[20] The Lydians were retrained by Cyrus the Great to be a commercial rather than a warlike people (I.155–157), which, as Shelley observes, was (if true) an unusual instance — "contrary to the received opinion" — of the power of government to influence the "manners of an extensive nation."

The "if true" has been added above to indicate Shelley's interest in the historicity of Herodotus' account — a subject that concerned Herodotus himself, though it did not stop him from retelling a good story.[21] Shelley, for example, seizes on one anecdote about Croesus (III.36) to suspect that he is a fictitious rather than a historical character. He questions the first account of how Darius' groom arranged for him to be chosen king of the Persians (III.86). On the other hand, Shelley draws

20. See SC 473, Commentary, fn. 1.

21. For example, at II.123 Herodotus writes: "Any person to whom such things appear credible may adopt the accounts given by the Egyptians; it is my object, however, throughout the whole history, to write what I hear from each people" (*Herodotus; A New and Literal Version from the Text of Baehr* by Henry Cary, London, 1882, p. 144). All translated passages are quoted from Cary's translation (first published in ?1847) in this Bohn's Classical Library edition. Henry Cary (1826–1868) was the son of Henry Francis Cary (1772–1844), translator of Dante.

SC 487 on Herodotus' attested observations to infer that "there were elder Poets than Homer" (page 621), to suggest a possible key to Egyptian hieroglyphics (page 621),[22] to total the tribute of Darius (page 623), and to note that the caste system existed in Sparta as well as in India and Egypt (page 624).

Above all, however, Shelley has singled out instances of human nobility in speech and heroism or self-sacrifice in action, whether historically grounded or mythical. Shelley notes Herodotus' accounts of the battles of Marathon (VI.100 ff.) and Thermopylae (VII.204 ff.) but not — except for an aside about the soothsayer Hegesistratus, who had earlier escaped from Sparta by cutting off his foot — that of the Battle of Plataea, which was decided partly by a series of accidents and partly because there was greater treachery and cowardice by the Persians' allies than by the allies of the Athenians and Spartans. He notes two anecdotes that showed the Spartan leaders' contempt for wealth (III.148 and V.51). He lists the (legendary) speeches of Otanes, the Persian who argued in favor of establishing a democracy rather than reinstating the kingdom (III.83), and of Sosicles of Corinth, who berated the Spartans for attempting to set up tyrannies in their dependent states, when they themselves would not submit to such a form of government in their own (V.92). He notes the self-sacrificing actions of Prexaspes, who told the truth to the assembled Persians and then committed suicide rather than become a tool of an imposter (III.75 ff.), and of Zopyrus, the Persian aristocrat who mutilated himself as part of a ruse to enable Darius and the Persians to recapture Babylon (III.153 ff.). And Shelley observed, probably with great satisfaction, where the sympathies of Herodotus of Halicarnassus lay; "equality of rights," wrote the historian, "shows, not in one instance only, but in every way, what an excellent thing it is. For the Athenians, when governed by tyrants, were superior in war to none of their neighbours; but when freed from tyrants, became by far the first; this, then shows that as long as they were oppressed they purposely acted as cowards, as labouring for a master; but when they were free every man was zealous to labour for himself."[23] Sentiments

22. On Shelley's interest in hieroglyphics and reference to them in *Prometheus Unbound*, see Donald H. Reiman, "Roman Scenes in *Prometheus Unbound* III.iv," *Philological Quarterly*, XLVI (1967), 69–78.
23. Herodotus, V.78; translated by Cary, pp. 335–336.

SC 487　such as this were, for Shelley, both poetry and truth — the synthesizing vision that harmonizes human experience into a will toward greater social and ethical good. This vision and the living language that embodies it — not the retailing of the fabulous — made Herodotus, along with Plutarch and Livy, a poet.

SC 488　P. B. SHELLEY, "ON LOVE," JULY 20–25, 1818

MANUSCRIPT (transcript), in the hand of Mary Shelley, 2½ pages. Double sheet, 4to (8.8 x 7.2 inches).
Laid paper. Watermark: [posthorn in crowned shield]| [cipher] *T & S*|.
Notations (printer's markings): 1. (upper left corner, page 1): *2*|; 2. (upper right corner, in pencil, page 1): *Preface by Mrs Shelley*|; 3. (upper left corner, page 2): *2*|; 4. (page 2, line 46, compositor's mark indicating the end of page 48 and gathering "D" in *The Keepsake*, between *as* and *the type*): [|; 5. (page 2, lower left corner, compositor's note indicating the beginning of page 49 and gathering "E" of *The Keepsake*): *49| E*|; 6. (upper left corner of page 3): *3*|.
Addition: manuscript inlaid in larger sheet, presumably from an album.

One Love
By Percy Bysshe Shelley

　　What is Love? Ask him who lives what is life; ask him who ~~worships~~ adores, what is God.

5　　　*I know not the internal constitution of other men, nor even of thine whom I now address. I see that in some external attributes they resemble me, but when misled by that appearance, I have thought to appeal to something in common and unburthen my inmost soul to them, I have found my language misunderstood, like one in a distant and savage land. The more*
10　*opportunities they have afforded me for ~~b~~ experience, the wider has appeared the interval between us, and to a greater distance have ~~they~~ the points of sympathy been withdrawn. With a spirit ill-fitted to sustain such proof, trembling and feeble through its tenderness, I have every where sought, and have found only repulse and disappointment.*
15　　　*Thou demandest what is Love. It is that powerful attraction towards all we conceive, or fear, or hope beyond ourselves, when we find within our*

[633]

SC 488 *own thoughts the chasm of an insufficient void and seek to awaken in all*

things ~~which~~ *that are, a community with what we experience within ourselves.*

20 *If we reason we would be understood; if we imagine we would that the airy*
children of our brain were born ~~un~~ *anew within another's; if we feel, we*
would that anothers nerves should vibrate to our own, that the beams of their
eyes should kindle at once and mix and melt into our own; that lips of
motionless ice should not reply to lips quivering and burning with the
25 *heart's best blood. This is Love. This is the bond and the sanction which*
connects not only man with man, but with every thing which exists. We are
born into the world, and there is something within us, which from the instant
that we live, more and more thirsts after its likeness. It is probably in corre-
spondance with this law that the infant drains milk from the bosom of its
30 *Mother; this propensity developes itself with the developement of our nature.*
We dimly see within our intellectual nature, a miniature as it were of our
entire self, yet deprived of all that we condemn or despise, the ideal protertype
of every thing excellent and lovely that we are capable of conceiving as be-
longing to the nature of man. Not only the portrait of our external being,
35 *but an assemblage of the* ~~minut~~ *minutest particles of which our nature is*
composed[x]: *a mirror* ~~upon~~ *whose surface reflects only the forms of purity and*
brightness: a soul within our own soul that describes a circle around its
proper Paradise, which pain and sorrow and evil dare not overleap. To this
we eagerly refer all sensations, thirsting that they should resemble and corre-
40 *spond with it. The discovery of its Antitype: the meeting with an understand-*
ing capable of clearly estimating our own; an imagination which should
enter into and seize upon the subtle and delicate peculiarities which we have
delighted to cherish and unfold in secret, ~~wh~~ *with a frame, whose nerves*
like the chords of two exquisite lyres, ~~stum~~ *strung to the accompaniment of*
45 *one delightful voice, vibrate with the vibrations of our own; and a combination*
of all these in such proportion as the type within demands: this is the invisible
and unattainable point to which Love tends; and to attain which, it urges
forth the powes of man to ~~exert~~ *arrest the faintest shadow of that without*
~~which~~ *the possession of which there is no rest nor respite to the heart over*
50 *which it rules. Hence in* ~~solut~~ *solitude, or that deserted state when we are*

Shelley, "On Love"   *July 20–25*, **1818**

SC 488   *surrounded by human beings and yet they sympathize not with us, we love the flowers, the grass, the waters and the sky. In the motion of the very leaves of spring, in the blue air, there is then found a secret correspondence with our heart. There is eloquence in the tongueless wind, and a melody in the*

55   *flowing brooks and the rustling of the reeds beside them, which by their inconceivable relation to something within the soul awaken the spirits to dance of breathless rapture, and bring tears of mysterious tenderness to the eyes, like the enthusiasm of patriotic success, or the voice of one beloved singing to you when alone. Sterne says that if he were in a desart he would love some*

60   *cypress.—— So soon as this want of or power is dead, Man becomes a living sepulchre of himself, and what yet survives is the mere husk of what once he was.*

---

x *These words are ineffectual and metaphorical. Most words are so— No help!*

line 12. *ill-fitted*: Mary Shelley uses the double hyphen that resembles a colon.

line 21. *un*: possibly *an*.

line 28. *correspondance* (sic).

line 30. *developes* (see also *developement*): alternative spelling.

line 32. *protertype* (sic).

line 40. *Antitype*: the *i* is not dotted and may be an *e*, though the dot may have been obliterated by the crossing of the two *t*'s.

line 48. *powes* (sic): for *powers*.

line 59. *desart*: contemporary spelling.

line 60. *of*: may be simply *p*.

COLLATION.

B: Bodleian Ms. Shelley adds. e. 11, pp. 1–9.

B²: Bodleian Ms. Shelley adds. d. 8, pp. 151–154.

K: *The Keepsake for 1829* (London, 1828), pp. 47–49.

M: Thomas Medwin, *The Shelley Papers* (London, 1833), pp. 21–24.

E: *Essays, Letters from Abroad, Translations and Fragments*, ed. Mrs. Shelley (London, 1840), I, 164–167.

F: *The Prose Works of Percy Bysshe Shelley*, ed. H. B. Forman (London, 1880), II, 267–270.

J: Shelley, *Complete Works* [Julian Edition] (London and New York, 1929), VI, 201–202.

C: *Shelley's Prose*, ed. David Lee Clark (University of New Mexico Press, 1954), pp. 169–171.

Omnia indicates agreement of all of the above.

line 3. Love?] Love?— *B*
        love? *M, E, J, C*
   Ask] ask *B*
   lives] lives, *M, E, F, J, C*
   life;] life— *M*
      life? *E, J, C*
   ask] Ask *C*

line 4. adores,] adores *B, B², K*
   God.] God? *E, F, J, C*

line 5. I know] *no new paragraph in M*
   men,] men. *M*
   nor . . . address.] omitted from *M*
   nor] or *B, B²*
   even of thine] even thine, *E, F, J*
        even yours *C*

SC 488

line 7. me,] me; *M*
    when] when, *K, M, E, F, J*
    appearance,] appearance *B, B², C*

line 8. common] common, *M, E, F, J*
    and] & *B*
    unburthen] unburden *C*
    soul to them, I] soul to them I *B*
               soul, I *M*

line 9. misunderstood,] misunderstood *B, B², C*
    and] & *B*

line 10. experience,] experience *B, B²*

line 11. and] & *B*

line 12. With] *begins a new paragraph in M*
    ill-fitted] ill fitted *B, B², M, E, F, J, C*
    proof,] proofs, *M*

line 13. and] & *B*
    through] thro *B*
    every where] everywhere *M, E, F, J, C*
    sought, and] sought   & *B*
          sought and *B²*
          sought sympathy, and *E,*
              ⌊*F, J*
          sought sympathy and *C*

line 14. have found] and found *C*
    repulse and] repulse & *B*
    disappointment.] dissappointment. *B*

line 15. <u>Thou</u>] *no new paragraph in B or M*
        Thou *M, C (all other texts give*
        Thou *in italics, as the underscore*
        prescribes)
    demandest] demandest, *M, C*
    what] What *M, C*
    Love.] love? *M, E, J, C*

lines 15–19. It is . . . ourselves] *omitted from M*

line 16. all we conceive,] all that we concieve *B*
        all that we conceive,
              ⌊*B², E, J, C*
    fear,] fear *B*
    ourselves,] ourselves *B, B²*
    our] ~~our~~ *B*

line 17. void] void, *B², K, E, F, J*

line 19. are,] are *B, C*
    community] ~~community~~ *B*

line 20. reason] reason, *M, E, F, J, C*
    understood;] understood: *M*
    imagine] imagine, *M, E, F, J, C*

line 21. within another's;] within anothers, *B*
          within another's, *B²*
          within another's: *M*
    feel,] feel *K*

line 22. that anothers] that anothers' *B*
        that another's *B², K, M,*
              ⌊*E, F, J, C*
    own,] own,— *M*
    their] her *M*

line 23. once] once, *M*
    and mix and] & mix & *B*
          and mix & *B²*
    own;] own, *B, B², E, J, C*
        own,— *M*

line 25. heart's] hearts *B*
    blood. This] blood:—this
          food. This *M*
    Love. This] love;—this *M*
    and] & *B*

line 26. man with man, . . . thing] the two
        ⌊sexes, but everything *M*
          man with
        ⌊man but with everything *C*
    which exists.] that exists. *M*
    We] *begins a new paragraph in M*

line 27. world, and] world & *B*
    within us, which] within us which *B, B²*
        within us which, *M,*
              ⌊*E, F, J, C*

lines 27–28. instant that we] instant we *M*

line 28. live, more and more thirsts] live & move
           ⌊thirsts *B*
          live more
        ⌊and more thirsts *B²*
          live and
        ⌊move, thirsts *M*

lines 28–30. It is . . . Mother] *marked with a mar-*
        ⌊*ginal line in B*
        omitted from M

lines 28–29. correspondance] correspondence *B,*
        ⌊*K, E, F, J, C*

line 30. Mother;] mother. *B*
        mother; *K, E, F, J, C*
    this] This *M*
    developes] develops *K, E, J, C*
    developement] development *K, E, J, C*
    nature.] nature— *M*

SC 488 .lines 31–38. We dimly see . . . overleap] *omitted*
⌊*from M*

line 31. dimly see] see dimly see^x *B*
intellectual nature,] intellectual nature
B, B², E, F, J, C

line 32. protertype] prototype *B, K, E, F, J, C*

line 33. and lovely] or lovely *B, E, J, C*
conceiving] concieving *B*

line 34. being,] being *C*

line 35. particles] particulars *B*

line 36. composed:] composed; *E, F, J, C*
*An indication that Shelley's footnote
should be keyed to* composed *first appears
in B² and is followed in all subsequent
texts except M; B indicates that the note
should follow* see dimly see *in line 31.*
purity and] purity & *B*

line 37. brightness:] brightness; *E, F, J, C*
our own soul] our soul *B, B², E, J, C*

line 38. Paradise . . . evil] Paradise which pain
⌊& <sorrow> or evil *B*
Paradise which pain
⌊and sorrow and evil *B²*
paradise, which pain,
⌊and sorrow, and evil *E, J*
paradise which pain,
⌊and sorrow, and evil *C*

lines 38–39. To this we eagerly] to this eagerly *M*

line 39. sensations,] sensation, *B*
sensations *M*
resemble and] resemble or *B, B², M, E,*
⌊*F, J, C*

line 40. Antitype:] antitype: *B, B²*
antitype; *K, E, F, J*
antetype— *M*
anti-type; *C*

line 41. estimating our own;] estimating the de-
⌊ductions of our own, *B*
estimating the de-
⌊ductions of our own— *M*
estimating our
⌊own, *B²*

lines 41–42. should enter into and] should enter
⌊into & *B*
can enter
⌊into, and *M*

line 42. subtle and] subtle & *B*

line 43. cherish] cherish, *M*
and] & *B*
secret,] secret— *M*
secret; *E, F, J, C*
frame,] frame *B, B², M, E, F, J, C*
nerves] nerves, *B, K, M, E, F, J, C*

line 44. lyres,] lyres *B, B², M*

line 45. vibrations] vibration *M*
own;] own— *M*
and a] and of a *B, M, E, F, J, C*

line 46. demands:] demands,— *M*
demands; *E, F, J, C*

line 47. and unattainable] & unattainable *B*
Love] love *M*
and to] & to *B*
attain which,] attain which *B, B², M*

line 48. powes] powers *Omnia*
that without] that, without *K, E, F, J*

line 49. the possession of] the posession of *B*
omitted from M
which there] which, there *K*
rest nor] rest or *B, B², M*

line 50. Hence] Hence, *M*
or that] or in that *B, B², M, E, F, J, C*

line 51. beings] beings, *M, E, F, J, C*
and yet] & yet *B*
sympathize] sympathise *B, E, J*

line 52. flowers, the] flowers the *B*
flowers, and the *M*
grass, the] grass & the *B*
grass and the *B²*
grass, and the *M, E, J, C*
waters and] waters & *B*
waters, and *K, M, E, F, J, C*

line 53. spring,] spring *B, B²*
spring— *M*
air,] air *B, B², M*
is then found] is found *M*

line 54. heart.] heat. *B*

lines 54–56. There is . . . the soul] *omitted from M*

line 54. wind, and] wind & *B*

line 55. flowing brooks] flowing of brooks *B*
and] & *B*
them,] them *B*

lines 55–56. inconceivable] inconcievable *B*

SC 488   line 56. soul] soul, *E, F, J, C*
             awaken] that awakens *M*
             to dance] to a dance *B, B², M, E, F, J, C*
         line 57. and] & *B*
             bring] brings *M*
             eyes,] eyes *B*
         line 58. patriotic success,] patriotic success *B, B²*
             voice of one] voice one *B²*
         line 59. Sterne] *begins a new paragraph in M*
             says] says, *M*
             that] that, *M, E, J, C*
             desart] desert *K, F*
                 desert, *M, E, J, C*
         line 60. cypress.—] cypress ... *B*
                 cypress— *B²*
                 cypress. *K, M, E, F, J, C*

Man] man *Omnia*
a living] the living *B, M, E, F, J, C*
line 61. sepulchre] sepulche *B²*
    and] & *B*
    husk] wreck *M*
    was.] was.—— *B*
lines 62–63. These words inefficient & metaphor-
    ⌊ical– Most words so– No help– *B*
    These words are ineffectual and
    ⌊metaphorical. Most words are
                ⌊so,—no help! *K*
Omitted from M
See collation to line 36.

DATING

The difficulty of dating Shelley's prose has long been an obstacle to arriving at an informed appraisal of Shelley's mature ideas. Until recently, the chief method employed to determine the date of a particular essay or fragment had been to compare its ideas and language with those of poems and essays of known date. This practice, at best a risky one, proved to be virtually useless in Shelley's case because his language and many of his ideas remain relatively consistent through a large portion of his short career. But since the Shelley-Rolls bequest to the Bodleian in 1946, the availability of Shelley's notebooks provides an opportunity to ascertain objectively and sometimes within rather narrow limits the dates at which a number of those essays and fragments were written. Such is the case with the essay that Mary Shelley called "On Love."

Shelley's original fragment, untitled in the draft, is written clearly with many legible cancellations on pages 1–9 of Bodleian Ms. Shelley adds. e. 11. This notebook draft of "On Love" is followed by sketches of trees (page 10), notes on Herodotus, Book I, chapters 7–14 (page 11), five blank pages (pages 12–16; there are actually two canceled words on page 15), and then (pages 17–41) by Shelley's essay entitled in the draft "A Discourse of the manners of the Antient Greeks relative to the subject of Love." The rest of the notebook (which now has a total of

Shelley, "On Love"   *July 20–25,* **1818**

SC 488   166 numbered pages) contains drafts for various poems, including *Julian and Maddalo, Prometheus Unbound* (at least parts of II.i, III.iv, and the Preface), "Stanzas written in Dejection, near Naples," Shelley's fragmentary drama on Tasso,[1] and a few lines that seem to be a fragment of "Lines written among the Euganean Hills." All these works are known to have been written in the period from the summer of 1818 through the summer of 1819.[2] On page 124 *reverso* appear financial calculations in Shelley's hand and a receipt in Italian in an unfamiliar hand for a month's wages (six scudi) which is dated "April 20, 1819," and signed "Vincenzo Gavita."[3] The notebook Shelley adds. e. 11 itself is a vellumbound pocket book of Italian manufacture. The sequential relationship between "On Love," the notes on Herodotus, and the "Discourse of the manners of the Antient Greeks relative to the subject of Love" strongly suggests that Shelley wrote "On Love" at Bagni di Lucca during the summer of 1818, probably soon after he had translated Plato's *Symposium* (July 7–20).[4]

When Shelley wrote to Godwin on July 25 he had already begun to write his "Discourse."[5] "On Love" can, therefore, be dated with some assurance between July 20 and July 25, 1818. It should be read as Shelley's response to Plato's *Symposium* and may possibly be the false start of an essay introductory to his translation.

TRANSMISSION OF THE TEXT

Mary Shelley's transcription of "On Love" presented above was, as the collation and printer's notations indicate, the copy of the essay that went to the press for its first publication in *The Keepsake for 1829*

1. G. M. Matthews suggests that this fragment (pp. 166–161 *reverso*) may have been the first thing written in the notebook. (See "A New Text of Shelley's Scene for *Tasso*," *Keats-Shelley Memorial Bulletin*, XI, 1960, 39–47.)

2. Bodleian Ms. Shelley adds. e. 11 also contains (pp. 154–128 *reverso*) the draft of the fragmentary essay entitled by Shelley "A Future State." This essay also belongs to the 1818–1819 period and cannot be dismissed as a juvenile effort.

3. The name is undoubtedly that of the servant Vincenzo whom Mary Shelley mentions in her Journal for February 28, 1819.

4. Mary Shelley, Journal. For a summary of information on the translating of "The Banquet of Plato" see Notopoulos, *Platonism*, pp. 381–386. Notopoulos, using Jones's edition, *Mary Shelley's Journal*, has dated the translation July 9–20. For Shelley's reading of Herodotus in 1818, see sc 487 and Commentary.

5. Shelley, *Letters*, II, 22.

SC 488 (*K*). The essay was almost immediately reprinted in *The Mirror of Literature, Amusement, and Instruction*[6] and soon appeared in translation in a French periodical.[7]

For the text in *Essays, Letters* (*E*), Mary sent to the printer a fair-copy book in which she had years earlier transcribed several of Shelley's prose works and from which she may earlier have copied sc 488. This transcript, Bodleian Ms. Shelley adds. d. 8, pp. 151–154 (*B²*), is closer to Shelley's original draft (*B*) in a few substantive features. One must conclude that Mary copied sc 488 from *B²*, introducing a few additional errors into this copy. This would date Bodleian Ms. Shelley adds. d. 8 at least before 1828. The transmission of the text of "On Love" was probably as follows:

1. *B*   Shelley's draft, written at Bagni di Lucca, 1818.
2. *B²*   Mary Shelley transcribed from *B*, probably 1822–1824.
3. sc 488 Mary copied from *B²*, 1828.
4. *K*   First printed version in the *Keepsake*, set directly from sc 488.
5. *E*   Set directly from *B²*.
6. *F*   *The Prose Works of Percy Bysshe Shelley*, ed. Harry Buxton Forman (London, 1880), II, 267–270, printed from *E*; collated with *K*.
7. *J*   Shelley, *Complete Works* (Julian), based on *E*, collated with *K*.

The text of "On Love" in Thomas Medwin's "Memoir of Percy Bysshe Shelley" in *The Shelley Papers* (*M*)[8] presents special problems: It differs from all other texts, omitting phrases and clauses found in *B* and containing many other variants from both *B* and Mary Shelley's transcripts. One might at first assume that *M* was merely a corrupted version of *K*, the only text publicly available by that date. Medwin is known to have transcribed inaccurately, and he also wrote in a difficult hand, which may have caused compositorial errors. But collation of

---

6. XII (No. 344, Supplementary Number, 1828), 370–371. On p. 373 the editor, speaking of the poetry in *The Keepsake for 1829*, says that among the poetic fragments are "three by Shelley" which "are very beautiful."

7. "Nouvel Essai sur l'Amour: Fragment traduit de B. Shelley" in *Le Voleur, Gazette des Journaux, Revue des Sciences, de la Littérature et des Théâtres*, No. 9 (February 15, 1829), pp. 34–35. I am indebted to Professor Burton R. Pollin for this information.

8. London, 1833, pp. 21–24.

Shelley, "On Love" — July 20–25, 1818

SC 488   Medwin's text with B and with B^2, sc 488, K, and E reveals that in a few significant instances M returns to Shelley's readings in B that are not found in any of Mary's versions,[9] and peculiarities in B itself are sufficient to explain in most instances how Medwin could have developed his version from Shelley's draft.[10] It is not impossible that Medwin discussed some features of the essay with Shelley and omitted some sentences on Shelley's authority, but it is more likely that B^2 and M represent simply two independent attempts to derive a text from B and that Shelley's draft itself provides the sole textual authority.

SHELLEY'S CHANGING CONCEPT OF LOVE

Viewed as Shelley's response to Plato's *Symposium*, "On Love" takes on greater significance than has often been attributed to it. Forman, noting that "Mrs. Shelley seems to regard this brief effusion on Love as in a manner cognate with Shelley's Platonic labours," continued: "It seems improbable however that it belongs to so late a period of his activity. The style appears to me rather that of 1815, or even earlier, than that of 1818."[11] Forman (like Rossetti before him) seems to have thought that the ideas in the fragment were immature, not realizing that they had parallels in the works of leading eighteenth-century moral philosophers like David Hume, Thomas Reid, and Dugald Stewart. David Lee Clark identified these sources of Shelley's ideas, but held to the argument for an early date (1814–1815).[12] Only Notopoulos, who was searching for Platonic influence, accepted Mary Shelley's linking of "On Love" with the translation of *The Symposium*.

9. See, for example, the collation of lines 15, 28, 28–30, and 41. On the meaning of Mary's footnote to the Preface of *Essays, Letters*, see Roland A. Duerksen, "Unidentified Shelley Texts in Medwin's *Shelley Papers*," *Philological Quarterly*, XLIV (July 1965), 407–410.

10. A remark in one of Shelley's letters indicates that Medwin took an exceptional interest in Shelley's translation of Plato's *Symposium* (and perhaps, therefore, Shelley's original prose associated with it). On August 22, 1821, Shelley wrote to Medwin, then in Geneva, adding in a postscript: "I think you must have put up by mistake a Ms translation of the Symposium of Plato. — If so pray contrive to send it me" (Shelley, *Letters*, II, 342). Whether Medwin had actually taken — or mislaid — the manuscript of Shelley's translation (which Shelley did not rediscover until July 1822, during his last visit to Pisa), Shelley's statement leaves no doubt that Medwin had the manuscript in his possession at some point before he left Pisa in February 1821.

11. *Shelley's Prose Works*, II, 266.

12. *Shelley's Prose* (University of New Mexico Press, 1954), p. 169.

SC 488   Yet, though Notopoulos and Mary Shelley are correct in linking "On Love" with Shelley's translation of *The Symposium* ("The Banquet of Plato"), Forman, Rossetti, and Clark are correct in seeing in it ideas that Shelley discarded in his last works. What has not been recognized before is that in the midst of Shelley's poetic career — after the publication of *Alastor* and *The Revolt of Islam* and the writing of *Rosalind and Helen* — he radically revised his entire conception of love and, at the same time, his view of the role of creativity and poetry in human life.

Shelley's "On Love" is a critique of the doctrines of love in *The Symposium*, or an alternative to them, rather than an endorsement of any of them. Many ideas from the brief fragment are echoed in a paragraph of Shelley's "Discourse on the Manners of the Antient Greeks Relative to the Subject of Love."[13] This paragraph also contains Shelley's most candid and detailed analysis of the role of sexual activity in love. If "On Love" is the false start of an introduction to *The Symposium*, I believe that Shelley abandoned it and began "A Discourse" on a different note because he felt that he had to approach a discussion of sex more obliquely. It was rhetorically more effective to discuss Greek civilization beginning with the greatness of Periclean Athens than to plunge immediately into the more controversial aspects of the subject. "On Love" is written, moreover, in the impassioned, poetic prose of *A Defence of Poetry* and embodies the rhetorical tone of the speeches in *The Symposium*. It may be said to constitute a fragment of Shelley's own speech in praise of love.[14] "A Discourse," on the contrary, attempts to explain the nature and role of love within Athenian society.

Shelley begins "On Love" (lines 3–4) by emphasizing the difficulty or even impossibility of defining love, comparing it to the problem of defining life or God. This difficulty is increased by a problem of communication, for Shelley (or the speaker, if one wishes to consider this a

13. See the paragraph beginning, "Let it not be imagined that because the Greeks were deprived of its legitimate object, [they] were incapable of sentimental love..." (Notopoulos, *Platonism*, pp. 408–409).

14. If Shelley revised this "speech" while Medwin was with him in 1820 or 1821, he may have done so as part of his plan to write "a Symposium of my own," as he mentioned to Gisborne on October 22, 1821 (Shelley, *Letters*, II, 363). In that case *M* could be the fragment of a more ambitious work, with Shelley in 1821 recognizing that his essay on love of July 1818 represented only one, limited viewpoint.

Shelley and his Circle : Manuscripts

SC 488   dramatic fragment) has found that he does not think as other men do — that there is a subtle barrier between himself and others (lines 5–14).

As the next paragraph explains, love arises when a person, feeling isolated, attempts to awaken in other beings a response to his own inner world. In this inner world there develops a self-idealization, a *beau idéal* of the self, incorporating all one's good qualities and excluding the sins or shortcomings. This "soul within the soul" provides a standard image against which to measure not only one's own external image and actions, but those of all other creatures. The goal love seeks, "the invisible and unattainable point to which Love tends," is complete harmony between the external world and this inner ideal. And, says Shelley, when one cannot find sympathy from other human beings, he turns to the vegetation and even inanimate nature and imagines a sympathy between them and himself.

There are obvious correspondences between this idea of a *beau idéal* within the soul and the "human form divine" that becomes the universal model in Blake's poetry. But Shelley's conception is more limited than Blake's, for Shelley begins with the recognition that his desire for a universal harmony is not, in fact, answered. Every individual has his own self-idealization, and these are not *necessarily* congruent with one another, with nonhuman creation, or with any supernatural power. Shelley's own self-idealization relates, as he reveals in his essay "On a Future State," to the desire for immortality:

This *desire* to be forever as we are; the reluctance to a violent and unexperienced change, which is common to all the animated and inanimate combinations of the universe, is, indeed, the secret persuasion which has given birth to the opinions of a future state.[15]

Love is a desire for harmony and sympathy, but one cannot say that this desire reflects any reality, any more than the desire for continuity and the resistance to change prove that there is a future state.

Shelley expresses his conception of love in terms common to the eighteenth-century doctrine of sympathy,[16] and he places the "beautiful," the real object of love, within the individual lover's own soul, rather

---

15. Shelley, *Complete Works*, VI, 209.

16. See Roy R. Male, Jr., "Shelley and the Doctrine of Sympathy," *University of Texas Studies in English*, XXIX (1950), 183–203.

SC 488   than in other people or external nature. Each external embodiment of this *beau idéal* fails the lover, because nothing external seems quite to conform to this ideal.

Shelley had dealt with the problems raised by this doctrine of love in *Alastor* and *The Revolt of Islam*. The Youth in *Alastor* is destroyed because he seeks in a mortal form the embodiment of his dream vision — the externalization of his inner ideal. Many commentators on *Alastor* have condemned the Youth's love quest as narcissistic; Shelley himself makes clear that it *is* narcissistic, and he sees it as misguided and wasteful, not because it is morally wrong, but because it is self-defeating and impossible of fulfillment. In *The Revolt of Islam* Shelley showed that the way out of the narcissistic trap was through service to one's fellow man. But even in this poem about sacrificing self for the larger benefit of humanity and posterity, the reward that Laon and Cythna reap in this world takes the form of a love that harmonizes with the fragment "On Love," for Laon and Cythna take turns molding each other's opinions. This theme suggests why Shelley chose as his wives and confidants young girls who were his disciples and, perhaps, why he idolized them, considering himself a passive suppliant before their radiance. He was worshiping, not a young lady, but what he believed to be an embodiment of his own internal ideal.

Such a doctrine of love has its frustrations, as Shelley's half-defeated beginning of "On Love" hints. Even before he wrote this fragment, Shelley may have recognized the essential instability of relationships based on such a symbolic use of other people. In his Dedication "To Mary" of *The Revolt of Islam*, he spoke of the sorrow of his early experiences in which love had been "a blight and snare."[17] But as long as he and Mary retained the illusion of a near-perfect harmony — "two tranquil stars" that "can look from [their] tranquillity/ Like lamps into the world's tempestuous night,"[18] Shelley could hold fast to his original conception of love. Only the rupture of the sympathy between Mary and himself forced him to reexamine his thinking on this all-important subject.

The first clear signs of the collapse of his old conception appear in his more or less personal poems written between late 1818 and August

17. See "Dedication," lines 46–54.
18. "Dedication," lines 122–124.

SC 488 of 1819 — "Lines written among the Euganean Hills,"[19] "Stanzas written in Dejection, near Naples," and *Julian and Maddalo*.[20] Not that these primarily concern love or that the themes and structures of these quite different poems are governed by consideration of the nature of love. They simply reflect Shelley's loss of certainty on the question and foreshadow the most important change in his mature thinking.

By the time Shelley wrote *A Defence of Poetry*, he had inverted his definition of love: "The great secret of morals is love; or a going out of our own nature, and an identification of ourselves with the beautiful which exists in thought, action, or person, not our own."[21] No longer must the external world respond or conform to the ideal within the self; rather, the self seeks the beautiful without. This statement in *A Defence* conforms almost exactly to the nature of love as expounded by Socrates in Plato's *Symposium*: "Love, therefore, and every thing else that desires anything, desires that which is absent and beyond his reach, that which it has not, that which is not itself, that which it wants; such are the things of which there are desire and love."[22] This emphasis on beauty outside the self, which attracts the lover because of *its* qualities rather than merely reflecting his own aspirations, remains fairly consistent in Shelley's discussions of love till the end of his life. It governs, for example, "The Sensitive Plant," as when Shelley writes:

> . . . the Sensitive Plant which could give small fruit
> Of the love which it felt from the leaf to the root,
> Received more than all, it loved more than ever,
> Where none wanted but it, could belong to the giver,–
>
> For the Sensitive Plant has no bright flower;
> Radiance and odour are not its dower;
> It loves, even like Love, its deep heart is full,
> It desires what it has not, the Beautiful![23]

19. Especially lines 1–44. On this poem, see Donald H. Reiman, "Structure, Symbol, and Theme in 'Lines written among the Euganean Hills,'" *PMLA*, LXXVII (September 1962), 404–413.

20. Especially lines like these: "There is one road/ To peace and that is truth, which follow ye!/ Love sometimes leads astray to misery" (lines 347–349). On the dating of *Julian and Maddalo*, see SC 531, Commentary.

21. Shelley, *Complete Works*, VII, 118.

22. Shelley's translation, Notopoulos, *Platonism*, p. 440.

23. Shelley, *Poetical Works* (OSA), p. 590.

The Carl H. Pforzheimer Library

Shelley, "On Love"   *July 20–25, 1818*

SC 488   In the late lyric beginning "One word is too often profaned" that Mary Shelley published in *Posthumous Poems*, Shelley seems to have shifted his ground still farther, comparing his conception of love to:

> The worship the heart lifts above
>   And the Heavens reject not, —
> The desire of the moth for the star,
>   Of the night for the morrow,
> The devotion to something afar
>   From the sphere of our sorrow. . . .[24]

Here the beautiful object or goal of the lover is not only independent of him but completely unattainable and recognized to be so. It is a distant beacon, and since it can never be reached, can never disappoint, can never leave "a heart high-sorrowful and cloy'd,/ A burning forehead, and a parching tongue."[25] This is a view corresponding much more closely to the later parts of the doctrine of love that Socrates attributes to Diotima in *The Symposium* — the love characteristic of those who "ascend through these transitory objects which are beautiful, towards that which is beauty itself."[26]

Shelley sets forth his mature doctrine of love most fully in *Epipsychidion*, and a full discussion of his ideas would necessarily include a detailed explication of that poem, as well as of passages in *Adonais*, *The Triumph of Life*, and several of the late lyrics.[27] Such an analysis is obviously beyond our present concern, which is simply to indicate the place of Shelley's fragment "On Love" in the development of his ideas. In summary, "On Love" states clearly the conception of love that Shelley held at least until the last months of 1818. This view grew out of the doctrine of sympathy as it was developed by various eighteenth-century philosophers. Probably a personal crisis — a serious quarrel between Mary and himself following the death of either their daughter

---

24. Shelley, *Poetical Works* (OSA), p. 645.

25. Keats, "Ode on a Grecian Urn," lines 29–30.

26. Shelley's translation, Notopoulos, *Platonism*, p. 449.

27. For brief accounts of structure and meaning of these works, see Donald H. Reiman, *Percy Bysshe Shelley* (New York, 1969), pp. 125–161.

SC 488   Clara (September 24, 1818) or their son William (June 7, 1819) — forced
Shelley to rethink the feasibility and relevance of his view of love. Inasmuch as this renewed examination of his theory of love coincided with
serious study of works of Plato, Dante, and Petrarch, it is not surprising
that his view of love became more "Platonic"; love came to mean an
identification of the self with the beautiful existing in "thought, action,
or person, not our own" and — eventually — pursuit of a beautiful unattainable in mortal existence.

Shelley clearly did not completely abandon his belief in the soul
within his soul, the *beau idéal* that he describes in "On Love." Rather,
it came to fulfill a different function in his thinking. Instead of the man
seeking to impose this pattern on a beloved person, the poet seeks to
embody the ideal in his creative works. In *A Defence of Poetry*, *Epipsychidion*, and *Adonais*, Shelley evolved his conception of poetry as the most
complete embodiment of this inner ideal; the creative experience of the
poet marked the nearest conjunction of the inner ideal and external
reality — though even this "record of the best and happiest moments of
the happiest and best minds" cannot capture all the meaning of the experience that produced the poem. Love and poetry thus interact in
Shelley's mature theory, with "poetry" (or creative activities generally)
fulfilling the basic psychological need — of giving external form to man's
inner ideals — that Shelley had originally seen as love's primary function. Shelley came to consider love primarily the guide, with creativity
producing much of the temporal sense of fulfillment that sympathy had
failed to provide.

SC 489   LORD CHANCELLOR'S ORDERS, JULY 25, 1818

DOCUMENT (transcript), 3 pages. Double sheet, 4to (10.1 x 8 inches).
Laid paper. Watermark (on each leaf): TOWGOOD'S SUPERFINE|.
Notations, in the hand of Harry Buxton Forman; see Textual Notes.

PROVENANCE: Harry Buxton Forman; Elkin Matthews, March 1947.

SC 489

Lord Chancellor
Saturday   25th July 1818
Eliza Ianthe Shelley and Charles Bysshe
Shelley Infants by John Westbrooke their
Maternal Grand Father and next friend
. . .   Plaintiffs Elizabeth Westbrooke
Spinster John Higham Esquire Percy
Bysshe Shelley Esquire Sir Timothy
Shelley Baronet and John Westbrooke
Defendants

.   .   .   .   .   .

His Lordship doth Order that the Report of the said Master Mr Alexander
dated the 28th day of April 1818 be confirmed and it is Ordered that the said
Infants Eliza Ianthe Shelley and Charles Bysshe Shelley be on or before the
20th day of August next placed by the Defendant John Westbrooke under
the care of the said Thomas Hume and Caroline his Wife and there continue
during their respective minorities or until the further order of this Court
and it is ordered that the interest of the said £2000 Bank £4 per Cent An-
nuities from time to time as and when the same shall be hereafter received
be paid by the said Eliza Westbrooke and John Higham to the said Thomas
Hume in part discharge of the annual sum of £200 to be allowed to him for
the maintenance and education of the said Infants subject to the further
order of this Court and it is Ordered that the said Percy Bysshe Shelley do
pay to the said Thomas Hume the sum of £120 annually by quarterly pay-
ments until the further order of this Court so as to make up with the said
Interest the annual sum of £200 and it is Ordered that the said Defendants
John Westbrooke and Elizabeth Westbrooke be at liberty to visit the said
Infant Plaintiffs at the house of the said Thomas Hume once in every month
and the last named Defendants are to be at liberty to apply to the Court in
case they shall be desirous to have other intercourse with the said Infant
Plaintiffs and it is Ordered that the said Defendant Percy Bysshe Shelley
be at liberty to visit the said Infant Plaintiffs once in every month in the
presence of the said Thomas Hume and Caroline his Wife or one of them
or if the said Defendant Percy Bysshe Shelley shall prefer it his visits may

SC 489   *be in case he proposes to got out of England according to his convenience so that they do not exceed 12 in the course of a year and the said Percy Bysshe Shelley is also to be at liberty to apply to the Court in case he should be desirous to have other intercourse with the said Infant Plaintiffs and it is ordered that the said Defendant Sir Timothy Shelley and his family have such intercourse with the said Infant Plaintiffs ~~and it is ordered that the said~~*

40   *~~Defendant S~~ as the said Sir Timothy Shelley shall desire and any of the parties are to be at liberty to apply to this Court as there shall be occasion*

B. 1817. Fo: 1487. T.W.

All Notations are in pencil in the hand of Harry Buxton Forman. Each page of the transcript was numbered by Forman when he sent this copy to press. Included here are pages 64, 65, 66. Above and to the left of line 1 is the notation *7 Piper.*

line 1. *Lord Chancellor:* preceded by *The* and followed by *'s Order dated* (in the hand of For-

man), which is triple-underscored and connected by a stroke to line 2, which is also underscored three times.

line 3. *Eliza . . . Defendants* (line 10): canceled with vertical pencil strokes. The line of dots which follows has also been canceled.

line 34. *got* (sic): *t* canceled in pencil.

line 39. The words are canceled in pencil.

TRANSCRIPTIONS of several major documents in the Chancery suit for custody of Ianthe and Charles Shelley (usually referred to as "Westbrook vs. Shelley") were owned by Harry Buxton Forman, who published texts of them in an appendix to his edition of Medwin's revised *Life of Percy Bysshe Shelley.* These transcripts that Forman sent to the press are now in The Carl H. Pforzheimer Library.[1]

It is unnecessary to reprint all of these transcriptions. (Perhaps some scholar thoroughly versed in the law of Chancery should take a fresh look at the original documents that record the case.) We are, however, reprinting the final transcription in Forman's series both to call attention to the whereabouts of the copies Forman used[2] and to add some information about Dr. and Mrs. Thomas Hume.

1. See Medwin, *Shelley,* pp. 182 n., 463–486. Of the nine documents printed by Forman, the texts of the two affidavits of "Elizabeth Westbrooke," January 10 and 13, 1817, are in Forman's hand — taken, he says, from "Mr. Wetherells brief." The other seven, in the hand of a legal secretary or clerk, were copied for Forman in the 1870's or 1880's. (Medwin, *Shelley,* pp. 182 n., 468 fn.) Forman has numbered the pages of these transcripts from 1 to 66; SC 489 represents pp. 64–66.

2. According to Shelley, *Letters,* I, 524 fn., "the various Chancery documents are printed in Appendix III of Medwin's *Life of Shelley.* . . . An additional document was printed by White (ii.508–17). The original MSS are in the Luther A. Brewer collection of the University of Iowa Library." Jones is correct about the document printed by White but mistaken about the others.

The Carl H. Pforzheimer Library

SC 489   The Lord Chancellor's order of July 25, 1818, was a hollow victory for Shelley — a victory because the chancellor put Ianthe and Charles under the care of the candidate advanced by P. W. Longdill, Shelley's solicitor, but hollow because by the time the decision was made Shelley had left England and never was to return to see his children again. This directive of July 25, 1818, remained in force only until January 1822 — when the attorneys for the Westbrooks and Sir Timothy Shelley cooperated to transfer the children to the care of a clergyman and his wife in Chelsfield, Kent. After Shelley's death Sir Timothy became the official guardian of Charles Shelley, while Ianthe was placed in care of John Westbrook and Eliza Westbrook Beauchamp.[3]

An interesting but unexplored aspect of the Chancery suit is the identity and character of the successful candidates for the role of foster parents to Ianthe and Charles Shelley. Dr. Thomas Hume, who acted in that capacity from 1818 to 1822, was not only the Thomas Hume, M.D. (?1769-1850) listed in the *DNB*, but also the Thomas Hume who was the early close friend of Thomas Moore, a correlation that has escaped students of Moore and Shelley.

Thomas Hume was born in Dublin about 1769.[4] He attended Trinity College in that city, receiving the degrees of B.A. (1792) and B.Med. (1796). In 1804 he was awarded the degree of D.Med. from University College, Oxford.[5]

Hume was already in London in 1799 when young Thomas Moore, fresh from his own degree at Trinity College, Dublin, made his first assault on the capital. In a letter to his mother on May 15 of that year, Moore described Hume as a "very pleasant acquaintance" and "a man of considerable talent."[6] Before the end of 1799 "Mr." (not yet "Dr.") Hume undertook negotiations that led to the publication of Moore's

---

3. Ingpen, *Shelley in England*, pp. 511-512. See also Ursula Orange, "Shuttlecocks of Genius: An Enquiry into the Fate of Shelley's Children," *Keats-Shelley Memorial Bulletin*, VIII (1957), 44.

4. See *DNB*, but the account in *Alumni Oxonienses* would place his birth in 1773 or 1774.

5. *Alumni Oxonienses* describes Hume as the son of Gustavus Hume, a doctor, but in the preceding column of the same work appears a Gustavus Hume, just a few years older than Thomas, who is listed as the son of Gustavus Hume of Dublin, "gent." The younger Gustavus Hume — possibly an elder brother of Thomas — matriculated at Trinity College, Oxford, in April 1781 at the age of nineteen and took his B.A. in 1785.

6. Moore, *Letters*, I, 6.

SC 489 translation of *Odes of Anacreon,* even arranging for the book to be re-viewed.[7] On July 28, 1800, in another letter to his mother Moore wrote of Hume: "I never met with any one more capable of friendship, or more adapted to cherish it. He has a peculiar delicacy . . . never to touch upon any thing grating to one's feelings. I could write a volume about him . . ."[8]

The warm friendship between Tom Moore and Tom Hume con-tinued until 1806, when it foundered as a result of Moore's quixotic duel with Francis Jeffrey. Hume acted as Moore's second in the affair (having himself, Moore later wrote, "been once, I think, engaged in mortal affray")[9] and it was Hume who was entrusted with loading the pistols that Moore borrowed for the occasion. The police intervened before a shot was fired, but gossip later spread that Jeffrey's pistol had no bullet in it. Francis Horner, Jeffrey's second, signed a sworn statement that he had seen Hume load the gun, but Hume himself (Moore wrote) "took fright at the ridicule which had been brought upon the transaction, said that he did not like to expose his name . . .; in short, he refused to sign the paper." This episode prevented Moore from publicly clearing his name, and indirectly led to Moore's later quarrel with Byron over *English Bards and Scotch Reviewers.* Moore exaggerated in saying that Hume's "conduct on that occasion caused a severance between us for more than thirty years,"[10] for Moore's journal and letters show him having a dinner celebrating his own birthday "with Hume at his cottage at Hanwell" on May 28, 1819,[11] and enjoying other friendly encounters with him in 1826, 1828, and frequently from 1834 on.[12]

In Moore's diary for 1844 there are references to Hume's "clever, warm-hearted wife" and Hume's "handsome wife."[13] These favorable

7. See Moore, *Letters,* I, 16.

8. Moore, *Letters,* I, 22.

9. Moore, *Memoirs,* I, 202.

10. For Moore's retrospective account of the affair, see *Memoirs,* I, 199–214.

11. Moore, *Memoirs,* II, 314. Moore could conceivably have seen Shelley's children or heard about them on this occasion, but he records nothing of them.

12. Moore, *Memoirs,* V, 79–80, 300; VI, 64; and especially VII, 26–27 and following. The references to Thomas Hume are difficult to distinguish in this edition because the index conflates mentions of David Hume (IV, 260, 265, 303, 338); Dr. John Robert Hume (VI, 45–46; see *DNB*); and Joseph Hume, M.P. (IV, 75, 88, 317; V, 60, 294; see *DNB*) with the references to Thomas Hume.

13. May 14 and June 3, 1844, Moore, *Memoirs,* VII, 370.

The Carl H. Pforzheimer Library

SC 489   judgments are Moore's only surviving estimates of Caroline Hume, who was "the last descendant of the mathematician, Dr. John Wallis."[14]

Even if we grant that the evidence we possess is still scanty, it suggests that Roger Ingpen's scathing denunciation of Thomas and Caroline Hume was unwarranted.[15] Ingpen based his judgment solely on the account submitted to the Lord Chancellor by the Master in Chancery of the educational plan the Humes would follow in raising Shelley's children — a plan probably drawn up by Shelley's solicitor Longdill to fulfill what he deemed to be the requirements of the Chancery court. The written plan, a document of litigation, tells nothing about the personality or character of Thomas or Caroline Hume. We must assume that, though Shelley apparently never met Hume,[16] he had been satisfied by Longdill (who was Hume's neighbor at Hanwell) that Dr. and Mrs. Hume were qualified by temperament, intelligence, and education to give Charles and Ianthe a sound and reasonably liberal upbringing, by the standards of the day.

Besides Dr. James Lind, Shelley's early mentor and a strong inflence on his liberal thinking,[17] several physicians were friendly with Shelley. One thinks, for example, of Dr. William Lawrence, Dr. Pope, the Quaker doctor Shelley knew at Bishopsgate, Dr. John Bell, and Dr. Andrea Vaccà Berlinghieri. Many members of the medical profession in Shelley's day were more liberal than their contemporaries in the other leading professions — the army, the clergy, and the law — partly because in those days medicine attracted men of humanitarian sensibility and partly because the scientific thought underlying medical procedures made the discipline as a whole far less tied to tradition or hostile to change than were the other professions.

---

14. For John Wallis (1616–1703), one of the leading English scientific thinkers of the seventeenth century, see *DNB.*

15. See *Shelley in England,* pp. 506–511.

16. See Shelley to Hume, February 17, 1821, Shelley, *Letters,* II, 264.

17. For Lind, see sc 117, Commentary (II); W. G. Bebbington, "A Friend of Shelley: Dr. James Lind," *Notes and Queries,* CCV (March 1960), 83–93; and Desmond King-Hele, "Shelley and Dr. Lind," *Keats-Shelley Memorial Bulletin,* XVIII (1967), 1–6.

SC 490 P. B. SHELLEY TO BROOKS, SON & DIXON, JULY 31, 1818

AL signed *Percy Bysshe Shelley.*, 1 page. Single sheet, 4to (9.6 x 7.2 inches).
Laid paper. Watermark: [cherub holding aloft banner with inscription]|
ALMASSO|.
Additions: 1. (recto): two large marks made with a flourish resembling a large
4; 2. page has been torn from a double sheet.
Docket, verso: *P B Shelley| 31 July 1818|.*

PROVENANCE: Edward T. Ingpen; Roger Ingpen; Clinton N. Rutan; Seven
Gables Bookshop, March 1961. *De Ricci 386* (p. 23).

Gentlemen
    I think I excepted especially a note of Fifty Pounds given to Mr Godwin
from those which I requested you not to pay.— If otherwise I beg you would
have the goodness now to pay it, & to explain on my part to Mr Godwin
5 *how the matter stands.*
    I would thank you also to transmit to me the present state of my accounts.
                  I remain, Gentlemen,
                    Your obliged Servant

Bagni di Lucca
10   *Percy Bysshe Shelley.*

    July 31· 1818.

[Address, verso]
Messrs Brookes & Co
by favour of W. Godwin Esqr

O N MARCH 12, 1818, Shelley had written from Dover to his bankers
Brooks, Son & Dixon to honor only four bills,[1] each of which he
identified by addressee, amount, and due period. One of these four was
£150 to Godwin dated at one month. In that March 12 letter, Shelley
writes that he had given various other bills but requests that "payment
be refused, as they depend upon conditional engagements with friends
in England who ought to be prepared to meet them."

1. See Shelley, *Letters*, I, 599. A bill was a promise to pay a named person a stated amount within a
specified period of time. See sc 61, Commentary (I).

Shelley to Brooks, Son & Dixon *July 31, 1818*

SC 490 Of those additional bills, Shelley had probably intended to pay three to Horace Smith — presumably in repayment of a loan[2] — and had simply forgotten to include them on the list of March 12. He wrote to Brooks to rectify this error on July 25, doubtless after receiving notice from Smith that payment had been stopped.[3]

The question arises whether Shelley made an error in the case of this £50 bill to Godwin, or whether this was one of those bills on which he specifically wished to stop payment. The latter seems more likely. With all the difficulties between Shelley and Godwin over money in the winter of 1818,[4] it is most improbable that Shelley would overlook any of his financial dealings with his father-in-law. The letter of March 12 may well have been written for the sole purpose of invalidating one or more bills drawn to Godwin that Shelley had been prevailed upon, against his better judgment, to write before he left London.

Shelley apparently discussed financial matters in a letter to Godwin written at Leghorn on May 13 but no longer extant.[5] We can gauge its contents only from the unpublished opening of Godwin's letter to Shelley of June 8, 1818:

I read your letter of the 13th of May with great pain. Let us therefore correspond no more on such subjects. If ever we meet again, perhaps something satisfactory may be arranged. But, since a certain period, you seem never to take up a pen on these matters, without being converted, as by a sort of spell, into a kind of being at which my nature revolts. If any great calamity suddenly overtakes me, I shall not fail immediately to communicate ^by that letter, either to you or Mary.

Meanwhile, ~~unless your mind is entirely alienated from me~~, there are a thousand subjects, which may be made the ^matter ~~subject~~ of a variety of agreeable letters. ~~Only touch not on the word money.~~ You are in a new country [etc.][6]

2. See sc 430 and Commentary.

3. Shelley wrote to Smith on July 26, according to Mary's Journal, and the letter to Brooks may also have been written that day. See Shelley, *Letters*, II, 27 and fn.

4. See especially sc 454 and Commentary.

5. Mary's Journal (which, unlike the published *Journal*, contains a separate entry for each day in May) does not note this letter. Perhaps Shelley wrote to Godwin without Mary's knowledge.

6. Abinger Manuscripts, Pforzheimer Microfilm, reel V, file 7. The text of the remainder of this letter, beginning with "You are in a new country," is printed in *Shelley and Mary*, I, 281–283, and excerpted in Shelley, *Letters*, II, 21 fn.

Shelley to Brooks, Son & Dixon   **_July 31, 1818_**

SC 490   Because Godwin canceled three and a half of the most biting sentences in the letter he sent to Shelley, one might suppose that he had repented of the language of his remonstrance. But in addition to the original letter, the Abinger papers also contain a holograph fair copy of this same letter that Godwin kept for his own reference in which the offending words have *not* been canceled. It appears, then, that the cancellations made in the copy sent to Shelley were merely for rhetorical effect. (Godwin made no attempt to either obliterate the words or make them illegible.)

In spite of Godwin's admonition to Shelley to avoid the subject of money and his own practice of this precept in his letters to Mary of June 20 and July 7, 1818, it seems likely that Godwin himself was the first to break silence on the subject. According to Godwin's Journal he wrote to Shelley on July 10, called on "Brooks, banker" on July 15, and wrote to Shelley again on July 17. We know nothing of the content of these letters, but it is likely that they mention the beginning of the latest and greatest Godwin financial disaster to trouble Shelley during his lifetime.[7] On June 23 Godwin recorded in his Journal: "clerk from Tilson, w. notice to quit." This is probably one of the earliest references to the struggle that Godwin undertook to remain rent-free in his house on Skinner Street.[8]

Whether motivated by a renewed sense of Godwin's past greatness, hopes for the future of the answer to Malthus on which the philosopher was then engaged, the warmer tone of Godwin's recent correspondence, feelings of guilt, or simply determination to do all that he reasonably could to extricate his father-in-law from financial distress, Shelley wrote this letter to Brooks of July 31 in such a manner as to leave his original intentions toward Godwin tactfully ambiguous. The letter is written on a quarto leaf torn from a double sheet, and has at least two sets of folds. It has never been sealed. Shelley or Mary probably wrote a note to Godwin on the conjugate leaf, which provided the address sheet for this letter.[9] That would have saved postage and enabled Godwin to read Shelley's avowal of his good intentions.

7. Apparently the letters do not survive. The Abinger collection contains no surviving entire holographs of Godwin letters to the Shelleys between the dates July 7, 1818, and March 5, 1819.

8. For a history of this case and its unfortunate conclusion, see Brown, *Godwin*, pp. 339–346, 349–355. *Johnstone's Guide* (p. 132) lists "Tilson & Preston, Solicitors, 29 Coleman St."

9. Note that the address of Shelley's letter informs Brooks that it is delivered "by favour of W. Godwin."

SC 491   P. B. SHELLEY TO T. L. PEACOCK, AUGUST 16, 1818

AL signed *P B Shelley*, 3 pages. Double sheet, 4to (9.6 x 7.3 inches).
Wove paper. Watermark: [cherub holding aloft banner with inscription]|
POLLET|; countermark: AP|.
Seal: wax, red.
Postal fee: 2/4.
Postmarks: 1. LUCCA|; 2. (Foreign Post Office stamp, London): FPO| SE 1| 1818|;
3. (evening duty stamp, London): c| SE| 1|·818|.
Notations: 1. (page 1, top center, probably in Peacock's hand): *Not printed.*|;
2. (page 3, sideways, in right margin): *p. 245, a*|.
Additions: 1. two repaired seal tears; 2. paste and paper adhering to page 4
from letter having been tipped into an album; 3. two cellophane stamp hinges
on page 4 from letter having been mounted in a second album.

PROVENANCE: Thomas Love Peacock (Sotheby, June 11, 1866, lot 751); Harvey;
a "Gentleman" (Sotheby, February 12, 1874, lot 81); Henry Huth (Catalogue,
1880, V, page 1703; his sale, Sotheby, June 12, 1911, lot 205); Quaritch, May
1923. *De Ricci 387* (p. 209).

No 7.

Bagni di Lucca
Aug. 16. 1818

My dear Peacock–

5   *No new event has been added to my life since I wrote last—*
at least none which might not have taken place as well on the banks of the
Thames as those of the Serchio. I project soon a short escursion—of a
week or so– to some of the neighbouring cities, & on the tenth of September
we leave this place for Florence, where I shall at least be able to tell you of
10   *some things which you cannot see from your windows which look to the quoit-*
ing place.

I have finished— by taking advantage of a few days of inspiration-
-which the Camenæ have lately been very backward in conceding— the little
poem I began sending to the press in London— – Ollier will send you the
15   *proofs. Its structure is slight & aery- its subject ideal. The metre corresponds*
with the spirit of the poem, & varies with the flow of the feeling.   I have
translated & Mary has transcribed the Symposium, as well as my poem; &
I am proceeding to employ myself on a discourse upon the subject of which

SC 491 *the Symposium treats considering the ~~subject~~ it with reference to the difference of sentiments respecting it existing between the Greeks & modern nations. A subject ~~by~~ to be handled with that delicate caution which either I cannot or I will not practise in other matters, but which here I acknowledge to be necessary. — Not that I have any serious thought of publishing either this discourse or the Symposium— at least till I return to England when we*
25 *may discuss the propriety of it.*

Nightmare Abbey finished. Well, what is in it? What is it? You are as secret as if the priest of Ceres had dictated its sacred pages. However I suppose I shall see in time; when my second parcel arrives. My first is yet absent.   By what conveyance did you send it?

30 *Pray are you yet cured of your Nympholepsy? 'Tis a sweet disease but one as obstinate & dangerous as any– even when the Nymph is a* <u>Poliad</u>. *~~W~~ Whether such be the case or not I hope your nympholeptic tale is not abandoned.   The subject if treated with a due spice of Bacchic fury & interwoven with the manners & feelings of those divine people— who in their*
35 *very errors are the mirrors as it were in which all that is delicate & graceful contemplates itself— is perhaps equal to any. What a wonderful passage there is in Phædrus– the beginning I think of one of Socrates's speeches in praise of poetic madness & in definition of what poetry is, & how a man becomes a poet. Every man who lives in this age & desires to write poetry*
40 *ought– as a preservative against the cold & false & narrow systems of criticism which every poetical empiric vents— to impress himself with this sentence— if he would ~~nu~~ be numbered among those to whom may apply this proud tho' sublime expression of Tasso—"*<u>Non c'e in mondo che merita nome</u> <u>di ~~poet~~ creatore, che Dio ed il Poeta.</u>"

45 *The weather has been brilliantly fine– & now among these mountains, the autumnal air is becoming less hot, especially in the morning & evenings. The chesnut woods are now inexpressibly beautiful– for the chesnuts have become large & add a new richness to the full foliage. We see here Jupiter in the East, & Venus (I believe) as the evening star directly after sunset.*
50 *More, & better in my next– M & C. desire their kind remembrances*
Most faithfully your friend
P B Shelley

Shelley to Peacock   **August 16, 1818**

SC 491 [Address, page 4]
      Thomas Peacock Esq
         Great Marlow
  55   *Bucks*
    Inghilterra
    Angleterre

line 5. *added*: probable reading.

line 7. *escursion*: possibly *exursion*.

line 19. *considering*: as is common in Shelley's writing, the *ing* ending is more symbolic than precise.

line 31. *obstinate*: probable reading.

line 32. *nympholeptic* (sic).

line 37. *there*: written through indecipherable letters.

line 44. *Dio*: slightly affected both by seal tear and repair of seal.

line 47. *chesnut*: contemporary alternative spelling; see also the plural form on the same line.

line 52. *P B Shelley*: followed by a paraph.

line 57. *Angleterre*: written sideways on address sheet.

As the "No. 7" at the top of this letter indicates, sc 491 is the seventh letter that Shelley addressed to Peacock from Italy. Of these, all but one (written, Mary's Journal records, on June 15 from Bagni di Lucca) survive in at least printed texts.[1] Shelley's July 25 letter had described his mode of daily life at Bagni di Lucca. He, Mary, and Claire had gone riding and walking. They had visited the Casino, where the fashionable English and Italian visitors congregated and where there was a ball every Sunday.[2] Shelley had been translating Plato's *Sympo-*

1. The five earlier surviving letters include three written from Milan on April 6, April 20, and April 30; one from Leghorn, dated June 5; and one from Bagni di Lucca, dated July 25, 1818. The first four, which are in the Bodleian Library, were published by Mary Shelley in *Essays, Letters* (1840). The letter of July 25 was published by Peacock in *Fraser's Magazine* (1860) but the manuscript has not surfaced since it was sold with his books and manuscripts in 1866.

2. Details about the activities and services available at Bagni di Lucca in Shelley's day are to be found in a twenty-three-page pamphlet entitled *Regolamento Per Il Servizio E Buon' Ordine Dei Bagni di Lucca* printed at Lucca in 1815 by Francesco Bertini. (While at Bagni di Lucca, the Shelleys stayed at the Casa Bertini, and it is not unlikely that Bertini owned the house rather than G. B. Chiappa, as Dowden speculated.)

According to the *Regolamento*, the season at the Bagni was from May 1 until the end of September. Besides the Baths themselves (under the superintendence of a physician and twenty-eight bath attendants, half of them men and half women), the Casino provided games of chance and billiards (pp. 21–23), and sponsored a ball every Sunday during July and August (p. 8). Mail was carried daily between Lucca and Bagni di Lucca by two messengers (p. 9).

SC 491   *sium*, reading Herodotus, and bathing daily in a pool under a waterfall.[3]
During this period Shelley really had seen little that Peacock could not
enjoy at his new house "facing the Coiting Place, in West Street" at
Marlow.[4]

Although nothing in his daily life had changed since July 25,[5] Shelley
had by August 16 overcome the writing block that he had lamented in
his letter of that date.[6] The Camenae (prophetic nymphs of springs in
ancient Italy who later became identified with the Greek Muses) had
granted him enough inspiration to finish *Rosalind and Helen* (lines 12–14).
It would be of interest to know which parts of that poem Shelley had
written in England and which were added in Italy, but this could be
determined only by detailed analysis of manuscripts of *Rosalind and
Helen*, coupled with a bibliographical analysis of the first edition to ascertain which gatherings were printed before Ollier received the completed
manuscript. We need observe only that Shelley's opinion of the poem
was not especially high. Beginning the poem when he was too closely involved emotionally in the strained relations with David and Isabel
Booth and William Baxter at the end of 1817,[7] Shelley never achieved
proper aesthetic distance from his subject. For it seems obvious that
once his anger had cooled, he had little interest in completing *Rosalind
and Helen*. In a letter to Ollier also written on August 16, he writes:
"Voici the conclusion of my little poem, which I took advantage of ten

3. See Shelley, *Letters*, II, 23–27.

4. Peacock to Shelley, July 19, 1818, Peacock, *Works*, VIII, 200. The spellings "quoit" and "coit"
both appear in the *OED*.

5. In both the present letter and that of July 25, Shelley's astronomical observations were incorrect.
In answer to our query, Paul B. G. Twomey, Scientific Assistant at the Hayden Planetarium in
New York, wrote as follows:

> After plotting the planetary positions for the dates, July 25, 1818, and August 16, 1818, the fol-
> lowing becomes evident:
>
>   1. a. The star in the east at sunset, July 25, 1818, was Saturn, not Jupiter as supposed.
>   b. The year before (c. August 3, 1817) Venus was a morning "star," visible only
>   before sunrise.
>   2. On August 16, 1818, Venus was an evening "star," but the planet in the east was
>   still Saturn.
>   . . . Jupiter . . . would have been quite conspicuous in the southwestern sky on both dates, and
>   very near Venus on the 16th of August.

6. "I have lately found myself totally incapable of original composition." (Shelley, *Letters*, II, 26.)

7. See SC 432, SC 434, SC 440, and SC 441 and Commentaries.

SC 491   days of dubious inspiration to finish — the tone of your reproaches and the printer's wonder operated as Muse on the occasion. You will observe that the fabric of the composition is light and unstudied — and that if it have little merit it has as much as it aspires to."[8]

Shelley gave Mary credit for persuading him to finish *Rosalind and Helen*, a distinction which she also claims in her "Notes On Poems Written In 1818" in her edition of Shelley's *Poetical Works* (1839). The poem remained a favorite of Mary's, and her preference for the bland sentimentalities of *Rosalind and Helen* over *Prometheus Unbound*, *Adonais*, and *The Triumph of Life* indicates that her judgment was not based on prejudice against Shelley's "romanticism" (as that word was defined by the Victorians), but resulted either from pride in her own role as midwife to this poem or else simply from an inability to appreciate Shelley's greatest imaginative and architectonic achievements. *Rosalind and Helen* was a poem such as could have been written by a number of later poets who imitated Shelley's superficial manner without comprehending his poetic vision.

Turning to Peacock's writings, Shelley expresses good-natured annoyance at Peacock's failure to describe *Nightmare Abbey* in any detail. Peacock's reason for not doing so seems obvious enough, if one accepts the traditional identification of Scythrop as a caricature drawn from Shelley's enthusiasms and foibles. Peacock must have told Shelley more about his plans for a poem on the subject of nympholepsy. In notes on Shelley's letters to him, Peacock remarked that he had "not now the most distant recollection" of what Shelley's remark on "a Poliad" referred to (line 31). As has been pointed out,[9] a "Poliad" was obviously a "city nymph," a coinage natural enough after Hunt's catalogue in "The Nymphs" (see SC 469, Commentary). Shelley's reference to Peacock's "Nympholepsy," that "sweet disease," probably refers to Peacock's real or supposed infatuation with some young lady in London. The identity of this woman was quite the kind of thing that the older and staider Peacock was likely to have forgotten, but we can examine the allusion briefly.

One person who can be eliminated immediately is Jane Gryffydh,

8. Shelley, *Letters*, II, 31.
9. Dowden, *Shelley*, II, 188 n.

SC 491   who lived in Merionethshire far from any city. Though Peacock had referred to her in 1810 as "the Caernarvonshire nymph,"[10] he had not seen her for seven years, and she can hardly have been uppermost in the mind of Shelley, who had never seen her. Marianne de St. Croix, with whom Peacock carried on a long and sometimes stormy romance,[11] was probably intended. Though her family's home was at one time in Homerton (a village just slightly less far to the north northeast of the City of London than Hunt's rural retreat at Hampstead was from the Grosvenor Square area), we do not know where Marianne was living in 1818. Peacock saw her brother William and his new bride several times during the summer and fall of 1818, and corresponded with both Marianne and Sarah de St. Croix (perhaps a sister).[12] What is more relevant is Shelley's linking of Marianne and Peacock, illustrated the following spring by a postscript to a letter to Peacock: "Pray tell me how Marianne St. Croix is?"[13] It seems likely, then, that Shelley was alluding to her as Peacock's "Poliad." And since later remarks indicate that the Shelleys did not get on well with Marianne,[14] Shelley may have been half-serious in describing nympholepsy as a dangerous disease, as well as a sweet one.

On March 20, 1818, Peacock had written to Hogg (sc 468): "When I have finished the novel [a never-completed novel set in London] I shall write another Pagan poem." During his study of classical superstitions for *Rhododaphne*, Peacock probably read widely on nympholepsy and discussed with some of his friends his plan to write a poem about it. Peacock later noted that he had "abandoned this design on seeing the

---

10. To E. T. Hookham, June 12, 1810, Peacock, *Works*, VIII, 185.

11. For the full course of Peacock's relations with the St. Croix family, see H. F. B. Brett-Smith's "Biographical Introduction" to *Works* (I, xii–ccxii), and especially those references cited in the Index. See also *Shelley and his Circle*, I, 100–102.

12. See the diary that Peacock kept from July 7 to September 26, 1818 (*Works*, VIII, 435–444). William de St. Croix was married on Saturday, July 11, 1818; Sarah may have been his new bride.

13. Shelley, *Letters*, II, 95.

14. When Shelley wrote in May 1820 to congratulate Peacock on his marriage to Jane Gryffydh, he added: "If you had married Marianne *I* should never have seen much of you, & now I have at least a chance" (manuscript in The Carl H. Pforzheimer Library). There is some indication, however, that Marianne shared some of the literary interests of Peacock's circle. Frank Hogan once owned a copy of Mary Shelley's *Frankenstein* signed "Marianne de St. Crois [*sic*], Jany 4, 1818" (Parke-Bernet, April 25, 1945, lot 646), and in a 1946 Sotheby sale there was a copy of Shelley's *The Revolt of Islam* inscribed "To Marianne St. Croix with the Authors best compliments, Jan. 22, 1818" (Sotheby, July 29–30, 1946, lot 371).

SC 491 announcement of Horace Smith's *Amarynthus the Nympholept*." He had obviously urged Shelley to silence about the details for his plan, for on October 8, 1818, Shelley wrote of Byron's *Childe Harold*: "You saw those beautiful stanzas in the 4th Canto about the Nymph Egeria. Well, I did not whisper a word abo[ut] nympholepsy, I hope you acquit me. — And I hope you will not carry delicacy so far as to let this suppr[ess] any thing nympholeptic."[15]

The truth is that nymphs were at this period "in the air" of the literary world. Besides Byron's passage on Egeria in *Childe Harold* (IV.cxvi–cxxvii) and Hunt's "The Nymphs" in *Foliage*, there are also Keats's explorations of medieval variants of the superstitions about nympholepsy in "La Belle Dame sans Merci" and "Lamia." Horace Smith, in the Preface to his anonymously published *Amarynthus, the Nympholept: A Pastoral Drama, in Three Acts, with Other Poems* (London: Longman, etc., 1821), cites some of the classical authorities — Plutarch, Ovid, and Propertius — and summarizes the core of the superstition: "The Νυμφόληπτοι of the Greeks, and the Lymphati or Lymphatici of the Romans, were men supposed to be possessed by the Nymphs, and driven to phrensy, either from having seen one of those mysterious beings, or from the maddening effect of the oracular caves in which they resided" (page v). The student of Shelley's poetry will think at once of Panthea's speech that opens Act II, scene iii of *Prometheus Unbound*:

> Hither the sound has borne us — to the realm
> Of Demogorgon, and the mighty portal,
> Like a volcano's meteor-breathing chasm,
> Whence the oracular vapour is hurled up
> Which lonely men drink wandering in their youth,
> And call truth, virtue, love, genius, or joy,
> That maddening wine of life, whose dregs they drain
> To deep intoxication; and uplift,
> Like Mænads who cry loud, Evoe! Evoe!
> The voice which is contagion to the world.

Shelley, who had been reading the classics with Peacock, may well have had in mind the oracular caves of the nymphs (cousins of the prophetic Camenae mentioned earlier in this letter) as the root source of his more universal myth of the powers and dangers of youthful inspiration.

15. Shelley, *Letters*, II, 44.

Shelley to Peacock   *August 16, 1818*

SC 491   Shelley associates Peacock's projected nympholeptic tale with the
passage on poetic madness in Plato's *Phaedrus*[16] and with the sentence
attributed to Tasso (in Serassi's *Vita di Torquato Tasso*)[17] which may be
translated, "None deserves the name of creator, except God and the
Poet." While at Marlow Hogg, Hunt, Peacock, and Shelley had all tried
to make themselves less forlorn by reanimating within their circle stories
of the Greek demi-gods. But for Peacock the classical myths that he
exploited in *Rhododaphne* were merely superstitions to be retold for entertainment; they possessed no shadow of reality. For Shelley, who had in
his youth sought for ghosts and on whom the awful shadow of an unseen
Power had descended more than once, the supernatural was not a dead
issue, available only for analytic inquiry or historical reconstruction. He
and Peacock had doubtless debated these questions across their years of
intimacy, and it seems right to think of Shelley's praise of poetic madness,
with justification from Plato and the mad poet Tasso, in the context of
that debate. Peacock does not comment on this — or on his own poetic
aspirations — in his surviving correspondence during the remainder of
1818, but *Nightmare Abbey* embodies a critique of poetic madness (among
other things), and once Peacock had committed himself to a career of
practical affairs at the East India Company, he carried to the public his
thoughts on contemporary poetry and poets, with appropriate self-irony,
in *The Four Ages of Poetry*. There, and in Shelley's answering *Defence
of Poetry*, formal and impersonal rhetorical structures replace the epistolary mode, and temperamental predilections transform themselves into
philosophic arguments that are as relevant to twentieth-century America
as they were to nineteenth-century Europe.

16. Peacock's note to this letter (*Fraser's Magazine*, LXI, March 1860, 304) identifies and translates
the relevant passage as follows:

> "There are several kinds," says Socrates, "of divine madness. That which proceeds from the
> Muses taking possession of a tender and unoccupied soul, awakening, and bacchically inspiring
> it towards songs and other poetry, adorning myriads of ancient deeds, instructs succeeding
> generations; but he who, without this madness from the Muses, approaches the poetical
> gates, having persuaded himself that by art alone he may become sufficiently a poet, will find
> in the end his own imperfection, and see the poetry of his cold prudence vanish into nothing-
> ness before the light of that which has sprung from divine insanity." — *Platonis Phædrus*,
> p. 245 a.

17. See sc 479 and Commentary.

SC 491   To return to this letter: Shelley's announced intention of seeing the art treasures of nearby Tuscan cities during August remained unfulfilled because of a sudden change in plans that is discussed below in SC 494, Commentary.

SC 492   P. B. SHELLEY TO CHARLES OLLIER, AUGUST 16, 1818

AL signed *Percy B.Shelley*, ½ page. Double sheet, 4to (9.6 x 7.3 inches; strip *ca.* 3.5 inches deep cut away from top of first leaf).
Laid paper. Watermark: [cherub holding aloft banner with inscription]| POLLET|; countermark: AP|.
Seal: wax, red.
Postal fee: 1/11.
Postmarks: 1. LUCCA|; 2. (British Foreign Post Office stamp)*:* FPO| SE 1| 1818|.
Additions: 1. (page 1)*:* random ink blots, perhaps from another, newly written sheet placed upon SC 492; 2. (page 4)*:* four diamond-shaped impressed marks of various sizes—perhaps made by a matched set of heavy paperweights.

PROVENANCE: Charles Ollier (?Puttick and Simpson, July 19, 1877, lot 66); Charles W. Frederickson (Bangs, May 24, 1897, lot 2347); W. R. Benjamin; Henry Cady Sturges (Anderson Galleries, January 16, 1923, Part IV, lot 232); W. R. Benjamin; City Book Auction #503, November 11 and 18, 1950, lot 328. *De Ricci 390* (p. 193).

Dear Sir

Oblige me by honouring a draft of £20 that will be presented to you signed A.B. If there ~~the~~ sh^d be any mistake with the Bankers it shall be rectified by return of Post, but I earnestly intreat you to pay the draft.

5   *Of course these letters are put to my Account.*

~~tr~~   Your's very truly
Percy B.Shelley

I had just sealed my other letter when I discovered the necessity of writing again ————

[Address, page 4]

10   *Messrs Ollier   Booksellers*
    3. Welbeck S^t
        Cavendish Square
            London
            Angleterre

Shelley and his Circle : Manuscripts

Shelley to Ollier   **August 16, 1818**

SC 492   line 4. *Post,*: the comma is difficult to distinguish because of the random blottings.
                  intreat: obsolete spelling.

IN EXAMINING this brief note, one enters into what is perhaps the least clear and least discussed of the several biographical problems connected with Shelley. The known facts are few and easy to state. On June 28, 1818, Shelley wrote "in great haste" to Ollier from Bagni di Lucca as follows:

> I write simply to request you to pay ten pounds on my account to a person who will call on you, and *on no account* to mention my name. If you have no money of mine still pay it at all events and cash the enclosed at the bank.
>
>   Ever most truly yours,
>   P. B. Shelley.
>
> The person will bring a note without date signed A. B. It is of so great consequence that this note shall be paid that I hope if there is any mistake with Brookes you will pay it for me, and if you have none of mine in your hands, that you will rely on my sending it you by return of Post.[1]

This June 28 letter exhibits several interesting features. First, Shelley does not indicate, and does not indeed seem to know, who the "person" applying to Ollier for the money will be. This person, in turn, does not know the identity of "A. B.," whose note will elicit ten pounds from Messrs. Ollier, Booksellers;[2] Ollier is to keep Shelley's name out of the affair.

It seems as though the draft was to be cashed by someone unknown to Shelley at the instigation of a third party, someone with whom Shelley was in correspondence or personal contact while he was at Bagni di Lucca. As both Shelley and Mary indicate in their letters from the Bagni that they knew no one there, the intermediary must have been a correspondent.

SC 492 was probably written on Sunday, August 16, 1818. It was postmarked in London on September 1, 1818. Mail required between two

1. Shelley, *Letters*, II, 19.

2. The designation "A. B." was, as one could imagine, a common one during this period for those who wished to remain anonymous. Certain personal and situation wanted ads in the *Morning Chronicle*, for example, ask respondents to address "A. B." in care of this or that lawyer or bookseller. Howard Robinson records in *British Post Office* how a grafter by the name of Peregrine Treves was paid £350 per year from 1781 to 1787 under the designation "A. B." (pp. 150–151). In March 1815 Shelley — or perhaps Claire, as Dowden surmised (*Shelley*, I, 518) — carried on a correspondence over the designation "A. Z." (Mary Shelley, Journal, March 20, 1815).

The Carl H. Pforzheimer Library

SC 492   and three weeks to get from Italy to London during the summer months, and SC 491, which Shelley wrote to Peacock on Sunday, August 16, is also postmarked in London on September 1. Shelley also wrote another letter to Ollier dated August 16, enclosing the conclusion of *Rosalind and Helen*, but the postmarks of this letter are unavailable.[3] Shelley's statement about sealing this other letter suggests that he wrote this one also on August 16, and the Lucca postmark assures us that it was mailed before he and Claire left the Duchy of Lucca sometime August 17 or 18 on their way to Venice via Florence.

What could have necessitated Shelley's second note to Ollier, asking that the bookseller pay the stranger another £20?[4] Mary's Journal for August 16 reads: "Finish transcribing S's eclogue — Shelley is not well — he reads Lucan — Another letter from Elise —." The word "Another" alludes to "a letter from Elise" that Mary records receiving on Friday, August 14. These two letters presumably caused Shelley to alter the plans he mentioned to Peacock (SC 491, lines 7–11) for visiting museums in the Tuscan cities. Instead, on Monday, August 17, Mary noted in her Journal, "S & C depart for Venise."

One's first thought is that, inasmuch as Elise's letter seems to have been Shelley's only contact with the outside world on this Sunday, that letter must somehow relate to his "necessity of writing again." This hypothesis would, in turn, lead to the speculation that the payment of £30 to someone in London might somehow relate to Shelley's Neapolitan child and the so-called "Hoppner scandal." This may, however, be a misleading assumption. Though Mary's Journal records no other letters, Mary would not have been the person to receive or pick up the mail, and if Shelley were trying to be secretive, he may well have intercepted another letter — possibly from London — that Mary knew nothing about. Or, Mary may not have recorded the arrival of a letter from a regular correspondent that contained no such pressing news as Elise's letter obviously did. This routine letter might include a reminder to pay a debt that Shelley did not wish to have made a matter of public gossip in London.

Shelley included in the first August 16 letter to Ollier "6 pieces of

3. Shelley, *Letters*, II, 30–31.

4. The top third of pp. 1–2 of SC 492 has been cut away, presumably because it contained a bank draft on Brooks, Son & Dixon that Ollier could use to reimburse himself for the £20.

SC 492 writing" (the additions to *Rosalind and Helen*) and "a letter which you will oblige me by putting in the twopenny post immediately." Did this sealed letter for the London post contain the draft for £20 signed "A. B."? If so, one must assume that it was addressed to someone who would not arouse Ollier's suspicion or curiosity — that is, someone to whom it was so natural for Shelley to write that Ollier would have no reason to associate this correspondent with the mysterious bearer of the draft signed "A. B." Most of those potential correspondents can be eliminated. It could not have been Peacock (beyond the range of the Twopenny Post), or Hunt (from whom Shelley almost despaired of hearing), or Hogg (to whom, as is clear from surviving letters, Shelley did not write for long periods of time). The one London friend with whom Shelley was in correspondence at this time and whose activities cannot be traced is Horace Smith. Possibly Smith was the person who received instructions from Shelley, together with the drafts signed "A. B."; he may have executed whatever commission Shelley had specified and sent a third party to collect the necessary money from Ollier. This would have been perfectly feasible, because Smith was a stockbroker, undoubtedly used to carrying out confidential business and having connections with messengers who could be trusted to carry out such transactions discreetly.

Having constructed the above hypothesis, I hesitate to go further into the realm of conjecture and speculate on the nature of the business that was being transacted for Shelley. White suggests that these letters were "possibly connected with some quixotic charity or some petty money-lender with whom he did not wish to be connected by name, or more probably with Shelley's recent instructions to his bankers not to pay certain claims."[5] If White is correct in any one of these suggestions, there is no reason to interest ourselves further about the unsolved mystery. It seems clear, however, that on at least one and probably two later occasions, Horace Smith arranged for the anonymous publication in England of poems by Shelley. Smith tells in his "Graybeard's Gossip about His Literary Acquaintance" how he arranged for the publication of *Œdipus Tyrannus; or, Swellfoot the Tyrant* in 1820.[6] And discovering that Shelley's "Ode to Naples" first appeared in the *Military Register and*

5. White, *Shelley*, II, 555, fn. 61.
6. *New Monthly Magazine*, LXXXI (November 18, 1847), 293.

SC 492 *Weekly Gazette* for October 1 and 8, 1820, White conjectured that Shelley may have simply included the poem when he sent the manuscript of *Swellfoot the Tyrant* to Smith and that this publication came from Smith's copy, either with or without Shelley's knowledge.[7]

It would be well, then, for students of Shelley to keep their eyes open to the possibility that while Shelley was in London in the early weeks of 1818, he left with Horace Smith a manuscript, poetry or prose, and that Smith arranged for its anonymous publication, with Shelley paying for the printing and other costs by means of these two drafts signed "A. B." No such anonymous publication is known, but if one is some day identified, the survival of these two mysterious but seemingly inconsequential notes to Ollier concerning the payment of £30 may be regarded as a matter of some importance.

7. White, *Shelley*, II, 223. For the text of the early printing of "Ode to Naples," see Judith Chernaik, *The Lyrics of Shelley* (Case Western Reserve University Press, 1972).

SC 492A P. B. SHELLEY TO BROOKS, SON & DIXON, AUGUST 16, 1818

AUTOGRAPH CHECK signed *Percy Bysshe Shelley.*, 1 page.
Single sheet (3.5 x 7.3 inches).
Laid paper.
Additions: 1. spindle hole; 2. two acid holes, one above and one below signature, caused by blots of corrosive ink; 3. check has been tipped in to a first edition of the Shelleys' *History of a Six Weeks' Tour* (London, 1817), which contains a bookplate of Christine Alexander Graham.

PROVENANCE: The Willis King III Library (Sotheby, October 5, 1971, lot 367).

> *Bagni di Lucca*
> *Aug. 16. 1818.*
>
> *Gentlemen*
> *You will oblige me by paying Mr Ollier*
> 5   *or bearer Twenty Pounds.*
>
> *Percy Bysshe Shelley.*
>
> *Mess^s Brookes & C° Chancery Lane*
> *£20.0..0   London*

SEE SC 492 and Commentary, especially footnote 4.

Shelley and his Circle : Manuscripts

Trelawny to White   *August 18–20, 1818*

SC 493   E. J. TRELAWNY TO AUGUSTA WHITE, AUGUST 18–20, 1818

AL signed *Trelawny*, 2¼ pages. Double sheet, 4ᵗᵒ (8.8 x 7.3 inches).
Wove paper. Watermark: Bᴀᴛʜ| 1816|.
Notations, in pencil: 1. (page 1): *1819–*; 2. (page 4): *Edward Trelawny*|;
3. (page 4): *Augˢᵗ 20ᵗʰ| 1818*|; 4. (page 4, in a modern hand): *18 Aug 1819*|.
Addition: series of pin-holes down left margin, indicating that manuscript was
once sewn with others into an album.

PROVENANCE: Augusta White Draper; Misses Kathleen and Molly Draper of
Montreal; Gannon, 1943.

August 18–19 or 20ᵗʰ
The <u>Farm</u>

> *"He travels, and expatiates as the bee*
> *From flow'r to flow'r — so he from land to land;*
> 5   *The manners, customs, policy of all,*
> *Pay contribution to the store he gleans;*
> *He sucks intelligence, in every clime*
>   *the honey of his deep research*
> *And spreads ᴧ~~intelligence, in every clime~~,*
> 10   *At his return — a rich repast for thee,"*

*Have been wandering as is now my chief delight & solace from
retrospection,*

*"May it be reserved for us Dear Crust'a to be distinguished by the honour
of establishing the worship and the alters of Friendship and Fidedelity!*
15 *Instructed by us, may the individuals of each sex learn that there is but one
road to happiness and but one mode of persuing it; singly they can never
reach their object, but sweetly journying in pairs they will find themselves
led into her presence without toil or difficulty"!——*

I send thee Crust a peace offering fror my long silence but in
20 *truth my absence, was the cause, how do you get on in this justling world,
you are an unhappy disposition, not contented with the ills which are inseperable from Life's eventful history, but ever on the look out for emaginary
ones, —— Shame say I on the good sence you posses — should be so perverted,—"tis in ourselves we are thus – or thus— rest assured it ill becomes*

[669]

SC 493　*you — and that tis not visionary emaginings,— but common worldly sence,*
which is valuable tis the only current coin! so look to it well –

　　　　Tis true, I as <u>you</u> would say I am inconstant but not in reallity —
　　　　　　"Yet still in hours of Love or strife
　　　　　　I've scap'd the weariness of Life;
30　　　　　　*Now Loving friends — now hating foes,*
　　　　　　~~I've scap'd the weariness of Life;~~
　　　　　　I Loath'd the Languor of repose;"

　　　　Thanks for not forgetting my Little Mary Ann in thy remem-
brances— tell her she is garnered up in my heart— and when tis her
35　*pleasure I will be in Town, nor marvel at this Crust, "My Motto is!——*

　　　　　　'He who loves but one alone,
　　　　　　Loves full power hath never known.
　　　　　　Only he true bliss, can tell,
　　　　　　Who <u>often</u> loves, and <u>always</u> <u>well</u>.

40　　　*And my enemies must allow I've ever fulfilled this motto;——*
　　　　So cherish me in thy heart sweet Crust and you shall reap a
plentious harvest— thy seed will not be scattered on a barren soil but the scions
of Friendship will luxuriantly shoot forth from the heart of
　　　　　　　　　　　　　　　　Trelawny——

[Address, page 4]
45　*Crust A——*

line 14. *Fidedelity!*: probable reading.　　　　line 19. *fror*: probable reading.

As we saw in SC 473, Trelawny retreated from London to a rural cottage in the vicinity of Pinner, Middlesex, in the spring of 1818. Datelined simply "The Farm," the present letter would seem to postdate SC 473, but we cannot with absolute certainty place it in 1818, for we know nothing definite of Trelawny's whereabouts between April 1818 and February 28, 1821, the date of his final letter to Augusta White before she left England. If one imagines Trelawny's wanderings as occupying

Trelawny to White   **August 18–20, 1818**

SC 493 months instead of weeks, this letter could have been written in August of 1819 or 1820, but in any case, it cannot be earlier than August 1818.[1]

In this letter Trelawny attempts to keep Augusta's feelings for him away from the disaster areas of love and hate; in a melange of quotations and/or paraphrases, he urges that they set an example of friendship and fidelity. That he succeeded in keeping Augusta's friendship while avoiding more entangling alliances is evidenced by the survival of these letters and by his later correspondence with Mrs. Augusta White Draper. In an ill-chosen quotation from Iago's famous speech to Rodrigo,[2] Trelawny chides Augusta for her "unhappy disposition," admonishing her for her attitudes rather than sympathizing with her difficulties. He quotes Byron's *Giaour*[3] and while telling her that Mary Ann (perhaps Augusta's younger sister?) "is garnered up in my heart" he makes another appeal for friendship. Trelawny's letter is, in fact, a tissue of contradictory sentiments, most, apparently, culled from his reading — a kind of epistolary commonplace book.[4] Among the literary works that appealed to Trelawny, it is clear that Byron's Mediterranean poetic romances beginning with *The Giaour* (1813) played an important part in shaping his self-image. The Shelley-Byron circle in Italy noticed the resemblance between Trelawny's tales of adventure as an Oriental pirate and the Giaour, Conrad of *The Corsair*, or Lara. *Adventures of a Younger Son* shows that he also identified himself with Selim in *The Bride of Abydos* and Hugo in *Parisina* insofar as they are sons (or supposed sons) mistreated by their fathers.

In Trelawny's later years, he apparently told youngsters like the American poet Joaquin Miller that "Lord Byron made him the hero of more than one wild poetic tale. He was 'Conrad,' 'Lara,' and the like."[5] Miller, who in 1893 wrote a memoir of his London conversations with

1. Notation 3, which dates the letter "Augst 20th 1818" (see Bibliographical Description), is written in a nineteenth-century hand, probably that of Augusta White Draper in later years.

2. Shakespeare, *Othello*, I.iii.322 and ff.

3. *The Giaour*, lines 984–987. Trelawny is quoting from memory; line 986 should read: "Now leagued with friends, now girt by foes."

4. The first paragraph of Trelawny's letter is a quotation from Cowper's *The Task* (IV.107–113). Trelawny evidently copied this quotation directly from the text since the only change in his transcription is the logical substitution of the final word "thee" for "me."

5. Joaquin Miller, *Trelawny with Shelley and Byron* (Pompton Lakes, N.J., 1922), p. 10.

SC 493   "Old Tre," did not stop to check the dates of Trelawny's first meeting with Byron. But Trelawny himself obviously played on the credulity of English society throughout the years of his lionization. He also told Miller that he had landed on the coast of California in his early years — a story that Miller, a Californian, found extremely significant.[6] What "Old Tre" did, it seems, was tailor his adventures to the temper of his auditors. It is not surprising, therefore, that while associating in Switzerland with Williams and Medwin, fresh from service in India, he should embroider the account of his adventures in the Far East,[7] or that, having moved on with them to Byron's circle in Pisa, he elaborated these adventures and his own character into parallels with the plots and the protagonists of Byron's early poetry. Thus, what to Miller seemed a clear-cut case of literature recording human life was a classic example of literature shaping human character and action.

6. Miller, *Trelawny*, p. 10.

7. See Lady Ann Hill, "Trelawny's Family Background and Naval Career," *Keats-Shelley Journal*, V (1956), 28.

SC 494   P. B. SHELLEY TO M. W. SHELLEY, AUGUST 23–24, 1818

L (copy) signed *PBS.*, in the hand of Mary Shelley, 3½ pages. Double sheet, 4to (9 x 7.4 inches).
Wove paper (see Commentary, fn. 10, below). Watermark: [Prince of Wales feathers]| *J & M*| 1823|.

PROVENANCE: *De Ricci 389* (p. 240).

> *To MWS. at the Baths of Lucca.*
>   *Venise. Sunday Morning*
>   *August 23^d—1818*

My dearest Mary

5   *We arrived here last night at twelve o'clock, and it is now before breakfast the next morning. I can of course tell you nothing of the future, and though I shall not close this letter till post time, yet I do know exactly when that is. Yet if you are very impatient, look along the the letter and you will see another letter date when I may have something to relate.*

x   x   x   x

Shelley and his Circle : Manuscripts

SC 494

We came from Padua hither in a gondola, and the gondolieri among ~~a~~ other things—without ~~at~~ any hint on our part began talking of L.B. he said he was a giovanotto Inglese with a <u>nome stravagante</u>, who lives very luxuriously, and spent great sums of money. This man it seems was one of L.B.'s gondolieri. No sooner had we arrived at the inn than the waiter began talking

15 *about him– said that he frequented Mr Hoppner's converzazioni.*

Our journey from Florence to Padua contained nothing which may not be related another time. At Padua, as I said, we took a gondola– and left it at 3 o'clock. These gondolas are the most convenient and beautiful boats in the world. They are finely carpeted and furnished with black and painted

20 *black. The couches upon which you lean are ~~un~~ extraordinarily soft and are so disposed as to be the most comfortable to those who lean or sit. The windows have at will either Venetian plate glass flowered, or venetian blinds, or blinds of black cloth to shut out the night. The weather here is extremely cold, indeed sometimes very painfully so, and yesterday it began to rain.*

25 *We past the laguna in the middle of the night in a most violent storm of wind rain and lightning. It was very curious to observe the elements above in a state of such tremendous convulsion and the surface of the water almost calm– for these lagunas, though five miles broad– a space enough in a storm to sink any gondola, are so shallow that the boatmen drive the boat along*

30 *with a pole. The sea-water furiously agitated by the wind, shone with sparkles like stars. Venice now hidden and now disclosed by the driving rain, shone dimly with its lights. We were all this while safe and comfortable— except that C—— was now and then a little frightened in our cabin. — Well adieu, dearest—I shall, as Miss Byron says, resume the pen in the ~~morning~~*

35 *evening.*

Sunday-(Monday) night– 5 o'clock
in the morning.

Well I will try to relate every thing in its order. After breakfast we took a gondola and went to the Hoppner's. C– went in first, and I, who had no

40 *idea of calling, sate in the gondola. Soon, a servant ~~came d~~ came down and requested me to go up stairs. I found Mr H. and C.—, and soon after Mrs H. a most agreable and amiable lady.*

x   x   x   x

[673]

The Carl H. Pforzheimer Library

sc 494   *At three o'clock I called on L.B. He was delighted to see me, and our*
first conversation of course consisted in the object of my visit. ——

                              x   x   x   x

45   *Well, my dear Mary, this talk went off, for I did not see in that moment*
how I could urge it further, and I thought that at least many points were
gained in the willingness and good humour of our discussion. So he took
me in his gondola – much against my will, for I wanted to return to C—
at the Hoppner's— across the laguna to a long sandy island which defends
50   *Venice from the Adriatic. When we disembarked we found his horses waiting*
for us, and we rode along the sands of the sea talking. Our conversation con-
sisted in histories of his wounded feelings, and questions as to my affairs,
and great professions of friendship and regard for me. He said that if he
had been in England at the time of the Chancery affair, he would have
55   *moved heaven and earth to have prevented such a decision. We talked of*
literary matters, his fourth Canto, which he says is very good and indeed
repeated some stanzas of great energy to me. ~~When we returned to his~~
~~palace——~~

                              x   x   x

     Well but the time presses. I am now going to the Bankers to send you
60   *money for the journey which I shall address to you at Florence, post office.*
Pray come instantly to Este, where I shall be waiting with C— and Elise,
in the utmost anxiety for your arrival. You can pack up directly you get this
                                                          o'clock
*letter, and employ the next day in that. The day after get up at four*ᴀ*and go*
65   *post to Lucca, where you will arrive at 6. then take* ~~vetter~~ *vetturino* ~~to~~ *for*
Florence and arrive the same evening. From Florence to Este is three days
veturino journey, and you could not I think do it quicker by the post. Make
Paolo take you to good inns, as we found very bad ones, and pray avoid
the Tre Mori *at Bologna, perche vi sono cose inespressibile nel letto. I*
70   *dont think you can, but* try *to get from Florence to Bologna in one day. Dont*
take the post for it is not much faster and very expensive. I have been obliged
to decide on all these things without you. —I have done for the best and my
own beloved Mary, you must soon come and scold me if I have done wrong,
and kiss me if I have done right — for I am sure I do not know which

Shelley to Shelley   **August 23–24, 1818**

SC 494   *and it is only the event that can shew. We shall at ~~leave~~ least have formed*
an acquaintance with a lady who is so good, so beautiful, so angelically mild,
that were she wise too, she would be quite a M—— But she is not very accom-
plished. Her eyes are like a reflection of yours, her manners are like yours
when you know and like a person.

80   *Do you know, dearest, how this letter was written —by scraps and*
patches and interrupted every minute. The gondola is now come to take us
to Fusina. Este is a little place and the house found without difficulty. I
shall count 4 days for this letter– 1 day for packing —f 4 for coming
here– on the ninth or tenth day we shall meet.

85   *I am too late for the Post– but I send an ~~ex~~ express to overtake it–*
Enclosed is an order for £50.— If you knew all that I had to do!

    Dearest love, be well– be happy– come to me and confide in your own
constant and affectionate

PBS.

90 *Kiss the blue-eyed darlings for me and dont let William forget me. <u>Ca</u>*
cannot recollect me.

line 11. *talking*: altered from *talked*.

line 12. *giovanotto*: altered from *giovonotto*.

line 15. *converzazioni* (sic).

line 42. *agreable* (sic).

line 62. *directly you get* (sic).

line 67. *veturino* (sic).

line 69. *inespressibile* (sic): should be plural: *in-espressibili*.

As we have seen, Shelley told Peacock in his letter of August 16
that he intended to visit "some of the neighboring cities" and that
on September 10 he would leave Bagni di Lucca for Florence (sc 491).
But the arrival of Elise's letter from Venice on the same day[1] changed
all these plans. It set in motion a train of events that within six weeks
had resulted in the death of Clara Shelley.

    The letters from Elise that reached Bagni di Lucca on August 14
and August 16 obviously alarmed Claire. Although their contents can
only be conjectured, they apparently reported, among other things, that
Allegra had been banished from Byron's residence at the Palazzo Mocenigo to the home of the British consul in Venice, Richard Belgrave

1. See sc 492, Commentary.

SC 494   Hoppner and his wife.[2] Hoppner, the son of John Hoppner, the portrait painter, had been appointed consul at Venice soon after the initial fall of Napoleon.[3]

Iris Origo notes that Hoppner later stated that he and his wife were not "particularly fond" of Byron's child (or of Elise).[4] In any case, it seems likely that Elise painted a dark picture of the new situation in which she and Claire's child found themselves. Claire insisted on going to Venice to see to Allegra's welfare, and Shelley agreed to accompany her. Nor need Shelley's motives for making the sudden journey have been entirely altruistic. Without raising the question of Shelley's emotional (or, possibly, sexual) involvement with Claire[5] — or, as a more recent theory has it, with Elise[6] — one may safely say that Shelley was bored with Bagni di Lucca (as he indicated to Peacock in SC 491) and that the prospect of seeing Venice and Lord Byron held great attractions for him simply as a means of intellectual stimulation. This letter itself reflects something of his renewed excitement after the journey and his initial meeting with Byron in Italy.

Shelley's and Claire's sudden flight to Venice, unfortunately, left Mary alone with her two children and two servants (Milly Shields and Paolo Foggi) in a town where she, knowing no one socially, was just as bored as Shelley had been and far more lonely. She immediately wrote to Maria Gisborne on August 17, explaining that "Shelley and Clare are gone (they went today) to Venice on important business and I am left to take care of the house—now if all of you or any of you would come and cheer my solitude it would be exceedingly kind—"[7] The Gisbornes arrived at Bagni di Lucca on the twenty-fifth. Before that, however,

2. See Marchand, *Byron*, II, 747.

3. Hoppner is so listed in the *Royal Kalendar* for 1815 (published in 1814). This publication continues to list him in that post through the volume for 1825. In the 1826 edition, the space for the consul-general at Venice has been left blank and the volume for 1827 gives the consul at Venice as "W. T. Money, esq. FRS." See also C. S. B. Buckland, "Richard Belgrave Hoppner," *English Historical Review*, XXXIX (July 1924), 373-385. For John Hoppner (1758–1810), see *DNB*.

4. *Allegra* (London, 1935), p. 39 fn.

5. Claire has generally been regarded as the leading candidate for the mother of the Neapolitan child that Shelley registered as his in February 1819.

6. See Ursula Orange, "Elise, Nursemaid to the Shelleys," *Keats-Shelley Memorial Bulletin*, VI (1955), 24.

7. Mary Shelley, *Letters*, I, 56.

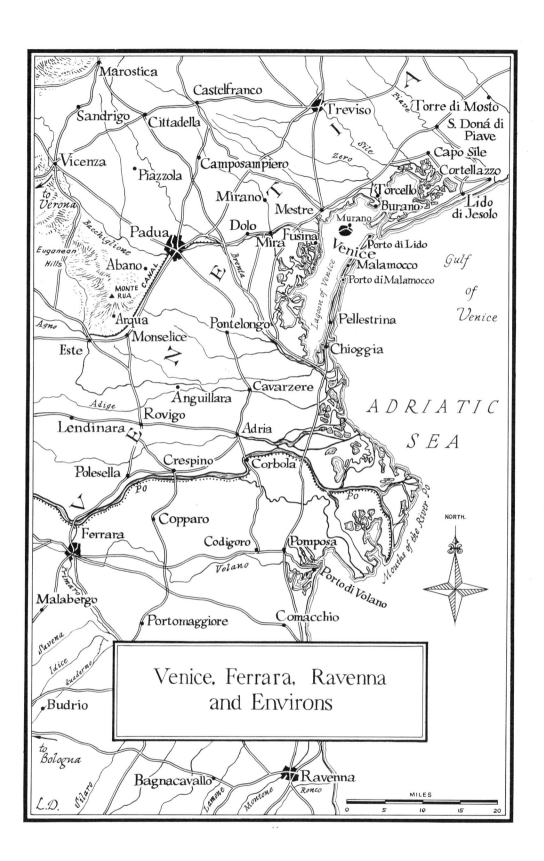

Venice, Ferrara, Ravenna
and Environs

SC 494   both Mary and the infant Clara had suffered a couple of days of bad health. On Friday, August 28, Mary noted in her Journal: "Finish reading the Symposium to Mrs. G—walk out in the evening—a letter from Shelley—consultation."

The subject of the "consultation" was the original of this letter, now in the Bodleian.[8] In sc 494, Mary has left out several personal references to Claire, Allegra, Elise, and the Hoppners, and Byron's negative opinion of Hunt's *Foliage*. She has retained the portions that have the tone of a travel letter of the period and some portions showing Shelley as devoted husband and father. Mary obviously wrote out this transcript with an eye to publication. One might guess that it was the copy for the first published version of this letter in Shelley's *Essays, Letters from Abroad, Translations and Fragments*.[9] Collation of the text of the original letter and the version in *Essays, Letters* with sc 494 shows, however, that the text in *Essays, Letters* omits different passages and makes different changes from Shelley's original. sc 494 was not the source of the text in *Essays, Letters*. There would have been no reason for Mary to make such a transcript after the publication of the 1840 text, but a probable date would have been the time of the publication of Shelley's *Posthumous Poems*, in 1824, when Mary was preparing for the press a companion volume of Shelley's prose (stopped before publication by Sir Timothy Shelley).[10]

On August 19, Shelley had written to Mary from Florence, outlining Claire's latest plans for approaching Byron (she was to remain at Padua

---

8. Shelley, *Letters*, II, 34–38.

9. II, 134–138.

10. The 1823 watermark of the paper is consonant with this speculation, though we have been unable to locate any of Mary Shelley's letters or other datable manuscripts on this paper. The paper itself is unusual; it is wove paper, resembling the linear paper of sc 386 in having either water-ruled or, more likely, folded margins, circa 1.4 inches wide on the left-hand edges of pp. 1 and 3 (right-hand edges of pp. 2 and 4) and circa .7 inches wide on the right-hand edges of pp. 1 and 3. In addition to sc 494, The Carl H. Pforzheimer Library has two other manuscripts with the same watermark and similar margins as well as three others with the same watermark, but without the margins. All are transcripts by Mary Shelley of Shelley's letters that would have been available to her in 1823–1824. Though three of these five other transcripts are tipped into a (rebound) copy of *Essays, Letters*, in each case, as with sc 494, the text of the transcript differs substantively from the text printed in *Essays, Letters* and cannot have been its source. On Sir Timothy Shelley's suppression of Mary Shelley's proposed edition of Shelley's prose and letters in 1824, see Charles H. Taylor, *The Early Collected Edition of Shelley's Poems* (Yale University Press, 1958), p. 9.

SC 494   or Fusina, while Shelley went to Venice to talk with Byron) and urging Mary to keep up her spirits.[11] Shelley and Claire left Florence about noon on Wednesday, August 19, and slept the first night at an inn on the road, the second night, August 20, at Bologna,[12] the third night (August 21) at Padua, and traveled, as Shelley here describes, from Padua to Venice by gondola (via a canal and the River Brenta, past Mira and Fusina) in about nine hours. (For the route, see The Shelleys' Wanderings in Italy, page 544, and Venice, Ferrara, Ravenna, page 677.)

In portions of this letter that have been omitted from Mary's transcript, Shelley outlined his reasons for asking Mary and the children to hurry to Este. Byron, supposing that Claire, Mary, and the children were together at Padua, agreed to let Allegra visit them, and offered to lend the Shelleys I Capuccini, a villa at Este that he had rented from Hoppner but in which he never actually lived.[13]

The most important literary consequences of the experiences described in this letter are to be found about a year later in Shelley's *Julian and Maddalo*.[14] More immediate results included Mary's trip from Bagni

11. Shelley, *Letters*, II, 32. Jones is certainly correct in thinking that Shelley's dating of this letter as "Thursday" is an error, but he himself errs in redating the letter "Tuesday" (August 18). The correct date of Jones's letter #478 should be, I believe, Wednesday, August 19, 1818. Various facts point in this direction: (1) Though Shelley does later tell Mary that she can travel from Bagni di Lucca to Florence in one day, he also says that she will have to get up at four o'clock in the morning to do so, and there is no evidence that he and Claire rose so early or departed so abruptly; (2) Shelley's reference in his letter from Florence to "yesterday's journey" being performed in "a one-horse cabriolet" assumes that Mary did not *know* his means of transportation for "yesterday," and hence that he had hired that carriage at Lucca; (3) Shelley describes the journey that lies ahead of them as "190 miles," which they intend to travel in three and a half days from the time of writing (Shelley, *Letters*, II, 33). According to *Itinerario Italiano*, the distance from Florence to Bologna was sixty-three "miglie" (p. 95) and that from Bologna to Venice ninety-eight "miglie" (p. 174), with the total travel time between Florence and Venice estimated as thirty-three and a half hours. Thus it seems clear that Shelley was planning on three and a half days of traveling time from Florence to *Venice* (not Padua, as Jones supposed). For a description of the road from Florence to Bologna, see fn. 12 below.

12. According to W. A. Cadell's *Journey in Carniola, Italy, and France in the Years 1817, 1818* (Edinburgh, 1820): "From Bologna to Florence the road is mountainous, over the Apennines, and the distance about seventy English miles. The Vetturini generally have their coaches drawn by mules, and go in two days" (I, 148). According to the *Guide des Voyageurs en Italie* (Florence, 1817), the actual traveling time from Florence to Bologna was fourteen hours and thirty-five minutes (p. 23); according to *Itinerario Italiano*, the same route took sixteen hours and thirty-five minutes (p. 95). Neither of these guides recommends the Tre Mori hotel in Bologna, where Shelley and Claire seem to have encountered bedbugs or lice ("unmentionable things in the bed").

13. Byron, *Letters and Journals*, IV, 166–167 and note.   14. See sc 531, Commentary.

SC 494   di Lucca to Este. Mary was unable to make the journey as rapidly as Shelley suggested but the trip was still too tiring for little "Ca" (Clara Shelley). She had been ill, Mary's Journal records, on Friday, August 21. Mary herself was "unwell" and "very unwell" on the two succeeding days. There is no indication in Mary's Journal that Clara was ill on Friday, August 28, when Shelley's letter reached Bagni di Lucca. On Saturday, Mary sent Paolo to Lucca, perhaps to reach an accommodation with the landlord of their rented house at the Bagni (a detail that Shelley, characteristically, forgot to mention). Sunday, August 30, which was Mary's birthday, was spent in packing. On August 31, Mary traveled with Maria Gisborne as far as Lucca, and parting with Mrs. Gisborne there, she and her group proceeded to Florence, where they arrived "late." Mary remained at Florence throughout the day and rode "about the city," presumably while Paolo Foggi was arranging for passports and hiring a *vetturino* for the trip into Venetia. On Saturday, September 5, after a journey of four days and three nights from Florence, Mary reached Este, with Clara "dangerously ill." There she also found Shelley "very unwell from taking poison in Italian cakes."[15]

Shelley in this letter remarks that, though he has been forced to make plans, he does not know whether he has done right or wrong "and it is only the event that can shew" (lines 71–75). From the viewpoint of the welfare of his marriage and his terrestrial happiness, the event proved him wrong (see sc 498 and Commentary), but the trip to Venice and the stimulation of Byron's conversation initiated Shelley's most productive poetic year, among the products of which were *Julian and Maddalo*, "Lines written among the Euganean Hills," *Prometheus Unbound*, and *The Cenci*, not to mention several fine lyrics and several equally fine letters to Peacock describing the tourist attractions of Italy. Shelley noted this paradox more than once in his poems of this period:

> "Most wretched men
> Are cradled into poetry by wrong,
> They learn in suffering what they teach in song."

> Our sweetest songs are those that tell of saddest thought.

15. Mary Shelley, Journal.

SC 495 WILLIAM GODWIN TO JAMES BROUGHTON, SEPTEMBER 1, 1818

AL signed *William Godwin*, 1 page. Double sheet (9 x 7.4 inches).
Laid paper. Watermark: [posthorn in crowned shield]| *JB*|.
Seal: wafer, green.
Notation, page 4, in pencil: *Life of Chaucer*|.
PROVENANCE: Sotheby, July 18–19, 1966, lot 544.

> *Dear sir*
>   *It would give me pleasure to see you. I believe I have told you before, I am almost always at home at nine in the evening. It might be a source of gratification to both, if we were now & then to talk over the matters*
> 5 *which seem to have engaged your attention.*
>   *I will with pleasure read over the manuscript Tamburlaine, if you wish it; though I am not vain enough to think that my doing so will be of any advantage.*
>   *I thank you for the Massacre at Paris.*
> 10   *very truly yours*
>   *William Godwin*
>
>   *Skinner Street,*
>   *Sep. 1, 1818.*
>
> [Address, page 4]
> *James Broughton, Esq*
> 15   *Clement's Inn*
>
> *g*

line 16. *g*: possibly *G*; there is little distinction between Godwin's upper- and lower-case *g*.

THE ABOVE NOTE provides a glimpse into part of Godwin's life that is often overlooked. Godwin's Journal shows that he carried on an active intellectual correspondence and social life with a wide variety of artists, thinkers, and men of letters — many of them younger men who, since they made no great stir in the world, remain rather shadowy figures. Such a man was James Broughton of Clement's Inn.

     Broughton's name appears in Godwin's Journal at scattered inter-

The Carl H. Pforzheimer Library

Godwin to Broughton   *September 1, 1818*

SC 495   vals. From the date of the Shelleys' departure from London, there are Journal references to Broughton on April 1, June 16 ("Broughton & E White sup"), July 1, August 24, August 28, and August 31. On September 1, the night Godwin sent this note, Broughton again supped with him, but there is no further Journal reference to Broughton in September or October.

James Broughton was not, obviously, one of Godwin's intimate friends or disciples. He was co-editor and then editor of a short-lived London periodical called the *British Stage and Literary Cabinet* (1817–1822). A contemporary manuscript note in one set of that journal identifies James Broughton (and his co-editor James Pulham) as of the East India House.[1] His interests — as the above note testifies — included Christopher Marlowe, for *Tamburlaine* and *The Massacre at Paris* are two of Marlowe's plays.[2] He is probably, then, the same James Broughton who in 1830 published five articles on Marlowe in the *Gentleman's Magazine* under the general title, "Of the Dramatic Writers Who Preceded Shakespeare."[3] These papers have claimed the favorable attention of students of Elizabethan drama down to our own day.[4]

One might suppose that, since he had an interest in early English drama, Broughton was acquainted with Coleridge, Hazlitt, or at least with his fellow clerk in East India House, Charles Lamb. There is, however, no reference to him in their published letters or in biographies of them. Clement's Inn, Strand (Plan of London, C2, Front Endpapers), was one of the Inns of Chancery, attached to the Inner Temple. Here was another possibility for association with Lamb, whose "connection with the Temple was fairly continuous until 1817."[5]

1. Robert W. Lowe, *A Bibliographical Account of English Theatrical Literature* (New York and London, 1888), p. 317. Of the editions of the *Royal Kalendar* available to us, those for 1812 and 1813 omit the list of East India Company clerks. However, editions dating from 1815 through 1830 list James B. Pulham as a clerk under the "Military Secretary for conducting the Military Correspondence with India" and James Broughton as clerk under the "Clerk to the Comm. of Shipping."

2. It is not clear from Godwin's cryptic note whether he is alluding to actual texts of the Marlowe plays or — more likely — to Broughton's essays on them.

3. Broughton's articles appeared in the January, February, March, April, and June issues of the *Gentleman's Magazine* (1830).

4. See *DNB* and *CBEL*, under Marlowe, and Felix E. Schelling, *Elizabethan Drama, 1558–1642* (Boston, 1908), II, 466.

5. Lamb, *Works*, II, 362.

Dear sir

It would give me pleasure to see you.
I believe I have told you before, I am almost always
at home at nine in the evening. It might be a
source of gratification to both, if we were now & then
to talk over the matters which seem to have engaged
your attention.

I will with pleasure read over the manuscript Tamburlaine, if you wish it; though I am
not vain enough to think that my doing so will be of
any advantage.

I thank you for the Massacre at Paris.
very truly yours
William Godwin

Skinner Street,
Sep. 1, 1818.

William Godwin to James Broughton, September 1, 1818
(SC 495), page 1

SC 495   What Broughton wished to discuss with Godwin must remain con-jectural. It is not unlikely that Godwin's *Life of Geoffrey Chaucer* (1803) and *Lives of Edward and John Philips, Nephews and Pupils of Milton* (1815) had given the Skinner Street philosopher some reputation as a historian and biographer and that Broughton wished to consult him on some problems in his study of Marlowe and his times. For further evidence of Godwin's interest in Elizabethan drama, see Godwin to John Payne Collier, February 6, 1819 (SC 511).

SC 496   T. L. PEACOCK TO T. J. HOGG, SEPTEMBER 7, 1818

AL signed *T. L. Peacock*, 3 pages. Double sheet, 4to (9 x 7.3 inches). Wove paper. Watermark: BASTED MILL| 1817|.
Seal: wax, red: [peacock]|.
Postal fees: 1. 7; 2. 1/1.
Postmarks: 1. (mileage stamp): MARLOW| 33|; 2. (morning duty stamp, London): C| 8 SE 8| 1818|.

PROVENANCE: Thomas Jefferson Hogg; Prudentia Hogg Lonsdale; John Ewer Jefferson Hogg; Major R. J. Jefferson Hogg (Sotheby, June 30, 1948, lot 101).

Marlow, Septr 7, 1818.

My dear Hogg

      It gave me great pleasure to hear of you again after so long an interval and had not the inproba Siren Desidia the pilotess of the Idle Lake

5   *seated herself too pertinaciously at the helm of the Vaga I should have re-scribed redeunto posito. I began to think that the heat of the courts had resolved you into a dew and that I should meet your ειδωλον some evening floating an uncooled fog-smoke on the surface of the river between the church and the abbey of Bisham. I can only attribute your preservation to the*

10   *indurescent and antisolvent qualities of the Attic salt with which you are so well seasoned, and which will make you a second* <u>Bacon</u>. *I have not yet had an opportunity of thanking you for El Ingenioso Hidalgo. I cannot yet*
                             of leisure and energy
*command enough in conjunction*ᴧ*to encounter him in the enchanted armour*

15   *of his original language: but I have gone through Jarvis's translation with great delight. I have lately read through the Thebais of Statius which is well worth reading though too much upon stilts on occasion. However it has very*

[684]

SC 496   *many beauties and the narration is interesting and well combined. I read*
         Nonnus occasionally but my progress was interrupted by a catalogus Ancum;
20   *which extends nearly through two books. This is rather too much though*
         there is much saving grace and sound piety in his invoking Homer at the
         outset.

     Ου γαρ εγω τοσα φυλα δεκα γλωσσησιν αεισω,

     Ου δε δεκα στοματεσσι χεων χαλκοθροον ηχω,

25   'Οπποσα Βακχος αγειρε δορυσσοος· αλλα λιγαινων

     'Ηγεμονας, και 'Ομηρον αοσσητηρα καλεσσω

     Ευεπιης ὁλον ὁρμον· επει πλωτηρες αληται

     Πλαγκτοσυνης καλεουσιν αρηγονα Κυανοχαιτην.—*L.XIII*

Your comparison of Rabelais to the court fool is most correct: he is indeed
30   *the court fool of Olympus: the chief jester of Jupiter: a genuine incarnation*
         of Momus.

    From the exiles I have had two letters both from Lucca but at the date
         of the last Augt 16 they were preparing to leave that place for Florence.
         Shelley says he wishes the wings of imagination could have enabled him to
35   *join our walks of which I gave him an account. He had seen nothing in its*
         kind so beautiful as Virginia Water. – I think there can be little in the
         "bel paese" to compensate the trouble of visiting it: still less the expence:
         least of all the loss of Greek incurred in travelling from inn to inn and hearing
         bad Italian spoken by ugly and filthy people. I have myself no aspirations
40   *that way and had rather sail the Vaga over Pont-y-casyllty than spur up*
         my flea-bitten over the Appenines. – I shall look forward with pleasure even
         to November as it will bring you back to the south when I hope I shall see
         your Homeric physiognomy in this gelid valley which we have consecrated
         to the only true gods to whom I hope you continue to pour libations and sing
45   *Dithyrambics. Write soon and in the meantime beuvez frais. Farewell. In*
         the name of Pan. Yours most sincerely   —   T. L. Peacock

[Address, page 4]

T. J. Hogg Esqr

    Norton

    near Stockton-upon Tees.

Peacock to Hogg   *September 7, 1818*

SC 496   line 19. *Ancum;*: this reading is doubtful.   line 43. *Homeric*: *H* written through *h*; *m* written
line 39. *no*: written on paper adhering to seal.   through another *m*.
line 40. *Vaga*: *a* written on paper adhering to
seal.

IN SPITE OF the "long interval" — three months — that has elapsed
since Peacock's last extant letter to Hogg, we are not without news of
his activities and his mode of living during one of those golden summers
that are, in England, so much the exception. His letter to Shelley of
July 5[1] is packed with personal and political detail. The bustle and results
of the recent Parliamentary election are much in his thoughts; "we have
been very tranquil in our rotten borough." That the abuses of the electoral system held a lively interest for Peacock can be seen in his novel
Melincourt (published by March 22, 1817)[2] wherein the City of Novote
and the Borough of Onevote afford a satire no less acute than the election
of the highly intelligent but speechless ape Sir Oran Haut-ton. He gives
Shelley some individual results, and pillories Wordsworth for backing
the wrong candidate in Westmorland and for actually asserting "that
the Commons ought to be chosen by the Peers." (Shelley's reply is
classic: "What a beastly and pitiful wretch is that Wordsworth! That
such a man should be such a poet!")

Further news is that he has completed *Nightmare Abbey*,[3] and is
about to move house. As for his other correspondent, "Hogg has passed
a week with me, and we had some long walks — one to Virginia Water;
one to Cromwell's House and *Velvet lawn*, which Hogg said must be one
of the folds of Parnassus transplanted to Buckinghamshire."

It also happened that two days after writing to Shelley, Peacock
suddenly began to keep a diary, which lasted, as a kind of summer holiday
task, from July 7 to September 26.[4] The first entry was, as forecast in the

1. See sc 485, Commentary.

2. Carl Dawson, *His Fine Wit: A Study of Thomas Love Peacock* (University of California Press,
1970), p. 192. The first review of *Melincourt* appeared in the weekly *Literary Gazette* for March 22,
1817 (Bill Read, "The Critical Reputation of Thomas Love Peacock . . . February, 1800, to June,
1958," unpublished dissertation, Boston University, 1959, p. 150).

3. Shelley's response to the news was to send Peacock a quotation from Ben Jonson, which was
duly used as a motto.

4. Printed in full in Peacock, *Works*, VIII, 435; original manuscript in British Museum.

SC 496   letter, "July 7. Moved into our house in West Street." Peacock, his mother, the piano, his own and Shelley's books, had settled in another Marlow home. After that, the laconic entries build up a picture of tranquil sun-warmed days spent on the river in his boat, the *Vaga*, sometimes on an evening trip with a sociable party, more often, and more happily, alone with his books. When he at last stirs from the "Idle Lake" to write to Hogg, the letter is a clear reflection of his summer leisure; out of the heat mist comes the whim of his seeing the substantial Hogg so liquified by the suffocating law-courts that "I should meet your *eidolon*[5] some evening" (line 7) afloat on that stretch of the river he most favored. The books he comments on to Hogg are all mentioned in the Journal as his daily reading.

Apparently Hogg had given him *El Ingenioso Hidalgo* — noted, without the titular flourish, in his diary: Monday, July 13, "Read part of 3rd vol. of *Don Quixote*." Thursday, July 16, "Finished Don Quixote. Jarvis's Translation."[6] The *Thebais* of Statius[7] is noted as his text for Sunday, August 2; but Nonnus, as he hints to Hogg, supplied him with intermittent reading of the *Dionysiaca*, which went on the river with him more than once.[8] Its Homeric echoes were possibly the attraction: the poem describes the progress of the god Dionysus to India. It introduces the catalogue of people and gods who joined the expedition to impose his worship on the Indians. In so doing, Nonnus uses the same expressions as Homer used in the *Iliad* when introducing his catalogue of ships that sailed against Troy. The invocation to Homer quoted by Peacock (lines 23–28) reads as follows:

> For I could not sing such great hosts with ten tongues,
> Nor with ten mouths pouring forth a voice like brass,
> As many as warlike Bacchus gathered together. But singing

5. Specter or phantom.

6. *El Ingenioso Hidalgo Don Quixote de la Mancha*. Charles Jarvis' translation from the original Spanish, with a Life of Cervantes, was first published in 1742 (London: Tonson and Dodsley, 2 vols.). Deliberately toned down, with omissions to suit its audience, it was readable and popular and went into many editions during the eighteenth and nineteenth centuries.

7. Statius, Latin poet of the post-Augustan age, ca. A.D. 45–96. His *Thebais*, on the old Theban story, is an epic in twelve books which, according to its author, took twelve years to compose. This and his other epics were popular in the Middle Ages; Dante, in the *Purgatorio*, recounts an interview with Statius.

8. For Shelley and Nonnus, see sc 433 and Commentary.

The Carl H. Pforzheimer Library

SC 496

> The leaders, I shall call, as my helper, on Homer,
> The whole harbour of eloquence, since sailors off course
> Call on the Dark-haired One to save them from their wandering.[9]

In his essay on *The Four Ages of Poetry*, Peacock chose, as one of the four classical periods, the brazen age of Nonnus.

What Peacock keeps from Hogg but hints at in his diary is that another theme was pushing its insistent way through Greek and Spanish epics and accompanying his idle drifting in the *Vaga*. Creation had taken hold of him: August 6, "Could not read or write for scheming my romance. Rivers castles forests abbies monks maids kings and banditti dancing before me like a masked ball." He was soon to be reading songs and ballads about Robin Hood; all these elements were to take shape as *Maid Marian*. This prospective adventure, along with the summer delights of his friendly river, may add something to the positive repulsion he feels for the "beautiful country" of Italy where even the local people, to his fastidious mind, speak bad Italian.

All he elects to picture is the dirt of the inns and the discomforts of, presumably, a flea-bitten ass or mule (the Shelleys had tried both in 1814) as laborious transport over the "Appenines." It was better for one of Peacock's temperament to sail at leisure in the *Vaga* — a sentiment Shelley himself might have applauded. The two had in common a love of boats, from the sailing of paper fancies on a lake to the practical pioneering plans for passenger steamboats. What Shelley attempted in that line with young Henry Reveley, Peacock was afterward to put into effect on a far bigger scale as the advocate of what the India Office affectionately called his "iron chickens" for an improved and speeded voyage to India. It was on his recommendation, too, that the great rivers began to be used as a means of transport: his plans for the Euphrates may well have germinated from thoughts during idle, but productive, hours on the Thames.

Meanwhile, on land or water, he was scheming out *Maid Marian* while he sent his advice to Hogg to "*beuvez* [or *buvez*] *frais.*" *Drink cool* appears to have been his lifelong preference and advice: in *Gryll Grange*

---

9. *Dionysiaca*, XIII.47–52. This passage, together with other Greek terms in the correspondence between Peacock and Hogg, has been translated for the present editor by Miss Caroline Read.

SC 496   Dr. Opimian (whose name was itself a wine),[10] being offered hock and claret, "pronounced both wines excellent and deliciously cool." On a later occasion, when the doctor had a different host, "they dined well as usual, and drank their wine cool."[11]

10. See sc 468, Commentary.

11. See Peacock, *Complete Novels*, II, 790, 810, where a Greek motto from Diphilus, used as a chapter heading, is translated:

> Cool the wine, Doris. Pour it in the cup
> Simple, unmixed with water. Such dilution
> Serves only to wash out the spirit of man.

SC 497   P. B. SHELLEY TO LORD BYRON, SEPTEMBER 13, 1818

AL signed *P B Shelley*—, 1 page. Double sheet, 4to (9.3 x 7 inches). Laid paper. Watermark: *P G* [letters written on banner held aloft by cherub]|. Seal: wax, red: [Judgment of Paris]|. Postal fee: 3. Postmarks: 1. ESTE; 2. VENEZIA| 17 SET|.

PROVENANCE: Lord Byron; Lord Broughton (John Cam Hobhouse); Lady Dorchester; Sir John Murray; A. S. W. Rosenbach. *De Ricci 391* (p. 33).

My dear Lord Byron

I have been four or five times on the point of setting out to Venise & have been always dissappointed by some unexpected circumstance.– Mary & the children arrived last Sunday & my little girl has
5 *since then been dangerously ill— so am detained an anxious prisoner here, for four or five days longer. She is now better, & I hope to be able to see you at the end of the week.———.   We have domesticated ourselves unceremoniously here, & ⟨-⟩ find it– as I think you would find it, a most delightful residence.*

10 *Mary desires her kind remembrances—Clare her love. Allegra is quite well, & whenever she is drest calls for Papa–.   William & she are grown fast friends ———*

Most sincerely yours
P B Shelley—

15 *Este— Sep. 13. 1818.*

The Carl H. Pforzheimer Library

Shelley to Byron   **September 13, 1818**

SC 497 [Address, page 4]
To the Right Hon—
    Lord Byron
    Venezia

line 3. *dissappointed* (sic).

line 8. ⟨?&⟩: smudged out by large blot.

line 11. *Papa–.*: Shelley seems to have made an extra loop on the final *a*.

line 15. *Sep. 13.*: *3* written through indecipherable numeral.

THE SECOND SENTENCE in this letter makes clear that Shelley, Claire, and Allegra had arrived at Este before Mary and — more important — that Shelley had, before this, dropped his fiction with Byron that Mary, Claire, and Shelley's children had been waiting for him at Padua. What Shelley had gained by his equivocations was Byron's permission for Allegra to spend some time with Claire. Once this end had been achieved, he must have told Byron where Mary and Claire really were. The illness of Clara Shelley mentioned in the same sentence governs the mood of this period in the life of Shelley and Mary, but Shelley's sanguine hopes for Clara's recovery were not fulfilled (see sc 498).

Shelley's own illness from the "poison" in some Italian cakes persisted at least through Wednesday, September 16 (Mary Shelley, Journal), and may account for the interval between the date of the letter (September 13) and its arrival in Venice (postmarked September 17). Mary also records that Shelley began to write *Prometheus Unbound* sometime before September 14, and this work also confined him to Este. The discussion with Byron on freedom and circumstance depicted in *Julian and Maddalo* probably motivated Shelley to depict dramatically the interplay between moral freedom and necessity.

During Mary's first days at Este, she read plays by Count Vittorio Alfieri (1749–1803) and by Vincenzo Monti (1754–1828), whom Byron had met in Milan.[1] She began to translate Alfieri, either for practice in

---

1. According to a booklist dating from the autumn of 1819 (Bodleian Ms. Shelley adds. c. 5, folios 155–156), the Shelleys owned an edition of "Tragedie di Monti" (it appears twice on the list). Since this list includes only books the Shelleys left with the Gisbornes in Leghorn when they went to Florence in the fall and winter of 1819–1820, they may have owned an edition of Alfieri which they took with them.

Shelley and his Circle : Manuscripts

SC 497 Italian or with an eye toward possible publication. Charles Lloyd, the friend of Wordsworth and Coleridge whom Shelley later mentions favorably in a letter to Hunt,[2] had translated the complete *Tragedies of Vittorio Alfieri* (published by Longman's in 1815), but if — as Jones suggests — the Shelleys knew Lloyd's translation, there is no indication that they admired it.[3]

Shelley, meanwhile, renewed his reading of Dante. The *Commedia* may be a greater influence on *Prometheus Unbound* and other poems of this period than is usually recognized. As Shelley writes in a later letter, while speaking of the influence of *Faust* on *Adonais*, "Poets, the best of them—are a very camæleonic race: they take the colour not only of what they feed on, but of the very leaves under which they pass."[4]

I Capuccini, the "delightful residence" of lines 8–9 was, according to Mary's later description, "a villa built on the site of a Capuchin convent, demolished when the French suppressed religious houses. . . ."[5] She goes on to describe nostalgically the beauty and charm of the house and gardens in their setting, concluding: "After the picturesque but limited view of mountain, ravine, and chestnut wood at the Baths of Lucca, there was something infinitely gratifying to the eye in the wide range of prospect commanded by our new abode." Both this retrospective account and Mary's statement to Maria Gisborne in a letter of September 1818 — "The house at Este is exceedingly pleasant with a large garden and quantities of excellent fruit"[6] — show that Shelley's favorable report to Byron was not mere politeness.

2. September 27, 1819, Shelley, *Letters*, II, 122–123.

3. See Shelley, *Letters*, II, 468. Information on Mary's translations of Alfieri has been obscured by two curious errors, one in the published version of *Mary Shelley's Journal* and the other in a note to Shelley, *Letters*. In her Journal entry for September 14, Mary wrote: "Begin to translate A. Read Cajo Graccho of Monti & Measure for Measure." In Jones's edition this reads: "Begin to translate 'A Cajo Graccho' of Monti, and 'Measure for Measure.'" Subsequent Journal entries make clear that "A." was Alfieri, whose dramas Mary was systematically reading. In a note to Shelley's letter to Mary of September 22, 1818, Jones speaks of Mary's translation of "Ariosto's *Myrrha.*" The reference in the letter is, of course, to a translation of Alfieri's *Mirra.*

4. Shelley to the Gisbornes, July 13, 1821, Shelley, *Letters*, II, 308.

5. "Note on Poems written in 1818," Shelley, *Poetical Works* (1839), III, 160. See also Byron's favorable account of it in a letter to Samuel Rogers, March 3, 1818, *Letters and Journals*, IV, 207–208.

6. Mary Shelley, *Letters*, I, 58.

SC 498   P. B. SHELLEY TO CLAIRE CLAIRMONT, SEPTEMBER 25, 1818

AL signed *PBS.*, 1¼ pages. Double sheet, 4to (9.6 x 7.3 inches).
Laid paper. Watermark: ASI[ ]ARIO [letters written on banner held aloft by cherub]|; countermark: D. I. C.|.
Addition: bound in straight grain red morocco with four other letters from Shelley to Claire.

PROVENANCE: Claire Clairmont; Paola Clairmont (July 30, 1879); H. Buxton Forman (Sotheby, June 19, 1897, lot 342); Barker; Sotheby, July 29, 1898, lot 384; Franklin; Pearson (Catalogues 81, [1899], lot 512, I and 83 [1900], lot 472, I); Harry B. Smith (*A Sentimental Library*, Privately Printed, 1914); A. S. W. Rosenbach, May 1926. *De Ricci 393* (p. 40).

> Mr Hoppner's
> <u>Friday</u>.
>
> *My dear Clare*
>
>   *yesterday*
> 5   *We arrived at Venice˄about 5 o Clock. Our little girl had shewn symptoms of increased weakness and even convulsive motions of the mouth & eyes which made me anxious to see the physician. As she past from Fusina to the Inn she became worse. I left her on landing and took a gondola for Dr Alietti. He was not at home.— When I returned I found Mary in*
> 10   *the hall of the Inn in the most dreadful distress. Worse Symptoms had appeared. Another Physician had arrived. He told me there was no hope. In about an hour—how shall I tell you– she died—silently, without pain. and she is now buried. . .*
>
>   *The Hoppners instantly came & took us to their house.—a kindness*
> 15   *I should have hesitated to accept, but that this unexpected stroke reduced Mary to a kind of despair —She is better to day.—*
>
>   *I have sent a message to Albè to say that I cannot see him today—unless he will call here– Mary means to try & persuade him to let Allegra stay. All this is miserable enough—is it not? but must be borne. . . ⟨——————*
> 20   *——————⟩—— And above all– my dear girl take care of yourself.—*
>   *Your affectionate friend*
>   *PBS.*

[Address, page 4]
La Signora Clairmont

Shelley and his Circle : Manuscripts

SC 498   line 19. (*Meanwhile forget me & relive* [or *revive*] *not the other thing*): possible reading; sentence has been heavily canceled with the intention to obliterate completely in an ink at least very similar to that in which the sentence was originally written. The words were probably canceled by either Shelley or Claire.

IN HIS LETTER of September 13 (sc 497), Shelley had promised Byron that he would visit him at Venice as soon as possible. On Tuesday, September 22, Shelley and Claire went to Padua, where Claire was to see a doctor.[1] Finding at Monselice (see "Venice, Ferrara, Ravenna," page 677) "a favourable opportunity for going to Venice," Shelley went there to secure a place for Mary and little Clara to stay. He arranged to meet them in Padua at the Stella d'Oro inn at 8:30 on the morning of Thursday, September 24. On that day they proceeded to Fusina — probably by road rather than by canal.[2] There Austrian soldiers tried to prevent the party from crossing the lagoon to Venice because the Shelleys had forgotten their passports. Shelley, however, overbore this resistance in his great concern for Clara's safety, and they proceeded to an unidentified inn at Venice.[3]

Dr. Francesco Aglietti (1757–1836), the physician whom Shelley sought (line 9), was a friend of Byron and — according to Byron's repeated testimony — not only the leading physician of Venetia, but one of the most deservedly celebrated men in all Italy.[4] Aglietti lived in the Palazzo Giustiniani-Lolin, a seventeenth-century edifice on the Grand Canal, almost directly opposite the Accademia di Belle Arti. Besides being a physician and collector of art, he was a Councillor of State for

1. Information in this paragraph, unless otherwise noted, comes from Shelley's letter to Mary, September 22, 1818 (Shelley, *Letters*, II, 39–40), and from Mary Shelley's Journal entry for September 24.

2. Though Shelley and Claire had, on their initial journey to Venice, traveled by boat from Padua, Mary's susceptibility to motion sickness may have militated against this mode of transportation. In 1844 Mary wrote of her return journey to Venice: "we proceeded along the banks of the Brenta to Venice. . . . this road was as distinct in my mind as if traversed yesterday . . . not a palace, not a tree of which I did not recognise, as marked and recorded, at a moment when life and death hung upon our speedy arrival at Venice" (*Rambles in Germany and Italy*, London, 1844, II, 77–79).

3. The soldiers' attempt to stop the Shelleys at Fusina was described by Mary in her "Note on the Poems of 1818" in a paragraph that first appeared in the one-volume second edition of *The Poetical Works of Percy Bysshe Shelley* (London, 1840), p. 229.

4. See especially Byron, *Letters and Journals*, IV, 223–224 and note.

SC 498   Venice and was at one time editor of a medical journal.[5] These activities, combined with an active social life, undoubtedly took Aglietti away from home so frequently that Shelley's failure to find him there was certainly not singular.

Without knowing more about the symptoms of Clara's illness, it is impossible to speculate on the cause of her death. Her burial — prompt in a city frequently endangered by epidemics — was in a cemetery for foreigners on the almost-deserted Lido.[6] The next year, Byron, musing on epitaphs, wrote to Murray of "the foreigners' burying-ground at the Lido, within the fortress by the Adriatic," as the place where he wished to be buried.[7]

The Hoppners' kindness during this period of bereavement touched the Shelleys deeply. This is the chief reason that they continued to hold the British consul and his wife in high regard long after the Hoppners had become biased against them, had failed to answer their letters, and were actually circulating slanders about them.[8]

In the final paragraph, Shelley assures Claire that he and Mary are not so lost in their own grief as to forget their responsibility to her. They will try to persuade Byron to let Allegra remain at Este a while longer. Shelley, according to Mary's Journal, was even better than his word, for he saw Byron on September 25, the day he wrote this letter. Byron could not and would not, in the wake of the Shelleys' personal tragedy, deny Shelley's request on Claire's behalf.

Shelley and Mary remained at the Hoppners' house in Venice through Monday, September 28. On September 29, they returned to Este, only to find that Claire had taken Allegra and William to Padua. Claire and the children returned to I Capuccini the next day, and all remained at Este until October 11, when the Shelleys returned to Venice. For an account of this and subsequent events, see SC 502 and Commentary.

5. See Lord Broughton (John Cam Hobhouse), *Recollections of a Long Life*, ed. Lady Dorchester (London, 1909), II, 61.

6. See Dowden, *Shelley*, II, 231, and the text of Mary's poem "The Choice" in Grylls, *Mary Shelley*, pp. 297–301.

7. Byron, *Letters and Journals*, IV, 314–315; see also IV, 310. The fortress to which Byron refers was probably the Forte di San Nicolo at the north end of the Lido, which guarded the channel called the Porto di Lido between the lagoon and the sea.

8. The entire course of relations between the Hoppners and the Shelleys will be discussed in a later volume.

SC 499   THOMAS HUME TO BROOKS, SON & DIXON, OCTOBER 12, 1818

> AUTOGRAPH CHECK signed *Tho. Hume*, 1 page. Single sheet (3.9 x 7 inches). Wove paper.
> Addition: Left end of check form, apparently containing a printed armorial design, has been torn away.
> PROVENANCE: Maggs, December 1958.

>   25
> Nᵒ   Chancery Lane   London *12 Oct.* 18*18*
> Messʳˢ Brooks & Dixon
>   Pay *Myself*———or Bearer
> 5   *Thirty Pounds.*   on *Accᵗ*
>   of *P. B Shelley* Esq
> £*30*   *Tho. Hume*

line 1. The portions of SC 499 in roman type are printed on the check in an elaborate script.

DR. THOMAS HUME, the friend of Thomas Moore, has been fully identified in SC 489, Commentary. As court-appointed foster parents to Ianthe and Charles Shelley, Dr. Hume and his wife, Caroline, received £200 annual interest — £80 from a trust fund set up by John Westbrook and £120 paid by Shelley in quarterly installments. The method used by Hume — simply writing a check on Shelley's account, using his own signature — was probably the same employed by Peacock to draw his annuity from Shelley.[1] Among the Brooks papers sold at Hodgson's on December 15, 1916 (lot 225) were "six cheques by T. L. Peacock *on account of P. B. Shelley Esqre*" (de Ricci, page 20).

Shelley's children were to be placed under Hume's care on or before August 20, 1818. The above check is probably the second drawn by Hume on Shelley's account. This pattern was repeated four times each year, until the beginning of 1821, when Shelley's financial situation became confused. When Hume then wrote such a bill, it was not honored, and he evidently protested the oversight, either by a letter of his own or through P. W. Longdill, his friend and Shelley's solicitor. Although Shelley responded on February 17, 1821, in a conciliatory letter to Hume, this by no means ended his troubles.[2]

1. See SC 307, Commentary (IV).   2. For further details, see White, *Shelley*, II, 285 and notes.

SC 500 LEIGH HUNT TO T. J. HOGG, OCTOBER 13, 1818

AL signed *Leigh Hunt.*, 3½ pages. Double sheet, 4to (8.9 x 7.2 inches).

Wove paper. Watermark: M & J LAY| 1816|. Gilt edges.
Seal: wax, red*:* [angel with olive branch, following serpent]|.
Postal fee: 1/1.
Postmark: (evening duty stamp, London)*:* oc| 14| ·818|.
Notations, in pencil: 1. (page 3)*:* υ above ω of 'υπερπετοωναι| (line 50); 2. (page 4, in hand of T. J. Hogg)*:* *Bl. Sc. H.*| *Sp.*| *Br.*| *Ra.*|.
Addition, pages 3 and 4: upper outer quarter of the page torn and separated, but intact.

PROVENANCE: Thomas Jefferson Hogg; Prudentia Hogg Lonsdale; John Ewer Jefferson Hogg; Major R. J. Jefferson Hogg (Sotheby, July 26, 1948, lot 276).

13. October 1818
8. York Buildings.

My dear Hogg,

    I sit down with your letter before me, at last, to
5 *answer it, & dare only catch the date by glimpses. You let your French*
lady's maxim apply, I hope, to answers of letters, as well as the letters them-
selves; for upon this principle I should double the virtue of self-denial, &
say that I had two reasons for _{not} *bearing to think of friends, who are delightful*
10 *correspondents as well as companions.— But seriously speaking, I beg your*
pardon for not having sooner acknowledged your unexpected & voluntary
kindness, which has given me additional wishes to have you back again.
Business is but a bad excuse on such occasions, or as Sir Philip Sydney says
of a merely contemplative life, "only a laborious title to idleness." Such as it
15 *is however, I may plead it, having never been so much occupied, I think,*
since I got into my studious or chrysalis state, & had a brain to spin wrapping
fancies out of. You see what Platonic vanities you have put into my head
with your quotation. I have been writing verse, & prose, & I believe neither
one thing nor t'other,—all of which you shall see on your return. Above all,
20 *you will be pleased to hear that I have been looking into Plato himself, &*
that I am going to get his works. I have been long yearning after him at

SC 500 *intervals, & your quotation sent me on the wing. What a truly Divine Writer!
What a manner at once lofty & unpretending, enthusiastic & placid, oracular & sympathetic! He seems to me to write what others have not only in*
25 *general <u>not</u>* ~~combined~~ *but what they fancied should be kept asunder,— the*
(above: *united,*)
*dignified & conscious superiority of the sage, with an intense relish of the
beauties all about him;— or rather, he affects no superiority; he does not even
speak in his own person; he would elevate himself no doubt, but then it is in*
30 *company with humanity. He talks with such an air & tone of deep & beautiful consciousness in his imagination, that he* ⟨——⟩ *to have a power from*
(above: *appears*)
*Nature to dispense with proofs & with logic. He communes with us like
a spirit in love. He seems to give a meaning and an utterance to the whispers
of evening winds & to the earnest look of the stars.— But where am I getting?*
35 *—I shall be writing an essay to you, instead of a letter. I agree with the whole
philosophy of yours, general & particular,— not excepting your Northern
Lights. You must not even talk of Nature's having denied us grapes, for she
not only, according to credible historiuncales, gave them to our modern cyder*
40 *countries some centuries ago, but what is better, they have abounded in all
our common stalls & baskets this month past.— Your nest in the garden is
truly delightful,— eye, nose, ear, & mind all in a state of enjoyment. So this
is the way you <u>divide</u> your time, is it? and manage to be a studious lawyer?*
45 *You return every year from the black spirits of Westminster—ₐto your ripening
apples & ripened eyes, as Adonis did from Acheron to Venus;—*
(above: ~~*to your ripening apples and ripened*~~   *Hall*)

              οι
       Παρ μεν ωρια κειται ʽοσα δρυος ακρα φεροντι,
       Παρ δ'απαλοι καποι·
50   ʽοι δε τε κωροι ʽυπερπετοωνται Ερωτες.

*It is lucky my new house has been blossoming into curtains & carpets, or I
should not know how to receive you out of your world of luxuries. We must
make the Lares suffice instead of the Dryads. We are pretty well settled, &
the place really puts on a little bit of a graceful as well as comfortable air.*
55 *To give you portrait for portrait, I am now writing in the back-drawing
room with candle & fire, my table covered with poets & philosophers of all*

Hunt to Hogg   *October* 13, 1818

SC 500   *sorts, Greek & English (there is a clever people of that name), & my face*
(mirabile visa) almost running into that of a lady, which happens however,
unluckily, to be made of plaister. It is a bust of Isis, who, you know, repre-
60   *sented Nature, & is the loveliest, I think, I ever saw,—overlooking & intel-*
lectual about the eyes, breathing & genial about the mouth. ~~and~~ *Two thick*
locks hanging on each side to the neck, & the hair running up on the forehead
         diadem &
into a kind of ₍ₐ₎apex, give her a goddess-like & worshipful look without taking
65   *away the natural beauty. It is to go over my study-door, on the top of which*
is already inscribed out of Davenant "To study quiet Nature's pleasant
law." You, who have perhaps only Greek friends, will say that the inscrip-
tion should have been in Greek; but I who have friends that Love Greek, I
may say, without knowing it, (which Sir Thoˢ Brown in other matters justly
70   *thinks the highest kind of faith) ought not to make them sensible that they do*
not know it;—& you will think so, I am sure. The alteration of my study
window has hindered the room from being finished yet, but I trust it will all
be furnished & inhabited this week. The garden also has been waiting for
the autumn, before the new trees could be planted; but the gardener is prepared,
75   *& this too, I trust, will be completed at the same time. In the garden however,*
at best, I can promise you but little; but in the study, I hope & believe, we
shall pass many a snug, quiet, & happy winters evening, over a little wine,
less tea, & a few divine old books. Believe me most sincerely & expectantly
yours,
80   *Leigh Hunt.*

[Page 3, upper part]
I have been writing to day to Thomas Moore to day, who is coming to see
me in November. You will like him much,— as you would naturally conclude.

[Address, page 4]
To

     Thomas Jefferson Hogg Esqʳᵉ
85   *Norton*
            near Stockton upon Tees,
         Durham.

Hunt to Hogg

SC 500

line 17. *vanities*: *i* written through *?n*.

line 32. ⟨———⟩: word heavily canceled through.

line 39. *cyder*: variant spelling.

line 43. *you*: written on paper adhering to seal.

line 45. *You*: written on paper adhering to seal.

line 51. *blossoming*: first *s* written through *?o*.

line 61. *mouth.*: period written over comma.

   Two: *T* written through *t*.

line 73. *garden ... Hunt.* (line 80): written on the top of page 1, above and then to the left of lines 1–2.

line 81. *I ... conclude.* (line 82): written on three lines in the top right corner of page 3 and partially enclosed in a right-angle bracket.

As WE HAVE previously seen,[1] a favorite recreation of Thomas Jefferson Hogg during his late-summer visit to his family home at Norton was writing long letters to his London-area acquaintances. Inasmuch as he seems to have employed considerable effort in this pursuit and faithfully preserved many letters by his correspondents, he would doubtless be disappointed to learn that, for the most part, they did not keep his. Though Hogg's letter to which sc 500 responds is no longer extant, its substance and tenor can easily be inferred from Hunt's remarks.

Leigh Hunt enters with gusto into Hogg's epistolary game of literary allusion, and for Hunt the tone is not forced or foreign.[2] Hunt seems also to have enjoyed Hogg's account of his garden at Norton, and he replies in kind with a description of the scene at York Buildings.[3] Hogg has, as usual, been quoting and recommending Greek authors; Hunt's expressed enthusiasm for Plato — whose works he had apparently neglected (lines 19–22) — might have persuaded Hogg that he had made a complete convert, had not Hunt reminded him that the English in general (and several British poets and philosophers in particular) were also "clever."

In what Hunt doubtless prized as a "pretty conceit," he compares Hogg's respite from his legal duties and his annual visit to his home and garden in the county of Durham to Adonis' seasonal freedom from Acheron, the realm of shades, to revisit the Venus, the goddess of Nature.

1. See, for example, sc 424 and Commentary.

2. Among the references to English authors, the allusion to the concept of faith espoused by Sir Thomas Browne (line 69) refers to section IX of *Religio Medici*, and the quotation is from Sir Philip Sidney, *The Countess of Pembroke's Arcadia*, Book I, chapter IX (London, 1590), p. 38.

3. Describing one's familiar surroundings was a firmly established epistolary convention of the period. See Hunt to Shelley (sc 486), Shelley to Peacock (sc 491), Keats to George and Tom Keats (sc 444), and especially Shelley's verse "Letter to Maria Gisborne" (Shelley, *Poetical Works*, OSA, pp. 363–365), lines 15–105.

The Carl H. Pforzheimer Library

Hunt to Hogg *October 13, 1818*

SC 500 The Greek fragments are from the Fifteenth Idyl of Theocritus (lines 112–113, 120). Within their contexts — parts of a song addressed to Aphrodite — they have been translated by Andrew Lang as follows:

"Before him [Adonis] lie all ripe fruits that the tall trees' branches bear, and the delicate gardens, arrayed in baskets of silver and the golden vessels are full of incense of Syria. . . . Here are built for him shadowy bowers of green, all laden with tender anise, and children flit overhead — the little Loves — as the young nightingales perched upon the trees fly forth and try their wings from bough to bough."

Hunt himself, no longer living in a rural setting such as he had enjoyed at Hampstead in 1816 or with Shelley at Marlow during the summer of 1817, must now content himself with the Lares, household gods, rather than woodland Dryads (line 53).

Hunt's postscript about Thomas Moore bears on the interesting question of their long-term relationship. Their acquaintance began while both were still struggling for recognition as authors and as liberals. But for several years Hunt was somewhat better established in London, first as a journalist and soon after as a political martyr and a poet. The first record of their association is a correspondence initiated by Moore in September 1811. The tone of Moore's early letters gradually shifts from that of a slightly obsequious suppliant for attention to that of a friend aware of his correspondent's (Hunt's) higher professional standing.[4] On March 3, 1814, Moore wrote to his mother: "I wish I could send you Hunt's Feast of the Poets, just republished, where I am one of *the four* admitted to *dine* with Apollo; the other three, Scott, Campbell, and Southey. Rogers, very unfairly, is only 'asked to tea'. I am particularly flattered by praise from Hunt, because he is one of the most honest and candid men I know."[5] In May 1816, Moore wrote to Francis Jeffrey, all but requesting a favorable notice of Hunt's *The Story of Rimini* in the *Edinburgh Review*.[6]

Relations between Leigh Hunt and Thomas Moore were outwardly cordial, then, at the time Shelley's friendship with Hunt began in 1816.

4. For these letters of 1811–1816, and for Moore's cordial mentions of Hunt to other correspondents, see Moore, *Letters, passim.*

5. Moore, *Letters*, I, 309.

6. Moore, *Letters*, I, 395.

Shelley and his Circle: Manuscripts

SC 500 It is likely that Hunt was responsible for suggesting a correspondence between Shelley and Moore and that Hunt encouraged Shelley to suggest Moore to a publisher as an appropriate reader for *Laon and Cythna* in 1817.[7]

During the years 1816–1818, however, Moore's feelings for Hunt seemed to have cooled somewhat. Though Hunt expected that he would have an opportunity to introduce Keats and Hogg to Moore during Moore's visit to London in November and December 1818, he himself did not even see Moore.[8] Tom Moore spent much of his time at Holland House, a society that Hunt had earlier declined to join (see sc 387 and Commentary). Reading back into Moore's correspondence, we find that Moore's changed feelings toward Hunt emerge as early as September 1816 in an equivocal remark to his mother about Hunt's review of Byron's *Monody on the Death of Sheridan*, in which Hunt describes Moore as a "refined Bacchanalian" poet who could never be "a very grave one."[9] The next piece of evidence is a letter Byron wrote to Moore on June 1, 1818; Byron begins a long discussion of Hunt's character, talents, and taste by writing: "Hunt's letter is probably the exact piece of vulgar coxcombry you might expect from his situation."[10] It is uncertain whether "Hunt's letter" was a published one, a personal one written to Moore or to another acquaintance of Byron and Moore (Samuel Rogers or Horace Smith, for example), or a business letter involving some misunderstanding like that with Taylor and Hessey. Byron's attack on Hunt (and *Foliage*) in the June 1 letter seems, in any case, to respond to gossip about Hunt retailed by Moore. An entry in Moore's diary for January 19, 1819, shows his mixed feelings toward Hunt: "A review of my poetical character in the 'Examiner;' good-naturedly meant, but I had much rather Hunt would *let me alone*."[11] This passage explains Moore's slightly

7. See sc 435 and Commentary.

8. See Moore, *Memoirs*, II, 219–238. Keats had looked forward to meeting Moore at Hunt's; see Keats, *Letters*, II, 11. It was not that Moore had forgotten Hunt. On October 5, 1818, he wrote to his publisher James Power that "Hunt has promised an article on the subject" of the *Irish Melodies*. (The manuscript of this unpublished letter is a recent acquisition of The Carl H. Pforzheimer Library.) Actually the *Examiner* for October 4, 1818, had noticed the seventh number of *Irish Melodies*, and it was in a letter of October 10 thanking Hunt for that publicity that Moore told him that they *must* meet in November (Moore, *Letters*, II, 467).

9. Moore, *Letters*, I, 405 and fn.; Hunt's review is in the *Examiner*, September 22, 1816, pp. 602–603.

10. Byron, *Letters and Journals*, IV, 237 ff.   11. Moore, *Memoirs*, II, 255.

The Carl H. Pforzheimer Library

SC 500   petulant letter to Hunt on January 21, 1819, in which, after thanking Hunt for his "very kind notices" and regretting his failure to see him during his "short & busy visit to town," Moore discusses the *Examiner*: "You . . . are always right in *politics* — &, if you would but keep your theories of religion & morality a little more to yourself . . . you would gain influence over many minds that you now unnecessarily shock & alienate."[12]

Thomas Moore and Hunt drifted further apart as Hunt committed himself more and more to the sweeping political, social, and ideological reforms advocated by men like Shelley and Hazlitt, whereas Moore became increasingly identified with Whig magnates like the Marquis of Lansdowne and Lord Holland. They could agree on reform of the Parliament, Catholic emancipation, and a few other basic political changes, but Moore — who had earlier (1803) accepted a government post and turned it into a sinecure[13] — was not an ideological reformer.

Relations between Leigh Hunt and Tom Moore further deteriorated at the time of the founding of the *Liberal*, with Moore joining the chorus of those who feared the influence of Shelley and Hunt on Byron. Hunt first attacked Moore vigorously under the reference "son of a grocer" in the Preface to *Ultra-Crepidarius* (1823). This attack also related to Moore's efforts to sabotage the *Liberal*. The quarrel continued in Hunt's *Lord Byron and Some of His Contemporaries*, where Hunt, after outlining his early pleasant associations with Moore, accuses Moore of urging Byron to disassociate himself from the *Liberal* because "there was 'a taint' in it"; Hunt suggests that Moore had sacrificed his "free sentiment on the fat altars of aristocracy."[14] Moore, in turn, retaliated in a poem entitled "The Living Dog and the Dead Lion"[15] and Hunt's attacks goaded John Murray into sponsoring Moore's edition of *The Letters and*

---

12. Moore, *Letters*, II, 471–472.

13. See L. A. G. Strong, *The Minstrel Boy* (London, 1937), pp. 88–96; Howard Mumford Jones, *The Harp That Once* (New York, 1937), pp. 61–62, 67–74, 206–208, and 335, note 6.

14. See *Lord Byron and Some of His Contemporaries*, pp. 57–58, 168–169.

15. *The Poetical Works of Thomas Moore*, ed. A. D. Godley (Oxford University Press, 1910), p. 600. Hunt replied to Moore's poem with one of his own entitled, "The False Lion & the Real Puppy." The poem was apparently unpublished in Hunt's lifetime, but the text appears in full in *The Novello Cowden Clarke Collection* (The Brotherton Library, University of Leeds, 1955), pp. 15–16.

Godwin to Booth   *October* 14, **1818**

SC 500   *Journals of Lord Byron: with Notices of His Life.*[16] According to Howard
Mumford Jones, in June 1841 Moore finally sought a reconciliation by
writing Hunt a letter "begging him to forget their quarrel over Byron."[17]
Earlier Moore had subscribed for five copies of Hunt's *Poetical Works*
(London: Moxon, 1832) after tactfully asking Mary Shelley whether it
would displease Hunt.[18] Hunt, in turn, included a compliment to the
"wit and festivity" of Moore's poetry in the Preface to that volume
(page lii). Tom Moore's eagerness to join the subscribers recalls Hunt's
generous offer to sell his piano to start a subscription for Moore, whose
deputy in Bermuda had absconded, leaving Moore with a £6,000 debt.[19]

No two men who valued good-will and the esteem of their contemporaries as highly as did Moore and Hunt could have carried on their
quarrel forever. In Leigh Hunt's *Autobiography*, published after Moore,
broken by the deaths of his children, had sunk into senile dementia,
Hunt explained away the origin of the great differences between himself
and Moore.[20]

16. Smiles, *John Murray*, II, 306 ff.

17. *The Harp That Once*, pp. 313–314. Jones is not specific about the source of his information, and
no letter to Hunt of this period appears in Moore, *Letters*.

18. Blunden, *Leigh Hunt*, p. 245; Moore, *Letters*, II, 742–743.

19. See Jones, *The Harp That Once*, pp. 206–208.

20. See Hunt, *Autobiography*, II, 84–89 (chapter XVIII).

SC 501   WILLIAM GODWIN TO DAVID BOOTH, OCTOBER 14, 1818

AL signed *William Godwin*, 1 page. Double sheet, 4[to] (8.7 x 7.2 inches).
Laid paper. Watermark: T EDMONDS| 1811|.
Seal: wafer, brown.
Postmarks: 1. (receiving house stamp, London): Newgate St.| 3 py P. Paid|;
2. (delivery stamp, London): 4 o'Clock| oc 14| 1818 EV.|; 3. (delivery stamp,
London): [   ]Clock AfNoon| oc 14| 1818| Two Penny P. Paid|.
Notation, page 4: *1818*|.

PROVENANCE: Isobel Stuart; "A Gentleman living at Leamington," Sotheby,
March 15, 1912, lot 310; Maggs, September 1922.

> *My dear sir*
>   *You say, you like to receive a letter by the post; so do I.*
> *"Hope deferred, maketh the heart sick." If you could vary the dull uniformity*

Godwin to Booth   *October 14, 1818*

SC 501   *of day after day in which no Booth appears, by a line now & then, bidding*
me, "Expect with cheerfulness—Booth has not forgotten me; Booth proceeds
by a line a day at least; the longest journey has an end"—or any of the like
said-saws, you cannot think how it would encourage me.

very sincerely yours
William Godwin

10   *Skinner Street,*
Oct. 14, 1818

[Address, page 4]
*M*ʳ *David Booth*
Homerton

line 8. *sincerely*: second *e* written through *l*.

GODWIN AND David Booth[1] had not only become close friends, but
Booth was assisting Godwin with the answer to Malthus that
Godwin was writing at this time. In the Preface to *Of Population*, Godwin
cites his

obligations to one friend in particular, Mr. David Booth, formerly of Newburgh
in the county of Fife, now of London. Without the encouragement and pressing
instances of this gentleman my work would never have been begun; and the
main argument of the Second Book is of his suggesting. . . . The reader will find,
annexed to the end of the Second Book, a Dissertation on the Ratios of Increase
in Population, and in the Means of Subsistence, which that gentleman had the
goodness to supply to me.[2]

Booth's "Dissertation," which appears on pages 243–288 in the first
edition of Godwin's *Of Population*, examines Malthus' basic arguments
about geometrical expansion of population and the mathematical increase in food production in order to show the fallaciousness of Malthus'
assertions. Booth argues more factually and exposes Malthus' logical
and mathematical inconsistencies more sharply than does Godwin's own
presentation. Though Godwin's Book II and Booth's appended dissertation pursue similar lines of reasoning, Godwin writes like a man who has

1. For Booth, see SC 432, 434, 440, and 441 and Commentaries.
2. *Of Population: An Enquiry Concerning the Power of Increase in the Numbers of Mankind, Being an
Answer to Mr. Malthus' Essay on that Subject* (London: Longman, 1820), pp. xi–xii. It has been reprinted in photographic facsimile (1964) by Augustus M. Kelley in the Reprints of Economic
Classics series.

SC 501 received assurance from a specialist, whereas Booth writes with the conviction of his personal investigations. It may be assumed, then, that David Booth wrote his "Dissertation on the Ratios of Increase in Population and in The Means of Subsistence" before Godwin completed Book II of his answer to Malthus.

Godwin's Journal for 1818 and the extant letters in which he mentions his reply to Malthus show that he actually began writing the work late in June, composed about forty pages by July 19, and then suspended writing for a long interval while he read (or reread) the fifth edition of Malthus' essay.[3] This reading continued intermittently through October 18. Then Godwin began to make notes in preparation for continuing his own writing.

On August 3 — during a lull in which he had almost ceased even to read Malthus — Godwin encountered David Booth, who dined with him the following day. In the following months, Godwin saw Booth — often at dinner — on September 6, 16, 20, 22, and 26; October 3, 21, 25, and 29; and November 5, 9, and 10. On November 11, Godwin noted: "Call on Booth (Malthus)." The following day, November 12, he began once more to compose his answer to Malthus. References in Godwin's Journal clearly indicate that in November he was at work on Book II — the section for which he gives special credit to Booth.

With the foregoing background, it becomes evident that in his note to Booth of October 14, Godwin is requesting news of Booth's progress on the "Dissertation" that was to lay the foundation for the continuation of his own reply to Malthus. In his good-humored appeal, Godwin employs Biblical phraseology and quotes Proverbs XIII:12 (line 3).

The address of this note indicates that on October 14 the David Booths were still living with W. T. Baxter and his family at Homerton. Godwin had earlier written to his wife that the Booths were planning to move to Hackney on Michaelmas (September 29).[4] On October 25, Godwin dined with Booth at Hackney (Journal). Thus, the two households did separate, but not as soon as Booth had originally planned.

3. T. R. Malthus, *An Essay on the Principle of Population; or, A View of Its Past and Present Effects on Human Happiness; with an Inquiry into Our Prospects Respecting the Future Removal or Mitigation of the Evils Which It Occasions. In Three Volumes. The Fifth Edition, with Important Additions* (London: John Murray, Albemarle-Street, 1817).

4. See SC 440, Commentary.

SC 502　P. B. SHELLEY TO LORD BYRON, OCTOBER 17, 1818

AL signed *P B. Shelley*, 1 page. Double sheet, 8ᵛᵒ (7.2 x 4.8 inches).
Laid paper. Watermark: D. I. C.|.
Seal: wax, red: [Pan and a satyr]|.
Notation, page 4: three illegible smeared letters written *reverso*.
Additions: 1. manuscript acid-stained throughout; 2. strip (now 1.5 inches deep) pasted along top edge of pages 1 and 4 so that manuscript could be inserted in album.

PROVENANCE: Roderick Terry (American Art Association–Anderson Galleries, May 2–3, 1934, I, lot 245); W. T. H. Howe; Audrey Wurdemann (Mrs. Joseph) Auslander; John Fleming, February 1954.

My dear Lord B.

*　　　I am so dreadfully sleepy that I cannot come to night— Will you have the goodness to send us— the "Fudge Family" the "Quarterly" and my Plato...*

5

Faithfully Yours
P B. Shelley

Between sleep & awake
*　　Oct. 17· 1818·*

[Address, page 4]
Right Hon—Lord Byron
10　　*Casa Nova Moncenigo–*

line 7. This line and the next are smeared and the entire text of the letter is blotted. Shelley evidently wrote the note hastily and folded it before the ink dried.

line 10. *Moncenigo–* (sic).

SHELLEY, MARY, Elise, and little William traveled to Padua on October 11 and to Venice on October 12 because William was ill and they wished to be near a good doctor.[1] During their stay at Venice from October 12 through October 31, the Shelleys did not live with the Hoppners, but rented accommodations within sight of the Rialto Bridge,

1. Mary Shelley, Journal; Mary Shelley to Maria Gisborne, November 2, 1818, Frederick L. Jones, "Mary Shelley to Maria Gisborne: New Letters, 1818–1822," *Studies in Philology*, LII (January 1955), 46.

Shelley and his Circle : Manuscripts

SC 502   very likely at the Hotel Grande Bretagne.[2] They did see the Hoppners frequently, dining with them almost daily.

Shelley often spent the evening at Lord Byron's residence — the middle one of three adjacent Mocenigo palaces on the Grand Canal, about halfway between the Rialto and Dr. Aglietti's Palazzo Giustiniani-Lolin. Mary later wrote of these days, "Often I expected S.'s return from Palazzo Mocenigo, till two or three in the morning. . . . Then I saw, as now I see, the bridge of the Rialto spanning the canal."[3] Obviously, Byron's nocturnal habits interfered with Shelley's regular hours, as they did again in 1821 when Shelley visited Byron at Ravenna.[4] Thus we find Shelley apologizing for his fatigue and asking for some books. Thomas Moore's pseudonymous *The Fudge Family in Paris* provided some part of the inspiration for Shelley's *Peter Bell the Third* and supplied the Shelley circle with a private nickname for the Reverend "Colonel" Robert Finch.[5] In a catch-up journal entry covering the period from October 14 through October 20, Mary records reading *The Fudge Family* and notes that Shelley "begins the Republic of Plato," which may well have been contained in the volume of Plato mentioned in line 4.[6]

The issue of the *Quarterly Review* to which Shelley alludes is probably that dated January 1818 (volume XVIII, number xxxvi), which printed reviews of *Frankenstein* and of Hunt's *Foliage*, the latter including two passages that attack Shelley. Apparently Byron either had not quite finished with the issue, or had lent it to Hoppner, for Mary records

2. See Byron, *Letters and Journals*, IV, 266–268; Lord Broughton (John Cam Hobhouse), *Recollections of a Long Life* (London, 1909), II, 59; and Lady Morgan, *Italy* (London: Henry Colburn and Co., 1821), II, 454.

3. *Rambles in Germany and Italy* (London, 1844), II, 81.

4. See Shelley, *Letters*, II, 330.

5. In *The Fudge Family in Paris, Edited by Thomas Brown, the Younger* (London: Longmans, 1818), "Colonel" Calicot, the distinguished-looking suitor of Biddy Fudge, turns out to be nothing but a "vile linen-draper." On Finch as "Colonel Calicot," see Elizabeth Nitchie, *The Reverend Colonel Finch* (Columbia University Press, 1940), pp. 1–6.

6. According to Notopoulos, Shelley used Edmund Massey's *Platonis de Republica* (Cambridge, 1713) for his fragmentary translations from *The Republic* (*Platonism*, pp. 42 fn., 60, 62, 493–496, 564). Shelley took only three volumes of his Bipont edition with him to Italy (see sc 473, Commentary). His "Plato" could have been one of the above four volumes or, perhaps, the "folio Plato whose incredible contractions & abominable inaccuracy," Shelley later wrote, "torment me to death" (to Hogg, October 22, 1821, Shelley, *Letters*, II, 361), for he may have purchased this volume at Venice.

SC 502 reading the *Quarterly* on Saturday, October 24, after dining at the Hoppners'. On November 24, 1818, Byron protested to Murray about an "oblique and shabby" attack on Shelley in the *Foliage* review that he presumed Southey had written.[7] Shelley also attributed the attack to Southey and was much angered by it, as can be seen in his December letter to Hunt from Naples.[8]

On Saturday, October 24, Shelley left Venice and on October 29 returned, bringing Allegra back to the city. (Claire, presumably, remained at Este or Padua.) Two days later, the Shelley party left Venice and reached Este on November 1. After three days of resting and packing, they began their journey toward Ferrara, Bologna, and thence — along the Via Flaminia — to Fano, Spoleto, Rome, and, ultimately, to Naples. Shelley's impressions of this journey are recorded in the long letters he wrote to Peacock on November 6, 9, 20, and December 17 or 18.[9] See also sc 510 and Commentary.

7. Byron, *Letters and Journals*, IV, 272–273.

8. Shelley, *Letters*, II, 65–66. The actual author of the review was probably Shelley's Eton schoolfellow John Taylor Coleridge. See sc 486, Commentary.

9. Shelley, *Letters*, II, 45–64.

Shelley and his Circle : Manuscripts

PEACOCK IN LEADENHALL STREET

THE CANDIDATE

FEW AMONG THOSE who study Peacock as novelist, literary essayist, and poet have penetrated far into the specialized world he entered in the East India Company's service. Strictly, it has appeared irrelevant, not only to the stream of English literature, but also to the particular eddy of social satire mingled with classical learning that is Peacock's own. The Romantic writers of his day usually hoped to make a full-time job of entertainment or instruction by their published writings. The exception is Wordsworth, whose not too onerous post as Distributor of Stamps for Westmorland secured him a basic income without noticeably impeding his flow of verse. With Peacock — neither a veritable Romantic nor so cold a scholar as claimed — the situation was different. Despite the conventional narrative poems of his early years, he had never been driven compellingly by the ardor of creation, and was often content to read and study his favorite Greek authors. In 1815 the break into fictional satire with *Headlong Hall* (dated 1816) was a new incentive that sent him rollicking through *Melincourt* (1817) and then *Nightmare Abbey* in the discovered delight of tilting at his friends and the intellectual poses then in vogue. He was now in the vein; the same year, 1818, he saw that gossip about the present age could be insinuated into a medieval setting: *Maid Marian* was nearing its close when it came to an abrupt halt, not to be taken up and finished for another four years.

The plain fact was, and is, that unless authorship brings in material returns, the man with a living to earn and a realistic outlook begins to see it as an idle hobby in which it is foolish and risky to indulge. This was precisely Peacock's case. He was not satisfied for Scythrop-Shelley to be helping him financially;[1] his keen practical judgments were — as both he and others appreciated — of a type that could be put to work on some existent project even in the fields of commerce where a fresh outlook and an unrusted intellect were more important than a long apprenticeship to tradition and prejudice.

Just such an opportunity arose in the old-established East India Company. The office of the Examiner at its London headquarters in Leadenhall Street (Plan of London, E2, Back Endpapers) was suffering

---

1. See sc 307, Commentary, fn. 6 (IV, 591), sc 424, Commentary, fn. 9, and sc 499, Commentary.

The Carl H. Pforzheimer Library

Peacock in Leadenhall Street

from acute staff shortage. This department dealt with all the Indian correspondence. No routine promotion of clerks was considered adequate to cope with the increasingly complex questions of administration in the company's Indian trade-possessions. A "higher than ordinary standard of qualifications"[2] was required. Peacock was appointed to one of the vacant or newly created posts in May 1819 after he had been through a course of training in the company's offices.

In the fall of 1818 Peacock's name had been put forward by his friend Peter Auber as the type of man liable to be of service, though at that time without specific knowledge of Indian affairs. The directors' first idea seems to have been to test his capacity for absorbing some technical problems of administration, weighing up the pros and cons, and coming to an independent conclusion. This is what Peacock does in the essay which follows. The company, as may be gathered from his first paragraph, handed out a bulky literature of reports and correspondence, of administrative details and controversial plans, of rival systems and their advocates, all employing the terms taken over by the British company from native officials.

It was a challenge that Peacock met with interest and alacrity. The test could lead to a regular salaried post which, in its turn, would justify him in remembering a girl in North Wales, Jane Gryffydh, as a possible bride. He and his mother had in July moved into a new house in Marlow. Here the uncompleted *Maid Marian* was put aside while he took up an entirely new profession. At thirty-three, with a keen flexible intellect fostered by Greek studies, he appears to have had no difficulty in mastering his subject and the jargon of it; nor — and this was important — in disentangling the essential principles from the network of controversy that had confused the issue.

Peacock had in fact been asked to explore no mere academic question to which the examiners already know the answer when they test the candidate. Not only were the authorities in disagreement but at this period there was little approach to a solution whether by preference or compromise. Lacking any contemporary statement as to why this live coal of a thesis was presented to an innocent and amateur outsider, one

2. Report of Committee of Correspondence, May 12, 1819, quoted in Peacock, *Works*, I, xciv. See also William Foster, *The East India House* (London, 1924), pp. 193 ff.

Shelley and his Circle : Manuscripts

Peacock in Leadenhall Street

may guess at two separate, if interwoven reasons. First, as a historian of the subject has it, the "most formidable task that confronted [the British Government] was the re-organization of the Land Revenue Administration."[3] It was a subject from which there was no escaping, either in Leadenhall Street, in reports given to the House of Commons at Westminster, or among the governing bodies of the several Anglo-Indian provinces — to say nothing of the village landholders and tenants who were primarily affected.

To study this question historically, economically, argumentatively, at however safe a distance from the trouble centers, would mean familiarizing oneself with a very substantial area of the East India Company's affairs. If Peacock were later to enter the Examiner's office he would be dealing in correspondence largely concerned with revenue collection and the detail of alternative systems. To equip himself for writing this one essay would be an unrivaled preliminary training for his work. His tackling of it would go far toward showing what aptitude he was likely to have for Indian affairs.

Secondly, it is surely not fantastic to suggest that the London office might itself gain something. If Peacock had the "higher than ordinary" standard of intelligence because of which Peter Auber had recommended him, he had also the merit of bringing a fresh mind to a question that had been chewed and wrangled over for some twenty years by men with a strong bias. By Peacock the issue could be judged coolly on the intrinsic merit of each system, carefully weighed up. The "cold scholar" was eminently capable of such detachment.

At the same time (though this was no concern of the company's) his satiric taste would appreciate, even enjoy, the display of acrimonious prejudice that met him in the material handed out. Knowing our Peacock, we may be pardoned for suspecting a whispered irony in his opening paragraph, demure and modest as it looks on the surface. He places his own "total inexperience" against "the great mass of talent, and of information founded on personal survey," and — here is the prick of the stiletto — "the division of opinion among so many able men who have given to it a long, dispassionate practical investigation."

3. B. H. Baden-Powell, *A Short Account of the Land Revenue and its Administration in British India; with a Sketch of the Land Tenures* (Oxford, Clarendon Press, 1894), p. 46.

The Carl H. Pforzheimer Library

Peacock in Leadenhall Street

Practical knowledge of their own districts they did have; able and talented men they no doubt were; dispassionate they were not. So let us credit this opening paragraph to Peacock the social satirist, here discreetly veiled. After that, the subject absorbs his discriminative faculties to the full; he is perfectly straightforward in analysis, summary, and conclusion. And he is certainly dispassionate. During his later career with the East India Company he was to show fruitful enthusiasm over steam navigation, shipping routes, especially river communications, and the building of boats from iron instead of wood. Peacock's "iron chickens" became a byword in East India circles.[4] But he was not again to play so active, if theoretical, a part in the question of land revenue collection. It might even be said that, as a friend of the Romantics, he preferred the poetry of ships and riverways and communications to the prose of tax collecting. This paper shows him mastering the prose.

REPRESENTATIVE METHODS OF TAXATION

To sketch in the background to "Ryotwar and Zemindarry Settlements" (see sc 503, line 1, textual note) and make it reasonably intelligible to the general reader, it is necessary to look back very briefly over the history and development of the East India Company. This company, which was, of course, the origin of what was to become in 1858 the British government's dominion over India, had begun as a private trading enterprise, receiving a royal charter of incorporation from Queen Elizabeth I in 1600. It was thus granted "the sole right of trading with the East Indies" — a right soon transferred to the Indian mainland, and retained in spite of disputes and skirmishes with the rival Dutch. After several renewals of charter, the company received from Charles I an immense increase of power with "the right to acquire territory, coin money, command fortresses and troops, form alliances, make war and peace, and exercise both civil and criminal jurisdiction."[5]

To all intents and purposes, this British-chartered company had the right and the task of managing those territories of India that came

---

4. Legend has it that Peacock was "the first man to say that iron would float."

5. *Encyclopædia Britannica* (14th edition), article on East India Company. For an extended account of the East India Company by Peacock's friend and sponsor, see Peter Auber, *Rise and Progress of the British Power in India* (London: Wm. H. Allen, 1837, 2 vols.).

Shelley and his Circle : Manuscripts

Peacock in Leadenhall Street

successively under its authority. The first "presidency" established was Bengal, to which had been added the Madras presidency and then that of Bombay. During the next century and a half the East India Company not only made big trading profits but grew to be the dominant power in India, responsible to its own "home government" in Leadenhall Street, London, for the administration of large populations spread over wide areas and living under variant conditions.

One of its most important and, as it was to turn out, most tricky assignments was the regular collection of land revenue from the cultivators of the soil in every village. It had always been recognized that the state should take a direct share of the produce. The administrative problems were concerned with the amount that should be taken — that is, the assessment of revenue — and the manner of its collection.[6] When the company took over the government of Bengal it also took over the system developed by the Mogul ruler Akbar whereby the local *rajahs* or officials served as "revenue farmers." A district official, literally described as "holder (dar) of land (zamin)," became known as a "zamindar" (or "zemindar"). They were empowered to collect from the village cultivators, known as "ryots,"[7] and under obligation to hand over a required sum to the government. The plan was somewhat haphazard, no firm principle of assessment having been established. The zemindars, unchecked, tended to enlarge their share and their pretensions, extracting all they could get for themselves as tax collectors for their villages.

In 1765 the company, having obtained the financial administration (known as "diwani," "dewannee," or "dewanny") of Bengal, sought to impose its own pattern of administration on this unformalized procedure. Various Hindu, Mohammedan, and British conceptions merged in a mist of confusion that blurred the issues. In fact, the working of the system was "looked on as a sort of mysterious craft which no outsider could presume to understand."[8] To effect a settlement it was necessary to survey the value of each estate according to yield and richness of soil, and thereby

---

6. For an account of the revenue systems, see Baden-Powell, *A Short Account of the Land Revenue*, pp. 33–50.

7. The individual cultivator, whether under a landlord or independent, is called "ryot," or "ra-iyat," an Arabic word meaning "protected" or "subject." (Baden-Powell, *A Short Account of the Land Revenue*, pp. 74–75.)

8. Baden-Powell, *A Short Account of the Land Revenue*, p. 47.

The Carl H. Pforzheimer Library

Peacock in Leadenhall Street

fix a rent payable by the ryot. This rent might be redetermined at intervals, according to the current value of the holdings; or it might be settled once for all. The company, through its advisers, concluded in favor of establishing a permanent settlement, or "fixed standard of assessment" (line 65), as Peacock expresses it, based on a single unchanging valuation of the land. It was believed that this would simplify the transaction for both collectors and cultivators, leaving the ryots free from the possible tyranny of extortionate zemindars.[9] Accordingly, after a preliminary investigation, a settlement of the land tax was drawn up in 1793 under the governor-generalship of the first Marquis Cornwallis, who declared it to exist in perpetuity. It became known as "the Zemindary (or Landlord) Settlement of Bengal."

Almost at once this form of settlement had its critics. Not only were the ryots failing to benefit as intended — or announced; but the zemindars had undergone a change, based partly on the English tendency to think in terms of landlords and tenants. While originally revenue agents, they had already, as noted, been acquiring power as estate-owners, and their position had now become hereditary. Under Cornwallis' permanent settlement the Bengal zemindar, in his entrenched position, had to be officially acknowledged as landlord, while the ryot or cultivator was seen by opponents of the system to have lost his security of tenure.

The settlement brought further disadvantages. Under native rule the executive official, besides collecting revenues, had played a large part in the affairs of the community as the government's local representative. He had held magisterial powers and police control. It followed that this native official was in close touch with the affairs of his district, able to provide information and to interpret the people's views. This was altered by the Bengal settlement, which took all authority out of native hands. It administered the law through a series of courts and appointed its own collector, whose office was debased into that of a mere fiscal agent for gathering in the revenues from the zemindars. He had little contact with or understanding of either cultivators or landlord class.

---

9. In practice, the result could be precisely opposite: The zemindar was responsible to the government for a fixed, unchanging land tax in return for landlord rights that enabled him, if unscrupulous, to dun the cultivator or seize his land for unpaid arrears of rent.

Shelley and his Circle : Manuscripts

Peacock in Leadenhall Street

The government's most powerful representative was now the district judge, who also functioned as magistrate and police chief. This over-worked compendium of officialdom spent his day in court and was no freer to go among the people than was the collector, adding up revenue figures in his office. As these posts were held by officials of the company, the Indians found themselves almost totally excluded from responsible positions. Instead of the Western rulers earning the trust and friendship of their subjects, the rift between British and Indian outlooks was per-ceptibly widening.[10] So persistent was this alienation that a faulty admin-istration was later claimed to be a leading cause of the Indian Mutiny in 1857. The company's government had become almost inaccessible to Indian opinion.

Finally, the economic result of the zemindary settlement was com-pletely unsatisfactory. As one scrutinizer reckoned in later days, ze-mindars and middlemen annually "receive about *13* millions sterling, besides expenses of collection and management from the ryots. This amount, then, and the Government's expenses of collection . . . constitute the real charges which are incurred for the collection of only four millions sterling."[11]

These formidable drawbacks were not at once perceived by those in authority in Bengal. The Marquis Wellesley (elder brother of the Duke of Wellington), who became governor-general in 1798, strongly advocated the Bengal system for all the company's territories, beginning with Madras. At home he was backed by Henry Dundas, president of the Board of Control.[12] However, it had to be admitted that a system suited (if it *was* suited) to one district might be inapplicable to other territories, and especially to South India where there were different conditions of soil, of land tenure, of population, and in the ratio of landholders to cultivators. The Court of Directors had become skeptical about the work-ings of the permanent zemindary settlement after its five-year trial.

---

10. The situation following the permanent settlement of Bengal is mainly summarized from C. H. Philips, *The East India Company 1784–1834* (Manchester University Press, 1940; reprinted 1961).

11. R. H. Hollingbery, *The Zemindary Settlement of Bengal* (Calcutta, 1879), I, 54.

12. A Board of Control, representing the ministry, was created under Pitt's India Act of 1784. The Court of Directors, numbering twenty-four, represented the company; it was elected by the share-holders or "Proprietors." Board and directors were frequently at variance. As will be noticed, they had an odd way of exchanging their relative policies over revenue systems.

The Carl H. Pforzheimer Library

Peacock in Leadenhall Street

Though they were anxious to restrain Wellesley from extending it without their approval, Dundas pressed so hard that they reluctantly agreed to let Wellesley go ahead.

Now a new voice came in; one that was soon to give direction and urgency to the discussion by creating a specific alternative. This new line of argument came from Madras. At first the harassed directors, already insecure in their reluctant policy, stood silent while the Board of Control refused to listen to Lord William Bentinck, the governor of Madras. Knowing the conditions in his own territories, Bentinck made out a strongly argued case against applying the zemindary settlement to the Madras presidency, but other difficulties in Madras led to his removal from office. The front was cracking, however; when Sir George Barlow, the next governor-general, took over Wellesley's zemindary policy, the directors bluntly opposed it. In May 1807 there was a London showdown. The directors protested to the board that the extension of their policy was causing unrest in the Madras presidency by its exclusion of Indians from government posts. The board now began to appreciate that the directors had a cogent argument.[13]

Then, in 1808, Colonel Thomas Munro came home on leave from Madras with a tale similar to Bentinck's, but more detailed, explicit, and constructive. He was dead against the Bengal system, the supremacy of the district judge, the ignorance and subordination of collectors. He had himself put forward and worked out another system in one region of Madras, eliminating zemindars and all other middlemen between the village cultivators and the government. It came to be known as the "Ryotwary Settlement." By this system each individual cultivator paid his rent directly to the state, which acted as landlord, an assessment of his holding having been made through a preliminary survey. Rent collecting was in the hands of a native commissioner who was usually the village headman. This official and his assistants supervised all administrative work. Further, they had magisterial powers to try and punish petty offenders and to settle law cases that under the Bengal system would have gone to the revenue courts to await the delayed attention of a district judge. The collector became virtually the local representative of the government, was conversant with his district, and was a friend to the

13. For much of this history, see Philips, *The East India Company*, p. 201.

Peacock in Leadenhall Street

people.[14] Thus he became a useful liaison officer between state and cultivator, Briton and Indian.

Such a settlement could, like the zemindary system, be made on a basis of permanent assessment (we shall see Peacock discussing the merits of permanence as applicable to both); but in practice a temporary form of settlement for a term of years became a feature of the ryotwary system, as being fairer and more flexible although it involved constant reassessment.

Munro's evidence, given before a select committee of the Commons, confirmed the directors in their anti-Bengal leanings and encouraged them to stand out against any further extension of the Bengal settlement. At last the board, under Lord Buckinghamshire, a former Madras governor, was as keen as the directors and ready to send orders out all over British India, Bengal excepted, to adopt the system advocated by Colonel Munro (who, as Sir Thomas Munro, was himself to become governor of Madras in 1819).

Now it was the directors who began to play cautiously, setting up a committee to compile a revised system. But in 1812 they also sent out a commission headed by Munro, requiring the Madras government to reintroduce the ryotwary settlement and transfer authority back to the collectors.[15]

So much for Madras. Bengal remained a problem, bogged in its permanent zemindary settlement, with district judges crushed under an ever-growing pile of lawsuits. The prime urgency was to prevent the rot from spreading. Lord Moira, succeeding as governor-general in 1812, was forbidden by the home government to sanction a permanent settlement in any of the company's new provinces. There was talk of reform in Bengal. This was delayed for years through "pressure of political business." One feature of the rivalry is that all who governed in Bengal

14. Philips, *The East India Company*, pp. 203–204.

15. The first report which publicly called into question the principle of permanent assessment of the revenues was *The Fifth Report from the Select Committee of the House of Commons on the Affairs of the East India Company*, dated July 28, 1812. It was reprinted over a century later: edited with Notes and Introduction by the Ven. Walter Kelly Firminger, Archdeacon of Calcutta (Calcutta: R. Cambray, 1917–1918, 3 vols.). Peacock studied the *Fifth Report* closely and his page references (in the margins of sc 503, lines 244, 265, etc.) are still serviceable, since the original page numbers are inserted in the text of the reprint.

The Carl H. Pforzheimer Library

Peacock in Leadenhall Street

preferred the Bengal system with its deficiencies, injustices, and lack of interracial contacts.[16] Man's natural aversion to tackling the difficult course when on the spot may partly explain this attitude. It was so much easier to work with a fixed and unrevisable rate of payment than to be constantly obliged to reassess. It was also easier to treat the ryots as one impersonal rent-paying entity than to examine each one's individual circumstances.

Nor was the ryotwary system a supreme solution. As we shall see Peacock noting in his essay, it is hard to insure against the fallibility of persons, against bribery and dishonesty, simple miscalculation, or the paying off of old scores by denouncing enemies. In the sixth section of his inquiry Peacock goes into the matter of collection with a lively sense of the personal factors. Using England as analogy, he remarks how certain costly and wasteful branches of revenue collection are retained as being "agreeable to the habits and inclinations of the people." He notes (from the reports he had studied) the "great trouble and inconvenience in collecting rents from individuals," as alleged by the opponents of the ryotwary system, the danger of erroneous assessment, complicated by "the dishonesty of the curnums [village accountants] who never give true accounts of the land in cultivation, and the consequent necessity of annually sending out examiners" who may themselves inflate the trouble.[17] The avoidance of all this detail is, he comments, a leading argument in

16. But there were other supporters. One was Thomas Law, collector and magistrate for Bahar, who had concluded a zemindary type of settlement before Cornwallis' general Bengal settlement and later printed a plea for it that was mainly an attack from several angles on the Ryotwar system. (See *Correspondence of the Honourable Court of Directors of the East India Company and of the Governor General in Council respecting the Permanent Settlement of the Land Revenue*, Privately Printed, 1825.) Another voice in favor of the zemindary system was John Hodgson, who wrote a memoir on the "Advantages of a Permanent Zemindarry Settlement" in three parts in 1806. His account was included in *The Fifth Report*, published in 1812.

17. Peacock takes his argument about land in cultivation from a letter of September 30, 1802, written by Colonel Munro, who states frankly, against his case, that an individual settlement, "if the curnums accounts could be depended upon, would naturally be the best. . . . But, as the curnum's accounts are always false, to begin with fixing the rents of the cultivators, would not only be the most tedious, but the most unequal of all settlements. Every single cultivator objects to his own assessment." (Quoted in Firminger, *Fifth Report*, III, Appendix 20, 213.) Munro is also quoted as saying, "Perhaps there is no Curnum who, in any one year, ever gives a perfectly true statement of the cultivation of his village, and it is only the fear of removal or suspension that can make him give such accounts as are tolerably accurate." (Thomas Law, *Correspondence of the Honourable Court of Directors*, p. 36. Law was of course eager to quote Munro against his own system.)

Peacock in Leadenhall Street

favor of the zemindary system. Only, as he goes on to point out, the detail is not avoided but postponed and transferred to the law courts.

Thus did the company's officials debate the pros and cons of their unending controversy; and thus did Peacock, studying their arguments and grouping the subject in its several aspects, arrive at a tentative judgment of the merits of the two systems.

THE EXAMINATION

In the fall of 1818, when Peacock was studying the reports and weighing the evidence, the situation was that at home both board and directors were favoring a ryotwary, temporary form of settlement and strongly opposing any extension of the Bengal system. Whether or not Peacock drafted his essay with this in mind, there is no hint of his attempting to please the authorities by a bias in their present favor.[18] Apart from a test of his own ability to handle the subject, they required a disinterested judgment from a front-rank intellect. Peacock provides it in the essay now published for the first time. He was not "in the know" as were the experienced veterans in India; rather, he was sitting over a game of chess, with zemindary and ryotwary chessmen moving over squares of permanent or temporary settlement. The result of his cerebration is that the ryotwary system wins on points. Peacock judged the systems according to six principles: on three of them, the systems were "nearly balanced"; on the other three, the ryotwary system held "a decided advantage." Since he was dealing with the office in Leadenhall Street and not with certain dogmatic officials in Bengal, his findings may well have brought "a decided advantage" to himself.

The paper was officially approved, probably by George Canning, the

18. James Mill, soon to be a fellow-worker with Peacock in the Examiner's Office, had published his influential *History of British India* in 1818. In this work he expressed his preference for the democratic, or ryotwary, system as giving the cultivators a secure living from the soil and a protection against the landlord class. Peacock, however, seems not to have begun reading Mill's *India* until the following year, when he mentions to Hogg on October 2, 1819 (sc 542) that he has read through the first volume at home. Peter Auber, retrospectively at least, also favored the ryotwary settlement. We may note in passing that a key paper advocating the ryotwary settlement was written in 1806 by William Thackeray (an uncle of William Makepeace Thackeray), who seems to have rendered more positive service to the East India Company and the people under its charge than had *his* father, the first William Makepeace Thackeray. See Auber, *British Power in India*, II, 410–430, and Gordon N. Ray, *Thackeray: The Uses of Adversity* (New York, 1955), pp. 24–42.

The Carl H. Pforzheimer Library

Peacock in Leadenhall Street

future Prime Minister, then president of the Board of Control. It was Canning's vitalizing influence that had induced the directors to reorganize the important Examiner's department. He is thus the main arbiter of Peacock's future career. The immediate consequence was that by the following January Peacock had moved to London and was studying Indian affairs in Leadenhall Street in hopes of receiving an appointment. His granddaughter Edith Nicolls Clarke records that " for his preparation for examination for the East India Company's service, he was allowed a school period of six weeks, and his passing papers were returned to him with this brief but high compliment: 'Nothing superfluous and nothing wanting.'"[19]

On January 13, 1819, he wrote to Shelley from 5 York Street, Covent Garden, about his expected employment. "It is not in the common routine of office, but is an employment of a very interesting and intellectual kind, connected with finance and legislation, in which it is possible to be of great service, not only to the Company, but to the millions under their dominion." He expects to be "an integral portion of Leadenhall Street for fifteen years to come." (In fact he was in the company's service from 1819 to 1856.) In the same letter he continues, "'Admirable' Coulson[20] dined with me last Sunday, I thought to puzzle his omniscience with a question concerning Indian finance; but I found him quite at home in the subject, and he talked as fluently of Zemindars, Ryots, Mokuddims [head cultivators], Putwarries [village accountants, known as Curnums in the Madras Provinces] &c, as if he had thought of nothing else for the last half-year."[21]

It is apparent that Peacock felt the fascination of these Indian terms. On October 2, 1819 (sc 542), he will be found excusing himself to Hogg for his lack of general news on the ground that there are "so few nooks of my brain untenanted by zemindars ryots adawluts[22] and cu<rnums>."

19. Peacock, *Works*, I, xcii.
20. On Coulson, see sc 418 and sc 426, Commentaries. The nickname "Admirable" derives from the sobriquet applied to James Crichton (1560–?1585), the Scot who — thanks to James Barrie's completely irrelevant play-title — still ranks as the most famous child prodigy in the annals of the English-speaking nations. See Patrick Fraser Tytler, *Life of James Crichton of Cluny, Commonly Called The Admirable Crichton* (Edinburgh and London, 1819) and, especially for Crichton's works and fictional works based on his meteoric career, *DNB*.
21. Peacock, *Works*, VIII, 215.
22. For "adawluts" see textual note to line 381 of sc 503.

Shelley and his Circle: Manuscripts

Peacock in Leadenhall Street

By that date he was in full employment with the East India Company, having been appointed in May 1819 as Assistant to the Examiner, in conjunction with Edward Strachey, James Mill, and J. J. Harcourt. In 1830 he became Senior Assistant to the Examiner (who was now James Mill), being responsible for the more important revenue dispatches; and on Mill's death in 1836 he succeeded to the post of Examiner, which he held until his retirement in March 1856.

ECHOES

Since the battle over zemindary versus ryotwary settlements was to continue throughout Peacock's career in the company's service, it is not irrelevant to take a glance at the subsequent moves. At home, the board and directors went on wrangling, not so much over the intrinsic merits of the rival systems as over their suitability for given districts. When the board sent sweeping orders for the Madras system to be established everywhere, the directors countered that no system had been or could be uniform throughout India, that in fact Cornwallis' Bengal settlement contained as much good as evil, that there was no reason to make a permanent settlement in any other province, and that a survey of rights was an essential preliminary to any long-term settlement. So they put a brake on ryotwary enthusiasm.

Compromise held no appeal for the Bengal government, which clung obstinately to its plan of imposing the permanent zemindary settlement on the more recently acquired Bengal provinces. Only in 1821 did the home government manage to turn it aside from this intention.[23] But again the board and directors were at variance, the latter pressing for a permanent settlement while the board upheld the principle of a variable annual assessment until a survey of rights should be completed. So reactionary did the Court of Directors now become that the board had to prevent it from reestablishing Cornwallis' regulation that denied to collectors all judiciary and administrative powers.

The ding-dong battle fought its way gradually towards a general victory for the ryotwary type of settlement and district administration. Despite its wrangles — or perhaps, as with any parliamentary body, by their benefit — some sense of balance and fair judgment that could never

23. Philips, *The East India Company*, p. 212.

The Carl H. Pforzheimer Library

Peacock in Leadenhall Street

have come from the India-based officials urged it toward the more equitable, and more profitable course. Finance will usually precede morality as a determining motive, but when the two are outstandingly compatible success builds on a broad and comforting base indeed. It has been said that the company's home government performed its best and most beneficial work in ensuring that the Madras system of administration should become the accepted mode throughout the Indian provinces.[24] In the company's last years from 1855 to 1858 when the government of India was transferred to the crown, a revision of all the early settlements was called for; but it was not until 1882 that the secretary of state declared the policy of permanent settlements *discarded*.[25]

A final word on Peacock's adroit essay. The editors of the Halliford Edition (1934), in deciding not to print it, stated somewhat glibly that it "was composed as a specimen of the author's ability, and had served its purpose when it helped to secure his appointment at the India House."[26] We have already hinted that it may have served the company as well as serving Peacock. There is some evidence to support the guess. If these editors looked carefully at the title page of the manuscript they would have seen on it, written faintly in pencil, the words, "ask Sir Bartle Frere's Opinion."

Henry Bartle Edward Frere, the distinguished colonial administrator, was born in 1815; he was thus only three years old when Peacock was writing "Ryotwar and Zemindarry Settlements." In 1835 he became a writer in the Bombay civil service, was assistant collector in Poona, and the following year set out to investigate and rectify the system of land assessment in Indapore. More important posts led to his developing the province of Sind as chief commissioner in 1850. For his admirable services during the Mutiny he received the K.C.B. in 1859. In 1862 Frere was governor of Bombay, improving and developing the province till his return to England in 1867.[27]

When was the suggestion made that he should look at Peacock's

24. Philips, *The East India Company*, p. 304.

25. Like many governmental policy decisions, the discarding of permanent tax settlements was easier to *declare* than to effectuate. According to the *Report of the Indian Taxation Enquiry Committee, 1924-25* (Calcutta, 1926), the inequities of land taxation in various parts of India were still much in evidence at that time.

26. Peacock, *Works*, VIII, Appendix VI, 461.   27. *DNB*.

Shelley and his Circle : Manuscripts

Peacock in Leadenhall Street

essay? As he is named here with his title, it cannot have been until after the Mutiny, when in 1859 the K.C.B. had been awarded. It could have been as late as 1867 when he returned from Bombay. If we take the earlier, more probable, date, Peacock had already been retired for three years from the East India Company; yet his theoretical preliminary essay seems to have retained significance enough for its recommendation to a highly notable authority on Indian administration. Whether or not Sir Bartle Frere *did* read and give an opinion on it cannot be said for certain. What can be said is that the essay was looked on as a contribution to its subject and no mere academic test for an aspirant. In common with reports from Indian provinces and debates between board and directors, it had become — or so we read the signs — a paper to be filed and referenced, a factor to be reckoned with in the company's affairs.

For a poet, classical scholar, and satirical novelist, this 1818 essay was no mean entry into the world of economics. Three years later Shelley wrote from Italy, in one of his moods of revulsion against literary vagabondage, to sound Peacock on the chances of an Indian career for himself. Peacock's answer of October 1821 was bluntly discouraging: "it is altogether impossible. The whole of the Civil Service of India is sealed against all but the Company's covenanted servants, who are inducted into it through established gradations, beginning at an early period of life..."[28]

It was perhaps a little unkind of Peacock not to admit that his case had been exceptional; but as he felt that the "Indian project... would agree neither with your mind nor body," he no doubt justified his flat negative. He would have held it good for Shelley (whom he suspected of hallucinations) to follow "some interesting matter connected with the business of life, in the tangible shape of a practical man";[29] but not in the East India Company — where indeed Charles Lamb toiled at accountancy from 1792 to 1825 with a rising salary but no other marked distinction. For thirty-seven years Peacock was a practical man pursuing the business of life and reaching the highest position in his department. From a strictly materialistic point of view, "Ryotwar and Zemindarry Settlements" was the herald of far solider achievements than was that other innovation, *Headlong Hall*.

S.N.

28. Peacock, *Works*, VIII, 225.   29. Peacock, *Works*, VIII, 226.

The Carl H. Pforzheimer Library

SC 503 T. L. PEACOCK, RYOTWAR & ZEMINDARRY SETTLEMENTS, NOVEMBER 2, 1818

HOLOGRAPH MANUSCRIPT signed *T. L. P.*, 18¾ pages. 1 double sheet enveloping 19 single sheets, folio (13 x 7.8 inches).

Laid paper. Watermark, double sheet: [East India Company cipher]| VEIC| 1818|; countermark: S & C WISE|; watermark, single sheets 1, 4, 5, 6, 10, 12, 13, 15, 17, 19: [Britannia in crowned oval]|; watermark, single sheets 2, 3, 7, 8, 9, 11, 14, 16, 18: F| 1816|.

Additions, double sheet: 1. hole .3 inches in diameter in left margin; 2. severe staining and discoloration of paper, with damage along the fold and edges; additions, single sheets: 1. series of 3 small holes in the left margin of each sheet, indicating that the pages were once joined together and then attached to covering sheet; 2. paper slightly discolored and right edges of pages curled and damaged in places.

Notations: 1. (page 1, in faint pencil): *Ryotwar Zemindarry [Settlements]|*; 2. (page 1, in red pencil): *1818| ask Sir Bartle Frere's Opinion|*; 3. (leaf 19, verso, along right margin): *Chairman|*.

PROVENANCE: Edith Nicolls Clarke; Mrs. K. Hall Thorpe (Sotheby, November 15, 1949, lot 479).

Ryotwar & Zemindarry Settlements
T. L. P. 1818.

	Ryotwar and	
	Zemindarry	*It cannot be supposed that, in my total inexperience*
5	*Settlements.*	*of the affairs of India, I should feel justified in offering*
		anything like a decided opinion on the important question
		of the comparative advantages of the Ryotwar and Zemin-
		darry systems in the settlement of a permanent land reve-
		nue: more especially when I consider the great mass of
		talent, and of information founded on personal survey,
10		*which are brought to bear upon this question in the re-*
		ports with which you have furnished me, and the division
		of opinion among so many able men who have given to it
		a long, dispassionate, practical investigation.
		The desire to ascertain, by the most assiduous en-
15		*quiry, the mode of raising a permanent land revenue on a*

Ryotwar and
Zemindarry
Settlements.

It cannot be supposed that, in my total inexperience of the affairs of India, I should feel justified in offering anything like a decided opinion on the important question of the comparative advantages of the Ryotwar and Zemindarry systems in the settlement of a permanent land revenue: more especially when I consider the great mass of talent, and of information founded on personal survey, which are brought to bear upon this question in the reports with which you have furnished me, and the division of opinion among so many able men who have given to it a long, dispassionate, practical investigation.

The desire to ascertain, by the most assiduous enquiry, the mode of raising a permanent land revenue on a basis the most equitable and beneficial to the people, is worthy of an enlightened and liberal government. The question involves many points of great intricacy, even treated as an abstract question in Political Economy: but it involves many additional difficulties, when considered with relation to any particular people, whose habits,

T. L. Peacock, Ryotwar and Zemindarry Settlements,
November 2, 1818 (SC 503), page 1

Ryotwar and Zemindarry Settlements.

Manners, customs, institutions, ancient laws, land-tenures, and greater or less facility of communication with the supreme power, must all be taken into account. Long and exclusive attention, devoted to a minute examination of all the materials of knowledge at present existing in relation to the country and its inhabitants, would be an indispensable preliminary to the delivering a decided judgment on either side of the question: there are however some general principles which are universally applicable, and to which, under such modifications as the nature of circumstances may require, all questions of this nature must be ultimately referred.

General principles.

The principles of equitable taxation appear to be six:

1. Self-limitation.
2. Fixed standard of assessment.
3. Equality.
4. Convenience of time.
5. Encouragement of industry.
6. Facility of collection.

Principle of limitation.

1. The principle of self-limitation, or difficulty of extension beyond the abilities of the payer, is necessarily inherent in all taxes on consumption, in which an increase of rate often produces a

*T. L. Peacock, Ryotwar and Zemindarry Settlements,
November 2, 1818 (SC 503), page 2*

SC 503   *Ryotwar and*   *basis the most equitable and beneficial to the people, is*
          Zemindarry   *worthy of an enlightened and liberal government. The ques-*
          Settlements.   *tion involves many points of great intricacy, even treated*
                              as an abstract question in Political Economy: but it in-
20   *volves many additional difficulties, when considered with*
                              relation to any particular people, whose habits, manners,
                              customs, institutions, ancient laws, land-tenures, and
                              greater or less facility of communication with the supreme
                              power, must all be taken into account. Long and exclusive
25   *attention, devoted to a minute examination of all the ma-*
                              terials of knowledge at present existing in relation to the
                              country and its inhabitants, would be an indispensable pre-
                              liminary to the delivering a decided judgment on either
                              side of the question: there are however some general prin-
30   *ciples which are universally applicable, and to which,*
                              under such modifications as the nature of circumstances
                              may require, all questions of this nature must be ulti-
                              mately referred.

          General   *The principles of equitable taxation appear to be six:*
35   *principles.*   *1. Self-limitation.*
                                    2. Fixed standard of assessment.
                                    3. Equality.
                                    4. Convenience of time.
                                    5. Encouragement of industry.
40   *6. Facility of collection.*
          Principle of   *1. The principles of self-limitation, or difficulty of*
          limitation.   *extension beyond the abilities of the payer, is necessarily*
                              inherent in all taxes on consumption, in which an increase
                              of rate often produces a decrease of revenue, as the con-
45   *sumer, regulating his expenditure by his means, limits his*
                              consumption in articles of necessity, and often drops it
                              altogether in articles of luxury: but it is as necessarily ex-
                              cluded from the very nature of land-revenue, in which an
                              exaggerated assessment, or an ill-regulated mode of collec-

[727]

The Carl H. Pforzheimer Library

SC 503   *Principle of limitation.*

tion, will infallibly ruin the cultivators: thus it becomes necessary to restrain the assessment within the limits of a certain proportion to the capacities of the land, and to arrange a system of efficient checks in the collection that shall secure the equal rights of every individual contributor. A scheme of settlement in perpetuity, in which the government voluntarily renounces all additional claims for ever, creates for itself a species of limitation as effectual as the inherent self-limitation of taxes on consumption: and even if the government should reserve to itself a right of increasing revenue with increasing cultivation the assumption of an invariable standard of proportionate assessment would answer the same purpose. This principle, as far as it can be thus made to act, seems to belong equally to both systems.

Fixed standard of assessment.

2. A fixed standard of assessment, which leaves no power of discretionary imposition to either the collector or the farmer of revenue, seems also to belong equally to the Ryotwar and to the Zemindarry settlements. There still remains a question, Under which is it least likely to be violated? Which of these two modes of settlement contains in itself the most efficient check to the probability of such violation? If the zemindar had the power of raising his rents, there would of course be no check whatever upon him in this respect, but since he has not, he is so far on a par with the collector in relation to the fixed standard of assessment. The zemindar, whose office is hereditary, and who will naturally desire to transmit his office and property to his children not only unimpaired but improved, has certainly a greater interest in the prosperity of the ryot than the collector, whose office is temporary, and who neither has, nor can have, any permanent personal interest in the land. Though the relation between the zemindar and the ryot be not exactly that between landlord and tenant, the

SC 503 *Fixed standard of assessment.*

ryot having a perpetual proprietary right in the soil as long as he pays his rent, yet it approaches more nearly to it than that between the ryot and the collector does. It never can be the interest of a landlord to drain the country of its resources, or to drive his tenant to other lands by any act of oppression: and this may always hold true of favorable

90

seasons: but in bad seasons, the zemindar, whose lands may be sold to make good the deficiency of his stipulated contribution, has more at stake than the collector, and will be inclined to go greater lengths for the preservation of his property. A complete and detailed survey being the basis

95

of a ryotwar settlement, the means of accurate knowledge in the case of a violation of this fixed standard on the part of a collector, are more readily within the reach of the judicial authority than in the case of a similar violation on the part of a zemindar, to whose local knowledge much

100

is conceded in the original formation of the settlement, on the ground of saving expence and difficulty in the minuteness of survey and in the operation of official checks. This circumstance, of a more accurate and accessible criterion of judgment, is a very manifest advantage of the

105

ryotwar system. The question of remissions necessarily belongs to this head: for in a country where the seasons are extremely variable from very great abundance to very great scarcity, either the standard of assessment must be taken very low at first, or must vary from year to year, or must

110

be subject to remission in the unfavourable seasons. Admitting the standard to be fixed from an average of a number of past seasons, and to include the principle of remission, to whom shall the remission go? to the ryot or to the zemindar? It must necessarily go to the cultivator. Shall

115

it go to the cultivator immediately from the government, or mediately through the zemindar? If through the zemindar, without discretionary power, I can conceive no advantage

SC 503   *Fixed standard*
         of assessment.

120

125

130

135

140

145

150

that would not at least equally result from its being made through the collector: if with discretionary power, there is at once a direct infringement of a principle which ought to be as carefully observed in remission as in exaction. But it may be said, the discretionary power must be equally entrusted to a collector, who will be more likely to abuse it: that is, not having so great an interest in the prosperity of the ryots, nor being so good a judge of the soil and the people, as the zemindar, he would not and could not enter so minutely into the merits of each individual case. But the detailed preliminary survey, in the ryotwar system, would give the collector ample materials of knowledge; and if the remission were at a fixed proportion to the fixed standard of assessment, there would be no discretionary power, and consequently no more danger of abuse in remission than in exaction: for the one is only an inversion of the other, and the same standard and rules of proportion will apply equally to both. If the standard of assessment be fixed from the average of seasons, excluding remission altogether, the zemindarry settlement will appear to have the advantage. A fixed and invariable revenue can be better raised mediately from the ryots through the zemindars, than immediately from the ryots by agents of government or collectors: because the cultivators, in very bad seasons, would not be able to pay the specified sum; and in very good seasons, their superabundant produce being comparatively valueless to them from the want of a market, they would not be able to employ their superfluity in such a manner as to be a resource in the bad seasons, which the zemindar might be able to do; all great capitalists having confessedly a very superior power to small ones in averaging one year with another and making the redundance of plenty the harvest of scarcity. A settlement, that includes the principle of remission, may with perfect justice be

SC 503 *Fixed standard of assessment.*

155

160

Principle of equality.

165

170

175

180

185

made at a higher standard of assessment than one that excludes it. It would seem, then, that if the principle of remission be included, the ryotwar settlement will be most advantageous to the government and to the people, and that, if it be excluded, the advantages of a ryotwar settlement, as far as they are connected with the fixed standard of assessment, are not so great as to counterbalance the multiplicity of detail, and consequent expence and inconvenience, which the zemindarry settlement would avoid.

3. Equality. Every member of the state should contribute equally to the exigencies of the state in proportion to his means. This, though for the convenience of arrangement I have placed it third, is in point of importance the very first principle of equitable taxation. It belongs essentially to the nature of the ryotwar settlement: but the zemindar system tends to the creation of a number of privileged capitalists, whose contribution, relatively to that of the cultivator, becomes less and less in proportion as their respective districts become improved. If a whole province be divided into zemindarries, each comprising a quantity of cultivated and waste land, and if the land revenue of each zemindarry be unalterably fixed in perpetuity at a specific sum of money, it becomes the interest of the zemindar to extend the cultivation of his district as much as possible, since with every such extension of cultivation his own revenue is increased and his stipulated payment more easily made: the state also has its advantage in this greater facility of payment, and in the increase of population, though the sum total of revenue remain unchanged: such a tenure too seems to bind the interest of the zemindar very closely to that of the state, as he would naturally conceive that with any change of government the contribution required from him to the supreme power would be increased in proportion to his augmented means: but, nevertheless, if every ryot

SC 503 *Principle of equality.*

190

195

Convenience of time.

200

205

210

215 *Encouragement of industry.*

through the district contributes a fixed proportion of his produce to the zemindar, the zemindar is obviously the only person decidedly enriched by the progress of cultivation: his revenue is continually increasing while the revenue of the state and the relative condition of the ryots remains the same. These considerations include some reasons of expediency, which may, under particular circumstances, incline the preference to the zemindarry system: but they do not seem to admit of a doubt as to the superiority of a ryotwar permanent settlement on the principle of equality of contribution.

4. Convenience of time. The tax should be paid at the most convenient time to the payer. A cultivator of land is better able to pay a larger sum after the harvest than a smaller sum before it; and it is equally injurious to himself and to the state, when he is reduced to the necessity of borrowing money at a heavy interest to make payments on anticipated produce. The zemindar cannot be a much better judge on this point than the collector, the proper time of collection being the same in every year, and ascertainable with extreme facility. If a fixed limit of time were included in the original settlement, neither the zemindar nor the collector could expect to infringe it with impunity, as all the requisite knowledge, to enable the judicial authority to determine on such infringement, would be still more easily within its reach, than in the case of a violation of the fixed standard of assessment after the most accurate preliminary survey. In this respect, therefore, it does not appear that either system has any marked advantage over the other.

5. Encouragement of industry. Taxes should always include a principle of encouragement to industry. An industrious will necessarily contribute more to the exigencies of the state than an indolent man, and his taxes should be so assessed as to give him his proportionate share in the

SC 503 *Encouragement of industry.*

225

230

235

240

Mr Hodgson.
245 *5th report.*
p. 937.

250

greater produce of his labor and skill. We have seen that in a permanent zemindarry settlement, in which the land revenue is unalterably fixed in perpetuity, the chief, almost the whole, advantages of improvement and increased cultivation go to the zemindar. In a permanent ryotwar settlement, in which the revenue is in like manner fixed in perpetuity, they are divided equally among all the cultivators, who will have a continual sense of bettering their condition with the progress of improvement and the extension of cultivation. Even in a ryotwar settlement not fixed in perpetuity, but yielding a progressive revenue with the progress of cultivation, this advantage might be so divided between the ryots and the company, as still to give the former the constant sense of improvement in their condition, and to form between both a bond of union founded on the sense of mutual prosperity. In both cases, every portion of land will pay a diminished assessment, and the waste will be cultivated under greater advantages. It is argued, that the want of capital would prevent the ryots from cultivating the waste, and that the creation of a great capitalist in the person of the zemindar would necessarily occasion the investment of his capital in the improvement of his zemindarry, and that this would be shewn "in the improved appearance of the country, in the building of substantial houses, the planting of gardens and topes, the making of roads, the erecting of choultries and bridges, and the building of pagodas." This would be assuredly a decided superiority in the zemindarry settlement, if it were certain that the extension of cultivation under the ryotwar system would not be attended with the same advantages: but it is to be questioned if the inhabitants of two wealthy villages, deriving any advantage from mutual intercourse, would not as readily make roads and bridges for their own accommodation as a zemindar would for them; or that a

[733]

SC 503   *Encouragement of industry*

wealthy farmer, under a system which assured to him the security of his property, would not build as substantial a house as he could inhabit; or that where public gardens and groves are a public comfort and advantage, the inhabitants themselves, or the collector under the authority of government to do so, would not plant them as willingly as

260   *the zemindar: indeed Mr Hodgson, the most strenuous advocate of the zemindarry system, admits, that "the ryot, when protected in the possession of his property, and not afraid to display it, will lay it out, first, in bettering his condition; secondly, in personal comforts; and thirdly, in*

265   *ubi supra.*   *local improvements, of the nature above described." As an incentive to industry, the ryotwar system appears in practice, under the Madras presidency, to have been attended with the most marked advantages, which were manifested in the improved condition of the cultivator, in the increase*

270   *of cultivation, in the civilization, obedience and content of*

5th report p. 124.   *the people, and in their universal regret on the departure of the principal collector. So far, then, as relates to the encouragement of industry, the superiority of a ryotwar permanent settlement appears sufficiently evident.*

275   *Facility of collection.*   *6. Facility of collection. The machinery of revenue should in all cases be as simple as the circumstances of the country will admit. The agents or middlemen between the payers of taxes and the government should be as few as possible, as every hand, through which a tax passes, rubs*

280   *off something from its amount. It is calculated that there are some branches of the revenue in England, in which not more than one third of the total sum collected is paid into the hands of government. They are retained in preference to others, of which the machinery would be more simple,*

285   *because they are in themselves, and in their mode of collection though more expensive and complicated, more agreeable to the habits and inclinations of the people; which in*

SC 503

Facility of
collection.

290

295

300

305

310

315

p. 121.

320

many cases, in all nations and in all conditions of society,
render it expedient to adopt or retain the more expensive
machinery of collection: but the knowledge connected with
this expediency, in the instance of any particular people,
can only be derived from experience.   It is alledged on the
one hand, that the ryotwar system involves great trouble
and inconvenience in collecting rents from individuals by
means of revenue officers; the constant and vexatious inter-
ference of the latter in all private transactions; great ex-
pence to government in maintaining them; the complication
of the original survey, involving the almost inevitable dan-
ger of error and unequal assessment, followed by an equally
complicated detail of collection, inextricably perplexed by
the dishonesty of the curnums who never give true accounts
of the land in cultivation, and the consequent necessity of
annually sending out examiners, whose conduct itself often
leads to long and vexatious investigation. On the other hand
it is contended, that the detail must be carried on by some-
body; that the ryotwar detail would not be very complicated;
that an equal assessment cannot be imposed without an
accurate survey; that an over-assessment will be naturally
complained of by the party aggrieved, and may with very
little difficulty be verified and rectified; that an under-
assessment will be promptly detected and made known by
the inhabitants of contiguous villages, "who have always
been found ready to give information on the subject, either
from jealousy at finding their neighbours thus favoured,
or from a hope of obtaining by this means a reduction of
their own burthens;" and that "when once the survey rent
is accomplished, and has been adjusted by the information
and experience afterwards acquired on the occasions which
annually occur of making the settlements, and by the aid
it receives from a variety of other co-operating causes,
among which the assistance of the inhabitants themselves

SC 503 *Facility of collection*

325

p. 123.

330

335

340

345

350

355

is not the least important, it becomes a less arduous and comparatively simple operation, the success of which principally and almost wholly depends on an active, uniform and unrelaxed exercise of superintendance and personal controul and inspection on the part of the collectors, over the different gradations of public servants employed under their authority." To avoid this minute detail, with which the ryotwar settlements must be founded and carried on, is one of the principal arguments for the zemindarry system. The zemindar stipulates to pay a certain revenue for his district, and is to raise this revenue, with additional advantage for himself, from the ryots, not arbitrarily but according to fixed and equitable rules of proportion: the ryot, who may consider himself aggrieved by undue exaction on the part of the zemindar, has his appeal to the judicial authority: but in every such appeal, the detail which it is proposed to avoid must be entered into, as far as relates to that particular case, before the cause can be determined; which must occasion perplexing and often ruinous delay to both parties; and if such complaints be numerous, the multiplicity of particular detail, thus made piecemeal and at random, will be more expensive and complicated than the complete general detail which is the basis of the ryotwar settlement, and at the same time will be always imperfect and always to be renewed in parts on every new difference between the ryot and the zemindar. It seems, indeed, that without such detailed survey there cannot be any effectual check upon the zemindar, and that with it there is no very evident necessity for his intervention: if discretionary power be entrusted to the zemindar to raise his revenue as he can, in reliance on the argument that it is the interest of a landlord not to oppress his tenants, then the machinery will be more simple than in the ryotwar system; but if it be not deemed either prudent or just to entrust him with this dis-

Peacock, Ryotwar & Zemindarry Settlements   November 2, 1818

SC 503 *Facility of*
collection

360

cretionary power, detail is not avoided but only postponed: it is particular and subsequent, instead of general and pre-liminary: it is undertaken for the purpose of settling dis-putes when they have arisen, instead of being made a groundwork to prevent them from arising: it is thus in every way more complicated and entangled, theoretically considered; and practically, it appears in many districts to have been attended with thousands of law-suits, the greater part of which could not be expected to be determined within the ordinary course of human life; an evil which the preliminary detail of the ryotwar system is so well cal-culated to obviate, as in practice it appears to have done.

365

Summary.

It would seem, then, that on the principles of limita-tion, of the fixed standard of assessment, and of the con-venience of time, the two systems are nearly balanced: but that on those of equality of contribution, of encouragement of industry, and of facility of collection, the ryotwar settle-ment possesses a decided advantage.

370

Modifications
375 *from par-*
-ticular
considerations.

These arguments, however, from general principles may be very much modified by particular considerations, of the nature of the land-tenures and ancient customs of India; of the disposition of the natives to obedience, whether to general government, or to particular personal hereditary authority; of the probable effects of the subdivision of prop-erty; of the system of police and the constitution of the courts of dewanny adawlut; of the total practical results of experience in both systems; and of the probable adapta-tion of either to permanency. On these points if you require it I shall be happy to give you my opinion when I am better acquainted with the minutiæ of the question.

380

385

November 2ⁿᵈ, 1818.

line 1. The title and date are written on the covering sheet which encloses the 19 single sheets. This outer sheet contains the cipher of the United East India Company, which required that the mark be included on all papers made for its use. (See Thomas Balston, *William Bal-*

SC 503   *ston, Paper Maker, 1759–1849,* London, 1954, pp. 166–167.)

line 1. *Zemindarry*: the *OED* lists the word with one *r*.

line 3. The marginal headings introduce each section of the essay and are repeated in the top left margin of each page of manuscript. In our transcript the subtitles will be repeated at the top of each new page to preserve the spirit of Peacock's arrangement. Peacock has also numbered each page in ink in the top right-hand corner, but we have omitted these numerals.

line 19. *as*: *s* written through *n*.

line 43. *in*: *i* written through *o*.

line 50. *thus*: written through *but*.

line 53. *checks*: to the left of this word (initial word in manuscript line) there is a penciled X.

line 62. *This principle . . . systems.* (line 64): this sentence has been added in a slightly smaller script, to squeeze it in under the last line of the section.

line 67. *also*: written below *seems*, which ends the last full line on page 3.

line 89. *favorable*: so here, but spelled with *our* in lines 110 and 314.

line 101. *expence*: contemporary spelling; see also lines 159 and 296.

line 116. *zemindar?*: *ar* written through indecipherable letters.

line 117. *conceive*: *n* originally written with an extra loop through which *c* was written.

line 157. *fixed standard*: *fixed* written through *rigid*; *st* written through ?⟨ ⟩*r*.

line 180. *remain*: *n* written through *ns*.

line 183. *government*: *nment* written through a very faint ?*nment*.

line 193. *zemindarry*: *rr* written through *r*.

line 242. "*in the . . . pagodas.*" (line 246): in this passage, as in all the other passages Peacock cites in this report, quotation marks begin each new line of manuscript, in accordance with the convention of the period. We have omitted these and included only the opening and closing marks.

line 244. *Mʳ Hodgson.*: marginal title added by Peacock in a small neat hand with a finer pen; so also with other marginal references to the *Fifth Report* (for full reference, see "Peacock in Leadenhall Street," p. 717, fn. 15).

topes,: in this reference the word means a mango grove. The name is also used for a Buddhist monument.

line 245. *choultries*: the word refers to a "covered public building, generally of hewn stone, often richly carved and ornamented, for the accommodation of travellers." It may also denote a covered colonnade in front of a South Indian temple. (See Firminger, *Fifth Report*, III, Glossary; for full reference, see "Peacock in Leadenhall Street," p. 717, fn. 15.)

line 281. *in which*: *in* written through smudged-out *f*.

line 286. *complicated,*: *ed* written through ?*ion*.

line 292. *alledged* (sic): here and throughout.

line 301. *curnum*: "Accountant of a village who registers every thing connected with its cultivation and produce, the shares or rents of the Ryot, with the dues and rights of government in the soil. It answers to the term Putwarry in the Bengal provinces." (Firminger, *Fifth Report*, III, Glossary.)

line 310. *that*: there is a short line and an X in pencil in the margin to the left of this word.

line 326. *controul*: obsolete spelling.

line 346. *in*: *i* written through *o*.

line 381. *courts of dewanny adawlut*: dewanny signifies financial administration, which in practice came down to revenue collection. Dewanny authority over Bengal and certain other provinces was conferred in perpetuity on the East India Company in August 1765. In 1772 civil and criminal courts were instituted for each provincial division or collectorship; the Dewanny Adawlut or Civil Court was for the cognizance of civil causes. The collector presided over the Civil Court on the part of the company in their quality of king's diwan, attended by the provincial native diwan and other officers of the collector's court (Firminger, *Fifth Report*, I, 3, 6).

SC 504   LEIGH HUNT TO P. B. AND M. W. SHELLEY, NOVEMBER 12, 1818

AL signed *Leigh Hunt.*, 4 pages. Double sheet, 4to (8.9 x 7.2 inches).
Wove paper.
Seal: wax, red: [angel with olive branch, following serpent]|.
Postal fees: 1. 1/11; 2. £1.3.4.
Postmarks: 1. (receiving house stamp, London): CRAWFORD STREET|; 2. (Foreign Post Office stamp, London): F 18| 86|; 3. (transit stamp): CHAMBERY|; 4. CORRISP^{ZA} ESTERA DA GENOVA| [fleur-de-lis]|; 5. 2 DECEMBRE|; 6. LIVORNO|; 7. NO 1818| 10 [D]IC|; 8. 4 [enclosed in elaborate red circle]|.
Notations, page 1, in ink: 1. *180* 2. [blot] *8*|.

$$\begin{array}{r} 5 \\ \hline 12)\overline{900} \\ \hline 75 \end{array}$$

PROVENANCE: Colonel Charles Shelley Leigh Hunt; Mrs. Beryl Dodgson (Sotheby, April 8, 1935, lot 205). See SC 414, Commentary.

8. York Buildings– New. Road
Thursday 12. November 1818.

     My dear friends,

         So I find, all of a sudden, why it is you do not write
5   *to me. I sent my last letter thoughtlessly by Mr Ollier's box, & they tell me to*
    my great chagrin that perhaps it may not have reached you yet. I had no idea
    of this, or I should have written to you again long before; & so I should at all
    events, had I not been daily devoured with printer's devils, & in expectation
    besides of hearing from yourselves. So Shelley has been hanging his head, I
10   *fear, & saying "Hunt is too careless;" & Marina has been looking sideways,*
    & thinking it not worth speaking about; & First Lady has consigned me over
    to the common character of mankind. Well I shall sit like Patience in a post-
    office, & wait for one of the kindest letters in the world.– What think you of
    my modesty as well as industry? I have been writing a Pocket-Book. ⟨————⟩
15   *it*
    The booksellers tell me ⌄will do exceedingly well; & Shelley will be at once
    pleased & surprised to hear that it is my own property, & that I mean to
    keep it so. It is entitled the Literary Pocket-Book or Companion for the

SC 504   *Lover of Art & Nature, & contains a long Calendar of the Months written by myself & interspersed with* ~~poetical~~ *quotations from dead & living poets,— Lists of men of original genius from the earliest times & the present,– of living authors of Europe, artists, & musicians,—& extracts from Bacon & others, & original poetry among which I have taken the liberty ("Hunt is too* ~~un~~ *ceremonious sometimes") of putting Marianne's dream, to the great de-*

25   *light of said Marianne, not to mention its' various M.S. readers. The names are not mentioned in this department of the book; but Shelley will be in good company,–at least I may speak for Keats, & Shelley will speak for some one else. I forgot, in my box-letter, to allude to the criticism in the Quart. Rev. upon Marina's book. Upon the whole, I congratulate her on it, as far as*

30   *they unde< >nd her. They have now been abusing Keats at a most f< >ious rate, since their abuse of Shelley; & it < > pleasant, on many accounts beyond the eyesight of such misereble half-witted critics, to see how the public disgust is increasing against them every day. I made no answer to Gifford myself, partly out of contempt, partly (I must really say) out of*

35   *something bordering on a loathing kind of pity, & partly for the sake of setting an example always praised but seldom or never practiced. I therefore instinctively paid a a friend like Shelley the compliment of feeling for him as I felt for myself;–but there are limits in forbearance, especially where the*

40   *task is not*_^ one of *self-revenge but of friendship; & as they have sent for his poem from Ollier's to criticise it, I mean, if they*_^ (Gifford or others) *do not take warning, to buckle on my old rusty resentments, & give them such a carbonado as I know I am* ~~capable~~ *able to give, & they most capable of feeling. I hope Ollier has told*

45   *you that Shelley's book sells more & more. God bless you all, & never think angrily or doubtingly of one who is just as sensitive to the opinion of those dear to him, as he ⟨——⟩ despises that of his enemies. Most affectionately yours, Leigh Hunt.*

50   *Marianne's all-but-very-best love.*_^ Bess requests to be put in by all means *Hogg, Keats, Novello, H. Robertson, & Coulson, sent their remembrances,– Hogg especial ones. I am now resuming my drama; & am going to propose to Constable, that when I have done it, I will undertake specimens of the Italian Poets from Dante to Metastasio.*

Hunt to Shelleys   *November 12, 1818*

SC 504   [Address, page 4]

        Percy B. Shelley Esqre

55

            ~~*alla cura dello Signor*~~

Poste restante

         ~~*Giovanni Gisborne*~~

     ~~*Leghorn*~~

          ~~*Livorno,*~~

60   ~~*Italy*~~   *Naples*   ~~*Italia.*~~

line 14. *Pocket-Book.*: period written through comma. Hunt broke his sentence in two by changing the punctuation, canceling the next word, and correcting *t* of *the* to *T*.

   ⟨————⟩: canceled word illegible.

line 29. *far as they unde⟨rsta⟩nd*: written on fragment of paper adhering to seal; bracketed letters affected by seal tear.

line 30. *at a most f⟨ur⟩ious*: written on fragment of paper adhering to seal; bracketed letters affected by seal tear.

line 31. ⟨*is*⟩: obscured by portion of seal and a seal tear.

line 32. *misereble* (sic).

line 37. *a a* (sic): last word on manuscript page 3 and first word on manuscript page 4. The first *a*, however, does not appear as a catchword.

line 47. *as . . . Hunt.*: words written in a very cramped hand on the final line of paper.

   ⟨————⟩: canceled letters illegible.

line 50. *Marianne's . . . Metastasio.* (line 53): written at the top of page 1, above and to the left of lines 1–2.

line 55. ~~*alla cura*~~: all the cancellations on the address page have been made with heavy slant strokes which affect (though they do not obscure) the readings on page 3 of the manuscript.

HUNT'S CONFESSIONS of his errors were almost always disarming. To the above letter, Shelley replied mildly that "a letter from you is always so pleasant that one never feels less inclined to complain of the long absence of such a pleasure than at the moment when it is conferred."[1]

Hunt reports that in keeping with Shelley's advice his latest literary effort, *The Literary Pocket-Book*, is entirely owned by him, rather than in partnership with his brother or some publisher. This publication, an annual pocket calendar and memorandum book containing some useful information (as such books do today) and some anecdotes, original prose, and original poetry (in the fashion of such books in that day), was published by Ollier and distributed by other booksellers.[2] Being practical

1. Shelley, *Letters*, II, 64–65.

2. Hunt was somewhat self-conscious with his "literary" friends about stooping to do such a book simply for money; see his letter to Charles Cowden Clarke (Clarke, *Recollections of Writers*, pp. 200–201). For a bibliographical description and survey of the contents of the five annual volumes dated 1819, 1820, 1821, 1822, and 1823, see T. J. Wise, *The Ashley Library* (London, Privately Printed, 1927), II, 196–199.

The Carl H. Pforzheimer Library

SC 504   and noncontroversial, *The Literary Pocket-Book* appealed to a wider public than Hunt's usual journalistic or belletristic publications;[3] being personal and annual, it was not lent out by circulating libraries or individual buyers, and therefore should have sold in larger quantities than many publications; being Hunt's copyrighted property, it earned some money for him; being ephemeral, it was frequently discarded and copies of the five volumes have become extremely rare.[4] The "Original Poetry" (pages 217–226) in the volume for 1819 included—besides the poem called "Marianne's Dream"[5] that Shelley wrote at Marlow about one of Marianne Hunt's dreams—two sonnets by Keats ("The Human Seasons" and "To Ailsa Rock"), two poems by Hunt, and two by Bryan Waller Procter (who wrote under the pseudonym "Barry Cornwall").

Although Hunt in this letter speaks up for Keats as good poetic company (lines 26–27) Keats himself, in a fit of revulsion against Hunt and his circle, wrote to George and Georgiana Keats that *The Literary Pocket-Book* was "full of the most sickening stuff you can imagine."[6] One should note, however, that in the same letter Keats admits that his personal distaste for Hunt had for him made "fine things petty and beautiful things hateful."[7]

For Hunt, oblivious of Keats's negative reaction toward him, the sole enemy was William Gifford. Hunt had obviously been stung by the *Quarterly Review*'s scathing attack on *Foliage*, which also attacked Shelley.[8] This was followed in the *Quarterly* for April 1818 by John Wilson Croker's savage review of *Endymion*.[9] Hunt in this letter trans-

3. See, for example, the favorable review in *Blackwood's Edinburgh Magazine*, VI (December 1819), 235–247.

4. Luther Brewer owned only the volume for 1822; see *My Leigh Hunt Library: The First Editions* (Cedar Rapids, Iowa, 1932), pp. 108–109. Fortunately, Shelley's own copies of the volumes for 1820, 1821, and 1822 are preserved in the Bodleian Library, Oxford (Bodleian Ms. Shelley adds. f. 2–4).

5. Shelley, *Poetical Works* (OSA), pp. 536–539.

6. Keats, *Letters*, II, 7. From this mention, we can ascertain that the volume had appeared by mid-December 1818.

7. Keats, *Letters*, II, 11.

8. *Quarterly Review*, XVIII (January 1818), 324–335 (published in June 1818). See SC 486 and SC 502, Commentaries.

9. *Quarterly Review*, XIX (April 1818), 204–208. On the authorship of this review, see Hill and Helen Chadwick Shine, *The Quarterly Review under Gifford* (University of North Carolina Press, 1949), pp. 61–62, and the letter from John Murray to J. W. Croker in Lyle H. Kendall, Jr., *A Descriptive Catalogue of the W. L. Lewis Collection, Part One* (Texas Christian University Press, 1970), pp. 80–81.

SC 504   lates his personal anger into righteous outrage at the abuse of his friends (lines 30–44). Characteristically, Hunt attributes the attacks to Gifford, not only as the editor of the *Quarterly* but as a personal enemy of Hunt and Hazlitt. (Shelley, on the other hand, blamed Southey for the mistreatment *he* suffered at the hands of the Tory journal.) Although Hunt did not strike back publicly until the autumn of 1819, when he replied to the *Quarterly*'s review of *The Revolt of Islam* (the "book" that "sells more & more," line 45), he had probably already buckled on his "old rusty resentments" and at least begun *Ultra-Crepidarius; a Satire on William Gifford*. When the poem was published in 1823 Hunt explained in the Preface that it had been written five years earlier. As SC 517 shows, Hunt was motivated not only by the *Quarterly*'s attack on *Endymion*,[10] but also by those on himself and Shelley in the earlier review of *Foliage*. There were at least two practical reasons why Hunt waited five years to publish his poem, besides his feelings of a "loathing kind of pity" for Gifford (line 35): First, Hazlitt had attacked Gifford in the *Examiner* for June 15, 1818, and he was soon to publish his expanded *Letter to William Gifford, Esq.* (1819), thereby carrying the attack to the enemy. (Hunt reviewed Hazlitt's pamphlet appreciatively in the *Examiner* on January 7, 1819.) Second, John and Leigh Hunt had in November 1817 threatened legal action against Baldwin, Cradock & Joy, London agents for *Blackwood's Edinburgh Magazine*, because of the scurrilous personal attacks on "The Cockney School of Poetry" in that journal. Their threats were taken so seriously by Robert Baldwin that his firm withdrew as agents for *Blackwood's Edinburgh Magazine*, being replaced by Cadell & Davies.[11] Naturally, the Hunts's legal (and moral) position vis-à-vis *Blackwood's* would have been weakened considerably had Leigh Hunt published his strong personal attack on Gifford at this juncture.

10. Edmund Gosse attributed Hunt's satire solely to the attack on Keats; see "*Ultra-Crepidarius*" in *Gossip in a Library* (London, 1891), pp. 285–291.

11. Robert Baldwin to William Blackwood, November 3, 1817, and November 11, 1817 (from photocopies of the original letters in the Blackwood Papers, National Library of Scotland, #4002). See Margaret Oliphant, *William Blackwood and His Sons* (Edinburgh and London: Blackwood, 1897), I, 133–139. In 1823 Cadell & Davies were similarly threatened with a suit by Hazlitt and John Hunt as the result of attacks in *Blackwood's Magazine*, but they resisted the pressure; see Theodore Besterman, *The Publishing Firm of Cadell & Davies* (Oxford University Press, 1938), pp. 67–73; Oliphant, *William Blackwood*, I, 274–277.

The Carl H. Pforzheimer Library

SC 504   The other literary efforts that Hunt in this letter says he is undertaking proved to be too ambitious. The drama he was resuming (lines
51–52) was his tragedy on the story of the Cid that was never acted.[12]
His plan to compile specimens of Italian poetry was partially realized,
after a delay of many years, in *Stories from the Italian Poets: With Lives
of the Writers* (1846), which Hunt dedicated to Sir Percy Florence Shelley.
But the later publication was changed in design (from excerpts in Italian
to English paraphrases) and reduced in scope to include stories from
only five Italian classic poets—Dante, Pulci, Boiardo, Ariosto, and
Tasso.[13]

Among those whom Hunt records as sending Shelley their greetings,
all have been fully identified in these volumes except Vincent Novello
and Henry Robertson.

Vincent Novello (1781–1861) was an original member of the Phil-
harmonic Society, a pianist and conductor of an Italian opera company,
an amateur actor in Shakespearean plays, and the host at many musical
evenings attended (with relish) by such people as Hunt and (with disdain) by Keats. He was a close friend of Hunt and Lamb,[14] and was
acquainted with many other London literary men. Charles Cowden
Clarke, a frequenter of his entertainments, married Mary Victoria Novello, his eldest daughter, and Clara Anastasia, his seventh child, became
a world-renowned soprano. A Catholic, Novello was from 1797 to 1822
organist of the Portuguese embassy chapel, South Street, Grosvenor
Square. In 1811 he had begun to publish "Novello's Sacred Music as
performed at the Royal Portuguese Chapel." He remained a prolific
composer of church music, examples of which can occasionally be heard
today. More importantly, his publications led to his son Joseph Alfred
Novello's founding of the important music publishing house of Novello
& Co., which still continues in London.[15]

12. See sc 486 and sc 529 and Commentaries.

13. Hunt characteristically shows a marked temperamental preference for Pulci over Dante because
the former had a "susceptible and most affectionate heart" (*Stories from the Italian Poets*, I, 283).

14. Lamb describes Novello's musical evenings in Elia's "Chapter on Ears" (*Works*, II, 38–41).

15. For further information on Novello, his family, and his circle, see *DNB*; Grove, *Dictionary*; the
letters of Hunt and Lamb; Charles and Mary Cowden Clarke, *Recollections of Writers* (London,
1878); Mary Cowden-Clarke, *My Long Life: An Autobiographic Sketch* (2nd edition, London, 1896);
Richard D. Altick, *The Cowden Clarkes* (Oxford University Press, 1948); and Averil Mackenzie-
Grieve, *Clara Novello, 1818–1908* (London, 1955). Additional unpublished manuscript material has

SC 504   Charles Cowden Clarke describes Henry Robertson—one of three brothers who were long-time friends of Hunt's—as "one of the most delightful of associates for good temper, good spirits, good taste in all things literary and artistic."[16] Robertson, an avid amateur musician in Novello's circle, was then (or later became) a Treasury Office clerk and the accountant of Covent Garden Theatre.[17]

been available since 1953 in The Novello-Cowden Clarke Collection in The Brotherton Library, University of Leeds; see *The Novello-Cowden Clarke Collection: A Hand-List* (58 pp., The Brotherton Library, 1955).

16. Clarke, *Recollections of Writers*, p. 17.

17. Clarke, *Recollections of Writers*, p. 18. See also Hunt, *Autobiography*, I, 130, and II, 225; Landré, *Leigh Hunt*, I, 75 and note, 112.

SC 505   WILLIAM GODWIN TO JOSEPH V. BEVAN, NOVEMBER 13, 1818

AL signed *W Godwin*, 1 page. Double sheet, 8vo (7.3 x 4.4 inches). Laid paper. Watermark: [crowned shield, upper portion]|.
Seal: wafer, green.

PROVENANCE: Carnegie Book Shop, May 1949.

> *Dear Sir*
>   *Would you do me the favour to look in upon me this morning, at any time between ten & two.*
>
>   *very sincerely yours*
>   *W Godwin*

5

> *Friday morning, Nov. 13,*
>   *half after nine.*

[Address, page 4]
Mr Bevan

G ODWIN'S JOURNAL ENTRY for June 11, 1817, reads "sup at Ogilvie's, w. Verplank & Bevan." This is the first record of Godwin's acquaintance with Joseph Vallence Bevan (1798–1830),[1] who had been one of James Ogilvie's[2] rhetoric students at the University of South Carolina.

1. For a biography of Bevan, see Ellis Merton Coulter, *Joseph Vallence Bevan, Georgia's First Official Historian* (University of Georgia Press, 1964).

2. See SC 405 and Commentary.

SC 505 It was to Bevan, an American not yet out of his teens, that Godwin addressed his small pamphlet, *Letter of Advice to a Young American on the Course of Studies it Might be Most Advantageous for him to Pursue*.[3]

The *Letter of Advice*, which focuses on a course of study "that shall make him who pursues it independent and generous,"[4] demonstrates anew Godwin's educational theory, which emphasized moral rather than intellectual development. Because Godwin believed that "the noblest part of man is his moral nature," he concentrated on the cultivation of the imagination rather than the accumulation of scientific and natural facts.[5]

Godwin's reading course, in addition to a general and marked avoidance of books of a scientific nature, specifically warns against overindulgence in new books or reviews. To cultivate the proper moral sentiments, Godwin first advises a study of the best models — ancient Greece and Rome — whose histories should be absorbed by reading their own historians either in original texts or in translation. After a study of classical times, Godwin suggests an investigation of the age of chivalry. For the formation of both intellect and feeling in the type of man Godwin wants to create, he also advocates a thorough knowledge of poetry; metaphysics, on the other hand, will provide "a disciplining and subtilising of the rational faculties."[6]

In addition, Godwin's program includes a consideration of language, which embraces the study of both foreign languages and English. For the English language he counsels reading the great authors of each successive age. Besides these readings, Godwin advises the young American to read extensively in English (modern, as opposed to ancient) history, both because of Bevan's own language and heritage and "because the English moral and intellectual character ranks the first of modern times."[7] The

3. For a history of the Godwin-Bevan relationship and an account of the genesis and printing of the *Letter of Advice*, see Jack W. Marken, "Joseph Bevan and William Godwin," *Georgia Historical Quarterly*, XLIII (September 1959), pp. 302–318. The *Letter of Advice* is reprinted in William Godwin, *Uncollected Writings (1785–1822)*, Introductions by Jack W. Marken and Burton R. Pollin (Gainesville, Scholar's Facsimiles and Reprints, 1968), pp. 429–444. All subsequent references to the *Letter* will be to this edition.

4. Godwin, *Letter of Advice*, p. 434.

5. Godwin, *Letter of Advice*, p. 432.

6. Godwin, *Letter of Advice*, p. 437.

7. Godwin, *Letter of Advice*, p. 441.

SC 505 pamphlet concludes with a caution against acceptance of any one authority and a plea for good study habits.

Godwin's *Letter of Advice* provides evidence of his educational role in the lives of young men.[8] Godwin had his *Letter of Advice* printed, he told Bevan, because other young men had often asked him for similar advice.[9] Having set down his reading plan, Godwin circulated it widely. The *Letter* was written, according to Godwin's Journal, between February 4 and 9, 1818, after Bevan had left London for a trip to Scotland and Ireland at the end of 1817, and it was issued on February 12 by M. J. Godwin and Co. After it appeared in Constable's *Edinburgh Magazine* for March 1818, it was reprinted in America by the *Analectic Magazine* (which also published five other letters written by Godwin to Bevan in 1818), *Port Folio*, *Robinson's Magazine*, and the *Georgia Journal*.[10]

Bevan returned to London from Ireland in the fall of 1818. His first reappearance in Skinner Street was on September 30, when he supped with Godwin.[11] Bevan and Godwin met a great deal in the final months of 1818, and though he did not "look in upon" (line 2) Godwin on November 13,[12] Godwin's Journal does record that he saw Bevan every day between December 13 and December 30 when he notes, "Bevan takes leave." The two continued to correspond after Bevan returned to Georgia, where he studied law and became the first official historian of his state.

8. For another of Godwin's advisory relationships, see sc 436 and Commentary. For an account of a different interest and role in education, see sc 508, Commentary.

9. Quoted in Marken, "Joseph Bevan and William Godwin," p. 304.

10. Pollin, Introduction to Godwin, *Uncollected Writings*, pp. xxiv–xxv.

11. Godwin, Journal.

12. Godwin notes in his Journal, however, that Bevan did call on November 12 and 15.

SC 506 LORD BYRON, CODICIL TO WILL, NOVEMBER 17, 1818

DOCUMENT signed *Byron*, 1¾ pages. Double sheet, folio (12.8 x 8.1 inches). Laid paper. Watermark: [lion rampant guardant, holding sword in left forepaw and three arrows or darts in right forepaw, in crowned oval]|; countermark: DUSAUTOY & C°| 1817|.

Seal (on page 2, beside Byron's signature, to authenticate it): wax, red: [crown]| B|.

Docket, page 4: *17th November 1818| Codicil to Lord| Byron's Will|*.

PROVENANCE: John Fleming, January 1962.

SC 506   *Codicil*

This is a Codicil to the last Will and Testament of me The Right Honourable George Gordon Lord Byron, I Give and bequeath unto Allegra Biron an Infant of about Twenty

5 *Months old by me brought up and–– now residing at Venice the Sum of – – Five thousand Pounds which I direct the Executors of my said Will to pay to her on her attaining the Age of Twenty one Years or on the Day of her Marriage (on Condition she does not marry with a Native of Great Britain)*

10 *which shall first happen And I direct my said Executors as soon as conveniently may be after my Decease to invest the said Sum of Five thousand Pounds on —— Government or real Security and pay— and apply the Annual Income thereof in or towards the Maintenance and Education of the said Allegra*

15 *Biron until she attains her said Age of — Twenty one Years or shall be married as aforesaid But in case she shall die before attaining the said ~~Marriage~~ and— without having been married Then I direct the said sum of Five thousand Pounds to become part of the residue of my — personal Es-*

20 *tate And in all other Respects I do confirm my said Will and declare this to be a Codicil thereto In witness whereof I have hereunto set my Hand and Seal at Venice this Seventeenth Day of November in the Year of our Lord one thousand Eight hundred and Eighteen*

25 *Signed sealed published and declared* ⎞   *Byron*   [seal]
      by the said Lord Byron as and for a ⎟
      Codicil to his Will in the presence of ⎟
      us who in his presence at his Request – ⎨
      and in the presence of each — other ⎟

30 *have subscribed our Names as Wit-* ⎟
      nesses ———— ⎠

       Newton Hanson
       William Fletcher

Shelley and his Circle : Manuscripts

Byron, Codicil to Will   *November 17, 1818*

SC 506   line 1. The entire document, except for the three signatures, is in a legal copying hand that closely resembles the signature of Newton Hanson.

line 5. *and—*: this dash, like all the others in the document, comes at the end of a line in the manuscript. The dash, therefore, is a means of filling out lines which do not extend to the right margin.

line 22. *Seventeenth*: in lighter ink. The word was evidently added at the time of signing; it is in the same hand as the whole manuscript.

Byron is known to have written at least four different wills, "on all major occasions" or in anticipation of "changes in his circumstances up to the time of the separation."[1] A will signed on June 14, 1809, when he was twenty-one and going abroad, made provision for his mother to possess Newstead Abbey *"for her life,"*[2] and a new will was made necessary by her sudden death on August 1, 1811. A third will was drawn up in 1813 when Byron believed that the sale of Newstead to Thomas Claughton was about to go through; "in it Byron divided his property between his cousin and heir to his title, George Anson Byron, and his half-sister," Augusta.[3] Byron did not draw up a new will at the time of his marriage to Anne Isabella Milbanke, on January 2, 1815, because the marriage settlement was arranged in accordance with existing wills on both sides, but he did sign one on July 29, 1815, when Newstead had been put up for auction. It was to this last will that he added the codicil of November 17, 1818.[4]

The basic provision of the 1815 will — "my dear wife Lady Byron and any children I may have being otherwise amply provided for" and George Anson Byron being quietly dropped — was that whatever could be realized from the sale of Byron's property after his death should go to Augusta Leigh or, after her death, to her children.

1. William H. Marshall, "The Byron Will of 1809," *The Library Chronicle*, Friends of the Library, University of Pennsylvania, XXXIII (Spring 1967), 97–114, from which much of the information in this Commentary has been drawn.

2. Marshall, "The Byron Will," pp. 103–109, prints the will of 1809 for the first time and surveys the later ones in the perspective it affords. At least one earlier will existed, before Byron's maturity, presumably drawn up by his mother through her solicitor, John Hanson.

3. Marshall, "The Byron Will," p. 101. On the proposed sale of Newstead to Claughton, see sc 567 and Commentary.

4. Both the 1815 will and the 1818 codicil were printed, almost verbatim in the case of the codicil, in an Appendix to Thomas Moore's *Letters and Journals of Lord Byron: with Notices of His Life* (London, 1830), II, 820–823.

SC 506 Byron's illegitimate daughter by Claire Clairmont, provided for in the codicil, was born on January 12, 1817, and named Alba by Claire.[5] Disapproving of the mother and her milieu — as well as of his own — Byron insisted upon the name used in the codicil, Allegra Biron. (Alba sounded uncomfortably close to Albé, Claire's nickname for Byron himself.) On the day after the child's first birthday he wrote a letter to his banker friend Douglas Kinnaird expressing, and disguising, his feelings in banker's terms:

Shelley (from *Marlow*) has written to me about my daughter, (the last bastard one), who, it seems, is a great beauty; and wants to know what he is to do about sending her. I think she had better remain till spring; but will you think of some plan for remitting her here, or placing her in England? I shall acknowledge and breed her myself, giving her the name of Biron (to distinguish her from little Legitimacy [Annabella's daughter, Ada]), and mean to christen her Allegra, which is a Venetian name.[6]

His idea was to have her educated "in a Venetian convent, to become a good Catholic, and (it may be) a *Nun*, being a character somewhat wanted in our family."[7]

When the child was one, Claire (for mixed motives, as Byron sensed) agreed to send her to him — thinking "How kind & gentle you are to Children!"[8] — and accepted the name he had chosen (adding a variant of her own), taking her to a London church to be baptized "Clara Allegra Byron" on March 9, 1818.[9] Byron, when she was brought to him in Venice in May, grew quickly fond: ". . . she is very pretty, remarkably intelligent, and a great favourite with every body; but, what is remarkable, much more like Lady Byron than her mother . . . very blue eyes, and that singular forehead, fair curly hair, and a devil of a Spirit — but that is Papa's."[10]

He nevertheless could see no happy future for her as English, whether in Claire's (and the Shelleys') society or in his own; so when she was

---

5. As soon as Shelley heard of Claire's pregnancy, he put her child into his own will (June 1816). For his probable reasons (and the will) see sc 333 and Commentary (IV), especially IV, 714.

6. Venice, January 13, 1818, Byron, *Correspondence*, II, 65.

7. To Augusta Leigh, May 27, 1817, Byron, *Letters and Journals*, IV, 124.

8. Claire to Byron, January 12, 1818, quoted in Marchand, *Byron*, II, 731.

9. Marchand, *Byron*, II, 732. See sc 437, Commentary.

10. Byron to Augusta, August 3, 1818, Byron, *Letters and Journals*, IV, 250.

SC 506   four, though he talked no longer of her becoming a nun, he did send her to school in a convent at Bagnacavallo, near Ravenna. He believed that ". . . to allow the child to be with her mother and with them and their principles would be like absolute insanity if not worse; that even her health would not be attended to properly. . . ."[11] (The deaths of the Shelleys' Clara in 1818 and William in 1819 had not inspired confidence.) He would not "give a *natural* child an *English* education, because with the disadvantages of her birth, her after settlement would be doubly difficult. Abroad, with a fair foreign education and a portion of five or six thousand pounds, she might and may marry very respectably. In England such a dowry would be a pittance, while elsewhere it is a fortune. It is, besides, my wish that she should be a Roman Catholic, which I look upon as the best religion, as it is assuredly the oldest of the various branches of Christianity."[12]

The will of 1815 and this codicil were in effect at the time of Byron's death on April 19, 1824, but Allegra had died almost exactly two years earlier at the age of five.[13] Thus the sum she was to have inherited from her father simply became, as he had directed, "part of the residue of [his] personal Estate. . . ."

A detailed account of the aggravation Byron experienced while cajoling and coercing John Hanson into delivering this codicil (together with other legal documents) to Venice for his signature would double the length of this commentary. The story unfolds in Byron's letters to Charles and John Hanson and to Douglas Kinnaird and Hobhouse, April 15, 1818, and following.[14] Most of the legal documents were, of course, drawn up in England, but where the codicil was drawn up is less clear. The paper upon which it is written is of English manufacture, though the watermark might at first suggest otherwise. John Abbott Dusautoy owned a paper mill in Hampshire in the 1790's and, though Shorter loses track of him in the early 1800's,[15] this example shows that

11. To Richard Hoppner, April 3, 1821, quoted in Marchand, *Byron*, II, 904.

12. Quoted in Marchand, *Byron*, II, 905.

13. April 20, 1822, Marchand, *Byron*, III, 992.

14. See Byron, *Letters and Journals*, IV, 225–268; Byron, *Correspondence*, II, 79–91.

15. Alfred H. Shorter, *Paper Mills and Paper Makers in England, 1495–1800* (Hilversum, Holland: The Paper Publications Society, 1957), pp. 172–173.

East India Company cipher (SC 503)

*Leigh Hunt's seal:
Angel with olive branch
following serpent (SC 474)*

Pan and a satyr (SC 502)   *Classical head (SC 419)*

*Shelley's seal:
Judgment of Paris (SC 407)*

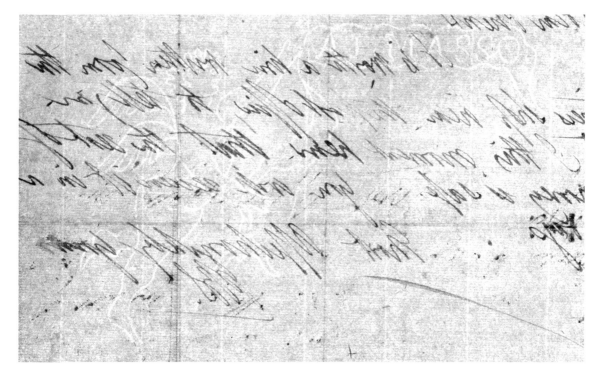

Cherub holding banner aloft (SC 553)

Byron's signature and seal (SC 506)

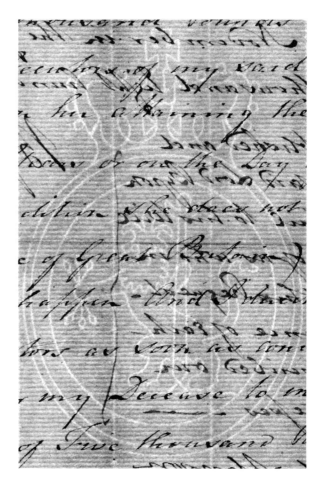

Lion in crowned oval (SC 506)

SC 506   the family remained in the papermaking business into 1817. This watermark (see page 753 for facsimile) had begun as the "Arms of the Seven
Provinces" of the Netherlands. In the eighteenth century, when Dutch
paper was the best in the world, other papermakers began to adopt — or
adapt — the standard Dutch watermarks, as here where the figure is
altered by reducing the number of "darts" (or arrows) in the lion's left
forepaw from seven (the number of the United Provinces) to three (for
England, Scotland, and Ireland).[16]

16. W. A. Churchill, *Watermarks in Paper . . . in the XVII and XVIII Centuries . . .* (Amsterdam: Menno Hertzberger, 1935), pp. 28–29.

SC 507   EDWARD DUBOIS TO T. L. PEACOCK, NOVEMBER 18, 1818

AL signed *Edw. DuBois–*, 2 pages. Double sheet, 4to (9.9 x 7.9 inches).
Laid paper. Watermark: W T| 1815|.
Seal (trace): ?wafer, red.
Notation, in pencil, page 4: *DuBois| 1818|*.
Additions: letter is badly stained and edges are curled.

PROVENANCE: Thomas Love Peacock; Edith Nicholls Clarke; Mrs. K. Hall Thorpe (Sotheby, November 15, 1949, lot 499).

Temple. Novr 18· 1818.

Dear Sir,

    *I was sitting here when I received your present, and I call Horace
Smith to witness whether my Chambers would at all disgrace any part of*
5   *Night-mare Abbey; and "woe to the inhabitants of the earth, for the Devil—."
that is, my door was open to any Attorney that might please to come in.
Every thing consistent and suitable, for no Attorney coming, I was, as Master
Mathew says "melancholy and Gentlemanlike," and perfectly prepared for
an incubus, except that my stomach was, by the absence of the Attorney & his*
10 *fee, rather empty.—With all this agreeable preparation for the enjoyment of
the Blue Devils, I was, but not grievously, disappointed—as thus: I read your
little work and it afforded me much entertainment   You have the advantage
of Shakespeare's Caller, for you called my spirits, which were sunk vastly
deep before, and they came. The best compliment I can pay you is one that*

DuBois to Peacock   *November 18, 1818*

SC 507   *has almost rusted in my keeping, for tho' I read and read, I rarely have cause or the heart to use it— I mean the wish for <u>more</u>.*

     The <u>Conclusion</u> of course displeased me, but not only for that reason, but because it is flat, and without that Castronerià or simplicité niaise, which would, under circumstances, have made a better wind up. I speak merely of

20   *what follows the second Lady's letter p. 217—I would have had it something in this way——*

       [The Letters dropping from his paralyzed ~~han~~ fingers, Scythrop fell into his chair, and fixing his eyes on the pistol, remained motionless, and deaf to the plaintive agony of his fond, distracted parent. The

25   *Abbey clock struck Ten. Suddenly starting from his seat he, at one and the same ~~time~~ moment, seized his father's hand with his right, and with his left a candlestick, and saying "Good night, Sir," went to Bed.]*

     In the former part of my correspondence, I feared that you had thought

30   *me rude, but I am as glad as any rogue could be on a different occasion, that I did you injustice. I envy you your literary retreat & devotion—as Pliny writes to Rufus "humiles et sordidas curas aliis mandas", or as Pope would have addressed you (<u>after dinner</u>) "<u>Awake</u> my St John, leave all meaner things &^c"*

35   *What you have done is well, but I believe you equal to "quid majus"— gird your loins, and put out your right arm— effinge aliquid et excude quod sit perpetuo tuum: nam reliqua rerum tuarum post te alium atque alium dominum sortientur. Nac nunquam tuum desinet esse. Scio quem animum, quod horter ingenium.*

40   *Vale.*
                 Edw. DuBois–

[Address, page 4]
For the Author of
      Nightmare Abbey.
By favor of T. Hookham Esqr

---

line 5. *Night-mare*: g written through indecipherable letters.

line 18. *Castronerià*: the accent should have been

omitted; both this word and the French phrase
signify stupidity.

line 31. *your*: y written through ?*ag.*

The Carl H. Pforzheimer Library

SC 507   ANY DISAPPOINTMENT that Peacock may have felt at Edward Du-
Bois' remarks on *Rhododaphne* (see SC 480, SC 481 and Commentary) did not dissuade him from sending DuBois a copy of his next
production. *Nightmare Abbey* had been printed by September 15, for in
a letter of that date Peacock tells Shelley how the two mottoes had been
arranged.[1] Peacock sent a copy to Shelley in a box dispatched about
November 12–14,[2] and perhaps he also instructed Hookham to send out
a few complimentary copies of the novel at that time.

   Nightmare Abbey was probably much to the taste of DuBois, him-
self best remembered for *St. Godwin* (1800; a parody of Godwin's *St.
Leon*); *Old Nick: A Satirical Story in Three Volumes* (1801); and *My
Pocket-Book* (1807; a satire on Sir John Carr's travels). But even though
DuBois may have been temperamentally disposed to prefer *Nightmare
Abbey* to *Rhododaphne*, his enthusiastic praise of Peacock's novel and
the hearty encouragement he gave the author to write more in the same
vein attests as well to his basic good taste.

   One feature of SC 507 that holds interest because of its unwitting
irony is DuBois' envy of Peacock's "literary retreat & devotion" (line
31). He exhorts the author of *Nightmare Abbey*, in words drawn both from
the opening of Pope's *Essay on Man* and from Pliny's letter to Caninius
Rufus,[3] to abandon all mundane concerns and devote himself entirely to
writing comic novels. Peacock, however, was — like DuBois himself —
feeling rather empty for the want of a fee (lines 9–10), and not too long
after he received this letter, he received equally heartening and far more
material encouragement to write more in the manner of "Ryotwar &
Zemindarry Settlements" (see "Peacock in Leadenhall Street" and
SC 503).

---

1. Peacock, *Works*, VIII, 204–205.

2. See Peacock's letter of November 29 (*Works*, VIII, 208).

3. *Epistles*, Book I, iii. The portions DuBois quotes (lines 32, 36–39) have been translated: "[leave]
the law and sordid pursuits of life to others . . . . Mold and fashion something that shall be really and
for ever your own. All your other possessions will pass on from one master to another; *this* alone,
when once it is yours, will for ever be so. As I well know the temper and genius of him whom I am
exhorting" (*The Epistles of Pliny, as Translated by William Melmoth*, ed. Clifford H. Moore, Boston:
The Bibliophile Society, 1925, I, 5–6).

SC 508   LADY BYRON TO REVEREND RICHARD WALLIS, NOVEMBER 27, 1818

AL signed *Al Byron*, 2½ pages. Double sheet, 4to (9 x 7.4 inches).
Laid paper. Watermark: T BARRATT| 1818|.
Seal: wax, black: *A I B*|.
Postal fee: 11.
Postmark: (mileage stamp): HINCKLEY| 100|.
Additions: 1. (pages 3–4): irregular tear, beginning at seal tear, two thirds
through leaf; 2. (top corners of page 3): two stickers in the shape of small red
hearts, used to attach manuscript to album leaf; 3. (corners of page 4): four
triangular paste marks.
PROVENANCE: Parke-Bernet, October 17, 1961, lot 32.

> *Kirkby*
> *Nov. 27th 1818.*

Dear Sir,

    I have had the pleasure of receiving your letter, and request you
5 *to appropriate the money to the purpose which you think most eligible, and*
which appears to me altogether desirable —
It gives me great satisfaction to find that the state of the School is so prosper-
ous, and approved by yourself & family — The instruction at night may be
very advantageous —— Margaret Johnston informed me that it had been
10 *suggested by Miss Wallis's as a desirable addition that prayers should be*
read when the School opened and closed. The idea was not new to me, though
I wished to defer the introduction of that regulation till I had observed its
effect on some similar institutions, and had learned the most judicious man-
ner of establishing it – for it is too often found that these duties are regarded
15 *as mere forms, unless the prayers are wisely adapted to the circumstances,*
and administered with due authority & impression. But I shall not forget
to make those enquiries, and shall hope to be assisted by your opinions —
    Something was also mentioned to me by the Schoolmistress respecting the
work– I should think that the arrangement which gave most satisfaction to
20 *the parents would be that most conducieve to the success of the School–*
    My father & mother join me in kind regards to your family circle, & be-
lieve me

> *My dear Sir, with every friendly wish,*
> *Yours very sincerely*
> *Al Byron*

25

Byron to Wallis *November 27, 1818*

SC 508 [Address, page 4]

North

> *The Revd R. Wallis*
>> *Seaham*
>>> *Castle Eden*

line 10. *Miss Wallis's*: perhaps Lady Byron in-tended to write *the Miss Wallises*.

line 14. *establishing*: first four letters written through smudged-out *?impre*.

line 15. *the prayers*: *e* of *the* written through *ey* which was erased.

line 20. *conducieve* (sic).

THIS LETTER of Lady Byron's from Kirkby Mallory in Leicestershire, her parents' home since the autumn of 1815, to the Reverend Richard Wallis, Vicar of Seaham — the place (see SC 250, III) which had been her home since infancy — supplies more evidence than hitherto known about her "design of establishing a village school"[1] at this time. "There is no record of her having then carried out the idea," states Ethel Mayne, though Annabella had written to William Frend about it.[2] But this letter indicates the existence of a school and schoolmistress sufficiently real to have been visited and consulted by Annabella and by the Wallis family. They have reported the school, still obviously in an experimental state, to be prospering. The vicar[3] is being granted some discretion in the outlay of funds supplied by Lady Byron, Kirkby, after all, being some 150 miles from Seaham;[4] and his daughters (the Miss Wallises?) have been encouraged to make suggestions, though these are rather coolly received; but Annabella is firmly in command and she writes as a practical educationist, preparing to investigate "some similar institutions" for pointers on regimen and method.

1. Ethel Colburn Mayne, *The Life and Letters of Anne Isabella, Lady Noel Byron* (London, 1929), p. 330, quoting William Frend's answer to a letter of Lady Byron's from Kirkby some time in 1818.

2. Mayne, *Lady Byron*, p. 330; she notes that Frend had established a Sunday school at Madingley, near Cambridge. It was not, though, "the first of all."

3. It had been Wallis who had baptized Anne Isabella Milbanke on May 17, 1792; he had assisted at the wedding, held at Seaham, January 2, 1815. The "Castle Eden" of the address was a sumptuous turreted mansion built by a banker's son in 1780. For an amusing account of a visit to it that year by Judith Milbanke, Annabella's mother, see Malcolm Elwin, *The Noels and the Milbankes* (London, 1967), p. 158.

4. Wallis has apparently indicated a "most eligible" purpose, and she is agreeing to it as "desirable."

Shelley and his Circle : Manuscripts

SC 508 The school in question cannot have been the simple Sunday reading class which it was fashionable for ladies bountiful to bestow upon the children of the poor. Annabella had or was developing ideas of vocationally utilitarian education on principles of social equality (with some blind spots). The "instruction at night" and arrangements to be made "respecting the work" of the children must be interpreted in the context of recent educational experiments about which Lady Byron's close adviser Henry Brougham had prepared an article for publication in the December issue of the *Edinburgh Review*.[5] Her own later article on the "History of Industrial Schools"[6] will take us to the heart of her interest in these experiments.

When the Swiss educator Henry Pestalozzi had recovered from his failure to become a preacher and had seen the economic collapse of his otherwise successful school for the orphans of Unterwalden, formed in 1798, his vision of a juvenile educational community "gave a distinct and tangible form to his deep inward longing to serve his fellow-creatures; it became the subject of his dreams and of all his plans, and he seized upon whatever promised to bring him nearer to the desired end with the eagerness of a shipwrecked mariner who grasps the frailest plank which the storm casts within his reach."[7] Thus Annabella interpreted the longings of Pestalozzi and his more orderly minded (and more Annabellan) co-worker Emanuel de Fellenberg of the Hofwyl school, which was the main subject of Brougham's article. She, too, in desperation after the failure of her efforts to reform a willful or insane husband and the wreck of their marriage, had grasped at the opportunity to serve her fellow creatures through education, and it was she — hardly the Swiss reformers — who looked upon it as, emotionally, a frail plank for her own survival.

In 1816 her form of respite from the battle of the separation had been, briefly, to join a clergyman's family in visits to "deserving cot-

5. With a sequel in October 1819. The *Edinburgh Review* "for December" would be issued some time in January, but the article must have been written before the date of Lady Byron's letter. For Brougham see *Shelley and his Circle*, IV, 643 ff.

6. Printed as Appendix IV in Mayne, *Lady Byron*, pp. 479–492; it was written after "the political events of 1845–1848" (p. 491).

7. Lady Noel Byron, "History of Industrial Schools"; Mayne, *Lady Byron*, p. 480.

The Carl H. Pforzheimer Library

SC 508   tagers.''[8] She had always had a streak of the pious — but also a tendency to contemn it as "pye-house"[9] when it was empty of practical good. After the devastating storm of Byron's death (in 1824) and her immediate devoting of herself to "help and comfort all (not connections merely) who need," she gave her attention, completely at times, to "much intercourse and correspondence with the prominent philanthropists, educational reformers, enthusiasts in the Co-operative Movement."[10] In 1828 she got to Switzerland, visited the Hofwyl school itself, and was so well impressed that she made arrangements to place as apprentice teachers two young Noel cousins.[11] On her return to England she first plunged into a cooperative scheme for the fishing village of Hastings, but that failed and she reached a separation from the Cooperative Movement a year later. Parties ran "too high!" Adults, perhaps, were immune to the modifications of human character which she still believed possible "in the first stages of life."[12] She settled for a while in London, taking a house at Hanger Hill, "with a large vacant room in which she proposed to set up a school," the children to be taught useful and delightful employments and to be freed from the caste of class, as would her own family, by association.[13] By 1834 she had mastered the essentials conducive to success, and the school for vagrant children that she established at Ealing Grove, Middlesex, throve until 1852.[14]

Pestalozzi's system of education was based on sense perception (*Anschauung*), but de Fellenberg, much to Lady Byron's liking, added action to perception, involving his pupils and teachers in physical, chiefly agricultural, work. To return to the 1818 letter, we must understand that the arrangements to be made with parents "respecting the work" refer not simply to schoolwork but to baking, churning, gardening, and so

---

8. Mayne, *Lady Byron*, p. 244; see also "'Fare Thee Well'—Byron's Last Days in England," *Shelley and his Circle*, IV, 642.

9. Mayne, *Lady Byron*, p. 244. Compare her reactions to speeches at a London meeting in 1820 on prison reform (pp. 291–292).

10. Mayne, *Lady Byron*, pp. 298, 326. At the news of Byron's death she felt "a *desert* spread before" her (p. 298).

11. Mayne, *Lady Byron*, p. 330.

12. Mayne, *Lady Byron*, pp. 328–329. The last quotation is from a letter of 1830.

13. Mayne, *Lady Byron*, p. 323.

14. Mayne, *Lady Byron*, pp. 330–331.

SC 508 forth as the particular parents might wish.[15] The intellectual part of education, if "wisely adapted to the circumstances," might or might not include daily prayers.[16] The essential principle, she came to stress, was "that the same means which renders the individual capable of self-support, namely his development as a worker, should be made the chief agent in his education. . . ."[17]

15. At the Hanger Hill school, children were to be taught, "besides the usual things, baking, churning, simple cookery, 'which, in rotation, would furnish delightful employments.'" (Mayne, *Lady Byron*, p. 323.) At Hofwyl, when de Fellenberg had developed both a school for the poor and a school for upper-class children, need arose for "various artizans such as wheelwrights, carpenters, joiners, blacksmiths, wood- iron- and leather-workers, mechanics, shoemakers and tailors; and the pupils of the lower school who were desirous of learning had therefore a wide field of choice open to them . . . without being obliged to abandon or neglect the other course of instruction." (Lady Byron, in Mayne, p. 487.)

16. For her view of morning and evening prayers as counterproductive in their effect on servants, see Mayne, *Lady Byron*, p. 338.

17. Lady Byron, "History of Industrial Schools," Mayne, *Lady Byron*, p. 489, italicized passage.

SC 509 T. L. PEACOCK TO T. J. HOGG, DECEMBER 15, 1818

AL signed *T. L. Peacock.*, 1 page. Double sheet, 4to (8.9 x 7.3 inches). Wove paper. Watermark: VALLEYFIELD| 1816|. Impressed stamp: [crown]| BATH|.
Seal: wax, black: [peacock]|.
Postal fee: 7.
Postmarks: 1. (mileage stamp): MARLOW| [33]|; 2. (morning duty stamp, London): c| 16 DE 16| 1818|.
Notation, page 4: *10/8.*

PROVENANCE: Thomas Jefferson Hogg; Prudentia Hogg Lonsdale; John Ewer Jefferson Hogg; Major R. J. Jefferson Hogg (Sotheby, July 26, 1948, lot 278).

My dear Hogg

I shall be most exceedingly glad to see you. I should have written before, but I purposed to write a long letter, in which the gods always frustrated my designs: and I was on the point of writing laconically to en-
5 *treat you to come down, when your letter very agreeably anticipated my purpose. You will find on your arrival here shoals of news from Shelley. Adieu*

The Carl H. Pforzheimer Library

Peacock to Hogg   *December 15, 1818*

SC 509 *till Saturday, when I shall listen for the wheels of the heavy, while the tea-kettle sings on the hob.*

Yours ever truly,

10 *Marlow– Dec– 15 – 1818.*   *T. L. Peacock.*
Bring the next Saturday's Cobbett with you. I have had all the others.

[Address, page 4]
T. J. Hogg Esqr
    1 Garden Court
      Temple
15   *London.*

line 4. *frustrated*: first *r* written through ?*or*. *designs*: the final *s* was originally only a thick stroke; then Peacock added a loop to make the letter more legible.

HERE IS another of Peacock's brevities, written in expectation of seeing his friend. The gods who frustrated his intention of writing a long letter would appear to have been gods of inventiveness, study, and brainwork. In the three months since his September letter to Hogg, Peacock had been very much occupied, exercising two different faculties of his mind. Transposing his element of contemporary satire into the medieval world, he had been busy on *Maid Marian*, and told Shelley on November 29, "I am writing a comic Romance of the Twelfth Century, which I shall make the vehicle of much oblique satire on all the oppressions that are done under the sun."[1] By the end of December he had written all but the last three chapters; and this was remarkable, considering the very different task he had faced and finished. Indian Land Revenue was a newer and more technical subject to tackle than the friars and outlaws of Sherwood Forest; and the unfamiliar terms connected with it had to be learned, rather than joyously invented after the manner of his "philotheoparoptesism" (which he annotates in *Maid Marian* as "Roasting by a slow fire for the love of God"). His success with this pragmatic undertaking has already been noted.[2]

With all this, Hogg was to have his usual welcome of a singing tea-kettle on its hotplate when — it being unseasonable for the long walk —

1. Peacock, *Works*, VIII, 209.
2. See "Peacock in Leadenhall Street," p. 709, above.

[762]

SC 509   he should arrive by the London coach. "Shoals of news from Shelley" is no exaggeration: Shelley had written to Peacock from Este, October 8; from Ferrara, November 6–7; from Bologna [November 9, undated]; from Rome, November [20]. These were all long descriptive travel letters, dwelling in detail on landscape, art and architecture, as well as giving personal news.[3] On the same day as this letter to Hogg was written, Peacock replied to the two letters from Bologna and Rome, delighting in the descriptions of paintings: "I read them to everyone who calls on me—not many to be sure . . ." He knew he would soon be reading them to Hogg. This was what Shelley expected, for he wrote to Hogg from Naples on December 21: "I consider the letters I address to Peacock as nearly the same things as a letter addressed to you."[4]

3. These letters, now in the Bodleian Library, were first published by Mary Shelley in Shelley, *Essays, Letters*, II, 141–168.

4. See sc 510.

SC 510   P. B. SHELLEY TO T. J. HOGG, DECEMBER 21, 1818

AL signed *PBS*., 3 pages. Double sheet, 4to (9.5 x 7.3 inches).
Laid paper. Watermark: NR| [written on banner held aloft by cherub]|.
Seal: wax, red: [Judgment of Paris]|.
Postal fees: 1. [indistinct]; 2. 1/11.
Postmarks: 1. NAP 1818| 22 DIC|; 2. ?*AP* [within double-rimmed oval]|; 2. (Foreign Post Office stamp, London): FPO| JA 9| 1819|; 4. [traces of two indistinct red postmarks or offsetting of stamps from another letter].
Notations, in pencil: 1. (page 1): *Copied?*|; 2. (page 1): *28*|; 3. (page 4): *Jan 9th 1819*|.

PROVENANCE: Thomas Jefferson Hogg; Prudentia Hogg Lonsdale; John Ewer Jefferson Hogg (Sotheby, July 27, 1922, lot 331). *De Ricci 398* (p. 134).

Naples Dec. 21· 1818

My dear Hogg

     I consider the letters I address to Peacock as nearly the same things as a letter addressed to you, as I know you see him at certain intervals,
5   *& they contain nothing but long accounts of my peregrinations which it would be wearisome to transcribe.— Since I last wrote to you I have been from Lucca to Venice, & from Venice, with the interval of a week at Rome to*

SC 510 *Naples, where I have at present a lodging opposite the sea. The more I see of*
this astonishing country the more do the wonders of nature the voluptuous
10   *softness of its climate, the wrecks of all that was most magnificent & lovely*
in antient art strike me with admiration. As Peacock will shew you I have
seen Rome, the bay of Baiæ, Vesuvius, the cataract of Terni; but Rome above
all delighted me, and from this Elysian shore surrounded by scenery at once
sublime and tranquil my thoughts point again to the majestic & eloquent
15   *desolation of what Corinna calls the "City of the Dead."*

     Are any of the Boinvilles returned, or do you hear any thing of them?
If the former, pray do not forget my remembrances to the respectable members
of the family. And Newton, is he come to Town? Tell him if you see him that
I should have much pleasure in seeing him on my return. I hear of you from
20   *Hunt. Do you often go there?*

     Your Kalleidoscope spread like the Pestilence at Livorno. A few weeks
after I sent your description to a young English Mechanist of that town, I
heard that the whole population were given up to Kalleidoscopism. It was
like the fever which seized the Abderites who wandered about the streets re-
25   *peating some verses of Euripides.   I saw Lord Byron at Venice; he is*
practising aphrodisaics at a great rate & I should think must be as tired as
Candide was of the mountain where the Deity is worshipped; but he will
not own it.

     The Opera house, St Carlos here, is very beautiful; but the boxes are so
30   *dear & the pit so intolerable that I fear we shall visit it but seldom. The*
scenery exceeds any thing of the same kind in theatrical exhibition I ever saw
before— The ballet is inferior to that of Milan, where that species of exhibi-
tion called a serious ballet is conducted with incomparable effect.-

     I do not like the Italian women; the men are, as the reviews say, ~~befo~~
35   *below critisism. They eat garlic; and are disgusting with ignorance & prosti-*
tution. There are towns, & classes in society where this, they say, is not the
case; & Florence is instanced; but Florence I have not visited & yet *in Naples*
I have no acquaintance—

40   *It will be difficult however to live contentedly in England again after the*
daily contemplation of the sublimest objects of antient art, & the sensations

SC 510 *inspired by the enchanting atmosphere which envelopes these tranquil seas &*
majestic mountains in its radiance. In Italy it is impossible to live con-
tented; for the filthy modern inhabitants of what aught to be a desart sacred
45 *to days whose glory is extinguished, thrust themselves before you forever.*
Adieu—   *We shall meet again soon*
Very affectionately yours
Pray tell me how your briefs   PBS.   *come in——*
N

[Address, page 4]
50 *T. Jefferson Hogg Esqr*
1 Garden Court
Temple
London
Inghilterra

55 *Angleterre*

line 21. *Kalleidoscope* (sic): see also line 23.
line 26. *aphrodisaics* (sic).
line 31. *kind*: the *d* seems to have been added later.
     in: *i* written through *I*.
line 35. *critisism* (sic).
line 36. *There*: *re* written through *y*.
     classes: may have been written *classess*.
line 38. *instanced;*: possibly semicolon is a comma.

line 42. *the*: *e* written through *?is*.
line 44. *filthy*: *y* written through and formed from some indecipherable letter.
     inhabitants: *i* written through *I*.
     aught (sic).
     desart: contemporary spelling.
line 49. *N*: probable reading; letter may be *F*. Shelley did not continue the word.
line 55. *Angleterre*: written perpendicularly to address in the left margin.

SHELLEY'S LETTERS to Hogg, Hunt, and his other English correspondents are nothing like his fine series of letters to Peacock that describe his journey from Este to Naples. Those descriptive letters were intended to serve as a permanent record of his impressions of notable artistic works and natural scenes along the way, as is clear from Mary's postscript to Shelley's letter to Peacock of November 9: "Take care of these letters because I have no copies & I wish to transcribe them when I return to England."[1] Having utilized two of Shelley's earlier travel letters to Peacock in *History of a Six Weeks' Tour*, the Shelleys may well

1. Shelley, *Letters*, II, 54.

SC 510   have thought of publishing parts of these letters of 1818. Peacock appreciated the value of the travel letters, for he wrote to Shelley:

> Your descriptions of painting are truly delightful; they make pictures more visible than I thought they could be made through the medium of words. I read them to everyone who calls on me . . . the general pleasure they give convinces me that if you bring home a journal full of such descriptions of the remains of art, and of the scenery of Italy, they will attract a very great share of public attention.[2]

With this enthusiastic encouragement, Shelley continued to send Peacock equally fine letters until the death of William Shelley, and he also began to make his notes on sculptures in the galleries of Rome and Florence.[3]

The mention of "Corinna's" description of Rome (line 15) alludes to Madame de Staël's *Corinne; ou l'Italie*, which Shelley and Mary read between December 12 and December 15, 1818.[4] The novel had been popular in England (there being at least two English translations by 1807[5]), and Shelley's rather oblique reference to it suggests that he assumed Hogg was familiar with it. (Perhaps both he and Hogg had read it early in their friendship as they had read Alfieri's autobiography.[6]) If, on the other hand, Shelley intended to mystify Hogg with pseudo-classical allusions, his reference to the Abderites reciting Euripides (lines 24–25) ought to have been successful, for it comes from C. M. Wieland's *Die Abderiten* (The Abderites), in which Wieland satirizes life in a small provincial German town under the guise of ancient Abdera.[7]

Hogg had sent Shelley a letter (no longer extant), which reached him at Leghorn, containing the description of a kaleidoscope. Henry Reveley (the "young English Mechanist") proceeded to build one. By

2. December 15, 1818, Peacock, *Works*, VIII, 211.

3. For Shelley's surviving notes, see Shelley, *Complete Works*, VI, 309–332, and 375–379.

4. Mary Shelley, Journal; Corinne refers to Rome as "la patrie des tombeaux" ("land of tombs") in her extempore effusion at the Capitol, Book II, chapter III.

5. The preface to the five-volume translation by D. Lawler (London: Corri, 1807) alludes to a rival translation already published.

6. See Shelley's review of Hogg's *Memoirs of Prince Alexy Haimatoff*, Shelley, *Complete Works*, VI, 177.

7. See Derek Maurice Van Abbé, *Christoph Martin Wieland (1733–1813)* (London, 1961), pp. 116–126. The Shelleys appear to have read the novel in French (Mary Shelley, *Journal*, pp. 97, 114).

Shelley to Hogg   **December 21, 1818**

SC 510   June 21, 1818, Maria Gisborne wrote to Mary, "Kaleidoscopism is at this moment with us in a most triumphant state . . .''[8] Shelley, who seems not to have written to Hogg since April 30 (SC 479), now belatedly thanks him for the information on the optical toy.

Shelley reiterates his negative reactions to Italian women (first expressed in SC 479), perhaps here to reinforce his criticism of Byron's "aphrodisaics" (line 26). Shelley expressed much more vigorous condemnation of Byron's encouragement of "sickening vice" in his letter to Peacock written three or four days prior to December 21,[9] and he may have softened his tone here because he was unsure that Hogg would share his own moral perspective on the matter. (One recalls Shelley's unfavorable comments on the views toward prostitution in Hogg's *Memoirs of Prince Alexy Haimatoff*.) Shelley may also have been brief simply because Hogg could read a longer account of Byron's behavior in Shelley's recent letter to Peacock.

The San Carlo opera house at Naples was, at the time of Shelley's visit, a controversial building less than two years old. The old San Carlo, opened in 1737, had been destroyed by fire on February 13, 1816. The new theater of the same name was opened on January 12, 1817. Stendhal, for one, had great hopes for the new opera house but was cruelly disappointed. On March 19, 1817, he wrote:

The *San-Carlo*, indisputably, has the status of a patriotic symbol for the good people of Naples. . . . But here is the truth, plain and unvarnished: the *San-Carlo*, considered as an *instrument for making music* bears absolutely no comparison with la Scala. Gradually, as the masonry dries out, its acoustics may grow less muffled; on the other hand, all the bright glitter of gilt-work which was applied too early to the still-damp surfaces of the rough-cast plaster ornamentation will soon grow hopelessly tarnished. The *décor* is the last word in banality, and moreover, offers no chance of improvement, since the effect is killed stonedead by the central chandelier. This same chandelier has another disastrous result: it throws the actors' faces into shadow.[10]

8. Gisborne, *Journals and Letters*, pp. 51–52. The kaleidoscope was invented by Sir David Brewster and patented in 1816; but because of a defect in the registration of that patent, the invention was pirated almost at once. In 1819 Brewster published *A Treatise on the Kaleidoscope* (see *DNB*).

9. Shelley, *Letters*, II, 57–58. G. Wilson Knight argues that Shelley's December letter hints at Byron's homosexuality (*Lord Byron's Marriage: The Evidence of Asterisks*, London, 1957, p. 224).

10. *Rome, Naples, and Florence*, trans. Richard N. Coe (New York, 1959), pp. 378–380.

Shelley to Hogg   *December 21, 1818*

sc 510 Stendhal, who knew more about opera houses than Shelley did, may have been right about the "beauty" of the Teatro San Carlo; he and Shelley were in agreement that the pit was intolerable.

The Shelleys seem to have been very lonely in Naples — as lonely as they had been during their early days in Turin and Milan.[11] The contrast between the conviviality of Lord Byron and the Hoppners in Venice and the Shelleys' relative lack of "acquaintance" in Naples (line 39) brought home more forcefully their isolation, as had a similar situation at Bagni di Lucca, when compared with the Gisbornes' society at Leghorn.

The Shelleys were not, of course, literally without all social communication during their three months at Naples (December 1, 1818–February 28, 1819). Charles MacFarlane records how as a young man he casually met Shelley in the Royal Museum at Naples (the "Studii" of Mary's Journal), and how the next morning he was introduced to Shelley by "Mr. Roskilly, an English medical practitioner who had married a Sicilian wife and settled down in Naples."[12] Mary Shelley's Journal for February 14, 1819, records: "Dr. Roskilly dines with us." Roskilly was almost certainly the "English surgeon" mentioned by both Mary and Shelley in letters of late January and February 1819, who was treating Shelley for "a disease of the liver."[13] The only house in Naples which the Shelleys are known to have visited was that of Madame Falconet, where they spent the evening of January 1 (Mary Shelley, Journal). M. Falconet was Shelley's banker;[14] Madame Falconet may have had soirées for the bank's foreign customers.

But even these brief social encounters at Naples came later than this

11. See Shelley to Peacock, April 20, 1818, Shelley, *Letters*, II, 6.

12. Charles MacFarlane, "Percy Bysshe Shelley" in *Reminiscences of a Literary Life*, ed. John F. Tattersall (New York, 1917), pp. 1–12. MacFarlane (December 1799–1858) would have been only eighteen when he met Shelley, and because he did not write these reminiscences until thirty-seven years later, we must exercise caution in using the details of his account.

13. Shelley, *Letters*, II, 76; Frederick L. Jones, "Mary Shelley to Maria Gisborne: New Letters, 1818–1822," *Studies in Philology*, LII (January 1955), 48. Jones's theory (Shelley, *Letters*, II, 76 fn.) that this was "Dr. J. Bell" is unsupported by any evidence that Dr. John Bell (1763–1820; *DNB*) was even in Naples at this time.

14. See Mary Shelley, *Letters*, I, 60.

Godwin to Collier   *February 6, 1819*

SC 510 letter.[15] By December 21 Shelley was obviously recalling nostalgically the companionship of Peacock, Hogg, and other friends in England. In this mood, Shelley's thoughts returned to John Frank Newton and the Boinvilles (lines 16–19), who were at the center of the first truly congenial intellectual society that he had known as an adult.

This letter to Hogg becomes, when its scattered members are seen aright, a unified meditation on the contrast implied in its first and expressed in its last paragraph: Italy's glories are its climate and those "wrecks of all that was most magnificent & lovely in antient art"; England, on the other hand, contains intellectually stimulating friends like Peacock, Hogg, the Boinvilles, John Frank Newton, and Hunt. English expatriates in Italy live among stupid people like the Abderites, who copy without comprehension the inventions emanating from England (lines 21–25), or among corrupt people like the Venetians, who are over-clouding Byron's sun-like soul.[16] Morally and intellectually, all Italy seemed to Shelley in December 1818 to be a "City of the Dead."

15. Writing to Sophia Stacey, March 7, 1820 (Mary Shelley, *Letters*, I, 98–99), a year after leaving Naples, Mary Shelley looked back on their visit there with some nostalgia:

> I told you that you would find Naples more gay than any town in all Italy—than in all the world, I do believe.... Both Mr. Shelley and I are much concerned to hear of your ill-health. I should have thought that the divine air of Naples would have thawed the cold you got in Via Valfonda and have revived you. I never found my spirits so good since I entered upon *care* as at Naples, looking out on its delightful Bay.... Its temperature and fertility would, if men were free from evil, render it a faery habitation of delight—but as a Neapolitan said of it, "È un Paradiso abitato dai diavoli."

16. Lines 25–28. See "Lines written among the Euganean Hills," lines 167–205.

SC 511 WILLIAM GODWIN TO JOHN PAYNE COLLIER, FEBRUARY 6, 1819

AL signed *William Godwin*, 1¼ pages. Double sheet, 4ᵗᵒ (8.8 x 7.3 inches). Laid paper. Watermark: T EDMONDS| 1811|.
Seal: wafer, green.
Docket, address page: *W. Godwin| Feby 6. 1819|*.
Notation, address page: *Literary Autographs|*.

PROVENANCE: Rosenbach and Co., February 1954.

The Carl H. Pforzheimer Library

SC 511   *Skinner Street,*
                                                           Feb. 6, 1819.

    Dear sir

        I find in the Edinburgh Magazine for December last, pub-
5 *lished by Constable, an article entitled, On the English Dramatic Writers*
who preceded Shakespeare, & signed J P C. Some impertinent fellow sug-
gested to me that these were your initials, & that no person was so likely to
write on the subject as yourself.

    In this article I find these words, "Mr Chalmers has lately produced
10 *to view a copy of a Historical Play by Christopher Marlow, printed in 1595,*
from which it is perfectly evident that Shakespeare derived the most important
materials out of which he has constructed his Henry VI, Part. 3."

    Now, waving the conjecture of the impertinent gentleman above-men-
tioned, & whoever is the author of the article, into which I have no right to
15 *enquire, the reason of my troubling you, is to say, that I have an insatiable*
curiosity in these matters, & that you would afford me much gratification if
you could inform me, 1. in what form Mr Chalmers has produced to view the
play in question, 2. how I could be admitted to partake in the view thus pro-
duced, 3. which question is superseded, if I obtain a satisfactory answer to
20 *my second, whether Christophers Marlow's name appears at full length in*
the title-page to the said play?

            I am, my dear sir,
              very sincerely
               your friend & servant
25   *William Godwin*

    [Address, page 4]
    John Collier, Esq
      Bouverie Street

line 4. *Edinburgh*: *b* written through *g*.   line 20. *my*: written through word beginning
                                                    with *o*, perhaps *our*.

To the general student of literature the above letter appears to
contain one of the first recorded confrontations between the pre-
varicating imagination of John Payne Collier, the noted Shakespeare

SC 511   scholar and forger, and the Spirit of Truth, personified for this moment in William Godwin. Although on June 15, 1819, Collier, a reporter for the *Times*, suffered a fate common to parliamentary reporters of the day when he was summoned before the House of Commons "for misreporting a speech of Joseph Hume to the prejudice of Canning," and bound over to the Sergeant-at-Arms for the night, there is no earlier record of his scholarly acumen and/or integrity being challenged in the field of Elizabethan drama, where he was to gain such fame and notoriety.[1]

The point at issue in Godwin's letter is whether Christopher Marlowe wrote the historical drama entitled *The True Tragedie of Richard Duke of Yorke*, first published in 1595 and reprinted in 1600 and either 1608 or 1619. The only extant copy of the 1595 edition (now in the Bodleian[2]) belonged at this date to George Chalmers (1742–1825), a noted Scottish antiquary living in London. Though the anonymous play is now regarded as a corrupt version of Shakespeare's *III Henry VI*, many scholars of this period believed it to be a source of Shakespeare's play. By 1807 Chalmers had already argued in print that *The True Tragedie* was a play by Marlowe and that it had influenced Shakespeare.[3] Edmund Malone (1741–1812), the greatest Shakespeare scholar of the day,[4] concurred, as can be seen in the variorum edition of Shakespeare begun by Malone and published in 1821 by James Boswell the younger.[5]

Godwin's inquiry was probably directed to Collier (whose family Godwin had known for years[6]) on behalf of James Broughton. As we saw in SC 495, Godwin had taken an interest in that man's study of Marlowe's works. On January 19, 1819, Godwin noted in his Journal, "Call on Broughton," and this rival scholar is almost certainly the gentleman (twice termed "impertinent," probably for rhetorical effect)

1. On Collier (1789–1883), see *DNB*.

2. It is known as the "Pegge-Chalmers copy." See The Carl H. Pforzheimer Library Catalogue: *English Literature, 1475–1700* (Privately Printed, 1940), III, 914, item 885.

3. William Beloe, *Anecdotes of Literature and Scarce Books* (London: Rivington, 1807), I, 365.

4. For Malone, see *DNB*.

5. Malone's view of *The True Tragedie* is found at II, 315 ff. of the Shakespeare variorum of 1821. For this reference, as well as perspective on J. Payne Collier, we are grateful to Professor Arthur Freeman.

6. Collier's parents were close friends of Henry Crabb Robinson, the Lambs, and others of Godwin's circle.

?R. W. Hayward, Legal Opinion   *ca. February* 17, 1819

SC 511 who suggested that Collier was the author of the article in Constable's *Edinburgh Magazine.*[7]

In SC 511 Godwin demonstrates his usual healthy skepticism of authorities by asking Collier for unambiguous primary evidence to support his assertions. In so doing, Godwin appears to us to have been unfashionably correct in his attitude. Godwin followed up his note of inquiry by calling on "J P Collier" on February 15, 1819. He and Collier met again on March 10 and March 21.[8]

7. Collier's article, the first of an intermittent series that continued through February 1821, appeared in the *Edinburgh Magazine* (a continuation of the *Scot's Magazine*) 2nd Series, III (December 1818), 525–531. It was signed "I. P. C." but some later articles in the series carried other combinations of initials — "J. P. C." and "C. P. J." The statement in Collier's article that aroused Godwin's (and probably Broughton's) interest reads as follows: "the commentators were not in possession of the information which has since come to light; neither the punctilious Capel, the self-conceited Malone, the industrious Steevens, nor any other note-manufacturer had seen what Mr Chalmers has since produced to view,—a copy of a Historical Play by Christopher Marlow, printed in 1595, from which it is perfectly evident, that Shakespeare derived the most important materials out of which he constructed his Henry VI. Part. 3. . . ." (p. 527).

8. Godwin, Journal.

SC 512 ?R. W. HAYWARD TO WILLIAM GODWIN, LEGAL OPINION, CA. FEBRUARY 17, 1819

DOCUMENT unsigned, 2 pages. Double sheet, 4to (8.9 x 7.4 inches). Wove paper. Watermark: C WILMOTT| 1816|. Docket, page 4, in pencil: *Observations| on the 2| Agreements|.*

PROVENANCE: H. Buxton Forman (Anderson Galleries, Part II, April 26, 1920, lot 383); Brick Row Book Shop, "A Catalogue of Percy Bysshe Shelley," November 1922, lot 228; Hodgson's, June 20, 1929, lot 195.

1st Agreement

    The meaning of this agreement seems to be that Messrs Constable & Co^y were to risk the expence of Paper & Printing of the work as well as 500 pounds to the writer of the Novel on condition that they should have half

5   *the Profits —allowing the Profits had been ever so small it does not appear that they retained any right of reimbursement. They stipulate only that they shall pay him no farther profit until his share shall have amounted to more than 500 pounds ————*

Godwin to Constable & Co. **February 18, 1819**

SC 512

2ᵈ Agreement –

Mess*ʳˢ Constable & Coʸ having bought half the Profits of the Novel for 500 pounds- as mentioned in the first agreement –now purchase ¼ Share more of these supposed profits for £250– Though it is not here expressed yet

                                               said by Mʳ Constable that

as this agreement refers to the former, it will be ~~but fair to suppose~~ the profits

15   *must amount to 750 pounds on the three fourths that is 1000 pounds in all– before Mʳ Godwin can claim any more money for his his remaining fourth*

                 is

Share.——— But this ∧matter of inference only and not borne out by this 2ᵈ agreement which is <u>as it appears</u> a perfect purchase of Three fourths

20   *Profits leaving Mʳ Godwin to claim one fourth —— In this claim or settlement between parties it will be convenient to supposes Messʳˢ C & Coʸ the Publishers to be different from the <u>Purchasers</u> and on whom both parties make their claim —— Let us take it in both ways———*

1ˢᵗ Messʳˢ Constables Statement	*2ᵈ Mʳ Godwins Statement*
£	
Profits *1109 –16..5*	*Profits —£1109 . 16 . 5*
Pᵈ by Mʳ C. *750..———*	*¼ Share is £ 277.. 9 . 1*
balᶜᵉ of which *359..16..5*	*which belongs to Mʳ G. to balᶜᵉ the Bill,*
Mʳ G. has ¼—£ *89..19..1*	*Mʳ C holds of him the Account Curᵗ*
	being balanced by the 750 pounds for
	which Messʳˢ Constable & Coʸ bought the
	³⁄₄ Profits

25

30

    In either view ¼ of the Copies on hand as well as ¼ of the Copy right remain the property of Mʳ Godwin ———

line 16. *his his*: the first *his* is a catchword at the bottom of page 1 of the manuscript.

line 18. *not*: written through *?out*.

line 19. *Three*: *T* possibly lower case.

line 21. *supposes* (sic).

line 29. *Curᵗ*: abbreviation for *Current*.

SC 513   WILLIAM GODWIN TO CONSTABLE & CO., FEBRUARY 18, 1819

AL (copy) unsigned, 1 page. Page 1 of double sheet, 4ᵗᵒ (8.9 x 7.4 inches), containing also SC 514.
Wove paper. Watermark: C Wɪʟᴍᴏᴛᴛ| 1816|.
Docket, page 4, in pencil: *Mandeville*|.

SC 513 PROVENANCE: H. Buxton Forman (Anderson Galleries, Part II, April 26, 1920, lot 383); Brick Row Book Shop, "A Catalogue of Percy Bysshe Shelley," November 1922, lot 228; Hodgson's, June 20, 1929, lot 195.

Messrs Constable & Co   *Feb. 18, 1819*
   Gentlemen
       I have examined the accounts left with me by Mr Constable when he set off for Scotland.

5   *The sum total of profits is stated*   *£*   *s*   *d*
       by you at at————————   *1071 . 11 . 5*
       To this is to be added — for a mis-
       take in the charge of paper—
       being 283 reams instead of
10   *253————————*   *38 . 5 . ——*
         making —— 1109 . 16 . 5
      One fourth part of which is ——— - 277 . 9 . 1^{1/4}
By the last agreement, signed between me & Mr Constable Dec. 4, 1816, this fourth part is mine, & I have to request therefore that you will place it to
15 *my credit.*

       I am at the same time gratified to perceive that this sum will fully cover the two bills of mine for £ 130–5–2 each, falling due March 24, & April 24 respectively, which are in your hands: & I write thus early, that you may have time to take them out of circulation without the trouble of
20 *renewing them.*

       I shall be glad to hear from you in course, with your approbation of this statement, & am,
         Gentlemen,
           Yours, &c

SC 514 WILLIAM GODWIN TO ARCHIBALD CONSTABLE, FEBRUARY 18, 1819

AL (copy) unsigned, 1 page. Page 2 of double sheet, 4to (8.9 x 7.4 inches), containing also SC 513.
Wove paper. Watermark: C WILMOTT| 1816|.
Docket, page 4, in pencil: *Mandeville*|.

Shelley and his Circle: Manuscripts

SC 514   PROVENANCE: H. Buxton Forman (Anderson Galleries, Part II, April 26, 1920, lot 383); Brick Row Book Shop, "A Catalogue of Percy Bysshe Shelley," November 1922, lot 228; Hodgson's, June 20, 1929, lot 195.

Feb. 18, 1819

My dear sir

  On the other side you have my letter of business, which I thought might as well not be mixed with my feelings towards my friend &
5 *the hospitable host of Craig Leith.*

  You stole a march upon us all, in the sudden way in which you left town in December last. I was grieved to find, on looking back, that I had not seen you for more than a fortnight previous to your departure. I hope & trust the illness of your young folks, which I believe was the cause that
10 *shortened your stay, has left no permanent effects behind.*

  Remember me, I pray, with kindness to all my friends, Mr Davis, Mr Cadel, &c, &c, &c. If you see Fairley, have the goodness to tell him, that I got his letter of the 3rd instant, in which he announces that I shall hear from him again in a day or two with some important documents for my
15 *Answer to Malthus, but that these documents have not reached me to the present hour.*   *Believe me, very faithfully yours*

THE COMMENTARY to SC 376 discussed relations between Godwin and Archibald Constable up to the time of Constable's second marriage, February 12, 1818. In the year between that time and the quarrel over the division of the profits from *Mandeville*, there seems to have been normal communication between them, but the tenor of their relationship is difficult to gage in the absence of most of the correspondence.[1]

  When Constable made his annual visit to London in November and December 1818, Godwin saw him frequently and also wrote him some letters.[2] It seems likely that the possibility of Constable's publishing

1. Godwin wrote to Constable on February 18, July 20, August 3, and August 24, 1818 (Godwin, Journal). Of these letters only part of that of August 3 (which is described as "a letter of condolence on the death of Mrs. Robert Cadell") is published in *Archibald Constable*, II, 97.

2. Constable called on Godwin or was a guest at Skinner Street on November 1, 11, 12, 18, 30, and December 1; Godwin called on Constable on November 7 and 20 and December 5 and 16. Godwin records writing to Constable on November 17 and December 6, 1818. (Godwin, Journal.)

Godwin to Constable   *February* 18, 1819

SC 514 Godwin's answer to Malthus (which Godwin says in his Journal was first advertised on December 8, 1818) was discussed during this period. If so, either Constable did not wish to handle the book at all[3] or else he and Godwin could not arrive at satisfactory terms. In any case, Godwin's two letters of February 18, 1819 (of which SC 513 and SC 514 are Godwin's copies) show that Godwin was struggling to maintain a cordial personal relationship with Archibald Constable while he pressed his case regarding the division of profits from *Mandeville*.

SC 512 is an opinion by a solicitor on the legal significance of the two agreements between Godwin and Constable and Company for the publication of *Mandeville*.[4] This legal opinion, along with a draft of the letter Godwin sent to Constable (of which SC 513 is Godwin's copy), was probably authored by R. W. Hayward, Godwin's solicitor, and was very likely written out by one of his clerks. In the week preceding February 18, 1819, Hayward called on or met Godwin three times, the last date being February 17.

In SC 513 Godwin responds to the account of Constable and Company on the sales, profits, and division of profits from *Mandeville*, which were listed in a statement Constable left in London before returning to Scotland in December 1818. The draft from which Godwin copied SC 513 was probably executed by Hayward after he and Godwin discussed the interpretation of the two *Mandeville* agreements, very likely during the week preceding Godwin's dual letters of February 18. If they were written on separate sheets or different pages of a double sheet, Constable may have treated them as two distinct letters, keeping the personal one, which was published by his son,[5] and filing the business letter with the firm's records.

Godwin, according to his Journal, wrote to Constable again on March 24 and on April 26, 1819. On May 3 Godwin noted in his Journal: "Menace from Constable." Constable's "menace" was, apparently, a threat to have Godwin arrested for failing to redeem the two promissory notes falling due on March 24 and April 24, to which Godwin refers in SC 513. Godwin's reaction can be found in SC 522 and SC 523. Godwin's

3. See SC 376, Commentary.
4. For the texts of these two agreements, see SC 324 (IV) and SC 376.
5. *Archibald Constable*, II, 98.

SC 514 letters of March 24 and April 26 (not, so far as we know, extant) were probably reminders that he wished the bills to be paid in full from his share of the proceeds of *Mandeville*. But, as a comparison of sc 512 with sc 513 shows, Godwin and his counsel did not expect that his claims to a full £277.9.1 would be accepted without question. This claim was a bargaining position.

Constable, on the other hand, either felt that he, too, needed the strongest possible bargaining position — by putting Godwin under threat of arrest — or else he, like Shelley, had grown tired of the spectacle of the radical philosopher begging for mercy and special consideration when he was unable to fulfill *his* side of a contract,[6] and then turning on the patient and understanding party with imperious demands as soon as he detected some weakness in his creditor's position.

We do not know how Godwin and Constable finally resolved their dispute. Presumably they arrived at some mutually satisfactory division of profits from *Mandeville*, for there is no evidence in Godwin's Journal of further threats of arrest or litigation from Constable. But Godwin may have alienated the powerful Edinburgh publishing magnate and all those influential writers and editors who clustered around him. One must understand the way in which William Godwin, however much respected he might be for his writings, generated antipathy in his financial dealings in order to appreciate why the literary world did not rally as a man when Godwin finally lost the lawsuit that made him pay rent for his house in Skinner Street.[7]

APPENDIX

Godwin and Polidori's Vampyre

Godwin appears in a more edifying role — as well as one more relevant to literary studies — in letters, now in the Henry E. Huntington Library, to William Sherwood (of Sherwood, Neely, and Jones[8]) and Henry Colburn. John William Polidori's story *The Vampyre*, coincident

6. For Godwin's delays in completing *Mandeville*, see sc 376, Commentary.
7. See Brown, *Godwin*, pp. 339–355.
8. See "The Composition and Publication of *The Revolt of Islam*," p. 156.

SC 514   with its appearance in Colburn's *New Monthly Magazine* as the work of
Lord Byron,[9] was published as a separate volume by Sherwood, Neely,
and Jones.[10] According to the title page of the volume, it was "Entered
at Stationers' Hall, March 27, 1819." On April 3, Godwin wrote to
William Sherwood:[11]

Sir
    I find in the Preface to a Tale said to be by Lord Byron, called the Vampyre,
& which I understand to be published by you this day, a passage full of the
grossest & most unmanly reflections on my daughter. I have to request you
would instantly stop the publication, & I have no doubt from your known
liberality that you will immediately consent to this. A very trifling alteration
will remove the injury of which I have so much right to complain.

I am, sir,
your obliged & obedient serv[t]
William Godwin

Skinner Street
    Saturday, Apr. 3,
       twelve o'clock

9. *New Monthly Magazine*, XI (April 1, 1819), 193–206.

10. Henry R. Viets, in "The London Editions of Polidori's *The Vampyre*" (*Papers of the Biblio-graphical Society of America*, LXIII, 1969, 83–103), provides an invaluable analysis of the extant issues of *The Vampyre*, in addition to an account of the Polidori-Colburn quarrel over the attribution of the story to Byron. Viets identifies the following published versions: "O," a state by "Colburn and Co.," of which Viets has found no copy, but which he posits as a state naming Byron as author; "I," another "Colburn and Co." state, of which Viets has identified two copies, with both Byron's and Polidori's names; "II," the first Sherwood, Neely, and Jones issue, with Byron's name on the title page; "III," the second Sherwood issue, with no author listed; "IV," a third Sherwood issue with omissions in signature "A" demanded by Godwin. However, a different interpretation can be offered. Since the differences among I, II, and III involve only their title and half-title pages, one could — instead of positing an earlier Colburn issue (O) — argue that I is actually the issue subsequent to II, made up as a trial replacement for the issue that claimed Byron as author. Polidori's letters of April 2 to Colburn and of similar date to the *Morning Chronicle* (Polidori, *Diary*, pp. 15–19), indicate that Polidori, upon learning of Colburn's deception, forced suppression of the Sherwood issue that attributed the work to Byron (II); Colburn may then have contemplated issuing the work instead under his own imprint with both Byron's and Polidori's names on the title page (I). In the final arrangement, Colburn and Polidori could have agreed to have Sherwood act as publisher with no author named (III). If this analysis is correct, Viets's state "O" is a ghost.
    We should note in passing that Byron's *Waltz*, published pseudonymously in 1813, had been first printed in proofs with John Murray as the declared publisher, but — perhaps to hide the authorship more securely — the poem was finally published by Sherwood, Neely, and Jones (*Biblio-graphical Catalogue of . . . Lord Byron*, London: The First Edition Club, 1925, pp. 24–26).

11. From a photostat of the Ms., quoted by permission of the Henry E. Huntington Library.

SC 514   Sherwood obviously responded promptly, asking for the specific point of Godwin's complaint and his suggested remedy. At two o'clock Godwin replied:[12]

> Sir
>   The most radical & at the same time the simplest remedy to the grievance of which I complain, ~~would~~ will be the omission of the whole of the last two or three pages of the introductory Letter to the publication of the Vampire, beginning from the words, p. xiv, "I must, however, free him from one imputation attached to him — of having in his house two sisters, &c.
>   From what follows it is impossible not to infer that these sisters are the two ladies named at the bottom of that page. Now, though the imputation is here contradicted, every one knows that the bare mention of such an imputation is a most horrible scandal. Can any thing be grosser than to say that my daughter & her sister were reported to have lived in sensual intercourse, & in the house with Lord Byron? The writer of the letter now stands out to the world as the author of this scandal in print.
>   Give me leave to add that my daughter is the wife of Mr Percy Bysshe Shelley, a circumstance that no one would surmise from reading this letter.
>   I request you to inform me, the moment you are able to inform me, that the injury of which I complain has been removed.
>   I also beg that you would not suffer any copies to get out to the public till this scandal has been redressed.
>   I am, sir,
>   your obliged & obedient servant
>   William Godwin
>
> Skinner Street
>   Apr. 3, Saturday,
>   two o'clock

The passage that Godwin found offensive appeared in the anonymous "Extract of a Letter from Geneva" printed both in the *New Monthly Magazine* (which, apparently, Godwin had not seen) and in the original printings of *The Vampyre*. Speaking of Byron, the correspondent declares:

I must, however, free him from one imputation attached to him — of having in his house two sisters as the partakers of his revels. This is, like many other charges which have been brought against his lordship, entirely destitute of truth.

12. From a photostat of the Ms., quoted by permission of the Henry E. Huntington Library.

SC 514   His only companion was the physician I have already mentioned. The report originated from the following circumstance: Mr. Percy Bysshe Shelly, a gentleman well known for extravagance of doctrine, and for his daring, in their profession, even to sign himself with the title Αθεος in the Album at Chamouny, having taken a house below, in which he resided with Miss M. W. Godwin and Miss Clermont, (the daughters of the celebrated Mr. Godwin) they were frequently visitors at Diodati, and were often seen upon the lake with his Lordship, which gave rise to the report, the truth of which is here positively denied.

(pp.xiv–xv)

There was also, on page xvi, a reference to "Miss M. W. Godwin" as conceiving the idea for *Frankenstein* on the same occasion as *The Vampyre*.

Henry Colburn, the publisher of the *New Monthly Magazine*, was responsible for Sherwood's publication of *The Vampyre*, and on Tuesday, April 6, 1819, Godwin was obliged to write to him as follows:[13]

Skinner Street, Tuesday
Morning, 11 o'clock,
April 6.

Sir
I had some communication with Mr Sherwood on Saturday respecting a passage of which I had thought I had just right to complain, in an introduction to a tale called The Vampire. I applied to Mr Sherwood, because I found the name of his house in the title-page. In answer he very obligingly desired me to state the particulars of my complaint, which he would forward to the party for whom the piece was published, & he had no doubt that what had offended me would be redressed. I accordingly wrote to him those particulars at two o'clock on Saturday.

To-day he informs me that you are the party for whom the piece is published, that he sent my letter to you, & that he has not yet heard from you. Give me leave therefore to request that you would consider my letter sent to you by Mr Sherwood as addressed from me to you, & that you would immediately oblige me with an answer.

You must be fully aware, sir, that the mention of any members of my family can be of no use to your pamphlet. If you hesitate about the expence of a cancel, I am very willing, though I should think it not quite fair, to take that expence on myself.

I am, sir,
your most obedient servant
William Godwin

13. From a photostat of the Ms., quoted by permission of the Henry E. Huntington Library.

SC 514 In his Journal for April 6, Godwin notes: "H Corry, from Colburn, calls." The difficulty was remedied by the expedient of reprinting the entire first gathering (including half-title and title page), omitting the offending passage quoted above, as well as the references to M. W. Godwin and *Frankenstein* on page xvi of the earlier issues. This revised version of the front matter (Viets's IV) continues to include the anecdote of how "Mr. P.B. Shelly" reacted in horror to a reading of Coleridge's *Christabel* at Diodati. The issue was that from which the Galignani piracy was printed in 1819, and all evidence suggests that — though copies of the version containing the names of Mary and Claire may have been circulated to the reviewers, as Viets suggests (page 96) — Godwin fairly well succeeded in suppressing the allusions to Lord Byron's revels[14] with his two daughters except for the original printing in the *New Monthly Magazine*.

14. Viets errs in identifying Shelley as the man who was falsely rumored to have had "two sisters as the partakers of his revels" (p. 102).

SC 515 P. B. SHELLEY TO CHARLES OLLIER, FEBRUARY 27, 1819

AL signed *Percy B Shelley.*, 1 page. Double sheet, 4to (8.5 x 6.8 inches).
Watermark: [very indistinct lion]|; countermark: [lion on pedestal above cipher]| [?T] B|.
Seal: wax, red: [Judgment of Paris]|.
Postal fees: 1. [indistinct]; 2. 1/11.
Postmarks: 1. NAP 1819| 2 MAR|; 2. ?AP [within double rimmed oval]|; 3. FPO| MR 20 [1]819|.
Notations: (page 1, in pencil, below line 7): *1819*|; 2. (page 4, on address flap, in ink): [three words obliterated]|.

PROVENANCE: Charles Ollier (Puttick and Simpson, July 19, 1877, lot 67); F. Harvey; Sotheby, March 12, 1903, lot 173; Pearson; Sotheby, June 1, 1905, lot 514; Quaritch; Maggs; Walter T. Wallace (American Art Association–Anderson Galleries, March 22, 1920, lot 1192); Brick Row Book Shop; Rosenbach and Co. *De Ricci 404* (pp. 193–194).

Dear Sir
  Pray let me hear from you (addressed to Rome) on the several subjects of my last letter, & especially to inform me of the name of the ship &

Shelley to Ollier   **February 27, 1819**

SC 515   *the mode of address by which my box was sent. As yet I have no tidings*
of it.

Your obliged Servant
Percy B Shelley.

Naples, Feb. 27. 1818.
N. B.

10   *If you do not write within three months after the receipt of this, address*
as before Mrs Gisborne, Livorno.

[Address, page 4]
          Mr C. Ollier
              Book Seller
          Vere St.   Bond St.
15   *London*

Inghilterra

Angleterre

line 8. *27.*: *7* written firmly through beginning   line 11. *M^rs*: altered from *M^r* or vice versa.
of *8*.
                                                          line 17. *Angleterre*: written to the left of and per-
      1818. (sic).   pendicular to the address.
line 9. *N. B.*: *N* resembles an *M*.

S HELLEY WROTE the above note on Saturday, February 27, 1819, the
eve of his departure from Naples to Rome. The Shelleys left it and
at least three other letters behind to be mailed by someone else — perhaps by the persons who took charge of Elena Adelaide Shelley.[1]

Shelley's chief reason for writing to Ollier concerned the "lost" box
of books and other items shipped by the publisher in August 1818. (This
box contained sc 486, the Hunts' long-delayed letter that they finished
on August 4.)

The record of the parcels shipped to the Shelleys in Italy is very
confusing — partly because of the lapses of time between their dispatch

---

1. Besides the present note to Ollier, a letter from Mary Shelley to Maria Gisborne, dated by Mary
February 19, but correctly redated by Jones February 26, 1819 (Mary Shelley, *Letters*, I, 62–63),
one from Shelley to Peacock, February 25, 1819, and another from Shelley to Brooks, Son & Dixon,
February 26, 1819 (Shelley, *Letters*, II, 77–82), are postmarked from Naples on March 2, 1819. We
intend to discuss at length the circumstances surrounding Elena Adelaide Shelley and the so-called
Hoppner scandal in later volumes of *Shelley and his Circle*.

Shelley and his Circle : Manuscripts

SC 515   and arrival. Peacock's letters provide a fairly detailed record of his activities in sending packages. The original plan was for Peacock to send a quarterly package containing the *Examiners*, Cobbett's *Political Register*, and such modern literary and political publications as would be of interest. He sent off the first "small box" to the care of John Gisborne before July 5, 1818.[2] In the July 5 letter Peacock informs Shelley that Ollier is also planning to send Shelley a "package." On September 15, 1818, Peacock mentions preparing "your Michaelmas box," and by November 29, 1818, he could write that he had "dispatched, more than a fortnight ago, the second box to the Ship Agents, with positive directions to send it by the first opportunity for Leghorn direct."[3] By January 22, 1819, the Gisbornes had received Peacock's first parcel and had forwarded its bill of lading to Naples. On that day Mary wrote to Maria Gisborne: "Another parcel is on its way, but we have not yet heard by what ship it sails."[4]

In his letter of September 15, 1818, Peacock had cautioned Shelley not to become too impatient about the slow arrival of his parcels: "I send these little packages by sea, and a vessel is sometimes three months on its voyage . . . ."[5] But Peacock at least informed the Shelleys by what ships his parcels had been sent so that they could inquire about their arrival. From Charles Ollier, Shelley heard nothing. On August 10 or August 16, 1818, Shelley wrote Ollier a letter (twice "discovered" in Berlin) from Bagni di Lucca in which he enclosed "6 pieces of writing," including the conclusion of *Rosalind and Helen*, as well as a letter for the Twopenny Post; he also inquired about the parcel that (he had learned from Peacock) Ollier was sending.[6] We know that Shelley sent Ollier the text of "Lines written among the Euganean Hills" for inclusion in the *Rosalind and Helen* volume. This poem, which cannot have been written before Shelley's stay at Este in September 1818, is probably

2. Peacock, *Works*, VIII, 192, 196.

3. Peacock, *Works*, VIII, 196, 205, 208.

4. Frederick L. Jones, "Mary Shelley to Maria Gisborne," *Studies in Philology*, LII (January 1955), 48.

5. Peacock, *Works*, VIII, 205.

6. Shelley, *Letters*, II, 30–31. The letter, first published in *Englische Studien*, LI (1917–1918), was discovered again by David Lee Clark, "An Unpublished Shelley Letter," *Modern Language Notes*, LX (May 1945), 330–331. See J. C. Maxwell, "A Shelley Letter: An Unrecorded Printing," *Notes and Queries*, XI (May 1964), 178–179.

SC 515   referred to in Shelley's one-sentence reproof to his publisher written on the back of a letter-cover addressed to Ollier in care of Peacock.[7] If so, the poem was sent from Naples, and since it cannot (the postal fee tells us) have been enclosed in sc 515, Shelley must have written Ollier a letter, now lost, sometime earlier in his stay at Naples — presumably in December 1818 or January 1819.

The postscript to sc 515, indicating that the Shelleys planned to stay in Rome about three months, is consistent with other statements of their original intentions. They wished at first to continue north to Florence for the summer,[8] but they later changed their plans several times. First they arranged to return to the Naples area for the summer and autumn, so that Mary would be under the care of Dr. John Bell.[9] In his April 6 letter to Peacock, Shelley indicated that they would leave Rome for Naples "in a month or six weeks."[10] But on May 11, Mary Shelley wrote to Maria Gisborne to tell her that they had decided to remain in Rome for yet another month.[11]

Remaining in Rome until the end of May proved to be a fatal error. About May 25 little William Shelley became ill. He remained so intermittently through June 3, when one crisis passed. He died on June 7, and the next day, just a week or two after they had originally planned to leave Rome, the Shelleys departed from the Eternal City forever.

7. Shelley, *Letters*, II, 101. References in Mary's Journal for December 18 and December 19 to copying "Shelley's poem" may refer to "Lines written among the Euganean Hills," rather than to *Prometheus Unbound*.

8. See Mary Shelley to Maria Gisborne, February 26, Mary Shelley, *Letters*, I, 62.

9. Shelley, *Letters*, II, 90; Jones, "Mary Shelley to Maria Gisborne," p. 50. For Dr. Bell (1763–1820), see *DNB*. Bell, like Shelley, had always been an antiestablishment maverick in Edinburgh medical circles and had suffered for his opinions. He was finally unable to attend Mary at the birth of Percy Florence Shelley because he became seriously ill, and died on April 15, 1820, at Rome, where his grave can be seen in the Protestant Cemetery not far from the graves of Keats and Severn.

10. Shelley, *Letters*, II, 92.

11. Jones, "Mary Shelley to Maria Gisborne," p. 52.

SC 516   P. B. SHELLEY, FRAGMENT FROM TRANSLATION OF PLATO'S *RE-PUBLIC*, MARCH 1819–MARCH 1821

HOLOGRAPH MANUSCRIPT (fragment), 2 pages. Single sheet, 4to (8.5 x 6 inches). Laid paper. Watermark: ANT FORTI (top half of each letter).

PROVENANCE: Walter T. Spencer, September 1922.

Shelley, Plato's Republic   **March 1819–March 1821**

SC 516 *desire; and what is to be found more intimately connected with wisdom than*

truth? Nothing   Can then the same nature ~~but~~ be at once philosophical &

prone to falshood! By no means. The true aspirant after knowledge ought

                                                                    the
5 *from his earliest youth to affect entire truth. Certainly   Whenever ~~certain~~*

affections   course of life
~~desires~~ violently impel a person to a certain particular ~~tendency~~   we know

that their strength is by so much the more remiss to any other tendency ~~in~~

~~proportion~~ as their stream having been diverted into another channel. Cer-

         He   a
10 *tainly. ~~Those~~ who has been impelled towards knowledge & ~~its~~ kindred*

discipline, seeks the ~~uns~~ pleasures of the soul ~~as within~~ as they ~~exists~~ within

itself, & omit the pursuit of bodily enjoyments; if indeed he be truly a phi-

losopher & not a fictitious resemblance of that character. Of necessity it must

be so. Such a person must be temperate, & in no manner a lover of money;

15 *~~for those things~~ for those things for the sake of which others devote their whole*

~~attention~~ powers at whatever expense to obtain wealth, he disregards; to ~~any as~~

                     can
him least of all mankind ~~would~~ there be any motive for accumulating wealth

20 *In addition, when you would distinguish a philosophical ~~disposition~~ na-*

ture from one which is not, ~~consider~~ observe————What?————Whether

it be servile or liberal; for all things a narrow littleness of ~~soul~~ ~~spirit~~ soul is

                    inauspicious
the most adverse to a mind aspiring to embrace that comprehensive circle of

25 *divine & human nature, beyond which nothing exists. For how ~~says~~ small*

*the   which
~~a~~ space ~~would~~ human life occupy in an intellect accustomed to the Magnificent

spectacle afforded by the contemplation of all time & all existence. Small in-

deed replies he   Could such a one consider death as terrible? Surely not

30 *A cowardly & illiberal disposition is incapable of participating in the doc-*

                              he who is
trine of true philosophy? Assuredly. But the modest free spirited & ~~gold~~

~~despising~~ a despiser of wealth, neither insolent nor cowardly would surely

neither be δυσσυμβολος nor unjust? Surely not.   And ~~in the consideration~~

35 *thus ~~by it~~ you may ~~discover~~tinguish a philosophical mind from one that is*

                                                          gentle
not so by observing from early youth whether its disposition is just & ~~mild~~,

or savage

The Carl H. Pforzheimer Library

SC 516 line 2. *truth?*: there appears to be a faint exclamation point between *h* and *?*, partially obscured by a long line crossing both *t*'s.

line 3. *falshood!*: obsolete spelling.

line 8. *strength*: Shelley originally wrote *ste*, then went back and squeezed in *r*.

line 11. *has*: written through *have*.

line 12. *they*: written through *it*.

line 14. *fictitious*: neither *t* is crossed.

line 17. *powers*: heavy line on verso gives *po* the appearance of having been canceled.

PLATO REMAINED a favorite author to whom Shelley returned again and again. Shelley is recorded as reading *The Republic* at Oxford (in French translation),[1] and (in Greek) during October and November of 1818, during the same months of 1819, and in September 1820. From evidence in the Bodleian notebooks, it seems clear that he was jotting down quotations from Book V late in 1821.[2] In addition, Notopoulos has posited that Shelley read *The Republic* at Marlow in 1817, about the time he was writing his "Essay on Christianity."[3]

It is, therefore, difficult to assign a precise date to any fragment of translation from *The Republic*. Inasmuch as Notopoulos, using internal evidence, dates Shelley's translations of fragments from *The Republic*, I–III, either March–April or October–November 1819,[4] it would seem unreasonable to assign this translation from Book VI to an earlier period without contrary evidence.

In all likelihood another leaf — perhaps conjugate with sc 516 — contained a translation of the opening passage of Book VI, which is only slightly longer than our fragment. When the paper was torn, the watermark was slightly mutilated, but with the aid of corroborating evidence from papers in the Bodleian Library, it can be determined that the existing portion of the watermark is ANT FORTI. Shelley used the same paper for writing a description of the Arch of Titus and for drafting his *Defence of Poetry* and a letter to the editor of *Ollier's Miscellany* regarding Peacock's *Four Ages of Poetry*.[5] The comments on the Arch of Titus must

1. See Hogg, *Shelley*, I, 121; Notopoulos, *Platonism*, p. 490 and note.

2. Notopoulos, in "New Texts of Shelley's Plato" (*Keats-Shelley Journal*, XV, 1966, 112), gives Shelley's Greek quotations from *The Republic*, 472d4–7 and 476c2–7, as found in Bodleian Ms. Shelley adds. e. 18. The adjacent material in the notebook suggests a very late date for these fragments.

3. Notopoulos, *Platonism*, p. 490.

4. Notopoulos, *Platonism*, pp. 492–493.

5. Bodleian Ms. Shelley adds. c. 4, folios 207–208, 232–246. There do not seem to be any Shelley letters in The Carl H. Pforzheimer Library that contain this watermark.

Shelley and his Circle : Manuscripts

Shelley, Plato's Republic   **March 1819–March 1821**

SC 516 date from Shelley's sojourn in Rome in the spring of 1819;[6] *A Defence of Poetry* was written between late January and March 1821. This fragmentary translation from Book VI of Plato's *Republic* probably dates from this two-year period.

That Shelley's interest in Book VI of *The Republic* was not ephemeral is clearly demonstrated in his letter to Hogg dated October 22, 1821, where in writing of Plato, he asks:

Do you know the ~~republic~~ Πολιτεια & especially the sixth book of it? His speculations on civil society are surely the foundations of true politics, & if ever the world is to be arranged upon another system than that of the several members of it destroying & tormenting one another for the sake of the pleasures of sense, or from the force of habit & imitation; it must start from some such principles.[7]

Like all of the rather arbitrarily divided "books" in *The Republic*, Book VI touches on several subjects. In the larger structure, Books V–VII constitute what is sometimes regarded as a digression from the discussion of the nature of the ideal or just city, which subject itself grows out of prior examinations of the nature of justice and the question of whether the just or the unjust man is happier. The "digression" in Books V–VII describes the "philosopher-kings" who must be rulers or "guardians" of the just city, a discussion culminating, at the opening of Book VII, with the famous allegory of the cave. At the end of Book V, Socrates had gained assent to his suggestion that the philosopher could be distinguished by his search for the *knowledge* of *truth*, whereas other men were content with *belief* in *opinion*. In Book VI he further argues that a love of truth implies besides wisdom, the other virtues he had earlier praised — justice, courage, and temperance. The middle of the book is devoted to Socrates' explanation to the skeptical Adeimantus of why, in the world around them, most so-called philosophers are either rascals or are useless to the state. The fault lies, Socrates asserts, in the false values of society, which prefers bad advice (which can lead to selfish gain) to the truth. But, Socrates affirms, there are mild ways of teaching the efficacy

6. Shelley, *Complete Works*, VI, 309. Shelley mentions the Arch of Titus in his letter to Peacock of March 23, 1819 (Shelley, *Letters*, II, 86), but in that letter he apparently confused the Arch of Titus with that which first commemorated Trajan and later Constantine.

7. Shelley, *Letters*, II, 360.

The Carl H. Pforzheimer Library

SC 516 of philosophy to the multitude, overcoming their prejudices. Socrates begins to discuss the education of the saviors of the constitution (preservers of the constitution), but this discussion leads almost immediately to the question of the nature of the good. Here Socrates confesses the difficulty of framing a satisfactory definition or description and turns to two similes in order to suggest the nature of the good. In the first simile, he likens the sun to the good and the eye to the human mind. In the second similitude, Socrates uses concepts from geometry to compare knowledge of the good to the mathematicians' hypotheses about perfect forms, and opinions about things to the actual lines and figures with which mathematicians must work. He concludes Book VI by enumerating four levels of knowing, which he assigns to four corresponding faculties in the soul: *reason* (intellection or knowledge of the abstract principles); *understanding* (the level of ordinary mathematical principles and hypothesis); *faith* (belief or conviction, dealing in opinions); and *perception* of shadows ("*picture-thinking*," conjecture, knowledge derived merely from the senses).

Western philosophy, wrote Whitehead, is "a series of footnotes to Plato."[8] And even those of us who have found Platonic influences on Shelley either overemphasized or misapplied come to realize, in reading such works as *The Republic*, that there are numerous direct parallels, not only in thought but even in language and images, between Shelley's poetry and prose and Plato's dialogues. Book VI of *The Republic* yields parallels that have not been pointed out in the obvious places like Notopoulos' massive study.

The passage in the translated fragment, though interesting as a point of comparison with Shelley's poetic description of his own youth and those of his heroes, does not call to mind any especially close verbal parallel in Shelley's poetry. On the other hand, in a subsequent section of Book VI (#491), Socrates says that the very qualities of human virtue — courage, temperance, and the like — as well as beauty, riches, bodily strength, and powerful connections in a city, all tend, in a corrupt social environment, to draw young men away from philosophy; he goes on to compare the growth of human virtue from good qualities to the growth of seeds that fail to receive their proper nutriment. This passage

8. Alfred North Whitehead, *Process and Reality* (New York, 1960), p. 63.

SC 516 closely resembles in imagery lines spoken by Rousseau in *The Triumph of Life*:

> And if the spark with which Heaven lit my spirit
> Earth had with purer nutriment supplied
>
> Corruption would not now thus much inherit
> Of what was once Rousseau . . . .[9]

Socrates contends (*Republic* VI, #500) that the philosopher "fixes his gaze upon the things of the eternal and unchanging order, and seeing that they neither wrong nor are wronged by one another, but all abide in harmony as reason bids, he will endeavour to imitate them, and as far as may be, to fashion himself in their likeness and assimilate himself to them. . . ."[10] Shelley's independence from Plato in basic thought is clear in *A Defence of Poetry* when he praises poetry and the arts above philosophy — images above abstractions. But he adapts Plato's description of the virtues acquired by the philosopher and applies them to the poet, even as he claims Plato himself for poetry:[11]

Poetry is the record of the best and happiest moments of the happiest and best minds. . . . A poet, as he is the author to others of the highest wisdom, pleasure, virtue and glory, so he ought personally to be the happiest, the best, the wisest, and the most illustrious of men. . . . the greatest Poets have been men of the most spotless virtue, of the most consummate prudence, and, if we could look into the interior of their lives, the most fortunate of men. . . .[12]

Plato's works, and particularly *The Republic* with its vindication of the sanity of true virtue and the happiness of the just man, were a great support to Shelley during the often lonely and frustrating years of his sojourn — or exile — in Italy. In the October 1821 letter to Hogg quoted above, Shelley himself stated the case succinctly: "I have employed Greek in large doses, & I consider it the only sure remedy for diseases of the mind. I read the tragedians, Homer, & Plato perpetually. . . ."[13]

9. Lines 201–204; Donald H. Reiman, *Shelley's "The Triumph of Life"* (University of Illinois Press, 1965), p. 162.

10. Paul Shorey, *Plato: The Republic* (Harvard University Press, 1963), II, 69.

11. "Plato was essentially a poet — the truth and splendour of his imagery, and the melody of his language, is the most intense that it is possible to conceive." (Shelley, *Complete Works*, VII, 114.)

12. Shelley, *Complete Works*, VII, 136, 138.

13. Shelley, *Letters*, II, 360.

SC 517   LEIGH HUNT TO M. W. SHELLEY, MARCH 9, 1819

AL signed *L.H.*, 7 pages. 2 double sheets, 4^(to) (9 x 7.3 inches).
Laid paper. Watermark (both sheets): **B. E. & S.**   1807   BATH [within decorative pattern]|.
Seal: wax, red: [angel with olive branch, following serpent]|.
Postal fees: 1. 3/10 double 1/6; 2. 3/10 [repeated]; 3. £2.[?73]; 4. 66.
Postmarks: 1. (Foreign Post Office stamp): F 19| 140|; 2. (transit stamp): ANGLE-TERRE|; 3. (transit stamp): CHAMBERY|; 4. [CORRISP^(ZA) ESTERA DA GENOVA]| [fleur-de-lis]|; 5. LIVORNO|; 6. 30 MARZO|; 7. 5 APRILE|.

PROVENANCE: Colonel Charles Shelley Leigh Hunt; Mrs. Beryl Dodgson (Sotheby, April 8, 1935, lot 205).

8. York Buildings – New Road
9. March 1819.

Marina Mia,

      I should have written much sooner but I have been in a
5 *world of doubts & difficulties. You know the difficulties which I foolishly*
suffered to remain upon me, when Shelley did that noble action. They have
latterly come pelting upon me, & thank God! the storm is pretty well over.
What pleases me much however, is, that these are old matters that have been
long coming, not new ones; & that both my economy & my resources have
10 *been increasing meantime. I have now the prospects before me, which I ought*
to have had on that occasion; & Shelley, when he returns, will have the
pleasure of seeing his kind intentions completed,– for all my comforts in this
respect will still have originated with him. You must know I have been writing
lately like a dragon: (nor is this simile so unlike as it seems, if we are to
15 *believe Emanuel Swedenbourg, who says that the devils have plays acted be-*
fore them, & that he saw critical dragons sitting in the pit). I hope the parcel
with the Pocket-Books has arrived by this time. I finished my tragedy the
week before last; & am now deep in translating passages out of the Greek
plays to make up the little volume commencing with Hero & Leander. What
20 *divine writers those Greek tragedians are! I should quarrel more with the*
unjust & shocking superstition about destiny upon which their writings are
founded, were they not perpetually yearning after every species of beauty,
moral & physical; & were there not even a lurking impatience & irreligion

SC 517 *against their own plots, which contain something more truly pious & wor-*
shipful to the "Spirit of Intellectual Beauty," than all the frightened com-
promises with bigotry in the world. "But what, Hunt, of Italy?" Ah, you see
I delay speaking of Italy.– I cannot come; I wish to God I could, & were
Shelley & you to be ill so as to want me to help comfort you, I feel almost
certain that I would;–but it is next to impossible. My brother John had for
30 *some months had an idea of retiring into the country, in order that his sons*
might be better furnished with means for entering into life; & just as I
wrote my last letter, he had finally determined upon it. He & my other brothers
dine with me tomorrow, previously to his departure, which takes place in a
couple of weeks; & then it will be more than ever necessary that I should
35 *be every Saturday at office, where my nephew Henry takes his place. Henry*
is a very nice ingenuous lad, who with his father's staider excellences, has
more imagination. He is going to live with Admirable Coulson, which appears
to me an excellent arrangement. The other day he surprised a company at his
father's with starting earnestly into conversation, his face all on fire, & mak-
40 *ing a zealous defence of Shelley whom some foolish person attacked. When he*
had done, he apologized for being so loud & abrupt, but "my uncle," said
he, admires & loves Mr Shelley, & this alone should excuse y me;"–upon
which his father added with evident delight, "My dear boy, you could not
have done better." Now all this, I conceive, is good & fine. I think it was
45 *Coulson who told me. Coulson is a good deal here; so are Hogg & Peacock,*
besides the Novellos &c. & a very nice couple, friends of theirs, a M^r & M^{rs}
Gliddon. We had a most glorious Twelfth-Night, with tea in the study at
                    (in the morning)
half past six_∧,*& the women all sparkling to the last. The Lambs also we see*
50 *at short intervals, & Alsager, & Hazlitt, who has just published a most bitter*
Γνωθι σεαυτον *Letter to Gifford,– which said Gifford by the bye, Shelley may*
be assured is his traducer, & not Southey. Southey is an honest man after a
                    does
fashion, & ~~will~~ not tell wilful lies.–   I have also made a very pleasant ac-
55 *quaintance in a young man of the name of Procter, who was a little boy at*
Harrow when Lord Byron was there, & who wrote the verses in the Pocket·
Book signed P.R.   Albeit bred up in different notions, he is a great admirer
of Shelley's book, & has a fund of goodness & good taste in general. Young

SC 517 *Curran too has been here three or four times; and there is a distant sort of endearment between me & the Lapwing— – I beg pardon. Somebody told Mr Godwin the other day that I said Milton was an atheist. So he wrote me a very polite letter to know ~~whether~~ what grounds I had for calling him so; & I answered & said, None,– having no grounds,ₐ*_{& never having so called him.}* *All that I had said was, that*

65 *Milton <u>latterly</u> never went to any place of worship or had any worship in his house; & it turned out that I could not prove even this, having confused my memory betwixt some words in the proving of his will & an assertion of Toland's to that purpose. Upon which Godwin sent me a very pleasant answer, stating that he thought this would be the amount of the matter, &*

70 *giving me a specimen of the way in which these things sometimes get into books. Hayley had said in his Life of Milton that Bacon was deformed; so Godwin (who tells me that he always makes a point of plaguing people on these subjects) wrote to him to know his authority; upon which Hayley returned for answer, that he had no authority, but that he conceived "he must*

75 *have mistaken Robert Cecil Earl of Salisbury for the Viscount St Albans;"— a pretty difference, between the crabbed politician, with a body as crooked as his soul, & the Hesperus of ₐ^{modern}philosophy.— Hogg & Peacock generally dine here every Sunday, when the former is not on the circuit; & we pass very*

80 *pleasant afternoons, talking of mythology, & the Greeks, & our old friends. Hogg, I think, has a good heart as well as wit. You have heard, of course, of Peacock's appointment in the India House; we joke him upon his new oriental grandeur, his Brahminical learning, & his inevitable tendencies to be one of the corrupt, upon which he seems to apprehend Shelleian objurgation. It*

85 *is an honour to him, that "prosperity" sits on him well. He is very pleasant & hospitable. He has told you, I suppose, that Mr Turner called on him the other day, & invited him & Hogg to dinner with his wife & Marianne at Kensington. Peacock asked me if I had any objection to meet them at his lodgings to dinner. I said I had, because ~~I~~ as I was not an old acquaintance*

90 *of theirs, ~~I~~ I could avoid their company, & ~~I~~ and would never meet a person who would not meet Shelley; but Hogg says that they are now very desirous of seeing him, & so my grandeur relented, & I shall shortly perhaps have to give an account of our confronting. Pray tell me in your next (for you will*

SC 517 *write again, ~~you~~ nymph of the sidelong looks, now I have done my epistolary*
duty) how you all are, & whether Shelley's Italian doctor has done him any
good. Didn't you go to Sicily while you were in the neighbourhood,— the land
of Theocritus, & Proserpine, & Polyphemus? I do not scruple to put the
one-eyed giant in such company, because he always appears to me a pathetic
rather then a monstrous person, though his disappointed sympathies at last

100 *made him cruel. What do you think of this Polyphemic theory of mine?– I*
have been for a long time in a state of remorse for not writing; & yet — But
I will not make bad excuses; for on such an occasion they m̲u̲st be bad. You
shall see how I will mend. There is not a day passes over my head, I assure
you, but what I think of Italy, & not for it's native productions, but it's

105 *foreign. Pray tell me how you are, & what you do, & where you go, & what*
you intend. Shelley says he should like to be walking about with me in the
Hampstead fields. It is what I repeat to myself every other day. If he were
here, I should walk as much agai< > as I do; & if he does not speedily q̲u̲i̲t̲e
restore his health, I sometimes think that my yearnings on this point may

110 *bring you over a little sooner than you contemplated. I am sure that if he*
lived at Kilburn or at some such place in the neighborhood, I should walk
there & back every day. God bless you. I am writing upon a little green
portfolio which you left in Russell St. & which I have usurped the use of ever
since. Remembrance to Clare. Marianne is writing out my tragedy, & so I

115 *have got Betsy Kent to write you a little more chit chat about us all. Ever*
most sincerely & affectionately L.H.

To Mrs Shelley, &c. &c. I should like to see Shelley & you in England,
again exceedingly, but of course not if it would do him harm. "Vain man!
& so you think your likings of consequence!

[Address, page 8]

120   *Double Letter.*

To

Percy B. Shelley Esqre

~~Alla cura del~~

Hunt to Shelley   *March 9, 1819*

SC 517 *Poste restante*

     Signor ~~Giovanni Gisborne~~,

   ~~Leghorn,~~

       ~~Livorno~~,

  ~~Italy~~.   *~~Italia.~~*

   Roma.

line 8. *is,*: written through indecipherable letters.

line 12. *this respect*: between these words is an ink mark that resembles, but is probably not, a hyphen or short dash.

line 19. *Leander.*: possibly *Leanders*.

line 30. *months*: *m* may be upper case.

line 37. *Admirable*: *A* possibly lower case.

line 84. *objurgation.*: period is a probable reading; punctuation may be a colon.

line 86. *M*ʳ: *M* written through *?T*.

line 87. *Marianne*: probable reading; not Marianne Hunt, of course, but Marianne de St. Croix.

line 106. *in the*: written on paper adhering to seal, as is *day* (line 107).

line 108. *agai<n>*: seal tear.

line 109. *may*: written through indecipherable letters.

line 110. *sure*: possibly followed by a comma.

line 111. *neighborhood,*: may be spelled *neighbourhood*.

line 117. *To Mᵗˢ . . . consequence!*: the postscript is written at the top of page 1 of the manuscript and occupies two and a half lines.

THERE IS a slight complication in the sequence of Hunt's letters to the Shelleys in 1818–1819. Hunt's letter of November 12, 1818 (sc 504), reached the Shelleys at Naples in mid-December,[1] and his next surviving letter to either Shelley or Mary is this one of March 9, 1819, which reached Rome (according to the postal date stamp) on April 5.[2] Yet Mary wrote to Marianne Hunt from Rome on March 12, 1819: "We had Hunt's letter at Naples e[x]pressing all his doubts & difficulties about the proposed jour[ney]."[3] This lost letter would, presumably, have been written in mid- or late January, as a reply to Shelley's letter of circa December 20, 1818, in which he proposed that Hunt should visit Italy on money to be borrowed from Lord Byron.[4]

Hunt's apology for delaying so long before writing this letter refers, therefore, to his earlier failure to state categorically whether or not he

1. See Shelley's reply to it, December [?20], 1818, Shelley, *Letters*, II, 64–68.

2. On April 6, 1819, Shelley wrote to Peacock that he had received letters from Hunt and Peacock "yesterday" (Shelley, *Letters*, II, 91–92).

3. Mary Shelley, *Letters*, I, 64.

4. Shelley, *Letters*, II, 67.

SC 517 would come to Italy.[5] John Hunt's retirement (lines 29–32) puts an end to the impractical scheme at this date, and only a more substantial proposal in the form of a journal by which Leigh Hunt was supposed to earn his living succeeded in luring the Hunts to Italy in 1821–1822.

Henry Leigh Hunt, John Hunt's eldest son, appears here in a favorable light as the defender of Shelley's good name, but he was later a principal in a less edifying dispute in which he and his father attempted to take away from Leigh Hunt and his family — then destitute in Italy — all interest in the *Examiner*.[6] A letter of December 21, 1820, from Henry L. Hunt to Marianne Hunt suggests that Henry's ill-will was directed not so much at his uncle as at Marianne Hunt and her careless extravagance.[7]

Whoever was primarily responsible, the Leigh Hunts were unable to balance their budget. To Hunt's half-shamefaced, half-proud account in the present letter of how, through his own labors and economy, he had overcome his creditors without additional assistance from the Shelleys, Mary replied dryly: "To tell you the truth both Shelley and I thought that we left you free and had easy minds upon that score—."[8] In thus challenging Hunt's posturing, Mary resembled her father, who had demanded to know Hunt's authority for his offhand statement on Milton's religious opinions (lines 60–62). Whatever personal faults Godwin may have had, disrespect for historial truth and scholarly accuracy were not among them. (See also SC 511.)

Leigh Hunt's most characteristic virtue, fully illustrated in this letter, was his acceptance of himself and tolerance of other people on their own terms. In this letter his expressions of good feelings begin, appropriately, with himself, literature, and the Shelleys. They extend first to his own family — his brothers John, Robert, and Stephen Shewell Hunt[9] and

5. The Shelleys had already concluded that he would not come; see Mary Shelley, *Letters*, I, 64. Perhaps their certainty came from a comment in Peacock's letter of January 13: "I do not see how he [Hunt] could visit Italy without being utterly ruined; for what in the interval would become of his paper?" (Peacock, *Works*, VIII, 215.)

6. See Brown, *Letters*, pp. 164–179, 190–199, 206–212, 215–220, 225–229, 242–249, 270–274.

7. The manuscript, which is in The Carl H. Pforzheimer Library, will appear in a later volume of *Shelley and his Circle*.

8. April 6, 1819, Mary Shelley, *Letters*, I, 65.

9. The most complete information on Leigh Hunt's siblings is to be found in Stephen F. Fogle's "Leigh Hunt's Lost Brother and the American Legacy," *Keats-Shelley Journal*, VIII, Part 2 (Autumn 1959), 95–101.

The Carl H. Pforzheimer Library

SC 517   his nephew Henry (lines 29–37) — and then to intimate friends like Walter ("Admirable") Coulson, Charles and Mary Lamb, William Hazlitt, Thomas Alsager, and Vincent and Mary Sabilla Novello.

Arthur and Alistasia Gliddon (lines 46–47) were also part of this circle. Arthur Gliddon is described in *Pigot's Metropolitan Directory* for 1828–1829 as a "tobacconist and importer of snuffs and segars," located at 42 King Street, Covent Garden. This shop figures in Hunt's essay, "Coffee Houses and Smoking," which appeared in the *New Monthly Magazine* in 1826.[10] In 1819 the Gliddon establishment, praised in one of Hunt's ephemeral "Harry Brown" poems in the *Examiner* of July 18, 1819, was probably at 31 Tavistock Street, Covent Garden, the address at which it is listed on the colophon of Hunt's *Indicator*, beginning with the issue of May 31, 1820. The friendship of the Gliddons and Hunts spread to the next generation. Thornton Hunt married Katharine Gliddon and Mary Florimel Hunt married John Gliddon, both children of Arthur's brother John.[11]

Hunt also introduces here the name of a young protégé named Bryan Waller Procter, whose mediocre poetry, published under the name of "Barry Cornwall," was to flourish for a few years and contribute to both Peacock's and Shelley's disgust at the bad taste of the contemporary reading public.

Hunt is not offended by Godwin and can tell the story of his own and William Hayley's errors with as little embarrassment as if Hayley had committed both blunders.[12] Hunt entertains Peacock (who had a low opinion of him) and accepts Thomas Jefferson Hogg in his eccentricity (line 81), Southey in his Toryism, and Polyphemus in his one-eyed monstrosity.[13] Hunt can accept the lapses of William Henry Curran, son

10. *New Monthly Magazine*, XVI (1826), 50–54; *Examiner*, #603 (July 18, 1819), p. 459; *Indicator*, I, No. XXXIV (May 31, 1820), 272.

11. For letters of Hunt to Arthur and Alistasia Gliddon, see Hunt, *Correspondence*, I, 192, 210, 211; see also Molly Tatchell, *Leigh Hunt and His Family in Hammersmith* (London, 1969), pp. 61–63, and Clarke, *Recollections of Writers*, p. 22. There is a letter from Alistasia Gliddon to Marianne Hunt in The Carl H. Pforzheimer Library.

12. On Hayley, a popular poet and prose writer of the day and the sometime friend and patron of William Blake, see Morchard Bishop, *Blake's Hayley; The Life, Works, and Friendships of William Hayley* (London, 1951).

13. Mary's reply again shows her sturdy independence of judgment: She declares that she had "written a book in defence of Polypheme" (*Frankenstein*) but that Hogg's "manners . . . always disgust me" and make his constant visits "absolutely intolerable." Mary Shelley, *Letters*, I, 66.

SC 517   and biographer of John Philpot Curran,[14] and can even be persuaded to accept an invitation to dine with Cornelia Boinville's husband, Thomas Turner, who was, one gathers, a constant enemy to Shelley.

Shelley takes up Hunt's remarks about the Turners in his letter to Peacock of April 6, written the day after sc 517 arrived in Rome. Shelley inquires about Mrs. Boinville, her daughter Cornelia, and her son Alfred, and he asks Peacock to tell Mrs. Boinville that "I have not forgotten her, or any of the amiable circle once assembled round her, & that I desire such remembrances to her as an exile & a *Pariah* may be permitted to address to an acknowledged member of the community of mankind." Shelley's interest in the Boinvilles continued, and he asked both Peacock and Hogg about them from time to time.[15]

Toward only one person does Hunt's constitutional benevolence fail him. For William Gifford, editor of the *Quarterly Review*, Hunt felt nothing but contempt and hatred. Hazlitt's *Letter to William Gifford, Esq.* had originally appeared, in briefer form, in the *Examiner* for June 15, 1818. On January 7, 1819, Hunt reviewed the expanded forty-four leaf pamphlet in the *Examiner*, and Keats quoted from it enthusiastically and at length in his letter to the George Keatses of March 12–13, 1819.[16] Hazlitt's attack — or rather answer to the *Quarterly*'s attacks on him — remains one of the classics of invective in the English language.[17] Hunt attributed to Gifford the abusive review of *Foliage*, with its attack on Shelley, whereas Shelley blamed it on Southey. Both were wrong, but neither altered his opinion on the authorship because each had other reasons for personal animus toward the man he suspected.[18]

---

14. The younger Curran is referred to as "the Lapwing," apparently because he, like his father before him, had a reputation as a promiscuous lover. For this use of "lapwing," see Shakespeare, *Measure for Measure*, I.iv.31–33, and Tennyson, "Locksley Hall," line 18. Fanny Imlay wrote to Mary on July 29, 1816, asking about Byron: "You must by this time know if he is a profligate in principle—a man who, like Curran, gives himself unbounded liberty in all sorts of profligacy" (*Shelley and Mary*, I, 108). John Philpot Curran, Godwin's best friend (see sc 461, Commentary), was at that time sixty-six years old. See also Leslie Hale, *John Philpot Curran* (London, 1958), p. 138.

15. Shelley, *Letters*, II, 92. For an extended account of the Boinvilles and Turners in later years, see Commentary to Shelley's letter to T. J. Hogg, April 20, 1820, which will appear in Volume VII of *Shelley and his Circle*.

16. Keats, *Letters*, II, 71–73, 74–76.

17. The phrase Γνωθι σεαυτον (line 51) is the well-known injunction of Socrates to "know thyself."

18. See sc 486 and Commentary, and sc 504, Commentary.

SC 517   Hunt's general good humor — in spite of Gifford — resulted in large part from his sense of accomplishment at the moment.[19] He had not only warded off the dragons of financial difficulty, but had also been "writing like a dragon."[20] Completing his tragedy on the Cid,[21] Hunt had begun translating Greek dramatic poetry to publish with *Hero and Leander*. He later changed his plan, for in 1819 Ollier published a volume that included only *Hero and Leander* and *Bacchus and Ariadne*.

19. In her reply of April 6, Mary remarked on Hunt's "good spirits" (Mary Shelley, *Letters*, I, 65). The "glorious Twelfth-Night" celebration at Hunt's house (lines 47–49) was mentioned by Peacock in his January 13 letter (Peacock, *Works*, VIII, 215) and is probably the one Mary Sabilla Novello recalls fondly in her letter to Hunt of October 19, 1823 (Hunt, *Correspondence*, I, 209).

20. Hunt's allusion to Emmanuel Swedenborg may derive ultimately from a passage in *The True Christian Religion*, translated by John C. Ager in Standard Edition, *Theological Works* (New York: Swedenborg Foundation, 1963, 30 volumes), I, 496. (This reference was obtained through the courtesy of Virginia Branston, Manager of the Swedenborg Foundation, Inc.)

21. See sc 486 and sc 529 and Commentaries.

SC 518   JOHN KEATS, POETIC FRAGMENT FROM "ISABELLA, OR THE POT OF BASIL," APRIL 1819

HOLOGRAPH MANUSCRIPT, 4½ lines. Fragment (.7 x 6.6 inches). Laid paper.
Addition: manuscript inlaid with cellophane tape in an album leaf, upon which has been mounted a note that reads: *From the M.S. of "Isabella or| the Pot of Basil"| John Keats| From papers left in the hands of| Joseph Severn|.*

PROVENANCE: Joseph Severn; Maggs, July 1948.

[From stanza xliii]

>   *And sing to it one latest lullaby*
> <   >*w her short absence might be unsurmized*
> <   > *her dream would try;*

[From stanza xlvi]

>   *Upon the fatal spot she seem'd to grow*
5 >   *Like to a native Lilly of the dell:*

line 2. *unsurmized* (sic).

Just as parts of the fair-copy manuscript of Shelley's *Laon and Cythna* were distributed by Mary Shelley and Leigh Hunt as examples of Shelley's autograph, so the holograph of Keats's "Isabella" was given

Keats, Isabella Fragment   *April* 1819

SC 518   out by Charles Brown and Joseph Severn. Brown seems to have been the first to have followed this course, for the W. Luther Lewis collection at Texas Christian University possesses the manuscript of the first six stanzas of the poem (written on a single double sheet) that has been mounted on another sheet containing this notation: "Autograph poem by Keats—given to me by *his* friend—*my* friend, C Brown Esq[r].— G.W."[1] But a sixteen-line fragment of stanzas xli and xliv that was sold at Christie's (July 1, 1970, lot 118) had been given to Robert Spence by Joseph Severn on December 6, 1850, and William H. Bond informs us that four other fragments of the manuscript in the Houghton Library, Harvard University, are traceable to Joseph Severn.

SC 518, though almost the smallest possible sample of a literary manuscript, has two verbal variants from the accepted text. To provide the context for comparison, we quote stanzas xliii and xlvi of "Isabella" as they appear in H. W. Garrod's Oxford English Text Edition.[2] (The lines appearing in the Pforzheimer manuscript are given in italics.)

xliii

When the full morning came, she had devised
   How she might secret to the forest hie;
How she might find the clay, so dearly prized,
   And sing to it one latest lullaby;
How her short absence might be unsurmised,
   While she the inmost of *the dream would try.*
Resolv'd, she took with her an aged nurse,
And went into that dismal forest-hearse.

. . . .

xlvi

She gaz'd into the fresh-thrown mould, as though
   One glance did fully all its secrets tell;
Clearly she saw, as other eyes would know
   Pale limbs at bottom of a crystal well;
Upon the murderous spot she seem'd to grow,
   Like to a native lilly of the dell:
Then with her knife, all sudden, she began
To dig more fervently than misers can.

1. Lyle H. Kendall, Jr., *A Descriptive Catalogue of The W. L. Lewis Collection, Part One: Manuscripts, Inscriptions, Art* (Texas Christian University, 1970), p. 63.
2. *The Poetical Works of John Keats* (2nd edition, Oxford: Clarendon Press, 1958), pp. 229, 230.

SC 518   Keats's composition of "Isabella" is dated by Walter Jackson Bate between March 25 and April 27, 1819.[3] The fair copy of these stanzas, which appear about two thirds of the way through the poem, was probably written toward the end of this period.

3. Bate, *Keats*, p. 310.

SC 519 P. B. SHELLEY TO BROOKS, SON & DIXON, APRIL 4, 1819

AL signed *Percy Bysshe Shelley*, 1 page. Double sheet, 4to (9.8 x 8 inches). Wove paper. Watermark: G S & C| [ ]7|.
Seal: wax, red: [Judgment of Paris]|.
Postal fee: 1/11.
Postmarks: 1. ROMA|; 2. (Foreign Post Office stamp, London): FPO| AP 24| 1819|.
Docket, page 4, in ink: *P B Shelley| 4 April 1819|*.

PROVENANCE: William Walker (Hodgson's, December 15, 1916, lot 225); Walter T. Spencer (Peck, *Shelley*, II, 388); Gabriel Wells; John E. Zahn (Rains Galleries, New York, April 21–22, 1936, lot 409); J. Howard Woolmer, June 1964. *De Ricci 406* (p. 23).

Gentlemen
                    for One Hundred Pounds
    *I have drawn a bill*ₐ*on Mess*^{rs} *Torlonia & C*^{o} *of this city, in which you will have the goodness to honour & place to my account.*
5   *I have the honour to be*
                                    Gentlemen
                                        Your obedient humb Ser^t
                                            Percy Bysshe Shelley

    Rome, April 4. 1819
    [Address, page 4]
10   *Mess*^{s} *Brookes & C*^{o}
        Bankers
        25 Chancery Lane
            London
            Inghilterra
15   *Angleterre*

[800]

SC 519   line 7. *Ser^t*: written on a fragment affected by the seal tears and now detached from the remainder of the manuscript.

line 15. *Angleterre*: written to the left of and perpendicular to the address.

IN CHOOSING his banker when in Rome, Shelley did as the other English in Rome did. He dealt with the house of Giovanni-Raimondo Torlonia (1755–1829), self-made founder of a banking empire and since 1809 the Duke of Bracciano. Torlonia was a subject of much discussion by the English and French travelers of the period, partly because of his meteoric rise to wealth and nobility and partly because the Duke and Duchess Torlonia were the greatest hosts to *conversazioni* and balls to which the foreign nobility and gentry might expect to be invited. Torlonia was described by an English visitor to Rome in 1814 as "a great personage here; he made a prodigious fortune by risking everything with the French, and having lately purchased large estates with a dukedom annexed, he is now the Duke of Bracciano, with two fine palaces in the town and two villas."[1] Frances, Lady Shelley, remarked snobbishly in her diary for December 26, 1816: "The Torlonias are *bourgeois*. His father was a *laquais de place* who, nobody knows how, made a fortune, turned banker, and becoming enormously rich, bought palaces and villas. He obtained a marquisate and later on a dukedom; meanwhile, he continued his business as banker. He gives fêtes, receives all Rome, and last night all London too. It was, however, a bad London assembly."[2]

To Shelley (as to Keats later[3]), however, Torlonia was simply a banker, for the Shelleys remained, in general, cut off from the English society that flourished in Rome. For Shelley's financial situation in 1819, see SC 545, Commentary.

1. *The Journal of John Mayne*, ed. John Mayne Colles (London, 1909), p. 164.
2. *The Diary of Frances, Lady Shelley, 1787–1817*, ed. Richard Edgcumbe (New York, 1912), I, 354.
3. H. Nelson Gay, "Keats's Last Bank Account," *Keats-Shelley Memorial Bulletin*, II (1913), 94, and Bate, *Keats*, p. 683.

SC 520   T. J. HOGG TO T. L. PEACOCK, APRIL 29, 1819

AL signed *T. Jefferson Hogg.*, 3 pages. Double sheet, 4to (8.8 x 7.3 inches). Wove paper. Watermark: C BRENCHLEY| 1818|.
Seal: wafer, green.
Postal fee: 11.

Hogg to Peacock *April 29, 1819*

Postmarks: 1. (dated mileage stamp): YORK| 29 AP 29| 1819| [   ]|; 2. (morning
duty stamp, London): [D]| 1 MY 1| 1819|.
Addition, page 4: seal tears mended with cellophane tape.

PROVENANCE: Thomas Jefferson Hogg; Prudentia Hogg Lonsdale; John Ewer
Jefferson Hogg; Major R. J. Jefferson Hogg (Sotheby, July 26, 1948, lot 273).

Black Swan Inn
York 29th April 1819

My Dear Peacock

      Extended on my back on a hard Sofa at an indifferent
5 *Inn, with but one picture in the room, & that represents Britannia staring*
at the King, in the dull city of York, where I know but one man, & he is a
Banker, how can I deny that there are many shapes of little Dæmons, that
πολλα δ'αελπτως κραινουσι Θεοι?—   *I had left home with the expecta-*
tion of being in London ere this, & had reached this place, when a Rheumatic
10 *Cold again seized me & still imprisons me most unwilling, feeding on boiled*
rice, quaffing "the Mixture as before," occupied in lying still & seeking
amusement in any other tense of the verb live, than the present. –
    I contrast my now lifeless life with what it was, when those verdant
walks clustered round us at divers periods, with that winter at Bishopsgate,
15 *wch was a mere Atticism, for we revelled in Greek, with the many folds en-*
compassing The velvet bottom with our well-earned sleep at the Jolly Crick-
eters, with the brightness of Virginia Water to one emerging from the Shades
of the Belvedere; when I think of these the most splendid hours of my exist-
ence (except some few glowing lights amidst boundless shadows, when I was
20 *young enough to be in love) I trust that I shall find a road, wch will lead back*
again to these good things & that some God will be to me a giver of them. –
After dinner fill your glass somewhat fuller than usual for my sake & drink
it off to absorb whatever anger any of the Gods may yet have against me & do
this without fear, as in your body such anger will be vain: and, if you wo^d
25 *do me another favor, call at my Chambers in your walk to the City & & tell*
my Clerk to say to all, who may ask for me, that I am unwell & at York, but
will be in town in a day, or two. There are no incidents here except that a
stranger sometimes, having opened the door & gazed around, says "I beg

Hogg to Peacock   *April 29, 1819*

SC 520 *pardon" & withdraws; last night a fat lady looked into the room & said,*
"I beg pardon, Sir, I mistook the door, as, at all times, especially in sickness
we sh^d have the simple & beautiful language of scripture on our lips I
answered immediately from my sofa with some animation in the words of
the Lamb, Madam, "I am the Door, enter into the sheepfold thro' me" she
fled in dismay; surely these comfortable words cannot be so appalling?——

35 *Conjuring you < > remember me kindly to the rustic of the New Road &*
to his shepherdess, I will conclude & lay down my head in search of conso-
lation from a scene or two of ΑΛΚΗΣΤΙΣ.
      With best comp^s to Mrs P. & Miss L.

                                          I am truly yours
                                          T. Jefferson Hogg.

40
    [Address, page 4]
    T. L. Peacock Esq.
        5 York Street
            Covent Garden
                London.

line 4. *at*: written through *in*.   line 34. *so*: written on fragment adhering to seal.
line 14. *us*: a long *s* is written through *t*.   line 35. *you < >*: seal tear.
line 16. *The*: *T* written through *t* or vice versa.   *New*: visible through seal.
line 25. *City & & (sic)*.

T‍HE "LONG INTERVAL" following Peacock's letter to Hogg of December 1818 (sc 509) is due not to estrangement but to proximity.
Early in the new year Peacock's India Office test had borne its fruit.
Though he had not yet received a definite appointment, he had been
called to London to undergo a period of training at Leadenhall Street.
From 5 York Street, Covent Garden, where he was still living at the
end of April, he had written on January 13 to tell Shelley of his present
situation, passing every morning in study at the India House with a
reasonable conviction that he would receive an appointment. Peacock
at Covent Garden and Hogg at the Temple, almost within a stone's
throw, could dispense with letter-writing. That Hogg, on his way back
from a family visit, should have been struck down at York by a rheumatic

Hogg to Peacock   *April 29,* 1819

SC 520   cold was a piece of bad luck. He faced it with Homeric philosophy; how could he deny, lying on his (probably horsehair) sofa in a bleak room graced by the dutiful patriotic picture, that "the gods accomplish many things contrary to expectation" (line 8)?[1]

To shorten the gloomy hours he falls to reminiscence of happier days, represented by "that winter at Bishopsgate." Hogg had been only a visitor; it was Shelley who in August 1815 took a furnished house at that eastern entrance to Windsor Great Park, and remained there until May 1816 when he went to Switzerland. For Shelley that was a moderately long tenure; and, as always with Shelley, he was the center of his circle, radiating interest and significance. "I was then living at Marlow," Peacock writes in his *Memoirs* of Shelley, "and frequently walked over to pass a few days with him."[2] Peacock continues, "The whole of the winter 1815–16 was passed quietly at Bishopsgate. Mr Hogg often walked down from London; and I, as before, walked over from Marlow. This winter was, as Mr Hogg expressed it, a mere Atticism. Our studies were exclusively Greek. To the best of my recollection, we were, throughout the whole period, his only visitors. One or two persons called on him; but they were not to his mind, and were not encouraged to reappear."[3] The only exception had been the Quaker Dr. Pope of Staines. And here, in this appropriate solitude, Shelley had written *Alastor.*

So here we have Hogg, already nostalgic after three years or so, coining the term "Atticism" that Peacock would pick out to quote when both were elderly. The beauty of lake and landscape, the nights spent at a more alluring inn than this cheerless Black Swan of York, struck Hogg in his mildly feverish condition as being his "most splendid hours." Again, as in Peacock's wistful letter of the previous March (sc 468), the unavoidable impression is that — allowing something to the classics and the sunlit lake — appreciation is inspired by Shelley. Even Hogg's subsidiary "glowing lights" may raise a question: when he was "young

1. Euripides' *Bacchae*, line 1389 (last but three of the play). Gilbert Murray's verse translation runs: "And many things God makes to be/ Past hope or fear."
2. Peacock, *Works*, VIII, 98.
3. Peacock, *Works*, VIII, 99–100. Peacock's reference to this letter of Hogg shows that he retained Hogg's letters to him at least until 1860. They were probably acquired by Prudentia Lonsdale after Peacock's death in 1866, for had Hogg (d. 1862) asked for them back during Peacock's lifetime, he would, presumably, have been obliged to return Peacock's letters to him, which were also sold by the Hogg heirs at Sotheby's in 1948.

SC 520   enough to be in love" (he is not very old, despite his rheumatism, in 1819), whom was he ever in love with? As Leporello[4] might have sung, "*Il catalogo è questo*": (1) Shelley's sister Elizabeth, by an effort, since he never met her; (2) Harriet, Shelley's newly wed first wife, by a natural instinct, when left alone with her in this very town of York; (3) Mary, the second and then unofficial wife of Shelley, by an immature agreement to share out in common. His fourth venture under Aphrodite, several years ahead, would be the lucky one, when in 1827 he collected and retained another of Shelley's leading lights, the "widowed" Jane Williams.

Meanwhile, coming back from dreams of love and Bishopsgate, he can ask the London-based Peacock to deliver a message for him. The final paragraph is an instance of pure "Hoggery" — an anticipation of the type of jest that was to fill out his *Life* of Shelley, and would creep, before that, into his continental travel-book *Two Hundred and Nine Days*.[5] There is no doubt that Hogg liked to indulge in a degree of harmless blasphemy; it is less certain whether he put it into action or kept it at the end of his fluent pen. In the present case, the chance is that he was civil enough to the encroaching lady, and thought out his "comfortable words" afterwards to embellish his letter. After closing his letter with greetings to Leigh and Marianne Hunt (lines 35–36) and to Peacock's mother and cousin Harriet Love (line 38), Hogg was ready to return to a solitary Atticism, reading scenes from Euripides' *Alcestis* (line 37).

4. During the opera season of 1817 Peacock persuaded Shelley to go with him to Mozart's *Don Giovanni*.

5. Published by Hunt & Clarke, March 1827; for the publishing partnership of Leigh Hunt's nephew Henry L. Hunt and Charles Cowden Clarke, see Richard D. Altick, *The Cowden Clarkes* (Oxford University Press, 1948), pp. 51, 63–64.

SC 521   LEIGH HUNT TO J. H. REYNOLDS, APRIL 30, 1819

AL signed *Leigh Hunt.*, 1 page. Double sheet, 8ᵛᵒ (7.2 x 4.4 inches).
Wove paper.
Seal (trace): wax, red.
Postal fee: 3.
Postmarks: 1. (Three Penny Post receiving house stamp, London, trace): PA[?DDINGTON]| [   ]| [   ]|; (delivery stamp, London): 12 oClock| 1 MY| 1819 [   ]|.
Addition, pages 2 and 3: letter patched in three places.

PROVENANCE: Walter T. Spencer, September 1922.

The Carl H. Pforzheimer Library

Hunt to Reynolds   *April 30, 1819*

> 8. *York Buildings– New Road*
> *30. April 1819.*

My dear Reynolds

     My nephew, young Henry Hunt, will see my brother
5 Robert to day or tomorrow, & tell him about the two pictures. I have also requested him to send you Frankenstein, which happened to be in his hands.–
Pray do not think of making excuses. Next to seeing you, I am always
happy to hear from you; & am not such an egotist in friendship as to quarrel
with you for a fit of absence, especially if you have been passing your time
10 comfortably.   Ever sincerely yours, Leigh Hunt.

[Address, page 3]
To

    J. H. Reynolds Esqre
    Little Britain.

line 3. The salutation (which may be followed by a comma) was heavily canceled, with the intention of obliterating the name of the addressee, when the letter was given away as an autograph — or later.

line 10. *yours*: there is a stray mark, possibly an apostrophe, following this word.

LEIGH HUNT, in his offhand praise of three "young poets" in the *Examiner* for December 1, 1816, linked forever the names of Shelley, Keats, and John Hamilton Reynolds. At that time Reynolds, though younger than Shelley by a full two years,[1] had already started a promising literary career. He had published a Byronic verse romance entitled *Safie. An Eastern Tale* (1814), *The Eden of the Imagination. A Poem* (1814), *An Ode* commemorating the fall of Napoleon (1815), and *The Naiad: A Tale With Other Poems* (1816). Reynolds also wrote regularly for John Scott's *Champion*, contributing poetry, literary essays, and drama reviews. Early in 1818, Keats, as we have seen, wrote two theatrical reviews for the *Champion* as a substitute for Reynolds, who was then at Exeter.[2]

1. Reynolds was born September 9, 1794. For the facts of his family, life, and literary career, see *Selected Prose of John Hamilton Reynolds*, ed. Leonidas M. Jones (Harvard University Press, 1966), pp. 1–7, and Robert Gittings, "The Poetry of John Hamilton Reynolds," *Ariel*, I (1970), 7–17; a list of writings by or attributed to Reynolds is appended to Jones's volume, pp. 427–443.

2. See SC 444, Commentary, which also identifies members of Keats's circle like Charles J. Wells.

Shelley and his Circle : Manuscripts

Hunt to Reynolds   *April 30, 1819*

SC 521   But John Hamilton Reynolds, like Charles J. Wells, was a man of divided will. Instead of pursuing passionately the vocation of poetry, as Keats did, Reynolds abandoned his literary efforts so that he could earn enough money to marry his long-time sweetheart, Eliza Powell Drewe of Exeter. On November 4, 1817, at the urging of James Rice (to whom Reynolds had introduced Keats), Reynolds was articled as a pupil in the law office of Francis Fladgate.[3] He enthusiastically pursued this new career, much to the disgust of Keats, who wrote to the George Keatses in December 1818: "I see very little of him now, as I seldom go to little Britain because the Ennui always seizes me there, and John Reynolds is very dull at home—."[4] On February 14, 1819, Keats repeated, "I see very little of Reynolds," and on March 18, 1819, he added: "Reynolds is completely limed in the law: he is not only reconcil'd to it but hobby-horses upon it—."[5]

     Inasmuch as Reynolds had almost lost touch with Keats (who had a few months earlier declared to him, "I have been getting more and more close to you every day, ever since I knew you"[6]), it was natural enough that he had also failed to keep up with Leigh Hunt and his circle of musical and literary dilettantes. sc 521 reveals that near the end of April 1819, Reynolds wrote to Hunt and apologized for having neglected him recently. He also called Hunt's attention to "two pictures"—probably paintings that Robert Hunt, who wrote art critiques, might wish to review in the *Examiner*.

     The date of Reynolds' renewed cordiality is significant. On April 21 Keats wrote to George and Georgiana Keats in America: "When Reynolds was here on Monday [April 19]—he asked me to give Hunt a hint

---

3. See sc 444 and Commentary. William Jerdan describes Fladgate as "one of the Sydney Smith species of wits (who are so rare), and was so prolific in piquant sayings, that, if all were remembered, they might fill a volume" (*The Autobiography of William Jerdan*, London, 1852, II, 172). *Johnstone's Guide* for 1817 lists Fladgate & Neeld, solicitors, 12 Essex, Strand.

4. Keats, *Letters*, II, 15. Little Britain, which was the home of Reynolds' father, a teacher at Christ's Hospital, ran from Aldersgate Street to the entrance of St. Bartholomew's Hospital (Plan of London, D1, Back Endpapers). Traditionally known for its printers and booksellers (see Wheatley, *London*, II, 405-407), Little Britain must by 1819 have been acquiring some of the flavor that Dickens conveys in *Great Expectations*, where the street is the site of Jaggers' law office (see, for example, chapter XX).

5. Keats, *Letters*, II, 60, 78.

6. July 13, 1818, Keats, *Letters*, I, 325.

[807]

SC 521   to take notice of his Peter Bell in the Examiner—the best thing I can do is to write a little notice of it myself" (which Keats proceeds to do in the body of his letter).[7] Notices of the two Peter Bells — Keats's on Reynolds' parody and Hunt's on Wordsworth's poem — appeared in the *Examiner* on April 25 and May 2, 1819, respectively. These articles, in turn, inspired Shelley in Italy to write *Peter Bell the Third*.[8] Reynolds' note very likely thanked Hunt for publishing the favorable account of his Peter Bell the second.

Given this occasion for Reynolds' letter, Leigh Hunt's response is certainly cordial. John Hunt's son Henry L. Hunt, now assuming his father's role at the *Examiner* office (see SC 517), will carry out Reynolds' suggestion about the "pictures" and send Reynolds a copy of Mary Shelley's *Frankenstein* (probably, Hunt's wording suggests, in response to Reynolds' request). But even in declaring himself to be no "egotist in friendship," Hunt verges on the self-conscious preening that nearly alienated Keats from him. Keats had written to Reynolds fourteen months earlier, "I will have no more of Wordsworth or Hunt in particular" because "we hate poetry that has a palpable design upon us—and if we do not agree, seems to put its hand in its breeches pocket."[9] Hunt seems to be very conscious of his own magnanimity in not being angry with Reynolds.

Charles Cowden Clarke later asserted that Reynolds was responsible for turning Keats against Hunt.[10] But it was early in 1818, when Reynolds was in Exeter, and late 1818, when Keats was seeing little of Reynolds, that Keats turned against Hunt most violently. Keats attributed his disaffection from Hunt to Hunt's egoism and bad taste and, incidentally, to his own tender ego.[11] If Reynolds was glorifying the legal profession and downgrading literature to Keats, he may have used Leigh Hunt as a convenient object lesson; but Keats was already disenchanted with Hunt and his circle — including Ollier, Novello, and Cowden Clarke

7. Keats, *Letters*, II, 93–94.

8. See Shelley, *Letters*, II, 134–135, and fn.

9. Keats to Reynolds, February 3, 1818, *Letters*, I, 224.

10. Keats, *Letters*, II, 11 fn.; see *The Novello Cowden Clarke Collection* (Brotherton Library, University of Leeds, 1955), pp. 8–9.

11. See his letters to the George Keatses, December 17, 1818, Keats, *Letters*, II, 11.

SC 521   himself.[12] We can note in closing that Keats's acquaintances among London's literary, artistic, and professional men divide themselves into two circles: Through Charles Cowden Clarke, his teacher and friend from the Enfield school run by Clarke's father, Keats met Leigh Hunt and his circle, including B. R. Haydon, Horace Smith, Charles Ollier, and Vincent Novello; through Reynolds, Keats met Benjamin Bailey, Charles Armitage Brown, Charles Dilke, James Rice, and John Taylor and Augustus Hessey, the publishers.[13] Charles Cowden Clarke's comment on Reynolds may reflect his suspicion toward the influence of Keats's other group of friends in general, rather than knowledge of any specific counsel that Reynolds may have given Keats.

12. Charles Cowden Clarke, of course, married Mary Novello.

13. *Keats Circle*, I, cxix.

SC 522   WILLIAM GODWIN TO ARCHIBALD CONSTABLE, MAY 5, 1819

AL (draft) unsigned, 1¼ pages. Single sheet, 4to (8.9 x 7.3 inches).
Laid paper. Watermark: [shield, lower part]| *JF*|.
Docket, page 2, in pencil: *Mandeville*|.

PROVENANCE: H. Buxton Forman (Anderson Galleries, Part II, April 26, 1920, lot 383); Brick Row Book Shop, "A Catalogue of Percy Bysshe Shelley," November 1922, #228; Hodgson's, June 20, 1929, lot 195.

May 5, 1819

　　Dear sir

　　　　I am utterly astonished at the letter I have just received from you. When you were setting out for Scotland at the end of last year, you left
5　*with me a statement of the accounts of Mandeville, by which it appeared that*
*the gross profits were £ 1071–11–5; or, after*ₐ*a correction of an error that I* (the)
pointed out in my letter to Edinburgh of Feb. 18 last, £ 1109–16–5. In that letter I stated to you my ideas of the debtor & creditor on that account, &
10　*claimed the fourth part of that sum as due to me, in terms of our agreement dated Dec. 1816. This sum I desired might be set off against the two acceptances then outstanding of £ 130 each. You express yourself not satisfied with this proposal, but you have made no statement on your side. The fourth*

SC 522   *part of £ 1109–16–5 is £ 277–9–1¼. If I am not entitled to the whole of*
this in your idea, to what part of it do you hold me entitled? I beg this may
be explained, & that the account may be put into a train of liquidation. It is a
very novel way of proceeding to threaten to arrest a man, before any statement
has been made by the party from whom the threat proceeded, how must it
is he claims as due to him. I am sorry you should have condescended to do
20   *this; & I am sorry you should have ~~been~~ seen any thing in my character,*
that should have induced you to think this was the way in which I was to
be led.

line 18. *must* (sic): for *much.*

SC 523   WILLIAM GODWIN TO ARCHIBALD CONSTABLE, MAY 5–6, 1819

L (draft), written as from Godwin and emended by him, 1 page. Single sheet,
4ᵗᵒ (9 x 7.3 inches).
Laid paper. Watermark: [shield, lower part]| *JF*|.
Docket, page 2: *Mandeville* [in ink]|; *Letters* [in pencil]|.

PROVENANCE: H. Buxton Forman (Anderson Galleries, Part II, April 26, 1920,
lot 383); Brick Row Book Shop, "A Catalogue of Percy Bysshe Shelley,"
November 1922, #228; Hodgson's, June 20, 1929, lot 195.

Skinner St. May 5ᵗʰ 1819

Dear Sir,

When you were setting out for Scotland at the end of last year,
you left with me a statement of the Accounts of Mandeville, by which it
5   *appeared that the gross profits were £ 1071.11.5; or, after the correction of an*
error that I pointed out in my letter to Edinburgh of Feb 18 last, £ 1109.16.5.
In that letter I stated to you my ideas of the manner in which this sum was
to be divided. If you think my division inaccurate, it is surely your business
                                            judge
10   *to state a division that you shall ~~think~~ ∧more equitableˣ. In expectation of*
your answer,

I am, Dear Sir,
Your most obedᵗ Servᵗ
W Godwin.

[810]

Byron to Guiccioli   *May 15, 1819*

SC 523   *x agreeably to the stipulations existing between us. If I am your debtor, it*

is fitting I should know the ~~amount~~ of your claim. If we mutually explain,

& know each other's minds, it is then, & then only, that we can come to an

amicable settlement.

20

May 6

A copy of this letter was sent by mistake yesterday, omitting the concluding lines.

line 1. Lines 1–14 written in an unidentified secretarial hand, except for the cancellation, interlineation, and *x* mark (lines 9, 10), which were inserted by Godwin.

line 15. In the manuscript lines 15–22 written in Godwin's hand, parallel to and then below the signature.

THE COURSE of Godwin's dispute with Archibald Constable in 1819 over the division of the profits from *Mandeville* was surveyed in the Commentaries to sc 512, sc 513, and sc 514. Here we need only add that Godwin's unsigned holograph draft answer (sc 522) appears to be his first hasty reaction to the legal steps taken by Constable; the calmer draft in an unknown hand was probably composed or dictated by R. W. Hayward, Godwin's solicitor.

From the additions in Godwin's hand, it appears that he sent a letter to Constable on May 5 transcribed from the draft supplied by Hayward, and then on May 6 he sent a revised copy, incorporating his later thoughts. This sequence is evidenced also in Godwin's Journal, for on May 5, 1819, he records: "Write to Constable," and on May 6: "PS to Constable."

SC 524   LORD BYRON TO TERESA GUICCIOLI, MAY 15, 1819

AL signed *Byron*, 1 page. Single sheet, 4ᵗᵒ (9.5 x 7.7 inches). Wove paper.

Notation, page 2, bottom quarter: *questa lettera è diretta alla Co. Gui̶c̶cioli| Teresa, nata Gamba|*.

Addition, page 2: four fragments of paper adhering to left margin, indicating that manuscript may have been mounted in an album.

PROVENANCE: J. A. Stargardt, Marburg, West Germany, November 29–30, 1966.

The Carl H. Pforzheimer Library

SC 524 *Signora Contessina Pregiatissima,*

       *Appena ricevuta la obbligantissima di lei lettera, Sig^a Contessina,
mi fo' un dovere di ~~rispondere~~ riscontrarnela collo stesso mezza, e di ringraziarla per i generosi sentimenti ch'Ella nutra a mio riguardo, nonché*
5 *pure ringrazio il Sig^r Cavaliere di Lei Marito, assicurandol entrambi, che
mi crederei onorato se potessi offerirle i libri ch'Ella— Sig^ra Contessina, con
tanta buona grazia mi chiede. — Debbo assicurarla non tener io presso di
me cosa veruna di mia penna, ne' a Venezia pure si trovano le mie opere,
perché in tal caso mi farei un pregio di servirla, accio avess'Ella ed il Sig^r*
10 *Cav^e una prova della mia obbedienza. – – – – –*
    *Non é fuor di proposito che dovendo io recarmi fra pochi giorni a Bologna
non passi anche a vedere la bella Romagna ed in ispecie le celebri antichita
di Ravenna, ed allora avrei il doppio piacere di baciarle rispettosamente la
mano, e riverire il Sig^r Cavaliere – a cui la prego far aggradire gl'ingenui*
15 *sentimenti della mia Stima ed amicizia. Intanto ho l'onore di' essere di Lei
Sig^ra Contessina*

             obb^mo ed umil^mo Ser^e
                 Byron
               P. d'Angleter< >

20 *Venezia. Addi 15 Maggio 1819.*

My dearest Madame Countess

    As soon as I received your most obliging letter, Madame Coun-
tess, I felt it my duty to reply to you by the same means, and to thank
you for the kind sentiments which you cherish in my regard, and I also
send thanks to the kind gentleman, your husband, assuring you both that
I would think myself honored if I could offer you the books which you,
Madame Countess, with such good grace requested of me. I must inform
you that I do not have with me anything from my pen, nor are my works
to be found in Venice either, because in that case I would do myself the
honor of serving you, so that you and your esteemed husband might have
a proof of my obedience.

It is not out of the question, since I must go to Bologna in a few days,
that I may also go to see beautiful Romagna and in particular the cele-

Signora Contessina Pregiatissima,

Appena ricevuta la obbli=
=gantissima di lei lettera, Sig.ª Contessina, mi fò un
dovere di *rispondere* riscontrarnela collo stesso mezzo,
e di ringraziarla per i generosi sentimenti ch' Ella nutre
a mio riguardo, nonché pure ringrazio il Sig.ʳ Cavaliere
di Lei Marito, assicurandol entrambi, che mi crederei
onorato se potessi offerirle i libri ch' Ella - Sig.ᵃ
Contessina, con tanta buona grazia mi chiede. — Debbo
assicurarla non tener io presso di me cosa veruna
di mia penna, né a Venezia pure si trovano le
mie opere, perché in tal caso mi farei un pregio
di servirla, acciò avess' Ella ed il Sig.ʳ Cav.ᵈ una
prova della mia obbedienza. — : — — —
Non é fuor di proposito che dovendo io recarmi
fra pochi giorni a Bologna non passi anche a
vedere la bella Romagna ed in ispecie le ce=
=lebri antichità di Ravenna, ed allora avrei il
doppio piacere di baciarle rispettosamente la mano,
e riverire il Sig.ʳ Cavaliere — a cui la prego far ag=
=gradire gl'ingenui sentimenti della mia stima ed amicizia.
Intanto ho l'onere d'esere di Lei Sig.ᵃ Contessina
Ab.ᵐᵒ ed umil.ᵐᵒ Serv.

Venezia. Alddi 15 Maggio 1819.

Lord Byron to Teresa Guiccioli, May 15, 1819 (SC 524), page 1

Byron to Guiccioli   **May 15, 1819**

SC 524   brated antiquities of Ravenna, and then I would have the double pleasure of most respectfully kissing your hand and of paying my respects to your honored husband — to whom I pray you will proffer the sincere expressions of my esteem and friendship. In the meanwhile I have the honor of being your most obliged and humble servant.

Byron
P[eer] of England

Venice. 15 May 1819.

Some of Byron's more common errors when writing in Italian include use of unnecessary apostrophes, omission of accents on final syllables, confusion of proper direction for accents, and mistakes in pronouns, verb forms, and gender. (See Iris Origo, "Byron's Letters in Italian," *The Last Attachment*, London, 1949, pp. 423–424.)

line 2. *lei* (sic): for *Sua*.

line 3. *fo'*: *o* written through *a*; the use of the apostrophe is incorrect unless Byron meant to write *fa'*, the imperative form.

    mezza (sic): for *mezzo*.

line 4. *nutra* (sic): for *nutre*.

line 5. *di Lei* (sic): for *Suo*.

line 7. *non tener io presso di me*: mistaken use of the infinitive *tener*; the phrase should read *che io non tengo presso di me*.

line 8. *ne'* (sic): for *nè*.

line 9. *perché* (sic): for *perchè*.

    accio (sic): should read *acciocchè* or *acciò che*.

    avess': the plural form *avessero* should have been used.

line 11. *é* (sic): for *è*.

line 12. *ispecie*: an archaic form of *specie* which Byron might have seen in Italian romances (Pulci, etc.).

    antichita (sic): for *antichità*.

line 14. *e riverire*: a more grammatical form would be *ed a riverire* or *e di riverire*.

line 15. *di Lei* (sic): for *il Suo*.

line 19. *P. d'Angleter<re>*: the final letters run off the edge of the paper; *P.* is an abbreviation for *Pair*.

line 20. *Addi* (sic): for *Addì*; may be translated *on the day of*.

BEHIND THE banalities of this public letter — a letter designed to be read by that celebrated antiquity, Teresa's husband — lay a crisis of passion and circumstance which was confronting an adulterous affair scarcely in its second month.[1] The letter sounds vacuous largely because of what Byron was trying not to say, what he was trying to find out clandestinely, and what he was trying to make up his mind about so that he might follow his heart.

The poet and his "Italian Caroline Lamb, . . . prettier, and not so

1. For a vivid account of this longest of all Byron's affairs, see Iris Origo, *The Last Attachment: The Story of Byron and Teresa Guiccioli, as Told in Their Unpublished Letters and Other Family Papers* (London, 1949). See also Marchand, *Byron*, II, 773 ff.

SC 524   savage,"[2] had conversed at an after-theater party in Venice on the second or third day of April 1819 and had plunged deeply into love — and scandal. Not more than ten days had elapsed, and Byron had scarcely formed a confident opinion of the fifty-eight-year-old Count Alessandro Guiccioli's magnanimity toward admirers of his nineteen-year-old countess when the count announced suddenly to Teresa that they must leave Venice for their home in Ravenna, with a stopover at Cà Zen, Guiccioli's desolate estate at the mouth of the Po. Teresa responded with passionate chagrin, and Byron was willing to follow her, but he held back from uncertainties of many kinds: how matters really stood all round, what "Ravenna" would mean, and a foreboding that he was facing "an opportunity of settling for life."[3] On April 13 Teresa sent her first letter to her lover under cover to Fanny Silvestrini, a friend who had stayed behind in Venice to assist their correspondence, but it somehow failed to reach Byron until the twenty-second. He then posted his first letter to Ravenna in care of an obliging priest, Gaspare Perelli. "By the aid of a Priest, a Chambermaid, a young Negro-boy, and a female friend [Fanny], we are enabled to carry on our unlawful loves," he remarked in June.[4]

Her first letter does not survive, but his of April 22 reflects the outpouring it must have contained and assures her that for him "there is no other woman in the world."[5] But his next, April 25, indicates that difficulties abound. She has written from "the country," Pomposa, where the count had a new estate, but has given Byron only her Ravenna address. Fanny has gone off to Treviso. And Byron has begun to brood on how fatal his love has always been "to those I love—and to myself."[6] By May 3 Fanny was back with alarming news that Teresa had been ill on the journey from a cause she had not wanted to reveal to the doctors.[7]

2. Byron to Kinnaird, April 24, 1819, *Byron: A Self-Portrait*, ed. Peter Quennell (London, 1950), II, 445.

3. Byron to Hobhouse, April 6, 1819, Byron, *Correspondence*, II, 107.

4. Byron, *Letters and Journals*, IV, 319.

5. Translated in Origo, *The Last Attachment*, p. 45; original Italian text, pp. 425–426.

6. Translated in Origo, *The Last Attachment*, p. 48.

7. Byron to Lord Kinnaird, May 15, 1819, *Byron: A Self-Portrait*, II, 448. Iris Origo (*The Last Attachment*, p. 51 and n.) conjectures that a word erased by Teresa in Byron's letter of May 3, 1819, and replaced by the word "*ammalata*" (= ill), "must have been *avvortito* (for *abortito* = miscarried)." But if so, Byron would not have gone on in the same letter to wonder "if there were some other cause" of her illness besides "riding" and to ask her to tell him "the real reason "and "clear up the

SC 524 Mysteriously Teresa's letters from Ravenna, when they came, did not unambiguously confirm the invitation which her husband had formally given Byron to visit them in Ravenna. By May 15 Byron had been informed that Teresa had had a miscarriage, beginning at Pomposa, and might still be very ill. No wonder that her instructions for his coming to see her had been "a little confused."[8]

The present letter is partly a testing of the ground, though perhaps prompted by Byron's dissatisfaction with the roundabout conveyance of earlier letters. It opens the possibility of a direct visit, of a chance stopping in, or of a secret rendezvous in Bologna. His English friends had been filling his ear with rumors that Count Guiccioli had been known to assassinate troublesome persons. But the question of Teresa's ability to receive him was his more serious concern. On May 15, the day of this letter, he wrote also to Lord Kinnaird, the brother of his friend Douglas Kinnaird:

It was my intention to have left Venice tomorrow, on my journey to R. but the Lady has miscarried, and her recovery seems more remote than was expected, being still in bed. I have been ordered to come at all events, but what the deuce should I do in the mean time without the possibility of seeing her, or at least of seeing her to any purpose in her present state. However, on the mere chance of seeing her only, I shall set out about the 20th and leave the rest to the protecting deities.[9]

Actually it was June before he left Venice. He made a ten-day trip of it, via Bologna. But when he reached Ravenna, he stayed for dinner.[10]

mystery." Plainly it was still a mystery to him. The assumption that Byron knew of the miscarriage this early beclouds the Origo interpretation of the immediately ensuing correspondence.

8. May 26, 1819, to Lord Kinnaird, *Byron: A Self-Portrait*, II, 455.

9. *Byron: A Self-Portrait*, II, 448.

10. The Carl H. Pforzheimer Library has recently acquired a newly discovered cache of correspondence between Teresa and Byron that complements the Gamba papers on which Iris Origo based *The Last Attachment*. Portions of these papers will appear in subsequent volumes of *Shelley and his Circle*.

SC 525 EDWARD ELLERKER WILLIAMS, PRIVATE JOURNAL, MAY 28–JUNE 2, 1819

HOLOGRAPH MANUSCRIPT, 26 pages, occupying leaves 3–15 of a copybook consisting of 60 leaves (8.3 x 5 inches), including the stub of the first leaf of the sixth gathering. The copybook is gathered in sixes, with the first and last leaves

SC 525 pasted down as endpapers, and also contains pencil drawings, water-color drawings, and miscellaneous fragments in verse and prose, probably of a later date.
Bound in quarter red skiver leather and cardboard covered by red binding
paper; pages hinged at short side, half of front cover torn away. All edges
trimmed.

Laid paper. Watermark: [crowned lion on a pedestal, rampant and brandishing
a scimitar]| JK| [   ]ol| [&]| [   ]mp|.

PROVENANCE: Jane Williams Hogg; Prudentia Hogg Lonsdale; J. Wheeler Williams; H. Buxton Forman (Anderson Galleries, Part II, April 28, 1920, lot 1199);
Brick Row Book Shop, "A Catalogue of Percy Bysshe Shelley," November 1922,
#250; Clinton N. Rutan, March 1964.

Private Journal

 *After having shaken a few dear friends by the hand I quitted London
about half past 3 o'clock on the aftⁿ of Friday the 28th May 1819 with my
friend Cox as Compagnons du Voyage, and arrived at Brighton at ten the*

5 *same night, having traveled Post from Town. —*

*Saturday 29th. After viewing the Pavilion, and other buildings; &ca, we
embarked with some difficulty on board the boat that was to convey us to the
Packet, and after having been shifted from one boat to another finally sail'd
from the harbour at 8 o'clock in the Evening. The wind was fair but notwith-*

10 *standing this the Vessel was haul'd upon a wind and kept up along the
shore until about midnight— Having then made Buchy Head she was suffered to keep away a point or two, and before day break had made 3 most
unnecessary angles, because the Master could not think of going out of his
usual track, however favourable the breeze, and to gratify the caprice of these*

15 *fellows we were kept at least three hours longer than we otherwise should have
been, tossing about in a head sea, and rendering every one, unused to the
water, as sick as possible; when the motion would scarcely have been felt had
they kept, as they might have done, the direct course— It may, perhaps, be
as well to remark that should ladies be inclined to embark at Brighton, it is*

20 *strongly recommended that a Schooner rather than a Cutter should be selected, the motion of the last being considerably increased by the weight of the
boom, causing a most unpleasant sea-saw pitching—*

 *Not a creature on board but that hail'd the sight of the harbour of Dieppe,
with the greatest delight, and almost all the Passengers, about 12 in number,*

SC 525 *pale as death jumped into a little french ~~boat~~ pilot-boat that came along side,*
and which conveyed us to the beach—
Sunday May 30ᵗʰ.— No sooner had the keel grated upon the sand than the
boat was boarded sans cremonie, by three or four persons whose office, by
their manner & the quick demand for our passports it requir'd but little
30 *penetration to discover were of the Police & Customs; both departments of*
which seem to be uncommonly well arranged—   We were recommended by a
fellow sufferer in the Packet to the Hotel De L'Europe, teint a M. Roland,
and found it an uncommonly clean and well attended house— but Roland
himself was particularly attentive and it being ~~neccessary~~ necessary to ex-
35 *change the Passports we recᵈ in London for those of France, we found his*
interest, which he most willingly ~~useful~~ exerted, extremely useful—   Before a
person can consider himself settled with his Baggage around him, three hours
will have elapsed and the novelty of the scene—the confusion, which it causes,
and the incessant ~~opportun~~ importunity of the rabble which never fails to
40 *follow strangers render this an event "devoutly to be wished for."—*

It being Sunday when we arrived all was of course gaiety and rejoicing,
but independant of this, it was the Fête of Pentecost, and all appeared in their
best attire. Nothing will strike the stranger more, than the head-dress of the
inhabitants, which, it is said, has been worn in Normandy from time im-
45 *memorial—   It consists of a cap of extremely white linen, placed nearly*
perpendicularly upon the head, and generally from half a yard to two feet
in height; from the sides of which, and from behind extend two wings, of
most delicately plaited or striped linen; these wings by the assistance of ~~sta~~
starch, I imagine, are made to fit close to the head and neck at the sides, and
50 *to erect themselves from the back part of the head, just suffering the hair,*
which is neatly turned up in a body, to appear between them; the streets being
crowded with the inhabitants, this moving mass of white head dresses formed
a most novel and striking appearance.—   But their whole dress is singular—
Long waists terminating as much in a point as the figure of the person will
55 *admit, are set off to advantage, and contrasted by an artificial rotundity &*
protuberance both before and behind, truly whimsical— to effect this, stuffing
is made use of, and but for the looseness of the petticoat, which is generally
red or dark brown, one would declare they wore hoops. The waist if it may

Private Journal.

After having shaken a few dear
friends by the hand I quitted London
about half past 3 o'clock on the after-
noon of Friday the 28th May 1819 with my
friend Cox as compagnon du
voyage, and arrived at Brighton at
ten the same night, having travelled
Post from Town. —

Saturday 29th. After viewing the Pavilion,
and other buildings, &c, we embarked
with some difficulty on board the
boat that was to convey us to the
Packet; and after having been shifted
from one boat to another finally
sail'd from the harbour at 8 o'clock
in the evening. The wind was fair
but notwithstanding this the Vessel
was hauld upon a wind and kept
up along the shore until about
midnight — Having then made
Beachy Head she was suffered to
keep away a point or two, and
before day break had made 3
much unnecessary angles, because

Edward Williams' Journal, May 28–June 2, 1819 (SC 525), page 1

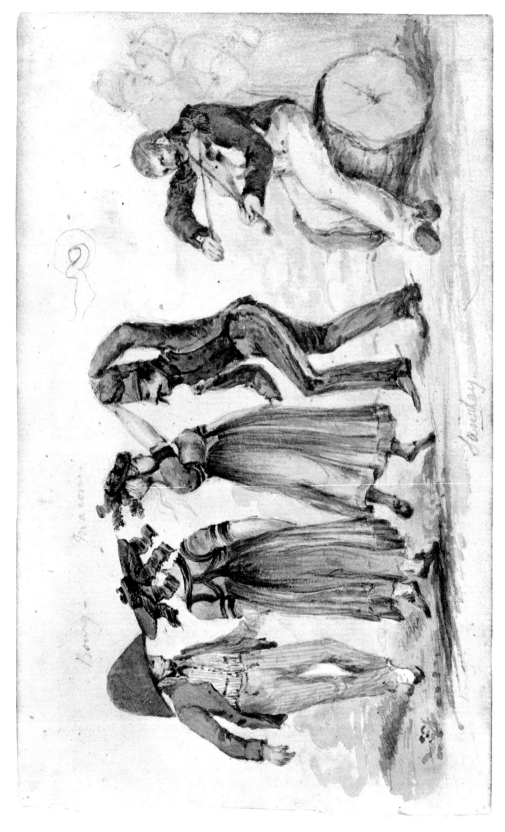

Pencil and watercolor sketch from copybook containing Edward Williams'
Journal (SC 525)

SC 525　be so called, reaching from the shoulders to the hips, after all their lacing is
but of a sorry shape; and is most commonly of a different color to the petticoat—　blue stockings upon thick legs, and shoes with buckles upon large
feet complete their dress; and yet, strange as it may seem, it is far from being
unpleasing–　During the day we went to Church or rather walked thro one,
and it being extremely full the long range of white caps looked still more
65　grotesque. In the evening we walked about a mile and a half into the Country
and witnessed a kind of Fete Champetre, which was held in what seemed to
us, an enclosed space with benches, resembling our Tea Gardens. Elevated
near a tree, some of the boughs assisting to support him, stood a fiddler, and
near him a boy with a drum, and in the midst of a crowd which surrounded
70　these musicians the white caps of the dancers were seen to glide thro' all the
mazes of what seem'd to me a most complicated figure; and in reaching the
spot, to my surprize I found these rustic's dancing a set of quadrilles with
all the ease and simplicity possible; & tho' their steps had not all the grace of
finish'd figurantés, their motions were far from being inelegant, and they
75　seem'd rather to sail along with winding inflections of the body, than to skip
about with ⟨——⟩ ~~feet~~ any activity of limbs; a style I always admired and
was consequently greatly pleased and amused—

In Dieppe as a Town there is nothing worthy attention– It is clean
and tolerably fortified; and their chief manufacturies in Ivory and laces–:
80　We left it on our way to Rouen on
Monday May *31st.* A description of the Diligence, a machine which we
ascended at *12* oclock, would be useless, no description could do justice to
this enormous vehicle ~~for travelling~~— On the road there is little to deserve
notice until we ~~descend~~ arrive at the summit of the hill about *2* miles from
85　the City; the view from thence is uncommonly grand. Manufactories upon the
largest and most splendid scale, of Silks– Paper– Linen's– &ca. will be
seen dispersed at distances throughout the fertile valley which bursts upon
the sight; having the appearance of so many palaces, in a vast & highly
cultivated amphitheatre. The road continuing at the foot of the range of hills
90　on the left, & through the midst of most exuberant foliage the Seine is at
intervals seen to wind, forming a coup d'œil highly picturesque.

No Englishman can enter Rouen without feeling a certain pride that

SC 525　*the City was once the seat of regency of his ancestors; and that all the principal*
　　　　buildings are the works of their hands. Indeed a great share of the blood of

95　*Normandy may be said to flow in our veins: not that this, by the by, ought*
　　　to be our boast, when we look at their degenerate state, but we may reflect
　　　with pleasure that the spirit of our Norman sires and Conquerors has been
　　　preserved in us untainted.

　　　Tuesday June 1st 1819. The Cathedral is the first building we visited this

100　*morning, which is a magnificent and extremely Gothic pile. ~~of building~~ Be-*
　　　sides the steeple, it has two towers— the square one on the left preserves the
　　　name of St Romain by whom it was erected in the year 623. to embellish
　　　the Cathedral which was built in 260. and enlarged by Archbishop Robert in
　　　942. The other tower is of most beautiful architecture, terminating in a gal-

105　*lery in the form of a crown. In the belfry of this tow'r was suspended the*
　　　largest bell in in Europe if we except that of Moscow. but this bell was taken
　　　down (not without destroying the interiors of the building,) during the Revo-
　　　lution; and together with all the brass which the ornaments on the ancient
　　　tombs afforded, was melted down and converted into money. Within the

110　*Church is a temple or rather a Chapel dedicated to the Virgin, the Altar*
　　　Piece of which is decorated with a very fine picture of the " Adoration of the
　　　Shepherds by Phip de Champagny, and considered his chef d'œuvre. There
　　　are also two splendid monuments— The one on the right is that of the Cardinal
　　　D'Amboise, a work of the fifteenth century, and astonishes by the perfection

115　*of the sculpture & the richness of its design. The other on the left is that of*
　　　the Seneschal of Brezé, Governor of Rouen— The ~~figure~~ recumbent figure
　　　of the naked Seneschal on the cenotaph is uncommonly fine, and has been
　　　　　　　　　　　　　　　Masters
　　　attributed to the first Italian ~~Masters~~; but it is, in th truth, the work of Jean

120　*Goujon the most admirable statuary of his age, and the best of the french*
　　　school. In the interior are several monuments, and among them, simply in-
　　　scribed on three square stones of black marble we learn that the heart of
　　　Richard Coeur du Lion is deposited, and that of his Brother Robert, and the
　　　Duke of Bedford— The lightness and strength of the architecture—the ele-

125　*gance & beauty of the windows of painted glass, and the stream of variegated*
　　　light which they afford, will, with the ornaments I have enumerated amply

SC 525   *repay the trouble of a visit to this splendid edifice. From this place we con-*
tinued our walk thro' the Boulevards, which, it is said, surpass those of
Paris; and arrived at the Convent of St Ursuline situated on an eminence
130   *on the skirts of the Town. We were accompanied in this excursion by a*
Mr Oliver, one of our fellow travellers in the Packet, whom we found to be an
intelligent and excellent companion. On passing the gates of the principal
entrance we learnt they were only opened to admit a Nun into her living
tomb, and for ever after closed upon her, until they should be reopened, that
135   *her corpse might pass on to the tombs " of all the capulets." I involuntarily*
shuddered at the horrible affects of bigotry and superstition, and walk'd on
in silence to the other gate, which was opened by a female whose habit ac-
quainted us, she was of the Ursuline Order, and who appeared to recognize
our guide, whose wife had had chambers within the walls one or two years
140   *since. During the Revolution the nuns were driven from this secluded abode,*
and were either imprisoned or dismiss'd; but after the cessation of civil
tumult and intestine broils, the Convent was again restored to them under
many proper, and well-judged restrictions and regulations; among which
were, that no nun should be confined to the cloister contrary to her inclination,
145   *but should have the power to quit it and mix with the world whenever she*
pleased; Another was, that the lady Abbess should receive and educate a cer-
tain number of pupils, as at a kind of school, the expences of which should
defray those of the Convent, or contribute to its support. It was the school
which we first visited, and the cleanliness and order which reign'd throughout
150   *astonished me. Each young lady has a private chamber; which are neatly*

each

furnished and form the two sides of a long corridor, at the end of which and
on other divisions was written " Silence" a meaning which seem'd strictly
observed. They are ushered to bed at a certain hour, and each retiring to her
155   *own chamber, the bolt wis turned upon her, and she wis thus confined during*
the night, having no communication whatever one with the other—— The best
Masters are provided and their improvement I am told is very rapid–

     On our way thro' the long galleries which form this part of the institution
we had occasion to pass the Convent Chapel, which forms one end of the one
160   *attended by the public, and divided at right angles from the Altar Piece by*

SC 525 *high iron gratings, before which a red curtain is drawn, to veil them from*
observation, so that during Mass or other prayers their voices are only heard
chaunting the responses–&ca. In this Chapel the Nuns were at prayer, and
had ranged themselves on either side the aisle; while the noviciates, in long

165 *white transparent robes, had seated themselves in a semi-circle* ~~around~~ near *the*
curtain. The last of the nuns who composed the line on the right, ~~hand~~ *was*
extremely pretty–indeed handsome.— She seem'd very earnest in her devo-
tions, and there was an expression of melancholy in her countenance which
bespoke all the serenity of a settled sorrow, and her whole appearance did not

170 *fail most powerfully to affect us. From the situation she held among her*
Sisterhood we concluded she was the last who had taken the veil, and if so,
she was the one whose history was related to us as we approached this spot.

Born of a family of the first respectabity, her beauty and riches had

175 *attracted the attention of a young Frenchman; her hand was engaged to him,*
and at the early age of 17. She was likely to become his wife. But who shall
calculate on happiness in this life – or delude himself with the promises of
Hope— Her father died, and his property was claimed by another branch of
the family, who were too successful in their claims, and a few months saw

180 *this poor girl, reduced from affluence to a state of comparative poverty— but*
this reverse of fortune was only of secondary consideration to the loss of her
parent, and when her bursting heart most needed consolation, and the tender-
ness which it is in the power of disinterested affection to afford, she found
her lover had also deserted her, and with her fortune, vanished his love.

185 *Unable to bear the weight which misfortune had heaped upon her, she*
retired from a world of misery to these cloisters, and took the dreadful oath
a short time since, being now in about her twentieth year.–

From this scene we retired to the garden where the tower in which Joan
of Arc was confined is still standing– It is of great antiquity, and ascended

190 *by a circular staicase, from the top of which a good view of the town may be*
had. The little cell in which she was chain'd is now a pigeon-house, and the
lower part is converted into a Wash-house for the use of the Convent. While
viewing the town from this height, and giving way to a train of reflections
which the place is likely to excite, the sound of a harp from one of the cell

SC 525 *windows of the Nunnery was heard, which recalling the poor Nuns history,*
completed a scene, and sensations ~~which~~ *I leave to the imagination. As to*
*our companion M*ʳ *Oliver, he poor fellow was quite overcome on looking from*
this tow'r into the chamber which his late wife had occupied– for independant
of the school, there are also some excellent rooms for boarders (as they are
200 *termed) which may be had unfurnishd for about £100 a year.*

    From the Convent we proceeded to Mont aux Maleade by a circuitous
and pleasant route. Having arrived at its summit and delighted ourselves
                               cottage
with the enchanting prospect it commands we entered a little ~~chateau~~*, which,*
205 *in a great degree, was conceal'd by the gardens* ~~which~~ *surrounding it and*
were regaled with some wine by the hospitable hostess– This cottage was
                    of the town
*the country retreat of some respectable person*ₐ*and was to be let at the mod-*
erate sum of 25 £ per year. with a tolerable garden and every convenience for
210 *domestic comfort. The following account will better give a description of its*
situation than I can, and the only inconvenience that would be felt, is, the
want of Society, that of Rouen being but very indifferent. "Les campagnes
environnantes du Mont-aux-Malades offrent des coteaux charmants qui in-
vitent à s'y reposer. Leurs richesses leur variété, le silence de ces lieux solitaires
215 *qui n'est troublé que par les chants de Philomèle, et des hereux habitants*
des airs, tout invite a s'y arrêter et à se livrer à la plus douce mèlancholie
sur ces pelouses émaillées de fleurs." I left this spot not without great re-
gret, and hastened to view the curiosities which the Town offers.– The first
which invited our attention was the house in which Corneille was born: it is
220 *ornamented without, with a bust of this author, and is now become a Cutler's*
shop– Passing on thro' the narrow, dirty streets of the Town we arrived
~~now~~ *at the "Place de' la Pucelle D'Orlean's." so called from her having*
been cruelly burnt at the stake in the centre of this square, by order of the
Duke of Bedford—the then Regent of France. A fountain is erected on the
                              one of
225 *spot of inferior design but of great utility to the inhabitants–*ₐ *The corner*
houses of the square has a small projecting room of very ancient appearance,
where she was exposed to public view as a Sorceress a short time previous to
                    general appearance
230 *her execution, and, no doubt, from its* ~~antiquity~~ *remains unaltered since that*

SC 525   *time; it is now a dirty Inn or rather* ~~*public house*~~ (cabaret (smoking house)) *, which is signified in writing under the window–   It is said that many of the houses, built of oak, which were erected in those days* ~~*and*~~ *are standing now, and their timber's but little*

235   *injured by time, and this from their curious structure I think is the case. If so it is a strong proof of the difference of our climates in their favour.*

     We next directed our steps to the Church of St Ouen, the architecture of which like the Cathedral is very gothic– light, and beautiful; and the interior if in point of elegance of structure and design, if it does not surpass may be

240   *certainly* ~~*t*~~ *said to equal it. During the Revolution it was shamefully despoil'd of its ornaments, and converted to the use of the Army,— Blacksmiths forges were erected between the pillars for the construction of arms– the smoke of which has entirely spoilt the appearance of what, once must have been, a*

245   *splendid organ; but it is rather remarkable that in other respects* (this organ) *it should have remained uninjured–: the windows too, beautifully painted with the representation of scriptural subjects– Saints &ca strange to say remaind unbroken, while the statues which adorned the pillars were* ~~*dis*~~ ⟨——⟩ (dislodged) ~~*broken*~~

250   *and in demoniac fury trodden underfoot. This Church was formerly belonged to a Monastery of Benedictines, and as scarcely a family of distinction but that had one or more children on its establishment, it became extremely rich, and commanded the first Interest.–   Near the Altar is a fine painting of the Visitation–   The railing of beautiful figurative design which formerly*

255   *surrounded the Communion table cost three millions of francs, but the greater part from it being of brass was melted down into money, like every other ornament of that metal. Many other Churches are worthy of attention–   The folding doors at the entrance to some of them being of solid oak, most wonderfully carved with the* <u>*Ascension*</u>*— the* <u>*Last-day*</u> *and other subjects, by some*

260   *religious devotees.— The size of one or two doors, (being of one solid plank,) which we measured must have been before* <u>*plaining*</u> *at least 6 feet in breadth– 15 in height and* <u>*6 or 7*</u> (inches) *in thickness——! Many Churches, eight or ten in number since the revolution, have been converted into receptacles for Public*

265   *Carriages– Stages– Waggons &ca.— Coach Builders have purchased some,*

Shelley and his Circle : Manuscripts

SC 525　— *upon the bases of others private buildings have been re erected–　I went into one which had become a Roulageoire, ~~and~~ into which the architecture had invited me, and found a very ancient and beautiful round painted window still standing— but the smell within was intollerable.——　We cannot reflect*

270　*on these changes without certain indiscribable sensations of ~~horror~~ regret at the conviction of a most impressive and inevitable truth. "Tempora Mutantur."–*

The Building which was a long time since a College of Jesuits is now a place where public business is transacted; the long line of cells in the corridor

275　*having been conveniently converted into offices. The stair case is very fine and will immediately attract the notice of the architect and stranger– There are also two long galleries of Pictures and of course in so large a collection a few will be found of the old Masters' to repay the trouble of finding them ~~out~~, among the rubbish of the french school which surrounds them. The last being,*

280　*by them considered the finest, are placed in the best light, to the great disadvantage of others– The inner gallery contains almost all scriptural subjects, many of the largest size–×One struck me particularly—and the subject appeared ~~to me~~ to be John in the wilderness, but bearing the marks of crucifiction– If it is intended to represent Christ, the design is bad indeed—at any*

285　*rate it seems to have been the Painters wish to picture a Saint rapt in the enthusiasm of entire devotion—the attitude—the upcast expression of the eyes– the clasped hands all denote that the artist understood the passion, and*

something of painting,ₐ^too and his production would in all probability have

290　*remained in happy obscurity, had he not introduced a Cherub appearing from the clouds and delighting the Saint with the harmony of a fiddle– One comment on pictures en passant. If Poets have been arraigned at the tribunal of Taste and Judgement, and have been condemned as impious in having mingled in their compositions too free descriptions of hereafter rewards and*

295　*punishments— who have heightened their language by bibliccal quotations, and been accused of sinning against religion; surely some bounds ought more properly to be placed on the pencil of the Artist who brings the working of his fanatical mind immediately before our view, leaving nothing to the imagination– and to gratify the ambition of priesthood these shocking productions are*

[827]

SC 525 *stuck in every corner of these churches, to please old women—frighten*
children & generally to disgust the reflecting and more religious part of man-
kind. of b which by the by, with all their mummery there are very few to be
found in this country—
Wednesday June 2nd—

305   *The first place we visited this morning was the Parliament House of*
William the Conqueror– It is now divided into various offices; but the Grand
Audience Chamber, the ceiling of which is very remarkable is appropriated
to many public uses. and the walls were entirely covered with placards and
other notifications– A man desiring to change his residence must here first
310 *publish his intention, that the Police may register his name elsewhere, and*
that no creditors may be swindled–   It is also requisite that the banns of any
persons wishing to be married should here be pronounced in a printed paper
and exposed on the wall.

           ×I have since learnt that this picture is by Domenichino and intended for
315 *St Francis & . . . . but not one line– not a syllable of my former opinion*
of it do I recant——

line 4. *Compagnons*: *s* canceled in pencil.

line 28. *cremonie*, (sic): for *cérémonie*.

line 42. *independant* (sic).

line 44. *from*: written through an indecipherable word.

line 66. *Fete Champetre*,: both words are missing circumflex accents. The first *e* in *Champetre* is written through *ai*.

line 72. *surprize*: alternate spelling listed in dictionaries of the period.

line 76. ⟨——⟩ *feet*: first canceled word illegible.

line 92. *Englishman*: altered from *English* with *man* crowded in under the beginning of *can*.

line 106. *in in*: the last and first words respectively on the recto and verso of a leaf.

line 112. *Phip*: possibly an abbreviation for *Philippe*.

line 122. *three*: written through *two*.

line 123. *Lion*: written over two smeared letters, the first of which is *a*.

line 136. *affects* (sic).

line 146. *Another*: *A* written through *a*.

line 155. *wis*: altered from *was*; *w* canceled; *i* written over *a*; the next *is* altered in the same way.

line 163. *chaunting*: obsolete spelling listed in *OED*.

line 164. *noviciates*,: alternate spelling listed in dictionaries of the period.

line 174. *respectabity*, (sic).

line 190. *staicase*, (sic).

line 194. *the place*: *e* written through *is*.

line 198. *independant* (sic).

line 200. *unfurnishd*: Williams usually puts an apostrophe in place of the *e* of *ed*, but the mark is missing here.

line 201. *Maleade*: should be plural.

line 203. *cottage*: interlined in pencil above *chateau* which is canceled in pencil.

line 205. *surrounding*: *ing* written through *ed*.

line 207. *of the town*: this interlineation and the caret on the main line are in pencil. The caret has been formed by adding a pencil stroke to an ink comma.

line 215. *hereux* (sic): for *heureux*.

Williams, Private Journal   **May 28–June 2, 1819**

SC 525

line 216. *invite a*: *a* should be written *à*.
　　　　mèlancholie: the accent should be acute.

line 222. *de'*: *d* written through *D*.

line 229. *general appearance*: interlined in pencil above ~~antiquity~~, which is canceled in pencil.

line 231. The words in this line are interlined in pencil above ~~public house~~, which is canceled in pencil.

line 240. *said*: probable reading.

line 244. *this organ*: interlined in pencil; caret and cancel line on main line are also in pencil.

line 247. *remaind*: *d* canceled in pencil.

line 249. *dis⟨——⟩*: canceled letters illegible.

line 264. *revolution,*: *r* may be *R*.

line 265. *Waggons*: alternate spelling listed in contemporary dictionaries.

line 269. *intollerable*. (sic).

line 270. *indiscribable* (sic).
　　　　~~horror~~: probable reading.

line 283. *crucifiction* (sic).

line 288. *too*: interlined in pencil; caret also in pencil.

line 295. *bibliccal* (sic).

line 301. *the*: written through *an*.

line 314. ˟*I have since ... recant*——(line 316): this note, apparently added after the text of the Journal was completed, occupies the final line of leaf 24, verso, as well as three lines squeezed in between each of the first three lines of manuscript leaf 25, recto.
　　　　Domenichino: written in pencil.

E DWARD ELLERKER WILLIAMS, Shelley's closest friend during the last year of his life, who shared the poet's fate when the *Don Juan* foundered off the Italian coast on July 8, 1822, was born in India on April 22, 1793. Edward was the son of John Williams (1741/42–1809), captain of the Second Battalion of Sepoys in the Bengal Army, and Jane Dale Williams (died July 29, 1798, aged thirty-three), the second of John Williams' four wives.[1] In 1805 young Edward was registered as a student at Eton, where Shelley had matriculated on July 29, 1804, and the two may have met there, though neither seems later to have recalled the other.

Williams did not remain long in the aristocratic confines of Eton, for by April 1807 he was a midshipman in the Royal Navy. As part of his training, the fourteen-year-old boy kept a log book, entitled in his hand: "A Journal of the proceedings of/ His Majesty's Ship Superb/ Donald McLeod Esq. Captain—/ Commencing the 18th of April 1807—/ and Ending the 22nd of December 1807—/ Kep't by Edwd Williams

---

1. V. C. P. Hodson, *List of the Officers of the Bengal Army, 1758–1834* (London: Constable, 1927–1947), III, 475–476. Captain John Williams was the author of the posthumously published *An Historical Account of the Rise and Progress of the Bengal Native Infantry, from Its First Formation in 1757, to 1796* (London: John Murray, 1817). In Hodson's opinion, Edward's name probably came from Major General Edward Ellerker of the Bengal Army. See Edmund Blunden, "The Family of Edward Williams," *Keats-Shelley Memorial Bulletin*, IV (1952), 50. According to Medwin, Williams was "a lineal descendant from one of Cromwell's daughters" (Medwin, *Shelley*, p. 312).

SC 525 Mid."[2] Although Trelawny's later record of his friend's account of his life is factually inaccurate, one statement he attributes to Williams — "I liked the sea, but detested the tyranny practised on board men-of-war"[3] — though it certainly expresses Trelawny's opinion, may also correctly reflect Williams' attitude and mark one bond between Trelawny and Williams. Whatever his motives for changing branches of the service, Williams next appears as cornet in the Eighth Dragoons (the King's Royal Irish Hussars), his appointment dated June 7, 1810.[4] He was promoted to lieutenant on April 28, 1813. He continues to appear on the lists as first lieutenant in the Eighth Dragoons through the Army List for 1817,[5] but he then disappears from that regiment to reappear (in the Army Lists for 1820 and 1821) as a half-pay first lieutenant in the 21st Foot regiment, with May 28, 1818, given as the date he went on half pay. The next information we have is found in the "Private Journal" now under examination.

Blunden has suggested that the liaison between Edward and Mrs. Jane Cleveland Johnson may have begun in 1818 and that they went together to the Continent late in that year.[6] In the "Private Journal," there is no suggestion that Williams was attached to Jane by June 1819. His traveling companion was, he says, his "friend Cox" (line 4), also mentioned in the better-known journal that Williams kept while he was with Shelley in 1821–1822.[7]

The accounts in this "Private Journal" and Williams' previously

2. This manuscript log book is in The Carl H. Pforzheimer Library (Shelleyana 153). Because it is completely impersonal, simply recording winds, weather, location, and movements of the *Superb* during a very uneventful tour of duty (the ship remained moored at Spithead from April 18 to June 13, 1807, and was moored at St. Helen's from November 18 through December 2, 1807, the date of the last full entry), we have not thought it necessary to describe it formally in *Shelley and his Circle*. It is interesting to note that Trelawny was a passenger on board the *Superb* from October 15 to November 19, 1805, while on his way to his first naval assignment. See Anne Hill, "Trelawny's Family Background and Naval Career," *Keats-Shelley Journal*, V (1956), 15–17.

3. Trelawny, *Records*, I, 136.

4. Robert H. Murray, *The History of the VIII King's Royal Irish Hussars, 1693–1927* (Cambridge, 1928), II, 705.

5. Blunden, following notes by Hodson, suggests that Williams went on leave to Europe in 1815 ("The Family of Edward Williams," p. 50).

6. Blunden, "The Family of Edward Williams," pp. 50–51.

7. This friend may have been George Cox, who was appointed cornet in the Eighth Dragoons on August 14, 1813 and who left the regiment sometime after September 1818 and before 1820.

SC 525 published Journal of 1821–1822 do not, however, jibe. (H. Buxton Forman noted this fact in pencil on a sheet loosely inserted in the "Private
Journal.") Williams says in his 1821–1822 Journal that he and Jane left
England together, landed at Dieppe, passed through Rouen and Versailles, and met Cox at Paris, where they remained some time, then
traveled through Troyes, Dijon, and Dole, spent three weeks at Lons-le-
Saunier (the capital of the Jura region), and finally settled for a year at
Geneva, where "on Sunday the 7th February 1820, at half past six in
the morning, my eldest child, Edward Medwin, was born, and christen'd,
by the Rev^d Mr. Rooke in June following."[8] The February 1820 birth-
date for Edward Medwin Williams suggests that the connection between
Williams and Jane must have begun by at least early June or July 1819.

There are two possible hypotheses that would harmonize the known
facts: (1) Williams and Cox may have begun the tour of France described
in the "Private Journal"; on or about June 2, Williams received word
from Jane Cleveland Johnson, with whom he had been having an affair,
that caused him to return to England, elope with Jane to France (by the
same route he and Cox had just followed), and proceed to Paris, where
they rejoined Cox. Or (2) the "Private Journal" may have been written
when Jane and Williams eloped to the Continent, but Williams chose
to disguise the identity of his companion because the "Private Journal"
was, in fact, the beginning of a travel book intended for publication.
The character of the "Private Journal" makes the second alternative at
least as likely as the first.

In examining the contents of this self-styled "Private Journal," we
find in it nothing private, but rather the staple stuff of the travel books
popular during this period. Comments on crossing the English Channel,
information on the passport and customs check, and remarks about the
hotel at Dieppe (lines 32–33) would have been appropriate, perhaps, for
either private reminiscence or public perusal. But it is difficult to imagine
an ordinary tourist, writing simply to record the highlights of his trip
to aid his own memory in later years, giving the history of the cathedral
of Rouen as Williams does (lines 99–127), or recording that the belfry of
the cathedral contained "the largest bell in Europe if we except that
of Moscow." It is equally unlikely that a man with a Welsh name and

8. Williams, *Journals and Letters*, pp. 101–102.

SC 525 Irish relations would, for his own private interest, glory in the supposition that "the spirit of our Norman sires and Conquerors has been preserved in us untainted" (lines 97–98). Williams' remarks share with many contemporary British travel diaries the characteristics of being chauvinistic, snobbish, and dull, and of containing numerous factual errors.

The strongest evidence that the "Private Journal" was really intended to be public resides, however, not in what it contains but in what it omits. The opening sentence, where he speaks of "having shaken a few dear friends by the hand" (line 2) is not in the nature of truly personal memoranda. Even laconic Godwin or Mary Shelley would at least have named names.

The Pforzheimer manuscript of the "Private Journal" gives every appearance of being a fair copy, perhaps taken at a later date from a more intimate account written at the time of the journey. The pencil and watercolor drawings in the back of the same copybook depict the local costumes of Geneva, Châlons, St. Gallen, the Jura region, Bourg, and Mâcon, and the notes and poetic fragments (obviously later than the "Private Journal") seem to relate to Williams' poetic drama *The Promise*, which we know Williams wrote in the early summer of 1821.[9] It seems clear that this copy of the "Private Journal" was made sometime after the trip through central France and into Switzerland (1819–1820) but before the trip to the south of France and to Italy in the fall and winter of 1820–1821.

In the H. Buxton Forman sale of 1920 there were eight of Williams' notebooks described as "Manuscript Journals, Sketch Books, and Memorandums," seven volumes in lot 1199 of Part Two of the sale (April 28, 1920) and Williams' midshipman's journal of 1807 in lot 1092 in Part Three of the sale (October 7, 1920). Of these eight notebooks, at least six can now be accounted for. Three — the present notebook containing the fair-copy "Private Journal" of 1819, the midshipman's log of 1807, and the fair-copy manuscript of *The Promise* — are in The Carl H. Pforzheimer Library. Williams' well-known journal of 1821–1822, edited and published by Richard Garnett in 1902 and by Frederick L. Jones in *Shelley's Friends* (1951), is with the Ashley Library in the British Museum. The Bodleian Library, Oxford, owns Williams' notebook (Shelley

9. Williams, *Journals and Letters*, p. 103.

SC 525   adds. e. 21) containing Sporting Sketches of his brief stay in "Hindo-stane," travel observations, some original verse, and extracts from his reading; in addition, it owns the manuscript of portions of *The Promise* with Shelley's corrections.[10] Perhaps in one of the missing notebooks there is the rough-draft version from which this fair-copy "Private Journal" was transcribed. For the moment, however, we must be satisfied with the brief public version of the beginning of Edward E. Williams' sojourn on the Continent.

10. This manuscript is described in Peck, *Shelley*, II, 365–380.

SC 526   WILLIAM GODWIN TO JOHN TAYLOR, JUNE 10, 1819

AN, third person, ½ page. Single sheet (*ca.* 6 x 7.3 inches).
Laid paper. Watermark: [F]ELLOWS|.
Additions: 1. paper trimmed to *ca.* two thirds of original quarto sheet; 2. remnants of yellow paste on three corners of verso.

PROVENANCE: Winifred Myers, June 20, 1969.

*M*ʳ *Godwin presents his compliments to M*ʳ *Taylor, &, if convenient to that gentleman, would do himself the pleasure to call on him for a few minutes' conversation, to-morrow, Friday, at two o'clock.*

> *Skinner Street,*
> *Thursday, June 10.*

5

[Address, page 2]

<   >*lor & Hessey*

<   >*t Street*

line 6. *<Messʳˢ Tay>lor*: trimming of paper has   line 7. *<Flee>t*: same as line 6, above.
removed portion of address.

SC 527   WILLIAM GODWIN TO JOHN TAYLOR, JUNE 14, 1819

AL signed *William Godwin*, 1 page. Single sheet, 4ᵗᵒ (9 x 7.4 inches).
Laid paper. Watermark: [posthorn in shield, lower part]| *JF*|.
Seal: wafer, orange.
Notation, page 2: (*N*ᵒ *43*)|.

PROVENANCE: Union Square Book Shop, June 24, 1930, #139.

Godwin to Taylor   *June 14, 1819*

SC 527   *Sir*

*Having maturely reflected on the conversation I had with you
on Friday last, & with Mr Hessey on Saturday, I feel so much discouraged
in my negociation, that I judge it most respectful to Mr Hazlit to drop it, &
5 proceed no further. I have therefore only to request the favour of you to return
to me the manuscript prospectus I left with Mr Hessey, I am,*

sir,

your most obedient servant

William Godwin

10   *Skinner Street,*
        Monday, June 14,
          one o'clock

[Address, page 2]
Mr *Taylor*
    Messrs *Taylor & Hessey*
15   *Fleet Street*

T HE ONLY years that June 10 fell on a Thursday and June 14 on a
Monday during the time that the firm of Taylor and Hessey was
located on Fleet Street were 1813 and 1819. References in Godwin's
Journal make clear that the above notes were written in 1819, and their
contents, in turn, breathe life into some otherwise meaningless entries
in the Journal.

The later note makes clear that Godwin spoke with John Taylor on
Friday, June 11 (keeping the appointment he made in the earlier note)
and with Augustus Hessey on Saturday, June 12, to negotiate on behalf
of William Hazlitt for the publication of a book. Godwin's Journal records the meetings with Taylor and Hessey, as well as calls on him by
Hazlitt on Thursday, June 10, and Sunday, June 13. At the second of
these meetings, Godwin and Hazlitt must have decided to break off the
discussions with Taylor and Hessey. The negotiations may have continued briefly,[1] but they came to nothing.

1. Godwin called on John Taylor again on Wednesday, June 16, and dined with Hazlitt on June 19
and on June 25.

Godwin to Taylor   *June* 14, 1819

SC 527   Taylor and Hessey, who specialized in *belles lettres*, had published
the second edition of Hazlitt's *Characters of Shakespear's Plays* (1818),
his *Lectures on the English Poets* (two editions, 1818 and 1819), and his
Lectures on the English Comic Writers (April 1819).[2] In September 1818
Hazlitt had quarreled with the firm because Taylor and Hessey would
not give him £200 for the last of these,[3] and it seems likely that he felt
his interests would be better served if the negotiations for his next book
were undertaken by a third party. Thus, Godwin presented Taylor and
Hessey with a "manuscript prospectus" and discussed terms with them.

The book described in that prospectus would seem, on first analysis,
to have been *Political Essays, with Sketches of Public Characters* published
by William Hone in August 1819. But by Hone's own testimony, he had
"concluded a bargain" for this work by February 3, 1819,[4] and Godwin's
letter can refer to *Political Essays* only if Hazlitt and Hone were seeking a
co-publisher. There is no evidence of this. The most likely subject of
Godwin's negotiation was Hazlitt's *Lectures chiefly on the Dramatic Literature of the Age of Elizabeth*, a series of lectures written from July to
September 1819, delivered at the Surrey Institution in November and
December 1819[5] and published in 1820 by Stodart and Steuart, 81 Strand,
and Bell and Bradfute, Edinburgh.[6]

It would have been natural to offer these lectures to Taylor and
Hessey (providing their terms were fair), because they had published
Hazlitt's previous two series given at the Surrey Institution. Keynes's
Bibliography (page 43) contains a clue to the failure of Godwin to bring
Taylor and Hessey to terms; although Hazlitt's *Lectures on the English*

2. See Geoffrey Keynes, *Bibliography of William Hazlitt* (London: Nonesuch Press, 1931), items 18,
33, 34, and 44.

3. Edmund Blunden, *Keats's Publisher: A Memoir of John Taylor* (London, 1936), p. 55.

4. Howe, *Hazlitt*, p. 251.

5. Howe, *Hazlitt*, p. 256. Keynes (p. 51) says the lectures were delivered in January 1820, but if so,
this would mark a second delivery of them — perhaps at the Crown and Anchor Tavern. See SC 471,
Commentary.

6. Keynes, *Bibliography of William Hazlitt*, item 51, pp. 50–51. Howe (p. 263) gives as the publisher
John Warren, who took over the sale of the book in 1821, reprinting the title page and selling this
second issue as a "Second Edition"; see Keynes, pp. 51–52. Robert Stodart had earlier published
Hazlitt's *A View of the English Stage* (1818), the remainder of which was also transferred to John
Warren in 1821 and issued with a new title page (Keynes, pp. 30–31). Perhaps Stodart's business
failed between 1820 and 1821.

SC 527 *Poets* had gone into a second edition, sales of the subsequent volume on the English comic writers apparently languished. More direct testimony comes from John Taylor himself, who on January 26, 1820, wrote to Michael Drury, his cousin who was a Philadelphia bookseller: "I should like to send over an Edition of 1000 Hazlitt's Lectures on the Poets, if I thought they would sell for more than waste paper, exclusive of the Freight, for we have overprinted that Work.—But perhaps we had better make a short End of them in our own hands.—[7]

One interesting footnote to Godwin's role in these negotiations is that Buchanan McMillan, the printer with whom Shelley struggled in his attempt to publish *Laon and Cythna*, was also the printer of Hazlitt's *Lectures chiefly on the Dramatic Literature of the Age of Elizabeth*. Perhaps Godwin recommended McMillan to Hazlitt as he had earlier done to Shelley.

Godwin attended at least four of Hazlitt's lectures when they were given at the Surrey Institution. His Journal indicates that he went on the following Fridays: November 5 (the first lecture in the series), November 12, November 26, and December 24 (the final lecture). He attended the theater on November 19, and on Thursday and Friday, December 16 and 17, he was scrambling about trying to get money ("Seek Curtis"; "Write, express, to Curtis, Camberwel"[8]) so that he probably did not attend a lecture.

On the two remaining Fridays during the series (December 3 and December 10), Godwin dined, met, or supped with some of the same people he notes as attending Hazlitt's lectures, and they may have gone there together without Godwin's noting the fact in his very selective Journal.

7. *Keats Circle*, I, 101.
8. See SC 447, Commentary and fn. 6.

SC 528 LEIGH HUNT TO T. J. HOGG, JUNE 30, 1819

AL signed *Leigh Hunt.*, 1½ pages. Double sheet, 8ᵛᵒ (6.7 x 4.2 inches). Wove paper.

PROVENANCE: Thomas Jefferson Hogg; Prudentia Hogg Lonsdale; John Ewer Jefferson Hogg; Major R. J. Jefferson Hogg (Sotheby, July 26, 1948, lot 276).

Hunt to Hogg   *June 30, 1819*

SC 528   *York Build^(gs)*
                                                        Wed^y Afternoon.

My dear Hogg,

   I am sorry I happened to be out the other evening when you
5 *called. I was at home not long afterwards. You will find me here as usual*
Saturday, Sunday, Monday, or Tuesday, & as usual truly happy to see you.
I shall write to Shelley immediately about this unfortunate loss. It is, luckily,
not the worst loss a man can have; but it must be terrible, like all real losses,
especially if the poor little fellow suffered. Pray come soon, when you do
10 *come, & let me have a long chat with you.*

          Most sincerely your's,
           Leigh Hunt.

THIS NOTE can be precisely dated once it becomes obvious that the "poor little fellow" of line 9 is William Shelley, who died in Rome on June 7, 1819. Shelley wrote this news to Peacock on June 8, requesting him to "tell all my friends, so that I need not write to them."[1] Shelley's letter was postmarked in London on Saturday, June 26, and probably delivered to Peacock the same day.[2]

Peacock, who saw Hogg frequently, doubtless notified him promptly. Hogg, in turn, probably called on Hunt either Sunday or Monday evening. Not finding Hunt at home, Hogg may have left the message with servants or children, but, in this case, he would more likely have sent Hunt a note, giving him such facts as could be garnered from Shelley's letter to Peacock. The present reply from Hunt to Hogg was written, then, Wednesday, June 30, 1819.

Hunt had at this time five healthy children (and a sixth on the way[3]); though his essay "Deaths of Little Children" refers to the "grave of one inexpressibly dear to us," the allusion is probably to his mother or his sister Mary, rather than to the death of any child of his own.[4] Hunt's

1. Shelley, *Letters*, II, 97.

2. For Godwin's reaction to news of the death of his grandson and namesake, see sc 530, Commentary.

3. Thornton, John, Mary Florimel, Swinburne, and little Percy Shelley Hunt were to be joined (September 28, 1819) by James Henry Sylvan Hunt. See sc 411, Appendix.

4. See *Indicator*, I (April 5, 1820), 202; Landré, *Hunt*, I, 21; Blunden, *Leigh Hunt*, pp. 5, 8–9.

The Carl H. Pforzheimer Library

SC 528 personal situation must be taken into account when evaluating his judgment — expressed both in this letter and in his essay — that the death
of a young child is "not the worst loss a man can have." Neither Fielding's Parson Adams nor Mary Shelley, Charles Ollier, William Wordsworth, and Thomas Moore, among Hunt's acquaintances, were able to
render so facile a judgment on the matter.

The Shelleys were not, of course, the only parents to lose children
in the epidemic that swept Rome in 1819 and the following two years.
In 1838 Professor Francesco Puccinotti (1794–1872) of Naples published a medical treatise in two volumes entitled *Storia delle Febbri
Intermittenti Perniciose di Roma negli Anni MDCCCXIX, MDCCCXX,
MDCCCXXI.*[5] In his Dedication Professor Puccinotti vents his continuing grief over the deaths of a young son and daughter in that epidemic almost twenty years earlier. This great outbreak of malaria also
struck Amelia Curran in 1819; her illness and William Shelley's grave-
stone were the primary topics of correspondence between her and the
Shelleys until Shelley's death. The Shelleys declined to invite her to
visit them in 1821, when her continuing illness might have been transmitted to Percy Florence Shelley.[6]

Although this Commentary is not the place to pursue such an argument in detail, it seems likely that some of the ideas and language in
Hunt's essay "Deaths of Little Children" suggested some passages in
Shelley's *Adonais*, written a year later. Shelley had seen at least some
numbers of the *Indicator* by October 1820.[7] Whatever consolation Hunt's
essay may have afforded the Shelleys in 1820 or 1821, Hunt did not try
to impose his acceptance of death on them in 1819. Neither, on the
other hand, did he write to them "immediately," as he promised Hogg.
True to his dilatory habits, he failed to write until spurred by the arrival
of a letter from the Shelleys telling of the tragedy. Then, in shame, Hunt
lied about the delay, picturing himself as too ill to write sooner (SC 529

5. History of the Pernicious Intermittent Fever of Rome in the Years 1819, 1820, 1821 (Naples:
Presso Puzziello Tipografo-Librajo, 1838). A new edition appeared in Naples in 1842, annotated by
G. Nicolucci. Both these editions are in The Carl H. Pforzheimer Library.

6. Shelley, *Letters*, II, 106–107, 158–160, 296; Mary Shelley, *Letters*, I, 73–74, 78–79, 93–94, 113–114,
142–143. For the most lasting link between Miss Curran and William Shelley — the portrait of
him she painted shortly before his death — see the frontispiece to this volume.

7. See Shelley, *Letters*, II, 239.

SC 528   and Commentary). His invitations to Hogg to visit him almost any day
show that he felt well enough on June 30 to write immediately, as he
proposed to do.

SC 529   LEIGH HUNT TO P. B. SHELLEY, JULY [8], 1819

AL signed *Leigh Hunt.*, 3½ pages. Double sheet, 4to (8.9 x 7.3 inches).
Wove paper. Watermark: BATH| 1816|.
Seal: wax, red.
Postal fees: 1. 1/11; 2. 18.
Postmarks: 1. (Foreign Post Office stamp, London)*:* F 19| 167|; 2. (transit
stamp)*:* ANGLETERRE|; 3. (transit stamp)*:* CHAMBERY|; 4. CORRISP^{ZA} ESTERA DA
GENOVA| [fleur-de-lis]; 5. 23 LUGLIO|; 6. (trace).
Notations, address leaf: 1. (in Leigh Hunt's hand)*: 8th July*|; 2. (in pencil)*: 108*|.

PROVENANCE: Colonel Charles Shelley Leigh Hunt; Mrs. Beryl Dodgson
(Sotheby, April 8, 1935, lot 205).

<blockquote>

York Buildings– July   1819.

My dearest friend,

　　*My letter would have come off to you before I received yours, had I
not been laid prostrate by a bilious fever, from which I am now recovering,*

5　*& which I think has left me in a condition to get better than I was before,
if I take care & take exercise;–which with me are nearly the same things. I
had received the news of your misfortune, & thought of all which you & Mary
must suffer. Marianne, I assure you, wept hearty tears of sympathy. He was
a fine little fellow, –was William; & for my part, I cannot conceive, that the*

10　*young intellectual spirit which sat thinking out of his eye, & seemed to comprehend so much in his smile, can perish like the house it inhabited. I do not
know that a soul is born with us; but we seem, to me, to attain to a soul, some
later, some earlier; & when we have got that, there is a look in our eye, a
sympathy in our cheerfulness, & a yearning & grave beauty in our thought-*

15　*fulness, that seems to say – our mortal ~~dre~~ dress may fall off when it will:–
our trunk & our leaves may go:– we have shot up our blossom into an immortal air. This is poetry, you will see, & not argument; but then there comes
upon me another fancy, which would fain persuade me, that poetry is the
argument of a higher sphere. Do you smile at me? Do you too, Marina, smile*

</blockquote>

The Carl H. Pforzheimer Library

SC 529   *at me? Well then,– I have done something at any rate. My dear friends, I affront your understandings & feelings with none of the ordinary topics of consolation. We must all weep on these occasions, & it is better for the kindly*

                   within

fountains ~~our~~ us that we should. May you weep quietly, but not long; &

25   *may ~~every~~ the calmest & most affectionate spirit that comes out of the contemplation of great things & the love of all, lay his most blessed hand upon you.– I fear this looks a little ~~a~~ like declamation; & yet I know, that he would be a very mistaken critic who should tell me that it was so.*

        I can do nothing with my tragedy,– at least not at present;– I may

30   *do something, when the new management at Drury Lane is settled, provided Kean likes it upon perusal. He has rejected it, in a manner, at present, without perusing; for in my letter to him I unfortunately said that there were <u>two</u> characters in it, either of which, it was thought, would suit him: and it turned out just afterwards, that he had a mortal antipathy to having any*

35   *second Richard in the field. He returned me a very polite answer, in which he said that his hands were full. I then sent to Covent Garden; & here it seems the manager lives in the house of a bad dramatist to whom he is under obligations, & who settles the destiny of all new comers. I had the honour to be rejected. You cannot suppose, of course, that I think my tragedy worse than*

40   *those which are recieved. I know it to be a great deal better; but between ourselves, I think I have hurt it for publication by k<   > in mind it's destination for the stage. At all events, I shall keep it <   > in hopes of future performance. What I most regret is, the waste of my <   > which I might have turned to more lucrative account; but I did my best & most*

45   *industrious.– The two little poems (Hero & Leand., & Bacchus & Ariad.) are out; & if Ollier (of whom every body, by the way, complains as well as yourself) does not bestir himself, I will make up a little packet next week, with these & one or two other ~~little~~ things in it. Perhaps I had better do so at once, if Peacock does not send.⟨—⟩ Is it possible that you have never*

50   *received even Ollier's first packet yet, with the portrait in it, which I thought, in my egotism, was to gratify you so ~~much~~? I guess as much by your silence*

SC 529   *about it.— You will see in the Examiner what I have said about your lovely poem of Rosalind & Helen, which is a great favourite of mine. I was rejoiced to find also that Charles Lamb was full of it. Your reputation is certainly*

55   *rising greatly in your native country, in spite of it's honest Promethean chains; & I have no doubt it will be universally recognized on it's proper eminence. I long, by the bye, to see Prometheus himself. I have no doubt you have handled his "wearied virtue" nobly. It is curious, but I had thoughts a little while ago of writing a poem myself, entitled Prometheus Throned; in*

60   *which I intended to have described him as having lately taken possession of Jupiter's seat. But the subject, on every account, is in better hands. I am rather the son of one of Atlas's daughters, than of Atlas himself.– I am glad you like the specimen of the Pocket-Book.– As my old chat refreshes you, I think myself especially bound just now to write often, & shall dispatch an-*

65   *other letter next week, addressed to Mary, which I hope will induce her to oblige me with one of those gigantic paragraphs which she entitles a letter also. Wont you write to me frequently too, if I write frequently?–God bless you, my dear, dear friends; & take care of your health & spirits if it be only for the sake of your affectionate   Leigh Hunt.*

70   *some time ago*
     *P.S. We are well. I persuaded Bessy Kent*ₐ*(who is a very good girl,) that you would like a letter from her, so she wrote one, & never sent it after all. So I have persuaded her, with a second persuasion, to send it now. If it should be old news, it at least tells you of old friends;– at any rate, I guess so.*

     [Address, page 4]

75   *P. B. Shelley Esqre*
          Presso al Signor Giovanni
                         Gisborne,
               Livorno,
                    Italia

80   *Leghorn,*
     Italie.   Italy.

The Carl H. Pforzheimer Library

SC 529

line 15. *dre*: probable reading.
line 16. *our trunk*: *our* written through *we*.
line 25. *every*: probable reading.
line 41. *k*<*?eeping*>: seal tear.
line 42. <   >: seal tear.
line 43. <*?time*>: seal tear.
line 48. *little*: probable reading.

line 49. ⟨*?so*⟩: possible reading.
line 51. *much?*: probable reading.
line 70. The postscript is written at the top of page 1, above and to the left of line 1.
line 80. This line and line 81 are written to the left of and perpendicular to the remainder of the address.

THE COMMENTARY to SC 528 outlines the sequence by which Hunt came to learn of the death of William Shelley. Shelley's letter to Hunt is no longer extant, but something in it aroused Hunt's shame at his own negligence in failing to write sooner. His excuse of ill health was, as we have seen, not candid. What is more, Shelley undoubtedly knew that Hunt's story was untrue when he read it, for Hogg, in his letter of condolence to Shelley, dated July 2, 1819, had written: "Hunt is very well— better than I ever remember to have seen him. . . ."[1]

When Hunt finally wrote, however, he evinced sympathy and expressed hope that was probably most welcome to the Shelleys — particularly Mary. Hunt was no philosopher, and his theory of the soul's growth — paralleling Keats's concept of the world as "the vale of Soul-making" and perhaps emanating from a common line of discussion in the London literary circles they both frequented[2] — is more poetry than argument. But he had the tact both to suggest this comforting hope of immortality and to admit that it was inadequate to mitigate the fact of death; it was merely a sign of his sympathy and concern for the bereaved parents.[3]

As we have seen,[4] Hunt had worked on his drama on the Cid for almost a year but this letter shows that his efforts would yield no immediate tangible results. Hunt's complaints at the unjustness of his treatment by the two theaters may have been warranted. During the 1818–1819 theatrical season at Drury Lane, Edmund Kean had shown himself self-centered and overbearing to playwrights, his fellow actors, and even the committee of the Drury Lane Theatre. He "often expressed

1. *Shelley and Mary*, I, 384.

2. See Keats, *Letters*, II, 101–104.

3. See Hunt's essay "Deaths of Little Children," *Indicator*, I (April 5, 1820), 201–204.

4. See SC 486, SC 504, SC 517, and Commentaries.

Hunt to Shelley   *July* **[8]**, **1819**

SC 529   his determination to play no secondary character whatever."[5] Thomas
Harris (*circa* 1740–1820), who had been a part owner of the Theatre
Royal, Covent Garden, since 1767 and the active manager since May 26,
1774, was noted for his series of short-lived favorites whose advice he
valued. John Howard Payne had held this position about 1816–1817, but
he had gone over to Drury Lane with his *Brutus* — performed by Kean
to loud applause in December 1818. A charge of plagiarism was leveled
at Payne, but the tempest subsided as soon as the story "was discovered
to have originated with the person who had taken the place of Mr. Payne
at Covent Garden. . . ."[6] Who Harris' advisor was in 1819 when Hunt
submitted his play, we have been unable to discover.[7]

In the passage already quoted from his *Autobiography*, Hunt related
how Elliston had suggested "an alteration in the third act."[8] From this
and SC 534 we know that Hunt did submit the play to Drury Lane
Theatre after Robert William Elliston, one of Hunt's favorite actors,
became its manager in the summer of 1819[9] and that Hunt withdrew the
play because he had portrayed the Cid "too after the beau-ideal of a
modern reformer, instead of the half-godlike, half-bigoted soldier that
he was." Hunt began, he wrote, "to recast the play, but grew tired and
gave it up."[10]

The scenes from the play that Hunt later published, with apologies,
in the *Companion*[11] may be those he had revised to make his character

5. *DNB*. The phrase, a "second Richard in the field," sounds very much like an echo of Shakespeare,
but the closest analogues we can discover are the struggle between two Harrys in *I Henry IV*,
V.iv.59–74, and "I think there be six Richmonds in the field" (*Richard III*, V.iv.11).

6. Gabriel Harrison, *John Howard Payne* (Philadelphia, 1885), p. 92; see also pp. 85–89.

7. Thomas Harris himself, treated briefly in the *DNB*, remains a shadowy figure. Hyder Rollins
notes that one obituary notice in the London *Courier* lists him as eighty-two years old at his death
(Keats, *Letters*, I, 199 fn.), but James Boaden, in *Memoirs of . . . John Philip Kemble* (London, 1825),
thought Harris to have died in "the 78th year of his age" (II, 568). Harris is, naturally, mentioned
by theatrical figures (e.g., Richard Brinsley Sheridan) in their letters, but students of the period do
not seem to have accorded him the attention due one who managed one of the two licensed London
theaters for forty-six years. See also *Public Characters of 1802–1803*, pp. 278–308.

8. See SC 387, Commentary.

9. For Elliston (1774–1831) see *Public Characters of 1806*, pp. 598–612; *DNB*; and Allardyce Nicoll,
A History of Early Nineteenth Century Drama (Cambridge, 1930), I, 219. Hunt's praise of his acting
is found in his *Critical Essays on the Performers of the London Theatres* (London, 1807).

10. Hunt, *Autobiography*, I, 167–168.

11. May 28 and June 4, 1828, pp. 289–303, 305–320.

SC 529 of the Cid conform to the legendary prototype. At least, it is difficult to find in the character there portrayed "the beau-ideal of a modern reformer." The Cid is caught in the familiar struggle between love and honor when he is forced to slay the father of his beloved Ximena for insulting the Cid's aged father. The dramatic blank verse, though imitative of Elizabethan plays, has more strength and virility than does most of Hunt's poetry. The excerpts in the *Companion* suggest that Hunt was realistic in evaluating his play as no worse than those accepted and better than many. What is more, had Hunt been encouraged by the acceptance of this play to write more neo-Elizabethan tragedies, his own poetry might well have been strengthened by the discipline of imitating the Shakespearean manner.

The high praise of *Rosalind and Helen* (lines 52–53) shows that Hunt's basic taste had not changed. He and Mary appreciated and tried to encourage Shelley's sense of pathos, preferring sentimental to philosophical poetry. Charles Lamb (who was not yet distancing his own feelings through the character of Elia) was one whose *Works* of 1818[12] also exhibit a marked penchant for the pathetic and sentimental. Shelley wrote to Hunt six weeks later, expressing admiration for Lamb's *Rosamund Gray*, which is a classic in the literature of quiet pathos and much more successful in that vein than *Rosalind and Helen*.

Shelley had informed Hunt in the now-lost letter of his progress on *Prometheus Unbound*. Hunt's reaction is typically gracious, but it baffles the imagination to conceive the reversal of literary history that would have occurred had Hunt told Shelley a few months earlier that *he* intended to write *Prometheus Throned*. Both may have been stimulated to the subject by Byron's "Prometheus," though, inasmuch as that poem was written at Villa Diodati in July 1816, Shelley's conversation may have inspired Byron on that occasion.[13]

Although Hunt promised to write to Mary the following week, he once again procrastinated until after the arrival of Mary's letter to Marianne Hunt, written June 29 and received in London on July 17.

12. *The Works of Charles Lamb* (London: C. and J. Ollier, 1818).

13. See Byron, *Poetry*, IV, 48–51; John Buxton, *Byron and Shelley* (London, 1968), pp. 45, 78, 261–263.

Shelley and his Circle : Manuscripts

SC 530   LEIGH HUNT TO M. W. SHELLEY, JULY [25–27], 1819

AL signed *L.H.*, 3½ pages. Double sheet, 4to (9 x 7.3 inches).
Wove paper.
Seal: wax, red*:* [woman's head, profile]|.
Postal fees: 1. 1/11; 2. 7; 3. 98.
Postmarks: 1. (receiving house stamp, London)*:* CRAWFOR[D STREET]|; 2. (Foreign
Post Office stamp, London)*:* F 19| 91|; 3. (transit stamp)*:* ANGLETERRE|; 4. (tran-
sit stamp)*:* CHAMBERY|; 5. CORRISP^ZA ESTERA DA GENOVA| [encircling fleur-de-
lis]|; 6. 11 AGOSTO|.

PROVENANCE: Colonel Charles Shelley Leigh Hunt; Mrs. Beryl Dodgson
(Sotheby, April 8, 1935, lot 205).

> *8. York Buildings– New Road*
> *July   1819.*

My dear Mary,

     I was just about to write to you, as you will see by my
5 *letter to Shelley, when I received yours. I need not say how it grieves me to*
see you so dispirited. Not that I wonder at it under such sufferings; but I
know, ~~that~~ at least I have often suspected, that you have a tendency, partly
constitutional perhaps & partly owing to the turn of your philosophy, to
look over-intensely at the dark side of human things; & they must present
10 *double dreariness, through such tears as you are now shedding. Pray consent*
to take care of your health, as the ground of comfort; & cultivate your laurels
on the strength of it. I wish you would strike your pen into some genial
subject (more obviously so than your last), and bring up a fountain of gentle
tears for us. That exquisite passage about the cottagers shews what you could
15 *do. Besides, to tell you the truth, I want an opportunity of speaking about*
your writings, having delayed criticising your novel so long for want of well
knowing how to handle it, that I know not what to be⟨–⟩ at in order to shew
you what I really feel. This is the whole mystery, I assure you,– if ever you
have a thought about it,– & not my old thief of a friend, delay, however he
20 *might have insisted on having a hand in the matter too. Then because I do*
not criticise the works of this friend, I do not criticise the works of this or
that acquaintance; & so I get into twenty dilemmas, which none but a
journalist can fully experience, & none but a very true friend, very clever

[845]

SC 530 to boot, can afford to pardon. And so, Madam, I fall in imagination at your
feet, & kiss the hands to your very illustrious Signoraship, hoping they will
soon furnish me with an opportunity of redeeming my character. Imagine
that in this sheet of paper, which your eyes are now engaged upon, you are
perusing my ~my~ petitioning face:– (don't take your hand from my chin:–) I
am sure there is enough sincerity in it to obtain my pardon,– & I hope

30 enough gaiety & good-humour to bring out a few little smiles from your own.
I wish in truth I knew how to amuse you just now, & that I were in Italy
to try. I would walk about with Shelley, wherever he pleased, having resumed
my good old habits that way; & I would be merry or quiet, chat, read, or
impudently play & sing you Italian airs all the evening. Pray is Shelley

35 still of opinion that a man ought to have time to write an essay between every
note in *Sul margine d'un rio*? I have lent somebody that beautiful little air
of Martini's he was so fond of, & cannot recollect whom; so that I often
miss it, with many internal execrations against the unknown. We are continually talking of you. Your names are truly "as familiar in our mouths

40 as household words. "I wish the Shellies were here!"– "What would Shelley
or Mʳˢ Shelley say to that?"—"I think Shelley would almo< > < > as
well with us here this fine hot summer weather, as in Italy."—I w< > I
had him writing here with me, & reading one another lectures upon being
dilatory & diaphragmatical."–"Mary would have been amused perhaps at

45 the opera tonight:"— & then we look up to your box, almost hoping to see a
thin patrician-looking young cosmopolite ~looking~ ^yearning^ out upon us, & a sedate-
faced young lady bending in a similar direction with her great tablet of a
forehead, & her white shoulders unconscious of a crimson gown. Apropos

50 (though the word is misapplied, as it happens to be really applicable) the
opera is not altogether so entertaining as it was during the God-gift dispensa-
tion (Fodor, i.e. Theodore), Mʳˢ Fine-Eyes (Bellocchi) being very coarse in
every other respect except her voice, & that is too sharp at top. She is the
oddest little hey-day lump you ever saw, fantastically dressed, & looking

55 alternately ~sad~ good humoured & sulky to an excess. Peacock has been reasoned by some mathematician out of his love for the opera, & is to read
Greek, they say, instead, on Saturday nights,– the Dithyrambic, of course,

SC 530   *to begin at seven precisely. What do you think of this debut of mine in scandal? But he glories in doing nothing except upon theory. He falls in love,*

60   *as it were, upon a gravitating principle. His passion,* ~~both~~ *literally as well as metaphorically, is quite problematical. Let B be Miss Jenkins, &c.— Hogg, from whom Shelley will have heard before this, has gone into the country for some weeks. I see a good deal of Lamb, Hazlitt, Coulson, the Novellos &c., but as much at their own houses as at mine, or rather more*

65   *just now. We give no dinners as we used. Our two other out-of-door amusements are the theatre (an involuntary one), & taking our books & sandwiches, & spending a day in the fields,– which we do often. Mr Lloyd, an old Lakist & friend of Lamb, & translator of Alfieri, has come to town, & speaks highly of Shelley, with whose poetry he is well acquainted. He laughs at those who*

70   *accuse him of having no principles, & says he is evidently full of principles, & as for that matter, of religion too. What do you think of this baulk in their teeth? L. is a man much shaken by sickness, but very acute-headed & metaphysical. Farewell till I write again, which shall be speedily. Tell me if I write with too great levity, and I will be as grave as my sympathy is sincere.*

75   *Try & walk, in spite both of bitter & sweet burdens. Marianne does, & is the better for it. Ever truly your's L.H.*

[Address, page 4]
P. B. Shelley Esqre
     Ferma in Poste,
         Livorno,

80   *Leghorn,*
            Italia.

    Italy.

    Italie.

line 8. *constitutional*: *titu* written through indecipherable letters.

line 16. *for*: written through illegible word.

line 17. ⟨-⟩: illegible letter.

line 27. *engaged*: corrected from *enaged*.

line 39. *"as familiar*: Hunt has distributed his quotation marks peculiarly in this passage.

     in our mouths: written on fragment adhering to seal.

line 40. *Shelley or M^{rs}*: written on fragment adhering to seal.

line 41. *almo*<*st*> < > : final two letters obscured by seal.

line 42. *with us here*: written on fragment adhering to seal.

     w<*ish*> : letters obscured by seal.

line 47. ~~*looking*~~: probable reading.

     upon: written through ?*at*.

The Carl H. Pforzheimer Library

Hunt to Shelley   **_July_ [25–27], 1819**

SC 530

line 55. *sad*: probable reading.

line 75. *does,*: the punctuation mark is uncertain.

line 76. *your's*: possibly followed by a comma; Hunt's writing on the final page of the letter is extremely small and cramped.

line 78. *Poste,*: for *Posta*.

line 83. *Italie.*: written to the left of and perpendicular to the remainder of the address.

Hunt's previous letter to Shelley, written on or about July 8, was date-stamped at Leghorn on July 23. The present letter to Mary was date-stamped on August 11; if it traveled at a similar pace, it was written about July 25–27. The opening lines make clear that it was written after the arrival of Mary's despairing letter of June 29, which was received in London on July 17, 1819.[1]

In this letter, Hunt attempts to rouse Mary from her depression and urges her to turn once again to writing. This advice calls to Hunt's associative mind his failure to review *Frankenstein* in the *Examiner*. Hunt is, no doubt, candid in saying that he did not know "how to handle" *Frankenstein*; the philosophical problems it raises were at once uncongenial to his characteristic habits of thought and dangerous to defend. Godwin's *Caleb Williams* had been an attack on "Things as They Are" in the political and social sphere, and *Frankenstein* was similarly subversive in the metaphysical and religious sphere. If Hunt understood this tendency (from his conversations with Shelley and Mary), he would have hesitated to point it out to the readers of the *Examiner*. If, on the other hand, he could not fathom the implications of the novel, he would have found it equally difficult to write intelligibly about them.

The rest of Hunt's letter consists of harmless chatter designed to relieve the condition that Mary described in her letter in these words: "I never know one moments ease from the wretchedness and despair that possesses me—."[2] Hunt's method is far different from Godwin's stern rebuke to his daughter's continuing depression:

I cannot but consider it as lowering your character in a memorable degree, and putting you quite among the commonality and mob of your sex, when I had thought I saw in you symptoms entitling you to be ranked among those noble spirits that do honour to our nature. Oh! what a falling off is here! . . . you have lost a child; and all the rest of the world, all that is beautiful, and all that has a claim upon your kindness, is nothing, because a child of three years old is dead![3]

1. Mary Shelley, *Letters*, I, 74–75.   2. Mary Shelley, *Letters*, I, 74.
3. September 9, 1819, *Shelley and Mary*, I, 410A.

Hunt to Shelley   *July* [25–27], **1819**

SC 530 Godwin's first response to Mary's bereavement is not extant, but that letter was perhaps kinder and more sympathetic. Godwin's Journal indicates that he received news of his grandson's death on Saturday, June 26. ("Letter of nepos," reads the laconic entry.) The next day Godwin recorded, following the list of his day's writing, reading, and social engagements, "Depression." By Tuesday, June 29, his spirits had revived: "Malthus, revise (animate). Write to Livorno." For the negative effect of some of Godwin's letters on Mary, see SC 531 and Commentary. There is, on the other hand, no evidence that Hunt's friendly chatter succeeded any better in rousing Mary's fallen spirits.

Hunt, besides mentioning things that he knew Mary liked, also abandons his attitude of universal benevolence (see SC 517 and Commentary) long enough to carp at Peacock, whom he knew Mary disliked.[4] Peacock may have been rude to Hunt in July to provoke Hunt's comments, or Hunt may simply be airing a long-felt resentment toward another of Shelley's beneficiaries from whom he was separated by basic temperamental differences. The mention of Peacock's "passion" and his mathematical attitude toward love points forward to his letter to Jane Gryffydh, proposing marriage. Had Peacock been advocating such a courtship in a discussion with Hunt? Or was he known to have been seeking a wife in London by a very calculating preferential process? In any case, the name "Miss Jenkins" (line 61) should be considered a Jane Doe designation and not the identity of a potential wife for Peacock.

That the Hunts no longer gave dinner parties (line 65) testifies to their straitened financial circumstances. Had another promising young poet been introduced to Hunt two years after John Keats was, he could never have received the same personal attention and encouragement that had been so vital to Keats's decision to pursue poetry.

Charles Lloyd (1775–1839), an early friend of Lamb and Coleridge who had published a translation of Alfieri's tragedies in 1815, had been periodically insane from about 1811 or 1812.[5] Lloyd was confined in an asylum near York from October 1815 to 1818, when he escaped and re-

4. See Mary to the Hunts, March 18, 1817, Mary Shelley, *Letters*, I, 24.

5. On Lloyd (and other members of his family), see *DNB* and E. V. Lucas, *Charles Lamb and the Lloyds* (London, 1898); SC 497, Commentary; and Southey, *New Letters*, II, 40–41, 134.

SC 530 turned to the Lake Country.[6] In May 1819, he escaped the vigilance of his family and went to London, where his wife decided to leave him in the care of a servant and under the friendly (but already overburdened) watchfulness of Charles Lamb.[7]

Hunt refrains from gossiping to the Shelleys about Lloyd's infirmity, alluding only to his having been "much shaken by sickness" (line 72).[8] But Lloyd's praise of Shelley should not be regarded as a breakthrough for Shelley's poetic reputation in London (as Hunt seems to suggest). Crabb Robinson, who knew of Lloyd's malady from a visit to the Lake Country in 1816, regarded him in November 1819 as "a poor sickly creature . . . in body and mind,"[9] and it is unlikely that Lloyd's recommendation of Shelley's poetry (or philosophical and religious principles) would carry much weight with his closest friends. Shelley, knowing nothing of Lloyd's insanity, was pleased with the account of him and returned Lloyd's compliment in his letter to Hunt of September 27, 1819, by praising a marginal notation in Lloyd's copy of Berkeley, which Southey had borrowed for Shelley's use while he was at Keswick in the winter of 1811–1812.[10]

The "sweet burdens" (line 75) that Mary and Marianne were carrying at this time were Percy Florence Shelley (born November 12, 1819) and James Henry Sylvan Hunt (born September 28, 1819).

6. *DNB*; Moorman, *Wordsworth*, II, pp. 231–232; *Minnow Among Tritons: Mrs. S. T. Coleridge's Letters to Thomas Poole*, ed. Stephen Potter (Nonesuch Press, 1934), pp. 74–75; Ernest de Selincourt, *The Letters of William and Dorothy Wordsworth: The Middle Years*, 2nd edition, revised by Mary Moorman and Alan G. Hill (Oxford: Clarendon Press, 1970, 2 vols.), *passim*.

7. See Lamb to Thomas Manning, May 28, 1819, Lamb, *Letters*, II, 246; *The Letters of Thomas Manning to Charles Lamb*, ed. G. A. Anderson (London, 1925), pp. 126–128.

8. Though unlikely, it is possible that Hunt was unaware of Lloyd's insanity. Southey in his *Life of Cowper* observed of Lloyd that "when in company with persons who were not informed of his condition, no one could descry in him the slightest appearance of a deranged mind" (Southey, *New Letters*, II, 440 and fn.), and Thomas Noon Talfourd, in a verbal portrait of Lamb's circle, pictured Lloyd discussing philosophy with Hunt (E. V. Lucas, *Life of Charles Lamb*, London, 1905, I, 373–374).

9. Robinson, *On Books*, I, pp. 187, 232, 237.

10. Shelley, *Letters*, II, 122–123.

SC 531 P. B. SHELLEY TO LEIGH HUNT, AUGUST 15, 1819

AL with signature cut out, 3 pages. Double sheet, 4ᵗᵒ (9.9 x 8.2 inches). Wove paper. Watermark: J Ru[s]e| 1817|; countermark: Bondon|. Seal: wafer, orange.

SC 531   Postal fee: 3/10.
Postmarks: 1. LIVORNO; 2. (Foreign Post Office stamp): FPO| AU·31| 1819|; 3. (delivery stamp, London): 12 o'Clock| AU·31| 1819 Nⁿ|.
Additions: 1. (page 3): closing and signature neatly cut out; 2. (page 4): two strips of paper pasted over seal tear.

PROVENANCE: Leigh Hunt; Alice L. Bird; Maggs, Catalogue 405, Summer 1921, #1264. *De Ricci 418* (p. 150).

Livorno   August 15·1819

My dear friend

      How good of you to write to us so often & such kind letters. — But it is like lending to a beggar– what can I offer in return?.

5   *Though surrounded by suffering & disquietude, & latterly almost over-come by our strange misfortune I have not been idle. My Prometheus is finished & ~~I have~~ am also on the eve of completing another work, totally different from any thing you might conjecture that I should write, of a more popular kind, &, if any thing of mine cᵈ deserve attention,, of higher*
10   *claims.—— "Be innocent of the knowledge dearest chuck till thou approve the performance."*

    I send you a little Poem to give to Ollier for publication but <u>without my Name</u>; Peacock will correct the proofs. I wrote it out with the idea of offering it to the Examiner, but I find that it is too long. It was composed
15   *last year at Este: two of the characters you will recognize, the third is also in some degree a painting from nature, but with respect to time & place, ideal. You will find this little piece, I think in some degree, consistent with your own ideas of the manner in which Poetry ought to be written. I have employed a certain familiar style of language to express the actual way in*
20   *which people talk with each other whom education & a certain refinement of sentiment have placed above the use of vulgar idioms. I use the word <u>vulgar</u> in its' most extensive sense : the vulgarity of rank & fashion is as gross in its way, as that of Poverty, & its cant terms equally expressive of base conceptions & therefore equally unfit for Poetry. Not that the familiar style*
25   *is to be admitted in the treatment of a subject wholly ideal, or in that part of any subject which relates to common life, where the passion exceeding a certain limit touches the boundaries of that which is ideal. Strong passion*

The Carl H. Pforzheimer Library

SC 531   *expresses itself in metaphor borrowed from objects alike remote or near, &*
casts over all the shadow of its own greatness——— But what am I about. If
30   *my grandmother sucks eggs, was it I who taught her.———*

      If you would really correct the proofs I need not trouble Peacock whom
I suppose has enough——— Can you take it as a compliment that I prefer to
trouble you?

      I dont particularly wish this Poem to be known as mine, but at all
35   *events I would not put my name to it– I leave you to judge whether it is best*
to throw it in the fire, or to publish it— So much for self self that burr that
will stick to one. I cant get it off yet. Your kind expressions about my
Eclogue gave me great pleasure, indeed my great stimulus in writing is to
have the approbation of those who feel kindly towards me.— The rest is mere
40   *duty. I am also delighted to hear that you think of us, & form fancies about*
us. We cannot yet come home. Poor Mary's spirits continue dreadfully de-
pressed. And I cannot expose her to Godwin in this state. ₍I wrote to₎ *This hard-*
hearted person, (the first letter I had written for a year) on account of the
45   *terrible state of her mind, & to entreat him to try to soothe her in his next*
letter. The very next letter, recieved yesterday, & addressed to her, called her
husband (me) "a disgraceful & flagrant person" tried to persuade her that
I was under great engagements to give him more money (after having given
him £4700) & urged her if she ever ~~would~~ *wished a connection to continue*
50   *between him & her to force* ~~her~~ ₍me₎ *to get money for him.— He cannot persuade*
her that I am what I am not, nor place a shade of enmity between her & me,
but he heaps on her misery, still, misery.— I have not yet shewn her the
letter— but I must. I doubt whether I ought not to expose this solemn lie;
55   *for such, & not a man is Godwin. but I shall, as is our custom, (I mean*
your's & mine), on the side of patience & endurance. I suspect my character,
if measured with his, would sustain no diminution among those who know
us both. – I have bought bitter knowledge with 4700. I wish it were all your's
60   *now!———*

      The title of your tragedy & the subject of it? And what dunces to accept
such things & refuse yours? No parcel, no pocke< > books, no po< >raits

Shelley to Hunt   *August 15, 1819*

SC 531   *are yet arrived? Just cross question Ollier about it— I know nothing from*
          Ollier— Is he yet friendly with you. You know the mind of most of the inhabi-
65   *tants of this eart< > is like the moon, or rather the wind, and if you know*
          it is thus to day it is no sign that it will be thus tomorrow– If reasons which
          you think good make you wish me to employ another bookseller, or not
          employ him— say so. & do so. Otherwise I have no wish to change even a
          lazy bookseller.

70   *No letter from Bessy or Marianne?— No news either of things Mary*
          wants. Now thats' not kind Marianne. However I send you my love & all
          of you

                                            <   >
          ⟨——⟩ *You see by what*   <   >
75   *I say about Godwin that I dont*
              shew this letter to Mary. ——

[Address, page 4]
Leigh Hunt Esqr
    N° 8.   York Street
            New Road
80   *London*
          Inghilterra

Angleterre

line 4. *return?*. (sic).

line 9. *attention,,*: Shelley added a comma immediately after *attention* because *of* was written too close to his first comma.

line 10. *dearest chuck*: probable reading; the *e* of *dearest* is obliterated by a hole from corrosive ink.

line 30. *was*: altered from *wh*.

line 32. *prefer*: *pre* written through indecipherable letters.

line 35. *judge*: *e* obliterated by a hole from corrosive ink.

line 36. *burr*: immediately following the second *r* is a hole caused by corrosive ink.

line 41. *cannot yet come home.*: a pencil line divides the line after this phrase and is drawn back under it. This line was probably a direction to the printer who set the preceding part of this letter for publication in Hunt's *Lord Byron and Some of His Contemporaries*.

line 45. *soothe*: *e* written through indecipherable letter or letters.

line 46. *recieved* (sic).

line 52. *me,*: punctuation mark may be a semicolon.

line 62. *pocke<t>*: *t* obliterated by seal.
          po<rt>raits: *rt* obliterated by seal tear.

line 63. *?*: probable reading.
          question: there may be something following this word but the seal obliterates the remainder of the line.

line 64. *friendly*: partially obliterated by seal.
          mind: possible reading, but the word seems to end in *ed*.

The Carl H. Pforzheimer Library

SC 531   line 65. *eart<h>*: *h* obliterated by hole from corrosive ink.

line 68. *Otherwise*: *O* written through *be*.

line 70. *?*: probable reading.

line 73. The signature and closing have been neatly cut out without affecting the text of the letter or its postscript. The missing text can be supplied from Hunt, *Lord Byron and Some of His Contemporaries*, p. 233: "Most affectionately yours,/ P. B. Shelley."

line 74. *⟨At⟩*: possible reading.

line 82. *Angleterre*: written to the left of and perpendicular to remainder of address.

SHELLEY MISADDRESSED this letter to "York Street" (where Peacock lived at No. 5) rather than "York Buildings,"[1] but it was apparently delivered to Hunt without incident. It is, perhaps, the most literary of all his surviving letters to Hunt, though nearly a third of even this is concerned with money and personal affairs — in this case, with Mary's depression and Godwin's renewed importunities. Hunt had set the tone in his last letter to Shelley (sc 529) by discussing the fate of his tragedy,[2] his other literary labors, and Shelley's *Rosalind and Helen* and *Prometheus Unbound*. Shelley's writing was, moreover, primary to him throughout 1819, his most prolific year as a poet.

Had Shelley remained in England during 1818–1822, he would almost certainly have participated in the political struggles of the day. It is difficult to imagine the author of two tracts on the Irish question, the *Letter to Lord Ellenborough*, and the two pamphlets signed "The Hermit of Marlow" remaining aloof from pamphlet wars during the year of Peterloo. Shelley's remoteness from news of daily political and social events saved him for poetry. When he responded most vehemently to the news (however much delayed) of these events, he could do so only in the timeless poetry of *The Mask of Anarchy* rather than in letters to the editor of the *Examiner* or the *Morning Chronicle*.[3]

Shelley's literary exertions in the spring and summer of 1819 were crowned by the completion of the first version of *Prometheus Unbound*

1. See the postscript to Shelley's next letter to Hunt, Shelley, *Letters*, II, 113.

2. Shelley is correct in noting (line 61) that Hunt had never specified, in any of the mentions of his tragedy, either its title or subject.

3. Shelley's letter to the *Examiner* on the trial of Richard Carlile (see *Letters*, II, 136–148) is the classic exception that proves the rule. Carlile's infamous trial and conviction occurred on October 12–14, 1819. Shelley began his letter to the *Examiner* on November 1 or 2 and mailed it from Florence on November 6. By the time the letter reached London, its subject was already over a month old, and the *Examiner* (for this or other reasons) never published it. Such an experience hardly encouraged Shelley to continue to spend his time in journalistic polemics.

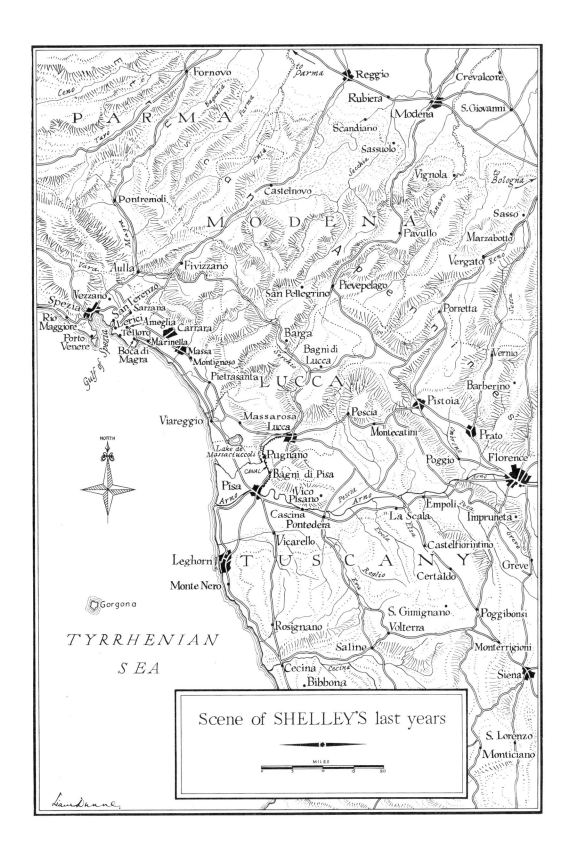

Scene of SHELLEY'S last years

MILES

0   5   10   15   20

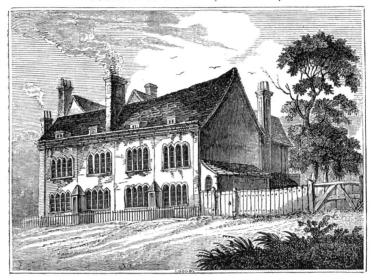

The earliest known illustration of Albion House

Villa Valsovano, Shelley's house near Monte Nero, outside Leghorn, from a photograph by W. Hall Griffin, reproduced in Roger Ingpen's Letters of Percy Bysshe Shelley (London, 1909)

SC 531 (in three acts) and *The Cenci*. As Shelley's remarks in his letters of
August through December show, he valued these two at their true
worth and was at some pains to arrange for them the best possible reception. Since he wished to submit *The Cenci* anonymously to Covent
Garden Theatre,[4] he did not want Hunt loudly whispering to all his
literary friends that Shelley had written a tragedy called *The Cenci*.
Here Shelley justifies his reticence by paraphrasing the words of Macbeth
to Lady Macbeth after he has plotted the deaths of Banquo and Fleance:

> Be innocent of the knowledge, dearest chuck,
> Till thou applaud the deed.[5]

The poem that Shelley sends (line 12) and here discusses is *Julian
and Maddalo*. H. Buxton Forman pointed out that Shelley first drafted
the portion of this letter dealing with the use of the familiar style in
one of his rough draft notebooks now in the Huntington Library.[6] Forman believed that Shelley always intended the paragraph for the letter
itself, rather than for the Preface to *Julian and Maddalo*. Another possibility is that Shelley included these remarks on style in the letter because
there was no logical place for them in the Preface, which is entirely
devoted to the *characters* in the poem. In several respects, what Shelley
tells Hunt about the date and occasion of the poem has been challenged
by recent scholarship, leading me to question whether other portions of
Shelley's letter might not also be premeditated set-pieces rather than
fully candid commentary.

Let us turn for a moment to the bitter paragraph on Godwin.
Shelley says that he and Mary cannot return to England because Godwin's importunities would further aggravate Mary's depressed spirits.
He goes on to describe how Godwin is, through his letters, attempting
to drive a wedge between Mary and Shelley, though he has not succeeded. Shelley adds to this charge of paternal callousness the more
common one of ingratitude. Yet, Shelley says, he will continue in pa-

---

4. See Shelley to Peacock, July ?20, 1819, Shelley, *Letters*, II, 101–103, as well as SC 537 and Commentary.

5. *Macbeth*, III.ii.44–46. Did Shelley purposely substitute "performance" for "deed" because of
his plans to have the play produced? If so, why did he change "applaud" to "approve"? In short,
did Shelley alter the quotation meaningfully or merely because his memory faltered?

6. Shelley, *Note Books*, I, 142–144.

[857]

The Carl H. Pforzheimer Library

SC 531   tience, not striking back at his father-in-law. Are the charges against
Godwin true? Very likely, although the crucial letters described by
Shelley do not, apparently, survive. Godwin's letter to Mary of September 9, 1819, exhibits a harsh, unsympathetic tone.[7] In the light of Shelley's comments, one can interpret Godwin's remarks as a renewed appeal
for Mary to persuade Shelley to help her father.[8] The only other surviving
letters from Godwin to Mary during this year (March 5 and October 15,
1819) are concerned almost exclusively with worries about his lawsuit.[9]
But what moved Shelley to attack Godwin at this time and in this way?
He was, of course, unable to tell his problems to anyone near at hand
(for Maria Gisborne was also Godwin's friend). So his outburst might
have seemed necessary simply as an outlet. But if, as has been repeatedly
argued,[10] Shelley and Mary had become somewhat estranged after the
deaths of Clara and William, by blaming Godwin Shelley also fulfilled
his need to externalize, as much as possible, the responsibility or guilt
for that estrangement.

   The problem of Shelley's putative estrangement from Mary also
brings into focus the basic questions about *Julian and Maddalo*. First,
where and when was it written? Shelley's statement (lines 14–15) that
"it was composed last year at Este" does not, G. M. Matthews argues,
agree with the evidence of the Bodleian rough-draft manuscript (Shelley
adds. e. 11).[11] Matthews concludes that although it may have been begun at Este, the draft gives evidence that lines 44 and following were
drafted "in or after December 1818" (page 65), and that "the likelihood
is . . . that substantial additions were still being made to *Julian and
Maddalo* as late as March 1819, if indeed, the whole poem were not
composed then" (page 66). I agree that the manuscript evidence indi-

---

7. *Shelley and Mary*, I, 410A. This letter is quoted, in part, in sc 530, Commentary.

8. In his letter of September 9, Godwin refers to Shelley as "the husband of your choice, to whom
you seem to be unalterably attached, a man of high intellectual endowments," but this can be
interpreted, not as a compliment to Shelley, but as part of the appeal to Mary to seek Shelley's
help for Godwin.

9. *Shelley and Mary*, I, 364A, 420A.

10. See White, *Shelley*, II, 46–49; Kenneth Neill Cameron, "The Planet-Tempest Passage in
Epipsychidion," *PMLA*, LXIII (September 1948), 961; Donald H. Reiman, *Percy Bysshe Shelley*
(New York, 1969), pp. 65, 69.

11. See Matthews, "'Julian and Maddalo': the Draft and the Meaning," *Studia Neophilologica*,
XXXV (1963), 57–84.

Shelley and his Circle : Manuscripts

SC 531   cates that the poem could not have been completed at Este and was probably written later. Why, then, does Shelley tell Hunt what he does? He may have wished to aid Hunt in identifying Byron as the other of the two recognizable characters (though the setting at Venice should have left no doubt). But a more meaningful explanation is that Shelley is attempting to dissociate the poem from Mary's recently articulated depression of spirits, as well as from his own mood mirrored in parts of SC 531. Shelley's reaction to the death of Clara was not outwardly severe (though the mood of the opening "Lines written among the Euganean Hills" and Shelley's comment on that poem in the Advertisement to the *Rosalind and Helen* volume belie this outward calm). In the following weeks, Shelley had written magnificent travel letters to Peacock about the journey to Rome and Naples. His single surviving letter to Hunt between the deaths of Clara and William gives no evidence of low spirits.[12]

Similarly, when Shelley describes the maniac as "in some degree a painting from nature, but with respect to time & place, ideal," he sounds much like the modern novelist claiming that resemblance to particular persons, living or dead, is purely coincidental. Even Shelley's interesting remarks about the familiar style (lines 19–29) may be read, in their context, not only as a rebuttal to some of Hunt's theory (and practice) of colloquial style and diction,[13] but as a disclaimer against the possible charge of copying life too closely. If someone else were to comment on the biographical identifications of the three characters, Shelley could reply that he had written the poem on a theory and had apparently been successful. In short, Shelley's remarks about *Julian and Maddalo* can be read as an attempt to hide the true facts of its composition from Hunt.

When Mary first published *Julian and Maddalo* in *Posthumous Poems* (1824), she dated it "Rome, May, 1819." In the first collected *Poetical Works* (1839), it appeared among "Poems written in 1820."[14] In the one-volume second edition (also 1839), Mary moved *Julian and Maddalo* to "Poems written in 1818"; in her note, after describing the

12. From Naples, December 1818, Shelley, *Letters*, II, 64–68.
13. See Hunt's Preface to *Foliage*.
14. III, 289–314.

The Carl H. Pforzheimer Library

SC 531   villa at Este, she added: "here also, as he mentions in a letter, he wrote
Julian and Maddalo . . ." (page 229). The letter referred to is the portion
of the present one (sc 531) that Leigh Hunt had first published in *Lord
Byron and Some of His Contemporaries* (1828).[15] Mary had, apparently,
come upon this reference while she was collecting Shelley's letters for
publication in *Essays, Letters from Abroad, Translations and Fragments*
(1840). In those volumes the same portion of Shelley's letter that appears
in *Lord Byron and Some of His Contemporaries* was reprinted, with
Mary's own, more correct notes (II, 220–223). Hunt, we must assume,
had not shown Mary the text of the entire letter, with its strong attack
on Godwin, out of respect for Shelley's wishes implied in his postscript.

Mary Shelley, however, knew *Julian and Maddalo* long before Shelley's death, for in the table of contents to the fair-copy notebook at
Harvard, the first entry (in Mary's hand) is "Maddalo and Julian" —
a poem that was at one time copied into that book.[16] The Harvard
Shelley notebook seems to have been used by Shelley chiefly at Florence
late in 1819 and Pisa in 1820. Mary may have dated the poem "1820"
in the four-volume *Poetical Works* (1839) because it had once been in
the fair-copy book.[17] It is not known whether it was Shelley or Mary
who copied *Julian and Maddalo* into the Harvard copybook, but Mary
had earlier transcribed lines 1–107 of the poem in one of Shelley's rough-
draft notebooks,[18] and she would at least have seen the transcription in
the Harvard notebook when she copied other poems into it. Thus Mary

15. Pages 232–233.

16. The transcription once in the Harvard safe-keeping copybook was undoubtedly removed by
Mary and used (probably after Mary had added punctuation and otherwise styled it for press)
as printer's copy for the first publication of *Julian and Maddalo* in *Posthumous Poems* (1824). It
seems to have been lost or destroyed, like the rest of Shelley's press copy from which the firm of
C. H. Reynell printed. Shelley's own fair copy, carefully styled for press and sent to Hunt in this
letter, remained in Leigh Hunt's possession until his death, when it passed into H. Buxton Forman's
hands and provided the copy-text for Forman's text in his four-volume edition of the poetry (III,
101–130). In the sale of Forman's library, the manuscript was purchased by The Pierpont Morgan
Library, where it remains. The drafts and Mary's partial fair copy in the Bodleian notebooks are
discussed below.

17. Charles H. Taylor, Jr., in *The Early Collected Editions of Shelley's Poems* (Yale University Press,
1958; see especially pp. 35–36, 72–73, 88), has shown that the 1839 text of *Julian and Maddalo* is
based on that in John Ascham's pirated edition of 1834. Dependence on this text does not, however,
explain why Mary dropped the date given in *Posthumous Poems* ("Rome, May, 1819"), which
Ascham's edition faithfully includes.

18. Bodleian Ms. Shelley adds. e. 12, ff. 177–171 *reverso*.

SC 531   clearly knew the complete text of *Julian and Maddalo* by 1820. Because, however, she dated the poem first at Rome in the spring of 1819 before William's death and later dated it 1820, either she herself did not associate the poem with her own and Shelley's depressed spirits after the deaths of Clara and William, or else *she* purposely tried to alter the date of composition so that others would not associate these tragedies with *Julian and Maddalo*. The evidence suggests that Shelley or Mary or both of them were anxious to conceal from the outside world the time that *Julian and Maddalo* was written.

G. M. Matthews argues, partly from the proximity of what he believes to be the first version of the famous lines 541–546 (concluding, "Most wretched men/ Are cradled into poetry by wrong,/ They learn in suffering what they teach in song") to "the unfinished Scene I of Shelley's *Tasso* drama," that the relation of the maniac to Shelley's conception of Tasso may be as close as that suggested by Carlos Baker.[19] Without denying that Shelley's attempt to write a drama on the life of Tasso may have contributed to both the language of *Julian and Maddalo* and, in particular, the character of the maniac, we must recognize that Shelley's evasiveness in discussing the poem's date and occasion strongly suggests that elements in the poem — besides the undisguised portraits of Byron and Shelley — reflect personal matters between Shelley and Mary that Shelley felt must be concealed both from her and from his closest friends. Matthews' determination of a later date for most of the poem does not in itself invalidate the hypothesis that the root cause of dissension between Shelley and Mary was the death of Clara Shelley. The later composition might help to explain how Shelley was able to achieve a proper aesthetic distance from his personal problems and to so objectify the *persona* of his suffering self that his contemporaries did not recognize the maniac as in any part a self-portrait, and modern critics have variously identified the maniac as Shelley, Tasso, and Byron.[20] But it might suggest that elements of Shelley's and Mary's

19. See Baker, *Shelley's Major Poetry* (Princeton University Press, 1948), pp. 124–138; Baker, "Shelley's Ferrarese Maniac," *English Institute Essays, 1946* (Columbia University Press, 1947), 41–73.

20. For arguments that the maniac portrays Byron and his marital difficulties, see G. Wilson Knight, *Lord Byron's Marriage* (London, 1957), pp. 223–224, and J. E. Saveson, "Shelley's *Julian and Maddalo*," *Keats-Shelley Journal*, X (Winter 1961), 53–58. Had the maniac been such a portrait,

The Carl H. Pforzheimer Library

SC 531 later fits of depression that followed the death of *William* Shelley played a part in the composition of the poem.

Shelley's decision that Ollier should publish *Julian and Maddalo* anonymously may be another clue to the personal origin of this poem. Only *Epipsychidion*, among Shelley's later volumes of verse, appeared without his name. Again, Shelley's injunction to Hunt "to judge whether it is best to throw it in the fire, or to publish it" and his remarks about "self" as a "burr that will stick to one" are uncharacteristic of his remarks about his other published poems. These differences may derive merely from Shelley's self-portrait as Julian, but his vehemence suggests that his feelings about the poem and its theme went beyond interest in the rather cool and objective picture of Julian. (Certainly he showed no similar self-consciousness about the more idealized, even sentimentalized, portrayal of Lionel in *Rosalind and Helen*.) Shelley's tone in this passage about *self* is sustained through the subsequent sentences about poetry as his duty, about Mary's "dreadfully depressed" spirits, and about Godwin's attempts to drive him and Mary apart.

Matthews, analyzing the Bodleian draft of *Julian and Maddalo*, argues that both the beginning and concluding narrative passages (lines 1–299 and 547–617) "were written first, as a completed framework enclosing a dozen or so blank pages on which the Soliloquy could later be improvised."[21] The approximately 150 lines of the poem for which no draft has been found include much of the maniac's soliloquy.[22] When one considers the passages of the soliloquy that *are* present in Bodleian Ms. Shelley adds. e. 11,[23] one realizes that these lines differ from those for which there is no surviving draft and which, according to Matthews, must have been composed later. Accepting Matthews' conclusions about the order of composition of the various parts of *Julian and Maddalo*,

---

however, Shelley would have had no reason to mislead Hunt or Mary about the time of writing the poem. His shift of the date of composition back to his time at Este would have suggested rather than shielded Byron, and if this had been his intention, he need not have said that the portrait was "with respect to time & place, ideal." There are other reasons, both in the text of *Julian and Maddalo* and in everything we know about Shelley's character, why the maniac could *not* be a portrait of Byron in the way G. Wilson Knight contends, but there is no need to argue this matter here.

21. Matthews, "'Julian and Maddalo,'" p. 63.

22. Matthews (p. 61 and note) lists the missing lines as 287–293, 300–336, 377–383, 408–510.

23. Lines 337–376, 384–407.

SC 531   I should like to hypothesize quite a different explanation for this order and present a somewhat new interpretation of the interaction between Shelley's relationship with Mary in 1818–1819 and the growth of *Julian and Maddalo*.

Shelley had been thinking of the life of Tasso as a subject for a dramatic poem since his arrival in Italy.[24] By the time he reached Venice, the idea had grown cold, and Byron's second treatment of Tasso, in the fourth canto of *Childe Harold*, must have been a further deterrent to Shelley's continuing his efforts in that direction. While at Venice, however, Shelley had visited the dungeons of the Doge's palace, and he and Mary had both seen a madhouse in the Venetian lagoon, probably from Byron's gondola and with their host's comments on the inmates.[25] Later, at Ferrara, Shelley visited the cell in which Tasso had been imprisoned and saw examples of Tasso's handwriting, which once again stirred his imagination.[26] It is quite possible that Shelley and Byron had discussed the life and art of Tasso during their meetings in Venice, but in any case Shelley already knew from the publication of Byron's *Lament of Tasso* that his ideas differed sharply from Byron's on the significance of Tasso's life.[27] Shelley may, therefore, have attempted to embody his views on Tasso in the dramatic form of a debate between himself and Byron, imagining a figure like Tasso to be an inmate of the Venetian madhouse. Such a character would have been "a painting from nature, but with respect to time & place, ideal."

Newman Ivey White has posited an estrangement between Shelley and Mary in October and November 1818. But outside the poetry, there is no evidence of such estrangement at this time.[28] Mary was undoubtedly deeply upset by Clara's death, but her later remarks on their stay in Venice and Este[29] give no indication that she looked back on that period as one troubled by dissension in her marriage, however much troubled it was by external circumstances. The death of William Shelley was the

24. See Shelley to Peacock, April 20, 1818, Shelley, *Letters*, II, 8; and sc 479 and Commentary.

25. See Mary Shelley, *Rambles in Germany and Italy* (London, 1844), II, 86–87, 99.

26. See Shelley to Peacock, November 6, 1818, *Letters*, II, 47–48.

27. See sc 419 and Commentary.

28. The most explicit passage is "Lines written among the Euganean Hills," 24–44.

29. See "Notes on Poems of 1818" in *Poetical Works* (1839), and *Rambles in Germany and Italy*.

The Carl H. Pforzheimer Library

SC 531 event that drove Mary to despair, and only after July 1819 does Shelley begin to admit to outsiders that he cannot share everything with Mary. This letter of August 15, 1819, to Hunt is the first one from Italy in which Shelley speaks, behind Mary's back as it were, about possible problems in his marriage.

If, then, the portions of *Julian and Maddalo* drafted in Bodleian Ms. Shelley adds. e. 11 were written in the spring of 1819, before the death of William Shelley, they may reflect chiefly (if not exclusively) Shelley's conversations with Byron in Venice and his continuing interest in Tasso as the type of the sensitive, poetic soul driven to madness by unrequited love and an unfeeling world. On the other hand, the portions of the maniac's speech *not* found in the drafts contain all the passages that White and others believe reflect most explicitly Shelley's personal tribulation. These could have been written *after* the death of William Shelley and, by being incorporated into the story inspired by Tasso and by others like him throughout history, these disjointed utterances would gain aesthetic distance even as they intensified the tone of the poem.

The hypothetical sequence that I have outlined explains why Shelley kept no drafts of the interpolated passages (so that Mary would not realize that they had not been original parts of *Julian and Maddalo*). It accounts for Shelley's self-consciousness about the poem in his letter to Hunt and yet shows why he felt able to send the poem at all. It explains why Shelley pushed the date of composition back to the fall of 1818. It explains both why Shelley allowed Mary to copy lines 1–107 in Bodleian Ms. Shelley adds. e. 12, and why he postponed showing her the entire poem until they were at Florence (and, probably, until Mary's depression had passed after the birth of Percy Florence Shelley). It helps to explain how Shelley could so successfully distance and structure a coherent poem that reflects his deep personal feelings, as he had been unable to do in *Rosalind and Helen*. It accounts for the proximity of the poem's early draft to drafts for the drama on Tasso and also explains why the most personal passages in *Julian and Maddalo* are so emotionally echoed by Shelley's comments on his own situation in sc 531.

Most of the weaknesses in White's explanation of the biographical significance of *Julian and Maddalo* arose from his literal acceptance of Shelley's statement to Hunt that the poem had been written at Este in

SC 531 the autumn of 1818. At that period there exists much stronger evidence for Shelley's interest in Tasso than there does for any estrangement between Shelley and Mary. Matthews' new evidence on the dating of the extant draft of *Julian and Maddalo* indicates that the parts of the maniac's soliloquy that may reflect Shelley's personal experience postdate the death of William Shelley, and hence were written in a period during which there is marked evidence of tensions between Shelley and Mary.

SC 532 P. B. SHELLEY, DEDICATION OF *THE CENCI* TO LEIGH HUNT, AUGUST [16–19], 1819

HOLOGRAPH MANUSCRIPT signed *P.B.S.*, 4⅔ pages. 3 single sheets (5.5 x 3.5 inches), containing also sc 536 and sc 548.
Laid paper. Watermark, leaves 2 and 3: [portions of shield]‖ .
Notation, page 5, lower third: curved stroke in left margin enclosing lines 74–79, and some indistinguishable letters written above the line, both in red pencil.
Addition: pages of manuscript have been removed from a notebook and hinged in three separate inlays of a volume bound in gold-tooled blue levant morocco by Sangorski and Sutcliffe.
PROVENANCE: Thornton Leigh Hunt; Walter T. Spencer (September 1922).

My dear friend
    In   Accept this
        Permit I inscribe with your name, from a distant Country, and after an absence whose months have seemed years, this the latest of my literary
5   *efforts.*
        Every thing which I have already written has I believe it is not the custom for friends to ask each permission when one graces his pages with the name of another but if it were, your portrait is before me, an admirable & most a & faithful portrait of you, were where every thing is imitated but
10 *the spirit of deep & earnest sweetness of the which is the spirit of within which the spirit of man's finest nature sometimes looks out of your eyes— your portrait is before me, & it smiles an imperfect approbation.*
                                    The writings
        The drama which I present to you is a sad reality. What I have ever

SC 532

 hitherto   a   presented to the world   which
~~published as yet has been visions of ideal excellence the picture of should &~~

⟨————⟩ contained ⟨ ⟩
~~may be~~ have ~~been the~~ impersonations of My own persuasion of what is

                    ⌊they are
20 beautiful & just; a kind of visions, which are not, but should be.

These belonged of right to you, who
    They have many literary defects. but I am yet young.
The drama which I now present to you is a sad reality

                    ~~dark~~
25 It ~~This~~ is a picture of human nature; I lay aside the presumptuo⟨ ⟩
    attitude of an instructor, & only paint, ~~as I~~ from the colours which my
    own heart furnishes what has been

        I feel ~~an~~ pride greater perhaps than is morally justifiable at
        ~~since my residence~~

30   'Tis   or some of its drowsy nurses
        ~~They~~ say that wise baby the World have been piping ~~its~~ half articulate cen-
                                    their
        ~~But for its a greater regard to its~~   since ⟨   ⟩
    sures of ~~you & me~~ us. You who have been virtuous & I who have been un-
35 fortunate posess a prescriptive right to this sort of ~~tribute~~ homage. It is the
    tribute which the ~~ver~~ excellent & the unhappy pay to the ~~prospero~~ & the pros-
                                    perverse
    perous for ~~being not~~ being ~~the~~ most unlike that which they cannot or that
    which they would not be

40   I hope ~~I ha~~ that no feeling so harsh as contempt is mingled with my smiles
                            good
    Alas my dear Hunt ~~of~~ what benefit ~~pleasure~~ would my testimony of your
                do
    excellencies ~~give~~ you. ~~I know it gives you pleasure that I should say so~~
45   and
    That my deep sense of them gives you pleasure I well know; ~~and~~ it is for my
                            that
    own ~~sake that I~~ satisfaction ~~that I~~ declare; if I had known a person more
                    alone
50 endowed with all that it becomes a man to posess I would have solicited for
    this ~~lit~~ work the honour of his name. One more gentle, honourable & ~~true,~~
                                innocent
    brave & true, one of more exalted toleration for all ~~evil~~ who are evil, & yet
    himself more free from evil; one who knows better both how to recieve & to

P. B. Shelley, six-line fragment from *Prometheus Unbound*, II.iii.82–89,
?*November–December 1819* (SC 548) and his "Dedication" to *The Cenci*,
August [16–19], 1819 (SC 532), pages 1–2

P. B. Shelley, "Dedication" to *The Cenci*, August [16–19], 1819 (SC 532),
pages 3–4

P. B. Shelley, "Dedication" to The Cenci, August [16–19], 1819 (SC 532),
page 5, and a draft stanza from The Mask of Anarchy, September 6–23, 1819
(SC 536), page 1

SC 532   *confer a benefit though he must ever confer more than he can recieve, ~~one who excuses all~~ of simpler & in the highest sense of the word, of purer life & manners I never knew.—and ~~Such is~~ My friendships had been already fortunate when your name was added to the list—*

60   *the*
        an
In ~~that contention against tyranny & fraud~~, in unyielding & irrecon-
                        (let me not say the opposition)
cileable enmity to the oppressions ~~in which we are both engaged~~ to which we
                                      and is in you
65 *have both pledged ourselves, and whose first fruits ~~the public h~~ should be ~~and I~~*
        is   *him*   *conforting*
~~hope are~~ the personal excellence of ~~those~~ who cherishes it, let us ᴧlive &
each other in our task
die.

70   *All happiness attend you my dear Hunt—*
                    Your affect. friend
                        P.B.S.

                                    with
        In that patient & irreconcible opposition ~~to~~ tyranny domestic & po-
                    the tenor of your life
75 *litical tyranny & imposture which has illustrated ~~your~~ life & which ~~which~~*
had I health   *& talents should illustrate mine*
⟨———⟩ ~~is~~ ⟨————⟩ and ⟨   ⟩ ~~purpose of mine~~, let us comforting each
other in our task, live & die

line 1. This line is written to the left of the final line of sc 548, which occupies the first third of page 1 of the manuscript.

line 6. *Every*: *Ev* written through a fainter *Ev.*

line 7. *when*: *w* written through *to.*

line 10. *the spirit*: *the* altered from *that.*

line 14. *present*: altered from indecipherable word.

line 16. *has*: *s* written through *ve* at the same time that Shelley changed *visions* to the singular form and inserted *a.* Later he returned to this section and canceled the whole phrase.

line 17. ⟨———⟩ *contained* ⟨ ⟩: words are cramped and illegible.

line 18. *have*: altered from *has* when *which* (*writings*) (lines 15, 13) replaced *picture* (line 16) as the subject.

line 20. *visions, which are*: *s* of *visions* added later; *are* was altered from *is* at the same time.

line 21. *These . . . reality*: written on the lower third of page 3 of the manuscript, along with *what has been* (line 27) and *I feel . . . at* (line 28). Shelley evidently first wrote pages 1–2 and then added material relevant to the last portion of page 2 at the bottom of the contiguous page. The words *what has been*, which occupy the last line of page 3, follow directly from *furnishes*, which is the final word on the last line of page 2. *I feel . . . at* occupies one and a half lines above *what has been* and below *These . . . reality*. All three segments are ruled off from the rest of page 3, which begins with a phrase Shelley later rejected, *since my residence.*

line 31. *have*: *ve* written through *s.*

line 33. ⟨*we parted*⟩: probable reading.

Shelley, Dedication of Cenci　　　　　　　　**August [16–19], 1819**

SC 532　line 35. *posess* (sic): see also line 50, below.
　　　　　　　　this: *is* written through *?eir*.

　line 38. *or*: written through *&*.

　line 42. *testimony*: *sti* written through *?m*.

　line 54. *recieve* (sic): see also line 55.

　line 55. *confer more*: *con* written through *rec*.

　line 57. *&*: written through *or*.

　line 63. *the*: altered from *those*.

　line 65. *and whose*: *and* written through *w*.

line 66. *conforting* (sic).

line 67. *cherishes*: *es* added later.

line 74. Lines 73–79 are marked off in the left margin by a curved stroke in red ?pencil.
　　　　　irreconcible (sic).

line 78. ⟨——⟩ *is* ⟨*?the goal*⟩: the line is written in a very cramped hand and is almost illegible.
　　　⟨　⟩: letters are illegible.

I N THE undated letter to Hunt in which Shelley tells of the arrival of Ollier's long-awaited parcel containing Hunt's portrait, Shelley declared: "I have written something & finished it—different from anything else & a new attempt for me,—& I mean to dedicate it to you. I should not have done so without your approbation, but I asked your picture last night & it smiled assent—"[1] This passage suggests that Shelley had already drafted the above Dedication of *The Cenci* to Hunt before he wrote the letter. Since Shelley had, clearly, not done so before the portrait arrived (and for a discussion of that date, see sc 533, Commentary), he must have drafted the Dedication either the same day he wrote to Hunt and Ollier or the previous evening, when the parcel arrived. It is not likely that, when Shelley saw his friend's gift to him and read Hunt's long and charming, albeit year-old letter (sc 486), his warm and friendly reaction was given form in the draft transcribed above.

The Bibliographical Description indicates that the three leaves containing this draft must have been separated from one of Shelley's rough-draft notebooks by Mary Shelley or Lady Jane Shelley and given to Hunt. The top recto of the first leaf also contains a few lines of draft for *Prometheus Unbound*, and a stanza drafted for *The Mask of Anarchy* appears on the verso of the third leaf. These leaves were once part of one of the notebooks given by Lady Jane Shelley to Richard Garnett and now in the Huntington Library, the "Note Book II" of *Note Books of Percy Bysshe Shelley* edited by Harry Buxton Forman in 1911 (now Huntington Ms. 2177). The three leaves were cut out from between the

1. Shelley, *Letters*, II, 112.

SC 532   leaves now numbered 6ᵛ and 7ʳ.² Folio 6, verso, contains drafts for lines from *Prometheus Unbound* (II.iii.81–85), which are continued on the top of the first page of SC 532. (For reasons why we believe that this passage for *Prometheus Unbound* was drafted later than the Dedication to *The Cenci* and after the composition of *The Mask of Anarchy*, see SC 536, Commentary.) Folio 7, recto, of the Huntington notebook contains, at the top, lines of pentameter verse, the only three uncanceled lines of which, beginning "Come, thou awakener," are published as "Fragment: Zephyrus the Awakener."³ At the bottom of the page is a draft of the first stanza of *The Mask of Anarchy*, and drafts for that poem continue (though the stanzas are not at all in their final order) on the subsequent folios.⁴

The impromptu nature of the draft of the Dedication is attested to not only by the many cancellations and the confused arrangement of the portions that were selected for the final form, but also by the very personal nature of the sentences later deleted. In revising the Dedication for publication, Shelley removed the passage on Hunt's portrait (lines 6–12), perhaps partly because he told Hunt himself much the same thing in the letter of August [?17–19]. Besides revising what he had drafted for the following paragraph, Shelley in the printed version assumed a more modest tone and deleted such bitter passages as that beginning, "They say that wise baby the World" (line 31).

In making these revisions, Shelley transformed a candid personal letter into a graceful public dedication not open to the kind of criticism that the *Quarterly Review* directed at Hunt's Dedication of *Foliage* to Sir John Swinburne.⁵ And while thus changing the nature of the document, he also assigned it a new date much earlier than the date of its actual composition. At the end of the Dedication, as printed in the first edition, appears: "Rome, May 29, 1819."

The date May 29 must have seemed appropriate to Shelley, and our problem is to discover why. The absence of any letters by Shelley

2. For many helpful courtesies over the years, we are grateful to the staff of the Henry E. Huntington Library and Art Museum, especially Herbert C. Schulz, formerly Curator of Manuscripts; Miss Jean F. Preston, Curator of Manuscripts; and Robert R. Wark, Curator of Art Collections.

3. Shelley, *Poetical Works* (OSA), p. 660.

4. See Shelley, *Note Books*, II, 21–82.

5. See *Quarterly Review*, XVIII (January 1818), 325.

SC 532   between April 6 and June 8 forces us to turn to the secondary sources of Mary Shelley's and Claire Clairmont's journals. From these laconic accounts, the fact that presents itself most forcefully is that May 29 was one of the last days when William Shelley's health seemed to be improving after the illness that struck on Tuesday, May 25. Mary's Journal notes for Friday, May 28: "William gets better in the evening"; Mary made no further remarks on William's health until June 2, when she wrote: "William becomes very ill in the evening." Claire's journal confirms this sequence. On May 28 Claire writes, as she had in earlier entries, "William ill"; on May 29, after what Mary describes as improvement in the evening, Claire records, "William better," a notation she repeats on May 31. For June 2, Claire like Mary writes, "William very ill."[6]

With the clue afforded by the two journals, we can suggest the factors that may have been operative in Shelley's choice of May 29 as the date of his Dedication. In the first place, Rome was not only the chief setting of the tragic story of the Cenci family, but Rome inspired Shelley to begin the play and, so far as we know, he may have conceived, though not executed, the entire drama by the end of May.

According to the Julian editors, Shelley "began to write his tragedy on March 4, 1819, at Rome."[7] The date is clearly impossible, for on March 4 the Shelleys were still traveling from Naples to Rome. At Leghorn in May 1818, Mary Shelley had transcribed the manuscript history of the Cenci family lent her by John Gisborne.[8] The next reference to the Cenci family occurs in the journals of both Mary and Claire, when on April 22, 1819, they record a visit to the Palazzo Colonna; both mention seeing the (supposed) portrait of Beatrice Cenci.[9] The next

---

6. Claire's account of William's illness is fuller than Mary's (see Claire Clairmont, *Journals*, p. 113), for she records the visits of Dr. John Bell (1763–1820), the Scottish surgeon who was caring for William. On June 2, immediately after the phrase, "William very ill," Claire adds, "Mr. Bell calls three times—" For Dr. Bell, see *DNB*. His grave is near Keats's in the Protestant Cemetery in Rome.

7. Shelley, *Complete Works*, II, 416.

8. The relevant portions of the entries in the Journal (not published by Jones) read as follows: "Saturday [May] 23rd Copy Mr G's Manu M.S."; "Sunday 24th copy"; "Monday 25th Finish copying the Cenci M.S."

9. The two journal entries suggest that the subject of La Cenci may already have been of special interest to the household by that date, but inasmuch as Shelley (in his letters) and Claire (in her journal) almost always single out the paintings by Guido Reni for special mention, this visit to the

SC 532   relevant entry occurs in Mary's Journal for May 11, where she records: "Visit yᵉ Casa Cenci." On May 14, Claire writes, "Read Manuscript of the Cenci Family," while Mary notes, "S writes his Tragedy—"

Shelley probably did not actually compose the bulk of *The Cenci* until June when he was settled at the Villa Valsovana, near Leghorn, but he did not then take pleasure in the process of writing the play. Whereas creative activity usually buoyed his spirits, the death of his son, coupled with Mary's depression, caused the composition of *The Cenci* to produce the opposite effect. On August 24 Shelley observes to Peacock, "I have been much better these last three weeks—my work on the Cenci, which was done in two months, was a fine antidote to nervous medicines & kept up, I think, the pain in my side, as sticks do a fire. Since then I have materially improved."[10]

The available evidence—none of it, unfortunately, close to definitive—suggests that Shelley dated his Dedication May 29, 1819, for two reasons: because *The Cenci* was conceived and begun in Rome during May, as well as set there, and because the last respite before the second, fatal illness of William Shelley marked the last time before the play was printed that Shelley's heart was really in his work. As he remarked to Hunt on August 15 (sc 531), "my great stimulus in writing is to have the approbation of those who feel kindly towards me.—The rest is mere duty." Shelley wished to date his heartfelt Dedication back to the period before composition was "mere duty."

Palazzo Colonna may mark the beginning of revived interest in the Cenci story. Interest in the painting, attributed to Guido, may have kindled Shelley's interest in the manuscript that Mary had copied a year earlier. Mary's note on the poem (1839) seems to support the latter possibility.

10. Shelley, *Letters*, II, 115. For further information on the writing, printing, and publication of *The Cenci*, see sc 537, Commentary.

SC 533   P. B. SHELLEY TO CHARLES OLLIER, AUGUST [17–19], 1819

AL signed *P B Shelley*., 1½ pages. Single sheet, fragment of 4ᵗᵒ sheet (8.3 x 2.3 inches).
Wove paper.
Notation, page 2, lower part, written in black ink, *reverso: 11443|.*
Addition: spindle hole.

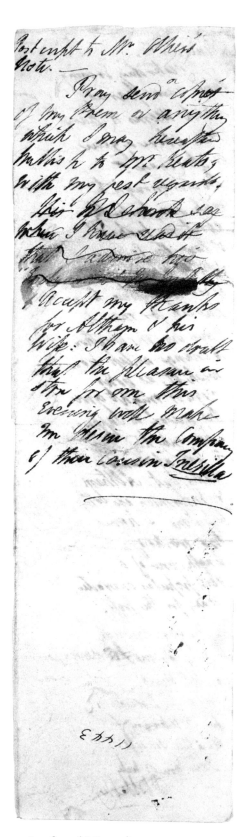

P. B. Shelley to Charles Ollier, August [17–19], 1819 (SC 533), pages 1–2

The Carl H. Pforzheimer Library

Shelley to Ollier   *August [17–19], 1819*

SC 533 PROVENANCE: Charles Ollier (Puttick and Simpson, July 22, 1878, lot 132); Naylor; Sotheby, February 27, 1882; Dolg; Rosenbach Foundation, February 1954. *De Ricci 419* (p. 195).

To Mr Ollier
> Dear Sir
>> Yesterday Evening came your parcel, which seems to have been above a year on its voyage?

5   Be good enough to write ~~soon~~, instantly about my books &c & how the Eclogue sells, & whether you wish to continue to publish for me. I have no inclination to change unless you wish it, as your neglect might give me reason to suppose. I have only had time to look at Lamb's works, but Altham & Endymion are both before me. I have two works of some length, one of a

10   very popular character ready for the press.
> Be good enough to pay for me £5 seven pounds to Mr Hunt.
> With best wishes for yr literary & all other success.
>> I am. Yours truly
>> P B Shelley.

15   Postscript to Mr Ollier's Note. ———

> Pray send a copy of my Poem or anything which I may hereafter publish to Mr Keats; with my best regards.
>> ~~This I I should say when I have read it that I admire his Endymion~~

20   ~~It probably~~
> Accept my thanks for Altham & his Wife: I have no doubt that the pleasure in store for me this evening will make me desire the Company of their Cousin Inesilla

line 1. *To Mr Ollier*: written in a larger hand, in the right margin of page 1 of the manuscript, perpendicular to the rest of the text. Shelley used a small, rather cramped hand for the remainder of the text of the letter. See facsimile, page 875.

line 3. *seems*: s written through w.

line 8. *had time*: nearly obliterated by spindle hole which has been mended.

line 11. *seven pounds*: added later in another hand.

line 17. *copy*: y written through *ies*.

line 19. *This ... probably*: probable reading.

line 21. *no*: n possibly written through n or another letter.

Shelley and his Circle : Manuscripts

SC 533   THE ABOVE NOTE to Ollier was written on the bottom edge of the second leaf of Shelley's undated letter to Hunt that was post-marked in London on September 3, 1819.[1] Since neither letter is dated, one must determine the time they were written from the arrival date of Ollier's parcel at Leghorn and from the time needed to send the dual letter of acknowledgment to England. Shelley's letter to Hunt of August 15 (sc 531) shows that the long-awaited parcel had not reached Leghorn by that date, whereas Mary records the arrival of Hunt's picture (sent in that parcel) in her catchall journal entry for August 12–20. Since Shelley tells Ollier that the parcel arrived "Yesterday Evening" (line 3), the earliest it could have reached Leghorn was August 15 after sc 531 had been mailed. But that was a Sunday, and it seems more likely that the parcel would have been delivered between Monday, August 16, and Thursday, August 19. Of six letters sent by Shelley to London between July 6 and September 21, 1819, that have both date of composition and an FPO postmark, one traveled from Leghorn to London in fifteen days, four went in sixteen, and one took twenty days.[2] A journey of fifteen to seventeen days would set the date of sc 533 between August 17 and 19, 1819.[3]

In the accompanying letter to Hunt, Shelley had asked Hunt always to send his letters by post rather than within parcels (as Hunt had sent sc 486 to save postal charges). There Shelley also reminded Hunt of some commissions that Mary had earlier given Marianne — chiefly a request that Marianne send a layette for the baby Mary was expecting.

1. Shelley, *Letters*, II, 111–113. We have examined a photocopy of the original manuscript of the letter to Hunt. It would appear that both sc 533 and the now missing first postscript to the Hunts could have occupied the portion cut from the letter to Hunt. For literal transcriptions of the letter to Hunt and the other Shelley manuscripts in the Lewis collection, see Lyle H. Kendall, Jr., *A Descriptive Catalogue of the W. L. Lewis Collection: Part One: Manuscripts, Inscriptions, Art* (Texas Christian University Press, 1970), pp. 94–127.

2. Godwin's letter of July 30 from London reached the Shelleys at Leghorn in fifteen days. Though this letter is not extant, the day it was written can be established from Godwin, Journal, and the date of its receipt from sc 531.

3. Although Shelley in a September 6 letter to Ollier states that "I received your packet with Hunt's picture *about* a fortnight ago" (Shelley, *Letters*, II, 116, italics added), one must emphasize the qualifying word; literally, a "fortnight" before September 6 would have been August 23, but that date is impossible. Even a date as late as August 20 (which Shelley, *Letters*, assigns as the date for sc 533 and the undated letter to Hunt) would presume an unusually quick fourteen-day journey from Leghorn to London (where the letter was postmarked on September 3).

Shelley to Ollier   *August [17–19], 1819*

SC 533   Tactfully, Shelley in the present note, which Hunt is to deliver to Ollier, requests Ollier to pay Hunt either five or seven pounds[4] on Shelley's account to cover the expenses involved.

In spite of Shelley's long frustration (see SC 531 and Commentary), he is both courteous and frank with his unobliging publisher. He asks about the success of his "Eclogue" (*Rosalind and Helen*), mentions two works, one likely to be popular (*The Cenci — Prometheus Unbound* being the other), and leaves with Ollier the decision whether or not to terminate their relationship. Ollier, who was not enjoying notable success as a publisher, had responded promptly, however, to Shelley's request of August 1 for a special copy of *Rosalind and Helen* by sending a letter and three posted packets that reached Shelley on September 5 — probably as early as Hunt would have delivered the above note to Ollier.[5] Apparently Ollier excused himself for not writing to Shelley earlier by telling him that his poems sold very slowly, that *Laon and Cythna* had been attacked in the *Quarterly*, and that he had remained silent because there was little cheerful that he could report. Shelley replied that, good news or bad, he still wanted his publisher to write to him: "I believe the truth is, I write less for the public than for myself."[6]

Shelley's critical reaction to Lamb's *Works* (1818), Keats's *Endymion* (1818), and Charles Ollier's own *Altham and His Wife* (1818) can be found in his mid-August letter to Hunt and his September 6 letter to Ollier. He praises the works by Lamb (especially *Rosamund Gray*) and Ollier, but, though he recognizes Keats's talent, he says of *Endymion*: "if he had printed about 50 pages of fragments from it I should have been led to admire Keats as a poet more than I ought, of which there is now no danger.—"[7] This later reaction makes all the more interesting Shelley's struggle, evidenced by the canceled lines in this note (lines 19–20), to compliment Keats on *Endymion*. The postscript seems to

---

4. It is not clear who changed Shelley's "£5" to "seven pounds." Was it Mary Shelley or Marianne Hunt?

5. See Shelley's response to Ollier, September 6, 1819 (Shelley, *Letters*, II, 116–118).

6. Shelley, *Letters*, II, 116. Some unobservant critics have taken this and other statements out of context to argue that Shelley actually did care little for public opinion. But Shelley's next sentence, ordering Ollier to rush him a special copy of the *Quarterly's* review of his poem, refutes such a contention.

7. Shelley, *Letters*, II, 117.

SC 533   have been written later, and the canceled words suggest that Shelley had read *Endymion* — or part of it — in the interim. He seems to be searching for the correct words in which to convey a mild compliment to Keats, without praising something he really did not like. Thus he begins "I *should say* . . . that I admire his Endymion" (italics added), instead of stating flatly that he does, in fact, admire it.[8] In the end, he simply asks Ollier to send the younger poet copies of his publications.

    Charles Ollier's second novel, *Inesilla* (line 23), was announced by 1818 for early publication; it did not appear until 1824.[9] In his Advertisement to *Inesilla* (dated December 1823), Ollier explains that the delay had been caused by the death of his eldest child.

8. Compare Shelley's equivocal phrasing in his letter to Hogg, November 28, 1817 (sc 431 and Commentary).

9. INESILLA,/ OR/ THE TEMPTER,/ A ROMANCE;/ WITH OTHER TALES./ BY/ CHARLES OLLIER,/ AUTHOR OF "ALTHAM AND HIS WIFE."/ [rule]/ LONDON/ PRINTED FOR E. LLOYD AND SON,/ HARLEY-STREET; AND/ WILLIAM BLACKWOOD, EDINBURGH./ [short rule]/ 1824/. Both Shelley, *Complete Works* (VIII, xlvii) and Shelley, *Letters* (II, 110 fn.), erroneously give this publication date as 1821, and the latter includes it in the list of Shelley's reading.

SC 534   LEIGH HUNT TO P. B. AND M. W. SHELLEY, AUGUST [23], 1819

AL signed *L.H.*, 3½ pages. Double sheet, 4to (8.8 x 7.2 inches).
Wove paper.
Seal: wax, red.
Postal fees: 1. 1/11; 2. 19.
Postmarks: 1. (receiving house stamp, London): CRAW[FORD STREET]|; 2. (Foreign Post Office stamp, London): F 19| 261|; 3. (transit stamp): ANGLETERRE|; 4. (transit stamp): CHAMBERY|; 5. [CORRISP^{ZA} ESTERA DA GENOVA]| [fleur-de-lis]|; 6. 8 SETTEMBRE|; 7. (trace).
Addition: drawings of foliage, probably by Shelley, on one flap of address leaf.

PROVENANCE: Colonel Charles Shelley Leigh Hunt; Mrs. Beryl Dodgson (Sotheby, April 8, 1935, lot 205).

> *8. York Buildings– New Road*
> *Augt 1819.*

My dear friends,
    Whenever I write to you, I seem to be transported to your presence.
5   *I dart out of the window like a bird, dash into a southwestern current of air, skim over the cool waters, hurry over the basking lands, rise like a lark over*

The Carl H. Pforzheimer Library

SC 534   *the mountains, fling like a swallow into the vallies, skim again, pant for breath – there's Leghorn– eccomi!– how d'ye do?*

         I wish you would encourage my epistolary virtues by writing to me
10   *every Monday morning;– I would write on the same day myself,–say at nine o'clock; & then we should have the additional pleasure of knowing that ~~were~~ we were occupied on the very same thoughts, & almost actually chatting together. I will begin the system at any rate; & if you do not help me to go on with it,–why I will heap Christian coals of fire on your heads by en-*
15   *deavouring to go ∧ᵒⁿwithout you.– There is the same continued sunshine this season, as last year. Every Saturday, when I go to office, I seem to walk through vallies of burning bricks, the streets and pavement are so intensely hot; but then there is a perpetual~~ly~~ fanning of fresh air in the fields, & you*
20   *may imagine I am oftener there. Sometimes I ramble about in them, some-times take my meals, sometimes lie down & read. The other day I had a delicious sleep in a haycock. These green fields & blue skies throw me into a kind of placid intoxication. Are there many moments more delicious than the one in which you feel yourself going to slumber, with the sense of green*
25   *about you,∧ᵒᶠ an air on your face, &∧ᵒᶠ the great sky arching over your head? One feels, at such times, all the grandeur of planetary consciousness without the pain of it. You know what I mean. – There is a sort of kind & beautiful sensuality in it which softens the cuts & oppressiveness of intellectual per-*
30   *ception.— Certainly a country so green as England cannot well be equalled by any other at such a season; & did not the less pleasant causes of that green return, I should try my utmost to induce you to come back again; for at this identical moment, I do not think you would be more comfortable any where than in such a place, with a book or two, a basket of fruit, and (oh*
35   *vain flattered friend!) Leigh Hunt. Shelley does indeed flatter me, when he writes to me as the "best friend" he has left behind. I heartily wish he had any better, for I am sure that they would go through a dozen fires for him; & as for that matter, so would I. In no race of friendship would I be the last, if my heart broke for it at the goal. But enough of this at present.– Pray do*
40   *not let Shelley be uneasy about my pecuniary affairs. It was he that enabled*

[880]

SC 534   *me to throw off the weight of them at first, & I should think it an ill return*
if I did not at least exert all the faculties which he set free. You know what
I told you of my remaining difficulties. Sir John Swinburne, in the best
manner helped me to manage with these; when unfortunately, our stationer,
45   *with whom we began upon credit, & who was always glad for the large sums*
we punctually paid him, to let us liquidate a heavy arrear at our leisure,
failed. The consequence was, that the assignees came upon us for payment,
which we could only effect after all by instalments; & these instalments
have taken several pounds which I could ill spare, out of my weekly income.
50   *However I have again lessened & squared my expenditure to it:– the landlord*
of our new house has given me permission to let it; & at Michaelmas, after
Marianne's confinement, we shall again live in a smaller one. Elliston, who
has just become renter & manager of Drury Lane, has got my tragedy, &
there are some symptoms of his not rejecting it, if the personal or political
55   *feelings of his patrons do not interfere. But my great reliance is on the*
Examiner, which I am happy to tell you is rising considerably at a season
of the year when in common with all other papers it used to fall. I exert
myself much for it; & to say nothing of the additional profits, it is not un-
pleasant to see the unequivocal proofs of one's strength of hand, in the eff
60   *results of the effort. We have also a scheme about book-advertisements, which*
we intend to put in practise the approaching bookseason, & which all our
friends reckon most promising;– so we shall do very well, believe me, however
annoyed at the moment.– I guess by Shelley's question about the Euganean
hills that he has not seen my criticism yet in the Exam^r, for surely, I spoke
65   *there of a poem which I admire beyond measure, for thought, imagination,*
music, every thing. He has a great admirer here from the Lakes, who has
come to London for his health,– Lloyd, one of the earliest Lake poets. More
of him in my next. God thrice bless you, Shelley mio, Marina mia.

Ever mo. affectionately your L.H.

70   *We are all well, though a little ailing occasionally, when we do not walk, or*
sit up too late, &c. Marian & Bessy beg their loves, & wish you to do all
sorts of wholesome things, & write & feel all sorts of pleasant ones;– they
mean, in books & poems. Your letters to us must be of course as lively or sad

SC 534   *as you are disposed to make them at the moment. It will be our business to rejoice with the one & condole with the other.–*

                           Once more most affectionately your's, L.H.

Shelley's little namesake is one of the kindest homuncules in the world.

[Address, page 4]
        Italie.

   P. B. Shelley Esqre

80   *Ferma in Posta*

         Livorno,

  Leghorn,

        Italia.

   Italy.

line 7. *vallies,*: common spelling of the period, recorded in *OED* and *Bailey's Dictionary*. Shelley used it in *The Esdaile Notebook* (sc 372, "The Voyage," IV, 996) and in discarded openings of *The Triumph of Life* (see Donald H. Reiman, *Shelley's "The Triumph of Life": A Critical Study*, University of Illinois Press, 1965, p. 235, line 24). See also line 18.

line 34. *two,*: following this word there was an ampersand which has been carefully erased.

line 44. *to manage*: written on fragment of paper adhering to seal.

line 48. *instalments;*: alternate spelling.

line 70. The postscript is written on page 1 of the manuscript, first above and then to the left of lines 1–2.

ALTHOUGH THIS letter lacks a date and although Shelley's letter to which this one was an answer is not extant, sc 534 should probably be dated August 23, 1819. It was evidently written on a Monday (lines 9–13) and reached Leghorn on September 8.

Hunt's letter centers upon contrasting images of fire and heat, on the one hand, and green-and-blue coolness, on the other. In threatening to "heap Christian coals of fire"[1] on Shelley by writing weekly, Hunt is reminded of the hot summer (the second one to Shelley's taste since he left England). He picks up the imagery again in testifying to his friendship, swearing that if Shelley had friends better than himself, "they would go through a dozen fires for him." (Hunt, of course, has been complaining of the "vallies of burning bricks" that he must traverse on his way to work, line 18.)

1. See Romans 12:20.

Hunt to Shelleys   *August* [23], 1819

SC 534   Leigh Hunt wrote his letters not so much by plan as by free association. A mind like Shelley's could take up Hunt's random remarks,
plumb their implications, and transform the thought into coherent poetic
images with philosophical insight. Consider, for example, Hunt's remarks
about the beauties of "green fields & blue skies" (line 22). When Hunt
qualifies his praise with "& did not the less pleasant *causes* of that green
return" (lines 31–32), he was, no doubt, thinking of England's rain and
dampness, which had been so harmful to Shelley at Marlow. Shelley, a
year and a half later, recognized as the "*causes*" behind the green of the
fields and the blue of the sky the distortion and mutability that underlie
all human experience:

> As long as skies are blue, and fields are green,
> Evening must usher night, night urge the morrow,
> Month follow month with woe, and year wake year to sorrow.
>
> .   .   .   .   .
>
> Life, like a dome of many-coloured glass,
> Stains the white radiance of Eternity. . . .
>
> .   .   .   .   .
>
> The fire for which all thirst; now beams on me,
> Consuming the last clouds of cold mortality.[2]

Hunt remarked in his letter of July [8] that he was no Prometheus,
like Shelley, but that he was "rather the son of one of Atlas's daughters,
than of Atlas himself."[3] This contrast between Shelley the Fire-bringer
and Hunt the descendant of the Atlantides (the Pleiades and Hyades,
who presided over the rainy season) seems to be borne out by the contrasting values in the imagery of their mythopoeic poetry.[4]

After reiterating his friendship for Shelley, Hunt turns to his current
financial crisis.[5] The "remaining difficulties" about which Hunt had told
the Shelleys were, no doubt, those that he had mentioned in his letter
of March 9, 1819 (sc 517). These unspecified debts, which apparently

2. *Adonais*, stanzas xxi, lii, liv (lines 187–189, 462–463, 485–486).

3. sc 529, line 62.

4. E.g., Hunt's "The Nymphs" and Shelley's *Prometheus Unbound*, with its "volcano's voice"
(see G. M. Matthews, "A Volcano's Voice in Shelley," *ELH: A Journal of English Literary History*,
XXIV, 1957, 191–228).

5. The passage, "You know what" (line 42) through "however annoyed at the moment" (line 62),
was omitted by Thornton Hunt from Hunt, *Correspondence*, along with most other references to
Leigh Hunt's financial difficulties.

The Carl H. Pforzheimer Library

SC 534   remained even after Shelley had given him a large sum of money and after Shelley had induced Ollier to advance him £200,[6] were paid by Sir John Swinburne.

In his *Autobiography*, Hunt gives Sir John Edward Swinburne, sixth baronet, brief but high praise:

Great disappointment and exceeding viciousness may talk as they please of the badness of human nature. For my part, I am now in my seventy-fourth year, and I have seen a good deal of the world, the dark side as well as the light, and I say that human nature is a very good and kindly thing, and capable of all sorts of virtues. Art thou not a refutation of all that can be said against it, excellent Sir John Swinburne? another friend whom I made in prison, and who subsequently cheered some of my greatest passes of adversity. Health, as well as sense and generosity, has blessed him; and he retains a young heart at the age of ninety-four.[7]

Sir John, born in 1762, lived on to the age of ninety-eight, dying in 1860, the year after Hunt's death. Hunt named his fourth son Swinburne in honor of this patron, dedicated *Foliage* (1818) to him, and throughout his career sent inscribed copies of his works to Sir John.[8]

Sir John Edward Swinburne has another significant tie with English literature as the grandfather of Algernon Swinburne, who described him as a French-educated gentleman of the old school, ultraliberal in politics, a friend of Mirabeau, a patron of the arts, and "most kind and affectionate to me always as child, boy, and youth."[9]

In spite of the increased circulation and influence of the *Examiner*, one of the most powerful voices of liberal opinion during the reform agitation of 1819, difficulties with the assignees of the paper's bankrupt stationer have once again circumscribed Hunt's income and driven him to new economies, such as leaving the house the Hunts had taken on a seven-year lease little more than a year before.[10] The Hunts did not take

6. See SC 539, line 36.

7. Hunt, *Autobiography*, II, 13.

8. Copies inscribed by Hunt to Swinburne of *Amyntas* (1820), *The Town* (1848), and Hunt's *Autobiography* (1850) were sold at Sotheby's, November 22, 1967 (lots 450, 454, 456).

9. See Edmund Gosse, *The Life of Algernon Charles Swinburne, The Bonchurch Edition of the Complete Works* (London, 1927), XIX, 3.

10. See SC 486 and Commentary.

SC 534   up their new residence at 13 Mortimer Terrace, Kentish Town, at Michaelmas (September 29), for Hunt's letter to Hogg on October 26 (sc 544) and that to Shelley on December 2, 1819 (sc 552) are dated from York Buildings, New Road. The Shelleys, expecting the Hunts to move to a new address, sent several letters to Hunt in care of the *Examiner* office, 19 Catherine Street,[11] and did so even after Bessy Kent had written them a letter dated January 6, in which she gave news of Hunt's affairs. The first surviving letter addressed by Shelley to Mortimer Terrace, Kentish Town, was his letter of April 5, 1820.[12] It is possible that the Hunts spent a few weeks or months living with some friend or relative (as they had lived with the Shelleys at Marlow) between houses.

On Robert William Elliston (line 52) and the reception of Hunt's play by Drury Lane, see sc 529 and Commentary; on Charles Lloyd (line 67), see sc 530 and Commentary.

Shelley in his lost letter must have asked Hunt if his "Lines written among the Euganean Hills" had reached London safely and whether or not it had been published. Shelley had also inquired about the manuscript in a note sent to Ollier in care of Peacock about mid-July,[13] and on August 1, he sent another note to Ollier — this one, perhaps, attached to his missing letter to Hunt — in which he asked that the *Rosalind and Helen* volume be sent to him by return mail "for a particular purpose."[14] Shelley may have wished to see the volume to ascertain, in the absence of mention by his correspondents, the fate of "Lines written among the Euganean Hills." Hunt had not only praised "Euganean Hills" in his review of *Rosalind and Helen* (*Examiner*, May 9, 1819), but also reprinted the entire text of the poem in a footnote to his review.[15]

---

11. See Shelley's letters to Hunt of September 27, November 2, November 13 (Shelley, *Letters*, II, 121–123, 134–136, 150–151), November [16] (sc 551), and December 23 (sc 555), 1819; see also Mary Shelley's letter to Hunt of September 24, 1819, and her letters to Marianne Hunt of November 24, 1819, and February 24, 1820 (Mary Shelley, *Letters*, I, 80–82, 83–86, 95–98).

12. Shelley, *Letters*, II, 179–182.

13. See Shelley, *Letters*, II, 101.

14. Shelley, *Letters*, II, 106.

15. See White, *Unextinguished Hearth*, p. 153 and note.

SC 535   LEIGH HUNT TO P. B. AND M. W. SHELLEY, SEPTEMBER 6, 1819

AL signed *L.H.*, 3½ pages. Double sheet, 4to (8.3 x 6.8 inches).
Wove paper. Watermark: JOHN HALL| [18]17|.
Seal: wax, red.
Postal fees: 1. 1/11; 2. 7; 3. ?91.
Postmarks: 1. (receiving house stamp, London)*:* CRA[WFORD STREET]|; 2. (Foreign
Post Office stamp, London)*:* F 19| 197|; 3. (transit stamp)*:* ANGLETER[RE]|;
4. (transit stamp)*:* CHAMBERY|; 5. CO[RRISP^ZA ESTERA DA GENOVA]| [fleur-de-lis]|;
6. 2[2 SET]TEM[BRE]|.

PROVENANCE: Colonel Charles Shelley Leigh Hunt; Mrs. Beryl Dodgson
(Sotheby, April 8, 1935, lot 205).

Monday– Sept. 6. 1819.

   My dear friends,

         We have as genuine a delight as you in your receipt
of the portrait, for we are delighted with your delight. How & why it delights
5 *me in particular, I need not say. But you tell us nothing of* pictures in return.
I would not have you go to any expense, but a sketch– a drawing– might
easily be managed. Indeed I do not suppose that expense on such an occasion
would be thought of. What is it then? Is it a modesty, you rogues, vainer
than my vanity? Shelley will answer unanswerably, I am sure, for one of
10 *you against yourselves; & as to* himself, *let him plant himself opposite the*
         glancing
artist, ~~looking~~ *neither to the right hand nor to the left,* ⟨——⟩ *& look him*
strait forward in the face, and if a spirit came down from the planet Mercury
to sit still a little & look at me, the thing could not be finer. I grant you that,
15 *as somebody said, the best thing in a face is what is not to be found in a*
portrait;– you say as much of my own;– but I send you what I can:– the
rest you have in your hearts; & do you think my heart is not as good a
painter? I have always thought as you do, Shelley, of Michael Angelo com-
pared with Raphael,– at least as far as I can recollect, or have thought at all.
20 *Yet I think highlier of him perhaps in some other points of view,– as in his*
ideas for instance of the old prophets & sybils, his picture of the soldiers
                                          is
hurrying out of the water, & in a creation of Eve, which∧*almost Raphaelian,*
if I may judge by the engraving. But as to the horrible picture you mention,

SC 535   *you have admirably described it. That figure of Christ in particular is every*

way a mistake & a monstrosity— Do you remember Raphael's Christ in te ~~be~~

miraculous draught of fishes, – that wonderful figure containing ~~almost~~ all

negative   at least,

the ∧beauty∧ of his doctrine without ~~the~~ any of the deformity of the faith which

30   *swallowed it up,–that self-sustained excess of gentleness,– that extreme of*

weakness, meeting, on the very strength of it's extreme, with power,– that

passive obedience made paramount,– & neutralizing slavishness by disarming

despotism,– making a part, as it were, of the aerial element about it,– a

thing issuing from out the air,– & if it were to be carried away by it, ~~subm~~

35   *looking as if it would submit & so resume itself. I scarcely know what I am*

writing, but I have a meaning in the core of it all; & having a meaning, you

will find it out, especially one of such a nature. I did not intend to ~~half~~ write

half so much on the subject any more than yourself; for I longed to thank

(*your* dedication)

40   *you for your proposed dedication. It∧ is one of the greatest honours as well*

as pleasures, of which my nature is susceptible. My spirit walks the higher

on the strength of its' approach; & as an Italian poet would say, più superbo

va. Nor do I say this laughingly, though I do; if you understand that paradox.

I am so serious upon the subject, that a smile comes to my relief. ⟨————⟩

45   *Where the reason & the imagination, the vanity, the heart, the private spirit*

& the public, are all gratified at once, one's enjoyment may well be a little

ineffable.— Pray tell me whether you would like your anonymous poem to

go to press directl⟨ ⟩ whether you would not rather wait till the next

book-season. ⟨ ⟩ wish at all for either of us not to remain with Ollier.

50   *I think ⟨ ⟩ does not improve him; but he was bred in a banker's, &*

he is — a bookseller. What should one expect? He is infinitely more intelligent

than the tribe in general, & in theory at least infinitely more liberal;– his

very laziness perhaps is a little bit of saving grace to him, & shews he is not

the ready slave of every possible penny;– & all things considered, it is

something to be

55   ~~better to ⟨————⟩who~~ *with one who at least understands one a little better than*

others.– Marianne, partly in penitence, & much in affection, is very busy

with Marina's orders. We pack up a box tomorrow, in which I shall put

such delicæ quædam as I can manage.– I need not say I thank you for your

SC 535   *kind wishes about Thornton; but after going on most promisingly with his drawing, he has shewn more & more latterly such a decided preference for letters & books, that ⟨————⟩ with great pleasure on my part I have let him have his way, & so ~~he~~ he is not to be a great painter, but a great journalist & philosopher, ~~majo~~ melior avis. He is always reading, & speculating on*

65   *what should be done for mankind. Young Henry Hunt has already taken his father's place in the Examiner; & though I cannot well conceive when I should leave off writing in it, I look forward with pleasure to the time when Thornton may join with his cousin, & relieve my regular labours,– for such they are to the spirit ⟨————⟩, & not unfrequently to the body.– God bless*

70   *you.– I shewed Lamb that passage about his Rosamond, upon which he said with the greatest air of sincerity–"I am proud of it."– Next Monday a letter as usual; & I hope Marina will write speedily. Pray make her.*

Ever your L.H.

[Address, page 4]

Italie.

75   *To*

P. B. Shelley Esqre

Ferma in Posta,

Leghorn,   Livorno,

Italy.   Italia.

line 12. ⟨————⟩: canceled letters illegible.

line 23. *creation*: *c* possibly *C*.

line 26. *te*: probable reading, for *the*.

line 33. *aerial*: probable reading.

line 43. *understand*: *and* written through indecipherable letters, possibly *ood*.

line 44. ⟨————⟩: two or three canceled words are illegible.

line 48. *directl*<*y or*>: seal tear.

line 49. <   >: seal tear; perhaps the words were *I don't* or *I have no*.

line 50. <*trade*>: possible reading; parts of letters missing because of seal tear.

     bred: probable reading.

line 52. *the*: written through indecipherable letters.

line 56. ⟨————⟩: canceled letters illegible.

line 62. ⟨————⟩: canceled word illegible.

line 63. *he*: possible reading.

line 69. ⟨————⟩: canceled word illegible.

Part of this letter, like Shelley's letter of August ?17–19 which it answers,[1] is anachronistic. Shelley had written in response to Hunt's

1. Shelley's letter is dated by Jones "[c. 20 August 1819]" (Shelley, *Letters*, II, 111–113). On the dating, see sc 533, Commentary.

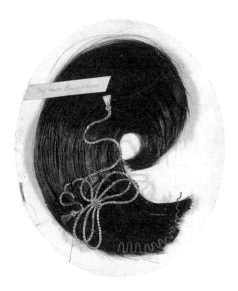

*Silhouette portrait of Shelley and lock of his hair, contained in a double frame
locket of red leather; the gold rim surrounding the lock of hair bears the
inscription, "In Loving Memory of My Dear Husband Percy Bysshe Who
Was Taken From Us July 8th 1822."*

SC 535   portrait and to the letter from Hunt begun about July 14, 1818, and completed August 4, 1818, that had taken over a year to reach Italy in Ollier's parcel. In it Hunt had questioned Shelley about Italian art, literature, and music.[2] Shelley replied in his letter of August ?17–19, 1819, by referring Hunt to his descriptive letters to Peacock and by stating his decided preference for Raphael over Michelangelo, and his negative opinion of the latter's "Last Judgment" in the Sistine Chapel.

Hunt replies with his customary tolerance, here extended both to Shelley's opinion and to Michelangelo's art (lines 18–26). The subject and manneristic style of "The Last Judgment" were foreign to Shelley's aesthetic experience and antithetical to his philosophy. There is no evidence that Shelley had studied the life of Michelangelo Buonarotti (1475–1564); had he done so, he might have gained appreciation for that great man's public artistic triumph over his enemies in the Sistine fresco. Shelley himself was in less than three years to utilize comparable elements of the grotesque to good effect in *The Triumph of Life*.

Hunt employs another method of turning Shelley back to Michelangelo's art, reminding him of Michelangelo's more idealized works, including especially the ceiling fresco in the Sistine Chapel, with its prophets and sybils and the story of Creation. These exhibit the vision of ideal beauty that Shelley missed in "Moses" and "The Last Judgment"—works that had contributed more to his opinion of Michelangelo's art because he was more familiar with them than with the artist's other works.[3] Hunt agrees with Shelley (lines 25–35) that the conception of Christ in "The Last Judgment" is inferior to that in "The Miraculous Draught of Fishes" of Raphael's cartoons,[4] and this preference was not only natural to men of their humanistic outlook but was certainly a viable opinion in the art criticism of the late eighteenth and early nineteenth centuries.

2. See sc 486.

3. One must remember that Shelley had not yet visited Florence to see "David" or the other masterpieces there. He had contemplated the style of "The Last Judgment" not only at the Sistine Chapel itself, but at the Royal Museum in Naples, which owned Michelangelo's original study for the Vatican fresco (see Shelley, *Letters*, II, 80–81). It seems likely that Shelley's visits to the Sistine Chapel were such that he did not have a chance to study the ceiling frescos in any detail.

4. This cartoon had been put on display at the British Institution in 1816 "for studying and copying" (see Ian Jack, *Keats and the Mirror of Art*, Oxford University Press, 1967, p. 97).

SC 535   Hunt's other remarks are more timely. He is suitably gratified by Shelley's expressed intention to dedicate his new work to him, and he asks Shelley how he wishes *Julian and Maddalo* (the "anonymous poem") to be published.[5] He urges the Shelleys to send their *portraits* (lines 5–14), implying in his argument that Shelley did not have a flattering profile.[6] In a response to a postscript by Mary, Hunt brings the Shelleys up to date on Thornton's career aspirations.[7] He also mentions in passing that Marianne has not yet sent the box of baby clothes that Mary had been awaiting for some months.

In her letter of June 29, 1819,[8] Mary mentions and strongly re-iterates her earlier request (in a letter now lost) that Marianne send her some baby clothes. From Mary's letter of August 28 it seems clear that Marianne had written about the commission, but had yet done nothing.[9] Shelley's tact in providing Hunt with money to cover the expenses (sc 533) ought to have moved the Hunts to quick action, but (to pass over some intervening cries of anguish[10]) Mary wrote a postscript to Shelley's letter to Hunt, November 2, 1819: "At the end of August Hunt wrote to say that my parcel was to be sent the next day—Sept. 12th he said his letter had been put off that he might give us news of it yet not a word of news did he give—nor has since—"[11] Actually, Hunt did finally send the box about October 11 (see his letter of September 20, sc 540), but Mary received the most urgently needed things in a box from Peacock that reached Florence before November 25, while Hunt's parcel was still in transit from Genoa to Leghorn.[12] Mary inquired about Hunt's parcel again about December 2,[13] and apparently

---

5. See sc 531, sc 532, and Commentaries.

6. Shelley, Claire, and William had sat for their portraits to Amelia Curran in Rome, April–May 1819. Shelley's portrait remained unfinished at his death (White, *Shelley*, II, 91). In January 1820, Claire records that "Mr. Tomkyns takes Shelley's likeness" (Claire Clairmont, *Journals*, pp. 115–116). For a facsimile of a silhouette portrait of Shelley, see page 889.

7. See sc 486 and Commentary.

8. Mary Shelley, *Letters*, I, 74.

9. Mary Shelley, *Letters*, I, 77.

10. Mary Shelley, *Letters*, I, 81.

11. Shelley, *Letters*, II, 135.

12. See Mary Shelley, *Letters*, I, 85.

13. Mary Shelley, *Letters*, I, 87.

SC 535 received it about December 13, when her final comment to Maria Gisborne was: "We have received our box—it contained no books—it was a silly expensive affair—but that was not my fault—I did the best I c[oul]d & that you know is a consolation—"[14]

One timely topic is conspicuous by its absence from Hunt's letters of August and September 1819.[15] Nowhere does he, as Peacock did in his August letter,[16] mention the Manchester massacre or the political turmoil in England. Did he refrain from doing so intentionally, because he feared that such subjects would only increase Shelley's and Mary's depression? The national crisis was certainly very much on his mind, as his numerous articles on it in the *Examiner* testify. One can identify Leigh Hunt's contributions to the paper by his signature of a pointing hand. This symbol must be distinguished from a hand pointing at two crosses, which may have been used for a time by Henry L. Hunt.

14. Mary Shelley, *Letters*, I, 90. Compare Shelley, *Letters*, II, 151, note 2.
15. SC 534, SC 535, SC 539, SC 540.
16. See SC 537, Commentary.

SC 536 P. B. SHELLEY, *MASK OF ANARCHY*, DRAFT STANZA, SEPTEMBER 6–23, 1819

HOLOGRAPH MANUSCRIPT, ½ page. Page 6 of 3 consecutive single sheets (5.5 x 3.5 inches), containing also SC 532 and SC 548.
For further details, see SC 532, Bibliographical Description.

The spirit

An red mist like the steam of gore
His quick footsteps rolled before
rove

5 *Upon And beneath his*
The And the

Shelley, Mask of Anarchy, Stanza   **September 6–23, 1819**

SC 536

> ~~Cried out like~~
> *And the earth whereer he went*
>
>   *cry*
> *A Like a trampled infant sent*
> ~~A piercing~~ *scream ~~of~~ ⟨——⟩ loud lament*

10

line 1. *The spirit*: appears in the upper left-hand corner. The remainder of the text of sc 536 occupies the lower half of the page.

line 11. ⟨——⟩: three-letter fragment, possibly beginning with *dr*.

THE SO-CALLED "Peterloo Massacre" took place on August 16, 1819, when in unheroic travesty of Waterloo, a group of mounted militiamen and hussars rode, sabers swinging, into a crowd of several thousand men, women, and children who had peacefully assembled in St. Peter's Field, outside Manchester, to hear a speech on reform by Henry "Orator" Hunt (no relation to Leigh Hunt). In the melee six people were killed and more than eighty wounded by sabers or trampled by the charging horses or by others in the crowd attempting to flee. Shelley first learned of the event from Peacock's letter that arrived shortly before September 6, 1819 (see sc 537 and Commentary), though his comments to Charles Ollier in a letter of that date do not suggest any decision to compose a poem.[1] But he must have begun very soon, because he completed a draft and wrote out an intermediate fair copy and Mary transcribed a final copy for the press that was mailed to Hunt on September 23.[2]

The above fragment appears on the verso of the third of three leaves that were removed from one of Shelley's notebooks by either Mary Shelley or Lady Jane Shelley (see sc 532 and Commentary). The meter and content of the lines reveal that the fragment is the first draft of a stanza intended for *The Mask of Anarchy* but not included in the later versions of that poem. A fair copy of this stanza in Mary's hand appears on folio 25, verso of Huntington manuscript 2177:

1. Shelley, *Letters*, II, 117.

2. The first draft of *The Mask of Anarchy* is in Huntington manuscript 2177; Shelley's holograph intermediate fair copy of the poem, now in the Ashley Collection at the British Museum, was reproduced in facsimile by The Shelley Society in 1887, with an Introduction by H. Buxton Forman; the press copy, in Mary's hand with Shelley's corrections, which was sent to Hunt in 1819 and used by him when he finally published the poem in 1832, is now in the Library of Congress.

The Carl H. Pforzheimer Library

SC 536

> A red mist like a steam of gore
> His quick footsteps rose before
> And the earth whereon he went
> Like a trampled infant sent
> A piercing scream of loud lament.

Forman, in discussing this stanza, notes that the only other words on the page are "The spirit" (in ink at the top of the page) and (in pencil at right angles to the fair copy of this stanza) "exempli gratia." Forman thinks "The spirit" (in Mary's hand) to be a heading for the stanza, indicating that the stanza relates to stanzas xxviii–xxxii, which describe the appearance of a "Shape" that conquers Anarchy, whereas Shelley's words "exempli gratia" "do not appear to bear any relevancy to the poetry."[3]

If it was Mary Shelley who removed the leaf containing Shelley's draft of the stanza from the notebook, she may have copied the stanza onto folio 25, verso (which was almost empty and follows the pages devoted to *The Mask of Anarchy*) to preserve in the notebook the text of the only stanza of *The Mask* that she was giving away. Mary, on the other hand, may have recopied the stanza in 1819 while she was engaged in transcribing the press copy of the poem simply to call Shelley's attention to a stanza that he had omitted from *his* intermediate fair copy. If that were true, Shelley's "exempli gratia" could be read as an elliptical comment on why he decided not to include the stanza: because the poem as he had fair-copied it was already supplied with enough similar details.

There remains another possibility. Shelley may originally have drafted the stanza to include earlier in *The Mask of Anarchy*, in the description of the triumphal progress of Anarchy (stanzas x–xiii). As Forman observes, the notebook draft lacks stanza viii that describes Anarchy's white horse, and the "quick footsteps" of sc 536, line 3, may have been meant to be those of Anarchy, unmounted. In this case, when Shelley elected to depict Anarchy as "Death on the Pale Horse,"[4] he

---

3. Shelley, *Note Books*, II, 40.

4. The large painting with this title by Benjamin West (1738–1820) was exhibited at the gallery attached to West's house, 14 Newman Street, London. Leigh Hunt, who had lived in West's house while a schoolboy (Mrs. West being the aunt of Leigh Hunt's mother), writes in his *Autobiography* (I, 97) of the strong impression this painting made on him. Keats, who with Charles Jeremiah Wells saw the painting in December 1817, was disappointed by its lack of intensity (Keats, *Letters*, I, 192), and Hazlitt criticized it severely (*Complete Works*, XVIII, 138). The subject should have interested Shelley, but we have no record of his opinion of the painting.

SC 536   would necessarily have omitted this picture of Anarchy as a striding
giant, an image that would draw a sharp parallel between Anarchy and
the avenging "Shape."

SC 537   P. B. SHELLEY TO T. L. PEACOCK, SEPTEMBER 9, 1819

AL signed *P. B. S.*, 1 page. Single sheet, 4to (9.9 x 8.2 inches).
Wove paper. Watermark: BONDON|.
Seal: wax, red: [Judgment of Paris]|.
Postal fees: 1. 1/11; 2. 4/9.
Postmarks: 1. LIVORNO; 2. (Foreign Post Office stamp, London): FPO| SE·25|
1819|.
Notations: 1. (page 1, top center, probably in Peacock's hand): *Not printed*| (see
also SC 491); 2. (address flap): *4/9*|.
PROVENANCE: T. L. Peacock (Sotheby, June 11, 1866, lot 756); Waller; Puttick
and Simpson, April 25, 1888, lot 929; Pearson; Alfred Morrison (Sotheby, Part
III, December 9, 1918, lot 2024); Sabin; Maggs, Catalogue 411, Autumn 1921,
#2276. *De Ricci 424* (p. 213).

Livorno Sep^t 9· 1819

My dear Peacock

    *I send you the Tragedy, addressed to Stamford S^t fearing lest it
might be inconvient to recieve such bulky packets at the India House.—*
5 *You will see, that the subject has not been treated as you suggested, & why
it was not susceptible of such treatment: in fact it was then already printing
when I recieved your letter; and it has been treated in such a manner that I
don't see how ithe subject forms an objection. You know Œdipus is performed on the fastidious French stage, a play much more broad than this.*
10 *I confess I have some hopes, & some friends here persuade me that they are
not unfounded.*
    Many thanks for your attention in sending the Papers which contain
                                                     distant
the terrible & important news of Manchester. These are as it were the thunders
15 *of the terrible storm which is approaching. The tyrants here as in the
French Revolution have first shed blood may their execrable lessons not
be learnt with equal docility:*

The Carl H. Pforzheimer Library

SC 537   *I still think that there will be no coming to close quarters until financial*
affairs decidedly bring the oppressors & the oppressed together.. Pray let
20   *me have the earliest political news which you consider of importance at this*
crisis

Yours ever most faithfully

P. B. S.

I send this to the India House—the tragedy to Stamford S^t

[Address, page 2]

25   *T. L. Peacock Esqr*

India House

London

Inghilterra

Angleterre

line 1. *1819*: there is a short slant stroke beneath *18.*

line 4. *inconvient* (sic).
      recieve (sic).

line 7. *recieved* (sic).

line 9. *stage,*: *ag* written through indecipherable letters.

line 16. *their*: Shelley appears to have added an extra loop between *e* and *i*.

line 17. *docility*: punctuation is crowded in at the edge of the page; Shelley may have meant to write a period. The next sentence is only slightly indented and may not have been intended as a new paragraph.

line 29. *Angleterre*: written to the left of and perpendicular to remainder of address.

THIS BRIEF but significant letter points in two directions. Its first paragraph marks the end of Shelley's main efforts on *The Cenci*, as Shelley sends a copy to Peacock to submit to the manager of the Theatre Royal, Covent Garden. The second paragraph, thanking Peacock for sending Shelley his first news of what the *Examiner* of August 22 called "Disturbances at Manchester," signals Shelley's renewed interest in English politics and the cause of reform that would lead him into a new poetic vein in *The Mask of Anarchy* (see SC 536) and related political lyrics, as well as into "the great sandy desert" of political prose, culminating in his *Philosophical View of Reform* (SC 546).

Shelley's first written account of his plan to write a drama on the

SC 537 Cenci story is his long late-July letter to Peacock.[1] At that time Shelley stated, "I have written a tragedy," implying that the main efforts of composition were behind him. He asked Peacock if he would attempt, without revealing the name of the author, to get the play accepted for production at Covent Garden, where Shelley hoped that Eliza O'Neill would play Beatrice Cenci.[2] Shelley sent with that letter a copy of Mary's translation of the Italian manuscript account entitled "Relation of the Death of the Family of the Cenci."[3] Peacock read it and in his lost August letter offered Shelley some suggestions on how to treat various parts — particularly Count Cenci's incestuous passion for Beatrice. Though Shelley's Preface — especially its final sentence — mentions the "manuscript" in such a way as to show that the Preface was written as an introduction to the "Relation,"[4] no part of the "Relation" was, in fact, included in the first edition. When Shelley decided to have *The Cenci* printed in Italy — sometime before Peacock's letter arrived (lines 6–7) — he did not, apparently, have a second copy of the translated "Relation" to send to the printer. Shelley may have been in such a hurry to print and ship *The Cenci* to England that he could not wait until he, Mary, or Claire had time to translate again the "Relazione" that Mary had copied at Leghorn in May 1818.

The fate of both Mary's original transcript of the Italian "Re-

1. Though Jones dates this letter ca. July 20 (Shelley, *Letters*, II, 101–103), it cannot have been written before July 22 and should probably be dated July 25. In the first paragraph, Shelley mentions receiving Hogg's July 2 letter (manuscript in the Abinger collection), which was addressed to Shelley in care of John Gisborne and date-stamped at Leghorn on July 21. Shelley could not, therefore, have received Hogg's letter until at least the evening of July 21. Shelley's letter to Peacock is postmarked in the London Foreign Post Office (FPO) on August 10; since the minimal time for Leghorn-to-London letters in the summer months was fourteen to sixteen days, the letter could have been written as late as July 26 or 27, but it was most likely written on July 25. Shelley's letter to Hogg of that date seems to have been written at the same time.

2. Even had Miss O'Neill (1791–1872) been anxious to play the part, her marriage in 1819 to W. Wrixon-Becher, M.P., of Ballygiblin Castle, County Cork (created baronet in 1831) ended her stage career (Ward, *Men of the Reign*, p. 689). For the Shelleys' reaction to news of her retirement, see Mary Shelley, *Letters*, I, 94.

3. "The translation which I send you is to be prefixed to the play, together with a print of Beatrice—" (Shelley, *Letters*, II, 103). The FPO postal fee of five shillings ninepence is three times the usual fee for a single letter, indicating that *something* was enclosed, though if this was the "Relation," it must either have been written in a very minute hand or have been greatly abridged.

4. Shelley's intention is even clearer when we compare the final Preface with the draft. See Shelley, *Note Books*, II, 87–98.

The Carl H. Pforzheimer Library

SC 537   lazione" and the translation sent to Peacock is unknown.[5] A notebook contains a translation in Mary's hand of the "Relation," with certain omissions.[6] This transcript served as press copy for the text printed after Mary's "Note on the Cenci" in the one-volume second edition of Shelley published by Moxon in 1839–1840.[7] In the *Indicator* for July 19, 1820, Leigh Hunt began his review of *The Cenci* with a summary account derived, he told Shelley, "out of the M.S. about the Cenci."[8] Although in the *Indicator* Hunt describes his source as a manuscript "copied by an Italian gentleman from a library at Rome,"[9] he may actually have used the translation Shelley had sent to Peacock as the basis of his account, perhaps sending parts of it to press as copy. Thereafter the first translation (by Shelley or Mary) was discarded or lost. Inasmuch as comparison of Hunt's quotations in the *Indicator* with Mary's translation in the Bodleian shows them to be independent translations of the same version of the story, Mary's surviving translation in the Bodleian may be a second translation done late in 1819 or 1820, perhaps for inclusion in a later edition of *The Cenci*.

Shelley declared in the late-July letter to Peacock that he had already written *The Cenci* and that "the play will be ready to be sent" by the time Peacock's return-of-post reply could reach him — that is, in about a month. So far as composition and transcription were concerned, Shelley kept within that schedule. Mary's Journal, which she resumed on August 4 (Shelley's twenty-seventh birthday) after a lapse of two months, records that Shelley was writing the play on August 4 and 7 and that on August 8: "he finishes his tragedy." On August 11

---

5. See fn. 3, above.

6. Bodleian Ms. Shelley adds. e. 13.

7. Truman Guy Steffan errs in saying that the Bodleian transcript omits passages that appear in Mary Shelley's second edition of Shelley's poems ("Seven Accounts of the Cenci and Shelley's Drama," *Studies in English Literature*, IX, 1969, 603).

8. Hunt to Shelley, August 23, 1820; manuscript in The Carl H. Pforzheimer Library.

9. *Indicator*, No. XLI, July 19, 1820, p. 322. The Carl H. Pforzheimer Library has recently acquired a manuscript of the "Relazione della morte della Famiglia Cenci" that is the same version of the story as that from which Mary's translation is taken. At the end, the transcription is said to be "dal Manuscritto originale nel Vaticano." The free endpaper of the notebook (of English manufacture) is signed "A Colyar 1818/Roma." For an analysis of the variant manuscript accounts of the Cenci story, see Steffan's article cited in fn. 7, above.

Shelley to Peacock   **September 9, 1819**

SC 537   Shelley was copying the play but on August 20, the next entry after a nine-day gap, Mary was copying "S's Tragedy." In a cumulative entry covering the week September 5–12, Mary wrote that "on friday [September 10]— S sends his tragedy to Peacock."

In what form did the play first go to England — fair copy, corrected proof-sheets, or final printed text? Shelley says (lines 6–7) that the play was "already printing" when he received Peacock's letter and he speaks of it being sent in "bulky packets" (line 4), but neither of these statements really casts much light on the problem: *The Cenci* was a long enough work to make up into more than one bulky postal packet either in manuscript or printed version,[10] and we might dismiss Shelley's comment about the drama having gone to press before Peacock's letter of advice arrived if we read it as an excuse to salve Peacock's feelings while rejecting his counsel. In his next letter to Peacock (September 21), Shelley clarifies the situation by saying that he had "printed in Italy 250 copies" both because costs were lower and because he believed "that the seeing it in print wd. enable the people at the theatre to judge more easily."[11]

In Mary's note on *The Cenci*, she mentions another reason Shelley had the poem printed in Italy: "to insure its correctness; as he was much annoyed by the many mistakes that crept into his text, when distance prevented him from correcting the press."[12] Still another, unstated reason was that sending the printed play to Peacock probably saved time, for had Shelley mailed the fair-copy manuscript to London, he or Mary would have been forced to transcribe another fair copy (like the Esdaile notebook or the Harvard notebook) to preserve the drama in case it should be lost in the mails. Because Shelley was, moreover, anxious to stage *The Cenci* before anyone else utilized the story, he obviously feared the loss of time that would result if his only press-ready fair copy went astray.

Shelley, for all these reasons, sent at least proof-sheets, and possibly the final printed text (less Dedication and title page) by September 9

10. Ollier, we note, sent the clipped pages of *Rosalind and Helen* to Shelley in four such packets (see Shelley, *Letters*, II, 106, 116).

11. Shelley, *Letters*, II, 119.

12. Shelley, *Poetical Works* (1839), II, 279.

SC 537   or 10. The sequence of events would, then, seem to be as follows: Shelley completed writing *The Cenci* on August 8. He began transcribing a fair copy almost immediately and Mary also joined in the work, perhaps copying the latter portions while Shelley was making arrangements and supervising the printing of the early acts.[13] The printing of the text was probably completed by September 9, and the entire book, including the Dedication and Preface, was in print, ready to be shipped to London by September 21.

    The second half of Shelley's letter looks ahead. Peacock in his August letter had enclosed press clippings on what came to be termed the "Peterloo Massacre" at Manchester on August 16 (see SC 536, Commentary). This letter could not, then, have been written before August 17 or 18.[14] Shelley had received it at least by September 6[15]; it could have been sent as late as Monday, August 23, which would have permitted Peacock to clip the story from the *Examiner* and other weekend papers. We do not know which clippings Peacock sent to Shelley, but they may have included those from the *Morning Chronicle* and *Cobbett's Political Register*.[16]

13. Though we do not yet have conclusive evidence, *The Cenci* was probably printed by the firm of Glauco Masi (successor to Tommaso Masi) in Leghorn. Dowden (*Shelley*, II, 279) suggested this possibility but without evidence other than the kinds of books Masi printed and sold. We have compared the types used in *The Cenci* with those of a volume printed by Glauco Masi the same year, *L'Italiade* by Angelo Maria Ricci. It seems clear to us that the title pages of the two volumes, the italic type used for stage directions in *The Cenci* and in *L'Italiade*, the type used for the text of Shelley's play and for the front matter of *L'Italiade*, and even the swell rules seem to be identical in the two books. Signor Fernando Vallerini, an antiquarian bookdealer in Pisa, has confirmed the idea that Glauco Masi was the printer of *The Cenci*.

14. Peacock's letter does not survive. Peacock evidently sorted out and destroyed all of his letters to Shelley that contained personal matters he preferred not to have made public. These included all reference to Shelley's financial support of him. It is quite likely that the missing Peacock letter of late August (and, probably, the lost letter of July also) contained an allusion to Shelley's subsidy. Perhaps Peacock was by this time thanking Shelley for his help and informing him that he no longer required that assistance. After Shelley's death, Peacock probably exchanged with Mary Shelley the thirteen Shelley letters to him from Italy that Mary published in *Essays, Letters from Abroad* for a similar number of his letters to Shelley.

15. See Shelley, *Letters*, II, 117.

16. Peacock may have sent Shelley clippings only from the *Examiner*, #608, August 22, 1819, which not only published its own news stories and commentaries on the riot and its aftermath but also reprinted accounts "From the *Times*" and "From the *Star*."

Shelley to Peacock   **September 9, 1819**

SC 537   Shelley's reaction shows both anger and restraint. To Ollier he had
written three days earlier, "the torrent of my indignation has not yet
done boiling in my veins."[17] But in the present letter, he expresses the
wish that the people may not learn from their "tyrants" to shed blood
as easily as the French did in their revolution (lines 15–17). What may
seem surprising to those who have a superficial knowledge of Shelley
is his prediction that the British people will not rise in open rebellion
("coming to close quarters") until the country's "financial affairs"
reach a state of insoluble chaos (lines 18–19). For Shelley's considered
ideas on the relationship between economic and political activities, see
SC 546.

Shelley responded to this crisis in British politics with several kinds
of writing. First, he wrote *The Mask of Anarchy* and a group of political
lyrics directed at the common people and designed to channel their
anger into nonviolent responses of firm passive resistance. Second, he
wrote a letter to the editor of the *Examiner*, a defense of freedom of the
press in the form of an extended analysis of the issues in the trial of
Richard Carlile on the charge of blasphemous libel for selling Paine's
Age of Reason.[18] Third, he began a treatise fully outlining his political
philosophy, *A Philosophical View of Reform* (SC 546). Because during
the same period he also managed to compose the fourth act of *Prometheus
Unbound*, several of the shorter poems published with it (including "Ode
to the West Wind"), and *Peter Bell the Third*, one can hardly say that
Shelley was completely preoccupied with English politics during the last
four months of 1819. But the news of Peterloo did engage Shelley's
maturing perspective in the practical affairs of his country in a way that
events had not since 1817, when he had written the two "Hermit of
Marlow" tracts.

17. Shelley, *Letters*, II, 117.

18. This case had first been brought to Shelley's attention by Hogg, who discussed it at length in
his July 2 letter to Shelley (Abinger Manuscripts, Pforzheimer Microfilm, reel IV, file 5). It should
be noted that in his letter on Carlile's trial, Shelley may have been attempting to duplicate the feat
of William Godwin, whose essay entitled *Cursory Strictures on the Charge Delivered by Lord Chief
Justice Eyre to the Grand Jury, October 2, 1794* (first published in the *Morning Chronicle*) changed
the course of English judicial history. See "William Godwin," *Shelley and his Circle*, I, 11, and
Herschel Baker, *William Hazlitt* (Harvard University Press, 1962), pp. 87–92.

SC 538 WILLIAM GODWIN TO ?JOHN RICHARDSON, SEPTEMBER 11, 1819

> AL signed *William Godwin*, 1 page. Double sheet, with ¾ of address page cut away, destroying address and part of docket; 4to (9.1 x 7.2 inches).
> Laid paper. Watermark: Ruse & Turners| 1817|.
> Seal: wax, black.
> Notation, page 1, upper left corner, in pencil: *author of "Political Justice" &c|*.
> Docket, page 4, in ink, partially torn away: *1819| S^t 11 Sept| Wm Godwin|*.
> Additions: four pieces of black wax adhere to page 4 and the two right-hand corners of page 1 are pasted down onto a leaf in a large album.
> PROVENANCE: Sotheby, February 2, 1963, lot 490.

Skinner Street,
Sep. 11, 1819.

Dear sir

You had the goodness, when I had the pleasure to see you in Skinner
5 *Street, to desire me without scruple to apply to you, in any question where*
it might be easily in your power to render me a service. The question of the
inclosed is a trivial matter, but till I recollected your kindness, I felt some-
what at a loss how to proceed respecting it. May I beg the favour of you to
cause my bill to be presented for acceptance? I expected a bill on London for
10 *this sum, & then perhaps I should have felt inclined to turn it into cash*
before it became due : perhaps you would be_so_obliging as to tell me how to
proceed respecting the bill as it is. I learn from the London Coffee House,
that you will probably be back here again in a week.

15 *May I beg you to excuse my troubling you in this petty affair, & to*
believe me to be,

Dear sir, your much obliged & obed^t servant
William Godwin

MARY JANE GODWIN vacationed from time to time, and when she did, Godwin had to take charge of the bookselling business on Skinner Street. Godwin's Journal shows that Mrs. Godwin was out of London in August and September of 1819. On Saturday, August 21, Godwin, his wife, and some friends took the steamboat to Southend, with Godwin (and several friends) returning to London on the following Monday (August 23). Godwin made one more weekend trip to Southend

Shelley and his Circle : Manuscripts

SC 538 (September 4–6); Mary Jane Godwin did not return to London until Friday, September 17.

At Skinner Street, Godwin recorded in his Journal only his usual activities — his reading, progress in writing his reply to Malthus, letters sent, and visits of David Booth and other friends. Though he does not comment in his Journal on the affairs of M. J. Godwin's Juvenile Library, he sent Mrs. Godwin reports on business in his frequent letters to her. Fortunately, many of these letters survive in Lord Abinger's collection, and the one written on Saturday, September 11, contains in two paragraphs a complete explanation for what would otherwise be an incomprehensible letter to an unknown correspondent.

My dear love

I have this morning received from Husley a bill for £40; but it is unfortunately a bill upon Liverpool, & not upon London, & drawn at sixty days *after sight*. Not knowing therefore what else to do with it, I shall send it by this day's post to Richardson of Liverpool, requesting him to have the goodness to cause it to be presented for acceptance, & then perhaps he will do me the further favour to give me cash for it. I sent to inquire at the London Coffee House, & was told that he would perhaps be in town in a week.

. . . . .

I should have mentioned above, that Husley excuses himself for not having sent the full amount of your invoice, & says, "By the next vessel that leaves the island, I will send cash; or a bill, for the remainder." His letter is also accompanied by another order, which I think should by all means be executed.[1]

In the first paragraph, Godwin tells us who the bill is from — one Husley, probably a bookseller (rather than a schoolmaster, the other principal class of M. J. Godwin's customers[2]). From the subsequent paragraph, we learn that Husley lived on an island. This must have been the Isle of Man, both because Liverpool was its chief English port of commercial connection and because it is the only island off the west coast of England (Ireland excluded, of course) large enough to support a bookseller who would owe more than £40 to M. J. Godwin.

1. Abinger Manuscripts, Pforzheimer Microfilm, reel IV, file 6.
2. In his letter of August 28, Godwin tells his wife that "the school-orders have been numerous, but small: two from Dr. Richardson, the largest £7.10, one from Miss Wheatley £4.10—, the rest trivial" (Abinger Manuscripts, Pforzheimer Microfilm, reel IV, file 6). Husley, to pay £40 and to owe more, must have been a bookseller. This "Dr. Richardson" (a schoolmaster) is fairly obviously not the "Richardson of Liverpool" mentioned in Godwin's September 11 letter and addressed in sc 538.

SC 538   Among the Richardsons listed in the Liverpool section of *Pigot's Directory*, the most likely candidates for recipient of this letter are two listed in the category "merchants": James Richardson, "21, New Quay," and John Richardson, "17, Water Street (and Isle of Man and Greenock Steam Packet Office)." The second, because of his connections with the Isle of Man and with the steam packet, seems to be the more likely prospect, although either merchant might make regular trips to London and stay at the London Coffee-house.

The London Coffee-house (1771–1867) on Ludgate Hill (extending east from Fleet Street toward St. Paul's Cathedral, Plan of London, D2, Back Endpapers) had long been a favorite inn of Americans and philosophical radicals. There in its early years had met the informal club for philosophical discussions which listed Priestly, Price, and Franklin among its members.[3] The inn has been mentioned earlier in these volumes as Shelley's letter-drop when, in the autumn of 1814, he was hiding from bailiffs.

One might conjecture that Mr. Richardson — James or John — was a man of about Henry Crabb Robinson's age who had in youth been impressed and influenced by the writings of Godwin and who, on a business trip, had made a pilgrimage to Skinner Street. In any case Godwin recorded in his Journal that "Richardson of Liverpool" called on him on July 23 and July 24, 1819.

3. Wheatley, *London*, II, 426.

SC 539   LEIGH HUNT TO M. W. SHELLEY, SEPTEMBER 12, 1819

AL signed *L.H.*, 3½ pages. Double sheet, 4to (9.3 x 7.4 inches).
Laid paper. Watermark: J & M| 1815|.
Seal: wax, red.
Postal fees: 1. 1/11; 2. 7 Pagato il Porto a Livorno; 3. ?91.
Postmarks: 1. (Foreign Post Office stamp, London): F 19| 73|; 2. (transit stamp): ANGLETERRE|; 3. (transit stamp): [CHAMBERY]|; 4. [CORRISP^{ZA} ESTERA DA GE-NOVA]| [fleur-de-lis]|; 5. 6 OTTOBRE|; 6. LIVORNO|; 7. 12| OTTOBRE|.
Notation, in the hand of P. B. Shelley, page 1, beneath postscript:

> *190*
> *190*
> ―――
> *380*   *300*

Shelley and his Circle : Manuscripts

SC 539 PROVENANCE: Colonel Charles Shelley Leigh Hunt; Mrs. Beryl Dodgson (Sotheby, April 8, 1935, lot 205).

Monday– Sept. 12. 1819.

York Buildings— New Road.

I will tell you, Marina, what I meant by "gigantic paragraphs;"–
short letters written in large characters. Count the number of words in one
5 *of my letters, & in one of yours, & see which has the greater. Thus you write*
The characters I write in are
a long letter, it is true, but not a full one. ~~Mine is~~ ⁁like the devils in Pandæ-
monium who shrunk themselves to pigmies that they might all get in;– yours
are the leaders of them, in secret conclave,– mightier. but not so numerous.
10 *Do not suppose I complain, though of course you could not object to ̶h my*
wishing as crammed letters as possible; & now I recollect, you have written
some long letters of the interlined sort. In general however they are such as
I say; but the last was in every respect an excellent one, & we thank you for
it most heartily. We thank you for your account of the podère; we thank you
15 *for that of the dancing; we thank you for the length of the letter; & if you*
so many
must still shed⁁tears (which are better too than shedding none), we thank
you for mingling with them the thought of your friends. We rejoice that you
can find the least passing refreshment from that drop, even in so bitter a cup.
20 *But the tears will come into our own eyes, & we want to diminish yours. –*
There is a divine passage in the Meditations of Marcus Antoninus,– a man
patient,
whose necessity for being ~~comforted~~ joined to an amiable temper, rendered
him a kind of mitigated Stoic. He advises people who wish to rejoice them-
25 *selves, to call to mind the several virtues or gifts of those they are acquainted*
with,– as the industry of this person, the good nature of that, &c. So, you
see, you are to beatify yourself any time at a moment's notice by reflecting
on Shelley's ardour of benevolence, Marianne's paper-cutting, or my per-
formance of a Venetian ballad,– on any thing, in short, great or small,
30 *which is pleasurable & belongs to your friends. But the notion is beautiful,*
is it not? There is another noble passage in him, which you & Shelley will
admire when you see the Pocket-Book, where I have quoted it. And this

SC 539 *reminds me that I must ask you, Shelley, to give me a few verses, if you have any to spare, for the next Pocket-Book, which will be speedily going to press. I have already begun to write the new matter. And what do you think? You remember the £200 which Ollier was prevailed upon by you to advance me before you left London. The first number of the Liter. Pocket-Book has sold so well, & promised so <u>better</u>, that I have liquidated the debt by selling him the copy-right for that sum. I only retain the Editorship, which had he not asked me to do I should have stipulated for, seeing this new channel of opinion opened to me. I am writing, for the 2d number, a new Calendar divided into the four seasons, in each of which I describe what the mere idler <u>sees</u> about him, what the bigot, what the money getter, &c. & what the observer of nature,– shewing the infinite ~~pleasure~~ superiority which the last has over the others in wealth of enjoyment. What a delightful description you give us, Marina, of the podere! You justly think I should enjoy the original. I have a poem of Tansillo's in the Parnaso Italiano, called Il Podere, in which he says*

I pavimenti miei sien fiori ed erbe,
<　　>*otti l'arche, ove il tesoro io serbe.*

⟨————————————————————————————

The botti of course imply the grapes.
————————————————⟩ *But what used to delight me in prison was a little poem which follows it by one Baldi, called <u>Celeo</u> o l'<u>Orto</u>; ⟨——⟩ because I had a little modicum of a garden there which I dressed up with trellises & a handful of turf, & some flowers, & in autumn ~~some~~* with *festoons of scarlet beans in default of grapes; & all this used to make me read with an anti-bilious transport a passage where Celeo exclaims —*

Mio picciol orto,
— – a me città, palazzo, e loggia,
A me sei vigna, e campo, e selva, e prato.

I have seen the brown ruddy-tinged legs you mention in pictures by Bassano and others. They look as fine & vital, in my ⟨ opinion, *⟩ as the red stems of the vine, where the ~~vine~~* wine *seems already circulating. As we must certainly move,*

Hunt to Shelley   *September 12, 1819*

SC 539   *we have made up our minds to move to Kentish Town, which is a sort of compromise between London & our beloved Hampstead. The London end*

70   *of it touches so nearly to Camden Town, which is so near to London, that Marianne will not be afraid of my returning from the theatres at night; & the country end is extremely quiet & rural, running to the wood & the slopes between Hampstead & Highgate. Hallo! the slopes are running away with me. I forget I am at the back of my letter.) You will see in my last letter that*

75   *I have anticipated what you say about the pictures: — so what have you to say still?— God bless you. I expect Marianne to be in bed every day, as she will tell you; but setting aside an the feelings inevitable on such occasions, I have no sort of actual fear about her, for she brings her children into the world*

I do firmly believe, by the bye, that the previous exercise

80   *almost as easily as one of your vine-dressers at Naples.*ₐ*Bessy joins in kindest*

she always takes, helps her amazingly.

remembrances. I feel nearer to you now I write every week; & when I hear as often, the neighbourhood will be doubled.

Yᵣ *affectionate L.H.*

85   *(You will see by a letter which you will receive the day after this, that it was kept back to tell when the box had gone off.)*

[Address, page 4]

Italie.

P.B. Shelley Esqʳᵉ

Ferma in Posta,

90   *Livorno,*

Leghorn,

Italia

Italy.

Firenze.

---

line 3. *paragraphs;"*–: quotation marks appear directly above semicolon.

line 7. *it*: appears to be underscored in blue ink.

line 8. *pigmies*: alternate spelling listed in contemporary dictionaries.

line 9. *mightier. but*: the period may have been intended as a comma.

line 49. *sien*: mistranscribed for *fien*. In the *Parnaso Italiano* text, the double letter *fi* is broken and looks like long *si*, a double-letter combination that appears frequently in the edition.

line 50. *<E b>*: seal tear.

line 51. The brackets in lines 51 and 53 indicate one and one-third manuscript lines which are canceled and illegible.

Hunt to Shelley   *September 12, 1819*

SC 539   line 55. ⟨*in whi*⟩: probable reading.   line 85. (*You will . . . off.*): postscript written at
          line 65. ⟨——————⟩: canceled letters illegible.   the top of page 1.
          line 77. *an*: probable reading.
          line 79. *believe,*: it is difficult to tell whether or   line 94. $\overline{Firenze.}$: the letter was evidently redi-
          not the comma is present.   rected by a postal employee who also canceled
                                                            lines 90 and 91.

T HIS LETTER is an immediate response to Mary Shelley's letter of
August 28, which reached London on September 11.[1] Mary began
by saying she could "write nothing to amuse" and complained several
times about her many vexations, but her letter is long and entertaining
nonetheless. Hunt's efforts to revive her spirits were bearing fruit. She
concludes her letter by asking what Hunt meant by referring (in sc 529)
to her letters as "gigantic paragraphs." Hence, his reply begins with an
explanation.

To those who must transcribe, proofread, and comment on them,
Hunt's letters to Italy do seem to be something out of Pandæmonium,
indeed. His neat but fine handwriting marches on, page after page, and,
though he seldom crosses his writing, he returns to the first page and to
any available room along the margins to add postscripts (see facsimile,
page 607). Social correspondents like Samuel Rogers and Thomas Moore
dashed off hundreds of insipid yet polished notes containing invitations,
thanks, compliments, and regrets.[2] Hunt, in these years, was not that
kind of correspondent; he would delay writing for days or weeks until
he felt either the desire to converse with a friend or a twinge of conscience for not having conversed earlier. Then he would pour himself
into the letter. The quality of Hunt's correspondence with his close
friends is (if one accepts his jaunty vein) very high, and the overall
quality of his letters before his journey to Italy in 1822 is especially good
because in those years, satisfied with himself, he considered most of his
acquaintances his friends.

True to another aspect of his character, however, Hunt — though in

1. Mary Shelley, *Letters*, I, 75–78. (Part of the letter is missing.)

2. Thomas Moore, in 1836, contrasted Southey's letter-writing habits with his own: "Southey, . . .
like myself, makes a point of answering all who write to him; but, unlike me, devotes the better and
fresher part of his day (the morning) to this task; whereas I minute myself, during the last hour
before dinner, to despatch as many of my answers to correspondents as I can scribble through in
that interval" (Moore, *Memoirs*, VII, 148).

SC 539   this instance moved to write promptly — procrastinated in mailing the letter for over a week (lines 85–86).

Two interesting passages in Mary's letter concerned the bad style of Italian ballroom dancing and the *podere* — literally, farms; but as Mary describes Tuscan agriculture, "like our kitchen gardens with the difference only that the beautiful fertility of this country gives them."[3] Hunt first alludes to the topics (lines 14–15) and later takes up the theme of the *podere* by quoting from Luigi Tansillo (1510–1568):

> I pavimenti miei fien fiori ed erbe,
> [Rami i tetti, e negre elci i marmi bianchi,]
> E botti l'arche, ove il tesoro io serbe. . . ,[4]

and Bernardino Baldi (1553–1617), whose Celeo exclaims, in the best tradition of pastoral romance, "My little garden will be my city, palace, and balcony, my vineyard, and field, and wood, and meadow."[5] In describing the Tuscan farmers at work in the *podere*, Mary spoke of "their brown legs nearly the colour only with a rich tinge of red in it with the earth they turn up"; again, Hunt turns to art for his analogue — the paintings of Bassano.[6]

Leaving the subject of art, Hunt tells the Shelleys the location of the new residence of his family — in Kentish Town, out of the high-rent district (lines 68–69).[7] Hunt finds much good in the move forced by his reduced income, as well as in deeding the copyright of the *Literary*

---

3. Mary Shelley, *Letters*, I, 76.

4. See *Parnaso Italiano*, XXIII, 283 (*Il Podere*, chapter III). The tercet of which Hunt gives the first and third lines may be translated: "My pavements will be flowers and grass,/ My copper roofs and white marble [will be] dark woods—/ And my coffers, the casks where I would preserve my treasure . . . ."

5. Hunt repeats and translates part of the Baldi quotation in chapter XIV of his *Autobiography* (II, 9).

6. Like Bach, Bassano was the cognomen of a large family of artists (the family name really was da Ponte) plying a single trade — in this case, painting. Works by Francesco (1540–1592), Giovanni Battista (1553–1613), Girolamo (1566–1621), Jacopo (1510 or 1516–1592), and Leandro (1557–1622) da Ponte, all painters from Bassano del Grappa, near Vicenza, appear in the index of artists in *Roma e Dintorni, Guida D'Italia del Touring Club Italiano* (1962). Hunt was probably referring to Jacopo or his son, Leandro, the two members of the clan who contributed most to Venetian painting.

7. The Hunts eventually moved about the end of 1819 to 13 Mortimer Terrace, Kentish Town (see SC 534 and Commentary). In 1824, Jane Williams and Mary Shelley — widows living on limited resources — also moved to separate dwellings in Kentish Town, Jane to 12 Mortimer Terrace, near the Hunts' old address (see Mary Shelley, *Letters*, I, 293, 297).

SC 539   *Pocket-Book* to Ollier to pay off an old debt (lines 38–39).[8] His "miti-gated" Stoicism in the face of these retrenchments adds example to his precept to Mary, still depressed in the wake of her bereavement, to cheer up according to a prescription in *The Meditations* of Marcus Au-relius Antoninus. Hunt's cultural orientation can be assessed by con-trasting his off-hand references to Tansillo, Baldi, and Bassano with his apparent need to characterize, if not fully identify, the masterwork of the "philosophic monarch" from the zenith of whose reign Gibbon traced the decline and fall of the Roman Empire.[9] If the reader who recalls Marcus Aurelius' stately *Meditations* also finds a disparity be-tween the powerful opening book of that work (in which the emperor rejoices by recalling in gratitude the virtues of his family, friends, and even slaves — many of them dead) and such Huntian analogues as "Marianne's paper cutting," he will only be acknowledging that Leigh Hunt was no Marcus Aurelius, nor was meant to be. But then, that emperor would not have devoted much time to an attempt to cheer up a friend like Mary Shelley.

Hunt's ingenuous comparison of his wife's ease in childbearing to that of Neapolitan peasant women (lines 78–80) may have appeared to the Shelleys less complimentary than Hunt intended it to be; he knew Neapolitan peasants only from romantic paintings, songs, and stories.

8. On the *Literary Pocket-Book*, see sc 504, Commentary. According to Hunt's statement in lines 35–39, Charles Ollier, rather than Horace Smith or Sir William Knighton, finally advanced Hunt the £200 to meet the financial crisis that had been threatening him in November 1817. Compare sc 412, sc 454, and sc 455 and Commentaries.

9. See, especially, chapter III, *History of the Decline and Fall of the Roman Empire*, ed. J. B. Bury (London, 1909), I, 85. "Marcus Antoninus" appears on a list of books Shelley ordered, in December 1812, probably from Hookham (Shelley, *Letters*, I, 343), and Shelley joins his name with that of Cicero in *Queen Mab* (II, 179). Shelley may have encountered the *Meditations* either in Greek or in Latin translation at Eton and probably read them in the original Greek before he took up the lesser works in that language that he read during his stay at Marlow in 1817 (see sc 407, sc 424, and sc 433).

SC 540   LEIGH HUNT TO P. B. AND M. W. SHELLEY, SEPTEMBER 20, 1819

AL signed *Leigh Hunt.*, 3½ pages. Double sheet, 4to (9.3 x 7.4 inches).

Laid paper. Watermark: [fleur-de-lis]|.
Seal: wax, red.
Postal fees: 1. 1/11; 2. 18; 3. 6.

Shelley and his Circle : Manuscripts

SC 540   Postmarks: 1. (Foreign Post Office stamp): F 19| 107|; 2. (transit stamp): [ANGLE]-
TERRE|; 3. (transit stamp): CHAMBERY|; 4. [CORRISP^ZA ESTERA DA GENOVA]| [fleur-
de-lis]|; 5. [ ] N[OVE]MBRE|; 6. 6| NOVEMBRE|; 7. (trace of circular red postmark).
Notations, page 1, written with a sharp quill in light ink: 1. (below *we* of line
12): *By*|; 2. (below *things* of line 13): *Tint*|.

PROVENANCE: Colonel Charles Shelley Leigh Hunt; Mrs. Beryl Dodgson
(Sotheby, April 8, 1935, lot 205).

> *8. York Buildings– New Road*
> *Monday Sept. 20.*

    My dear friends,

        Marianne, the jade, made me keep my last Monday's letter in
5 *order that I might tell you in a postcript when the box had gone off; & lo!*
the box is not off till to-day; so that you will receive two Monday's letters
at once. It is not her fault however that the box did not go earlier. Some little
circumstances prevented it, which could not be helped.
      Bad news!   The box cannot go, till some things in it are made up.
10 *So says the man at the office, & accordingly Bessy has returned with it in a*
coach, & it must be regulated & divided ~~accordingly~~ *in two. We will make*
all the haste we can. Marianne, who expects to be confined daily, has some
things of her own in preparation, which she can send; & we hope & trust
they will yet be in time. May the little Italian repay you for what you have
15 *suffered in Italy! If on no higher account, I should be sorry that you came*
away from such a country without some pleasant associations, <u>*human*</u> *as*
well as inanimate. You know, I suppose, that Smollett was buried at Livorno.
There were some things about ~~*him*~~ ^{*his writings*} *very unpleasant; but he was an honest*
20 *man, & an independent one, & is understood to have done immense good to*
the poor wounded sailors in naval fights by those pictures of pitiless surgery
& amputation in Roderick Random. It is a curious coincidence that our
other chief novelist, Fielding, lies buried at Lisbon. We have no poet out of
our green earth. But Chaucer as well as Milton paid a visit to Italy; so did
25 *Gray; so did Drummond, Donne, & the Earl of Surrey. There is a fine*
ghastly image in a poem of Donne's on the subject, which will please you.
He is dissuading his wife from going with him (he went on a political mis-

SC 540 *sion) & hopes that she will not start in her sleep at night, & fancy him*
slain;–

30
<blockquote>

'*Crying out "Oh! Oh!*
Nurse, O my love is slain! I saw him go
O'er the white Alps alone; I saw him, I,
Assailed, taken, fight, stabbed, bleed, fall, & die."
</blockquote>

I am tempted, for other reasons, to copy out the beginning of this poem for
35 *you, which with the exception of a little coarseness which got into the grain*
of this writer's strong intellect, is very intense throughout.

<blockquote>

By our first strange & fatal interview
By all desires, which thereof did ensue,
By our long striving hopes, by that remorse
40 *Which my words' masculine persuasive force*
Begot in thee, & by the memory
Of hurts, which spies & rivals threatened me,
I calmly beg. But by thy father's wrath,
By all pains which want & divorcement hath,
45 *I conjure thee: and all the oaths, which I*

And thou have sworn to seal joint constancy,
I here unswear, & overswear them thus;
Thou shalt not love by means so dangerous.
Temper, O fair love! love's impetuous rage;
Be my true mistress, not my feigned page.
I'll go, & by thy kind leave, leave behind
Thee, only worthy to nurse in my mind,
Thirst to come back.
</blockquote>

She could not accompa<   > him, it seems, openly; & wished to do so in the
disgu<   > of a page. Do you k<   > Donne? I should like to have some
more talk with yo<   > about him. He was one of those over-metaphysical
headed men, who can find out connexions between every thing & any thing, &
50 *allowed himself at last to become a clergyman, after he had (to my conviction,*
at least) been as free & deep a speculator in morals as yourself. (I am
talking to Shelley, you see, Marina; but you are one flesh.) Are not those
three words "I calmly beg," very grave & lovely? And all the rest,– is it
not fine, & earnest, & "masculine-persuasive"?

55   *I am refreshing myself, when I can snatch a holiday hour, with*
translating that delightful compromise ~~with~~ of Art with Nature, Tasso's
Aminta. For I have now a new periodical work in ~~contemplation~~ hand, in
addition to the Examiner. My prospectives come out in a week or two, & the
first number follows the week after. It is to be called the Indicator,– after a
60 *bird of that name who shews people where to find wild honey; & will in fact*
be nothing but a collection of very short pieces of remark, biography, ancient

SC 540

fictions, &c. In ~~fact~~ short, of any ~~ideas~~ that come to hand, & of which I
shall endeavour to extract the essence for the reader. It will have nothing
65   *temporary whatsoever in it, political or critical; & indeed will be as pleasant*
labour to me as I can have, poetry always excepted. Will you throw me a
paragraph or so now & then, as little startling at first as possible to vulgar
prejudices? It will come out every Thursday, price Twopence,— the accom-
70   *plished specimen, you see, of the "Twopenny Trash". If it succeed, it will*
do me great service, being my sole property; & I am weary with writing
every day & making nothing of it to put an end to my straitnesses, though
the Examiner increases too. Ever your affectionate Leigh Hunt.

Oct. 20. 1819.

75   *You will see, by the date underneath, that this letter has been kept back just*
a month. I speak of this delay in the letter accompanying it. The box did
not go, after all, till Monday week; but we hope, by what your letters tell us,
that it will still be in time. Heaven send it may. Many thanks for your
Monday letters. I have finished the Aminta. I find I have mentioned the
80   *Indicator to you in the present letter.*

[Address, page 4]

To   *Italie.*

  P. B. Shelley Esqre

Ferma in Posta,
~~*Appresso al Sig^r Giovanni Gisborne,*~~

85   *Florence,*   *Firenze,*
~~*Leghorn,*~~   ~~*Livorno,*~~
  Italy.   *Italia.*

line 5. *postcript* (sic).

line 11. *divided*: *vi* written through indecipherable
letters.

line 29. *slain;*: semicolon is smeared and may
have been intended as a colon.

line 45. *conjure thee:*: *e thee* written on fragment
of letter adhering to seal.

line 46. *not accompa<ny>*: seal tear; *not ac-
compa* written on fragment of letter adhering to
seal.

line 47. *disgu<ise>*: obliterated by seal.

  Do you k<now>: seal tear; *Do you k*
written on fragment of letter adhering to seal.

line 48. *yo<u>*: obliterated by seal.

line 72. *end*: probable reading.

line 75. *You will . . . letter.* (line 80): postscript
is written above and to the left of lines 1–2 on
the first page of the manuscript.

line 85. *Florence,*: the letter was probably re-
directed by one of the Gisbornes.

The Carl H. Pforzheimer Library

SC 540   AGAIN, HUNT tries to renew his promise to write every Monday to the
Shelleys (see sc 534), and again he delays sending the letter —
this time for a full month. This letter reached the Shelleys at Florence
on November 6. The second letter mentioned in Hunt's postscript is
not extant, but in it Hunt reported the birth of James Henry Sylvan
Leigh Hunt (September 28), to whose birth Shelley alludes in his reply
(sc 551).

We have robbed the reader of the suspense associated with the
Hunts' mission to send infant's clothes to the Shelleys by mentioning
in sc 535, Commentary, that the box finally arrived too late to do Mary
or Percy Florence Shelley much good. The unaccountable delay of that
very important errand, together with Hunt's later neglect of his side
of the correspondence, had depressed the Shelleys by the end of the year
almost as much as his letters of July through September had cheered
them.[1]

Strangely — almost prophetically — Hunt's letter turns by free association from the forthcoming birth of the Shelleys' child to their previous
bereavements and then to the graves of Smollett at Leghorn and Fielding
at Lisbon. For Hunt to write in 1819, "We have no poet out of our
green earth," seems almost, to modern eyes, a request for volunteers
that would soon be filled by the poets most closely associated with him —
Keats in 1821 and Shelley a year later.[2] Once they were laid to rest in
Rome — and once Byron had died in Greece, though brought home
again — dying abroad became almost fashionable for English poets. Later
in the century, Clough, Landor, and Elizabeth Barrett Browning joined
Keats and Shelley in Italian graves.

Free association next carries Hunt from his incipient catalogue of
the graves of famous poets to a list of English poets who visited Italy
and thence to John Donne's "Elegie XVI: 'On His Mistris.'"[3] Shelley,
in his reply of mid-November, fails to answer Hunt's question, "Do you

1. See sc 555 and Commentary.

2. Actually, there were already a few significant English poets buried abroad — most, like Crashaw
(buried at Loreto), being English Catholics driven abroad by politico-religious conflicts of the sixteenth and seventeenth centuries.

3. In the lines Hunt first quotes (lines 30–33) from the closing of the poem, he introduces an error
that may suggest he has written them without actually copying them from a text of Donne; line 33
should read (preserving Hunt's forms of accidentals): "assailed, fight, taken . . . [etc.]."

SC 540 know Donne?," and this oversight robs us of a trifle of literary information that has many ramifications, especially for the history of taste in our own century. Shelley might have replied, "Yes, I've read and admired Donne's poetry for years. From him I've acquired my taste for paradox and his 'Songs and Sonnets' have contributed markedly to my own ideas on love." If Shelley had expressed such an opinion of Donne, their poetry would not have been chosen so often and so artificially as marking two poles in poetic method. But Shelley's silence on the subject, coupled with a lack of evidence in his reading lists and prose that he knew Donne's works, suggests that the quotation in this letter from Hunt may have been one of Shelley's few tangential encounters with the poetry of the Dean of St. Paul's.[4]

Hunt was reading Donne, clearly, while rifling his library for material for the *Indicator*. That periodical (referred to by Hunt as "Two-penny Trash" because of William Cobbett's political journal that bore both that price and that name) began publication on Wednesday, October 13, 1819, and continued under Hunt's editorship through the issue of Wednesday, March 21, 1821,[5] which Hunt closed with "The Indicator's Farewell." The periodical was continued in a "new series" by someone else, writing under the name of Onwhyn, beginning Wednesday, March 28, 1821, and continuing through Thursday, August 30, 1821. A note to the first issue explained, "we have carried on the number and folio of Mr. Hunt's Indicator." Hunt's explanation of the title is elaborated in a long epigraph that appears in the first seven numbers of the journal; he identifies the bird as an African species, "the *Cuculus Indicator* of Linnæus, otherwise called the Moroc, Bee Cuckoo, or Honey

4. On Friday, February 27, 1818, Coleridge gave the tenth lecture of his 1818 series at the Philosophical Society of London, Fleur-de-Luce Court, Fleet Street, on "Donne, Dante and Milton." According to H. N. Coleridge, "Nothing remains of what was said on Donne in this lecture." (*Coleridge's Miscellaneous Criticism*, ed. Thomas M. Raysor, Harvard University Press, 1936, p. 131, note.) Henry Crabb Robinson wrote that the lecture "was on Dante and Milton — one of his very best. He digressed less than usually and really gave information and ideas about the poets he professed to criticize." (Robinson, *On Books*, p. 220.) Shelley was in London on February 27. Mary's Journal records only her quiet day; Claire notes "Hogg & Peacock dine," but does not say how Shelley spent the evening. Shelley may have heard the lecture, especially since he was about to embark on a full reading of Dante's *Commedia* in the original.

5. It is clear that Hunt's letter, with the exception of the postscript, was completed on September 20, or before the day of publication of the *Indicator* was changed from Thursday (projected) to Wednesday (actual).

SC 540   Bird." His own search for sweets to be included in the early issues took him to the Shelleys' letters even before they had received his request for help. For example, in the second number, for October 20, 1819, Hunt included a paragraph on the "Autumnal Commencement of Fires" that draws cleverly on Mary's complaints about cold weather in Italy in her letter of September 24 (postmarked in London on October 9).[6] Actually, the concept of the indicator bird, showing men where to find honey and sharing the spoils with them as a kind of junior partner, is in many respects a just emblem of Hunt's most important role in English letters. He led the younger Keats, Shelley, and even Byron to certain poetic subjects and to great literary masters of Italy and the English Renaissance, as well as to music and art; he led the middle-class reading public to these things, as well as to the works of Keats and Shelley, and (to a much lesser degree) Byron and Wordsworth.

Besides writing on both politics and the arts for the *Examiner* and launching the *Indicator*, Hunt was industriously translating Tasso's *Aminta* (lines 56–57). His translation, *Amyntas*, appeared in 1820.[7] The load of work Hunt undertook in 1819–1820 was greater than that he had carried in previous years. No longer could he be charged by his friends — as Horace Smith had done on January 3, 1818 — with failing to help himself while calling on his friends for assistance.[8] Hunt devoted himself so fully to his work that by 1821 his health was weakened and he had to give up the *Indicator*.[9]

6. See the *Indicator*, I, 9–10; Mary Shelley, *Letters*, I, 80.

7. This book, published not by Ollier but by T. and J. Allman, was dedicated: "To John Keats, Esq. This translation of the early work of a celebrated poet, whose fate it was to be equally pestered by the critical, and admired by the poetical, is inscribed, by his affectionate friend, Leigh Hunt."

8. Hunt, *Letters*, pp. 117–119. See sc 412, Commentary.

9. See Hunt to Shelley, March 1, 1821, and July 10–11, 1821, Hunt, *Correspondence*, I, 161–167.

SC 541   T. J. HOGG TO T. L. PEACOCK, SEPTEMBER 26, 1819

AL (DRAFT) signed *T. J. H.*, 4 pages. Double sheet, 4^(to) (9 x 7.3 inches). Laid paper. Watermark: [posthorn in crowned shield]| [cipher] *TG*|.

PROVENANCE: Thomas Jefferson Hogg; Prudentia Hogg Lonsdale; John Ewer Jefferson Hogg; Major R. J. Jefferson Hogg (Sotheby, July 26, 1948, lot 273).

Hogg to Peacock   *September 26, 1819*

SC 541   *Norton Septr 24th 1819.*
                                              6

My Dear Peacock

       When I assure you that ~~I have intended to write to you~~
5   I have ~~reso~~ determined to write to you
every day for ~~these~~ two months∧you will ~~rather~~ wonder that you receive any
                 rather   a letter   how
~~letter from me~~∧than ~~that it arrives~~ so late ~~for~~∧many thousand things have you
resolved to do every day ~~for~~ these last thousand days & how many myriads
                 will remain undone at
10 of them ~~are still to be postponed till~~ the great day of Nisi prius when Hermes
                                              to coerce
shall ⌒come⌒first ~~to coerce~~ with his golden wand∧your reluctant shade?
                    if   of much
15   ~~If~~ My employments ~~have~~ not ~~been~~ profitable ~~they~~ have at least been
                              ∧
constant & I cannot remember one idle hour since we parted . – I will give
you some account of them & will ask in return the same from you.

                                              only remark
       ~~I went~~ Of the ~~cur~~ circuit & sessions ~~of w^{ch}~~ I will ~~give you no other account~~
20   hardly to be borne
       heat of ye was ~~most~~   write   with diplo-
~~than that the courts were dreadfully hot~~ lest you sh^d in revenge ~~speak~~ at length
matic fluency
of ~~Eastern Affairs of~~ men with barbarous names & of their ~~actions~~ still
                        actions
25 more barbarous∧but now if you play fair you can only say that Leadenhall
                                                          have
street was orientally hot. ~~I have cultivated my legs by~~ Some long walks∧&
                   εσια
30 cultivated my legs   & ἡ κυνηγησις περδικοκτόνος occupies them in
~~I keep them in practice by~~ pervading stubbles transgressing hedges & struggling with bushes ~~in shooting~~. ~~You will readily believe that I have not for-~~
                                                          are not forgotten
~~gotten~~ Our exertions in keeping pace with the indefatigable Coulson∧I often
35 wish that I co^d join your Sunday walks & I live in hopes that when I return
your pedestrianism will still flourish for the winter as we have experienced
hardly ~~as~~ less   propitious than
is ~~nearly as favorable to such pursuits as~~ the summer & if we start at ten
                                       with ye intervent^n of Tea
40 ⌒before five or six in the evening⌒we shall ~~have~~∧described ⌒a good circumference⌒
~~tea having intervened~~ nor shall we avail ourselves of our dinner wch at that

SC 541   *season is doubly welcome with diminished alacrity. — I have read Hecuba*

& ~~several~~ those *books of the Odyssey ~~especially those~~ w^ch ~~follow~~* after *the return of Ulisses*

45   *to Ithaca; w^ch* they *are not sufficiently known or admired the gradual increase of*

the ragged begars influence & ~~the development of his~~ powers though ~~of a~~ less

50   ~~*brilliant*~~   *bright*   scenes *some ~~rays~~* reflected in: *~~by~~ beauteous mirror are not less ~~worthy of~~*

~~*more unassuming nature*~~ *than ~~other parts of that~~ work are ~~not less masterly~~.*

~~*observation*~~ *faithful*

— I long sought for some one who had read Plato's Republic & who co^d

55   in vain
therefore give me some account of it but ~~I found no one~~ & I thought at last

that it wo^d be much easier to read it through than to discover any one who

had done so . — I accordingly set to work I am at present just half way

whatever is most remarkable seems to have been borrowed freely *from the Institu-*

60   without any acknowledgement
tions of Lycurgus & ~~Plato seems to have been of this Opinion for he does~~

~~not once mention the Spartans~~ at least as far as I have read. I have found

Some unintelligible   striking
many fine passages: ~~There is~~ nothing very ~~excellent~~ in the matter the manner

65   *uniformly excellent*
~~is exquisite~~ The Greeks are as much superior ~~to all the world~~ in the ~~compo~~

~~writing~~ of Dialogues as in all other compositions . — I was surprized to

find that ~~the~~ Plato had attracted the attention of the Quarterly reviewers I

read the long article ~~wch is~~ at the beginning of the last number. it is sufficiently

70   ose
perverse. According to th~~at~~ ingenious gentlemen Aristophanes wrote the

Comedy of the Clouds because there were no such Universities at Athens as

such an
there are in England & that we have no reason to suppose that ⟨ ⟩ ~~such an~~

75   *"inimitable & untranslatable piece" ~~as they terms it~~ will be written in England*

so long as
~~because~~ whe have two such Almæ matres or by any mothers son of them. You

will hardly believe this but if you will take up the review you will find it

Gymnastic   observing
80   *stands thus. After speaking of Music & ~~Atheletic~~ ˄exercises &˄ that the*

learnt
Attic boys ~~were taught~~ to fiddle & to box & that ~~not~~ unlike our commoners

SC541

& fellow commoners ~~they were unwilling to with this &~~, ~~because~~ there were
[*above: not content / sa / since*]

no colleges & halls in wch their understandings ~~w~~ their morality & especially

their piety might be carefully laid by & so preserved from injury viz. from

wear & tear for rust is academically speaking no injury ~~then~~ ~~Therefore~~ the
[*above right: they were not*]

90 Sophists came to teach them ~~desirous~~ something worse than nothing (the art
[*above: content with these accomplishments. We are told that thus discontented*]

of teaching nothing as there ~~being~~ no Universities ~~not~~ being then‿known)‿
[*above: were   un-   &*]

95 ~~thereby offended~~   who in this Comedy attacked them &c., &c.
[*above: therefore*]

Aristophanes, ~~therefore supposing that Socrates was a Sophist & a teacher
of what was worse than nothing~~ attacked ~~him by means of this Comedy~~.

The Universities therefore ~~if I read aright~~ secure to us the blessings of a

Quarterly Review & ~~guarantees~~ us against a second Aristophanes   our

100 friend S. who is an Oxonian & thinks A. coarse must rejoice at this.— I

have read Grotius de Veritate Religionis Christianæ. It is the only Gentleman
[*above: lately*]

like book I ever ~~read~~‿on that subject & for that reason & for many others &
[*above: met with*]

105 also because it is the shortest I like it ~~the~~ best. It is a learned work. The style

is that of an advocate who thinks that he has but a bad cause but must make

the best of it & who seems to feel that if he fails ~~he~~ it ~~trusts~~ will be allowed

that he has only done his duty‿~~in~~ & ~~without overstepping the~~ rules of good-
[*above: & as earnestly / as rationally‿as is consistent with an unreasonable*]

110 breeding It often reminded me of Cicero when he is writing ag^t his own

opinion w^{ch} ~~is~~ ~~not~~ uncommon with him & wch he co^d do as he well knew
[*above: a thing by no means*]

better than any man.
[*below: ‿*]

115   I have partaken largely of Botanical works & books on other

branches of Nat^l Hist^y. they make the country more ~~pleasing~~‿add to the
[*above: agreeable*]

pleasures of a walk &‿form a habit of observing ~~with~~ minute attention. a
[*above: help to   things*]

120 habit as valuable as it is rare. Things are but little ~~att~~ observed in these

days & consequently <u>words</u> are in due proportion misunderstood & mis-

applied.—

Hogg to Peacock   *September 26, 1819*

SC 541

> *Pray write soon tell me what you know of S. H. & C. Tell H. I will*
> *write to him in a day or two & that I am most grateful for the E. —   Re-*
125 *member me ~~most~~ very kindly to C. & with Comps to Mrs P.*

believe me yrs sincerely

T. J. H.

ᛁᚤᚦᛦ·ᛐᛦ·ᚤᛁᚠ ᛐ·ᛦ·ᛐᛁᚤᛐ *Cleasby.*

T. L. Peacock Esq
130   *East India House*
                London

line 15. *My*: *M* written through *m*.

line 19. ~~cur~~: probable reading.

line 26. *but*: squeezed in between the caret and *now*.

line 34. *Our*: *O* written through *o*.

line 48. *begars* (sic).

line 49. *in:*: followed by marks — possibly a word or two in Taylor shorthand.

line 56. *than*: written through *that*.

line 66. *is*: probable reading; word is blotted as well as canceled.

    in: written through *an*.

line 68. *reviewers*: *ers* added later.

line 71. *gentlemen*: *men* altered from *man* when *that* was changed to *those*.

line 74. ⟨ ⟩: false start.

line 75. *they*: *t* and *y* added to *he* and the *s* of *terms* canceled at the same time; then Hogg returned to cancel the entire phrase.

line 87. *preserved*: *pre* written through *per*.

line 99. *Aristophanes our*: *Aristophanes* is the last word on page 3; *our* is the first word on page 4.

line 102. *Religionis*: *R* written through *E*.

line 106. *but*: written through indecipherable letters.

line 109. *is*: altered from *was*.

line 111. *reminded*: *ed* written through *s*.

line 118. *things*: the underscore cancels *with* in the line beneath.

Hogg, AGAIN spending his summer vacation with the family, drafted another letter as a literary composition, taking a peculiar pride and pleasure in recasting and rearranging the clauses, as well as altering his expressions. Since his alterations begin with the date, it may be guessed that he wrote the first draft on September 24 and made his corrections two days later. In spite of them, the letter remains a heavy composition. In the first paragraph he mixes legal terms with Greek mythology without achieving an acceptable blend. *Nisi prius*, literally "unless before," was in English law a court panel that went to the various county towns to hear evidence on cases that would go to trial in the courts of Westminster during the ensuing term, *unless before* that

Shelley and his Circle: Manuscripts

Hogg to Peacock   **September 26, 1819**

SC 541   inquiry, the case had already been tried by an assize court.[1] Hogg uses the legal metaphor in connection with the mythological one in which Hermes — "the star of Lethe," as Keats calls him — guides the souls of the dead to Hades.[2]

The summer of 1819 seems to have been warm enough to warrant an attempted joke about the "oriental" heat of Leadenhall Street, as the headquarters of the East India Company in London. In spite of it, Hogg has been for some long country walks over rough ground in the interest of partridge-hunting (line 30), remarks about which, on his second thoughts, he translates into Greek. The customary account of his reading (presumably *Hecuba* is Euripides' play) leads to a sudden give-away: It is surprising that so arduous a Greek scholar has not yet read Plato's *Republic*; not even, apparently, in translation, which would have given him the general account he was hoping for. He now finds the best ideas in it borrowed from the Institutions of Lycurgus.[3] Hogg is perhaps unfair to Plato here, since Lycurgus is a half-legendary figure. His reputed constitutional reforms are said to have been unknown to historians and philosophers up to the time of Plato, whose ideals of law and government were then represented as operative facts in Lycurgus' day. Hogg may have been, if unconsciously, adhering to this tradition when claiming Lycurgus as the origin of Plato's ideas on the State. Naturally he would find no "acknowledgment" by Plato!

His involvement in Aristophanes' *The Clouds*, the *Quarterly* reviewers, and the English universities works out tortuously to a fair conclusion. *The Clouds* had satirized the Sophists and followers of Socrates, whose discipline had been shown as perverting the already doubtful morals of a young pupil. Although the book reviewed in the *Quarterly Review*, XXI (April 1819), 271–320, is *Lectures on the History of Literature, Ancient and Modern, from the German of Frederich Schlegel* (Edinburgh, 1818), the running head, "*View of Grecian Philosophy. — The Clouds, &c.*," more nearly gives the subject of the essay. (Shelley calls it "an attack on the character of Socrates."[4]) The reviewer was Thomas

1. See John Gifford, *The Complete English Lawyer* (London, n. d.), pp. 124–125.

2. Keats, *Lamia*, I, 81.

3. Lycurgus, date uncertain, 10th to 8th century B.C., was the reputed founder of the Spartan constitution.   4. Shelley, *Letters*, II, 145.

Peacock to Hogg   *October 2, 1819*

SC 541 Mitchell (1783–1845), a graduate of Christ's Hospital and Pembroke College, Cambridge, an acquaintance of Hunt, Byron, and Moore, and later the translator of Aristophanes (*DNB*). Surprisingly, Hogg fails to mention another article in the same issue of the *Quarterly* that proved to be of great interest to Shelley: the scurrilous attack on *Laon and Cythna*.[5]

At the moment Hogg is all for tolerance and good manners, as evidenced in Grotius' *De veritate religionis Christianæ*, which had the additional merit of being short.[6]

Hogg's postscript consists apparently of a runic inscription that he copied on one of his rural walks near Cleasby, East Gilling, in the North Riding of Yorkshire, eleven miles northeast of Richmond, Yorkshire, and three miles southwest of Darlington in the county of Durham.

5. See sc 543 and Commentary.

6. Hugo Grotius (Huig van Groot), 1583–1645, Dutch jurist and statesman, wrote dramas and treatises in Latin. He entered the religious controversy between Catholic and Protestant to preach toleration, but soon took an active part in party campaigns and was imprisoned. Escaping through the ingenuity of his wife, he became for a time Sweden's ambassador to France. His *De veritate religionis Christianæ*, 1627, was an effort to reconcile Protestant and Catholic by forming a common code of Christianity irrespective of doctrinal differences. The treatise earned a wide popularity, was used in Protestant colleges, and was translated for missionary purposes into Arabic, Persian, and Chinese. (*Encyclopædia Britannica*, 14th edition.)

SC 542 T. L. PEACOCK TO T. J. HOGG, OCTOBER 2, 1819

AL signed *T. L. Peacock.*, 2¾ pages. Double sheet, 4to (8.6 x 7.2 inches).
Laid paper. Watermark (East India Company cipher): VEIC| S & C WISE| 1816|.
Postmark: (evening duty stamp, London): B| OC| 2| ·819|.
Addition: seal cut out, affecting text.

PROVENANCE: Thomas Jefferson Hogg; Prudentia Hogg Lonsdale; John Ewer Jefferson Hogg; Major R. J. Jefferson Hogg (Sotheby, July 26, 1948, lot 278).

India House, Octr 2, 1819

My dear Hogg,

I much marvelled what was become of you. It will give me much pleasure to hail the first day of Michaelmas term when you will cease

5 *to pursue the flying nymphs of the north and find yourself temptingly nipped in the fleshy part of the arm by the non-fugient damsels that celebrate the pervigilium Veneris under the classic arch of Temple Bar. I anticipate much pleasure and profitable Sunday pedestrianism during the corroborating gales*

Peacock to Hogg   *October 2, 1819*

SC 542   *of December and the valid frosts of January when we shall prognosticate our*
locality in the categories of time and place about an house beyond the setting
sun when our old altars will be fuming with much odor of roast beef. If your
κυνηγεσια περδικοκτονος should meet with the propitious leading of Artemis
you may bring up a leash or two in the name of Mahershalelhashbaz, which
Voltaire translates: Partagez vite les dépouilles. –

15   *I have been very busy here and I have read through at home the first*
                                with
volume of Mill's India, which,ˏsome articles in the Quarterly and one or
two fashionable books which every body reads and the Examiner and, ὑστερος
προτερος, Cobbett, constitute all my unofficial lections. Mill has accompanied
20   *me in many Sunday excursions and now that the days close in, we walk*
together every day from 4 till 6 which keeps us in health. Tomorrow the
steam-boat perorates for the season and I shall take my last view of Richmond-
bridge till the reseration of Favonius unless some splendid frosty sunshine
should tempt us so far.

25   *I have had several letters from Shelley who is still at Livorno. I have*
not seen Hunt since the first Wednesday in August. Coulson is rusticating
in the West of England. This letter is not a fair return for yours: but there
are are at present so few nooks of my brain untenanted by zemindars ryots
adawluts and cu<   > that I am already bankrupt in any <   >
30   *of unoriental intelligence, acq<   > since y<   > departure.*
                                                Yours ever faithfully
                                                        T. L. Peacock.

[Address, page 4]
*T. J. Hogg Esq*ʳᵉ
        Norton
35   *near Stockton-upon-Tees.*

line 5. *yourself*: *f* written through *ves*.
line 9. *valid*: written through another word.
line 20. *excursions*: middle syllable heavily written through another. Possibly Peacock began to
write *exercises* but did not finish the word.
line 22. *take*: altered from *takes*.
line 23. *reseration*: word means the act of opening
up; that which opens (*OED*).

line 27. *there are are* (sic).
line 29. *cu<rnums>*: seal cut out.
      <   >: seal cut out.
line 30. *acq<uired>*: seal tear at edge of paper.
      since y<our> departure: seal cut out;
top of *d* visible.

The Carl H. Pforzheimer Library

Peacock to Hogg   *October 2, 1819*

SC 542   IF, AS THE DATE indicates, this letter is a direct answer to Hogg's literary composition of September 26 (sc 541), its opening is a sufficiently oblique rejoinder. While Hogg has been protesting his purely classical and topographical occupations, Peacock mischievously cuts through to another of his friend's propensities, absent though it is from the account of his "employments." He evidently suspects that Hogg's botanical interests which "add to the pleasure of a walk" were, even at Norton, usually of the fair sex. He goes on to picture Hogg pursuing, not partridges but the flying nymphs of the north (line 5). The sequel in London will be still more material and far less fugitive. These far-from-elusive celebrants of Venus can only be prostitutes with a regular beat under the now-vanished arch of Temple Bar.[1] Hogg, walking between the Law Courts and his chambers in Garden Court, Temple, would have been exposed daily to nips in the arm.

Peacock, now living in the same area, had no doubt been subjected to some nips himself. He hopes, however, that he and Hogg will still keep up their Sunday walks, going out of town westward ("beyond the setting sun") to find the same good meals. A remark about Hogg's partridge-shooting (line 12; see sc 541) and its putative results sends him off on one of those Peacockian fancies that defy the annotator: "Mahershalelhashbaz" rolls off the tongue as solemnly as the "philotheoparoptesism" of *Maid Marian* (see sc 509, Commentary), and once again Voltaire's editor Dr. Bestermann (see sc 468, Commentary) declines to vouch for the quotation. Hurrying to divide the spoils was, however, a favorite pastime of Voltaire's royal patrons, Frederick and Catherine.

The end of the Thames steamer's season marks also the end of Peacock's excursions up the river as far as Richmond Bridge until the west wind (the Romans' Favonius, the Greeks' Zephyrus) returned in the spring. The allusion to the wind is interesting chiefly for coming in the same month as Shelley's more familiar reflections on the same subject (see sc 547).

1. See the late Latin poem *Pervigilium Veneris*, which treats spring rather than the autumn. Temple Bar, a gateway to the City of London designed by Sir Christopher Wren, was erected in 1672 on the site of an earlier structure. It stood at the junction of the present Strand and Fleet Street, over against the Law Courts. In 1878 it was removed, to be set up ten years later at the entrance to Theobalds Park near Cheshunt, Hertfordshire. A griffin on a pedestal took its place on the old site.

Shelley and his Circle : Manuscripts

Peacock to Hogg   **October 2, 1819**

SC 542   The fact is that Peacock is now metamorphosed from an idler on his Marlow waters into an India House official, not only hard working but constructively interested in the company's affairs and all that relates to them. He may employ lawyers' adjectives in describing gales and frosts to tease Hogg about the practical affairs of Michaelmas term, but it is important for *him* to read James Mill's *History of British India*, which had been published the previous year. Mill[2] was by this time Peacock's colleague as provisional Assistant to the Examiner of Indian correspondence at India House. His election had been influenced by the great success of his *History*. Peacock's relations with Mill are reputed, by some biographers, to have been less than cordial, yet this letter shows them enjoying daily walks and Sunday excursions together. On the subject of Peacock's test essay, "Ryotwar and Zemindarry Settlements" (sc 503), the two held somewhat similar views, with radical leanings. Peacock had, however, arrived at these independently; this letter reveals that he did not read Mill's *History* until nearly a year after his own essay was written.

Even so, Peacock lists Mill among his *un*official reading, in company with such cultural necessities as Hunt's *Examiner* and, "the primary one last" (lines 18–19), Cobbett. Of more general concern are his letters from Shelley, the most recent of which was sc 537, with Shelley's reaction to the news of Peterloo. (Shelley's letter of September 21 did not reach London until October 7.)

Finally comes Peacock's confession that his wayward letter is due to an obsession with the details of his job. Here are the terms that readers of Peacock's essay (sc 503) will have met with, all belonging to the systems of land revenue collection in the Indian villages under the company's authority. Peacock seems to enjoy displaying them to his uninitiated friend — "zemindars ryots adawluts and curnums"; that is, landholders, cultivators, revenue courts, and village accountants. Obviously the Indian correspondence, of which Peacock was an Assistant Examiner, continued throughout 1819 to dwell largely on this vexed and controversial matter of revenue settlements.

2. James Mill, 1773–1836, became Assistant Examiner in 1823, when his son, John Stuart Mill, entered the India Office as a clerk. In 1830 James Mill succeeded to the Examinership, Peacock and Edward Strachey being then appointed Senior Assistants until Mill's death in 1836, when Peacock became Examiner. See "Peacock in Leadenhall Street," p. 709, fn. 18.

The Carl H. Pforzheimer Library

SC 543   P. B. SHELLEY TO CHARLES OLLIER, OCTOBER 15, 1819

AL signed *P B Shelley*., 3 pages. Double sheet, 4to (9.5 x 7.4 inches).
Wove paper.
Seal: wax, red: [Judgment of Paris]|.
Postal fees: 1. 8; 2. 1/11.
Postmarks: 1. FIRENZE|; 2. (Foreign Post Office stamp, London): FPO| OC 30|
1819|.

PROVENANCE: Charles Ollier (Puttick and Simpson, July 19, 1877, lot 70); re-
sold to Beet at Ollier's second sale at Puttick and Simpson, July 22, 1878, lot
166 A; Alfred Morrison (*Catalogue of the Collection of Autograph Letters and
Historical Documents Formed Between 1865 and 1882 by Alfred Morrison*, VI,
Privately Printed, 1892, 120); Maggs, Catalogue 411, Autumn 1921, #2275.
De Ricci 430 (p. 196).

Florence, Oct. 15. 1819

Dear Sir

   *The droll remarks of the Quarterly & Hunts kind defence arrived
as safe as such poison, & safer than such an antidote usually do.*

5   *I am on the point of sending to you 250 copies of a work which I p̶
have printed in Italy; which you will have to pay 4 or 5 pounds Duty upon,
on my account; Hunt will tell you the kind of thing it is, & in the course of
the winter I shall send directions for its publication, until the arrival of
which directions I request that you would have the kindness not to open the
10   Box, or if by necessity it is opened, to abstain from observing yourself, or
permitting others to observe what it contains. I trust this confidently to you,
it being of consequence. Meanwhile assure yourself that this work has no
reference direct or indirect to politics or religion, or personal satire, & that
this ̶p̶e̶r̶e̶-̶c̶ precaution is merely literary.*

15   *The Prometheus, a poem in my best style whatever that may amount to,
will arrive with it, but in Mss.— which you can print & publish for the
season—— It is the most perfect of my productions.——*

   *Southey wrote the article in question, I am well aware ... observe the
impudence of the man in speaking of himself. The only remark worth notice*

SC 543 *in this peice, is the assertion that I imitate Wordsworth.– It may as well be said that Lord Byron imitates Wordsworth, or that Wordsworth imitates Lord Byron, both being great poets, & deriving from the new springs of thought & feeling which the great events of our age have exposed to view, a similar tone of sentiment imagery & expression. A certain similarity all*

25 *the best writers of any particular age inevitably are marked with, from the spirit of that age acting on all. ~~To the~~ This I had explained in my preface which the writer was too disingenuous to advert to.— As to the other trash, & particularly that lame attack on my personal character, which was meant so ill & ~~at~~ which I̲ am not the man to feel, tis all nothing. I am glad, with*

30 *respect to that part of it which alludes to Hunt that it should so have hap-*

               work
 pened, that I dedicate, as you will see, a ~~poem~~ which has all the capacities for being popular, to that excellent person— I was amused too with the finale, it is like the end of the first act of an opera, when that tremendous

35 *concordant discord sets up from the orchestra, & every body talks & sings at*

                   God
 once. It describes the result of my battle with their omnipotent, his pulling

         like Pharoah
 me under the sea by the hair of my head, my calling out like the Devil who

40 *was g̲a̲m̲e̲ to the last, swearing & cursing ~~all~~ in all comic & horrid oaths like a french postillion on Mount Cenis, entreating every body to drown themselves pretending not to be drowned myself when I < > drowned, & lastly b̲e̲i̲n̲g̲ d̲r̲o̲w̲n̲e̲d̲.——*

   You would do me a particular kindness if you would call on Hunt,

45 *& ask him when my parcel went, the name of the ship, & the name of the captain, and whether he has any bill of lading, which if he has, you would oblige me by sending together with the rest of the information by return of Post—— addressed to the post office Florence———*

   Make my best regards to your brother— What a pity it is he does not

50 *(or perhaps he does) pursue that style of critical writing which he once showed me in a county paper on Shakspear.*

               Yours very sincerely
                P B Shelley.

I have given a check on you for £2.10.0.

Shelley to Ollier   *October 15, 1819*

SC 543   [Address, page 4]
 Messrs Ollier &° C°
   Booksellers
    Vere Street
     Bond Street
 Angleterre   *London*

line 3. *defence*: probable reading; final letters imprecise.

line 14. *precaution*: *r* may have been altered from *e*.

line 16. *for*: written through *in* or vice versa.

line 20. *peice*, (sic).

line 22. *the*: possibly written through another word.

line 40. *cursing*: *c* written through indecipherable letters.

line 42. *themselves*: possibly followed by a comma covered by seal.

 pretending: *din* written on fragment adhering to seal.

 I <am>: obscured by seal.

line 49. *does*: *d* written through *h*.

line 51. *Shakspear*: there may be a very tiny *e* at the end of the word.

line 54. The postscript is written at the top of page 1.

THIS LETTER treats five topics — two important and three routine. The first of the small matters is Shelley's request that Ollier check up on unbusinesslike Leigh Hunt (lines 44–48), a variant of his frequent requests that Hunt or Peacock check up on unbusinesslike Charles Ollier. He hoped, no doubt, that both the bearers and the receivers of these messages would profit from the admonishment, but in this hope he seems to have been disappointed.

In the final paragraph, Shelley sends his compliments to Ollier's younger brother James, remarking on the latter's potential as a literary critic. Without Charles Ollier's letters to Shelley, we cannot determine exactly what prompted Shelley's remarks, but from this hitherto-unpublished paragraph we learn that James Ollier, like his brother Charles, had some literary aspirations.[1]

In the postscript Shelley calls upon Ollier, as he did from time to time, to resume his profession of banker.[2] Shelley, when he set out for the Continent, had left Brooks, Son & Dixon explicit instructions not to honor any checks or bills drawn by him except for a few that he spe-

1. See also sc 389, Commentary.

2. See sc 492 and Commentary.

SC 543   cifically exempted.[3] While in Italy he apparently felt that inasmuch as Ollier was collecting not only the booksellers' commission but the entire price of his poems, Ollier would have a small balance in Shelley's favor which could be drawn upon.[4] These small disbursements, coupled with the slow sale of his poems, apparently put Shelley in Ollier's debt by the time he finally asked for an accounting.[5] We do not know to whom Shelley would have written a check for £2.10, payable in London. Perhaps it was someone who had applied through Peacock or Horace Smith for the payment of a small debt.

The two major subjects of the letter are literary. First Shelley wants Ollier to print *Prometheus Unbound* and to accept (and pay duty on) the edition of *The Cenci*, without revealing Shelley's authorship. For if the play were accepted and produced at Covent Garden, Shelley feared that unless his anonymity were preserved, his enemies would destroy any chance of success.[6] As it turned out, Shelley need not have taken such precautions. Peacock submitted *The Cenci* to Thomas Harris of Covent Garden,[7] but that venerable gentleman — with, no doubt, the counsel of his favorite of the moment — "pronounced the subject to be so objectionable, that he could not even submit the part to Miss O'Neil for perusal, but expressed his desire that the author would write a tragedy on some other subject, which he would gladly accept."[8]

As we have seen, Shelley had kept Peacock informed of his progress on *The Cenci* and on September 9 had sent him the text of the play, presumably a printed copy, with which to try the theaters.[9] On September 21 Shelley informed Peacock that he had sent him *Prometheus Un-*

---

3. Shelley, *Letters*, I, 599.

4. Note, for example, his instructions to Ollier to pay Hunt a sum of five (or seven) pounds (SC 533 and Commentary).

5. See Shelley, *Letters*, II, 376–377, note 5, and 387.

6. See Shelley, *Letters*, II, 102; Mary Shelley, *Letters*, I, 78 n.

7. On Harris, see SC 529, Commentary.

8. Mary Shelley, "Note on *The Cenci*," Shelley, *Poetical Works* (1839), II, 279. Peacock himself did not like the play or its subject well enough to urge it upon anyone; see Shelley, *Letters*, II, 126. Peacock's letter arrived on Thursday, October 14, a day of the week when mail arrived from England (see also Mary Shelley's Journal) and hence Shelley's letter to Maria Gisborne, which mentions Peacock's letter, can definitely be dated October 14 rather than "October 13 or 14" (Shelley, *Letters*, II, 123).

9. See SC 537 and Commentary.

The Carl H. Pforzheimer Library

SC 543 *bound* in the care of Mr. Gisborne, the new work not "to be sent to Ollier for publication" until Shelley should give further instructions.[10] Perhaps Peacock declared himself too busy to take responsibility for *Prometheus*, or expressed doubts about its quality; or perhaps Shelley decided that Peacock was not the person to see that poem through the press and sent new instructions to Gisborne. In any case, Gisborne started back to Italy with it. In his October 14 letter to Maria Gisborne Shelley added in a postscript that the Gisbornes were to "send the Prometheus" to England along with the printed copies of *The Cenci*, "if Mr. G. is returned."[11]

The apparently inconsistent travel plans made for *Prometheus* become comprehensible if we assume that Shelley's postscript ordering that the manuscript be sent to Ollier back in England (before he had even looked it over again) was provoked by the combination of Peacock's unflattering letter (no longer extant), and by the arrival in the same mail of the *Quarterly Review*'s vicious attack on Shelley and his poetry (see below). True to his nature, Shelley was defiant rather than cowed in the face of negative reactions by friend and foe alike; he immediately determined to publish *Prometheus*, "a poem in my best style ... the most perfect of my productions" (lines 15–17). But whether because of lack of funds, their involvement in Henry Reveley's steamboat building,[12] or hesitation lest Shelley should again change his mind, the Gisbornes delayed in carrying out Shelley's instructions. Shelley, however, seems to have held to his first determination. Mary, in a postscript to her letter of November 4, thanks Mrs. Gisborne "for your

10. Shelley, *Letters*, II, 120. John Gisborne had gone to London to seek a position for Henry Reveley and to consult about selling and reinvesting the proceeds of his own and Henry Reveley's government bonds ("the funds"). He left Leghorn on September 12 (Mary Shelley, Journal) and returned there on or shortly before October 20, 1819 (Shelley, *Letters*, II, 129). Lawrence John Zillman has simply ignored the evidence when he states as a fact that "John Gisborne's plans were changed, and he did not go to England until the following May" (*Shelley's "Prometheus Unbound": A Variorum Edition*, University of Washington Press, 1959, p. 5). See especially Maria Gisborne's October 11 letter to the Shelleys, in which she describes her husband's journey (Gisborne, *Journals and Letters*, pp. 53–54), and Shelley's letter of October 21, 1819, in which he sends "congratulations to Mr. Gisborne on his arrival" (Shelley, *Letters*, II, 129).

11. Shelley, *Letters*, II, 126. Shelley probably received the news that his *Prometheus* was returning to Italy from the same letter in which Peacock criticized *The Cenci*.

12. See SC 545 and SC 553 and Commentaries.

SC 543 trouble about the Cenci."[13] Perhaps the Gisbornes had sent word that the 250 copies were now packed for shipping, or perhaps Mary was simply mentioning the work to remind the Gisbornes of Shelley's earlier request. It is clear, however, from a later letter that the ship on which the copies of *The Cenci* and the *Prometheus* manuscript were finally sent did not leave Leghorn until "the middle of December."[14]

The final — perhaps the chief — concern of Shelley's letter is the scathing review of *Laon and Cythna* in the *Quarterly Review* issue dated April 1819.[15] This review, like that of Hunt's *Foliage*, is now known to have been written by John Taylor Coleridge (1790–1876), nephew of Samuel Taylor Coleridge and a classmate of Shelley at Eton.[16] But Shelley, for reasons analyzed in detail by Kenneth Neill Cameron, was convinced that Southey was the author of both reviews (as well as the later *Quarterly* attack on Keats).[17]

The published correspondence from Southey to John Taylor Coleridge shows that, when Shelley later wrote his angry letters to Southey concerning the review, Southey asked Coleridge whether *he* had written it and sent Coleridge copies of Shelley's two letters and his own answers.[18] There is no published evidence that Southey earlier retailed stories about

13. Frederick L. Jones, "Mary Shelley to Maria Gisborne," *Studies in Philology*, LII (January 1955), 53.

14. Shelley to Ollier, March 6, 1820, Shelley, *Letters*, II, 174.

15. XXI, 460–471. A letter from John Murray to Croker shows Murray's intense dislike of Shelley. "I send you a most extraordinary Poem by Godwins now Son-in-law—pray keep it under Lock & Key—it is an avowed defense of *Incest*—the author is the vilest wretch in existence—living with Leigh Hunt—The book was published & he is now endeavouring to suppress it." (Hill and Helen Chadwick Shine, *The Quarterly Review Under Gifford*, University of North Carolina Press, 1949, p. 66.)

16. On the derogatory review of Hunt's *Foliage* in the January 1818 issue of the *Quarterly*, see sc 502, sc 504, sc 517, and Commentaries. *A List of Eton College, Taken at Election, 1808* (Eton, [1808]), shows that, although John T. Coleridge was born two years before Shelley, they were both in the Fifth Form, Upper Division, in 1808. In April 1809, Coleridge was elected a scholar at Corpus Christi College, Oxford, from which he graduated with many honors in 1812. One contemporary who seems to have known the identity of the *Quarterly* reviewer was John Gibson Lockhart, who in his review of Shelley's *Alastor* in *Blackwood's Edinburgh Magazine* for November 1819, attacks the *Quarterly* reviewer of Shelley and alludes slightingly to college rules at "Oriel or Exeter." Lockhart was a student at Balliol when John Taylor Coleridge was elected fellow at Exeter College, Oxford.

17. "Shelley vs. Southey: New Light On An Old Quarrel," *PMLA*, LVII (1942), 489–512.

18. See W. Braekman, "Letters by Robert Southey to Sir John Taylor Coleridge," *Studia Germanica Gandensia* [Ghent, Belgium], VI (1964), 117–118.

SC 543   Shelley to John Coleridge, and remarks in Southey's letters of this period suggest that Southey was disturbed about the harsh tone of many of the *Quarterly*'s articles — perhaps including this one.[19] Coleridge, who was called to the bar at the Middle Temple in 1819, could have heard of Shelley's problems, domestic and otherwise, from his fellow barristers — including Thomas Jefferson Hogg or *his* acquaintances.

Shelley had written to Ollier on September 6 to send him "the *Quarterly*'s article by the post," rather than in the slower freight parcel. Ollier (or Hunt) had exercised enough discretion to include with the review an antidote — Hunt's rebuttal published in the *Examiner* of September 26.[20] Hunt's attacks on the *Quarterly* reflect resentments harbored from a long series of provocations by the Tory journals. We have seen Hunt, angered by the *Quarterly*'s treatment of Shelley, Keats, and himself, threaten as early as November 12, 1818, "to buckle on my old rusty resentments, & give them such a carbonado as I know I am able to give" (sc 504). The three *Examiner* articles of September–October 1819 contain some most vigorous and powerful prose. Hunt is much more effective, I believe, in his attack on the *Quarterly*'s methods and reviewers than in his praise of Shelley (chiefly in the third part), where he does not escape a tendency toward sentimentality. In his rebuttals to the *Quarterly*, Hunt intimates that he knows the identity of the author of the offending review of Shelley. But it is clear from the following passage that Hunt believes the reviewer to be one of his old enemies, William Gifford or John Wilson Croker, just as firmly as Shelley believed Southey to be his tormentor:

19. See Southey, *New Letters*, ed. Kenneth Curry (Columbia University Press, 1965), II, 182, 184, 197–198. Other remarks, however, find Southey planning vicious attacks on his own personal and ideological enemies.

20. Hunt's defense continued in a similar vein in the *Examiner* for October 3 and October 10; these last two parts could not have reached Shelley before he wrote this letter unless Hunt had composed all three before publishing the first. From internal evidence, there is no reason to think that the three articles could not have been composed at one sitting, and this would explain why Elizabeth Kent copied (at least part) of the defense for Shelley, rather than simply clipping the relevant article from the *Examiner*, which would have been less costly to mail as well. But inasmuch as Shelley writes to Hunt on November 2, 1819, about the "third part" of Hunt's "observations on the Quarterly" and does not thank Miss Kent until mid-November 1819 for "writing out, in that pretty neat hand" Hunt's "kind & powerful defence" (see sc 551), one cannot be certain that more than the portion published in the *Examiner* for September 26 arrived from Ollier with the review from the *Quarterly*.

Shelley and his Circle : Manuscripts

SC 543   What is Mr. Shelley's private life to the *Quarterly Review*, any more than Mr. GIFFORD's or Mr. CROKER's, or any other Quarterly Reviewer's private life is to the *Examiner*, or the *Morning Chronicle*, or to the *Edinburgh Review*. . . .The Reviewer talks of what he "*now*" knows of Mr. Shelley. What does this pretended *judge* and actual male-gossip, this willing listener to scandal, this minister to the petty wants of excitement, now know more than he ever knew, of an absent man, whose own side of whatever stories have been told him he has never heard? Suppose the opponents of the *Quarterly Review* were to listen to all the scandals that have been reported of writers in it, and to proclaim this man by name as a pimp, another as a scamp, and another as a place or pulpit-hunting slave made out of a schoolboy tyrant?[21]

The final reference to a clergyman once a schoolboy tyrant might be a veiled allusion to Henry Hart Milman, but the reference is not at all clear. Neither Shelley nor Hunt (nor Byron, in his various remarks on *Quarterly* reviewers) gives any indication that they were aware that John Taylor Coleridge, who had been noted as a fighter at Eton,[22] wrote for the *Quarterly*. And whatever Coleridge's prowess as a schoolyard boxer, he showed little moral courage in allowing the misattribution of the offending review, first to his friend Southey and later to Henry Hart Milman, to go uncorrected until after his death.[23]

Besides Shelley's interesting remarks on poetic imitation and the spirit of the age in the present letter — ideas that he later incorporated in the Preface to *Prometheus Unbound* — and the energy that flowed from Shelley's anger into *Adonais*, the hostile review of his longest poem in the *Quarterly Review* had less positive results. Appearing as it did before the publication of *The Cenci* and *Prometheus Unbound*, the review badly hurt Shelley's chances of finding a sympathetic audience for his poetry during his remaining years. It drained off some of his energy into resentment against the reviewer, into attempts to identify the reviewer,

21. White, *Unextinguished Hearth*, pp. 147–148. The Reverend Henry Hart Milman had been in the Sixth Form at Eton with Shelley in 1808, and went to Brasenose College, Oxford, in 1810 at the same time Shelley went to University College.

22. Wasey Sterry, *Annals of The King's College of Our Lady of Eton Beside Windsor* (London, 1898), p. 212.

23. See Shelley, *Letters*, II, 299, 309; the identification of the author of this review of *Laon and Cythna* was not settled until, after the death of Coleridge, Archibald Milman (Henry Hart Milman's son) wrote to Lady Shelley to clear his late father's name (*Shelley and Mary*, II, 636–637).

The Carl H. Pforzheimer Library

SC 543 and into his polemic letters to Southey.[24] It even caused him to introduce into *Adonais* — otherwise certainly the most nearly perfect of Shelley's poems and, in my opinion, still his greatest achievement — what may be considered a touch of self-pity and self-justification. And the combined force of the small sales of his poems and Ollier's resultant neglect of him may have contributed to Shelley's reluctance to engage upon any major poetic effort that was not more or less topical or occasional until, in 1822, he began *The Triumph of Life*.[25] It would certainly have been better for Shelley had the *Quarterly Review* never treated *Laon and Cythna* and *The Revolt of Islam*; it may well have been to his advantage had he never seen the *Quarterly*'s attack. Charles Ollier, who could be counted upon to procrastinate whenever Shelley needed help or encouragement, was Johnny-on-the-spot with these bad tidings. Shelley, it is true, would eventually have encountered the *Quarterly* article in Italy,[26] but had Ollier not (perhaps to excuse the slow sale of Shelley's works, in part due to his own phlegmatic business practices) made a point of calling to Shelley's attention the imminent appearance of the *Quarterly* article and then rushing it to Shelley in an unusually prompt response to Shelley's request, Ollier would not have underscored the significance of one negative article. And, with more self-confidence, Shelley might have undertaken more works on the scale of *Prometheus Unbound*.

24. See Shelley, *Letters*, II, 203–205, 230–233.

25. Shelley's completed long poems that were begun after his reading of the *Quarterly*'s hostile review of *The Revolt of Islam* were *The Mask of Anarchy* (1819, published 1832) and *Peter Bell the Third* (1819, published 1839); "Letter to Maria Gisborne" and "The Witch of Atlas" (both 1820, both published 1824); *Œdipus Tyrannus; or, Swellfoot the Tyrant* (written, published, and suppressed 1820; republished 1839); *Epipsychidion* (written and published *anonymously* 1821); *Adonais* (1821, published 1821); and *Hellas* (1821, published 1822). The only important finished shorter poems of these years that were not lyrics or occasional were "The Sensitive Plant" and "Ode to Liberty," published with *Prometheus Unbound*. "The Witch of Atlas" was not strictly occasional (though, in a sense, it was a second answer to Wordsworth's *Peter Bell*), but it was written rapidly and does not represent a large-scale, sustained effort like *Queen Mab*, *The Revolt of Islam*, or *Prometheus Unbound*.

26. Medwin's story (*Shelley*, pp. 225–226) implying that Lord Dillon saw Shelley's first encounter with the review at Delesert's reading rooms in Florence is probably apocryphal. If that issue of the *Quarterly* first came to Hunt's attention in London between September 19 and September 26 (as he says in his first article), the issue is unlikely to have been on the shelves of a public reading room in Florence before October 15, when Shelley received the clipped article via the post.

SC 544 LEIGH HUNT TO T. J. HOGG, OCTOBER 26, 1819

AL signed *Leigh Hunt.*, 4 pages. Double sheet, 8ᵛᵒ (7.9 x 5 inches).

Laid paper. Watermark: [fleur-de-lis (upper part)]|.
Addition: discoloration of about one-half inch to one inch, along upper and right margins of page 1.

PROVENANCE: Thomas Jefferson Hogg; Prudentia Hogg Lonsdale; John Ewer Jefferson Hogg; Major R. J. Jefferson Hogg (Sotheby, July 26, 1948, lot 276).

York Build⁰ˢ New Road
Oct. 26. 1819.

My dear Hogg,

> *I am quite ashamed at not having answered your letter*
5 *sooner, & at writing you so shabby a one after all. I felt impelled, I assure*
you, more than usual, to write you a long & a grateful one; but the greatest
fatigue & hurry, not unaccompanied with illness, prevented me; for the diffi-
culties of which you have heard too true an account, have so worried & sad-
dened me, that among various other speculations how to get rid of them, I
10 *have set up another little weekly publication, – not political, though two-*
penny trash. It is a sort of chit-chat with the reader upon matters of taste,
fiction &c. and you will be happy to hear, promises excellently well. Three
numbers will have appeared by tomorrow, but I do not send them to you, as
they ~~will not~~ are not stamped like newspapers, & so will not go free. – My
15 *dear Hogg, I am most extremely sensible of your great kindness in writing*
to me as you have done about my difficulties, especially as the sympathy in
this particular instance, from you, brings with it a certain preventing gener-
osity, which is very ~~rare~~ rare. The least justice I can do myself however, is
to say, that I have always supposed you possessed of these feelings, or I
20 *could not have allowed even my false shame to remain silent towards you so*
long upon the subject of that obligation you helped me with,– a trifling one,
I am aware, to your spirit, but not to your bachelorship nor to my wants at
the time. My broken promises on that head have galled me many & many
a time: but I trust they will not remain broken very long. If I used to be
25 *negligent in money-matters formerly, my half-bruised brains will bear witness*

Hunt to Hogg   *October 26, 1819*

SC 544 *for me that I am not so any longer.– Yet I am not down cast, seeing how my*
friends bear with me. My prospects, thank Heaven, were never better, than
just now; whatever my immediate pressure is. A little while, & a good hard
struggle, and my wings, I trust, will be as free as ever.– You will find my
30   *new papers at your chambers when you return. I hope to meet you at Pea-*
cock's tomorrow week.– Believe me,

> *My dear Hogg,*
> > *Your ever-remembering friend,*
> > > *Leigh Hunt.*

35   *What an exquisite joke about the Riot Act, & how told! I made Coulson*
ready to die with it in the street, by Whitehall.

line 27. *Heaven,*: *H* may be lower case.

W HEN HOGG wrote to Peacock on September 26, he promised to
write to Hunt "in a day or two."[1] Hunt replies tardily, then, to
Hogg's apparently cordial letter from Norton after receiving an invitation
from Peacock for Wednesday, November 3, on the occasion of Hogg's
return to London after his summer holidays (lines 30–31).

The loan from Hogg obviously weighed heavily on Hunt — probably
because he knew that Hogg was not well-off. Hogg had, perhaps, lent
Hunt a sum early in the year when (as Hunt told Mary) "difficulties . . .
have latterly come pelting upon me."[2] By July Hogg may have grown
curious about the fate of this loan, for he fished for information in his
letter to Shelley of July 2: "Hunt is . . . I am afraid not getting rich.
You hear from him often, and no doubt of his affairs."[3] Shelley, however, was little help: "as I hear nothing from him of money difficulties
I hope that your conjecture in that respect is groundless."[4] When Hogg
finally mentioned to Hunt himself the rumors of his reverses, Hunt was
far more communicative about his "difficulties" (lines 7, 16).

1. SC 541.
2. SC 517.
3. *Shelley and Mary*, I, 384.
4. Shelley to Hogg, July 25, 1819, Shelley, *Letters*, II, 105.

Shelley to Brooks, Son & Dixon   *October* **30, 1819**

SC 544   Shelley had, of course, known something of Hunt's problems from references to them in several letters. But he and Mary had chosen to ignore Hunt's hints on the subject so that he would undertake his own rescue. Shelley would not have told Hogg anything about Hunt's finances for the same reason he told him little about his own; Hogg had no right to ask. Hunt had no such reticence about his private affairs, especially to one who had assisted him. But in this letter he emphasizes his own efforts to strengthen his fortunes by describing the *Indicator* (lines 10–12) and sending copies to Hogg's London lodgings in Garden Court, Temple, while — apparently — sending this letter to the Hogg family home at Norton.[5]

Hogg's "exquisite joke about the Riot Act" may have been a topical one growing out of the concern of English liberals over the repressive use of troops to break up peaceful public meetings like that at Manchester. The most recent such outbreak had occurred at Paisley, Scotland. According to the relatively objective *Annual Register* for 1819, after peaceful reform rallies at Leeds, Birmingham, and other places, had been watched but not interfered with by the government, "a very moderate attempt at interference on the part of the constituted authorities of Paisley produced opposite and highly disgraceful results."[6] There, when the magistrates ordered seizure of the reformers' slogan-bearing flags, a riot ensued. After several days of burning and looting, the disturbance was put down with the aid of cavalry from Glasgow. Perhaps Hogg's joke suggested that the Riot Act was an act designed to incite riots.

5. The letter as it survives gives no hint as to how it was sent to Hogg. It has no address and the sheet is not folded as many times as one would expect. I suspect that Hunt enclosed the letter in a copy of the *Examiner* (which we know from SC 541 Hunt was sending to him at Norton). This newspaper, as Hunt mentions (line 14), could be sent through the mails free and Hunt could save postage by enclosing this note in the latest issue of the *Examiner*.

6. "General History," *Annual Register* for 1819, p. 109.

SC 545 P. B. SHELLEY TO BROOKS, SON & DIXON, OCTOBER 30, 1819

AL signed *Percy Bysshe Shelley*, 2 pages. Double sheet, 4to (9.5 x 7.4 inches). Wove paper. Watermark: *PM*|.
Seal (trace): wafer, orange.
Postal fees: 1. 8; 2. 3/10.

The Carl H. Pforzheimer Library

Shelley to Brooks, Son & Dixon   *October 30, 1819*

SC 545   Postmarks: 1. FIRENZE; 2. (Foreign Post Office stamp): FPO| NO· 13| 1819|.
Notations: 1. (page 1): [large paragraph sign, top center]|; 2. (page 3, middle): *£47. 18. 5 Balance of Acct*

    50

   ~~*147. 18. 5*~~ *pᵈ Coutts &C*

    97. 18 5

    on acct of Florence Bʳ

Docket: *P B Shelley| 30 Oct 1819|*.

PROVENANCE: William Walker (Hodgson, December 15, 1916, lot 225); Walter T. Spencer; Gabriel Wells; Anderson Galleries, December 4, 1922, lot 380; Brick Row Book Shop; Jerome Kern (Anderson Galleries, January 21–24, 1929, lot 1105); Seven Gables, December 1952. *De Ricci 436* (p. 23).

Florence, Oct. 30.1819

   Gentlemen.

      I have this moment recieved a letter from Mʳ Peacock who gives me to understand ~~*who gives m*~~ *that I have drawn on you instead of on*

5 *Messʳˢ Coutts for some, but what portion, he does not say of the £400 credit I recieved from you in April. Should this have been the case it must have arisen from some informality which occurred respecting a bill of £175, & perhaps also one of £50, which were drawn from Livorno instead of Rome, & on that ground alone, the former protested by Messʳˢ Coutts. I drew a new*

10 *bill to indemnify the holder of the former, of the same amount, to which I think it possible, (but having no memorandum, cannot speak with certainty), that your names might have been attached.—*

    The funds therefore on which I counted, or such a portion of them as make up together with that in your hands, ~~*tha*~~ *what I know I have not drawn*

15 *for, remain at Messʳˢ Coutts— I beg you immediately to withdraw them, & send them together with the remainder of my money, to me at Florence in the simplest form & the most expeditious manner, & this letter shall be yours & their authority for complying with my request. And I should be indebted to you for the politeness of doing it without delay, this misunderstanding having*

20 *exposed me, as you will readily conjecture, to great inconvienience.— I inclose a note to Messʳˢ Coutts.*

    Trusting that at all events you will be so obliging as to pay immediate

[938]

Shelley to Brooks, Son & Dixon   *October 30, 1819*

SC 545   *attention to the subject of this letter, & that you will immediately place my*
         funds at my command

25   *I have the honour to remain,*
                                         Gentlemen, Your very obed. Sev.
                                              Percy Bysshe Shelley

         [Address, page 4]
                 Messrs Brookes & Co
                         Bankers
30   *Chancery Lane*
         Angleterre   *London*

line 3. *recieved* (sic): see also line 6.   line 20. *inconvienience.* (sic).
line 4. *m*: probable reading.   line 26. *Sev.*: probable reading.
line 15. *withdraw*: may have been intended as
two separate words.

THE SMALL misunderstanding reflected in the present letter to Brooks,
Son & Dixon is a foretaste of the problems Shelley was to encounter in 1820. This letter provides an occasion to outline Shelley's
known financial dealings in 1818 and 1819.

First, let us enumerate the known transactions involving Shelley's
account with Brooks, Son & Dixon from the time Shelley left England
on March 12 until February 26, 1819, when he asked them for a statement
of his account. The last letter Shelley wrote before leaving England was
an order to Brooks to pay bills totaling £327 that were to fall due from
fifteen days to four months after March 12, 1818, the date of the letter.[1]
In the last three quarters of 1818 Shelley apparently wrote only two
substantive letters to Brooks, Son & Dixon — both from Bagni di Lucca
in July. In one he asked his bankers to honor three promissory notes
for £50 each that he had earlier written to Horace Smith,[2] and in the
second (SC 490) he ordered them to honor a note to Godwin for £50.
Shelley had, in addition, written checks payable by Ollier for £10 and
£20 to the mysterious "A.B.," and had reimbursed Ollier by means of a

1. Shelley, *Letters*, I, 599.
2. Shelley, *Letters*, II, 27–28. See SC 430 and Commentary.

SC 545   check drawn on Brooks for at least the second sum.[3] He obtained money during his travels from local bankers,[4] apparently drawing upon a cash letter of credit, in which the money was deposited with a London banker and could be drawn on at correspondent banks in major Italian cities.[5] Presumably this money was the portion of the *post obit* loan from William Willats that remained to Shelley after he had given money to both Godwin and Hunt.[6]

Therefore, besides the £327 that Shelley (just prior to his departure) had asked Brooks to pay, he authorized £220 to £230 to Horace Smith, Godwin, and Ollier. In addition, Thomas Hume would have drawn a total £90 from Shelley's account after August 1818[7] and Peacock apparently received either £25 or £20 each quarter. From the time Shelley left England until he was about to leave Naples for Rome, his account would have received four quarterly payments of £250 from his father's banker — a total of £1,000 — against which Shelley, Hume, and Peacock are known to have drawn a total of at least £717 or £737.

On February 26, 1819, Shelley wrote to Brooks, Son & Dixon, requesting them to send him a letter of credit for £400 "in every respect similar to the last" in care of Torlonia at Rome.[8] (From the present letter, we learn that the £400 was transferred to Thomas Coutts & Co. and that the letter of credit was drawn in the name of that house, which was presumably better known in Italy than was Brooks.) Shelley's letter reached London on March 20, just before the deposit of his next £250 quarterly income, of which £200 was his to spend. Presumably Brooks complied both with Shelley's order for the letter of credit and with his request (in a postscript) for a statement of his bank balance. But before that letter of credit and statement reached Rome, Shelley, on April 4,

3. See sc 492 and Commentary and sc 492A.

4. See, for example, sc 494, lines 59–60.

5. See Shelley's request to Brooks, February 26, 1819, for "a letter of credit . . . in every respect similar to the last" (Shelley, *Letters*, II, 82).

6. See sc 454, Commentary.

7. Thomas Hume, of course, had begun drawing £30 per quarter from Shelley's account, probably in August 1818. If sc 499 was Hume's second quarterly payment, his next payment would have come due around January 12, 1819. See sc 499 and Commentary.

8. Shelley, *Letters*, II, 82.

SC 545   1819 — apparently in immediate need of funds — drew a bill for £100 on Torlonia payable by Brooks.[9]

Because Brooks, Son & Dixon had already transmitted to Coutts the £400 Shelley had requested in his letter of February 26, the hundred pounds he drew from Torlonia on April 4 was deducted not from that amount but from his balance at Brooks. When the letter of credit for £400 arrived from Coutts, Shelley apparently supposed that the £100 Torlonia had advanced him earlier was to be deducted from this. But Torlonia obviously received an additional credit of £100 from Brooks.

Brooks's statement of Shelley's account, which was already on its way to Shelley before he wrote on April 4, would show only the £400 debit and not the additional £100. Shelley apparently made his later calculations on the basis of Brooks's March statement and believed that he had drawn only £400 from his account at Brooks during the first half of the year.[10] His confusion was, no doubt, intensified by the haste with which the Shelleys departed Rome after William Shelley's death, obviously not pausing to put their affairs in order. From later correspondence we can ascertain that when Shelley left Rome, he had on deposit with Torlonia £100 more than he knew and with Brooks £100 less than he supposed. He undoubtedly also failed to calculate the losses from bank charges and currency exchanges.

On August 25 Shelley requested that Brooks send him £100 in four notes of £25 from Herries & Co.[11] When this money failed to reach him at Florence by October 14, Shelley borrowed £50 from a Florentine banker to advance to Maria Gisborne to help finance the steamboat designed by her son Henry Reveley.[12] On September 23 Shelley wrote to

9. Shelley informed Brooks of this in SC 519, which was received in London on April 24, 1819.

10. See Shelley, *Letters*, II, 161.

11. Postmarked in London September 14, 1819, Shelley, *Letters*, II, 116. According to Ralph Richardson, Herries & Co. had in 1772 joined with several other banks — including the Edinburgh banking firm of John Coutts & Co. (parent of London's Thomas Coutts & Co.) — to establish the London Exchange Banking Company "for the purpose of issuing promissory notes to travellers payable on the Continent" (*Coutts & Co., Bankers*, London, 1900, p. 69). *The Royal Kalendar* for 1819 lists Herries, Farquhar, Halliday, Chapman, & Halliday at 16 St. James Street. William Brockedon's practical *Road Book from London to Naples* (London: John Murray, 1835) recommends the bills of exchange of Herries & Co. as the most "convenient, safe, and independent" way of carrying money for the trip (p. 5).

12. See Shelley to Maria Gisborne, October 14 and October 21, Shelley, *Letters*, II, 124–126, 129.

SC 545   Brooks again, reminding them to send the £100 in Herries' "circular notes" and telling them that he had drawn a bill on them payable to the banking firm of Webb & Co. at Leghorn.[13] This £200, representing the amount Shelley could draw on his Michaelmas income (payable September 29), was intended to finance the completion of Henry Reveley's steamboat, which was to ply between Leghorn and Marseilles. When Brooks received this letter on October 9, they informed Peacock that they had not enough on deposit in Shelley's account to honor the bill for £200 drawn to Webb. Peacock wrote to Shelley explaining the situation, his letter reaching Shelley on Thursday, October 28.[14] Shelley looked over his records and wrote to Brooks two days later, in time to send the letter in the next mail headed toward England.[15]

In sc 545 Shelley explains that he had earlier (that is, before drawing the £200 bill to Webb which is the subject of the dispute) drawn bills at Leghorn (Livorno) for £175 and £50 upon his £400 credit with Coutts (he believed). Because in his haste to leave Rome he had neglected to inform Coutts of his change of address, his bill for £175 had not been accepted and he had redrawn it (lines 7–10). Shelley suggests that in redrawing this bill of exchange, he may have drawn by error on Brooks rather than Coutts. But this seems not to have been the case. Rather, it was the bill for £50 that he drew erroneously on Brooks (though if he *had* drawn on Coutts without allowing for their charges of £2.1.7, the bill would still not have been accepted). The notation shows (see Bibliographical Description) that Brooks and Coutts together had a total of £97.18.5 of Shelley's money.

Shelley had not depended upon his bankers alone. He informed Maria Gisborne on October 28, that he had also written "to private friends,"[16] and it was reliable Horace Smith who first came to Shelley's rescue. On December 7, 1819, Shelley wrote to Henry Reveley that, though he had as yet "received no satisfactory letter" from his bankers, he was sending Henry "the produce of £100" to be paid by Messrs.

13. Letter postmarked in London October 9, 1819, Shelley, *Letters*, II, 121. [   ] Webb of Leghorn and Charles F. Barry of Genoa were banking partners. For Byron's dealings with Webb and Barry see Byron, *Letters and Journals*, VI, *passim*, and Marchand, *Byron*, III, 1046.

14. See Shelley to Maria Gisborne, October 28, 1819, Shelley, *Letters*, II, 130.

15. For the Florentine postal service, see sc 551, Commentary.

16. Shelley, *Letters*, II, 131.

SC 545   Ward.[17] It is clear from the copy of the draft transcribed in Shelley, *Letters*, that H[orace] S[mith] Esqre validated the draft. He probably sent Shelley an order on Messrs. Ward, who were presumably *his* correspondents at Leghorn. Smith's intervention explains why Shelley drew on H. B. Ward rather than Webb & Co. and why, early in 1820, he put his finances in Smith's care.[18]

Though Shelley denied having received a *satisfactory* letter from Brooks, they *had* written to him, for Shelley also wrote to them on December 7, 1819.[19] The notation on sc 545 indicates that Brooks, Son & Dixon enclosed a bill of exchange for £97.18.5 payable to Shelley by a Florentine banker. This sum was the total in his accounts at Brooks and Coutts. From Shelley's letter of December 7, we learn that Brooks explained exactly what had happened to the rest of his money. But Shelley did not remember having drawn £100 on Brooks payable to Torlonia. (That he actually *had* done so, however, is evidenced by sc 519.)

At this point £200 was missing — the £100 in Herries' notes and the £100 at Torlonia's. The first £100 apparently arrived on December 14, 1819.[20] Shelley had received the final £100 from Torlonia and transmitted it to the Gisbornes on December 23.[21]

From the foregoing account, we conclude that in 1819 Shelley contributed at least £250 and possibly £350 to Henry Reveley's steamboat: (1) The £50 borrowed from the Florentine banker and sent to Maria Gisborne on October 21, 1819; (2) the £100 received from Horace Smith, sent to Henry Reveley on December 7; (3) the £100 in Herries' notes, *possibly* transmitted in Mary Shelley's letter to Maria Gisborne, December 14 (see sc 553, Commentary); (4) the £100 recovered from Torlonia, sent to the Gisbornes December 23. The only resources that we know Shelley had in addition to this total of £350, at least £250 of which went into the steamboat, was the £97.18.5 that Brooks transmitted to him in response to sc 545. Fifty pounds or more of this would

17. Shelley, *Letters*, II, 161–162.
18. See Shelley to Brooks, January 17, 1820, Shelley, *Letters*, II, 170.
19. Shelley, *Letters*, II, 161.
20. See sc 553 and Commentary.
21. Shelley, *Letters*, II, 165.

SC 545   have been required to repay the loan from the Florentine banker, leaving the Shelleys £100 in debt to Horace Smith and with something between £45 and £145 plus the £200 Christmas income to live on between the end of September and the end of March. During the four-month stay in Florence, Percy Florence Shelley was born and the Shelleys — besides maintaining themselves — entertained Charles Clairmont and Sophia Stacey and her companion Miss Corbet Parry-Jones, each for a few weeks.[22] It is small wonder, then, that Shelley was forced to sell his (or Thomas Charters') carriage sometime before leaving Florence on January 26, 1820.[23]

22. White, *Shelley*, II, 172–175.
23. See "Shelley's 'Chariot,'" *Shelley and his Circle*, III, 173–174.

SHELLEY'S TREATISE ON POLITICAL ECONOMY

SHELLEY'S POLITICAL PHILOSOPHY

A T TIMES during his career as a poet, Percy Bysshe Shelley looked longingly at the active life that he had been prepared for and imagined that political activity was more important to the world than any of the poetry he was writing.[1] He must often have wondered whether he could have exerted a greater influence for good had he feigned conformity on religious questions during his university career and assumed his father's seat in Parliament, instead of rebelling and becoming an apparently ineffectual poet, exiled in Italy. Shelley's feelings of isolation and his knowledge of the relative failure of his writings were brought home to him with added force in late 1819 and early 1820 by the stirring political events in England and by the neglect shown him by his English friends and his publisher. Sir Timothy Shelley did not stand for re-election to Parliament in June 1818,[2] and Shelley, who probably did not know why, may well have thought back to his own youthful plans: "My father is in parliament, and on attaining 21 I shall, in all probability, fill his vacant seat."[3]

Shelley's strong and continuing interest in English politics had expressed itself, after his expulsion from Oxford and the loss of his hopes to serve in Commons, in political speeches and writings that from the beginning combined an insider's knowledge of the actual power struc-

1. Note his plan to become a clergyman (Peacock, *Memoirs*, pp. 75–77) and his later one to go to India (see Shelley to Hogg, October 22, 1821, and Shelley to Peacock, January [?11], 1822, Shelley, *Letters*, II, 361 and note, 374).

2. Sir Timothy was succeeded as Member from New Shoreham in the next Parliament by James Martin Lloyd, who had formerly been a Member from Steyning, Sussex. Lloyd's election was uncontested. Sir Timothy either retired voluntarily or the new Duke of Norfolk, who controlled the seat, decided to replace him with one of his own followers. Charles Howard, the eleventh Duke of Norfolk, the patron of Sir Bysshe Shelley, had died on December 16, 1815, less than a year after Sir Bysshe himself. He was succeeded by his Catholic cousin Bernard Edward Howard (1765–1842). Timothy Shelley's single recorded speech in Parliament was a testimony in defense of the orderliness of a reform meeting held in Horsham on February 24, 1817, but lest it appear that he finally raised his voice in the House of Commons because he had broken with the new Duke of Norfolk and felt freer during his lame-duck session, it should be noted that Sir Timothy nominated the duke's candidate for the Horsham seat in Parliament in the first contested election after passage of the Reform Bill of June 7, 1832 (see William Albery, *A Parliamentary History of the Ancient Borough of Horsham, 1295–1885*, London, 1927, p. 283).

3. Shelley to Hunt, March 2, 1811, Shelley, *Letters*, I, 55.

Shelley's Treatise on Political Economy

ture in Great Britain and the motivations of its operatives with a firm grasp of ideal (or *theoretical*) political principles. Although, as David V. Erdman has shown, Byron's political sympathies were always at war with his aristocratic prejudices,[4] Shelley saw nothing particularly admirable in the ideals or practices of the Tory place-men and the Whig magnates who made up the governments and the chief Parliamentary "opposition" under George III and the Prince Regent. Only among the philosophical radicals of various denominations (whose numbers in the House of Commons were always very small during Shelley's formative years) did he detect any signs of disinterested advocacy of measures that would benefit the entire nation and its common people.

On the theoretical side, Shelley had early read the writers whose thought lay behind the French Revolution, including Montesquieu, Rousseau, Voltaire, Condorcet, and Volney, as well as Harrington, Algernon Sidney, Locke, Hume, Godwin, and Bentham. In Italy Shelley became especially interested in the political ideas of Plato. The general aim of all these authors was to argue to specific political actions from first principles grounded firmly on their theories of the nature of the universe, the nature of man, his relationship to God (if they felt capable of determining that), and his prospects for development. Shelley's political thought, like theirs, never generalizes from a small fraction of mankind in one country, having a peculiar history imposed by past decisions, compromises, habits, or accidents. When Shelley became interested in history, it was in history on a universal scale; he studied it to learn from the experiences of various civilizations what forms of government and social order were most successful in fostering human happiness, how these beneficent forms were instituted and sustained, and through what weaknesses they fell.

Shelley's political beliefs are consonant with his entire philosophical orientation. Shelley's metaphysics — or rather his *lack* of metaphysics — was based on his understanding of the epistemological problem. Having studied the works of Bacon, Locke, Hartley, Berkeley, Hume, and Sir William Drummond, he could not assent unconditionally to any precise explanation of the ultimate nature of the universe, because he

---

4. See "Lord Byron" and "'Fare Thee Well' — Byron's Last Days in England," *Shelley and his Circle*, III, 282–323 *passim*; IV, 638–653.

Shelley's Treatise on Political Economy

accepted a view of the human mind and of the sources of human knowledge that judged reason, finally, like the sensory data on which it operates, to be fallible and limited. He believed that the resulting skepticism was ethically beneficial, because self-doubt should stop men from destroying one another over differences of opinion. In "Mont Blanc" he declares that the lack of definite knowledge about God or "Power" can "repeal/ Large codes of fraud and woe" (lines 80–81).

Since Shelley believed that there could be no certitude about such matters as "the will of God," or "the law of Nature," or "the Divine Right," he saw both ethics and politics as instrumental to the welfare and happiness of the people (and other living creatures) that come within the compass of an individual's power (ethics) or within the scope of a social unit (politics). For Shelley, as for Pope, the proper study of mankind was not God, but man. Even in his early, more opinionated days, Shelley's greatest scorn was reserved for those who pretended to know the ultimate truth and who damned men for disagreeing with them: "how ridiculous in a foppish courtier not six feet high to direct the spirit of universal harmony, in what manner to conduct the affairs of the universe!"[5]

Inasmuch as Shelley believed the will of God was something that limited human beings could not know with certainty, he grounded ethics on a more mundane foundation. Shelley was very much a man of his time in accepting the hedonistic basis of values. He regarded human pleasure ("happiness") as the pragmatic value and the greatest good for the greatest number as the viable goal of political activity.[6] Thus far Shelley's ideas resembled the utilitarian ethics of Jeremy Bentham. But in *A Defence of Poetry* (1821) Shelley was careful to distinguish between different kinds of utility based on two kinds of pleasure — "one durable, universal and permanent; the other transitory and particular."[7] In this sense, he followed Godwin and foreshadowed John Stuart Mill's break with Bentham's "hedonistic calculus" by introducing qualitative distinctions rather than following to its logical conclusions a merely quantitative system in which push-pin is as good as Shakespeare

---

5. *An Address, to the Irish People*, Shelley, *Complete Works*, V, 217.
6. See *A Defence of Poetry*, Shelley, *Complete Works*, VII, 131–132.
7. See Shelley, *Complete Works*, VII, 132.

The Carl H. Pforzheimer Library

Shelley's Treatise on Political Economy

(or better than Shakespeare, if the simple game gives greater pleasure to a greater number of people). Shelley's hedonism, as one would expect from a person of his aristocratic upbringing and temperament, was impure. He wished all men to select the "higher" sources of pleasure that he believed to have greater value.[8]

Because Shelley viewed political organization as designed by and for men on earth (rather than God in Heaven), he believed men could change the existing systems in any way that would contribute to their welfare and happiness. But the aftermath of the French Revolution had taught him that not every change is an improvement and that the use of force turns the revolutionaries themselves into new tyrants. So Shelley's early political writings, without exception, advocate reform through discussion and education, through public meetings and the formation of educational and philanthropic associations, rather than through use of direct action, either violent or nonviolent.

The axioms of Shelley's *Declaration of Rights* (1812) distill ideas found at greater length in *An Address, to the Irish People* (1812) and *Proposals for an Association of those Philanthropists, who convinced of the inadequacy of the moral and political state of Ireland to produce benefits which are nevertheless attainable are willing to unite to accomplish its regeneration* (1812). In the *Declaration of Rights* Shelley recognizes the right of society to coerce violators of its laws (VII), denies the right of an individual "to disturb the public peace, by personally resisting the execution of a law however bad" (IX), and declares that "no man has a right to do an evil thing that good may come" (XVII). Yet the document is in other respects one of the most radical manifestos ever penned; it insists on absolute freedom of speech and press (XI–XIV), declares that "expediency is inadmissible in morals" and that "politics are only sound when conducted on principles of morality" (XVIII), and advocates more or less equal distribution of property (XXVII–XXIX). On

---

8. Shelley grapples with the problem in a more profound way than John Stuart Mill does by recognizing that, "from an inexplicable defect of harmony in the constitution of human nature, the pain of the inferior is frequently connected with the pleasures of the superior portions of our being. . . . Our sympathy in tragic fiction depends on this principle; tragedy delights by affording a shadow of the pleasure which exists in pain" (Shelley, *Complete Works*, VII, 132–133). Some modern readers might add examples from athletics, where the physical pain endured and overcome in long-distance running, swimming, and mountain climbing contributes to the pleasure of achievement in both competitive and noncompetitive sports.

Shelley's Treatise on Political Economy

war and the military, Shelley writes: "Man has no right to kill his brother, it is no excuse that he does so in uniform. He only adds the infamy of servitude to the crime of murder" (XIX).[9]

Shelley's youthful radicalism, like the more mature viewpoint expressed in his *Philosophical View of Reform*, demanded that there be no discrepancy between means and ends. If one opposes violence on the part of an oppressive government, he must not resort to violence as an antidote.[10] If one decries the widespread existence of ignorance, poverty, and vice, he should attempt to alleviate these problems on a personal basis by teaching, giving relief to needy people, trying to persuade men to abandon vicious habits and — above all — by himself avoiding vicious habits and actions.

Did Shelley believe, then, that social renovation depended upon a reform of individuals or of institutions? With a reform of both. Since men mold institutions, reformed individuals will create better institutions; but, since the wisdom and virtue of at least a minority always exceeds the quality of existing institutions, the enlightened group ought to press (peacefully, of course) for immediate improvement of those wanting institutions.[11] Shelley, in other words, recognized the phenomenon of "cultural lag." The enlightened minority could through improved social institutions improve the environment — educational and moral — to the point where the mass of the population would accept the improvement as natural and could grow amenable to the next set of improvements.

Shelley admired flexibility more than stability in all human institutions for the simple reason that he believed in "perfectibility" — the idea that products of the human intellect were capable of continuing and endless improvement.[12] This is why he praises the British Constitu-

---

9. Shelley, *Complete Works*, V, 271–275.

10. See *An Address, to the Irish People*, Shelley, *Complete Works*, V, 233.

11. Because the question has been disputed, I shall quote two relevant passages from *An Address, to the Irish People*: ". . . without individual amendment it is vain and foolish to expect the amendment of a state or government" (Shelley, *Complete Works*, V, 236); "The excellence of the Constitution of Great Britain, appears to me, to be its indefiniteness and versatility, whereby it may be unresistingly accommodated to the progression of wisdom and virtue. Such accommodation I desire; but *I wish for the cause before the effect*." (Shelley, *Complete Works*, V, 244n.; italics added.)

12. For the classic statement of this doctrine and the probable source of Shelley's belief, see Godwin's *Political Justice* (Priestley edition), Book I, chapter VIII, entitled "Human Inventions Susceptible of Perpetual Improvement."

Shelley's Treatise on Political Economy

tion for its "indefiniteness and versatility" (see note 11) and the American Constitution for its supposed provision that it had to be updated every ten years.[13] Nor did Shelley make exceptions of his own pet ideas to the doctrine that all institutions ought to be prepared to change with the times. When he advocated the formation of an association to work for reform in Ireland, he named the group an "Association of philanthropy, because good men ought never to circumscribe their usefulness by any name which denotes their exclusive devotion to the accomplishment of its signification."[14] In other words, when a group announces as its sole interest the combatting of a single evil (a disease like infantile paralysis, for example) or one humanitarian goal (prevention of cruelty to animals), there is danger either that the organization will perpetuate itself beyond the time when its purpose has been accomplished or that its members may circumscribe their activity by such a narrow sphere that they ignore other social evils at least as great.

Shelley suspected that all institutions, except the most general and amorphous, tended to limit and dehumanize men, stifling the imagination and natural sympathies and turning sensitive human beings into functional automatons or dead abstractions. He had witnessed and studied — as men have witnessed since — people who committed enormous crimes or who remained unmoved in the face of such crimes for the "good" of faith, nation, party, class, or family. Shelley's fear of the divisive and dehumanizing power of abstractions and the institutions devoted to them, as well as his belief in personal responsibility, led him to describe liberated man in *Prometheus Unbound* as "equal, unclassed, tribeless, and nationless,/ Exempt from awe, worship, degree, the king/ Over himself" (III.iv.195–197).

Shelley's political philosophy cannot be described by enumerating specific reforms that he advocated. All those set forth in *A Philosophical View of Reform*, such as the need for more equal representation in Parliament, abolition of the standing army in peacetime, and reduction of the unfair burden of taxation and inflation on the working classes, follow naturally from Shelley's few cardinal principles, the essence of which is the liberty and the responsibility of each individual to govern

13. See *A Philosophical View of Reform*, sc 546, lines 697–701, and note.
14. *Proposals for an Association . . .*; Shelley, *Complete Works*, V, 268.

Shelley's Treatise on Political Economy

himself. Like other radicals of his day — from Paine and Jefferson to Cobbett and John Stuart Mill — Shelley believed in reducing to a minimum the power and influence of institutions — especially national governments — over individuals.[15] Had he lived to see both the reform of Parliament and the growth of great corporations and other private institutions, he would probably have seen greater need for the popularly elected government — no longer the tool of a small oligarchy — to control the new instruments of that oligarchy. Shelley would be the first to say that circumstances alter cases, and that, though the ultimate goal of government should remain the greatest welfare and happiness for the greatest number of human beings, the means should be changed promptly to meet new conditions. Shelley's political philosophy, it seems to me, has enough vitality and universality to be relevant today and for the future. Its virtues include an awareness of human limitations, coupled with a hopefulness about improving the lot of all men; a refusal to mistake means — the machinery of even reformed institutions — for ends; and a willingness to work for reforms needed at the moment even while realizing that those very reforms will someday have to be replaced. In maturity Shelley seldom mistook the body of his political thought for its spirit. There are very few political theorists, from Plato to the present, about whom that can be said.

DATING THE MANUSCRIPT

Shelley began to write his essay on reform (which encompasses his ideas on political economy) as a direct result of his renewed interest in English politics precipitated by news of the Manchester (Peterloo) massacre (see SC 537 and Commentary). But he wrote several other works and did considerable reading before undertaking this major political treatise. At Leghorn in September 1819, Shelley's indignation gave impetus to *The Mask of Anarchy* (see SC 536 and Commentary). After moving to Florence at the beginning of October, he read systematically Clarendon's *History of the Rebellion* and Plato's *Republic*. But by the

15. Southey, as we have seen (SC 408, Commentary, fn. 9), was expressing a more conservative position by advocating that the government fight postwar unemployment by undertaking public works, whereas the liberals and radicals of this period urged instead a reduction in government spending.

The Carl H. Pforzheimer Library

Shelley's Treatise on Political Economy

end of that month the only writing by Shelley recorded in Mary's Journal was *Peter Bell the Third*, which was copied by Mary and sent to Hunt by November 2 — the same day that Shelley finished reading Clarendon's *History*.[16] Shelley composed at least one other poem with political significance — that published with *Prometheus Unbound* under the Wordsworthian title, "An Ode, written October, 1819, before the Spaniards Had Recovered their Liberty."

On November 3 Shelley began writing his lengthy letter to the Editor of the *Examiner* regarding the conviction of Richard Carlile on the charge of blasphemous libel for republishing works by Thomas Paine.[17] (Hogg had first called Shelley's attention to the case in his letter of July 2, 1819, before it came to trial.[18]) Shelley's defense of Carlile takes an interesting tack: He argues that English constitutional law requires that a man on trial be judged by a jury of his *peers*, and since Carlile is not a Christian, a jury of his peers must include at least some men who profess the same faith as Carlile — namely Deism. At one point, Shelley identifies himself as a Deist, qualified to sit on such a jury (though this may have been inserted partly to support the rhetoric of his argument).[19]

On November 6 Shelley wrote to the Gisbornes, by way of making excuses for not writing sooner, that he had "just finished a letter of five sheets on Carlisle's affair" and that he was "in hourly expectation of Mary's confinement." Later in this letter, while asking the Gisbornes about their reading in Portuguese and of Theocritus, he adds, "I have deserted the odorous gardens of literature to journey across the great sandy desert of Politics; not, you may imagine, without the hope of finding some enchanted paradise."[20] This has been regarded by com-

16. Edward Hyde, Earl of Clarendon, *The History of the Rebellion and Civil Wars in England, Begun in the Year 1641; with the Precedent Passages and Actions, That contributed Thereunto, and the happy End, and Conclusion Thereof by the King's blessed Restoration, and Return, upon the 29th of May in the Year 1660.* After the first edition appeared in 1702–1704 the work was republished frequently. Shelley could have read any of the eighteenth-century editions or ones published in 1807 or 1816.

17. On Carlile, see the *DNB* and sc 551, fn. 6. For the text of the draft of Shelley's letter, see *Letters*, II, 136–148.

18. See *Shelley and Mary*, I, 383–385.

19. See Shelley, *Letters*, II, 140, lower third of the page.

20. Shelley, *Letters*, II, 148–150.

Shelley's Treatise on Political Economy

mentators as Shelley's first reference to *A Philosophical View of Reform*,[21] but it seems doubtful that it is such a reference at all. First, Shelley is referring to reading, not writing, and he very likely means that he has been reading Clarendon's *History* and Madame de Staël's account of the French Revolution instead of literature.[22] If Shelley is referring to writing, he had that day completed his long letter on the illegality of Carlile's trial, which was a political as well as a religious argument.

Mary Shelley did not keep her Journal between November 9 and December 31, 1819 (Percy Florence was born on November 12). Neither Mary's nor Claire's journal (from which the last half of 1819 is lacking) mentions Shelley's work on a political treatise. Only three indisputable contemporary references to *A Philosophical View of Reform* occur, then, in Shelley's letters. In the first, to Charles Ollier on December 15, 1819, Shelley writes:

I am preparing an octavo on reform — a commonplace kind of book — which, now that I see the passion of party will postpone the great struggle till another year, I shall not trouble myself to finish for this season. I intend it to be an instructive and readable book, appealing from the passions to the reason of men.[23]

With this clear statement, we can recognize another reference to the work in Shelley's December 23 letter to the Gisbornes, where, after telling them that he has "finished an additional act to Prometheus," he adds "I am engaged also in a political work—".[24] Finally, five months later Shelley wrote to Hunt:

Do you know any bookseller who w^d publish for me an octavo volume entitled 'A philosophical View of Reform'. It is boldly but temperately written — & I think readable — It is intended for a kind of standard book for the philosophical reformers politically considered, like Jeremy Bentham's something, but different & perhaps more systematic. — I w^d send it sheet by sheet. Will you ask & think for me?[25]

21. See, for example, Shelley, *Complete Works*, VII, 332; Shelley, *Letters*, II, 150 fn.
22. See Mary Shelley, *Journal*, for November 5, 1819.
23. Shelley, *Letters*, II, 164.
24. Shelley, *Letters*, II, 165.
25. May 26, 1820, Shelley, *Letters*, II, 201.

The Carl H. Pforzheimer Library

Shelley's Treatise on Political Economy

These three brief quotations provide our only external information about when Shelley drafted the fragmentary essay and what he hoped for it. They also suggest that one reason he did not finish it was because he could not interest a publisher in it.[26] Nothing in the May 26, 1820, letter to Hunt indicates that Shelley was actually still drafting his treatise by that date. Rather, his statement suggests that he had been looking over his earlier work and that, if a chance to publish appeared, he would revise it to send "sheet by sheet."

The evidence of the manuscript and its contents is far from conclusive for setting either a beginning or a terminal date. We know that the passage on the political situation in Spain (sc 546, lines 1063 ff.) was drafted before news of the Spanish insurrection of January 1820 had reached Shelley. Most of his information and remarks are too general and could have come from too many diverse and perhaps unrecoverable sources to enable us to adduce specific dates for the *terminus a quo* or the *terminus ad quem*. The internal and external evidence both suggest the period from November 1819 to January 1820 as the probable time of composition, with the bulk of Shelley's work probably falling in December 1819, when he mentioned it in the letters to Ollier and the Gisbornes quoted above.

Given this general time period for at least the first burst of composition, one can detect in the lines in Shelley's letter to Hunt of November [16], 1819 (sc 551), the spirit that Shelley carried into the writing of *A Philosophical View of Reform*:

The great thing to do is to hold the balance between popular impatience & tyrannical obstinacy; to inculcate with fervour both the right of resistance & the duty of forbearance. You know my principles incite me to take all the good I can get in politics, forever aspiring to something more. I am one of those whom nothing will fully satisfy, but ⟨wh⟩o am ready to be partially satisfied by all that is ⟨practicable⟩.

Whether the commencement of *A Philosophical View of Reform* is dated in early, mid-, or late November 1819, this paragraph shows that Shelley had fixed the tone and aim of the entire work at the very beginning. He was responding calmly and reasonably to the recent inflammatory events

26. There is no evidence that Hunt ever responded to Shelley's request. His next surviving letter to Shelley is dated August 23, 1820 (manuscript in The Carl H. Pforzheimer Library).

Shelley's Treatise on Political Economy

in Great Britain, hoping to use them as a warning to prod the ruling classes into instituting progressive reforms rather than awaiting the deluge of violent revolution.

PREVIOUS TRANSCRIPTIONS AND EDITIONS

Shelley's manuscript of *A Philosophical View of Reform* had been examined and parts of it transcribed by at least five students of Shelley before work began on the present edition.

1 and 2. Sometime before 1839, Mary Shelley made a transcript of the uncanceled portions in a copybook into which she had transcribed other prose works by Shelley. In 1839 she removed most of the pages *except* those containing *A Philosophical View of Reform* to send as press copy for Shelley's *Essays, Letters*. Her transcription, never published in any form, remains in the copybook, now in the Bodleian Library, Oxford.[27] Thomas Jefferson Hogg read through Mary's transcript and interlined additions and corrections, but it is unclear whether he did so before 1839 at Mary's suggestion or after her death, when he was writing his life of Shelley. While Mary's transcription is readable and true to the spirit of Shelley's draft, she not only omits canceled passages and deletes or completes Shelley's unfinished sentences, but she also includes more legible canceled alternative readings instead of difficult-to-read but uncanceled interlineations. Like other editors, she occasionally mistranscribes individual words.[28] Yet, as would be expected in the work of one who was intimately acquainted not only with Shelley's handwriting and habits of composition, but also with his patterns of thought and expression, Mary's transcript, with Hogg's additions, is helpful as a corrective to other texts. While preparing our text for the press, we consulted a microfilm of Mary's transcript, and (through the courtesy of

27. Bodleian Ms. Shelley adds. d. 6. The following pages of copybook as numbered by Mary Shelley have been removed: 1–52, 55–111, 214–241, and several leaves after page 247. *A Philosophical View of Reform* thus occupies pages numbered 118–213 by Mary (in ink) and numbered by the Bodleian (in pencil) pp. 9–104.

28. Some examples of her variations from a literal text are her readings of *impelled* for *inhabited* (line 136), *violence* for *tyranny* (line 146), *temporary* for *compromizing* (line 245), *possessor* for *professors* (line 328), *abstract* for *political* (line 501), *connexions* for *concerns* (line 800), and — to cite a more extended and crucial example — *following acts upon the purer* instead of *futurity casts upon the present* (line 1502).

The Carl H. Pforzheimer Library

Shelley's Treatise on Political Economy

the Bodleian Library, Oxford) we have recorded in the notes the more important verbal variants between her transcription (MWS) and ours.

3. Edward Dowden, while working under the auspices of the Shelley family on his biography of Shelley, read and transcribed at least sections of Shelley's essay from the original notebook, which he describes and quotes from briefly in his essay in the *Fortnightly Review* entitled "Shelley's *Philosophical View of Reform*."[29] Though for his purposes Dowden might have relied on Mary Shelley's much more legible transcription, collation of the extracts he quotes shows that he transcribed (or checked his quotations) from Shelley's original. We have recorded the substantive variants between our transcription and Dowden's published excerpts. Dowden's article in the *Fortnightly* of 1886 was, by the way, the first attempt to correct the date of Shelley's prose fragment "On Life" to 1818 or later. Many Shelleyans have, unfortunately, persisted in dating it much earlier.

4. In 1894 Lady Jane Shelley gave the notebook containing *A Philosophical View of Reform* and "On Life" to the Reverend Stopford A. Brooke (1832–March 1916), a Shelley enthusiast and apostle of religious and political liberalism.[30] Shortly before his death in 1916, in a gesture consistent with his grief over the senseless carnage of World War I, he *apparently* removed from the notebook, and *certainly* contributed to a literary auction organized by Edmund Gosse for the Red Cross, the last gathering of ten leaves that contained Shelley's essay "On Life" and his fragment on contraception.[31] The notebook itself he bequeathed to his daughter Maud (Mrs. T. W. Rolleston), whose husband fulfilled Brooke's wishes by producing the first edition of Shelley's longest effort in prose, which was published in 1920, exactly a century after Shelley had hoped it would appear.[32]

29. *Fortnightly Review*, New Series, CCXXXIX (November 1, 1886), 543–562; reprinted in Dowden's *Transcripts and Studies* (London, 1888), pp. 41–74.

30. See the letter by Stopford Brooke that accompanies the manuscript of "On Life" in The Pierpont Morgan Library.

31. See L. P. Jacks, *The Life and Letters of Stopford Brooke* (London: John Murray, 1917), II, 671, 686. The fragment on contraception, occupying parts of three pages of the twenty in The Pierpont Morgan Library, has never, to my knowledge, been either published or alluded to in Shelley scholarship.

32. Percy Bysshe Shelley, *A Philosophical View of Reform*, with an Introduction and Appendix by T. W. Rolleston (Oxford University Press, 1920).

Shelley and his Circle : Manuscripts

Shelley's Treatise on Political Economy

Rolleston's edition was done without recourse to Mary Shelley's transcript; the editor could have used Dowden's published excerpts had he known of them, but though Rolleston (p. x) cites remarks on Shelley's treatise in Dowden's *Shelley*, he gives no indication that he knew Dowden's essay of more than thirty years before. Collation of substantive features suggests that Rolleston's transcription, as represented in his edition, was done *de novo*. Rolleston — though presumably not experienced in deciphering Shelley's manuscripts — did a creditable job of presenting the substance of Shelley's thought in the essay. He has not glossed over the difficulties, though he did not feel it necessary to attempt detailed transcription of canceled passages. There are, as might be expected, a number of verbal mistranscriptions and a few instances in which Rolleston has not arranged the parts according to Shelley's probable intention. But his edition was a good first public presentation of *A Philosophical View of Reform*.

5. In April 1921 Mrs. Rolleston sold her Shelley notebook at auction in London, and it was purchased by Carl H. Pforzheimer. Mr. Pforzheimer almost immediately made the notebook available to Dr. Walter E. Peck, the leading young American Shelley scholar of the period, and he permitted Peck to take the notebook to Wooster, Ohio, during the summer of 1923, where Peck examined it closely enough to finish an article entitled "Unpublished Passages from the Pforzheimer MS. of Shelley's *Philosophical View of Reform*."[33] Peck completed a new edition of the *Philosophical View of Reform* as his sole contribution to the three volumes of Shelley's prose in the Julian Edition.[34] In 1930, the same year that *A Philosophical View of Reform* was published in the Julian edition, an edition of fifty copies of the treatise was "Printed for Private Circulation for Carl H. Pforzheimer." This issue, edited by Peck, contains his text and notes exactly as they appear in the Julian Edition, except for the addition of a "Preface" and the rearrangement of the pagination of the notes.[35] The Pforzheimer issue has a colophon, not found in the

33. *PMLA*, XXXIX (1924), 910–918.

34. See Roger Ingpen's "Editor's Preface" to Shelley, *Complete Works*, VII, v.

35. The verso of fly-title "Editorial Notes" is blank in the Pforzheimer private issue, with the notes themselves beginning on the following recto, instead of on the verso of that fly-title, as in the Julian Edition (see Shelley, *Complete Works*, VII, 331–332).

The Carl H. Pforzheimer Library

Shelley's Treatise on Political Economy

Julian Edition, indicating that the printer was that favorite of Buxton Forman and T. J. Wise, Richard Clay & Sons of Bungay, Suffolk.

Walter E. Peck, whose colorful exploits have added so much spice to the history of Shelley scholarship (and whose unfortunate end was once adduced to me as a reason to stay clear of interest in Shelley), was quite a good scholar when he put his mind to his work. His editing of *A Philosophical View of Reform* is admirable, though unfortunately for Shelley (happily for those of us who have devoted months coming afterward to make repair), there remained a number of additions and corrections to be made — a few key ones suggested by Mary Shelley's transcript, which was not available to Peck.

EDITORIAL PROCEDURES

The uncanceled portions of Shelley's treatise have been adequately presented through Peck's improvement of Rolleston's text, and had the holograph manuscript been lost in 1931, an editor might — with some intelligent guesses — have pieced together from the surviving evidence in Mary Shelley's transcript, Dowden's remarks, and Rolleston's and Peck's editions, a close approximation of Shelley's latest intention before he abandoned the essay sometime early in 1821. But, like many of Shelley's notebook drafts, that of *A Philosophical View of Reform* has a great deal to teach us about Shelley's thought and — in this case particularly — his rhetorical method of presenting his ideas. Shelley had what I believe students of Coleridge have characterized as a tangential intellect, in which the connections of each subject to every other facet of human thought were so readily apparent that the author was in constant danger of being led from his ostensible topic to one of its ramifications. Shelley, in his published works at least, managed to resist this proclivity by expanding the main points of his argument and by exiling his tangential topic sentences to the footnotes. Many of the longer cancellations in sc 546 were removed not because Shelley wrote what he did not believe but because he had let the growth of a subtopic detract from the force of his central argument. In a few instances Shelley undoubtedly removed passages or phrases because he felt that the openness of his argument would offend the moderately liberal members of the

[958]

Shelley and his Circle : Manuscripts

Shelley's Treatise on Political Economy

land-owning, business, and professional classes who were his apparent audience. His rhetorical strategy was to unite all those who earned their living through their own skill or labor, rich or poor, against those whom he termed "drones" (lines 2438–2447) — the two aristocracies, the landed and the financial. And to this end he constantly modifies what he says about the inherent rights of equal property to make clear that he does not advocate the *enforcement* of a literally egalitarian society (see lines 3868–3915).

But there is no need, I think, to belabor the value of seeing Shelley's rough drafts in their original order and with all their cancellations transcribed. In the case of *A Philosophical View of Reform*, the draft itself is also the sole textual authority (for where Mary Shelley or other editors have departed from it, purposely or otherwise, they have done so on the basis of inferences drawn also from the evidence of this manuscript), and as such, its accurate transcription is a *sine qua non* for an authoritative edition of the work. We have therefore transcribed the text of the manuscript, including cancellations, line by line and page by page, as literally and precisely as we have been able to decipher it and present it in type.

The footnotes record, as our Textual Notes usually do, Shelley's errors or departure from conventional usage. In no Textual Notes do we record mere careless omissions of apostrophes in possessive forms, and in this long and complicated transcription we have also *excepted* from mention Shelley's repeated miswritings of the following words: *government* (often miswritten *goverment* or *govermnent*); *their* (often *thier*); *conceive*, *deceive*, and other words including *–cei* (usually misspelled *cie*); *allege* (often *alledge*); *privilege* (often *priviledge* or *priveledge*); *possess* and *possession* (often lacking one *s*). Where these words appear with unconventional spellings, we will ask the reader to trust that we have managed to shepherd through retypings and proofs Shelley's actual orthography. Here as elsewhere, if we cannot be reasonably certain that a word is misspelled or miswritten, we follow English common law by giving Shelley the benefit of the doubt and recording the correct spelling.

We have indicated when words are canceled or underscored, but inasmuch as reproducing multiple cancel lines would render our text illegible, we have noted the existence of *significant* second or third cancel

[959]

The Carl H. Pforzheimer Library

Shelley's Treatise on Political Economy

lines in the footnotes rather than in the text. Illegible words, both canceled and uncanceled, and false starts — a partially formed letter or syllable — are indicated by the usual wide-angle brackets, but only those upon which we have a substantive comment are recorded in the notes.

On the small pages of the notebook, Shelley was often forced to crowd his words at the right-hand edge of the page, and in interlining he has occasionally used small cramped letters or contractions (c^d for *could*, etc.). Except where we feel that one of these instances has special significance or might confuse scholars who later compare our transcription with the manuscript, we have not recorded such features in the notes.

Occasionally it is possible to ascertain that specific phrases or sentences were added to the text later, perhaps when Shelley was rereading a number of pages while preparing to resume composition. Sometimes the addition is written with a new or newly sharpened quill; sometimes the color or the proportion of pigment to water in the newly mixed ink is different from that used for the previous passage; occasionally the phrase will have blotted the opposite page when Shelley turned quickly on to the next leaf after writing an insertion or emendation. Where such evidence indicates the presence of late additions, we have recorded our thoughts in the notes, but we have not attempted to establish the sequence of composition for each revision or series of false starts; in most cases the evidence will be the words themselves, their relative position on the page, and whether they are canceled or uncanceled — evidence which is being presented to the reader.

We have transcribed as part of the text the few page numbers that appear to be in Shelley's hand. In addition, the notebook contains two independent sequences of numbers in pencil. Each leaf was numbered in the upper right-hand corner of the recto by the staff of The Carl H. Pforzheimer Library, and we have included these folio numbers in brackets at the beginning of each page as a key to guide future users of Shelley's notebook to a particular place in his text. The other incomplete sequence — page numbers in pencil on the bottom edge of recto pages and top of verso pages (that is, on the outer edge of each notebook *page*) — may have been added by Peck or Rolleston or, years ago, by someone at the Pforzheimer Library. The numbers do not appear to be contemporary with Shelley or Mary, and we have not transcribed them.

Finally, although we usually reserve factual and critical commentary on the manuscript being presented to follow the transcription, in this instance it seemed best to provide brief explanatory comments and factual annotation on particular statements by Shelley in the footnotes that also include both the textual notes and a selective collation of substantive variants from Mary Shelley's transcript, and the publications of Dowden, Rolleston, and Peck. For the selective collations we employ the following sigla:

MWS: Bodleian Ms. Shelley adds. d. 6, pp. 9–104.

Dowden: Edward Dowden, "Shelley's 'Philosophical View of Reform' (a Transcript)," *Transcripts and Studies* (2nd edition, London, 1896), pp. 41–74.

Rolleston: Percy Bysshe Shelley, *A Philosophical View of Reform*, with an Introduction and Appendix by T. W. Rolleston (Oxford University Press, 1920).

Peck: Shelley, *Complete Works*, VII, 1–55, 331–340.

D.H.R.

SC 546 P. B. SHELLEY, *A PHILOSOPHICAL VIEW OF REFORM*, NOVEMBER 1819–?1820

HOLOGRAPH MANUSCRIPT, 208 pages fully or partially occupied by text of the treatise; in notebook also containing sc 547 and sc 549. The notebook, which was composed of irregular gatherings, consists of 142 leaves (6 x 3.8 inches) excluding stubs of 16 torn-out leaves. (A gathering of ten leaves containing "On Life" and a fragment on contraception, once part of the notebook, is now in The Pierpont Morgan Library.) Bound in vellum over paper boards (6.2 x 4.3 inches), the notebook is sewn at short end and text runs parallel to the sewn end; binding covered by Shelley with ink drawings and calculations. Notebook housed in green levant morocco hinged case, with spine stamped in gold: *Shelley/ MS./ 9/*, lined with silk except for a central section of the inner top cover, which contains a notation: *Shelley's M.S./ Philosophical view of Reform*.
Laid paper. Watermark: [shield (center design trimmed away)]|.

PROVENANCE: Mary Shelley; Sir Percy Florence and Lady Jane Shelley; the Reverend Stopford A. Brooke; Maud Brooke (Mrs. T. W.) Rolleston (Sotheby, April 4, 1921, lot 729); A. S. W. Rosenbach.

SC 546   CONTENTS: pastedown endpaper, numerals, sketches, and notations; stubs of 3 torn-out leaves; leaf 1, recto (fragment only), sketches, calculations, notations; leaf 1, verso, outline of treatise; leaf 2, recto, to leaf 106, verso (excluding unnumbered stubs between leaves 63 and 64 [1], 69 and 70 [2], 70 and 71 [1], 92 and 93 [2]), occupied fully or partially by *A Philosophical View of Reform*, except for the following pages: leaf 59, verso, blank; leaf 74, recto, financial calculations; leaf 75, verso, blank; leaf 105, recto, blank; 1 stub between leaves 106 and 107; leaf 107, recto, to leaf 108, recto, blank; leaf 108, verso, to leaf 109 (fragment only), recto, Note on "Ode to the West Wind" (sc 547); leaf 109 (fragment only), verso, sketch; leaf 110, recto, sketch and notation; leaf 110, verso, to leaf 132, verso, blank (blank unnumbered stubs between leaves 111 and 112 [1], 112 and 113 [1], 114 and 115 [2], 124 and 125 [1]); leaf 133, recto, sketch; leaf 133, verso, to leaf 138, recto, blank (blank unnumbered stub between leaves 135 and 136); leaf 138, verso, written *reverso* (title only): *On the punishment of/ Death/*; leaf 139, recto, sketch; leaf 139, verso, and leaf 140, recto, fragments from *Prometheus Unbound*, IV, written *reverso* (sc 549); leaf 140, verso, to leaf 141, verso, blank; leaf 142, recto, notation; leaf 142, verso, blank; pastedown endpaper, sketches and calculations.

[LEAF 1, RECTO]		~~10~~ *17 power & wealth*	
Napo		*Grevances* *50*	
Bonaparte	1st	*Sentiment of the Necessity of change*	
~~*Napoleon*~~		*Probability Necessity*	10
Such a yell	2	*Practicability & Utility of such*	
[LEAF 1, VERSO]		⌊*change*	
100 50 ~~*cheeke*~~ *2050 Clocke*	3	*State of Parties as regards it—*	
The contest between men	4	*Probable mode— Desirable mode*	

Before leaf "1" in the Pforzheimer Library's sequence of numbers, there appear the following evidences of Shelley's hand: (1) the vellum front cover contains three to six undeciphered words, besides an elaborate sketch of a tree and rocks, possibly on a lake or river bank, with hills rising on the farther side of the water; (2) the front pastedown endpaper contains ten or more sketches of faces, besides some numerals and two words, one possibly *Frankenstein*, the other undecipherable (see facsimiles, page 1005); (3) undeciphered word fragments appear on two of three unnumbered stubs of leaves torn out of the notebook, apparently by Shelley.

Amid the sketches of trees are two large ink blots which — because of the corrosive quality of the ink — have caused holes in the paper. Other such ink blots on subsequent leaves have caused similar damage, occasionally affecting a letter or two of text. Unless these holes affect the legibility of words, we have not commented on them. In Shelley's day the common writing inks were made by mixing crushed gall-nuts ("Aleppo galls"), iron sulphate ("green copperas"), powdered gum arabic, and water. In some formulas chips of wood were boiled with the galls and a small amount of copper sulphate was added.

line 5. *Clocke*: *ke* runs off edge of page.

line 8. *Grevances* (sic).

line 13. *mode . . . mode*: MWS reads *modes . . . modes.*

Shelley, *A Philosophical View of Reform*   **November 1819–?1820**

SC 546

Let us believe not only that is necessary
because it is just & ought to be, but
necessary because it is inevitable & must
be

[LEAF 2, RECTO]

⟨   ⟩

A Philosophical View of Reform
20   ~~*considered with*~~
        ~~*It is acknowledged by all, excepting*~~
by those who imagine that
their personal interest is directly
or indirectly concerned in main
-taining the ~~unjust~~ power in
which they are clothed by the
existing institutions of English
Goverment do not acknowledge
the necessity of a material
30   *change in those institutions.—*
With this exception, there is no
                the British empire
inhabitant of ~~England~~ of Mature
age & perfect understanding
not fully persuaded of the
necessity of Reform.–
        ~~*It may be useful to recapi*~~
        ~~*tulate, in a popular manner*~~
        ~~*the grievances under*~~

[LEAF 2, VERSO]
    chap 1.   Introduction   40
From the dissolution of the
Roman empire, that vast &
successful scheme for the ~~slaver~~
enslaving & ~~duping~~ the most
civilized portion of mankind,
            two recent wars
to the epoch ~~of the Reforma~~
        have
tion, ~~there~~ succeeded a series
of schemes, on a smaller scale,   50
operating to the same effect.
            ⟨   ⟩ *Sacred*
~~*The names of religion were*~~
~~*The*~~ *names borrowed from the*
~~*reli*~~ *life & opinions of Jesus*
Christ were employed as
symbols of ~~emp~~ domination
& imposture; & a system of
~~*simple affec*~~ *liberty & equality*
for such was the system preached   60
        great   was
by that Reformer, perverted to
~~*cement*~~ *support oppression–. Not*

[LEAF 3, RECTO]
his doctrines, for they ~~can~~ are too
simple & direct to be susceptible

---

line 14. *Let us ... must be* (line 17): this epigraph, whether original or a quotation, reflects Shelley's concern with the laws of historical change and his belief (or hope) that a superhuman power of amelioration, a tendency like a moral law, was at work in history. Peck inserts this sentence after line 36, believing it to be a replacement for canceled lines 37–39. He then prints the whole of lines 22–36 and lines 14–17 as an epigraph or introductory thesis.

line 14. *that is*: MWS, Rolleston, and Peck all insert *it* after *that*, a superfluous addition because in Shelley's sentence *that* functions as a demonstrative rather than as a relative pronoun.

line 18. ⟨   ⟩: possibly four undeciphered words are crowded on top edge of page.

line 33. *Mature*: may be *mature*; *e* runs off edge of page.

line 46. *two recent wars*: MWS and Rolleston read *the French Revolution*; Peck reads *the present year*.

line 52. ⟨   ⟩ *Sacred*: possible reading; may be *secret*.

line 56. *as*: written through *of*.

line 60. *such*: MWS reads *that*.

line 60. *preached*: Rolleston reads *planted*.

SC 546

of such perversion— but the mere
names. Such was the origin of
the Catholic Church, which
together with the several dynasties

70   which then beginning to consolidate
themselves in Europe, means, being
    according
interpreted, ~~m~~ a plan ~~by~~ to
which the ~~few~~ cunning & selfish
  have
few employed the fears & hopes
of the ignorant many to the
Establishment of their own power
the ⟨ ⟩

80 and the destruction of the real
interest~~s~~ of all.

  The Republics & municipal
goverments of Italy opposed for
some time a systematic & effectual
resistance to the all-surroun

[LEAF 3, VERSO]

ding tyranny,.   The~~y~~ Lombard League
defeated the armies of the despot
in open field, and until ~~the~~
Florence was betrayed to those

90   *polished tyrants*
flattered traitors, the Medici,

Freedom had one citadel wherein
it could find refuge from ~~the its~~
a world which was its enemy.
Florence long balanced, divided
& weakened the strength of the
~~emperors & the Popes~~ Empire & the
Popedom.   To this cause, if to
   undisputed
any thing was due the ~~mani~~   100
~~-fest~~ superiority of Italy in
   over
literature & the arts ~~to~~ all
its contemporary nations, ~~the~~
    own
~~the irresistible energy of~~ that ~~energy~~
union of energy & of beauty which
distinguish from all other poets
the writings of Dante that

[LEAF 4, RECTO]

restlessness of fervid power which   110
expressed itself in painting &
  and in ~~architectural~~ rude but daring
sculpture & from which, ~~by a~~
architectural forms
⟨–⟩ conjointly from the creations
of Athens its predecessor & its
image, Raphael & Michel Angelo

line 70. *beginning*: *inning* written through *an*.

line 71. *means,*: a verb, its subject being *which* (line 68). An editor might clarify Shelley's correct syntax by enclosing either *together . . . Europe* or *being interpreted* in parentheses.

line 82. *The Republics . . . Popedom.* (line 98): Shelley's conception of Italian history comes from J. C. L. Simonde de Sismondi's *Histoire des Républiques Italiennes du moyen âge* (16 vols., 1807–1818). The Lombard League of northern Italian communes, under the leadership of Milan, defeated Frederick Barbarossa near Legnano in 1176, leading to the Peace of Constance (1183) that recognized the partial autonomy of the Italian city-states. In the later wars between the Guelph and Ghibelline parties — names that changed in significance but were used to designate the two sides of the struggle between the popes and the Holy Roman (German) emperors for authority in Italy — Florence held the balance of power. Shelley attributes the rise of Italian culture to the vitality released by the citizens' freedom from absolute political and ecclesiastical authority.

line 86. *tyranny,. They*: Shelley evidently inserted a period and altered *t* of *they* to *T* but forgot to cancel the comma.

line 102. *over*: MWS reads *above*.

line 108. *other poets*: MWS reads *the poets*.

line 109. *Dante*: punctuation after this word uncertain because paper is deteriorating.

Shelley, A Philosophical View of Reform November 1819–?1820

SC 546

120

which created
drew the ~~inspi~~ inspiration of What
        now those forms & colours
is the   astonishment of the world.
~~Our own~~ The father of our own
                wrought
                ~~carried~~
literature, Chaucer, ~~drew~~ from the
simple & powerful language of
a nursling of this Republic the
basis ~~of our own~~ literature. And
thus we owe, among other causes,

130

                belonging to
the exact condition ~~of our own~~
intellectual existence, to the
generous disdain of submission
which burned
exists in the bosoms of men
who filled a distant   & inhabited
of ~~another~~ generation & another
land.

[LEAF 4, VERSO]
            When this
140 ~~But this~~ resistance was overpowered
                then
~~Whilst another was yet maturing~~
        as what
(~~and no~~ resistance to fraud &
        has not   been   overpowered?
~~tyranny has been yet successful~~)
another was even then maturing.

The progress of philosophy & civiliz
ation which ended in that
imperfect emancipation of man   150
kind from the yoke of priests
& Kings called the Reformation,
had already commenced. ~~In~~
~~many parts of Europe~~ Exas
-perated by their long sufferings
inflamed by ~~p~~ the sparks
                flames
of that superstition from the ~~wretches~~
of which they were emerging, the
poor rose against their natural   160
enemies, the rich, & repaid with
bloody interest the tyranny of

[LEAF 5, RECTO]
ages. It seems as if any approa
ch to the temple of Freedom, were
fenced about with a wilderness
of misery & desolation. One of the
signs of the times was that the
                like
oppressed peasantry rose the ~~slaves~~
Negro slaves of a West Indian   170
Plantations, and murdered their
tyrants when they were unaware.
For so dear is power that
The tyrants themselves neither

line 123. *wrought*: MWS reads *fraught*.

line 124. ~~*carried*~~: probable reading.

line 126. *&*: written through *of*.

line 128. ~~*of our own*~~: here, as elsewhere in Shelley's drafts, he reinstates canceled passages by means of underlining; in this case, the underline was inadvertently made too short to restore the sense of the passage.

line 134. *burned*: Dowden reads *burnt*.

line 136. *inhabited*: MWS reads *impelled*.

line 143. *what*: MWS reads *whose*.

line 146. ~~*tyranny*~~: MWS reads *violence*.

line 154. *Exasperated . . . unaware.* (line 172): the reference is to the Peasants' War (1522–1525) in Germany.

line 163. *if*: *f* obscured by hole in page caused by deteriorating paper.

line 170. *Negro*: written through *of*.

line 170. *a . . . Plantations*, (sic).

SC 546   then nor now nor ever ha left
or leave a path to freedom
but thro their own blood. &
the desolation of all except
                which is
180   freedom valuable or ⟨   ⟩able in
the world. This had place in
France & Germany. The con
test then waged under the
                        have seldom
names of religion, which were no
        been anything more the only
the popular & visible symbols

[LEAF 5, VERSO]
        which express
of the degree of power in some shape
190   or other aimed at by or other
asserted by one party & disclaimed
by the other, ended; & the result
is though partial & imperfect
is perhaps the most anima

-ting that the philanthropist
            in the history of man
can contemplate. The republics
            has been
of Holland which was so long
an armoury of the arrows of   200
learning by which superstition
has been wounded even to death
was established by this contest.
What though the name of Repub
-lic & by whom but by conscience
stricken tyrants could it be extin
guished, is no more. The Republics
of Switzerland derived from this
event their consolidation & their
union. From England then   210

[LEAF 6, RECTO]
first began to pass away the
stain of conquest. The unre Religious
The exposition of a certain portion

line 175. *nor*: *r* written through *w*.

line 180. *freedom valuable or* ⟨   ⟩*able in*: canceled with a thick, dark stroke; ⟨   ⟩*able* may possibly be *reasonable*.

line 186. *anything*: MWS, Rolleston, and Peck read *any*.

line 197. *The republics . . . is no more.* (line 207): Shelley was thinking not only of Spinoza's writings but also of the numerous publications by French *philosophes* that were published (or purported to be published) in Holland during the seventeenth and eighteenth centuries. The Dutch Republic, established by the Union of Utrecht (1579), endured until 1795, when the French revolutionary armies established the Batavian Republic, which gave way — after various transformations — to a kingdom under Louis Napoleon (1806–1810), became part of the French empire (1810–1814), and — after the Hundred Days — was joined with what is now Belgium in the Kingdom of the United Netherlands.

line 205. *conscience*: written through indecipherable letters.

line 206. Rough sketch of small tree in left margin extending from line 206 to line 208.

line 206. *could*: Rolleston reads *would*.

line 208. *this event*: the Reformation.

line 210. *From England . . . conquest.* (line 212): this statement, linking the Reformation with an English retreat from conquest, is comprehensible only in terms of Shelley's Eurocentric view of history. He is referring to the end of the English attempts to conquer France encompassed in the Hundred Years' War (1337–1453). Calais, the last English stronghold on the Continent, fell in 1558, just before England's great expansion into overseas conquest and involvement in the slave trade.

line 213. *exposition*: Rolleston reads *exposure*; MWS transcribed *exposition*, but Hogg changed the reading to *exposure*. Shelley uses *exposition* either in its primary sense of *expulsion* (*OED* 1) or to mean *exposure* (*OED* 2). See facsimile, page 1006.

Shelley, A Philosophical View of Reform   November 1819–?1820

SC 546

of religious imposture, drew with
it an enquiry into political
imposture, and was attended
with an extraordinary exertion
of the energies of intellectual power
Shakespeare & Lord Bacon & the
220 *great writers of the age of Eliza*
beth & James the 1ˢᵗ were at
once the ~~causes~~ effects of this

[SKETCH OF TENTS AND TREES ON
BOTTOM ONE-THIRD OF PAGE]

[LEAF 6, VERSO]
new spirit in men's minds, &
the causes of its more complete
developement. By rapid grada
-tion ~~thos the st chure~~ the nation
was conducted to the temporary
abolition of aristocracy &
episcopacy, & the mighty example
230 *which " in teaching nations*
how to live," England afforded
to the world of bringing to
public justice t one of those

chiefs of a conspirasy of
priveledged murderers & robbers
                    has been
whose impunity ⟨——⟩ the consecration
            Note   The
of crime. [Th ~~In the true~~ maxim
that criminals ~~deserve condem com~~   240
should be pitied & reformed, not
detested & punished alone affords
a source of   ]
After ~~a renewed defeat~~ the selfish
                    compromizing
& ~~temporizing~~ passions & interests
of men had inlisted themselves
to produce & establish the ~~event~~
counter revo

[LEAF 7, RECTO]
            of Charl⟨ ⟩ the II unequal   250
~~called~~ the Restoration, the combat
was renewed under the reign of
        his successor
~~James the 2ᵈ~~ & that compromise
between the unextinguishable spirit
of Liberty, & the ever watchful
spirit of fraud & tyranny, called
the Revolution, had place.... [~~This~~

line 215. *political*: MWS reads *religious*.

line 218. *power*: word runs off edge of page.

line 222. *this*: *s* written through *?se*; final letter heavily blotted.

line 225. *By rapid . . . crime.* (line 239): Shelley's judgment on the English Civil War and the execution of Charles I is especially significant in view of his later attempt to write a drama entitled *Charles the First*.

line 234. *conspirasy* (sic).

line 237. The strokes canceling lines 260–262 on leaf 7, recto, have blotted beneath lines 237–240 on the opposite page and look like underscores.

line 237. ⟨of⟩: probable reading; *f* does not appear to have a descender.

line 243. *a source of*: Mary Shelley fills the space after this phrase with *regret*.

line 245. *compromizing*: MWS reads *temporary*, Rolleston reads *temporizing*, and Peck reads *compromising*.

line 247. *inlisted*: contemporary alternate spelling.

line 250. *Charl⟨es⟩*: paper worn away.

line 250. *unequal*: heavy blot obscuring *e*; *l* runs off the edge of page.

line 258. *Revolution,*: comma may be semicolon. The reference is to the Glorious Revolution of 1688 that replaced James II with Mary and William III (of Orange).

SC 546

with
event ~~was correlative to a new~~
~~æra in the history of the progress~~
~~of man.~~—] ~~At th~~ on this occasion
Monarchy & Aristocracy & Episco
pacy ~~were indeed es thoug~~ were
at once established & limited by
    Unfortunately   no more
law– ~~What~~ they lost₍in extent
    than
of power, they gained in security

270 of possession. Meanwhile, those
~~who~~ by whom they were established
acknowledged & declared that it
~~was~~ the will of the People ~~from~~
~~who~~ was the source from which
    in that instance,
these powers derived the right to
subsist; A man has no right
to be a King or a Lord or a

[LEAF 7, VERSO]
Bishop but so long as it is
    &
280 for the benefit of the People ~~that~~
~~he should be so, & s impersonate~~
⟨ ⟩ and so long as the People judge
that it is for their benefit, that
he should impersonate that character.
The solemn establishment of this
    our
maxim, as the basis of Consti-
-tutional law, more than any
290 ~~desirable~~ beneficial and energetic

application of it to the circum-
-stances of this æra of its pro-
-mulgation, was the fruit of that
    vaunted event.
~~victory over a bigotted tyrant~~
    series of events
Correlative with this event in
    the commencement of
England, was a new epoch in
the history of the progress of   300
civilization & society.
    I am unwilling to attribute
any great share in the improvement
⟨ ⟩ being so intellectual   as man
⟨ ⟩ mankind to a circumstance

[LEAF 8, RECTO]
so entirely accidental < > mechanical
as the invention of printing. This was
one among a multitude of causes ra
diating to a single centre
~~Milton was~~ That superstition which has   310
disguised itself under the ~~appellation~~
    name
    system
of the ~~religion of~~ Jesus, ~~and had~~
~~already by the religious~~ subsisted
under all its forms, even where it
had been separated from those
things especially considered as abuses
by the multitude, in the shape
    an   320
of ~~many~~ intolerant & oppressive

line 265. Remainder of this page is heavily blotted and words are formed with heavy dark strokes.

line 272. it: here, as elsewhere, Shelley neglected to cancel a word when he changed the syntax of the sentence.

line 277. A: written through indecipherable letters.

line 293. that: at written through ?e.

line 295. bigotted (sic).

line 305. ⟨of⟩ mankind: the beginnings of both this line and the interlineation are heavily written over. There are some indecipherable strokes written through the m of mankind.

line 306. <&>: paper worn away.

line 313. system: the underscore is uncertain; Shelley may have meant to cancel this word.

line 316. where: MWS reads when.

Shelley, *A Philosophical View of Reform* November 1819–?1820

SC 546

~~Protes~~ Catholics massacred Protestants & Protes
hierarchies. ~~How~~ The new Testament
tants proscribed Catholics, & extermination was the
is in every ones' hand & the few
    sanction of each faith within the limits of the
who ever read ~~the~~ it with the
    power of its professors
simple sincerity of an unbiassed
330 judgement, may perceive how distinct
from the opinions of any of those
        established
professions themselves ~~Christians~~, were
the doctrines & the actions of
Jesus Christ. At the period of

[LEAF 8, VERSO]
the Reformation this test was applied
        formed
& this judgement ~~applied~~ of then
then existing hierarchy, & the
340 same compromise was then made
between the spirit of truth & the
spirit of imposture. After ~~the~~ a
        which ploughed up the area of the
~~bloody & desolating~~ struggle,
    human mind
as was made in the particular

instance of England between the
spirit of freedom & the spirit
of tyranny at that event called the
Revolution. In both instances   350
the maxims so solemnly recorded
~~were the~~ remains as trophies of our
the difficult & ~~partial~~ incomplete
victory planted on the enemies
land
~~soil~~. The will of the People to
change their goverment is an
acknowledged right in the Consti
-tion of England. The protesting
against ~~certain dogmas declared~~   360

[LEAF 9, RECTO]
~~as true &~~ with respect to whatever
~~dogmas relating to the connexion~~
~~of the invisible cause of the~~ man X
            which
religious dogmas∧present themselves
to his mind as false is the ina-
-lienable ~~of rig recorded right~~ inalienable
prerogative of every human being. ——
            was marked by the
This new epoch commencement ~~with~~ of   370

line 323. *hierarchies*.: Shelley neglected to change this word to the singular when he replaced *many* (line 321) with *an*, above. In most instances we do not comment on such oversights when they seem to be obvious.

line 328. *professors*: MWS reads *possessor*.

line 329. *unbiassed* (sic).

line 330. *distinct*: MWS reads *distant*.

line 332. *established*: Rolleston reads *orthodox*; Peck reads *establishers*.

line 338. *of*: written through *to*.

line 346. *in*: written through *on*.

line 349. *that*: altered from *the* or vice versa.

line 349. *called*: MWS reads *of*.

line 353. *the*: perhaps Shelley attempted to cancel this word.

line 354. *the enemies*: MWS reads *our enemies*.

line 358. *Constition* (sic).

line 363. *man X*: the *X* at the end of the line indicates the placement of lines 383–393.

line 367. *inalienable*: badly crowded at edge of page; almost illegible.

line 370. *This*: altered from *Those*.

line 370. *commencement*: altered from *commenced*.

SC 546

en deeper enquiries into the forms
of human nature, than are com-
-patible with an unreserved
      of those
belief in any ^popular mistakes
          faith
     systems of ~~belief~~ with respect
upon which popular ~~religions~~
    ⟨   ⟩ to the ~~mysterious cause~~ agencies of the

380   with all their superstructure of
     universe
political & religious tyranny are

⎧
⎩ X   Regular & graduated systems
of alternate slavery & tyranny
by which all except the
lowest & the largest class were
to be gainers in the materials
of subsistence & ostentation at

[LEAF 9, VERSO]
the expense of that class, the

390   means being fraud or force
were established in the shape
of feudal monarchies upon the
ruins of the

built. Lord Bacon, Spinosa,

        ~~Descartes~~
Hobbes, Bayle, Montaigne
in ~~omitting the Poets who~~
deig⟨   ⟩ ~~Laid the found anato~~
~~mized the nature of social man~~
⟨   ⟩ regulated the reasoning powers   400
         past
criticised the history, exposed the
         by illustrating their causes
~~past~~ errors, and anatomized the
    & their connexion
inmost nature, of social man.
~~Hume began to know~~ Then
~~followed Locke~~ with a less
interval of time than of genius,
followed Locke, ~~who by~~ and   410
the philosophers of his exact

[LEAF 10, RECTO]
and intelligible ~~school~~ but super
ficial school. Their illustrations
of some of the minor ~~propos~~ conse
quences of the ~~enclyclopædic~~ doc
-trines established by the sublime
           correct
genius of their predecessors, were
popular, simple & energetic. Above

line 371. *enquiries*: Shelley may have miswritten the word as *enquires*.

line 371. *forms*: Rolleston reads *point*.

line 379. *to the mysterious cause agencies of the*: MWS reads *to the wonders of the*; Rolleston and Peck read *to the cause and agencies of the*.

line 383. *Regular . . . ruins of the* (line 393): to be inserted at line 363; this is the core of a sentence beginning (line 359) *The protesting against* and concluding (lines 366–368) *is the inalienable prerogative of every human being*. One word — *were* in line 391 — must be deleted to correct the syntax. This placement has been missed by Rolleston and Peck, who treat the passage as an incomplete footnote; MWS omits the entire passage.

line 394. *Spinosa,*: Shelley's spelling of Spinoza's name was a current variant, reflecting Latin usage that altered z to s. See also line 506.

line 396. *Bayle,*: Rolleston reads *Boyle*. Pierre Bayle (1647–1706) was the author of the skeptical *Dictionnaire historique et critique* (1695–1697) that exerted a great influence on French thought in the eighteenth century, as well as direct influence on Shelley and Byron.

line 397. *the*: written through *those*.

line 398. *deig⟨ ⟩*: possible reading; may be two words.

line 401. *past*: written with same fine quill in which *past* was canceled in line 404.

line 415. *enclyclopædic* (sic).

Shelley, A Philosophical View of Reform   *November 1819–?1820*

SC 546

all they indicated inferences the
most incompatible with the popular
religions, & the established goverments
of Europe. [Philosophy went forth
as the pioneer into the enchanted
forest of the dæmons of worldly
power, as the pioneer of the
overgrowth of ages.] Hartley
                         Hartley
                    in a later age
430 *Berkeley & Hume following the*
traces of these inductions have
clearly established the certainty
of our ignorance with respect to

                        obscure
those great questions which under
the name of religious truths
have been the watchwords of con⟨   ⟩

[LEAF 10, VERSO]
and the symbols of unjust power
since ever since they were distorted
by the narrow passions of the   440
immediate followers of Jesus Christ
from these that meaning to which
philosophers are even now restoring
them.– The writers of the French
The modern writers of
Montesquieu, Sidney, Harrington,

line 423. [*Philosophy . . . overgrowth of ages.*] (line 427): Shelley evidently planned to remove this sentence from *A Philosophical View of Reform* when he included a similar sentence in his fragment "On Life," which he drafted in back of this notebook (see page 956). Clearly the essay "On Life," insofar as it is completed, was an outgrowth of this section of *A Philosophical View of Reform*. Just as obviously, Shelley had passed this point in sc 546 before drafting "On Life." I would guess that Shelley drafted "On Life" about the time he wrote and canceled *Before it c^d build it must destroy* (line 479), which also parallels a sentence in "On Life." The word *pioneer* (line 426) is used in its root military sense of a soldier who clears a road for the main army (*OED* 1).

line 423. *forth*: very cramped; Rolleston reads *now*.

line 426. *the*: written through *these*.

line 428. Shelley's grouping of David Hartley, M.D. (1705-1757), George Berkeley, Bishop of Cloyne (1685-1753), and David Hume (1711-1776) is historically more coherent than the modern grouping of John Locke (1632-1704), Berkeley, and Hume. Shelley — like Godwin, Wordsworth, and Coleridge of the earlier generation — read Hartley's *Observations on Man, His Frame, His Duty, and His Expectations* (1749). Shelley's annotated copy of the fifth edition of Part One (1810) is in The Carl H. Pforzheimer Library.

line 437. *con⟨ ⟩*: MWS reads *contest*; Rolleston and Peck expand this to read *contention*.

line 439. *ever*: heavy blot obscures reading.

line 446. Shelley's grouping of Charles Louis de Secondat, Baron de la Brède et de Montesquieu (1689-1755), Algernon Sidney (1622-1683), and James Harrington (1611-1677) was apparently a false start of a section that would have traced political theories of the seventeenth and early eighteenth centuries as lines 394-444 had outlined the epistemological inquiries from Bacon to Hume. Montesquieu's great work *L'Esprit des lois* (1748) was the most influential political study of its time. Sidney's posthumous *Discourses concerning Government* (1698) was reprinted throughout the eighteenth century. Harrington's *The Common-wealth of Oceana* (1656), which Hume called the "only valuable model of a commonwealth," depicts England as an aristocratic republic in which agrarian reform limits the size of landed estates, and all the interests of the state are represented in a balance of power. In Shelley's eventual development of this section (lines 496-531 below), Harrington's name is omitted, perhaps because his work belongs to creative Utopian literature as much as to political theorizing.

SC 546 ~~Montesquieu, and~~ A crowd of writers
in France seized upon the most
popular topics of these doctrines,
450   developing
and ~~deducing the following~~ those
                 particular ~~doctrines~~ portions
~~train of peculiar inferences~~ of the
new philosophy which conducted
to inferences at war with the
dreadful oppressions under which
              country
that ~~nation~~ groaned, made familiar
to mankind the falshood of the
460   mediators
pretences of thier religious & political
oppressors. Considered as philosophers
                 have consisted
their error seems to ~~arise~~ chiefly
              ⟨ ⟩
from a limitedness of view; they

[LEAF II, RECTO]
told the truth, but not the whole
              might have
truth. This arisen from the terrible
470 sufferings of their countrymen inciting
them rather to apply a portion of

what had already been discovered to
to their immediate relief, than to
              ⟨ ⟩ ⟨   ⟩
pursue the abstractions of thought,
~~for~~ as the great philosophers who
preceded them had done, for the
sake of a future & more universal
advantage. ~~Before it c^d build it must de=~~
                                    └~~stroy~~
                 that   480
       Meanwhile Whilst ~~mental~~ philoso
              burying itself in the obscure parts of
-phy which‸regards the truth & falshood
our nature
of dogmas relating to the cause
of the universe, & the nature &
              relation
manner of man's ~~connexion~~ with
it, was thus stripping Power of its
darkest mask, Political philosophy   490
or that which considers the relations
of Man as a social being, was assuming
a precise form. This philosophy
indeed sprang from & maintained
[LEAF II, VERSO]
a connexion with that other, as its

line 447. *A*: written through *t*.

line 449. *topics*: Peck reads *portions*, omitting all other words between *popular . . . of the* (line 453).

line 458. *that*: written through *their*.

line 459. *falshood*: variant spelling common in Shelley's day and his preferred form; see also line 483.

line 460. *mediators*: Rolleston reads *mediaeval*.

line 466. *limitedness*: Rolleston reads *limitation*.

line 469. *This*: altered from *They*.

line 469. *arisen*: altered from *arose*.

line 470. *inciting*: middle letters of word very cramped; MWS, Rolleston, and Peck all read *inviting*; Dowden reads *inciting*.

line 472. *to to* (sic).

line 474. ⟨*ele*⟩ ⟨*entary*⟩: *elementary* would fit the context; Rolleston and Peck read *one interest*; MWS and Dowden omit the word(s).

line 479. *Before . . . destroy*: see first Textual Note to line 423.

line 482. *burying*: MWS reads *busying*.

line 493. *This*: written through *these*.

SC 546   parent. *What would* ~~Montesquieu &~~
Swift & Bolingbroke & Sidney
& ~~Montesquieu~~ *& Locke & Montes*

or
500   *quieu &* ⟨————⟩, *& even Rousseau*
political philosophers
not to speak of ~~Godwin~~, *the writers*
of our own age Godwin & Bentham
have been but for Lord Bacon

other
Montaigne & Spinosa, & the great
luminaries
~~writers~~ *of the preceding epoch? Some*
-thing excellent & eminent no doubt
510   *the least of these,* ~~but would have been~~
but some thing different from & inferior
to what they are. ~~The A~~ *A series*
with more or less success
of these writers illustrated the principles
of human nature as applied to man
in political society. A thirst for
accommodating the existing ~~insti~~
according
~~tutions of which govern~~ *forms* ~~into~~
520   are found   to
which mankind ~~are~~ *divided* ~~according~~

to
those ~~doctrines~~ *rules of freedom &*
were thus
of ~~co~~ *equality which have been*

[LEAF 12, RECTO]
discovered as being the elementary
principles according to which
the happiness resulting from the

social union ought to be produced
& distributed, was kindled by these   530
enquiries. ~~Europe exhibited a~~
~~frightful picture of successful in-~~
this
~~justice.~~ *Contemporary with* ~~these~~
condition of the intell
~~enquirers~~ *all the powers of man*
seemed, though in most cases under
forms highly unauspicious, to develop
themselves with uncommon energy.
~~All~~ *the mechanical sciences, &*   540
~~those which~~ *attained to a degree*
of perfection which though obscurely
foreseen by Lord Bacon it had
been accounted madness to have
prophesied in a preceding age. Com-
-merce was pursued with a perpetu
-ally increasing vigour, & the
same area of the Earth was perpe
compelled
-tually ~~made~~ *to furnish more &*   550
more subsistence. The means & sources
21

[LEAF 12, VERSO]
together
of knowledge were thus increased
with knowledge itself, & the instru
-ments of knowledge. The benefit of
this increase of the powers of man,
became in consequence of the
~~unjust and~~ *inartificial forms into*

line 496. Though Shelley had earlier begun this section (line 446) with an apparent intention of paralleling the development of "mental philosophy" with that of "Political philosophy," he decided to subordinate the latter, as he was to do also in his *Defence of Poetry* — though there with a different emphasis and a different list of key writers in each field. For Montesquieu, Sidney, and Locke, see notes above. Henry St. John, Viscount Bolingbroke (1678–1751), was the Tory politician whose philosophical ideas were versified by his friend Pope in *An Essay on Man*.

line 500. ⟨~~Voltaire~~⟩,: possible reading.

line 501. *political*: MWS reads *abstract*.

line 535. *intell*: MWS reads *intellectual exertion*; Rolleston and Peck read *intellect*.

line 536. *man*: Rolleston reads *mankind*.

line 552. *21*: possibly in Shelley's hand; in pencil at bottom of page.

SC 546

      continues to be
which society *is* distributed, an *ins*
             evil
trument of his additional ~~misery~~.
The capabilities of happiness were
increased & applied to the augmentation
            European
of misery. Modern society is thus
         assumed
    engine   *to be*

570   a ~~machine~~ ~~inves~~ ~~designed~~ for useful
purposes, whose ~~powers~~ force is
by a a system of subtle mechanism
           pitch
augmented to the highest, but
which instead of grinding corn
    water
or raising acts against itself &
                  wearing
~~destroys~~ ~~the~~ is perpetually w⟨———⟩ *grind-*
                     [*ing*

580   & breaking to pieces
away the wheels of which it is composed.
   The result of the labours of the
political philosophers has been the
establishment of the principle

[LEAF 13, RECTO]
of Utility as the substance & liberty

      as   *according to which the concerns*
& equality the forms of human
human life ought to be administered
~~society~~. By this test ~~relig~~ ~~legislation,~~
~~morality~~ the various institutions   590
       political ~~institutions~~ *society*
regulating ~~human~~ ~~society~~ have been
tried, and as the undigested growth
of the private passions errors &
interests of ~~un~~ barbarians and oppressors
have been condemned. And many
new theories more or less perfect
~~but all as being the result of~~
~~dispassionate have~~ but all superior
to the mass of evil which they   600
would supplant, have been given
to the world. ~~The one~~
   The system of Government in the
United States of America was the
first practical illustration of the
new philosophy. Sufficiently remote,
it will be confessed, from the accur
rancy of ideal excellence is that
representative ~~govern~~ system ~~of~~
which will soon cover the extent   610

[LEAF 13, VERSO]
of that vast Continent. But it is

line 560. *continues to be*: Rolleston reads *was*; Peck reads *came to be*.

line 561. *society*: Rolleston reads *mankind*.

line 568. *assumed to be*: probable reading. MWS omits the phrase, using instead the canceled ~~designed~~.

line 572. *a a* (sic).

line 572. *subtle*: MWS reads *subtlest*.

line 579. w⟨*orn*⟩: probable reading.

line 582. *The result . . . to the world.* (line 602): Shelley's conception of political utilitarianism was consonant with his skeptical epistemology; since man could not know an absolute standard of values, the only viable solution was to take the "happiness" of the greatest number of men as a working normative value. Shelley's political utilitarianism can be traced to such works as Hume's *Enquiry concerning the Principles of Morals* (1751), Bentham's *Introduction to the Principles of Morals and Legislation* (1789), and, most significantly, Godwin's *Political Justice* (1793), where Godwin argues for the ultimate utilitarianism of having the less valuable members of society sacrifice themselves for the more valuable.

line 588. *life*: replaced ~~society~~ (line 589) at the time of original composition; the rest of lines 586 and 588 were inserted later with a sharper quill, rendering superfluous *human* in line 587.

line 607. *accurrancy* (sic).

Shelley, A Philosophical View of Reform   November 1819–?1820

SC 546

scarcely less remote from the insolent
& ~~corrupting~~ contaminating tyrannies
           under
~~under whatever name,~~ ˄which with
         with
~~the exception~~ Some limitation of these
terms as regards England, Europe
groaned at the period of the successful

620   rebellion of America. ~~America has
neither kings nor to nobles nor priests~~
America holds forth the victorious
example of an immensely populous,
& as far as the external arts of
life are concerned a highly civilized
community administered according
to republican forms. It has no
King, that is it has no officer to
whom wealth & from whom corruption

630   hereditary oligarchy
flows. It has no ~~aristocracy,~~
that is ~~a set of men priveledged~~
       it ~~no~~ is it acknowledges no
order of men priveledged to cheat &
~~insu the r~~ & insult the rest of the

[LEAF 14, RECTO]

members of the state, & who inherit
    a
the right of legislating & judging
which the principles of human nature

640   compel them to exercise to their own
           detriment
profit & to the ~~prejudice~~ of those
           peculiar
not included within their ~~own~~ class.

It has no established Church, that
   it has
is no system of opinions respecting
the abstrusest questions ~~belonging
to h~~ which can be topics of human
thought, founded in an age of   650
error & fanaticism, and opposed
by law to all other opinions, &
defended by prosecutions ~~which induce captivity~~ ( )
sanctioned by enormous bounties
       it   idle priests
given to ~~that order of pestilential~~
    forced thro the unwilling hands of the
~~pr men whose profession is necess
cultivators~~ those who have an interest in the culti
~~-arily ( ) idleness~~ out of the hard   660
    vation & improvement of the soil
earnings of the labouring poor.
~~It is lastly~~ It has no false
representation, but a true repre
sentation whose consequences are
~~captivity and dungeons~~ captivity confis
cation infamy & ruin)

[LEAF 14, VERSO]

~~That is the executive~~ The will of
   many   represented by the few
the ~~people~~ is ~~represented in the~~   670
~~directly represented~~ in the assemblies
of legislation, & by the officers of
the executive entrusted with the
administration of the executive power,
almost as directly as the will
of one person can be represented
by the will of another. ~~The incal~~

line 654. *bounties*: MWS reads *contributions*; Rolleston reads *grants*.

line 655. The interlineations and cancellations in lines 655–661 were first done in pencil and then revised in ink. Most of the penciled words are illegible, and those that can be read (e.g., *Priests* and *idle*) seem to have been replaced by the inked interlineations.

line 657. *thro*: Rolleston reads *from*.

line 663. *It*: *I* written through *i*. The pronoun's antecedent is *America* (line 622).

line 665. *whose . . . ruin* (line 667): this clause, which Shelley marked off from what immediately precedes and follows, seems meant to follow *soil* in line 661. The ultimate antecedent of *whose* is *Church* in line 645.

SC 546 *culab* [*This is not the place for*
dilating upon the inexpressible
680 *advantages, (if such advantages*
require any manifestation) of
a self governing Society, or one
which in any approaches it
in the degree of the Republic of
the United States.] *Lastly*
it has an institution by which
it is honourably distinguished
from all other goverment which
ever existed. It acknowledges

[LEAF 15, RECTO]

690 *constitutionally acknowledges the*
progress of human improvement,
and is framed under the limitation
of the probability of improvement
new new vi more simple views
of political science being rendered
         human life
applicable to their work. There
is a law by which the Consti-
-tion is revised reserved for revision
700   *set of*
every ten years. Every other legis
legislator or institutor men who
   have   *office*
assumed the ⟨————⟩ *of legislating*
& framing institutions for future
ages, with far less right to such
an assumption than the founder

of the Am. Rep. assumed to them
-selves the idea that their work
was the wisest & the best that   710
could possibly have been produced,
: these illustrious men looked upon

[LEAF 15, VERSO]

       their species   28
the past history of man, & saw that
it was the history of his mistakes,
and his sufferings arising from his
mistakes, they observed the superiority
of their own work to all the works
which had preceded it, & they judged
it probable that in other political   720
institutions would be discovered bearing
the same relation to those which
they had established, which they
bear to those which have preceded
them. They provided therefore for
the application of these contingent
discoveries to the social state
without the violence & misery atten
dant upon such change in less
modest & more imperfect govern-   730
-ments. The United States, affords
        would   *been*
the example, as we should have expected
from theoretical deductions affords the
              an
example of a free happy s com
-pared with the old goverments of

line 678. [*This is not . . . States.*] (line 685): this sentence is bracketed for deletion.

line 697. *There is a law . . . every ten years.* (line 701): Shelley is probably conflating — perhaps misled by a misinformed writer on America — the provision for constitutional amendment (Article V) with the provision for reapportionment of the House of Representatives after each decennial census (Article I, Section 2, Part 3).

line 698. *Constition* (sic).

line 701. *ten*: MWS reads *two*.

line 704. ⟨*founder*⟩: possible reading.

line 704. *legislating*: Rolleston and Peck read *legislation*.

line 707. *founder*: apparently singular, though the plural would seem to be required.

line 720. *probable*: Rolleston reads *possible*.

line 721. *bearing*: Rolleston reads *having*.

Shelley, *A Philosophical View of Reform*   November 1819–?1820

SC 546   [LEAF 16, RECTO]

740

750

760

Europe & Asia of a free happy & strong
people. Nor let it be said that they
owe this superiority rather to their
situation than to their goverment. Give
them a King, & let that King waste in
luxury riot & bribery the same sum
~~with~~ which now serves for the entire
expenses of ~~it~~ their goverment. Give them
an aristocracy & let that aristocracy
legislate for the people. Give them
a priesthood, & let them ~~pay a tenth
of~~ bribe with a tenth of the produce
of the soil, a certain set of men to say
a certain set of words. ~~Give them as~~
        if you give them these things
~~you must, a certain st great standing
army to cut down the people if they~~
                        the larger
~~murmur.~~ ~~Give~~ Pledge ~~one~~ portion of
them by financial subterfuges
to pay the half of their property or

————— *Note* —————

Its error consists not in the not represen-
-ting the will of the People as it is, but
in not providing for the full develope-
-ment, ~~and the most~~ the most salutory
condition of that will. For two conditions

[LEAF 16, VERSO]
                theoretically
are necessary to a perfect goverment, &
                        ⌊one

                adequately
of these alone is fulfilled by the most
most perfect of ~~practically~~ goverment
the Republic of the United States. To   770
represent the will of the People as it
is. To provide that that will should
be as wise and just as possible. To
a certain extent the mere representation
        the   *will*
of public produces in itself a wholesome
condition of it, and in this extent
America fulfills ~~the~~ imperfectly &
indirectly the last & most important
condition of perfect government.   780

earnings to another portion, & let the
                        enjoy
proportion of those who ~~eat~~ the
fruits of the toil of other without toiling
themselves, be three instead of one
Give them, as you must if you give
them these things a great standing
army to cut down the people if they
murmur. ~~If any~~ ~~Whatever American~~
If ~~any~~ any American should see these   790
words, his blood would run cold at
                        a change
the imagination of such. He well

[LEAF 17, RECTO]
knows that the prosperity & happiness
of the United States, ~~would~~ if subjected
to such institutions, be ~~an~~ no more.

line 756. *portion*: altered from *part* with *ion* cramped in. Peck reads *part*.

line 759. The note (lines 760–780) should probably be keyed to *free happy & strong people* (lines 738–739).

line 763. *the*: written through *sa*.

line 763. *salutory* (sic).

line 768. *most most* (sic).

line 773. *To*: written through *In* or vice versa.

line 786. *Give them . . . no more.* (line 796): both Rolleston and Peck place this passage after the section extending from lines 797 through 812. MWS moves to the end of the sequence only two sentences: *If any American . . . no more.* (lines 790–796).

SC 546

Give them a Court of Chancery, & let
 & the interests in
the property, the liberty, ~~the possession~~
800   *concerns of life*
of the dearest ~~interests~~, the exercise
 of a social being
of the most sacred rights depend upon
 one of the most servile
the will of ~~th~~ a creature of the kingly
~~power which~~ & oligarchical ~~power~~
~~which to which~~ & priestly power
to which every man, in proportion as
he is of a ~~just~~ enquiring & ~~honourable~~
810 *philosophical mind, & of an sincere &*
honourable disposition is a natural
& necessary ~~enemy~~.
The just & successful Revolt of America,
~~& the establishment of its govern~~
ment corresponded with a state of public
opinion in Europe of which it was
 first
~~one of the earliest~~ results. The
 31
820 *French Revolution was the second*
The oppressors of mankind had had

[LEAF 17, VERSO]
enjoyed (O that we c^d say suffered)   *32*
a long & an undisturbed reign in France,
and to ~~pining~~ the pining famine,
the ~~naked &~~ shelterless destitution of
the inhabitants of that country,
had been added, & heaped up, insult

harder to endure than misery. For
the feudal system, (the immediate
causes & conditions of its institution   830
having becomes obliterated,) had degener-
ated into an instrument of not
only of oppression but of contumely;
and both were unsparingly inflic
-ted. ~~A numerous wealthy proud~~
 outraged
~~hierarchy insulted the common sense~~
~~of men. And,~~ blind in the possession
 strength
~~& exercise~~ of ~~power~~, drunken as with   840
the intoxication of ancestral greatness
the rulers percieved not that encrease
 subjects
of knowledge in their ~~people~~ which
 its exercise insecure.
made ~~their situation unsafe.~~ They called
soldiers to hew down the people when
their power was already past. They
[LEAF 18, RECTO]
tyrants were as usual the aggressors
 Then
~~And the And a scene of blo And~~   850
the oppressed having ~~the power to avenge~~
~~their injuries, being~~ having been rendered
brutal, ignorant, servile, and bloody,
 long
by slavery, having ~~been~~ had the
 in them
~~thirst of~~ intellectual thirst excited
by the progress of civilization, satiated

line 800. *concerns*: MWS reads *connexions*. The allusion is, of course, to the Chancery decision that deprived Shelley of the care of Ianthe and Charles Shelley; Mary Shelley's placement of this sentence as the climax of the rhetorical sequence of sentences beginning *Give them* indicates that she knew Shelley's feelings on this question to be at least as strong as his reaction to Peterloo, alluded to in lines 786–789.

line 805. *creature*: Rolleston reads *creations*.

line 819. *31*: in pencil.

line 827. *added,*: final *d* written through indecipherable letter.

line 828. *endure*: Rolleston reads *bear*.

line 842. *encrease*: alternative contemporary spelling.

SC 546

from fountains of literature poisoned
by the spirit & the form of monarchy
arose & took a dreadful revenge
on their oppressors. Their desire to
   wreak   to this extent
take this revenge, in itself a mis
take, a crime, a calamity, arose
from the same source as their other
                              affords
miseries & errors, & was an addition

870 *-al proof of the necessity of that*
long delayed change which it
accompanied & disgraced. If a
Revo just & necessary revolution
      could have
can been accomplished with as
little expense of happiness & order
in a country governed by despo
-tic as one governed by free

[LEAF 18, VERSO]
      equal
880 *laws, liberty & justice would lose*
their chief recommendations, & tyranny
      be divested of
its most odious revolting & terrific
attributes. Tyranny fortifies itself
with the wrecks Tyranny entrenches
itself within the existing interests

of that great mass   of the most refined
within the peace of domestic happiness
of the best & citizens of th a nation
   〈   〉   890
and says If you dare trample
upon these, be free. The world If
Though this terrible condition shall
not be evaded, the world is no longer
in a temper to decline the challenge.

The French were what their literature
   (excluding Montaigne & Rousseau,) & some
is weak, superficial, vain, with
   few leaders of the
little little imagination, & with   900
passions as well as judgements
cleaving to the external forms
of things. But they felt misery
& insult Not that are physi or
                    the inhabitants of the nations
ganically different from other men
who have become
at least as or rather not that

[LEAF 19, RECTO]
their organical differences whatever
they may amount to incapacite them   910
from the exertion attainment of
arriving at the exercise of the highest

line 860. *fountains . . . monarchy* (line 861): Shelley shared the contemporary English prejudice against French literature, often commenting on its debased qualities. The authors he most commonly excepts from these adverse generalizations are Rousseau, Montaigne, and Montesquieu (see line 897). In his mature years, he occasionally speaks well of Voltaire (but not of the other *philosophes*) but he does not mention Rabelais, Racine, Corneille, Boileau, Molière, Fénelon, Le Sage, Prévost, Saint-Pierre, Barthélemy — all of whom Shelley certainly read and whom he must here be classifying as more or less poisoned writers.

line 872. *disgraced.*: MWS places lines 896–923 (*The French were . . . in man*) immediately after *disgraced* (though she has failed to transcribe the unfinished interlineation *the inhabitants . . . become*, lines 905, 907). Lines 872–895 (*If a . . . decline the challenge.*) then follow. Rolleston and Peck retain the notebook order without rearrangement. I should think that Mary Shelley's decision was the better one in this case.

line 887. *of the most refined*: added later with a sharper quill.

line 897. (*excluding*: Rolleston reads *excepting*.

line 904. *Not that are*: *they* accidentally omitted.

line 910. *incapacite* (sic): for *incapacitate*.

SC 546

powers to be attained by man. Their
institutions made them what they were.
Slavery & superstition, contumalely &
the tame endurance of contumely, and the
habits engendered from generation to
generation out of this transmitted

920   inheritance of wrong ~~made them what~~ *created this thing*
which has extinguished
what has been called the likeness of God
~~which~~
~~they were.~~ /*in man.–* The Revolution in France
overthrew the hierarchy the aris
tocracy & the monarchy, & the
whole of that peculiarly insolent &
oppressive system on which they were
based. But as it only partially

930   extinguished those passions which
are the spirit of these forms a
reaction took place, which has
restored in a certain limited
degree the old system. In a degree

[LEAF 19, VERSO]

36

indeed exceedingly limited, & stript
its
of all ~~their~~ antient terrors; ~~& with~~
the lion

940   of the Monarchy of France with his

teeth drawn & his claws pared,
now
sits maintaining the formal ~~state~~
likeness
a
of most imperfect & insecure dominion.
The usurpation of Bonaparte, and
then the Restoration of the Bourbons
were the shapes in which this reaction
clothed itself and the heart of   950
every ~~lover of f~~ lover of liberty was
as with palsy
struck ~~cold~~ by the succession of
these events. [~~But though more was~~
~~desired than could be obtained,~~ ~~But~~
~~whilst the~~ But ~~the good~~ reversing
the proverbial expression of Shakes
it may be
peare, the ~~ill which~~ good which
the Revolutionists did lives after them   960
their "ills are interred with their bones"
~~But~~ But, the ~~pro~~ military project
of   goverment of the great tyrant
having failed, and their being

[LEAF 20, RECTO]

even no attempt ~~to set up the~~ and
if there were any attempt there being
not the remotest possibility of reestablis-
-hing the enormous system of tyranny

line 913. *to be attained by*: MWS reads *attributed to.*

line 915. *contumalely* (sic).

line 921. *which . . . in man.–* (line 923): late addition (in sharpened quill), partly written over drawn line. See note to line 872, above.

line 938. *antient*: a characteristic contemporary spelling and Shelley's usual one.

line 939. *lion*: Rolleston and Peck read *hope.*

line 940. *his*: altered from *this.*

line 942. *now sits*: MWS reads [   ] *its*; Peck reads *was its.*

line 944. *likeness*: MWS reads *shape*; Rolleston reads *witness.*

line 947. Shelley began writing this line with a newly sharpened quill, probably after reading over and correcting the previous pages.

line 952. *as with palsy*: added later with a duller quill.

line 964. *their* (sic): for *there.*

Shelley, A Philosophical View of Reform   November 1819–?1820

SC 546

abolished by the Revolution, France
is as it were regenerated. It's ~~has~~
~~a goverment~~ legislative assemblies
are in a certain limited degree representa-
                         will
-tions of the popular, & the executive
power is ~~hemmed~~ hemmed in by jealous
laws. France ~~in this respect~~
                      occupies in this
respect the same situation as was
occupied by ~~Char~~ England at the

980 *restoration of Charles the 2ᵈ. It has*
undergone a revolution, (~~how~~ unlike
in in the violence & calamities which
attended it, because unlike in the
abuses which it was excited to
put down) which may be paralled
~~With what our court writers~~ with
that in our own country which
ended in the death of Charles the
           The Authors of

990 *1ˢᵗ. Both revolutions proposed*

[LEAF 20, VERSO]

a great ~~& glorious object~~ er & more
glorious object than the degraded
passions of their countrymen permitted
them to attain. But in both cases
abuses were abolished which never since
have dared to shew their face. There
remains in the natural order of
human things that ~~France should~~
the tyranny & perfidy of the reigns

of ~~Jam~~ Charles the 2ᵈ & James the   1000
     (for these were less the result of the disposition
2ᵈ ~~under~~ perhaps under a
     of particular men, than the vices ~~engendered in~~
milder form & within a shorter
     which would have been engendered in any but an
period should produce the institution
     extraordinary man, by the natural necessities of
of a government in France which
     their situation)
may bear the same relation to   1010
the state of political knowledge exis
ting at the present day, as the
Revolution under William the 3ᵈ
bore to the state of pol. knowledge
existing at that period
     Germany, which is, among the

[LEAF 21, RECTO]

great nations of Europe, one of
the latest civilized, with the exception
of Russia, ~~which is~~ is rising
with the fervour of a vigorous   1020
youth, to the assertion of those
          for
rights ~~of~~ which it has that
     desire arising from   surest
knowledge ~~which is~~ the pledge
of victory. The deep passion &
          bold
the ~~profound~~ & Æschylean vigour
of the imagery of their poetry,
the enthusiasm however distorted   1030
     the flexibility & comprehensiveness of
of their religious ~~sentiment~~ &

line 970. *It's*: *'s* added after the following phrase was canceled. The incorrect use of an apostrophe in the possessive form of pronouns was common during Shelley's time even in published writings. See, for example, Hunt's use of it in sc 550.

line 975. *hemmed*: Shelley seems to have missed a loop in the second *m*.

line 985. *paralled* (sic).

line 991. *er*: after canceling *~~& glorious object~~*, Shelley wrote *er* to change *great* to the comparative degree (see facsimile, page 1006).

line 1001. (*for these . . . situation*) (line 1009): this parenthetical interlineation, though written late, should be inserted after *James the 2ᵈ* (line 1000).

line 1007. *necessities*: MWS reads *result*.

line 1031. *flexibility*: Rolleston reads *purity, truth*.

SC 546

their language which is a many sided mirror
political sentiments their severe
                    of ever changing thought
bold & liberal spirit of critisis
m, their subtle and deep philos
            mingling fervid intuitions into truth with
ophy however erroneous & illogical
1040   *obscure errors*
(for the period of just distinction
of is yet to come;) & their taste
& power in the plastic arts
prove that they are a great
People. And every great peop

[LEAF 21, VERSO]

nation either has or wa is or will
be free. The panic stricken ty
rants of that great country
promised to their subjects that
1050 *their governments should be*
administered according to repub

lican forms, they retaining
merely the right of hereditary chief
magistracy in their families.
This promise, made in danger
                dream that they can
the oppressors would have break
in Security. And every thing
                    wears
in consequence bears in Germany   1060
the aspect of revolution m rapidly
maturing revolution.
            Spain In Spain & in the depen-
-dencies of Spain, good & evil
            in the forms of Despair & Tyranny
are struggling foot to foot, and
an expence of bloo the but the
Victory is A traitorous That

[LEAF 22, RECTO]
great   22
glorious people has been delivered   1070

line 1033. *language*: Mary Shelley omitted this word, which was filled in later in MWS, probably by Hogg.

line 1034. *severe*: Rolleston reads *sincere*.

line 1035. *of ever*: MWS reads *of the ever*.

line 1036. *critisism*, (sic): note that in this and other rough-draft notebooks, Shelley splits words between two lines without regard for syllabic divisions (see facsimile, page 1007).

line 1045. *peop*: Shelley apparently had written this much of the word when he noticed that he had used *People* four words before and, without canceling the fragment, turned the leaf to write *nation*.

line 1047. Shelley alludes to such events as the "Appeal to my People" (*Aufruf an mein Volk*) that Frederick William III, King of Prussia, issued from Breslau, March 17, 1813. The *Annual Register* for 1813 contains English translations of the texts of similar appeals by King Louis XVIII to the people of France, February 1, 1813, inspired by news of Napoleon's disastrous retreat from Moscow; by King Frederick Augustus of Saxony, an ally of Napoleon, February 23, 1813, on his retreat from Dresden in the face of the advance of Russian armies; as well as the translation of a Manifesto by Francis I, Emperor of Austria, explaining why his people should support him against Napoleon; one by Frederick VI, King of Denmark, calling on his people for support against Sweden (which had joined Russia and the Allies in a treaty against Napoleon); even a "Proclamation addressed to the Hanoverians" (also subjects of the British crown), congratulating the Germans that they were no longer "groaning under the yoke of foreign rulers" (the French and Napoleon), but were "once more blessed by the paternal government of native princes." (This last was issued on behalf of the "Privy Counsellors of the King of Great Britain, appointed to the Electoral Ministry of Brunswick-Lunebourg.")

line 1066. *foot to foot,*: Mary Shelley wrote *fast to fast*, above which Hogg wrote *face   face*; Rolleston reads *face to face*.

line 1067. *expence*: alternate spelling listed in *OED*. See also line 2134.

line 1070. *has*: altered from *have*.

Shelley, A Philosophical View of Reform   *November 1819–?1820*

SC 546

bound hand & foot to be trampled
upon & insulted by a traitorous
                    a wretch
& sanguinary tyrant, who makes
credible all that might have been
doubted in the history of Nero,
Christiern, Muley Ismael or
Ezzelin—   The persons who have
thus delivered them ~~have~~ were that

1080 *hypocritical knot of conspiring*
tyrants, who proceeded upon the
credit they gained by putting down
the only tyrant among them who
                    not
was the ~~least of a~~ hypocrite, to

undertake the administration of
        arrondisements
those ~~systems~~ of consecrated
        injustice &
violence which they deliver to   1090
those who ~~most~~ the nearest
resemble them, under the name
of the " Kingdoms of the earth"——
                              41
        ~~Every patriot & philosopher~~

[LEAF 22, VERSO]
              42
This action signed a sentence of
death confiscation exile or
captivity against every philoso
pher & patriot in Spain. The   1100

line 1073. *wretch*: Rolleston reads *monster*.

line 1076. *Nero,*: comma added in pencil.

line 1077. *Christiern,*: *C* written through *M*. Christiern, or King Christian II of Denmark and Norway (1481–1559), was surnamed "the Cruel"; he conquered Sweden in 1520 and put to death the Swedish nationalists ("the Stockholm Blood-Bath"). Driven out of Sweden (1521) and deposed in Denmark (1523), he was finally imprisoned (1532) after he attempted to seize Norway. Muley Ismael (Moulay Ismail), "the Bloodthirsty," Emperor of Morocco from 1672 to 1727, tortured one of his sons to death and subdued his people with a bodyguard of elite Negro slaves, similar to the Janissaries of the Turkish empire. Ezzelino (or Eccelino) da Romano (1194–1259), "the Tyrant," son-in-law and vicar of the Holy Roman Emperor Frederick II, led the Ghibelline faction in Lombardy as lord of Verona, Vicenza, and Padua. His cruelty was proverbial; according to Sismondi, "Eccelino developed a thirst for blood and a lust of cruelty which seized every excuse for its gratification, and did not spare young or old, or even his own blood-relations; and he made his name an execration and an astonishment to the nations." In the *Inferno*, Dante sees Ezzelino in the Seventh Circle, where those punished for committing violence against others are immersed in a river of blood.

line 1079. *that*: altered from *those*.

line 1081. *the*: altered from *their*.

line 1083. *the*: written through *on*.

line 1083. *only tyrant . . . hypocrite*, (line 1085): Napoleon.

line 1087. *arrondisements* (sic): for *arrondissements*; here Shelley uses the word as a synonym of regions or provinces in a metaphorical phrase.

line 1088. *consecrated*: altered from *consecration*.

line 1093. *" Kingdoms of the earth"——*: Shelley draws upon all the negative associations from the story of Jesus' rejection of the temptation to inherit the "Kingdoms," as told both in the New Testament and in *Paradise Regained*.

line 1094. *41*: in pencil, probably in Shelley's hand.

line 1100. *The*: *e* written through *is*.

[983]

SC 546

Ferdinand, he
~~execrable~~ tyrant ~~allied himself~~
whose name is changed into a proverb
~~to the priests & the military~~
of execration
~~chiefs who by in and rendered~~
~~himself by intimidation &~~
~~imposture absolute master of a~~
all
1110   found natural allies in the
a few of the most dishonourable
priests & military chiefs of that
devoted country. And the conse
quences of military despotism,
of
and the black, stagnant,
arising from
~~wicked~~ venemous hatred &
envy &
1120   ~~jealousy of all mankind which~~
priests in common with eunuchs
seek every opportunity to wreak
upon the portion of ~~the~~ mankind
exempt
~~free~~ from their own unmanly

[LEAF 23, RECTO]
disqualifications
~~deprivations~~, is slavery. And
what is slavery . . . in its mildest
form hideous, & so long as one
in its victims   1130
amiable or great attribute survives,
rankling & intolerable, but in
exhibits itself
its darkest shape, it is ~~as now~~
in Spain, ~~insecurity of property,~~
~~prostration of conscience & of~~
~~understanding, no license to think~~
~~or write or speak torture~~ it is
the presence of all, & more than all the
evils   1140
for the sake of an exemption from
mighty
which, mankind submit to the ~~great~~
calamity   a system of
~~evils~~ of govermenent. It is ʌinsecurity
of
of property & of person, ~~its is~~ prostra
-tion of conscience & understanding,

line 1101. In 1808 the Spanish people had rejoiced when King Ferdinand VII had assumed the throne upon the abdication of his father, Charles IV, whose wife, Maria Louisa of Parma, and her favorite, Manuel de Godoy (called "Prince of the Peace"), had been immensely unpopular. But when Ferdinand was restored in 1814 after the fall of Napoleon, he so abused his power that by 1818 the liberals were even talking of recalling Charles IV (who died at Rome, however, on January 20, 1819). In June 1819 an army about to be shipped from Cadiz to reconquer Spain's South American colonies grew mutinous and had to be disbanded. Thereafter the government grew more oppressive, putting the Inquisition in charge of suppressing political dissent. Torture was used to exact confessions from those implicated by government spies. Shelley read accounts of events in Spain in the *Examiner* (for as Peck points out in a note, Hunt had been attacking Ferdinand since 1814), but being resident in Italy Shelley would have had more direct sources of information, Spanish and Italian politics being inextricably intertwined. Shelley's remarks on Spain show that he wrote this part of *A Philosophical View of Reform* before the successful bloodless revolution in Spain in January 1820.

line 1101. Main lines canceled and interlineations (lines 1101–1108) written later with a sharpened quill.

line 1103. *changed into*: Rolleston reads *is held*.

line 1113. *devoted*: Shelley uses this word in the sense of "doomed" (*OED* 3).

line 1118. *venemous* (sic).

line 1134. *is*: written through *it*.

line 1136. *&*: written through *of*.

line 1139. *presence*: Rolleston reads *essence*.

line 1143. *to*: written through *th*.

SC 546

      of
it ~~is~~ *famine heaped upon the
greater number & contumely heaped
upon all,* ~~it is torture~~ *defended
by* ~~precauti~~ *unspeakable tortures
employed not merely as punishments
but as precautions; by secret*

[LEAF 23, VERSO]
*death & captivity & the application
to political purposes of the* ~~most~~
    exccrated   *instruments*
~~abhorred~~ *& enormous* ~~abomations~~

1160   *of religious cruelty* ⟨–⟩ ~~All who
have given evidence of~~ *Those men of
understanding integrity & courage
who rescued their* ~~Native~~ *country from*
                  ⌊*one*
tyrant, one exiled from it by his
              &
~~enemy & rival~~ *successor his enemy*
    & their legitimate King.
~~& his most~~ ⟨ ⟩ *tyrants however they
may squabble among themselves have*

1170   *common friends & foes. The taxes* ~~of~~ *are
levied at the point of the sword.* ~~There~~
            occupy
are armed insurgents in ~~the~~ *all the*

defensible mountains of the country.
~~Women M~~ *The* ~~numerous~~ *dungeons
~~of that~~ which are peopled thickly,
~~with~~ ⟨–⟩ and* ~~torture~~ *persons of every
sex & age have the fibres of their
frame torn by subtle torments.
Boiling water (such is an article*   1180
in the last news from Spain) is
               noble
poured upon the legs of a ~~woman~~
Spanish Lady

[LEAF 24, RECTO]
*newly delivered, slowly & cautious
nes ly* ⟨–⟩ ~~until she~~ *that she may*
what she knows of a conspiracy against the tyrant
confess ~~her~~ *and she dies,* ~~cursing~~
                  as ~~one who~~ *as*
   the slave Epicharis   *constant*   1190
*impecrating curses upon her tor-
turers, & passionately calling upon
her children. These events, in the present
condition of the understanding &
sentiment of mankind are the rapidly
passing shadows, which forerun a*
~~resistance & change~~ *successful insurr
ection* ~~in those~~ *They lean looking
prophets whispering fearful change,*

line 1154. *merely*: MWS reads *only.*

line 1155. *secret*: Rolleston and Peck read *want.*

line 1156. *application*: word carelessly written; seems to be *applialtion.*

line 1159. ~~abomations~~ (sic).

line 1164. *one* (sic): for *are*; MWS reads *were*, Rolleston and Peck read *are.*

line 1173. *are . . . in*: Shelley apparently intended to alter the beginning of the sentence to read *Armed insurgents occupy all . . . .*

line 1187. *tyrant*: cramped in down right-hand margin of page.

line 1189. *as constant as*: MWS reads *enduring with the constancy of.*

line 1190. *Epicharis*: a slave implicated in a plot against Nero; she killed herself rather than reveal the names of her accomplices (Tacitus, *Annals*, xv.57).

line 1191. *impecrating*: Shelley first wrote *impercating* and then changed the *r* to *c* (leaving the appearance of *cr*) instead of correcting the *er* to *re.*

line 1193. *children.*: originally *child*; *ren.* cramped in later.

line 1198. *They lean . . . fear of change.* — (line 1203): this sentence, an excellent example of Shelley's allusive style, calls attention to the paraphrase from *Paradise Lost*, I.598–599 ("with fear of change/

SC 546   the ~~comets~~ ominous comets of our
great
republican poet perplexing monarchs
with fear of change.— Spain,
having passed through an ordeal
severe in proportion to the wrongs
kindled
& errors which it is ~~destined~~ to erase,
be renovation
Whose
1210   must of necessity. ~~The~~ country
~~which could have~~ produced Calderon
& Cervantes, what else did it,
but breathe thro the tumult of

[LEAF 24, VERSO]
46
the despotism & superstition which
invested them, the prophecy of
consummation
a glorious ~~destiny? They~~
The independents of South
1220   America are as it were already

free. Great Republics are about
to consolidate themselves in a
portion of the globe sufficiently
vast & fertile to nourish more
~~m~~ human beings than at present
occupy, ~~the~~ with the exception perhaps
of China, the remainder of the inha
bited earth— Some indefinite
arrears of misery & blood remain
to be paid to the Moloch of   1230
oppression   inflexibly
~~Monarchy.~~ These, it will exact
to the last drop & groan. But
its   enfranchized
not the less are ~~they~~ inevitably ~~free.~~
The Great Monarchies of Asia
~~h~~ cannot, let us confidently
remain
hope, ~~cannot~~ be unshaken by

the earthquake which is ~~crumbling~~   1240
shattering

Perplexes Monarchs") by alluding to "our republican poet" and also quotes Shakespeare's *Rich-ard II*: "The bay trees in our country all are withered,/ And meteors fright the fixed stars of heaven./ The pale-faced moon looks bloody on the earth,/ And lean-looked prophets whisper fearful change" (II.iv.8–11). More subtly, Shelley connects — either consciously or as a natural result of his literary sensitivity — the simile in *Paradise Lost* that describes Satan as being dimmed "as when the Sun . . . from behind the Moon/ In dim Eclipse . . . with fear of change/ Perplexes Monarchs" with Shakespeare's simile of the eclipsed sun in *Richard II* (III.iii.62–66) that, some scholars believe, underlay Milton's simile. (See John Milton, *Complete Poems*, ed. Merritt Y. Hughes, New York, 1957, pp. 226–227 and note.)

line 1201. *great*: a faint *g* precedes this word.

line 1207. *erase,*: probable reading; Rolleston, Peck, and MWS also read *erase*.

line 1208. *renovation*: the sentence requires that this word be changed to *renovated*.

line 1210. *The country*: it is unclear whether Shelley intended to cancel the second word. For this phrase, MWS reads *When it*, Rolleston reads *Spain*.

line 1220. *as it were*: it corrected from *at*.

line 1230. *Moloch*: Molech or Moloch, a god of the Ammonites in the Old Testament, received as burnt sacrifice children of his worshipers (II Kings 23:10; Jeremiah 32:35). Milton, who introduces Moloch as the bloodthirsty fallen angel in *Paradise Lost*, knew (and perhaps Shelley also knew) that the word in Hebrew meant "king."

line 1231. *inflexibly*: Rolleston reads *inflict by*, Peck reads *implacably*. The sentence should read: *These to the last drop & groan it will inflexibly exact.*

line 1238. *remain*: probable reading.

line 1241. *shattering*: *ng* obliterated by ink blot; Rolleston reads *shaking*, Peck reads *shatters*.

SC 546   [LEAF 25, RECTO]

to dust
the "mountainous strongholds" of th⟨ ⟩
tyrants of the Western world. ~~to nothing~~
~~Revolutions~~ in the political & religious
state of the Indian peninsula, seem
to be accomplishing, & it cannot
be doubted but the zeal of the
missonaries of what is called the
1250   Christian faith, will produce beneficial
innovation there, ~~what is here an en~~

even
~~cumbering crust of outworn~~ by the
dogmas & forms of what
application of ~~what is~~∧here an
outworn incumbrance. The Indians
have been enslaved ~~to the most &~~
~~severe~~ & cramped in the most severe
~~formal~~ & paralysing forms ~~of human~~
1260   by man⟨ ⟩ the   of his
~~soci~~ which were ever devised; some
intellect
new enthusiasm ought to be kindled
among them to consume it & leave
even
them free, and if ~~one opinion~~
~~relating to the natural equality~~
~~of men, ⟨   ⟩ of sense the docrtri~~
doctrines of Jesus ~~Chr~~ do not
1270   penetrate through the darkness

of that which those who profess to

[LEAF 25, VERSO]
be his followers call Christianity,
there will yet ~~be ar number of~~
~~ideas he suggested to them, or rather~~
~~forms imposed upon them~~ be a
number of social forms ~~substituted~~
modelled upon those European
feelings from which it has taken
its colour, substituted to those accor
ding to which they are at present   1280
cramped, & from which, when
the term for complete emanci
shall
pation ~~may~~ arrive, their disen
gagement may be less difficult,
& under which their progress
the
to it may be less imperceptibly
slow. ~~Of Persia we know little,~~   1290
~~but that it has been the theatre~~
~~of terrific contentions respecting~~
~~the change of dynasties.~~ ~~The~~
Many native Indians have acquired
it is said
a competent knowledge in

[LEAF 26, RECTO]
the arts & philosophy of Europe,

line 1242. *to dust*: appears to have been added when *to nothing* (line 1244) was canceled.
line 1243. *th⟨e⟩*: ink blot; see note to line 1241.
line 1245. *Revolutions*: canceled and then reinstated by underlining.
line 1248. *but*: probable reading; *u* is strangely formed.
line 1249. *missonaries* (sic).
line 1251. *encumbering*: Shelley seems to have missed one loop of the *m*.
line 1255. The caret is misplaced; either it should precede *is*, or else it refers to *even* in line 1252.
line 1260. ⟨ ⟩: illegible letters. Shelley's intention would seem to have been to interline a phrase (to follow *devised*) reading something like: *by man [for] the [destruction] of his intellect.*
line 1260. *his*: Rolleston reads *this*.
line 1268. ⟨——⟩: illegible letters were canceled before entire phrase was excised.
line 1282. *term*: Rolleston and Peck read *time*; MWS reads *term*.
line 1284. *disengagement*: MWS reads *disentanglement*.

[987]

SC 546

& Locke & Hume & Rousseau are
familiarly talked of in Brahmi
-nical society. But the thing
1300 to be sought is that they should,
as they would if they were free attain
to a system of arts & literature
of their own.— Of Persia we know
little but that it has been the
theatre of sanguinary ~~conon~~ contests
for power, & that it is now at Peace.
The Persians appear to be ~~a~~
~~beautiful refined~~ from organiza
tion a beautiful refined & im-
1310 caret
passioned people, & would probably
soon be infected by the contagion
of good.   The Turkish Empire
is in its last stage of ruin, &
it cannot be doubted but that
the time is approaching when

the deserts of Asia Minor & of
Greece will be colonized by

[LEAF 26, VERSO]
–50

the overflowing population of ~~the~~   1320
~~more wisely~~ a happier & a
~~wiser countries~~ countries less
enslaved & debased, & that the
climate & the scenery which was
the birthplace of th all that
is wise & beautiful ~~in the compass~~
forever   spoil
~~of our~~ will not remain the ~~prey~~
of wild beasts & unlettered Tartars,
~~whom~~ In Syria & Arabia &   1330
spirit
~~Ægypt,~~ the the ~~great questions~~ of
human ~~intellect~~ have aroused a
sect of people called the Wahabees
who maintain the Unity of God,

line 1303. The Persian empire had been involved with European politics at least since 1601, when the British helped Shah Abbas drive the Portuguese out of the Persian Gulf. During the early nineteenth century Napoleon had first encouraged a Russian invasion of India through Persia and then had offered the Russian province of Georgia to Persia if she would attack India. Without knowing the source of Shelley's latest information, we cannot tell to what events he alludes; *sanguinary contests for power* was a useful label that might be attached to almost any period of Persian history. During this period British military advisers were influential in Persia, helping her watch their mutual foes, Russia, Turkey, and Afghanistan.

line 1303. *Of:* O written through *o*.

line 1310. *caret:* written at an angle upwards through *tion*.

line 1327. *forever   spoil: the* from line 1328 belongs between these interlineations. MWS, not deciphering the interlineations, reads, *remain the prey of*.

line 1333. *have aroused:* MWS corrects Shelley's grammar to *has aroused*, Rolleston and Peck to *has roused*.

line 1334. The Wahhabi movement, the fountainhead of the modern history of the Arabian peninsula, had begun in the middle of the eighteenth century in east central Arabia as a puritan Islamic religious revival initiated by Muhammad ibn 'Abd al-Wahhab and sponsored by Mohammed ibn Sa'ud (died 1765) and his son 'Abd al-'Aziz (died 1802) and grandson Sa'ud. After the Wahhabis had sacked Karbala (in Iraq) in 1801 and had captured Mecca in 1802 and Medina in 1804, the Ottoman sultan deputized Mohammed Ali Pasha, viceroy of Egypt, to crush the Bedouins who followed the Wahhabi beliefs. In 1812 the Egyptians captured Mecca and Medina. In 1814 Sa'ud died and was succeeded by his son 'Abdullah. In 1818 the Egyptians besieged and took the heartland cities of the Wahhabis, capturing 'Abdullah, who was sent to Constantinople and beheaded. The Wahhabis continued to revive periodically throughout the nineteenth century, their political position vis-à-vis the Turkish empire resembling that of the *carbonari*, young Italy, and the Garibaldini vis-à-vis the

Shelley, A Philosophical View of Reform   November 1819–?1820

SC 546

& the equality of man, & their
must
enthusiasm (goes on, "conquering &
to conquer–") even if it must be
1340 repressed in its present shape. ~~In~~
The Jews, that wonderful people
which has preserved so long the
symbol of their union, may
reassume their Ancestral seats &
Ægypt having but a nonimal

dependence upon Constantinople
and is under the government
[LEAF 27, RECTO]
of Othman* Bey, a person of
enlightened views, who is introducing
European literature & arts &   1350
is thus beginning that change
which Time, the great innovator,
in
will accomplish ~~over~~ that degraded

Austrian empire. After World War I, the Wahhabis under Ibn Saud successfully overthrew the British-sponsored dynasty of Sharif Husain ibn 'Ali, to establish what is now Saudi Arabia. Thus Shelley was correct in identifying the indigenous Arabian movement of national liberation, even though he does not seem to be aware that the movement had been temporarily suppressed by the Egyptian campaign of 1818.

line 1337. *must*: MWS ignores this interlineation; Rolleston and Peck read *must go on*.

line 1338. In the sixth chapter of Revelation, after the Lamb opened the first of seven seals on the book, the Apostle beheld "a white horse, and he that sat on him had a bow, and a crown was given unto him, and he went forth conquering, and to conquer."

line 1341. *The Jews . . . seats &* (line 1344): crosswritten in two and a half lines from bottom to top of page. The passage, though obviously unfinished, shows Shelley advocating a national Jewish state in Palestine at a time when, because of the influence of Moses Mendelssohn, Zionism was at a low ebb in Western Europe.

line 1345. The Mameluke rulers of Egypt had been conquered by the Ottoman Turks early in the sixteenth century; Egypt was ruled until 1786 by Turkish pashas (and their dependent Mameluke beys), who maintained a great deal of independence from the Ottoman porte. After the French Revolution, Napoleon occupied Egypt, involving Egypt in struggles between the French and Egyptians on one side and the English and Turks on the other until the French withdrew in September 1801. The British withdrew from Alexandria in 1803, leaving in Egypt a three-cornered struggle for power among the Mameluke beys (favored by the British), the Turks, and rebellious Albanian (Arnaut) soldiers (originally in the service of the Ottomans) who were led by Mohammed (Mehemet) Ali. The last faction eventually gained control and Mohammed Ali became pasha of Egypt under nominal Ottoman rule. In 1811, while preparing for his first campaign against the Wahhabis (see note to line 1334), Mohammed Ali Pasha broke the power of the Mameluke beys, destroying the remnant of their power in 1816. He and his son Ibrahim Pasha were to play an important part in prolonging the Greek war for independence when the Egyptian fleet and army came to the aid of the Turks in 1824.

Othman Bey, whom Shelley mentions as ruler of Egypt, was surely not so, though he may have been an important official under Mohammed Ali Pasha. Though he could not have been Othman (or Osman) al-Bardisi, the famous Mameluke ally and rival of Mohammed Ali Pasha (for he had died in 1807), it remains possible that Othman Bey was an exiled Mameluke whose nephew announced that his uncle was the rightful ruler of Egypt. In any case, Shelley's information was almost surely gossip in Italy rather than news from England. (See lines 1368–1376.)

line 1345. *having*: altered from *has*; *ing* squeezed in.

line 1345. *nonimal* (sic).

SC 546

                means
   country   *by the same*
people – ~~and the~~ *and* ~~the sub~~ *its sublime*
~~sub~~ *enduring monuments may*
excite lofty emotions in the hearts

1360

of the posterity of those who now
contemplate them ~~stupidly~~ *without*
admiration ~~or emotion~~—*The Lastly*
      in
~~West the~~ *West Indian islands*
first from the ~~generous in~~ *disin*
terested, yet necessarily causes
measures of the English Nation

This person sent his Nephew to ~~Italy~~
          ⌊*Lucca*
to study European learning, & when

1370

his Nephew asked with reference to
some branch of study at enmity with
           ⌊*Maho*
metanism, whether he was permitted to
      51

engage in it, he replied— ~~Do any thing~~
You are at liberty to do any thing
which ~~doe~~ *will not injure another*

[LEAF 27, VERSO]

and then from the ~~unsparing &~~
~~terrible~~ *infection of the Spirit of*
Liberty in France, the deepest
stain upon civilized man is ~~str~~

1380

fading away. ~~There~~ *Two nations*
of free negroes are already esta
blished; one in pernicious mockery
         over
of the usurpation ~~in~~ *France, an*
empire, the other a republic; both
animating yet terrific spectacles
to those who inherit around
them the degradation of slavery
        peril

1390

& the ~~danger~~ *of dominion.*
   Such is a ~~picture~~ *slight sketch*
    general
~~of the condition of the hopes of the~~

line 1355. *means*: almost illegible.

line 1362. *Lastly*: written over extended line used to cancel *The*.

line 1364. In connection with the West Indies, Shelley alludes to (1) the Parliamentary acts of 1807 abolishing the slave *trade* (though not slavery itself) in British colonies and of 1811 making slave-trading a felony; and to (2) the dissemination of revolutionary principles in the French West Indian colonies, which led to the revolt of black Haitians under Toussaint L'Ouverture (who was betrayed by Napoleon and died in a French prison in 1803). In 1819 there were two black nations in Haiti — an "empire" in the north under Henri Christophe and a "republic" in the south under General Jean Pierre Boyer.

line 1366. *causes*: written through indecipherable word; MWS, Rolleston, and Peck read *cautious*, a reading that editors may wish to adopt as consistent with the sense of the passage.

line 1368. *This person . . . another* (line 1376): footnote keyed to asterisk, line 1348. The two final lines of this note (1375–1376) appear at the bottom of leaf 27, verso, in the manuscript. *Y* of *You* (line 1375) is written through an indecipherable letter.

line 1373. *51*: written in pencil.

line 1378. *infection*: *e* written through *l*.

line 1390. *peril*: Rolleston reads *spirit*.

line 1392. *sketch*: *k* written through *c*.

line 1394. *of the condition*: here and elsewhere in this complex sentence, Shelley's final intention is subject to editorial interpretation. I would read the sentence (lines 1392–1413) as follows: "Such is a slight sketch of the general condition of the hopes and aspirations of the human race to which they [i.e., *hopes and aspirations*] have been conducted, after the obliteration of the Greek republics

Shelley, A Philosophical View of Reform   November 1819–?1820

SC 546   ~~and aspirations of~~ the human race
to which they have been conducted
~~by the ⟨ ⟩~~ after the obliteration of
the Greek republics, by the successful

[LEAF 28, RECTO]

1400   ~~tyranny of Rome, ever after external~~
          its
tyranny of Rome, ~~their~~ internal
liberty having been first abolished,
and by those ~~events consequent~~
              consequent upon those
upon the miseries & superstitions which
                    has
   event
~~destroying the compelled those forced~~
compelled the human race to begin
1410   *its*
anew ~~the~~ difficult & obscure career
of producing, according to the forms
of society, the greatest portion of good.

     Meanwhile England, ~~which is~~ the
particular object for the sake of which

                   have been
these general considerations ~~were~~ stated
on the present occasion, has arrived
~~at a crisis~~, like the nations which
surround it, at a crisis in its destiny.   1420
     The literature of England, an
energetic devepement of which has
ever followed or preceded a great &
free developement of the national
will, has arisen, as it were from a
new birth. In spite of that low-
-thoughted envy which would ~~degrade~~

[LEAF 28, VERSO]

& undervalue, thro a fear of comparison
with its own insignificance, the
eminence of contemporary merit, it   1430
         ours
is ~~felt by the British~~ this is in ~~liter~~
intellectual atchievements a memorable
age and we live among such philoso
-phers & poets as ~~has~~ surpass beyond

by the successful external tyranny of Rome (its internal liberty having been first abolished) and by those miseries and superstitions which consequent upon [that] event ha[ve] compelled the human race to begin anew its difficult and obscure career of producing, according to the forms of society, the greatest portion of good." Shelley would undoubtedly have simplified this sentence before publishing his treatise, but its meaning is clear: Shelley has been tracing the renewal of human hopes and aspirations after the subjugation of liberty in Rome by internal tyrants, who then subjugated liberty in Greece; the consequent *miseries and superstitions* of the Roman Empire and the Dark Ages have compelled the human race to begin anew its attempts to develop the forms of a just society.

line 1398. The underline marked off space at the bottom of the page for the continuation of Shelley's footnote (see lines 1368–1376 above).

line 1400. *its*: the antecedent is, apparently, *Rome*, whereas Shelley may have first intended *their* to refer to *the Greek republics* (line 1398).

line 1422. *devepement* (sic).

line 1426. *In spite . . . age* (line 1434): An edited version might read: "In spite of that low-thoughted envy which would undervalue (through a fear of comparison with its own insignificance) the eminence of contemporary merit, ours is in intellectual achievements a memorable age. . . ." Compare Shelley's revised version of this sentence in the last paragraph of *A Defence of Poetry*. See Shelley, *Complete Works*, VII, 140.

line 1428. *undervalue,*: Rolleston reads *underrate*.

line 1430. *eminence*: may have been written *enimence*.

line 1433. *atchievements* (sic): MWS reads *inquirements*; Rolleston and Peck read *achievements*.

SC 546

*comparison any who have appeared
in our nation since its last struggle*
      For
for liberty. The most unfailing herald
1440 *of ~~or~~ companion, or follower, of an
universal employment of the sentiments
of a nation to the production of beneficial
change is poetry,   meaning by
poetry an intense & ~~impres~~ impassioned
power of communicating intense &
impassioned impressions respecting man
& nature. The persons in whom this
power takes its abode may often,
as far as regards many portions*
1450   correspondence with
of their nature have little ~~tendency~~

of   which   it   is   the   minister.
the spirit of good)
             *But although they
may deny & abjure, they are
   In this sense, Religion
may be called Poetry, though
distorted from the beautiful
simplicity of its truth– Coleridge
has said that every poet was*   1460
*religious, ~~orig~~ the converse, that
every religious man must be a poet
was a more true –*

[LEAF 29, RECTO]
*yet compelled to serve, that which is
seated on the throne of their own soul.
They are usually men, who having*

line 1438. *For*: though MWS omits this word, Shelley's addition of it is important to the thought of the passage, the causal relationship between the spirit of liberty and the rebirth of literature being an important point both here and in *A Defence of Poetry*.

line 1440. *of ~~or~~*: *of* written through indecipherable letters. Since Shelley canceled *or*, a comma should be inserted after *of*.

line 1450. *correspondence with*: probable reading; MWS reads *in common*. An edited version of lines 1449–1453 would read: ". . . as far as regards many portions of their nature, have little correspondence with the spirit of good of which it is the minister" ("it" referring to "power," line 1448). Compare the nearly identical sentence in the final paragraph of *A Defence of Poetry*.

line 1454. *But although . . . own soul.* (line 1465): Shelley also used this sentence, together with the more famous assertion in lines 1474–1475 (*Poets . . . world.*), in the peroration of *A Defence of Poetry*. See Shelley, *Complete Works*, VII, 140.

line 1456. *In this sense, . . . more true –* (line 1463): crosswritten from bottom to top of leaf in darker ink (see facsimile, page 1007). MWS places it as a footnote keyed to *nature* (line 1447).

line 1459. *Coleridge . . . religious,* (line 1461): the source of this particular quotation has eluded us, but Coleridge discussed the parallels between poetry and religion in "*Blessed are ye that sow beside the Waters*": *A Lay Sermon* (London, 1817, pp. 87–88). In the same pamphlet Coleridge traces all the evils of English commercialism (the "Spirit of Barter," as he calls it) to "the institution of the Funds in the reign of William the Third" (p. 84) and attacks public credit, paper money, and the national debt (pp. 97–113).

line 1464. *yet*: follows *they are* of line 1455 (before transcription of crosswriting).

line 1464. *that*: *t* written through either *&* or *w*.

line 1466. *They are usually . . . themselves.* (line 1471): notice how, in *A Defence of Poetry*, Shelley turns this negative judgment on the poetic temperament (which parallels the thought in his lyric published with *Prometheus Unbound* beginning, "Chameleons feed on light and air") into a more positive statement: "But in the intervals of inspiration, and they may be frequent without being durable, a Poet becomes a man, and is abandoned to the sudden reflux of the influences under which others habitually live. But *as he is more delicately organized than other men, and sensible to pain and*

Shelley, *A Philosophical View of Reform*   *November 1819–?1820*

SC 546

1470

an intense apprehension of all other
things have an intense apprehension
of their own pleasure & comfort, for
the sake of which they sell, or waste
themselves. And ~~they~~ whatever
systems their may professedly support,
they actually advance the interests of
Liberty. Poets & Philosophers are the
unacknowledged legislators of the world.
Before the F. R. a better state of public

⌊mind

The panic going away
All the great writing, full of hope
Not necessary to debate here on the

⌊grounds of

1480

Reform — that to come in next Cap.
It is impossible to read the productions
of our most celebrated writers
whatever may be their system
relating to thought or express^n

[LEAF 29, VERSO]
                56
without being startled by the electric
life which there is in their words.
They measure the circumference
or ~~sould~~ sound the depths of human

                                comprehensive   1490
nature with an ~~all embracing~~
    all–
& ⟨—⟩ penetrating spirit, at which
they are themselves perhaps the
most sincerely astonished for
it less their own spirit than the
spirit of their age. They are the
priests of an unapprehended inspiration
                    ⟨——⟩
                    forms   1500
the mirrors of ~~the~~ gigantic ~~shadows~~
    which futurity   casts upon the present
~~around them,~~ they ~~are like~~ words
which express what they conceive
not, the trumpet which sings to
battle and feels not what it inspires
the influence which is moved not
but moves. Poets & philosophers
are the unacknowledged legislators
of the world.   1510
But, omitting these more abstracted
considerations, has there not been

[LEAF 30, RECTO]
and is there not in England a
    desire
~~spirit~~ of change arising from the
profound sentiment of the ~~inefficiency~~

pleasure, both his own and that of others, *in a degree unknown to them, he will avoid the one and pursue the other with an ardour proportioned to this difference.*" (Shelley, *Complete Works*, VII, 139; italics added.)

line 1472. *professedly support,*: Rolleston and Peck read *have professed by support.*

line 1476. *Before . . . next Cap.* (line 1480): MWS puts these headings of Shelley's ideas in a footnote keyed to *Liberty* (line 1474).

line 1476. *F. R.*: French Revolution.

line 1477. *going away*: probable reading.

line 1480. *Cap.*: abbreviation for *Caput* (Chapter).

line 1481. *It is impossible . . . of the world.* (line 1510): this passage is almost the actual text of the last four sentences of *A Defence of Poetry* (Shelley, *Complete Works*, VII, 140).

line 1490. *comprehensive* and *all–* (line 1492): both words added later with sharper quill.

line 1502. *futurity casts upon the present*: MWS reads *following acts upon the purer.* Shelley's metaphor is expanded from a line in Thomas Campbell's "Lochiel's Warning," published with *Gertrude of Wyoming* (London, 1809), pp. 117–123, where the Wizard says: "... coming events cast their shadows before." Byron uses this and the previous line as the epigraph for his "The Prophecy of Dante" (published with *Marino Faliero* in 1821).

SC 546   *exceedingly inefficiency of the existing*
institutions to provide for the physical
& intellectual happiness of the people?

1520   *It is proposed in this work to ex*
     the present condition
state & examine,ₐthis desire. 2 to
elucidate its causes & its object
3 comprising to the shew the practi
cability & utility, nay the necessity
of change 4 to examine the state
of parties as regards it, & 4ᵗʰ to
state the probable, the possible, &
the desirable mode. in which it shᵈ

1530   *be accomplished*
    On the Sentiment of the
Necessity of Change
According
  By the principles of human nature
as modified by the existing opinions
& institutions of society, a man
a man loves himself with an

[LEAF 30, VERSO]
overweening love. The generous emotions
       to

1540   *of disinterested affection of which*
the records of human nature teach &
  ⟨   ⟩
our experience teach us that the human
heart is susceptible in the highest
highly susceptible, are confined and
rendered intense within the narrow
circle of our kindred & friends. &
are rendered for want   And therefore
there is a class of men considerable

1550   *from talents, influence, and station*
who of necessity are enemies to
beneficial innovation Reform. For

Reform would benefit the nation at
their expense instead of suffering
them to benefit themselves at the
expense of the nation.—If a reform
however mild were to take place, they
must submit to a diminution of those
luxuries & vanities in the idolatry
of which they have been educated   1560
trained. Not only they, but their
what perhaps in most cases is

[LEAF 31, RECTO]
would be esteemed a harder necessity,
their wives & children & dependents
     ⟨   ⟩
must be comprehended in the same
restrictions. That degree of pain,
which however it is to be regretted
is necessarily attached to the relinquis
hment of habit the habit of parti   1570
-cular persons at war with the general
permanent advantage, must be
inflicted by the mildest Reform.
It is not alledged that every person
whose interest is directly or indirectly
concerned in the maintaining things
as they are, is therefore necessarily
interested. There are rare individuals
who can be just judges even against
themselves, & by study & self knowledge   1580
have formed themselves to examination
   have established
a severe tribunal within themselves

It is of no avail that they call
this selfishness principle, or that
they are self deceived deluded by

---

line 1522. The caret, which is rather below this line, may be *x* or stray mark.

line 1530. *be accomplished*: probable reading; MWS reads *accomplish its end.*

line 1542. ⟨*?own*⟩: possible reading.

line 1549. *is*: *i* written through *a*.

Shelley, *A Philosophical View of Reform*　　November 1819–?1820

SC 546

the same sophism with which they w^d
decieve others. To attach another
name to the same idea, may puzzle

1590　the hearer, but can in no manner change
the import of it.

[LEAF 31, VERSO]
to which those principles ~~of justice~~
　　　　　　　　　　on which
~~the happiness of the greater number~~
which demand the advantage of the
　　　　　　　　　　　　⌊greater
number are admitted to appeal. But
these, even should they be many, would
yet be few among the many./All
public functionaries who are over

1600　paid either in money or in power
for their ~~t~~ public services, beginning
with the person invested with the
royal authority, and ending with
the ~~bailiff~~ turnkey who extorts
　　　　　shilling
his last ~~pittance~~ from a starving
prisoner. All members of the
House of Lords, ~~all the all~~ who
tremble ~~lest their hereditary power~~

1610　~~& their enormous~~ the duties
annihilation of their borough in

[LEAF 32, RECTO]
　　　　　　　　　　risk
terest might not involve the ~~peril~~
of their hereditary legislature power,
and of those distinctions which ~~are~~
~~advantag inasmuch~~ considered in
a pecuniary point of view are injurious
to those beyond the pale of their cast
in proportion as
~~as~~ they are beneficial to those within.　1620
~~As a moral evil The functionaries~~
~~of the established church~~ An im
mense majority of the members of
the assembly called the house of
Commons, who would be reduced, if
they desired to administer public
business, ~~to seek that popular favour~~
　　　　　to impo to exercise the legis
lative to consult the interest of their
　　　　and conform themselves　　　　1630
electors.　　　The functionaries of ~~the~~
~~established church, who religion~~ who
know that ~~their~~ their claims to several
　　　　　　yearly
millions∧of the ~~revenue~~ produce of
the soil for the service of ~~anouncing~~
certain dogmas, ~~which not certainly~~
　　　　　　　which ~~other men~~
　　true &
if necessary other men would ~~inculcate~~　1640

line 1587. *the same sophism . . . import of it.* (line 1591): this passage, which completes the footnote beginning at line 1584, is written at the bottom of leaf 31, verso, following the ruled line below line 1611. Shelley forgot to cancel this half of his footnote.

line 1592. This line follows directly in context line 1583.

line 1592. *those*: altered from *the*.

line 1617. *pecuniary*: *c* written through *n*.

line 1620. *those*: written through *these*.

line 1622. *An*: *A* written through *a*.

line 1632. *the established church,*: as elsewhere in Shelley's drafts, the underlining reinstates the canceled words.

line 1636. *anouncing* (sic).

SC 546

force as effectually for as many thous
ands would undergo a very severe

         61

[LEAF 32, VERSO]

         62

examination. The officers The numerous
lawyers civil The doctors proctors
surrogates of the civil law. The masters
   Lord
Chancellor with his dependent officers,

1650   *& the tribe of lawyers attornies &*
clerks to whom the enormous im
postures of that more than ecclesias
tical tyranny administer enormous
profits. These and many more

     With some it assumes the mask of
fear, with others that of hope——
     with all it is expectation
Two circumstances arrest the
attention of an those who turn

1660   *their mo regard to the present*
   political
condition of the English nation;
       almost
first that there is an universal
         approach
sentiment of the arrival of
        to be wrought
some change in the institutions

of the government, & secondly
the necessity & desirableness   1670

[LEAF 33, RECTO]

of such a change. And From the
first of these propositions, it being
matter of fact, no person addressing
the public can dissent. The latter
    a general belief in which
from which the former flows &
on which it depends, is matter of
opinion, but which to the mind
of all excepting those interested in
maintaining the contrary is a   1680
doctrine so clearly established that
they on do even they, admitting
that great abuses which exist
are compelled to impugn it by
insisting upon the specious topic
       by which they alone could be
of that popular violence would do
     remedied would
more be more injurious than
the contenance of these abuses.   1690
But as those who argue thus
   for the most ⟨   ⟩ part
derive great advantage &
convenience from the continu
ance of these abuses, their estima

line 1641. *force*: Shelley meant this word to be combined with the uncanceled *in* of *inculcate* in the previous line to read *inforce* (variant of *enforce*).

line 1643. *61*: written in pencil.

line 1650. *attornies*: contemporary spelling.

line 1652. *ecclesiastical*: Shelley originally miswrote the word; *asti* written through indecipherable letters.

line 1655. *With some . . . expectation* (line 1657): these lines are written with a sharper quill, in different ink.

line 1658. *arrest*: MWS reads *must meet*.

line 1671. *From*: altered from *To*; MWS reads *I omit*.

line 1673. *person*: MWS reads *one*.

line 1690. *contenance*: for *continuance* or possibly *countenance*; MWS, Rolleston, and Peck all read *continuance*.

SC 546 [LEAF 33, VERSO]

                                    temporary
tion of the mischiefs of popular
violence as compared with the
                        permanent
1700 *mischiefs of tyranical & ~~decieving~~*
fraudulent forms of goverment is
likely, from the known principles
of human nature, to be exaggerated.
Such an estimate
It comes too with a worse grace
from them, who if they would
in opposition to their own unjust
advantage, take the lead in
                        spare
1710 *reform, might ~~save~~ the nation*
from the inconveniences of ~~tem~~
the temporary dominion of the
~~people~~ poor, who ~~until in their~~
                very
by means of that₍ₐ₎degraded
condition which their insurrection
would be designed to ameliorate,
are sufficiently incapable of
                                genuine
1720 *discerning their own ~~true~~*
& permanent advantage, tho'

[LEAF 34, RECTO]
        surely
~~probably~~ less incapable than

those whose interests consist in
proposing to themselves an object
~~who~~ perfectly opposite & wholly
incompatible with that advantage.
        I meant the government party
        ~~We have no choice therefore but~~
These persons₍ₐ₎therefore propose   1730
to us the dilemma of submitting
to a despositism which is notoriously
gathering like an avelanche year
by year; or taking the risk of
something which it must be confessed
bears the aspect of revolution. To
this ~~dilemma~~ alternative we are
reduced by the selfishness of those who
taunt us with it. And the history
of the world teaches us not to hes   1740
itate an instant in the decision,
if indeed the power of decision be
not already past——
    The establishment of King

[LEAF 34, VERSO]
William III on the throne of England
has already been referred to as
a compromise between liberty &
despotism; ~~in The Long Parlia~~
~~ment whose proceedings had~~
~~prepared that ev~~ The Parliament   1750

line 1696. *temporary*: probable reading; Peck reads *uprisings*.

line 1699. *permanent*: probable reading.

line 1700. *tyranical* (sic).

line 1719. *genuine*: word added later with sharper quill.

line 1722. *surely*: MWS reads *scarcely*.

line 1726. *&*: MWS reads *or*.

line 1726. *wholly*: Rolleston reads *utterly*.

line 1728. *I . . . party*: careted in to follow *These persons* (line 1730); MWS places the clause within parentheses, changing *meant* to *mean*.

line 1732. *despositism* (sic).

line 1733. *avelanche* (sic).

line 1736. *bears*: MWS reads *wears*.

line 1750. *The Parliament . . . of the people.* (line 1755): King William III and Mary were recognized as sovereigns by a "Convention Parliament" that assembled on January 22, 1689, after William

SC 546

of *that* which that event was
the act, had ceased to be, in
                    an
the same emphatic sense, a repre
sentation of the people. *Since*
           dissolution
the meeting of the Long Parli
                 questionless
ament, *which it cannot be*

1760 *questioned* was the organ of
the will of all classes of people
in England since it effected the
complete revolution ⟨——⟩ in a tyranny
                          meet
       But the ⟨ ⟩ since *starting* its
consecrated by time, a great
       meeting, & since its dissolution
change had taken place in
England. Feudal manners &

1770 institutions having become ob

[LEAF 35, RECTO]

literated, monopolies & patents
having been abolished, property
having been rendered s & personal
liberty having been rendered secure,
the nation *advanced rapidly*
advanced rapidly towards the acq
-uirement of the elements of national
prosperity. ^X Population increased,
a greater number of hands
were employed in the labours of
agriculture & commerce, towns
sprang up arose where villages
had been, & the *number of*
proportion borne by those *by*
whose labour *the* produces the
materials of subsistence & enjoy
ment to those who claim for

1780

had virtually conquered England with the help of a group of key noblemen and generals and with the acquiescence of a large part of the English public. That Parliament, which was declared a regular Parliament on March 20, 1689, without standing for election, was not dissolved until October 1695.

line 1756. *dissolution*: possible reading; the word would not, in any case, be included in an edition that published only Shelley's latest intention.

line 1757. The "Long Parliament," led by Shelley's heroes Pym and Hampden, met from November 3, 1640, until late in 1648, when most of its members were expelled, leaving the "Rump Parliament." In April 1653 Oliver Cromwell expelled both the Rump Parliament and his Council of State and, after an unhappy experience with "Barebone's Parliament" (1653) — perhaps the most radical in England's history — Cromwell ruled as Lord Protector without Parliament (except for a brief attempted revival in 1656–1658) until his death. In 1659 Richard Cromwell reassembled the Rump Parliament, and finally General Monk recalled to the Rump those members of the Long Parliament who had been expelled in 1648. The revived Long Parliament, first assembled nearly twenty years before, dissolved itself and new elections were held, bringing in a "Convention Parliament" that recalled King Charles II from Holland.

Shelley asserts that the fact that the Long Parliament was able to effect revolutionary changes in English law is *prima facie* evidence that it enjoyed the support and was fully representative of the English people. The history of the full Long Parliament in resisting extremists of both absolutist and republican persuasions would support Shelley's contention that the Long Parliament was, at least, no party tool, as he considered the British Parliament of his day to be. In any case, his further assertion (lines 1765–1769) that there had been massive social changes in England since the dissolution of the Long Parliament is indisputable.

line 1763. *in*: written through *of*.

line 1764. *meet*: this word and *starting*, beneath it, are completely entangled.

line 1778. *prosperity.*: the *x* that follows this word indicates the point at which Shelley wished to insert lines 1795–1806 (*But for want . . .*) from leaf 35, verso.

Shelley, A Philosophical View of Reform   November 1819–?1820

SC 546
1790

*themselves a superfluity of these
materials began to increase
    fourth
indefinitely. A ~~third~~ class*

[LEAF 35, VERSO]

    made
  *began to arise appeared
therefore ~~arose~~ in the nation,*

*But for want ^X of just regula
  in
tions ~~for~~ the distribution of
~~these elements~~—which is indeed
the great problem of government,-
    ~~have~~
the elements of prosperity became
    & power
~~com~~ when combined the sources
of ~~that~~ despotism & misery.*

1800

*which ~~since the Revolution have~~
gradually
the unrepresented multitude.
~~Nor was it~~ Nor was it so much
that ~~towns arose~~ villages which
sent no members to Parliament
became great cities, & that
~~cities, from consid~~ towns which
had been considerable enough to
send members, dwindled, from
local circumstances into villages.
This ~~do~~ cause ~~had~~ no doubt*

1810

[LEAF 36, RECTO]

*contributed to the general effect
of rendering the Commons house
  a less complete
~~no longer~~ a representation of the*

1820

line 1793. *appeared*: MWS and Rolleston read *made its appearance.*

line 1795. *But . . . gradually* (line 1806): see note to line 1778.

line 1797. *the distribution*: Shelley appears to have started another word, beginning *es* after *the* before writing *distribution.*

line 1801. This line should read: *the elements of prosperity & power became*; the phrase *& power*, which is crowded between *prosperity* and *became*, slants downward.

line 1807. *the unrepresented multitude.*: continues the thought from line 1794. Notice how Shelley's comments on the rise of the proletariat foreshadow the concerns of Marx and Engels. Actually, the reputed role of the *sans-culottes* in the French Revolution, whether or not distorted by Royalist apologists (see George Rudé, *The Crowd in the French Revolution*, Oxford University Press, 1959), had given every student of history an example of the potential explosiveness of the disenfranchised urban poor.

line 1808. *Nor was it . . . into villages.* (line 1815): the enlarged cities that were unrepresented in Parliament in 1819 included Bradford, Leeds, and Manchester in the textile areas of Yorkshire and Lancashire, Stoke-upon-Trent and Wolverhampton in the Staffordshire pottery area, and Birmingham and Sheffield, in which the English metal-working industries were arising. Some of the more famous rotten boroughs in which a few electors — sometimes as few as one or two individuals — sent two representatives to Parliament included Old Sarum in Wiltshire, Grampound in Cornwall, Gatton in Surrey, and Bishop's Castle in Shropshire. In the last borough, for example, the members in 1819 were the uncle and the brother-in-law of the Earl of Powis. In *The Black Book; or, Corruption Unmasked* (London, 1820), John Wade calculated (p. 423) that, of 658 members of the House of Commons, 300 were nominated by peers, 187 by rich commoners or by the government itself, and only 171 were returned by popular elections of any sort (many of which were also influenced by the same rich and powerful individuals).

  It is, perhaps, noteworthy that New Shoreham, which Sir Timothy Shelley represented in Parliament until 1818, was not deprived of its two representatives by the English Parliamentary Reform Bill of 1832 (2 William IV, c. 45) but was merely modified to include some adjacent towns and areas.

[999]

SC 546

                         Yet
people. ~~But~~ had this been all,
tho it had ceased to be a legal
                    might
& actual, it ~~would~~ still have been
a virtual Representation of the
          a portion of the   *universally*
People. But ~~the nation~~ nation became
multiplied into a a denomination,

1830   *~~which not existing before, or rather~~*
~~existing only to a degree in which~~
~~its interests were sensibly interwoven~~

              which
~~with those who were directly represented~~
had no constitutional presence in
the state. This denomination had
not existed before, or had existed
only to a degree in which its
interests were sensibly interwoven
                    ⟨ ⟩ enjoyed ⟨ ⟩ constitution

1840   *with that of those who ~~were~~*   *presence*
directly represented. Thus, the
              which borne by
proportion ~~of the huma~~ English
men ~~who~~ who posessed a

[LEAF 36, VERSO]
                faculty
right∧of suffrage ~~to nominate to the~~
~~Representative assembly~~ to those
who were excluded from that

1850   *right faculty*
~~suffrage~~ at the several periods of

1641 & 1688 had changed ~~from~~
          by the operation of these causes from
1 to 5 to 1 to 20. The rapid
& effectual progress by which it
               1 to 20 to   *hundreds*
changed from∧one to many ~~thousands~~
in the interval between 1688
& 1819 is a process, to those

1860   *~~who regard the immense increase~~*
familiar with the history of
the political economy of that perid,
          which is
rendered by these principles suffi
-ciently intelligible. The number
therefore of those who have influence
on the government ~~although~~
                    even if
numerically the same as at the

1870   *was*
former period, ~~is~~ relatively different.
~~At presen~~ ~~At the one period~~
And ~~it is~~ a sufficiently just

[LEAF 37, RECTO]
~~barometer~~ is afforded of the
          measure
degree in which a country is
enslaved or free, by the consi-
-deration of the relative number of
individuals who are admitted

1880   *to the exercise of political rights.*
Meanwhile another cause was

line 1828. *But the nation*: at this point Shelley began to use a sharper quill.

line 1829. *a a* (sic).

line 1831. *to*: written through *in*.

line 1838. *a*: written through *in*.

line 1840. ⟨ ⟩ *enjoyed* ⟨ ⟩ *constitution*: written in a small cramped hand at the edge of the page; MWS, Rolleston, and Peck read *a constitutional presence*, which undoubtedly was Shelley's intention.

line 1854. *5*: written through *8*; MWS reads *five*, Rolleston and Peck read *8*.

line 1859. *is*: written through *in*.

line 1862. *perid*, (sic).

line 1867. *on*: written through *of*.

line 1878. *number*: MWS reads *manner*.

SC 546   operating of a deeper & more

who compose the

extensive nature. The ~~House of~~

advantage

Lords, must by the ~~nature~~ of

as the great landed pro

their situation, posess ~~an great~~ con-

⌊sider⟨

⟩

prietors

1890   influence over nomination to the

commons. This influence from an

the

original imperfection in ~~an~~ equal

distribution of suffrage, was always

enormous, ~~In 1641~~ but it is

only since it has been combined

with the cause before stated that

appeared to be

it has ~~been~~ fraught with

1900   consequences incompatible with

public liberty. In 1641 this

influence, was almost wholly

[LEAF 37, VERSO]

inoperative ~~upon the coun~~ to

pervert the counsels of the nation

from its own advantage. But

at that epoch the enormous tyranny

agents

of the ~~ministers~~ of the royal power

weighed equally upon all denomi

1910   nations of men, & united all counsels

to extinguish it, add to which,

~~that~~ the nation was in a very

as stated before

considerable degree fairly represented

in Parliament., ~~& that the &~~

oppressors

~~that the ministers of the crown~~

common danger which was

~~had~~ The ₌bond of union between the

people   1920

aristocracy & the ~~commons of the~~

destroyed

~~nation~~ having been ~~withdrawn~~

systematized their influence

the former ~~arrogated to themselves~~

~~power as they~~ through the

permanence of hereditary right,

whilst the latter were losing

power by ~~numerical increase~~

[LEAF 38, RECTO]

inflexibility of the institutions which   1930

forbade a

refused ~~to acco the~~ just accomo

dation to their numerical increase.

After the operations of these causes

accession

had commenced the ~~access~~ of

William the III placed a seal upon

forty years of Revolution.——

    The Govermnent of this country

at the period of 1688 was regal   1940

tempered by aristocracy, for

~~how~~ what conditions of democracy

one portion of which

attach to an assembly imperfectly

nominated by less than ~~one~~ a

people

twentieth part of the ~~nation~~, and

~~swallowed up the by the influence~~

~~of the nobles. This was the~~

~~epoch of the birth of that~~ power   1950

line 1884. *The*: because of the changed syntax caused by the interlineation, this word should be changed to *Those*.

line 1888. *consider⟨able⟩*: Shelley probably intended this word, but his writing runs off edge of page.

line 1903. *inoperative* and *to*: probably uncanceled, but the cancel mark drawn through the last line of leaf 38, recto, has blotted onto this page.

line 1918. *danger*: MWS reads *oppressor* at this point. It is possible that *danger* is canceled and the interlined *oppressors* two lines above may be its replacement; if so, *oppressors* should probably be read as the singular noun followed by a comma.

SC 546

another perfectly nominated by
the nobles? ~~It had been more agreable~~
~~to liberty that~~ Then ~~began three~~
For the nobility ~~ceasing to fear~~
~~the royal power, & being awa~~

[LEAF 38, VERSO]

70

~~kened to~~ having by the assistance
of the people imposed close limitations
upon the royal power, finding

1960   *that power to be ~~its~~ natural ally,*

            For the people
& the people, its (who from the increase
          acquired greater
of their numbers ~~had more~~ and
more important rights whilst the
         those right
organ thro which ~~they might be~~
asserted grew feebler ~~from as they~~
~~increased~~ in proportion to the increase

1970   *of*
of the cause of these rights & their impor
tance) its natural enemy, made the
Crown the mask & pretence of their
own authority. ~~Then was The~~
~~royal power~~   *despotism of the*
   At this period, began that ~~despotism~~
oligarchy of party, & representin
   under colour of administering
the executive ~~for~~ power lodged

1980   *in the King, represented in truth*
the interests of the rich, &

[LEAF 39, RECTO]

~~When it is said by~~ When it is
          speaking of the interval
said by political reasoners ₍ that
between 1688 & the present time
the royal power progressively
increased, they use an expression
      suggests
which ~~conveys~~ a very imperfect &
partial idea. The power which has   1990
increased is ~~merely~~ that entrusted
with the administration of affairs,
composed of men responsible to the
aristocratical assemblies, or to the
reigning party in those assemblies,
         orders of the nation
& which represents those ~~rich &~~
which are priviledged
~~the powerful, can will~~ & will retain
power as long as it pleases them   2000
& must be divested of power as
soon as it ceases to please them.
   The power which has increased therefore is the
~~Though less contumelio~~ The
   power of the rich.
name & the office of King is merely
the mask of this power, & is a
kind of stalking horse used to
conceal these "catchers of men" whilst
     Monarchy is only the string which ties   2010
they lay their nets.— Though less
   the robbers bundle
~~abhor~~ contumelious & abhorrent

---

line 1952. ~~*agreable*~~: the approved contemporary spelling, according to Bailey's Dictionary.

line 1953. ~~*three*~~: possibly *these*.

line 1969. *in*: written through *as*.

line 2005. *power*: tangled with *~~Though~~* in line above.

line 2009. *"catchers of men"*: though the strongest suggested allusion is Jesus' injunction that Peter and his colleagues become "fishers of men" (Matthew 4:19; Mark 1:17), Shelley's use of "catchers" gives the phrase Shakespearian overtones; the verb *catch* was used frequently and strikingly by Shakespeare (and Spenser) with predatory overtones, almost never in Milton's poetry, and only with much more benign connotations in Cowper and Pope.

line 2012. *robbers*: tangled with word above.

line 2013. *contumelious*: appears to end with *uous*.

Shelley, A Philosophical View of Reform   November 1819–?1820

SC 546   [LEAF 39, VERSO]

from the dignity of human nature
than an absolute monarchy, ~~the~~
an oligarchy of this nature exacts
more ~~from~~ of suffering from the people,
because it reigns both by the opinion
generated by imposture, & the force
2020   *which that opinion places within*
its grasp.

    At the epoch adverted to, ~~first~~
~~was applied~~ the device of public
credit, was first systematically
             ~~resource~~ instrument
applied ~~to~~ as ~~an engine~~ of govern
-ment. ~~The persons This last &~~
~~most successful~~ It was employed
at the ~~period~~ accession of William
2030   *III less as a resource for meeting*
the financial exigencies of the
              the bond
state, than as ~~an instrument~~ to
connect
~~bind~~ those in the possession of pro
        with
-perty ~~to who~~ who had by
~~an accident of party~~ taking ad
vantage of an accident of party,

[LEAF 40, RECTO]

acceded to power. In the interval   2040
elapsed since that period it has
accurately fulfilled the intention
of its establishment, & ~~it will~~
~~continue~~ has continued to add
              even
strength to the government, until
            ⌈*Now (afterwards*⌉
the present crisis.⌊   *But it* ⌋
           Now
This device is one of those execra   2050
ble contrivances of misrule which
overbalance the materiale of common
advantage produced by the progress
of civilization, & increase the
number of those who ~~do~~ are idle
in proportion to those who work.
    whilst it increases through the factitious wants
    of those indolent priveldged persons the quan-
             ⌊*tity of work to be done.*
The rich, no longer being able to
rule by force, have invented this   2060
scheme, that they may rule by
fraud.–   The most despotic govern
ments of antiquity were strangers
to this invention, which is a com
-pendious method of extorting from

line 2023. *public credit,*: the beginning of the "national debt" in England (according to the *National Cyclopædia of Useful Knowledge*, London, 1849, which embalms the liberal orthodoxy of the previous generation), was connected with the chartering of the Bank of England in 1693. This account gives the national debt at the accession of George I in 1714 as £54 million, at the peace of Aix-la-Chapelle in 1748 as £78 million; at the peace of Paris (ending the Seven Years' War) in 1762, the debt had reached £139 million, with annual interest of £4.6 million. The war for American independence raised the debt to £268 million; by the peace of Amiens in 1802 that total had increased £360 million, to an annual interest of almost twenty million pounds; and the subsequent wars to Waterloo added another £420 million, raising the total to £885 million, with an annual interest of £32 million.

    For a suggestion on Shelley's own sources for the information and attitudes reflected in lines 2022 ff., see Kenneth Neill Cameron, "Shelley, Cobbett, and the National Debt," *Journal of English and Germanic Philology*, XLII (April 1943), 197–209.

line 2026. *as*: changed from *an.*

line 2055. *idle*: *d* written through *n.*

line 2056. *work.*: the period lost its function when the interlineation was added.

line 2058. *priveldged* (sic).

SC 546

far more than
the people ~~what~~ prætorian guards
and arbitrary tribunals, & excise

[LEAF 40, VERSO]

(74

2070 officers created judges in the last
resort, could ever wring. ~~The Persian~~
                    Neither the
Persian monarchy nor the Roman
empire, ~~to w to~~ where the will of one
person was acknowledged as unappea
                extorted of
lable law, ever ~~collected a~~ twentieth
~~part of the proportion~~ now ~~collected~~
                        extorted
2080 from the property & labour of the
inhabitants of Great Britain. ~~When~~
Alexander found in the treasury
of Darius about three millions in
        utmost resources which had been collected
Gold, as the war treasury from an
    by sustaining a war
empire, which brought ~~cent invade~~

G with the exception of India
                comprehended
& China ~~embraced~~ the whole vast   2090
extent of the population & territory
of Asia about ~~The degradation~~
        Of the National Debt.
~~Taxes to It is a fraud & an imposture~~
w The precious metals have been from
the earliest records of civilization em
-ployed as the signs of labour & the
titles to ~~ine~~ an unequal distribution
of its produce. The ~~Government of~~

[LEAF 41, RECTO]

a a country is necessarily entrusted   2100
with the affixing to certain portions
of these metals a stamp, by which
to mark their genuineness; no other
is considered as current coin, nor can be
a legal tender. The reason of this, is
that no alloyed coin should pass

line 2067. *prætorian guards*: the imperial bodyguard at several periods during the history of the Roman Empire exercised brute force to impose tyrants on the people; for example, in A. D. 193, after murdering the reforming emperor Pertinax, they publicly sold the office of emperor at auction to the highest bidder. See Edward Gibbon, *Decline and Fall of the Roman Empire*, chapter IV.

line 2082. *Alexander*: we have seen in SC 487 how Shelley took an interest in Herodotus' account of the annual tribute paid to Darius I. Here, from a later historian — possibly from Plutarch, who in his *Life of Alexander* mentions the sum of the treasure at Susa as being 4,000 talents in gold and silver coin — Shelley was tempted to give a figure in pounds sterling as the sum exacted by Darius III.

line 2085. *Gold,*: G is large but not definitely a capital.

line 2085. *from*: written through *of*.

line 2086. *by*: possible reading.

line 2093. *Of the National Debt.*: written later with dark heavy strokes and actually superimposed upon *of the population & territory* (line 2091) as a heading for the next section (see facsimile, page 1008).

line 2095. *precious metals*: Shelley's interest in the return to the gold standard and specie payments was shared by many of his contemporaries, including David Ricardo. Silver was demonetized in 1816 and by 1819 the decision had been made to redeem Bank of England notes with gold in stages between 1820 and 1823. See Frank Whitson Fetter, *Development of British Monetary Orthodoxy, 1797–1875* (Harvard University Press, 1965), pp. 64–95.

line 2099. *produce.*: written through *profits*.

line 2106. *alloyed*: MWS reads *alledged*.

line 2106. *pass*: below this word appear minute numerals which seem to be *10* above *20*, or possibly *1020*.

Front cover of vellum notebook containing SC 546, SC 547, and SC 549 with an ink drawing by Shelley and the front pastedown endpaper of the same notebook, showing Shelley's doodlings

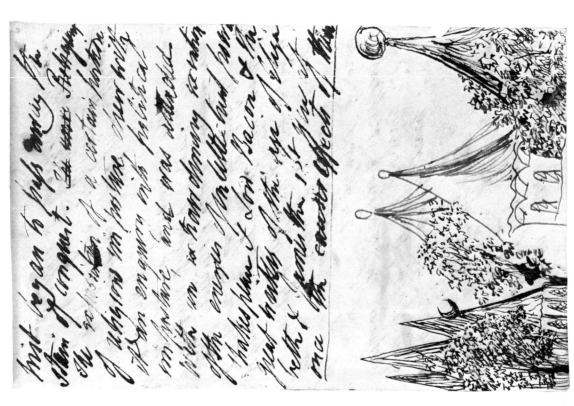

P. B. Shelley, *A Philosophical View of Reform*, November 1819–?1820, lines 211–222 with sketch and lines 991–1016 (SC 546, leaf 6, recto, and leaf 20, verso)

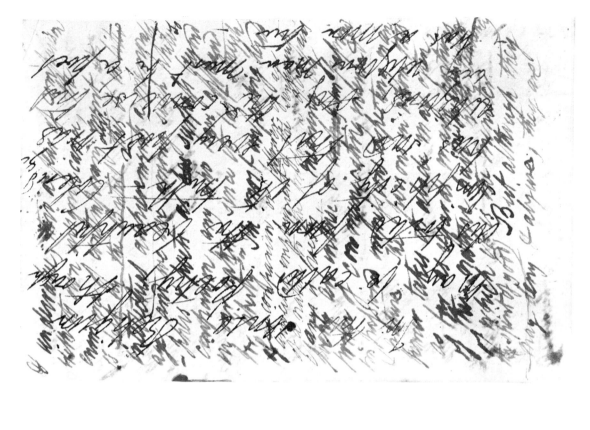

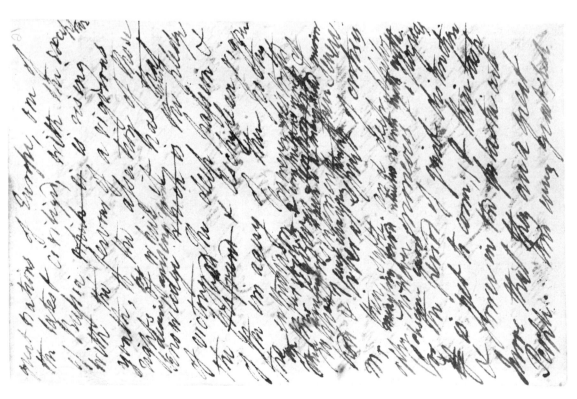

P. B. Shelley, A Philosophical View of Reform, November 1819–?1820, lines 1017–1045 and lines 1428–1463 (SC 546, leaf 21, recto, and leaf 28, verso)

P. B. Shelley, *A Philosophical View of Reform, November 1819–?1820, lines 2069–2099 and lines 2184–2217 (SC 546, leaf 40, verso, and leaf 42, verso)*

P. B. Shelley, *A Philosophical View of Reform*, November *1819–?1820*, lines
3661–3678 and lines *4963–4984* (SC 546, leaf 74, verso, and leaf 104, recto)

SC 546

current, & thereby depreciate ~~that~~
the
~~which is~~ genuine, & ~~on~~ by augmenting
2110   the price of the articles which are the
produce of labour defraud the
holders of that which is genuine of
the advantages legally belonging to
them.   If the Goverment itself
~~debases the metal~~ abuses the trust
reposed in it to debase the coin, ~~to~~
in order that it may derive advan
unlimited   this
-tage from the multiplication of it
2120   mark entitling its holder to command the
the gradations by which it sinks
labour & property of others
as labour rises to ~~its true valu~~
the level of
~~intrinsic value~~ their comparative
values produces, ~~as the price of~~
~~their~~ a public confusion & misery.

[LEAF 41, VERSO]
The foreign exchange meanwhile in-
⌊structs
the government how temporary was
2130   its resource. This mode ~~though rarely~~
~~resorted to, was~~ no of making the
distribution of the sign of labour, a
source of private aggrandisement
at the expence of public confusion &
loss, was not wholly unknown to the
nations of antiquity.
     ~~But this scheme of public credit~~
~~has the merit of novelty.— A gover~~
~~-ning party~~   But the moderns scheme

of public credit is a far subtler &   2140
more complicated contrivance of misrule.
~~It engages a number of persons to~~
~~trans The persons entrusted with the~~
~~government of the nation engage as~~
great
~~others~~   Where all∧transactions of
personal in England
∧property∧are managed by signs &
that is by ~~pieces of paper⟨ ⟩~~ the author-
⌊ity
of the possessor expressed upon paper,   2150
where ~~this slip of paper represents an~~
~~estate, this other a bale of goods,~~ this
other heap gold & silver represent

[LEAF 42, RECTO]
~~land & houses, & a slip of paper~~
~~represents gold & silver, & a persons~~
~~name attached to a small paper~~
~~represents his authority right to such~~
thus representing in a compendious
form his right to so much gold, which
represents his right to so much labour.   2160
~~it seems easy to prevent a complica~~
~~tion arising from the~~ A man may
write on a piece of paper what he
pleases; he may say he is worth a
thousand
~~million~~ when he not not worth a
hundred ~~thousand~~ pounds. ~~The great~~
~~merchants & bankers do this, &~~
~~this is what is called credit~~ If
he   ⟨ ⟩   2170
they ~~make~~ can make others believe this

---

line 2107. *current, . . . augmenting* (line 2109): parts of these lines smeared by ink blots from line 2093 on opposite page; these blots confirm that the heading was written later, while Shelley was rereading and revising.

line 2118. *this*: probable reading.

line 2139. *the*: altered from *this*.

line 2139. *scheme*: final letter runs off edge of page.

line 2166. *not not* (sic).

SC 546

     he
they has ~~their~~ credit for the sum
       his
to which ~~their~~ name is attached.
And so long as this credit lasts, he
can ~~buy & sell~~ act as if he
~~posessed this sum,~~ & can enjoy
all the advantages ~~arisin~~ which
2180 ~~are~~ would arise out of the actual
        of ~~it~~ the sum he is believed to posess.
possession. He can lend two hundred
to this man, & three to that

[LEAF 42, VERSO]
other, & his bills, among those ~~to~~
who believe that he possesses this
sum, pass like money.   Of course
in the same ~~degree that~~ proportion
as bills of this sort ~~operate~~ beyond
the actual goods or gold & silver
2190 possessed by the drawer, pass current
they defraud those who have gold
& silver ~~of the the ad~~ & goods of
the advantages legally attached to
     the   and they defraud the labourer &
their posession of them,∧by increasing
artizan of the advantage attached to labour &
the nominal price of ~~provisions~~
such a participation in them as their ⎰whilst
the products of labour,   ⎱and ⎰they
2200 industry command   and
add to the toil, ~~whilst~~ they render

     his wages fluctuating &
~~the uncertain the wages~~ of that
~~class by which they are produced~~
        the ~~pea~~ cultivator & the manufacturer
~~These are the persons to whom~~
the rulers apply for a loan of
Money ~~or rather~~   They lend no money
but they only write down their names,
or transfer that ~~fictitious credit~~   2210
which their friends & neighbours had

[WRITTEN CROSSWISE ON THE LAST FIVE
LINES OF LEAF 42, VERSO]
therefore from
the perpetual
tendency
of the rich
    de
inaquate

[LEAF 43, RECTO]
in them, to the government, which
in return ~~gives them~~ pledges the
faith of the nation to the payment   2220
of the amount. (The effects of a
base coin, a depreciated currency are
thus perpetuated in the currency of any
paper which shall be the symbols~~of~~
a transaction of this nature.) ~~A number~~
~~of~~ A number of persons however really
contribute their property to these loans,

line 2173. *has*: altered from *have*.

line 2185. *possesses*: MWS reads *has*; Mary probably purposely changed the word because *possess* and *possession* appear frequently just before this use.

line 2194. *and they defraud . . . industry command* (line 2200): a continuous interlineation, though Shelley dipped his quill again before writing *the advantage* (line 2196), the entire passage keyed by the caret to come between *them,* and *by* in line 2195.

line 2194. *defraud*: MWS reads *deprived*.

line 2196. *artizan* (sic).

line 2205. ~~*pea*~~: probably beginning of *peasant*.

line 2212. Lines 2212–2217, probably crosswritten after the next few leaves were canceled, were intended to follow line 2202 (see facsimile, page 1008). It was probably Shelley's intention to cancel line 2205.

line 2217. *inadequate*: *ate* written through indecipherable letters.

SC 546

2230 & recieve in exchange a ~~printed ack~~
~~-nowledgement called of~~ promise signed
by the authorized agents of the gover
ment that it shall be paid.—
                                    kind
            ~~A transaction of the nature, while~~
~~if they were aware of its real nature~~
~~would decieve no one, im~~ deludes the
nation ~~seduced~~ allured by the appearance
                                    appears
of good faith ~~that is~~ in the transaction
& in utter ignorance of its real
2240 meaning ⟩   The paper on which this
promise is written, has in the
existing instance of England

[LEAF 43, VERSO]
            now   80
~~completely~~ superseded the currency
of the legal & ordinary coin. ~~If~~
~~these promises were only issued~~ ⟨   ⟩
Then promises to pay, or Bank
notes are so many evidences in the
                        persons from whom
2250 hands of the holders that the ~~nation~~
            they receive them
~~is pledged to pay the~~ is indebted to
them to that amount Thus the
current coin of the nation has
been superseded by ~~the symbols of~~
pieces of paper whi~~ch import that~~
~~the gold which they~~ supersede has
~~been spent. They are the memorandum~~
~~of the debt; in the And they~~
2260 ~~who possess these~~ | ~~The whole nation~~

therefore have ~~been pledged repres~~
~~ent~~ each of whi~~ch represents a~~
~~portion~~   is an acknowledgement
of ~~the~~ a debt incurred by the
            of that paper
holder having ~~resigned his right~~
~~in the~~ transferred his right ~~in h~~
the amount of gold expressed
                        to the
upon ~~that paper~~ it The government   2270

[LEAF 44, RECTO]
person from whom he recieved it.
But ~~in m~~ as in many instances
neither gold nor any palpable sign
of ~~labour~~ the produce of labour ~~being~~
lent
given, ~~but the whole transaction being~~
~~a system of discounts~~ has been lent,
this ~~paper which stands in lieu~~ promise
to pay, would if actually paid in gold,
only reward, ~~by the speculations of~~   2280
            great   speculators
~~those who lent their credit~~ for this
            these wealthy impostors
~~who lent their names,~~ having nothing
else to lend to ~~the rulers of the day but~~
their signatures, & recieved ~~all~~ a signa-
                                    ⌊ture
in payment.

                                    not
    Yet, if these "promises to pay" have   2290
            a far greater
been issued in exact proportion that the
represents the amount
~~interest of~~ quarterly interest due

line 2239. &: written through indecipherable letters.

line 2244. *currency*: originally miswritten *currenly*.

line 2246. ⟨*I have*⟩: possible reading.

line 2261. *have*: written through *had*.

line 2282. *this*: possibly *the*.

line 2283. *these*: altered from *the*.

line 2289. *have*: altered from *had*.

line 2291. *that*: originally *to*; then miswritten *that* for *than*.

Shelley, *A Philosophical View of Reform*   November 1819–?1820

SC 546

even ~~to~~ on this ~~nominal debt~~ mass,
of part of which is real, & part
merely nominal debt; ~~it would have~~
~~constituted~~   ~~Here is the deciet~~
The government have taken advan
-tage of this necessary substitution
2300   of paper for coin ~~to perpetuate~~

[LEAF 44, VERSO]
consequent upon loans of this nature, to
   other
issue ~~more pieces of paper~~ promises
to pay, which represented no loan
      are
previously made, but ~~were merely~~
bills
    are merely
   This, and no other, has been the
2310   ~~This is~~
course pursued by ~~the existing Goverment~~
The ~~modern govern~~ existing Gover
      in substituting a currency of
nment of England has had no
paper to one of Gold.
need to depreciate the currency by
alloying the coin of the country, ~~but~~
they have merely⟨——⟩fabricated
pieces of paper on which they promise
2320   to pay a certain sum. The holders
of these papers came for payment
in some representation of property
universally exchangeable. They
then declared that the persons
who ~~under their authority~~ held the
office for that payment could not

be forced by law to pay. They
    subsequently
~~then~~ declared that these pieces

[LEAF 45, RECTO]
    legal   2330
of paper were the ~~current~~ coin
of the country. Every one possessing
these promissory notes ~~is evidently~~
a public creditor to what amount
in gold or in ex land, it is
~~difficult to determine~~ a difficult
calculation of circumstances to
determine. /   +
  ~~Of~~ this nature are all ~~such~~
~~tra~~ such transactions of companies   2340
& banks as consists in the
circulation of promissory notes
to a greater amount than
~~beyond~~ the actual property
possessed by those whose
~~names~~ names they bear. They have
the effect of augmenting the
prices of provision, and of
benefiting at the expense of ~~those~~
the community the speculators   2350
in this traffic.– ~~This system~~
~~of paper~~ One of the vaunted

[LEAF 45, VERSO]
effects of this system is to increase
the national industry. That is, to
increase the labours of the poor, &
    which they supply
those luxuries of the rich. To make

line 2300. *coin*: possibly followed by caret though nothing is interlined above it.

line 2317. *alloying*: MWS reads *depreciating*; as in line 2106 above, she apparently failed to decipher the word.

line 2327. *by*: written through *to*.

line 2330. *legal*: written indistinctly with insufficient ink.

line 2338. The cross apparently marks the spot to which Shelley wished to key a footnote, possibly lines 2370–2384.

line 2347. *augmenting*: *aug* written through *ag*.

line 2357. *those*: altered from *the*.

SC 546

2360

a manufacturer work sixteen hours
where he only worked eight. To ~~set~~
turn children into lifeless & bloodless
machines at an ~~per~~ age when otherwise
they would be at play before the
cottage doors of their parents. To
                      augment
~~increase~~ indefinitely the proportion
of those who enjoy the profit of
the labour of others, as compared
with those who exercise this labour
To screw ~~eff~~

2370

In a treatise devoted to general
considerations it would be superfluous
to enter into the mode in which
this has been done; those who desire
to see a full elucidation of that
made, may read Cobbets Paper against
gold. Our present business is

[LEAF 46, RECTO]

~~to~~ with consequences. I would

awaken, from a ~~view consi~~
                    that
consideration ~~of our~~ the present   2380
miseries of our country, are nothing
necessarily inherent of the stage of
civilization at which we have arrivd,
foresight & hope. ⌐   S. B.
                              4023.

                 in ~~one sense~~
These ~~notes are the representations~~ of
~~a debt which exceeds the~~
       The consequences of this transac-
                                  ⌊tion
has been the establishment of a   2390
new aristocracy, which has its basis
in fraud, as the old one has its
basis in force. The hereditary landowners in England derived their title
from royal grants, ~~dispensed~~ they
are fiefs bestowed by conquerors, or
                  ⌐Since usage has consecrated
church lands⌈ ~~By aristocracy~~
                  ⌊Let me be allowed

line 2361. *an*: changed from *a* after *per* was canceled.

line 2369. *screw eff*: Rolleston reads *screw up*; Shelley may have intended to write something like, "To screw efforts to their highest pitch"; in any case, the construction would have paralleled *To turn* and *To augment* above.

line 2375. William Cobbett's *Paper Against Gold* (London, 1815, 2 vols.) consisted of letters that had earlier appeared (1810–1812) in the *Political Register*. See Cameron, "Shelley, Cobbett, and the National Debt" (note to line 2023).

line 2376. *is*: written through *in*.

line 2383. *arrivd*, (sic).

line 2384. *S. B.*: inasmuch as we cannot discover that the letters *S. B.* have a relevant significance as an abbreviation, we think it possible that Shelley intended to publish *A Philosophical View of Reform* pseudonymously, reversing the initials for Bysshe Shelley. Of Shelley's eleven prose publications, only the two Irish tracts of 1812 were issued under his full name; six of his fourteen poetic publications in book form (including "Mont Blanc" in *History of a Six Weeks' Tour*) were issued anonymously or pseudonymously.

line 2390. *establishment*: altered from *established on*.

line 2392. *fraud,*: Rolleston reads *funds*.

line 2393. *landowners*: MWS reads *landholders*.

line 2397. *Since*: Rolleston reads *Long*.

line 2398. *church lands*: the thought is continued by lines 2420–2423 below.

line 2399. *allowed*: Peck reads *assumed*.

Shelley, A Philosophical View of Reform   November 1819–?1820

SC 546

a distortion of the wd aris from its primitive
to employ the word aristocracy in
          meaning
that ord– sense which signifies
[LEAF 46, VERSO]
that class of persons who ~~derive~~ possess
a right to the produce of the labour
of others, without dedicating to the
common service any labour in
return.– This class of persons, whose
existence is a prodigious anomaly

2410   in the social system, has ~~yet been~~
~~inseparab an~~ ever constituted an
                & there has never been
inseparable portion of it & ~~any no~~
    an approach in practise towards any
~~plans~~ of political society modelled
on equal justice ~~has ever~~ – at
least in the complicated mechanism
of modern life– ~~been brought to~~
~~practise. The most ardent~~

2420
                  bankers & merchants
or they have been bought by ~~merchants~~

from those persons. Now bankers &
merchants are persons whose

~~practical~~ ~~The human~~ Mankind
seem ~~to have given up~~ t to
acquiesce as, in ~~any~~ a necessary
condition of the imbecility of their

[LEAF 47, RECTO]
own will & reason, in the existence
of an aristocracy. With reference too
to this imbecility, it has doubtless   2430
                great
been the instrument of ~~immense~~
social advantage, although the
advatage would have been greater &
which might have been produced
according to the forms of a just
distribution of the goods & evils of
life.   The object therefore of ~~all~~
l all enlightened legislation, &
administration, is to enclose within   2440
the narrowest practicable limits

line 2400. *a distortion*: Rolleston reads *the abstraction*, Peck reads *the distinction*.

line 2400. *wd aris*: abbreviation for *word aristocracy* (see following line).

line 2401. *employ*: em seems to be written through illegible letters.

line 2402. *meaning*: a difference in inks makes it possible to ascertain that this word is not an alternative to *sense* below it, as its position would suggest, but follows *primitive* in line 2400.

line 2403. *ord- sense*: MWS reads *wide sense*; Rolleston and Peck expand to *ordinary sense*.

line 2414. *an*: possible reading.

line 2414. *practise* (alternative spelling): Shelley may have inserted this disclaimer about *practice* rather than *theory* being barren of examples tending toward equality because of his awareness of such abortive attempts to implement theories as the Pantisocracy scheme of Southey, Coleridge, and their friends.

line 2421. *or they . . . persons whose* (line 2423): this fragment continues the thought in line 2398 concluding with *church lands*.

line 2427. *imbecility*: Shelley uses the word here (and in line 2430 below) in its basic sense of weakness or feebleness.

line 2430. *to*: ?9 written below this word.

line 2433. *the*: altered from *that*.

line 2434. *advatage* (sic).

line 2439. *legislation,*: following and slightly below this word is a mark resembling 9.

line 2441. *practicable*: MWS reads *practical*.

SC 546

   drones
this order of ~~men~~*. The effect of*
the financial impostures of the
modern rulers of England has
been to increase the number of
the drones. Instead of one aris
tocracy the ~~inavoidable condit~~
condition which in the present

[LEAF 47, VERSO]

2450　*state of human affairs, the friends*
of justice & liberty are willing to
 subscribe as to
~~consider~~ *an inevitable evil, they*
  supplied　with
have ~~given~~ *us two aristocracies.*
  consisting
The one the great land proprietors
 prosperous
& ~~wealthy~~ *merchants,* ~~we admit~~
2460   *who exchange*
receive and ~~exchange the produce~~
~~of this country for the~~ *interchange*
the produce of this country with the
   in
produce of other countries; this
~~we su~~ *because all other great*
communities have as yet acquiesed
in it we acquiesce. ~~The other, a~~
   Connected with
2470 *the member of*
~~these~~ *this, is a certain generosity &*
refinement of manners & opinion,
which although neither philosophy

nor virtue ~~is a better substitute for~~
  has been that acknowledged
substitute for them, which at least
~~makes those ven~~ *is a religion*
which makes ~~the~~ *respected those*

[LEAF 48, RECTO]

   ⟨　⟩ *is an*
venerable names. But∧*the aristo*　　　2480
cracy of ~~attornies &,~~ ~~speculators~~
~~in the funds &~~ *attornies & excise*
-men, & ~~master manufa~~ *pensioners*
& bank directors, & ~~insurance~~
  government pensioners
~~office keepers & m~~ *usurers, stock*
  country bankers
jobbers, ~~which has arisen not~~
~~to the~~ *with their dependents &*
descendants. These are a set　　　2490
of pelting wretches ~~whos~~ *in whose*
employment there is nothing to
  their
exercise, even to ~~its~~ *distortion,*
the more majestic faculties of the soul.
~~They do nothing but cog, decieve~~
Though at the bottom it is all trick
there is something ~~magnificent~~
   frank & magni
ficent in the ~~hospitality~~ *chivalrous*　　2500
hospitality & the disdain of infamy
connected with a gentleman. There
is something to which—until you
see through the base falshood upon

---

line 2447. *Instead*: altered from *It*.

line 2451. *justice*: MWS and Rolleston read *virtue*.

line 2458. ~~*prosperous*~~: probable reading.

line 2467. *communities*: MWS reads *countries*.

line 2467. *acquiesed* (sic).

line 2479. ⟨ ⟩: this word is completely obliterated by ink blot cancellation. MWS, Rolleston, and Peck all supply *other*.

line 2483. *manufa*: master manufacturers meant "industrialists."

line 2495. *faculties*: probable reading; MWS reads *principles*; Dowden reads *forces*.

line 2496. *cog,*: verb meaning to practice certain tricks in throwing dice; fraudulently to control their fall; to cheat; to produce cunningly and fraudulently (*OED*).

Shelley, A Philosophical View of Reform   November 1819–?1820

SC 546 [LEAF 48, VERSO]
which all inequality is founded—
to which it is difficult for the
imagination to refuse its respect, in
the *pa* faithful & ~~substantial~~ &
direct dealings of the substantial
2510 merchant. [& ~~we~~] But in the
~~proceedings~~ habits & lives of this
new aristocracy created out of
    an increase   calamities
the public ~~debt~~, & whose existence
must be determined by their termination, there is nothing to qualify
       disapprobation
our ~~disgust~~. They eat & drink &
sleep, & in the intervals of those
2520   *being performed with most ridiculous*
~~actions~~, they cringe & lie. ~~Those~~
    ceremony & accompaniments
~~who only recieve such~~

—————————

As usual
The first persons decieved are those

who are the instruments of the
fraud, & the merchant & the
country gentleman may be ~~acquitted~~
~~of~~ excused for believing that
their existence is connected with   2530
[LEAF 49, RECTO]
the permanence of the best
practicable forms of social order

—————————

They poison the literature of the
age in which they live, by requiring
      anti
either the ~~proto~~ type of their own
mediocrity in books, or such
        distorted & inharmonious idealisms
stupid & ~~exaggerated⟨   ⟩harangue~~
~~of~~ as alone ~~may stir thier~~ have   2540
the power to stir thier torpid ima
ginations.   Their hopes & fears are
of the narrowest description. ~~If~~
~~they care Good name, Reputation,~~
~~love, They are full of all those~~

line 2510. [& ~~we~~]: first square bracket written through two indecipherable letters.

line 2520. *being*: Rolleston and Peck read *things*.

line 2520. *ridiculous*: Rolleston reads *vexatious*.

line 2522. *accompaniments*: s is doubtful.

line 2524. The sentence between lines 2524–2532 was apparently to be inserted after *merchant* (line 2510).

line 2525. *decieved* (sic): MWS reads *decried*; Rolleston reads *describes*.

line 2533. *They poison . . . personal advantage* (line 2554): Shelley's reaction to the nouveau riche was surprisingly violent, considering his own grandfather's role in establishing the fortune of Shelley's family. But his own family had long been part of the country gentry — and Sussex gentlemen, by reason of their proximity to London, were generally better informed and more in style than those of more distant counties.

    The present passage reinforces and helps to explain and focus some comments in the prefaces to Shelley's poems — particularly that passage in the Preface to *Alastor* where he speaks of those "morally dead" who are "neither friends, nor lovers, nor fathers, nor citizens of the world, nor benefactors of their country."

line 2535. *anti*: inserted later with a sharper quill.

line 2538. *inharmonious*: added later with a sharper quill.

line 2539. *exaggerated*: written through illegible word.

line 2539. ⟨—⟩: possibly *ex*.

line 2540. *have*: crowded into the margin, with *e* written below *v*.

line 2545. *all*: probable reading.

SC 546   ~~regards~~ Their domestic affections
are feeble & they have no others. They
              of any
think ~~of no~~ commerce with their
2550   species but as a means ~~of personal~~
~~what they call self interest, not~~
as never as an end. and as
a means to the basest ~~of~~ forms
of personal advantage
                   this
         If aristocracy had been

[LEAF 49, VERSO]
~~created by~~ ⟨————⟩ ~~what is~~
~~called the national debt~~ arisen
from a false & depreciated currency,
2560   ~~not~~ to the exclusion of the other;
its existence would have been a
                      a
moral calamity & ~~an everlasting~~
disgrace, but it would not have
~~been an oppression~~ constituted an
oppression.   But the ~~other~~ hered
              who held
itary aristocracy ~~had~~ the political
administration of affairs & it

took the measures which created   2570
     other
this, for purposes peculiarly its
own. Those measures were so
~~taken therefore as to~~ contrived as
in no manner to diminish the
⟨————⟩ wealth & power ~~of the rulers~~
the contrivers. The lord does not
spare himself one luxury, but
the peasant & artizan are amerced

[LEAF 50, RECTO]
     many needful things   2580
of ~~their necessities~~. To support the
~~existing~~ system of social order
according to its supposed unavoi
dable constitution, those from whose
              external accomodations which
labour all those distinguish a
civilized being from a savage arise
              before the institution of this
worked ~~before the establishment~~
     double aristocracy   2590
~~of this aristocr~~ eight hours. ~~in~~
~~order that the aristocracy might~~
~~la For this labour~~ And of these
only the healthy were compelled

line 2546. *regards*: probable reading.

line 2553. *means*: altered from *mean*.

line 2556. *If*: written through *This*.

line 2556. *aristocracy*: written in four units, *ar is to cracy*.

line 2556. *had*: *d* written through *s*.

line 2557. *by* ⟨————⟩: new word(s) written through old, rendering both illegible. The earlier phrase may have been *bad rulers*.

line 2564. *it*: written through *n*.

line 2575. *the*: altered from *their*.

line 2579. *artizan* (sic): Shelley normally employs the z to represent the voiced sibilant, and this, his preferred spelling, shows his pronunciation.

line 2579. *amerced*: Rolleston and Peck read *assured*; *to amerce* is to punish by exacting an arbitrary fine.

line 2583. *unavoidable*: Shelley uses this word where we might say "nonvoidable."

line 2585. *accomodations* (sic).

line 2586. *those*: altered from *that*.

Shelley, A Philosophical View of Reform   **November 1819–?1820**

SC 546

        labour
to ~~work~~, the ~~old the sick~~ efforts
of the old the sick & the immature
being dispensed with, & they
maintained by the labour of the
2600   *for such is the plain English of the*
sane, That labour procured
     poor rates
a competent share of the decen
cies of life, & society seemed to
extend the benefits of its insti

[LEAF 50, VERSO]

       94
tution even to its most unvalued
instruments. ~~Their~~ Although deprived
     resources
2610   *of those ~~refinements~~ of sentiment &*
knowledge, which might ~~be their~~

~~lot according~~ have been their lot
could the wisdom of the institutors
of social forms have established
an system of strict justice, yet
they earned by their labour a
competency in those external materials
of life, ~~&~~ which, & not the loss
of moral & intellectual excellence,
is ~~the~~ supposed to be the legitimate   2620
object of the desires & murmurs
of the poor. Since the institution
of this double aristocracy however
     appointed task   *ten*
their ~~have worked not eight~~ but
   twenty
~~sixteen~~ hours a day. Not that
they have all ~~rigidly worked~~ the

line 2596. *efforts of the old . . . of the poor.* (line 2622): Shelley, as an agriculturist, believed in the classical operation of the Poor Laws, in which working members of a small rural community paid to the parish a percentage of their incomes sufficient to support the few paupers — widows and orphans, aged and infirm. The rise of industrial cities, with their periods of mass unemployment, and the increase in the numbers of farm day-laborers, who (after the few prosperous years during the war when English agriculture was free of foreign competition) were often unemployed, caused a breakdown in this welfare system. The Poor Laws were attacked by the merchants, industrialists, and all tax-paying citizens of the new industrial towns, and their effects were decried by William Cobbett, champion of the rate-paying yeoman farmer (though Cobbett shifted the blame to the Tory government, London Jews, and assorted other scapegoats).

The Poor Laws that were in effect in Shelley's day dated from 1601 and had several features that were subject to abuse. (Churchwardens were, for example, empowered to apprentice orphans or children whose parents could not support them, and Crabbe's story of Peter Grimes, Letter XXII in *The Borough*, 1810, is the tale of one monstrous abuse of this provision.) But Shelley, as he shows here, feared that the alternative decided upon by the *drones* (as he calls them) who ruled the country might be to let the poor starve while they themselves continued to draw their sinecures and interest from the public treasury.

The actual Poor Law amendments, passed by the reformed Parliament in 1834, maintained the basic system of 1601 but modified the law's administration to reduce the burden on particular parishes and to discourage pauperism by making existence in workhouses as dehumanizing as possible.

line 2601. *procured*: MWS reads *produced*.

line 2602. *poor*: possible reading.

line 2613. *institutors*: Rolleston and Peck read *institutions*.

line 2620. *legitimate*: probable reading.

line 2621. *desires*: MWS reads *designs*.

line 2625. *their*: altered from *they*.

SC 546   [LEAF 51, RECTO]

2630
                   twenty
poor have rigidly worked ~~sixteen~~
hours, but that the worth of
               twenty
the labour of ~~sixteen~~ hours now,
        food
in ~~clo~~ ~~bread~~ & clothing is equivalent
             ten
to the worth of ~~eight~~ hours, ~~then~~
            twenty   *labour*
then. And because ~~sixteen~~ hours
2640
cannot be exacted from ~~any~~ those
                  from the nature of the human
who before performed ten, the aged
frame
& the sickly are compelled either to
work or starve. Children who
were exempted from labour are
put in requisition, & the vigorous
promise of the coming generation
blighted by premature exertion.
2650
Nor ~~is this enough~~ does this suffice
Men re~~lieve~~ ~~the wages of~~ certain
nomi~~nal wages, but~~ this mean~~s~~
noth~~ing~~. For fourteen hours
labour which they do perform

[LEAF 51, VERSO]

                   in
they recieve,—no matter ~~to~~ what
nominal amount— the price of
               less
seven. They eat ~~worse~~ bread, wear

worse clothes, are more ignorant   2660
immoral, miserable & desperate.

For the burthen on them is
twofold. They support this bastard
aristocracy, whose titles to their
                      the possession
labour consists in a false currency.
~~And these who eat the fruits of their~~
~~labour contribute no labour~~
               then is
This ~~being~~ the condition of the   2670
lowest & the largest class, from
whose labour the whole materials
~~of subsistence~~ of life are wrought,
~~of~~ of which the others are only
the receivers or the consumers. Although
               all other
But the condition of ~~the other~~
~~classes of society is not the~~

[LEAF 52, RECTO]

~~They are thus~~ They are more supers
titious, for misery on earth begets   2680
               expectation
a diseased ~~desire~~ & panic stricken
faith in miseries beyond the grave.
"God they argue rules this world
as well as that; and assuredly
since his nature is immutable &
his powerful will unchangeable
he rules them by the same laws.

line 2644. *are*: written through *is*.

line 2645. There is a minute sketch of foliage in right margin.

line 2649. *premature*: *pre* written through indecipherable letters.

line 2654. *perform*: Rolleston reads *perforce*.

line 2659. *bread,*: altered from *bred*.

line 2673. *are*: written through *is*.

line 2675. *Although*: added later with sharper quill.

line 2677. The context continues at line 2698.

line 2684. "*God . . . revengeful—* (line 2694): This passage provides a commentary on the psychological reaction of Beatrice Cenci in Shelley's drama.

Shelley, A Philosophical View of Reform November 1819–?1820

SC 546

The gleams of hope which speak
of Paradise, seem like the flames
in Milton's hell, only to make dark
ness visible, & all things takes its
colour from what surrounds them
They become revengeful—
            alibi

[LEAF 52, VERSO]
~~*less incompatible with* ⟨ ⟩ *miseries*~~
            either employed as recievers of the products
                            ⌊*of labour*
*classes of society*ᴧ*excepting those*
within the priveledged pale is
2700 *singularly unprosperous, ~~and even~~*
            ~~*The great consequences of a tyran*~~
~~*nical govermnent are thus*~~
~~*upon these the ac reaction the*~~
~~*The heathful circulation of the*~~
and even they, experience the
reaction of their own shortsighted
tyranny, in all those sufferings
& deprivations
which are not of a distinctly

physical nature, in the loss   2710
of dignity simplicity & energy
& in the possession of all those
qualities which distinguish a
slave driver from a proprietor.
      ~~*The great character of tyr*~~ ⟨ ⟶ ⟩*y*
~~*is an order*~~

[LEAF 53, RECTO]
~~*The great character of misgovern*~~
                  Right
~~*ment is stamped upon*~~ *Govern*
ment being an institution for   2720
the purpose of securing such a
moderate degree of happiness to
                  experimentally
men, as has been practicable,
~~*mis*~~*; the sure character of mis*
goverment is misery, & first
            and if that be despised
discontent, then insurrection, as
            legitimate
*the*ᴧ*expression of that misery.*   2730
            The public ought to demand happiness
~~*The best republic or monarchy or*~~

line 2695. *alibi*: Shelley uses the word in its earlier sense, as an adverb meaning "elsewhere"; that is, he intends to insert lines 2679–2694 elsewhere in the treatise.

line 2696. ~~*miseries*~~: probable reading.

line 2697. Line inserted later with sharper quill.

line 2697. *labour*: probable reading; Peck reads *work* and Rolleston failed to decipher the interlineation; Mary Shelley also left a blank, but Hogg filled it with *labour*.

line 2698. Shelley continues the thought from line 2677.

line 2698. The caret was written later with a sharper quill.

line 2699. *pale*: MWS reads *class* (added by Hogg).

line 2704. ~~*heathful*~~ (sic): for *healthful*.

line 2706. *shortsighted*: probable reading.

line 2708. *deprivations*: may be singular.

line 2715. ~~*tyr*⟨*anny*⟩~~: page is discolored, affecting text.

line 2723. *experimentally*: probable reading.

line 2725. *character*: MWS reads *characteristic*. Shelley here uses *character* to mean "a distinctive mark, evidence, or token" (*OED* 8, now archaic).

line 2731. *ought*: Rolleston reads *right*.

line 2731. *happiness*: Shelley used *happiness* and *happy*, not in the psychological sense, but in their more fundamental meanings of "good fortune, . . . prosperity" (*happiness*, *OED* 1) and "fortunate,

The Carl H. Pforzheimer Library

Shelley, A Philosophical View of Reform   November 1819–?1820

SC 546

By a fortunate law of nature the
~~All the rest are the means & the~~
labouring classes, when they cannot get food
~~form~~   Laws & assemblies &
for their labour, are ⟨   ⟩ to take it by force
courts of justice, & ~~represe~~ deleg
-ated powers placed in p balance or

2740

in opposition are the means & the
form, but public happiness is
the substance & the end of political
institution. Whenever this is
~~rendered insecure~~ attainted ~~not~~

[LEAF 53, VERSO]
                                    external
in a nation, not from ~~foreign~~
force, but from the internal
arrangement, & divisions of the
common burthens of defence &

2750

maintenance, then there is
oppression. ~~And then there is~~
~~need of Reform~~ And then arises
an alternative between Reform
~~or Revolution & Despo~~ the ins
titution of a military Despotism;
or a Revolution in which

various   one   an
~~two~~ parties striving after ill
digested   democracy
~~defined~~ systems of ~~equality~~, &   2760
the other clinging to the
outworn abuses of power, leave the
few ~~friends of rational~~ who aspire
to more than the ~~one~~, & who would
                              former
overthrow the latter at whatever
expense to wait until that
modified advantage which

[LEAF 54, RECTO]
results from ~~their conflict~~
produces ~~the~~ a small portion   2770
~~of that social improvement~~
which with the temperance & the
toleration which both regard as
a crime, might have resulted
from the occasion which they let pass
in a far more signal manner
                              which are the consequences
      The propositions to which the
Malthus   or the corollaries of
preceding reasoning seems to have   2780
conducted us are—

lucky, prosperous" (*happy*, *OED* 3). In other words, Shelley says that the duty of government is to protect men from the worst effects of ill-fortune — bad harvests, natural disasters, ill health, and the like.

line 2733. *By a fortunate . . . force* (line 2737): MWS omits this interlined sentence, probably intentionally.

line 2733. *law*: probable reading.

line 2737. *are* ⟨*certain*⟩: possible reading; Rolleston and Peck read *impelled*.

line 2756. *Revolution*: Shelley, though he has said (lines 2725–2730) that it is a law of nature that men should overthrow unbearable tyranny, never advocates armed rebellion as a cure for anything except despair. Notice how he exempts himself from those who would support either an *ill digested democracy* (unacceptable because ill digested) or the *outworn abuses of power*.

line 2757. *various*: possible reading; written through indecipherable word.

line 2768. *modified*: marred by ink blots from opposite page.

line 2769. Most of the canceled words in lines 2769–2771 seem necessary to the completion of the thought.

line 2775. This line must have been written after line 2776 and was presumably intended to follow it.

line 2777. Lines 2777 and 2779 were written with a sharp quill except for *Malthus*, line 2779, which was probably written as guide-note before line 2778.

[1022]

SC 546

majority
That the people of England are
destitute & miserable, ill clothed
~~in a severe & chang~~ ill-fed, ill-
educated.

being
That they know this, & that
they are impatient to procure
2790 a reform of the cause of their
abject & wretched state.

peculiar
That, a cause of this misery

[LEAF 54, VERSO]
is the unequal distribution which
under the form of the national

has been
~~debt~~ it is surreptiously made of
the products of their labour &
the products of the labour of
2800 their ancestors; for all property
is the produce of labour.

That the cause of that cause is a defect
in the c   government
~~That if they did not know~~
~~is, yet every member~~ of
~~the priveledged classes~~

~~That such a Reform is~~
being
~~not only the desire of the majority~~

~~of the suffering people, but also~~ 2810
~~of those of refined education~~
~~& enlightened minds. & being~~
That if they knew nothing
of their condition, but believed
that all they endured & all

[LEAF 55, RECTO]
were deprived of arose from the
unavoidable condition of
human life, this belief being
an ~~injustice~~ error, & the endurance
of enforces an injustice, every 2820
enlightened & honourable person
whatever may be the imagined
interests of his peculiar class, ought
to excite them to the discovery
of the true state of the case &
to the temperate but irresistible
vindication of their rights.

~~Those & A reform is thus proved~~
~~to be~~ A Reform in the England
is most just & necessary. What 2830
ought to be that reform.

of the present day
~~So.~~ A writer— (a priest of
course— for his doctrines are
those of a eunuch & of a tyrant.)

---

line 2793. *a*: superimposed on *the*.

line 2797. *surreptiously* (sic).

line 2797. *of*: probable reading; written below the line.

line 2802. Lines 2802–2803 written later with a sharp quill.

line 2805. ~~is,~~: written through *the*.

line 2809. ~~majority~~: *ty* crowded below line.

line 2815. *that all they*: smeared by ink blotted from facing page.

line 2826. *but*: *b* written through ?*sl*.

line 2829. *in*: altered from *is*.

line 2833. The writer referred to is Thomas Robert Malthus, who though a priest was hardly a eunuch (he sired a son and two daughters) or a tyrant.

Shelley's interest in Malthus and the Malthusian theory of population had been long and intense. He first attacked Malthus in his *Proposals for an Association . . .* (1812; see Shelley, *Complete Works*, V, 266–267). In a footnote to the Preface of *The Revolt of Islam* he declares that the later editions of Malthus' work, which allow for human moral restraint as a check on population, reduce

SC 546   [LEAF 55, VERSO]

has stated that the evils of the
poor arise from an excess of population, & that ~~they ought to~~
~~be restrained from the enjoyments~~

2840
     been
After they have stript naked
by the tax gatherer & reduced
to bread & tea & fourteen hours
    by their masters
of hard labour, & after the frost
has bitten their defenceless limbs.
        had
and the cramp has wrung like a disease within
          ⌊*their bones*
And hunger & the suppressed

2850
     has
revenge of hunger stamped the
ferocity of want like the mark
of Cain upon their ~~visage~~ countenance
that the last tie by which
Nature holds them to ~~the beau~~
      earth
~~tiful~~ & benignant ~~land~~ whose
plenty is garnered up in the

strongholds of their tyrants, ~~that~~
~~they are~~ is to be divided;   ~~The~~   2860
that the single alleviation of their
sufferings & their scorns, the one

[LEAF 56, RECTO]

thing which made ~~them equa~~
it impossible to degrade them
below the beasts, the ~~sole line~~
~~which divides~~ which ~~made~~
amid all their crimes & miseries,
      separated
yet ~~prevented~~ a cynical & unmanly
contamination, ~~from supers~~ & an   2870
~~un~~ antisocial cruelty from all
       harmonious
the soothing elevating & ~~harmonizing~~
gentlenesses of the sexual intercourse,
& the humanizing charities of
domestic ~~aff~~ life which are its
appendandages,—that this is to be
obliterated. They are required to
abstain from marrying ~~or~~ under
penalty of starvation. And ~~the~~   2880

"the *Essay on Population* to a commentary illustrative of the unanswerableness of *Political Justice*." But Shelley felt constrained to combat Malthusianism poetically both in *Prometheus Unbound* and *Œdipus Tyrannus* (C. E. Pulos, "Shelley and Malthus," *PMLA*, LXVII, March 1952, 113–124) and here in prose.

  Shelley's revived interest in Malthus was probably generated by reading a French translation — perhaps Pierre Prévost's version of 1809 — at Este in October 1818, when in a letter to Peacock he writes: "Malthus is a very clever man, & the world would be a great gainer if it would seriously take his lessons into consideration — if it were capable of attending seriously to any thing but mischief — but what on earth does he mean by some of his inferences!" (Shelley, *Letters*, II, 43.) Sometime in 1818 or 1819 Shelley jotted in a notebook (Bodleian Ms. Shelley adds. e. 12, p. 36) this note (in ink): "If Peace should ever return to me — / An Inquiry into in what degree the principle of population can affect the future hopes of mankind / Equality — Republicanism—." On the same page and the next one are drafts (in pencil) that are apparently for an early version of the struggle in *Prometheus Unbound*, Act III, scene i, between Demogorgon (called here "the serpent of being") and Jupiter, as reported in a dialogue between Asia and Panthea.

line 2848. *wrung like*: tangled with & *the* (line 2849) and written below *had*.

line 2848. *their bones*: runs down beside the following two lines.

line 2865. *beasts, the*: *the* written through *that*.

line 2873. *elevating*: probable reading.

line 2875. *charities*: first *i* altered from *a*.

line 2877. *appendandages*, (sic).

Shelley, A Philosophical View of Reform   November 1819–?1820

SC 546

⟨——⟩*it is threatned to deprive*
them of that property which is
as strictly their birth right as
a gentleman's land is his birth
right, without giving them

[LEAF 56, VERSO]
any ~~additional~~ *compensation*
~~for~~ *but the insulting advice*
      to
of conquering with un⟨ ⟩ ~~und~~
2890   ~~isciplined~~ *minds undisciplined in*
the habits of higher gratification
a propensity ~~on~~ *which persons of*
      consummate
the most ~~cultivated~~ *wisdom*
        contend
have been unable to resist. and
which it is difficult to admire a person for
   ~~The writer in question asserts~~
    having resisted—   *& an ⟨*   ⟩ *for*
2900   ~~these doctrines with the most~~
    which is perhaps guilty to be provided
~~violent~~ *violence* ~~If the doctrines~~
  ⟨ ⟩ *a* ⟨ ⟩ *are perhaps* ⟨ ⟩⟨ ⟩
~~of this writer~~ *The doctrine of this*
    is that
writer ~~as to~~ *the principle*
of population, when under no
dominion of moral restraint
outstripping the ~~pro~~ *sustenance*
2910   *produced by the labour of man,*
and that not in proportion

to the number of inhabitants;
but ~~perpetually~~ *operating as*
    equally
~~powerfully~~ *in a thinly peopled*
community as in one where

[LEAF 57, RECTO]
the population is ernormous,
being not a prevention, but a
        strange
check. ~~Now this is a novel~~   2920
view to take of the effects of moral
restraint, which has generally been
supposed & justly favourable to
population; one would at least
in the ordinary sense of moral
restraint & we are not instructed
~~by the w~~ *This whether its*
~~a just & an un~~ *i view of the*
subject whether right or wrong
and this is not the place for   2930
confuting at length a particu
lar writer, particularly as he
has now fallen within a
mighty grasp—is ~~Unless he~~
~~says consent to go~~ *So far a man*
might have been conducted by ~~the~~

[LEAF 57, VERSO]
    108
~~opinions whic~~ *a train of reasoning*
which though it may be shewn to

line 2881. *threatned* (sic).

line 2882. *that property*: Shelley refers to the rights of paupers to sustenance under the Poor Laws. (See note to line 2596.)

line 2896. *and which . . . resisted—* (line 2899): the interlineations are written with a sharper quill.

line 2899. *an ⟨*   ⟩: possibly *an example*.

line 2902. ~~doctrines~~: probable reading.

line 2903. The line is so tangled with the lines above and below it as to be virtually illegible to us.

line 2916. *one*: written through *a*.

line 2917. *is*: written through indecipherable letter.

line 2917. *ernormous*, (sic).

line 2934. *mighty grasp—*: an allusion to Godwin's *Of Population*, which Shelley knew to be in progress at least as early as July 25, 1818 (see Shelley, *Letters*, II, 22).

SC 546

be defective, would argue in the
reasoner no selfish & slavish feelings.
It is But he has the hardened
insolence to propose as a remedy that
~~the rich should be~~ the poor should
be compelled (for what except
compulsion is ~~the confiscation of that~~
        a threat of the confisca
tt tion of ~~that property~~ those funds which
by the institutions of their country ap-
        ⌊*pointed*

2950   had been set apart for their sustenance
in sickness or destitution) to abstain
from sexual intercourse, whilst the
rich are to be permitted to ~~produce~~
as add as many mouths to
consume the products of the labour
of the poor as they please. If
~~it be those~~ ⌈*The* rights of all men
are intrinsically & originally equal

[LEAF 58, RECTO]
& they forego the assertion of all
2960   *only*
of them, that they may the more
securely enjoy a portion⌉ If
                are found to
any new disadvantages attach
to the condition of social existence
those disadvantages ought not
to be borne exclusively by one
        class
~~denomination~~ of men, nor especially
2970   by that class whose ignorance
leads them to exaggerate the
advantages of sensual enjoyment,
whose callous habits render domes
tic endearments more important

dispose them to resist the suggestions to
to ~~prevent the crimes of~~ violence
        & cruelty
by which their situation ever exposes
                all
them to be tempted, & whose other   2980
enjoyments are limited & few,
whilst their sufferings are various
& many. In this sense I cannot
imagine how the advocates
of equality have so readily

[LEAF 58, VERSO]
could so readily have conceded thus
the unlimited operation of the
principle of population, affects
the ~~practicability of the~~ the
truth of their theories. On the   2990
contrary the more heavy & certain
are the evils of life, the more injus
tice is there is casting the burthen
of them exclusively on one order
in the community. ~~If it be~~
~~necessary that they should~~ They
seem to have conceded it merley
because their opponents have a~~ss~~
                Surely
insolently assumed it. It is enough   3000
            rich should
that the ~~persons who~~ possess ~~all~~
~~the other luxuries & enjoyments of~~
life to the exclusion of the poor
all other luxuries & comforts, &
wisdom & refinement the ~~most~~
least envied but the most

[LEAF 59, RECTO]
deserving of envy among all
their priveledges; ~~when a new~~

line 2957. The bracketed sentence is an aphorism that Shelley probably thought more suitable for another part of the paper, possibly as a footnote keyed to the word *right* in line 3393.

line 2978. *by*: written through *?by* or *?to*.

line 2993. *is there is* (sic): see also *merley* (sic) for *merely*, line 2997.

line 3000. *It*: a line through *It* evidently indicates alteration to lower case *I*.

Shelley, A Philosophical View of Reform   November 1819–?1820

SC 546   *error is discovered in the consti*
-tution of human nature /
[LEAF 59, VERSO, BLANK]

[LEAF 60, RECTO]
What is the Reform that
the We desire.—
          And here it be it remis
     Before
          We have aspire after no theore
tical & abstract perfection in
the amelioration of our political
state; before we appr can
3020 *approach to it is necessary that*
we possess those advantages
which the expe have been we
have been cheated of, & which
the experience of modern
times has proved that the
                    even
nations under the present
          1st   would
are susceptible. These We

[LEAF 60, VERSO]
          these   2d
3030 *would regain, & We would establish*
some form of goverment which

might secure them us against
such a series of events as have
conducted us to a persuasion
that the forms now accord
ing to which it is now admi
nistered are inadequate to
that purpose.
          We would abolish, the national   3040
debt.
          We would disband the standing
army. We would, with every possible re-
                              ⌊*gard*
to the existing interests of the holders, abolish sine-
                                          ⌊*cures*
          We would, with every possible
regard to the existing interests
of the holders, abolish tithes.
And make all religions, all
forms of opinion respecting the

[LEAF 61, RECTO]
origin & goverment of the   3050
Universe, equal in the eye of
the law.
                    cheap
          We would make justice⌃certain
& speedy; & would ap & extend
the institution of juries to every

line 3011. *of human nature*: probably underscored to indicate break in thought.

line 3012. *What . . . desire.—* (line 3013): Mary Shelley, probably correctly, treats these words as the heading to a new section of the treatise.

line 3012. *Reform*: *R* is broken and looks like *li*.

line 3014. *it*: first *it* altered from *is* or vice versa.

line 3015. *Before*: probable reading; end of word indistinct.

line 3018. *amelioration*: *l* written through *r*.

line 3028. *would*: inserted unnecessarily.

line 3030. *2d*: probable reading.

line 3040. *abolish,*: the use of a comma between the subject and predicate to indicate a pause was a standard practice advocated in both grammars and elocution manuals of Shelley's day.

line 3043. *We . . . sinecures* (line 3044): inserted later.

line 3044. *interests*: probable reading; word may be singular.

line 3044. *sinecures*: probable reading.

SC 546

        possible
to every ~~of~~ *occasion of jurisprudence.*
~~*Abolishing the court of Chancery*~~ *-x*

3060

    The national debt was ~~*contracted*~~
                          chiefly
contracted in two liberticide wars
    undertaken by
~~*by the rich, in order the first*~~
~~*by the rich that the*~~ *by the*
privelded classes of the ~~*nation*~~
country ~~*in order*~~ *the first for*
    ineffectual
the purpose of tyrannising

3070

~~*over a portion of their subjects*~~
over one portion of their subjects,
~~*the second in order to extinguish*~~
~~*the enthusi*~~ *the resolute spirit*

[LEAF 61, VERSO]
of attaining these rights in another.
    The labour which this money
represents, & that which is repre
sented by the money wrung for
~~*the purposes of the same detes*~~
table character, out of the people

3080

since the commencement of
the American war would ~~*have*~~
if properly employed, have
covered our land with monum
ents of architecture ~~*that might*~~
~~*have rivaled the*~~ *exceeding the*
    sumptuousness
~~*magnificence the*~~ *& the* ~~*grace*~~
             beauty
of Ægypt & Athens; it might

3090

have made every peasants cottage
surrounded with its garden
a little paradise of comfort,
      every convenience desirable in civilized life
with ~~*an assortmen*~~ *neat tables &*
                nice
chairs, & good beds, & a ~~*little*~~
collection of useful books

[LEAF 62, RECTO]
    ships
and our ~~*fleet*~~ *manned by*

3100

sailors well-paid & well clothed
might have kept watch round
this glorious island against the

line 3058. The final three words of this line are affected by ink blotting from leaf 60, verso, lines 3043–3044.

line 3059. The cancel line may have been intended as an underscore.

line 3062. *liberticide wars*: Shelley refers to the British wars to repress the American and French revolutions.

line 3066. *privelded* (sic).

line 3074. *attaining*: Peck reads *obtaining*.

line 3074. *these*: Peck and Rolleston read *their*.

line 3085. *the*: written through *m*.

line 3090. *peasants cottage* . . .: Shelley's firsthand knowledge of the contrasting *actual* condition of English peasant cottages came most recently from his visits of mercy among the peasants and lace-makers of the Marlow area in 1817.

line 3093. *every . . . life*: added later with sharp quill.

line 3093. *civilized*: MWS reads *cultivated*.

line 3098. *ships*: beginning *s* badly blotted.

line 3099. *our ships . . . prosperity.* (line 3106): British liberals of this period supported expansion of the navy (which defended the islands against outside enemies) above the maintenance of a standing army (which could be used to oppress dissenters at home). Thus the liberals appealed to patriotism in the name of Nelson, while the Tories made Wellington their hero.

SC 546

          assuredly
less enlightened nations which‸
would   until they could have imitated
~~might~~ have envied its prosperity.
But the labour which is expressed
          has been
by these sums ~~thus~~ diverted from these
3110 ~~genuine~~ purposes of human happiness
to the promotion of slavery or the
attempt at dominion, & a great
portion of the sum in question
is debt & must be paid.

───────────────────

          have
This sum cannot ~~amounted~~ to less
than two thousand millions; it
would be a curious problem in
political œconomy to calculate
3120 the precise degree of comfort
& of ornament– –
[LEAF 62, VERSO]
     The ~~sum of forty six millions~~,
                    ⌊*which*
~~is the interest of this debt, were~~
~~suffi alone more than sufficient~~
~~is paid out of the labour of~~
~~the poor.~~   Is it to remain
          eternal
unpaid forever, an ~~perpetual~~
          land
3130 rent charge upon the ~~earth~~ soil,
from which the ~~poor draw their~~
~~subs~~ inhabitants of these islands

          were
draw their subsistence?; this ~~is~~
to pronounce the perpetual
institution of two orders of aris
tocracy, & men are in a temper
to endure one with some reluctance.
          be
Is it to paid now, if so   3140
what are the funds; or when
and how is it to be paid?
The fact is that the ~~prin~~
~~-cipal~~ of the ~~debt~~ national

[LEAF 63, RECTO]
debt is a debt, not contracted
by the whole nation towards
a portion of it, but a debt
contracted by the whole mass of
the priveledged classes towards one
                    classes
particular portion of those. If   3150
~~the~~ principal where paid, the
whole property of those who
          must
possess property ~~ought to~~ be
valued & the public creditor
whose property would have been included in this
                    ⌊*estimate*
satisfied out of the proceeds.
          all
It has been said that ~~all the~~   3160
~~national~~ land in the national
is mortgaged for the amount
of the national debt. This is

line 3105. *until . . . imitated*: added later with a sharp quill.

line 3109. *these*: first *these* changed from *the*.

line 3116. *This sum . . . of ornament– –* (line 3121): apparently an incomplete footnote.

line 3116. *amounted*: *ed* and the interlineation in the line above were added later.

line 3128. *an*: *n* added later, when *eternal* replaced *perpetual*.

line 3129. *land*: Peck reads *sacred*.

line 3141. *what*: changed from *when*.

line 3144. *=cipal*: *al* written through *le*.

line 3151. *those.*: altered from *them*.

line 3157. *estimate*: crowded at edge of page below *this*.

SC 546

*a partial statement. Not only
all the land in the nation, but
all the property of whatever
denomination, all the houses*

[LEAF 63, VERSO]
116

3170   goods
 & the furniture & the ~~money~~
      clay
  every article of merchandise
& ~~the vanilla sugar &c of merc~~
   all the
*~~hants~~, & the property which is
represented by the very money*
   fund holder
*lent by the ~~public creditor~~, who
~~probabl~~ is bound to pay a certain*
3180   *whilst he is*
*portion as debtor, & ~~is entitled to~~ to
recieve another certain portion as
creditor:* ~~*In the To use the*~~
  *The property of the
~~whole nation~~ rich is mortaged
~~to let the mortgagee~~ to use
the language of the law, let the
mortgagee foreclose.*——
  ~~*This would profit the debtor*~~
3190 *If the principal of this debt,*
 were paid
  such
after due reductions had been made

        equal
*so as to make an ~~similar~~ value
taking corn for the standard
be given as was recieved, it would
be the rich ~~now~~ who ~~must~~*

[THERE IS A LEAF TORN OUT BETWEEN
LEAVES 63 AND 64]
[LEAF 64, RECTO]
     as   *they*
alone could, & justly ought to   3200
*pay it. ~~It would in fact be~~
~~a mere transfer among men of~~
  ~~But the interest of it~~*

          & ⟨   ⟩
*It would be a mere transfer among
persons of property., ~~a considerable
loss and change indeed to all~~, As it
is the interest is chiefly paid by
those who had no hand in the*
        are   3210
~~borr~~ borrowing & who ~~were~~ sufferers
   in other respects
*from the consequences of the trans
actions in which ~~they~~ money
was spent⌡Such a gentleman must
lose a third of his estate, such a
citizen a fourth of his money
in the funds; the persons who
borrowed would have paid, &
the juggling & complicated system*   3220

line 3172. *merchandise*: written through ~~*clay*~~, which was probably an alternative for ~~*money*~~ (line 3170).
line 3173. ~~*vanilla*~~: possible reading.
line 3182. *recieve* (sic): MWS reads *pay* (but Hogg has written in *receive* above Mary's line of text).
line 3185. *mortaged* (sic).
line 3189. ~~*profit*~~: possible reading.
line 3193. Rolleston treats lines 3193–3197 (*after . . . recieved*, [sic]) as a footnote.
line 3195. *an*: *n* added later, when *equal* replaced ~~*similar*~~.
line 3196. *standard*: *ard* written through *ing*.
line 3208. *the interest . . . borrowing* (line 3211): Shelley's argument here is that since the bulk of national revenues came from duties and various direct sales or purchase taxes, the burden of financing the debt was placed on consumers of such common items as tobacco, sugar, tea, and beer.
line 3213. *the trans*: *the* altered from *those*.
line 3218. *in*: altered from *it*.

Shelley, *A Philosophical View of Reform*   *November 1819–?1820*

SC 546

of ~~finance~~ paper finance be
suddenly at an end/The payment
of the principal of the

[LEAF 64, VERSO]
    what is called
National debt, which ~~the has be~~
it is pretended is so difficult
~~&~~ ~~tremendous~~ a problem, is only
difficult to those who do not
see who is the creditor & who

3230   the debtor, & who the wretched
sufferers from whom they both
wring the ~~luxuries~~ taxes which
under the form of interest is
given by the former & accepted
by the latter ~~because there is~~
~~a conspiracy between them~~
~~both to~~   This ~~a debt which~~
~~so that the principal if paid would~~
~~be paid by~~ It is ~~on the~~ from the

3240   labour of those who have no pro
perty that ~~the persons~~ all the
persons who posess property think
to extort the perpetual interest
        larger the whole of
of a debt ~~owed by one part of~~
~~them to another part~~ them to

[LEAF 65, RECTO]
the ~~smaller~~ part, ~~which the~~
latter know they could not ~~enf~~
  persuade
3250   ~~compel~~ the former to pay, but by
conspiring with them in an impos-

-ture which ~~shifts the burthen of~~
      labourers
makes the ~~third class~~ ~~pay~~ pay
what the first neither recieved by
their sanction nor spent for their
benefit, & what the second never
lent to them. They ~~labour of s~~
        would both
shift to the labour of ~~pres~~ the   3260
present & of all succeeding gener
    of the
ations ~~of the gre~~ the payment
of the interest of their own debt,
     from themselves & their posterity
because the payment of the
principal would be no more than
a compromise & transfer of
property between each other, by
which   *be spared*   3270
the nation would ~~save~~ forty
four millions a year, which

[LEAF 65, VERSO]
      120
now is paid to maintain in
luxury & indolence the ~~debtor~~
       to protect them from
public debtors & ~~the public creditor~~
the demand of those
One of the first acts of a reformed
govenment would undoubtedly be   3280
an effectual scheme for compelling
these to compromise their debt
between themselves.

[BLANK SPACE IN MANUSCRIPT]

line 3229. *is*: written through *are*.

line 3243. *extort*: MWS reads *extract*.

line 3254. *the*: written through *a*.

line 3276. *them*: written through indecipherable word.

line 3278. *those*: probable reading.

line 3283. *between*: MWS corrects the grammar to *among*; Shelley also used *between* a few lines above in a similar context.

SC 546

to protect them from the
demand of their creditors upon them,
who being part of the same body,
& owing as debtors whilst they
possess a claim as creditors, & willing

3290 to ~~unite to~~ *agree to* abstain from demanding
the principal which they must
all unite to pay, for the sake
of recieving an enormous interest
which is principally wrung out
of those who had no concern
whatever in the transaction

[LEAF 66, RECTO]

whose scope in society has a plebeian
& intelligible utility, everyman

When I speak of persons of property,
3300 not every man who possesses any *degree of property* & this will
I mean ₐthe rich   Every man
~~though he chance not to~~
whose personal exertions are more
valuable to him than his capital;
every tradesman who is not a
monopolist, all ~~clerks &~~ surgeons
& physicians, & ~~apothecaries &~~
all those mechanics
3310 p artists & ⟨————⟩ any persons

~~all clerks & editors &~~ ⟨   ⟩ men
~~whose skill & wisdom of whatever~~
~~profession &~~ farmers, all those
persons whose profits spring from
or strength
their own skill & wisdom in greater

[LEAF 66, VERSO]

honourably & honestly exerting
abundance than from the employment
of money ~~to command~~ take advant
the
-age of the necessity of starvation   3320
of their fellow citizens
for their profit are those who pay,
as well as those more obviously
understood by the labouring classes,
the interest of the national debt.
It is the interest of all these
persons as well as that of the
poor to insist upon payment
of the principal.   3330

For this purpose, the form ought
to be as simple & succinct as
possible. The operations ~~of fore~~
~~closing a mortgage, or buying~~
deciding
of ~~determining~~ who was to pay,
&
at what time, & how much, to

line 3284. *to protect them . . .*: continues Shelley's thought from *public debtors &* (line 3277), replacing interlineations above and below.

line 3297. The third of a page above this line is blank.

line 3297. *whose scope*: initial mark on this page and the mark following line 3302 indicate that *whose . . . everyman* should follow line 3302.

line 3298. *, everyman*: apparently written later with a sharper quill.

line 3299. *When I speak . . . the principal.* (line 3330): MWS treats the uncanceled portions of these lines as a footnote keyed to the word *themselves* in line 3283. It might also be keyed to the phrase *persons of property.*, in line 3206.

line 3300. *degree*: probable reading; MWS omits *degree of*; Peck and Rolleston read *right*.

line 3309. *all those mechanics*: may be underscored, rather than canceled.

line 3311. ⟨   ⟩: Peck, perhaps correctly, reads *literary*.

line 3317. This line was written later with a sharper quill.

line 3336. *determining*: canceled with the same sharp quill that was used to insert *deciding* (line 3335).

line 3338. *at what time,*: disfigured by blotting from opposite page.

Shelley, A Philosophical View of Reform   November 1819–?1820

SC 546

whom, are ~~readily determined~~
divested of financial chicanery
[LEAF 67, RECTO]
problems readily to be determined
         the common   may be invested
~~when the before~~ tribunals which may
    may
posess a legal jurisdiction to award
the proportion due upon the several
claims of each.
And this forbearance & regard have by
political institution usually been ac-
                 ⌊corded

3350   in an inverse reason from what is just
& natural. there
There are two descriptions of property,
which, without entering into the
subtleties of a more refined moral
theory as applicable to the existing
forms of society, are entitled to two
very different ~~meas~~ measures of
forbearance & regard. ~~The one is~~
~~that which produced whose found~~
3360   ~~ation which~~ Labour, industry, economy
~~industry,~~ skill, genius, ~~are the~~ or

any of ~~thes~~ similar powers honour
ably & innocently exerted are the
~~just~~ foundations of ~~property~~ one
description of property, and ~~it seems~~
~~every man whatever may be the~~

[LEAF 67, VERSO]
~~and in his discretion over the~~
~~property so acquired & so preserved,~~
all true political institution ought
to defend every man in the exercise   3370
of his discretion with respect to
the property so acquired. ~~These rights~~
~~are of the very highest order &~~
~~such is the property~~ Of this kind
is the principal part of the property
enjoyed by those who are but one
degree removed from the class which
              ⌈Yet
subsists by daily labour. ⌊and there
are instances of persons in this class   3380
who have procured their property by
fraudulent and violent means, as
theire are instances in the other
⌊as ~~Judges, mili~~ of persons who

line 3343. ~~when the~~: written with a sharper quill.

line 3346. Lines 3346–3347 were written with extra ink and have blotted on the opposite page (see note to line 3338); Shelley closed the notebook immediately after completing this sentence.

line 3347. *claims*: word may be singular.

line 3352. *There are*: this section is written with a sharper quill, in this case probably indicating the beginning of a new session of composition.

line 3360. *economy*: *c* written through *n*.

line 3363. *innocently*: MWS reads *usefully*. Shelley varies his adjectives from *honourably & honestly* that he had inserted at line 3317 above, probably while he was reading over the earlier text before beginning a new stint of composing.

line 3369. *institution*: Shelley frequently prefers, in this treatise and elsewhere, to use the generic singular form (rather than the plural) when naming such abstractions.

line 3370. *in*: *n* written through *s*.

line 3371. *with*: written through *in*.

line 3379. *subsists*: *b* written through *s*.

line 3379. *there*: written through *its*.

line 3384. The line drawn by Shelley down the left margin probably indicates that he wished to reconsider either the text or location of this passage (lines 3384–3543).

SC 546
/have acquired their property by
innocent or honourable exertion.
　　just
All ~~true~~ *philosophy* & political science
abounds with limitations & exceptions]

[LEAF 68, RECTO]

3390
Property thus acquired men leave
to their children. & ~~Though~~
　absolute　+
the ~~absolutions~~ right ~~is less in~~
becomes weakened by descent, ~~because~~
~~the apprehension of men~~ first because
　　　　greater
it is only to avoid the ~~worse~~ evil
of arbitrarily interfering with the discretion
that the great evil of admitting

3400
　　　　acknowledging
~~of any man~~ any person to have ~~a right~~
~~in matters of property~~　*an exclusive*
to property who has not ~~acquired~~
　　　　created
it by his skill or labour is admitted,
& secondly because, the mode of its
having been originally acquired is
forgotten, ~~the~~ and it is confounded with
property acquired in a very different

3410
manner, and ~~the rights upon ⟨ ⟩~~ prin
ciple upon which all property
justly rests, after the great principle
　　advantage　*thus*
of the general ~~good~~, becomes ∧*forgotten*
　disregard
& misunderstood. ~~Yet in~~ Yet the

priveledge
right of ~~will~~ disposing of property
by will is one necessarily connected
with the existing forms of domestic　3420

[LEAF 68, VERSO]

life, & ~~until it gro~~ exerted merely
by those who have acquired property
by industry, or who have preserved
it by economy, would never produce
~~such an inequality as would~~ any
great & invidious inequality of fortune.
A thousand accidents would perpetually
tend to level ~~among~~ the accidental
elevation, & the signs of property
would perpetually recur to those　3430
whose deserving skill might attract,
or whose labour might create it.
　　But there is another species of
property, which has its foundation
　　　　or
in usurpation & ~~conquest~~ imposture
or violence, without which, by the
nature of things, immense ~~accumu~~
　　　possessions of gold or land
~~lations~~ aggregations of ~~property~~ could　3440
never have been accumulated.
~~Mono Of this For how can a~~
~~man by fair~~

[LEAF 69, RECTO]

/Of this nature is the principal
part of the property enjoyed by

line 3389. *exceptions*]: the end bracket actually appears below this word, which crowds the edge of the page.

line 3393. *right*: the cross may mark the word to which Shelley intended to key the sentence on "rights of all men" that he bracketed on leaf 57, verso (see note to line 2957).

line 3397. *it is . . . admitted*, (line 3405): Shelley here, almost as an afterthought, shows why he could be a disciple of Godwinian anarchism but never one of Marxism. He could never justify physical, as distinguished from moral, enforcement of equality ("justice" in Godwin's sense).

line 3397. *the*: written through *a*.

line 3401. *of . . . property* (line 3402): thought follows *discretion* (line 3398).

line 3411. *all*: written through *th*.

line 3412. *rests,*: Rolleston reads *exists*.

line 3423. *have*: written through *?derive*.

Shelley, A Philosophical View of Reform   November 1819–?1820

SC 546 /the aristocracy & by the great
| fund holders, ~~whose ancestors never~~
                              great
                    the majority of whose
3450 | ancestors never either deserved it by
                    talents
| their skill & ~~genius~~, or acquired &
| created it by thier personal labour.
| ~~That they did not deserve it is~~
| ~~If they des If desert be the measure~~
| ~~They could~~ It could not be that they
| deserved it, for if ~~desert had been~~
                                      the
| ~~proper~~
3460 | ~~the measure~~ honourable exertion of
              most glorious imperial
| the ~~best~~ faculties of our nature had
| been the criterion of the possession of
| property, ~~Shake~~ the posterity of
| Shakspeare of Milton of Hampden
| of Lor   would be the wealthiest
| proprietors in England. It could not be
                              legitimate
| that they acquired it by ~~per honest~~
3470 | industry,— for besides that ~~it is the~~
              real
| m mode of acquisition is matter
| of history– an no honourable

[LEAF 69, VERSO]
                    127
| profession or honest trade, nor the
| hereditary exercise of it, ever in such

| numerous instances accumulated
                              so vast as those
| ~~the vast~~ masses of property enjoyed
| by the ruling orders in England.   3480
| They were ~~produ~~ either grants from
              abs   feudal
| the ~~despotic~~ sovereigns whose right
| to what they granted was founded
| upon conquest or oppression, both
| a denial of all right; or they were
| the ~~abbey la~~ lands of the antient
| Catholic clergy which ~~first of~~
| according to ~~all~~ the most acknow
| ledged principles of public justice   3490
| reverted to the nation at their
| suppression, or they were the
| products of patents & monopolies
| ~~by which~~ an exercise of sovereignty
| ~~the~~ most pernicious than
| direct violence to the interests

[LARGE STUBS OF TWO TORN-OUT LEAVES]

[LEAF 70, RECTO]
| ~~with respect to the legitimacy of~~
| ~~a public debt to be incurred~~
| ~~under whatever circumstances it~~
| is astonishing that political   3500
| theorists have not branded as the
| most pernicious & odious
          There are three sets of people

line 3461. *most glorious*: written with almost dry quill; *imperial* with pen newly filled.

line 3466. *of Lor*: MWS retains *of* followed by a blank; Rolleston omits *of Lor*; Peck gives *Lor[d Bacon]*.

line 3475. *profession*: *pr* written through indecipherable letters.

line 3478. *vast as those*: Rolleston reads *much as the*.

line 3487. *antient*: contemporary alternative spelling.

line 3495. *most pernicious than*: the *t* of *most* has been tinkered with, possibly changed to an *e*; *than* altered from *that*. Peck reads *that*; Rolleston omits lines 3495–3496. The editor should follow MWS in reading *more pernicious than*.

line 3497. The thought of leaf 69, verso (Shelley's page *127*), continues on leaf 70, verso (Shelley's page *128*). The relevance of the material on leaf 70, recto, is dubious. Probably its context was to be found on the two leaves that Shelley tore out between leaf 69 and leaf 70, and he might have removed leaf 70, recto, also if he could have done so without destroying leaf 70, verso.

SC 546   one who can place a thing to
another in an intelligible light;
another who can understand it
when so communicated, & a
third who can neither discover
nor understand it.

[LEAF 70, VERSO]

3510   *128*

of a commercial nation, or in later
times ~~they have been the~~ such
property has been ~~usurped not~~
                              accumulated,
          fair
~~not by talent & industry, but~~ by
dishonourable ~~tricks~~ cunning &
the taking advantage of a fictitious
paper currency to obtain an unfair
~~distinction~~ power over labour &
3520   the fruits of labour.
                              accumulated
          Property thus ~~acquired~~ being
transmitted from father to son,
                              the
acquires, as property of ~~a~~ more
legitimate kind loses, force &
sanction, but in a more limited
manner. For not only on an
3530   examination & recurrence to first
principles is it seen to have been
founded on a violation of all that

                              to
is ~~by~~ which the latter owes its

[UNNUMBERED STUB]

[LEAF 71, RECTO]

sacredness, but if is felt in its
existence & perpetuation as a
public burthen & known as a
rallying point to the ministers
of tyranny, having the property
of a snow ball, gathering as it rolls,   3540
& rolling until it bursts.—
          ~~With respect to the classes~~
          ~~The⟨ ⟩ Yet there are~~

~~The de⟨ ⟩~~
          ~~The purpose in stating~~
                              & skill
          First Labour & the immediate
wages of labour, & skill, ~~which~~
is a property of the most sacred   3550
          indisputable
& ~~inalienable~~ right, & the found
ation of all other property. And

[LEAF 71, VERSO]
          a man⟨ ⟩   *129*
the right ~~to this~~ property in the
exertion of his own bodily & mental

line 3512. *have*: written through indecipherable letters.

line 3520. *labour*: *la* written through indecipherable letters.

line 3528. *sanction,*: period changed to comma.

line 3528. *but*: written through *The*.

line 3528. *more*: Rolleston reads *very*.

line 3534. *latter*: refers to *property of the more legitimate kind* (lines 3526–3527). MWS reads *other*.

line 3535. *if*: MWS, Rolleston, and Peck correct the word to *it*.

line 3542. *classes*: written through *calsses*.

line 3544. *de⟨si⟩*: Shelley may have begun to write *desire* and broken off with a flourish.

line 3551. *inalienable*: Shelley may have replaced this word so as not to echo so obviously the American Declaration of Independence. See also line 3561.

line 3553. ⟨——⟩: possibly *enjoys*, with the *ys* left unwritten.

line 3554. *to*: canceled and then underlined.

Shelley, A Philosophical View of Reform   *November 1819–?1820*

SC 546 *faculties, or to the ~~immediate~~ und*
                          & free
          oubted produce, & reward ~~freely given~~
                                & for of
3560   *~~by others for & from~~ that exertion*
          is the most ~~inalienable of rights~~
          ~~It is certain~~ If however he ~~steals~~
          ~~or~~ takes by violence or appro-
                          through
          -priates to himself by fraudulent
          cunning or recieves from another
          property so acquired, his ~~possession~~
          ~~to~~ of ~~that property, however~~
          ~~from prudence others~~ his claim to
3570   *that property is of a far inferior*
          force. We may ~~submit to it from~~
          ~~pr motives of~~ acquiesce, if we
          evidently percieve an overbalance
          of public advantage in submission,
                          under
          in this claim; but if any ~~occasion~~
          ~~should arise~~ of public emergency should
                          might been
          arise, at which it ~~was~~ necessary ~~by~~

[LEAF 72, RECTO]

3580   *~~a tax on capital~~ as at present by*
          ~~a tax on capital so that~~ to satis
                  by a tax on capital
          fy the claims of a part of the
          nation by a contribution from such
          national resources as may with

the least injustice be appropriated
to that purpose, assuredly it would
not be on labour & skill the
foundation of all property; nor on
the ~~wages & undoubted wa~~ profits   3590
& savings of labour & skill, which
are property itself; but on such
possessions which can only be called
property in a modified sense, as
~~probably~~ have from their mag
nitude & thier nature an evident
origin in violence or imposture.

          Thus there are two kinds of
property.——

[LEAF 72, VERSO]

                  131   3600
The national debt as has been stated
                          the whole
is a debt contracted by ~~one portion~~
of the ~~p~~ a particular class in the
nation towards a portion of that
class. ~~But~~ It is sufficiently clear
that this debt was not contracted
for the purpose of the public advan
                  was
tage. Besides there ~~is~~ no authority   3610
in the nation competent to ~~this~~
                  a
measure of this nature. The usual
vindication of national debts is

line 3561. *of*: written through *&*.

line 3563. *or*: written through *&*.

line 3568. *to*: smudged with inked fingerprint.

line 3570. *of*: written through *a*.

line 3574. *of*: written firmly through smeared ink.

line 3580. *as*: changed from *at*.

line 3581. *so*: *s* written through *t*.

line 3595. *have*: written through *had*.

line 3597. *origin*: *in* written through indecipherable letters.

line 3605. *portion*: MWS reads *part*.

SC 546

in an overwhelming emergency
that they are are contracted, for
the purpose of defence against a
common danger, & that being contracted
for the vindication of the rights &

3620 *liberties of posterity & of the whole,*
it is just that posterity should
bear the burthen of payment.
This reasoning is most fallacious.
Nations The history of nations presents
us with a succession of extraor

[LEAF 73, RECTO]

dinary emergencies, & if any
  given their present imperfect organization their
existence is perpetually threatned
by new & unexpected combinations
  or internal

3630 *& developements of foreign force.*
Imagine a situation of equal
emergency to occur to England
as that which the ruling party
    at this ⟨   ⟩ war
assume to have occurred, as their
excuse for burthening the nation
      perpetual
with the payment of 45000,000

3640   *annually*   *suppose France &*
interest forever & ⟨———⟩ as it

& Austria
Russia were to enter into a league
against England
the first to revenge its injuries, the
second to satisfy its ambition, & the
      soothe
third to exercise its jealousy.
Could the nation bear 90,000,000
of yearly interest, the labourer   3650
work forty eat half as much
as now, & expose must there
be twice as many luxurious &
idle persons, must the labourer
      twenty eight
recieve for seven fourteen hours or

[LEAF 73, VERSO]

work what he now recieves for fourteen,
as he now recieves for fourteen
what he once recieved for seven?
But this argument   3660

[LEAF 74, RECTO, CALCULATIONS]

[LEAF 74, VERSO]
The

    What is meant by a Reform of
parliament?

line 3615. *emergency*: word very cramped. MWS left a blank, but Hogg filled in *emergency*; Rolleston and Peck read *measure*.

line 3616. *are are* (sic).

line 3627. *given . . . organization*: interlineation written later in different ink.

line 3627. *given*: probable reading; Rolleston and Peck read *thro*.

line 3628. *existence*: MWS reads *experience*.

line 3628. *threatned* (sic).

line 3630. *or internal*: written at the same time as *given . . . organization*, line 3627.

line 3642. *Austria*: possible reading; written upon canceled line above. Rolleston reads *Germany*; Peck, *America*; but MWS reads *Austria* (like France and Russia, a member of the Holy Alliance).

line 3652. *as now, & expose*: cancel line appears almost as underline.

line 3656. *or* (sic): for *of*.

line 3660. *argument*: remainder of leaf 73, verso, blank; leaf 74, recto, has financial calculations involving "crowns," and therefore probably related to Shelley's personal finances rather than to England's national debt.

Shelley, A Philosophical View of Reform   November 1819–?1820

SC546

The idea o We mean that the com-
        ⌊mons
house should be chosen,
The theoretical idea of the English
        its
Constitution is that his chief magi-
trate should be an hereditary King,
3670 served by responsible ministers,
    Until For a certain epoch, England
was gloriously distinguished from
the great Nations of the Continent
We desire that the House of Com-
        ⌊mons
should be chosen by the great body
of the lower orders of
    If England were a Republic
governed by one assembly; if

[LEAF 75, RECTO]
there were no hereditary aristocracy
3680 which who are as a permanent
representation of things established
who stand for all that par chamber
of hereditary aristocracy to check
and balance the ⟨   ⟩ attempts of the
    is
ma which was at once an actual &
a virtual representation of all who
claim through rank or wealth, super
iority over man their countrymen; if

there were no King who is as the
point rallying point of all the those
rich & the noble whose tendency is
at once to gather & to confer that
power which is consolidated at the
expense of the nation, then

[LEAF 75, VERSO, BLANK]
[LEAF 76, RECTO]
The advocates of universal suffrage
have reasoned correctly that the
        no
right of every individual who is
        can
governed to a direct share in the
government of the his country can
be deprived denied a direct share in
the government of his country without
supreme injustice; – But as reasoning
        inquiries
of an abstract nature would lead
us to conclusions systems of
social order, which If we pursue
the train of reasonings which have
conducted to the conclusion, we
discover that systems of social
order which the perverse & un
teachable passions of men render
totally at present wholly imprac
ticable   still more incompatible

3690

3700

3710

line 3672. *glorioussly* (sic).

line 3688. *claim*: Rolleston reads *attain*.

line 3691. *of . . . noble* (line 3692): *those* added and other phrases canceled later, in darker ink.

line 3693. *gather*: though lightly canceled, this word seems necessary to Shelley's thought.

line 3695. *nation, then*: the comma and *then* added later in darker ink.

line 3696. This leaf begins in the same dark ink used to correct leaf 75, recto. It probably marks a new day of composition.

line 3703. *denied*: badly written, resembling *deened*.

line 3709. *we pursue*: Rolleston reads *one pursues*.

line 3713. *perverse & unteachable passions of men*: though Shelley has canceled the phrase, it embodies one of his most striking statements of human moral imperfection. Compare Prospero on Caliban (*The Tempest*, IV.i.188–190): "A devil, a born devil, on whose nature/ Nurture can never stick, on whom my pains,/ Humanely taken, all, all lost, quite lost."

The Carl H. Pforzheimer Library

Shelley, A Philosophical View of Reform   *November 1819–?1820*

SC 546   than universal suffrage with

[LEAF 76, VERSO]

                  instant
any reasonable hope of accomplis-

3720   -ment ~~will~~ appear to be ~~founded~~

on ~~the indisputable elements of the~~

that which should result from a

just combination of the elements of

social life. If I do not unders

            why

tand, wherefore those reasoners

who propose at any price an

immediate appeal to universal

suffrage, because it is that which

3730   ~~they~~ it is injustice to withold, do

not insist on the same ground, on

     immediate   *(to*

the abolition ~~of m~~ for instance

⟨   ⟩

of monarchy & aristocracy, & the

levelling of inordinate wealth

          including the Parks & Chases of

& an agrarian distribution of

the rich

3740   the uncultivated districts of the

      ⟨   ⟩ *these measures* ⟨ ⟩

country. No doubt, the institution

of universal suffrage would by

necessary consequence ~~immediately~~

[LEAF 77, RECTO]

tend to the ~~temporary~~ abolition

of these forms; because it is impossible

that the people, having attained

the power, should fail to see, what

the demagogues now conceal from them

the legitimate consequence of the   3750

doctrines through which they had

      A Republic

attained it. ~~This abolition would,~~

however just in its principle, &

         glorious

~~great in its obj~~ animating in its

object, ~~could not fail to be tem~~

~~porary, or if not temporary~~ would

through ~~the~~ violence & sudden change

    which must attend it

~~be~~ incur a great risk of ~~perm~~   3760

being as rapid in its decline as

in its growth. ~~It is this vulgar~~

~~eagerness, this~~   The ~~conflict of~~

~~passions in which a new system~~

~~is engendered demands above~~

line 3719. *accomplis–* (sic).

line 3722. *from*: written through *of*.

line 3726. *wherefore*: possibly canceled with the same finely sharpened quill in which Shelley wrote *why*.

line 3730. *do*: *d* with *o* run off the page.

line 3733. *for*: blotted, possibly canceled.

line 3734. ⟨?*glaring*⟩: possible reading.

line 3738. *&*: smudged.

line 3741. ⟨*Lacking*⟩ *these*: possible reading; entire interlineation written in different ink.

line 3746. *impossible*: crowded down the right-hand margin.

line 3749. *them*: crowded into right-hand margin.

line 3752. *A Republic*: interlineation written later in sharpened quill; *blic* blotted from late correction on leaf 76, verso.

line 3755. *glorious*: written in sharpened quill at same time as *A Republic*.

line 3759. *change*: quill sharpened at this word.

line 3765. *new*: separately canceled earlier.

line 3766. *demands*: cancel line indistinct.

SC 546 all things caution & The great
                                          might
                    A civil war, which would be

[LEAF 77, VERSO]

3770 engendered by the passions atten
        -dant on this mode of reform,
                confirm
        would produce in the mass of
        the nation those military habits
        which have been already intro-
        duced by our tyrants, & with
        which nothing liberty is incom
        patible – A soldier is From the
        moment that a man is a soldier
3780 he becomes a slave. He is taught
        obedience; that that lesson so readily
        his will is no longer, which is
        the most sacred prerogative of man,
        guided by his own judgment.
                        ⟨———⟩
        He is taught to despise human
        life & human suffering; he is

⟨–⟩ this is the universal distinction
of slaves. the He becomes He is
more degraded than a murderer;   3790
he is like the bloody knife, which

[LEAF 78, RECTO]

has stabbed, and knows it not; a
fee scar feels not; a murderer we
may abhor & despise; a soldier
        by profession
is beyond abhorrence & below contempt.
These are the beings whom some
hold in   Inasmuch as the character
of a citizen

It is better that they should be instructed   3800
in the whole truth, than that they
should see the clear grounds of their
rights, the objects to which they
ought to tend; & be impressed
with the just conception of that
persuasion, that patience & courage
& reason & endurance, & a calm

line 3768. *might*: seems to be on a level with line 3767, but is actually a replacement for *would* in line 3769.

line 3770. *attendant*: *ant* written through *ing*; MWS, Rolleston, and Peck all read *attending*.

line 3775. *have*: possibly written through *are*.

line 3789. *slaves.*: semicolon altered to period.

line 3791. *bloody knife,*: Shelley varies a simile from Book IV, chapter VI, of Godwin's *Political Justice* (London, 1793), where in tracing out the implications of the doctrine of Necessity, Godwin makes repeated comparisons between a "murderer" and "the knife he employs" as being equally under the power of Necessity (see, for example, volume I, page 313). Though Godwin distinguishes the forces of causation that motivate men from those that impel inanimate objects, Shelley finds it at least rhetorically useful (whether or not his belief differed from Godwin's) to distinguish between a man's *will . . . guided by his own judgment.* (lines 3782–3784) and the soldier's will, completely subservient to the command of another.

line 3792. *has*: altered from *sta*.

line 3793. *feels*: second *e* altered from *l*.

line 3794. *abhor*: *a* written through *b*.

line 3797. *These . . . some*: canceled with almost dry pen.

line 3799. *citizen*: followed by blank space, equivalent to six lines.

line 3800. *instructed*: word obscured by ink blot from verso of leaf 78.

line 3805. *the*: written through *a*.

line 3805. *of*: separately canceled earlier.

SC 546 [LEAF 78, VERSO]
yet irresistible progress.
        Probable means
        ——————

3810 ~~That the House of~~ Commons should
reform itself, ~~seems a contr~~ unin
-fluenced by any fear that the people
~~public~~ would on their refusal as⟨   ⟩
to itself that office, seems a contra
diction. What need of Reform if it
expresses the will, & watches over
the interests of the public. And if,
as is sufficiently evident, it despises
that will & neglects that interest

3820 ~~Wherefore should~~ what motives
would incite it to institute a reform
which the aspect of the times renders
indeed sufficiently perilous but
          will speedily be
without which there is no longer
any thing in England to dis

[LEAF 79, RECTO]
tinguish it from the basest &
most abject community of slaves
that ever existed——.

3830   One motive

[LEAF 79, VERSO]
N ~~Yes I have made a⟨   ⟩~~
This is impossible in great nations, &
             ⌊the most
Enlightened theorists have therefore pro-
             ⌊posed the dividing
        great
them into a ~~vast multiplicity~~ of
        ⌊legitimate govern
        ⌊federated republics –
        ge
The great principle of ~~Reform in~~
             consists in
~~England is undoubtedly, that~~
every individual of mature age   3840
& perfect understanding ~~should~~
~~assist to~~ giving his consent to the
        continued
institution & the⌃existence of the
social system, which is instituted
for his advantage & for the
advantage of others in his situation.
~~Becaus~~ As in a great nation
this is practically impossible,
masses of individuals consent to   3850
qualify other individuals whom
they delegate to superintend

---

line 3813. *as⟨sume⟩*: probable reading, obscured by ink blot. So in MWS, Rolleston, and Peck.

line 3815. *it*: refers to *House of Commons*.

line 3818. *evident,*: MWS reads *demonstrated*.

line 3825. *is*: canceled later with same sharpened quill as used for interlineation.

line 3832. *This . . . republics* (line 3835): except for *legitimate govern* (line 3834) and *ge* (line 3836), these lines, written in pencil, were apparently added later. MWS and Rolleston place these lines after *situation* (line 3847); Peck, after *public* (line 3817).

line 3835. *federated*: MWS reads *federative*.

line 3838. *consists in*: this addition and cancellations in lines 3837, 3839, 3841 were written with a sharpened quill — perhaps after leaf 80, recto, lines 3860 ff.

line 3841. *should*: appears underscored. Shelley's probable intention was to cancel.

line 3842. *giving*: changed from *give* with sharpened quill.

line 3851. *other*: *o* written through *as*.

line 3852. *delegate*: *le* changed from *la*.

SC 546

their concerns. ~~These masses~~
~~aught to be equal~~
[LEAF 80, RECTO]
~~The body of~~ these delegates have
~~supreme authority~~, constitutional
authority to exercise the func
tions of sovereignty; ~~both in~~
im they unite in the highest
3860 *degree the legislative & executive*
                    ~~Yes I⟨ ⟩~~
functions. Any goverment that
is founded on any other basis, is
a goverment of fraud or force, and
aught on the first convenient
occasion to be overthrown——
            grand   political
The great principle of reform

is the natural & ~~in~~ equality
of ~~mankind~~ men; ~~not equality~~   3870
~~of property~~ not with relation
to their property, but to thier
rights.   ~~Equality in possessions~~
~~which   It is a~~ That equality
in possessions which Jesus
Christ so passionately taught

[LEAF 80, VERSO]
is a moral rather than a political
truth, & is such as ~~ins~~ social
institutions, cannot without mischief,
~~secure~~ inflexibly secure. Morals &   3880
politics can only be considered as
portions of the same science, with

line 3854. *aught* (sic): *OED*, *Bailey's Dictionary*, and various poetic concordances indicate that there was continuing confusion of the orthographies *aught* and *ought* up to Shelley's day, though the common transfer was to use the spelling *ought* for the substantive as well as for the verb.

line 3860. *degree the*: *degree* was first written with a very dull point; Shelley then sharpened or changed his quill, clarified the *ee* of *degree* and continued with the sharpened writing. Here one need suspect no extensive lapse of time between the writing of *degree* and *the*.

line 3861. *~~Yes I⟨ ⟩~~*: erased by smearing wet ink. *Yes* may possibly be *Yet*.

line 3864. *and*: written through *or*.

line 3865. *aught*: see note to line 3854 above.

line 3867. *grand*: probable reading; Rolleston reads *first*; Peck, *broad*; MWS reads *grand*.

line 3868. *principle*: *e* written over *es*.

line 3873. *rights.*: canceled semicolon precedes period.

line 3877. *moral . . . immediate practise.* (line 3926): the separation of *moral* from *political truth* was a formalized pattern in the philosophy of Shelley's day. Adam Smith, when he was professor of moral philosophy at Glasgow, had divided his subject into four series of lectures: (1) natural theology, including proofs of the being and attributes of God; (2) ethics, from which lectures Smith published his *Theory of Moral Sentiments* (1759); (3) the theory of political institutions which are founded on "justice," or jurisprudence; (4) the theory of the political institutions founded on expediency, from which Smith published his *Inquiry into the Nature and Causes of the Wealth of Nations* in 1776. The title of Godwin's *Enquiry concerning Political Justice* must have suggested to its first purchasers that it was to treat the area of Smith's third series of lectures, but Godwin's book actually encompassed a far wider range and advocated a close union of ethics, law, and political economy. Shelley and Godwin were both certain that if legal sanctions were imposed to attempt to enforce (*inflexibly secure*) an equal division of property, the society and its individual members would lose more "happiness" (the end of society) through the coercion and totalitarian spirit that would accompany the attempt than would be gained in happiness from the resultant leveling. Godwin's system was based not on coercion but on voluntary recognition of individual responsibility for the greater good.

SC 546 relation to a system of such abs
                    Moses
    olute   those ⟨   ⟩ble persons
~~tract~~ perfection as ~~Jesus Christ~~ &
                        &
~~other reasoners have~~ Plato & Rousseau
& other reasoners have asserted
& as Godwin has, with irresistible
eloquence, ~~& strength of r~~ systema
-tised & developed . . .   Equality in
posessions must be the last
result of the utmost refinements of
civilization; it is one of the
~~continued~~ conditions of that
system of society, towards which
with whatever hope of ultimate
success, it is our duty to tend.

[LEAF 81, RECTO]

3900 We may, & ought to advert to it,
as to the elementary principle, as
                        perhaps
to the goal, unnatainable ₍by us,
but which, as it were, we revive
in our posterity to pursue. We derive
tranquillity & courage & grandeur
            from
of soul ~~by~~ contemplating an object
which is, ~~to so fas~~ because we will

it, & may be, because we hope &   3910
desire it, & must be if succeeding
generations of the enlightened sin-
                    we should
cerely & earnestly seek it ⟨——⟩⟨——⟩
⟨ ⟩ with sincere & patient hope —
    But our present business is
with the difficult & unbending
                    actual
realities of life, & when we have
drawn inspiration from the great   3920
                    hope
object of our ~~aspirations~~ it becomes
us ~~to apply~~ with patience &
resolution, to apply ourselves to
accomodating our theories to

[LEAF 81, VERSO]

immediate practise. ~~The~~

    ~~The people it~~
        The ~~philosophical mind will~~
    readily ~~percieve that the instruc~~
    ~~tion & state of mind of the~~   3930
    ~~great~~ That Representative Assembly
    called the House of Commons, ought
    ~~wi~~ questionless, to be <u>*immediately*</u>
    nominated by the great mass of
    the people. The aristocracy &

line 3884. *Moses*: possible reading; written upon penciled phrase in line 3885. (Peck reads the word as *Christ*; MWS and Rolleston omit it.)

line 3885. *those* ⟨   ⟩*ble persons*: very indistinct pencil.

line 3886. *~~Jesus Christ~~*: canceled in pencil.

line 3887. *&*: in pencil.

line 3888. *Rousseau*: last two letters badly blotted.

line 3903. *unnatainable* (sic): written through (and perhaps distorted by) indecipherable word or words ending in *y*.

line 3905. *derive*: written through indecipherable word; MWS reads *drain*.

line 3914. ⟨——⟩⟨——⟩: canceled by smearing wet ink.

line 3915. *hope* —: Peck reads *aspi-[ration]*; MWS and Rolleston omit entire line.

line 3918. *actual*: intermixed with *life* (below) and descenders from *difficult* (above).

line 3921. *hope*: MWS, Rolleston, and Peck read *hopes* (probably because the top of the *t* in *aspira-tions* rising from below resembles an *s*).

line 3925. *accomodating* (sic).

Shelley, A Philosophical View of Reform   November 1819–?1820

SC 546

& the interests of those who unite in
the great cap the is sufficiently
their own persons the vast priveledge
conferred by the possession of inordante wealth

3940 represented by the House of Peers
& by the King. Those theorists
who admire & would put into
action the mechanism of the
what is called the British Constit
ution, would acquiesce in this view

[LEAF 82, RECTO]

of the question. For if the Hou
regal po the House of Peers be
a direct represen permanent represen
tation of the priveledged classes; if the

3950 regal power be the have, like all
powers powers, a perpetual tendency
towards its own aggrandisen be no more
form
than another form & a still more
jealously to be regarded
perilous one, of the same representation;

which
if the House of Commons be any
what it is, an Assembly chosen
no not chosen by the mass of the   3960
population, what becomes of that
democratic element, upon the
presence of which, it has been
the practis it has been supposed
waning
that the long superiority of England
over
to the surrounding nations has
depended.

[LEAF 82, VERSO]

Universal   10 ‾‾‾‾   3970
                  13300
The Any sudden attempt at
Universal suffrage would probably
produce an immature attempt
a
at a Republic; it is better that

line 3939. *conferred . . . wealth*: written vertically up left-hand margin from bottom to top of page; *inordante* miswritten for *inordate*. This line continues the thought of lines 3936 and 3938, which Shelley intended to precede *is sufficiently* (line 3937).

line 3941. *Those theorists . . . of the question.* (line 3946): Those who supported the concept of the "British Constitution" and formed constitutional societies and associations were conservatives of the established classes who based their conception of the British Constitution on the settlements of 1688 and 1714. Shelley is appealing to them (or goading them) with their own argument that the government ought to rest in a balance of the powers of king, nobility, and commons. Shelley includes plutocrats with the aristocracy rather than with the commons, as had been done in 1688.

line 3952. *aggrandisen*: probably incomplete for *aggrandisement*.

line 3955. *jealously*: Rolleston reads *advisedly*.

line 3957. *which*: Rolleston and Peck read *whilst*.

line 3960. *mass of the population,*: MWS reads *people*, probably to avoid the longer phrase so soon after *great mass of the people.*, lines 3934–3935.

line 3963. *has been*: ink changes here to a lighter brown ink in which Shelley also inserted *which* six lines above.

line 3965. *waning*: inserted in still another ink. Shelley seems to have been writing slowly and doggedly in the latter half of this manuscript, rather than writing long passages at one sitting. His handwriting is larger, better spaced, and more legible here than in much of the first half of the notebook.

line 3973. *probably*: written through indecipherable word.

line 3975. *a*: possible reading.

line 3976. *that*: changed from *than*.

SC 546

is of so inexpressible great &
~~such an~~ object should never have
  sacred
3980 been attempted that that it should
    be
  ~~have been~~ attempted & fail– It
  is no prejudice to the ~~boldes~~
  ultimate establishment of the boldest
  political innovations that we
  temporize so as, ~~to~~ when they
  shall be accomplished they may
  be rendered permanent.
      It would perhaps be advisable
3990 to begin, by establishing a suffrage
  which should be universal in

[LEAF 83, RECTO]
  ⟨   ⟩
  point of extension, & of rights
  rather than in point of numbers
        Considering the population of
                ⌊*England*
  ~~as~~ Great Britain & Ireland, as twenty
  millions & the ~~legislative~~ representative
  assembly as five hundred; each
  member ought to be the expression
4000 of the will of 40,000 persons; of
  these two thirds would ~~be children~~
  ~~livery servants idiots lunatics or persons~~
  ~~otherwise incapable of ex~~ women;
  ~~females~~ women & children, & persons
  under age; the actual number

of voters therefore for each member
would be 13,300. ~~It is supposed~~
~~that the~~   The whole extent
of the empire might be divided
    five hundred   4010
into electoral departments
~~composed in a combined~~ or
~~paris~~ parishes, and the

[LEAF 83, VERSO]
the inhabitants assemble on a
certain day to choose ~~a member~~
exercise their right of suffrage –
    ~~There is a general panic in~~
~~the minds of men~~
      ~~Many are strongly impressed~~
~~with the concep~~ fear, ~~lest the~~   4020
~~multitude, unused to the arts of~~
~~government, should elect men who~~
would ~~attempt some in ruinous~~
      ~~As a provisional measure~~
If ~~All~~ Mr Bentham, & other
writers have urged the admission
of females to the right of
suffrage; this attempt seems
somewhat immature. – Should
        my   4030
~~this Let the~~ opinion, be the result
of despondency, the writer of

[LEAF 84, RECTO]
these pages would be the last

line 3977. *inexpressible* (sic).

line 3980. *that that* (sic): for *than that*.

line 3986. *temporize*: Shelley uses the word in its now-archaic meaning to delay or await a more favorable time (*OED* 2).

line 3992. ⟨*regard*⟩: possible reading.

line 4000. *40,000*: *4* written through another number — probably *5*.

line 4007. *13,300.*: *oo* written through *33*.

line 4008. *extent*: MWS reads *entent*.

line 4013. *the the* (sic).

line 4017. *general*: a sketch of a cloud just above this word obscures the *l*.

line 4029. *Should ~~this~~*: written after ~~*Let the*~~ was canceled.

line 4032. *the*: altered from *this*.

SC 546   *to withold his vote from any system*
which might tend to an equal &
full developement of the capacities
of all living beings.——
The ~~system of ballot, is in my~~
~~judgement highly reprehensible;~~ –
4040   *The system of voting by ballot,*
which some reasoners have recom
mended, ~~has~~ is attended with obvious
inconveniences. ~~It withdraws the~~
     elector   regard
~~voter from the eye of his country &~~
~~his neighbours, & allows him~~ his
neighbours, & permits him to conceal
the motives of his vote, ~~when but~~
which if concealed cannot but be
4050   *dishonourable, when if he had*
known that he had to render

[LEAF 84, VERSO]
a public account of his conduct
he would have never permitted them
to guide him.– There is ~~also,~~ in
this system of voting by ballot
& of electing a member of the
R. A. as a church warden is elected
something too mechanical. The
elector & the elected ought to meet
4060   *one another face, to face, & inter*

             by actual presence
change the meanings   *~~& understand~~*
~~each other~~ share some common impulses
& in a degree, understand each other.
         the
There ought to be a common sym
-pathy, ~~there ought to~~ of their ⟨ ⟩
excitements of a popular assembly,
among the electors themselves.
The imagination would thus be   4070
strongly excited, & a mass of
generous & enlarged & popular

[LEAF 85, RECTO]
sentiments be awakened, which
would give the vitality of

That republican boldness of censu
ring & judging one another, which
has indeed exerted in England,
~~under the~~ under the title of "public
opinion," though perverted from its
true uses, into an instrument of   4080
prejudice & calumny would then be
applied to its genuine purposes –
~~Da~~ Year by year the people
would become more susceptible
of assuming forms of government
More simple & beneficial.

line 4040. *voting by ballot,*: Shelley means secret ballot as opposed to one's open declaration of his vote. Open voting was customary in Shelley's day.

line 4043. *~~It withdraws . . . country~~ &* (line 4045): canceled and later reinstated by underlining.

line 4057. *R. A.*: *Representative Assembly*, MWS, Rolleston, and Peck.

line 4061. *by*: possibly *of*; in either case there should be no comma after the first *face* in line 4060. MWS and Peck read *of*.

line 4067. *their*: probable reading.

line 4077. *has indeed exerted*: each editor repairs the sense in his own way; MWS reads *is indeed exercised*; Rolleston reads *had indeed existed*; Peck reads *has indeed [been] exerted*.

line 4079. *perverted*: *per* written through *pre*.

line 4080. *uses,*: MWS reads *purposes*.

SC 546 *It is in this publicity of the exercise*
of sovereingty that the difference
between the republics of Greece & the

[LEAF 85, VERSO]

4090 *Monarchies of Asia,* ⟨——⟩ *consisted.—*

$$\begin{array}{r} ^{1}3333 \\ 500 \\ \hline 2,0)\overline{6,666,50,0} \\ 333,3250 \\ 2 \\ \overline{6,666\,500} \end{array}$$

These assemblies ought at first
to be triennial, unless the
This universality of

4100 *If one of the consequences (as*
is exceeding by probable, if the
existing govern   *But*
If the existing government
shall compel the Nation to take
the task of reforming into its
own hands, one of the most
                  obvious
probable consequences of such a
circumstance, would be the abolition

4110 *of monarchy & aristocracy.*
               then
*Why, it will*ₐ*be argued, if the*

[LEAF 86, RECTO]

subsisting condition of social

---

forms is to be thrown into confusion
should these things be endured,
—of course in such an event they
would not be endured — In
contemplation of such an event,
         why do we now
there We endure them? because   4120
        Do we think   Is it, because we
we imagine not because we
                  hereditary
think that a King is cheaper &
                elected
*wiser than an*ₐ*President, or a*
House of Lords & a Bench of
              are essential
Bishops are promote the dignity
              are institutions modelled   4130
by the wisdom of the most refined
& civilized periods, beyond which
the wit of mortal man can furnish
nothing more perfect? Of It
course is because the In case
the subsisting Goverment should
compel the people to revolt

[LEAF 86, VERSO]

this question w to establish a repres
entative assembly in defiance of
them, and to assume in the defence   4140
of that assembly an attidute of resis

---

line 4087. *It is*: written through *If in*.

line 4088. *sovereingty* (sic).

line 4090. ⟨——⟩: word partially obscured because written over the calculations, in which Shelley has first multiplied 13,333 (voters per district) by 500 (number of electoral districts), then divided the result by 2 and finally multiplied again by 2 to check his division. These calculations obviously pertain to lines 3995–4011 (leaf 83, recto).

line 4090. *consisted.—*: MWS reads *existed*.

line 4105. *reforming*: *ing* canceled by smearing wet ink.

line 4112. *argued,*: MWS reads *enquired*.

line 4126. *an*: changed from *a* at same time *elected* was inserted above.

line 4126. *a*: seems to be followed by extra strokes, resembling *n* or *r*.

line 4134. *It*: written after *Of course* canceled and then later canceled with a very faint stroke.

line 4140. *defence*: in the absence of an alternative, the editor must reinstate *defence*, which Shelley may have canceled because *in the defence* suggests a false parallel to *in defiance* in the previous line.

line 4141. *attidute* (sic): for *attitude*.

Shelley, *A Philosophical View of Reform*   *November 1819–?1820*

SC 546

tance & defence, this question would
probably be answered *in a very summary*
manner:– *No friend of mankind*
& *of his country can desire that*
           suddenly
such a crisis should arrive; but
still less, once having arrived
     hesitate   under what banner

4150   can he ~~doubt~~ ~~on which party~~
       array his person & his power
to ~~stand~~ —— *At the peace the*
       people
~~Nation~~ *would have been contented*
with ~~moderate Reform; or perhaps~~
~~even with strict economy, & severe~~
strict economy, & severe retrenchment,
and some direct & intelligible
plan for producing that equili

4160   *brium between the capitalists &*
the landholders which is

[LEAF 87, RECTO]
delusively styled the payment
of the national debt had this
       system been adopted
~~measures~~ ~~taken place~~, *they proba*
-bly would have refrained from
exacting Parliamentary Reform,
the only secure guarantee that it
would have been pursued.– Two

4170   *years ago it might still have been*
possible to have ~~adopt~~ *commenced*

a system of gradual reform. The
people were then insulted, tempted &
betrayed, & ~~the petitions of a million~~
of men rejected with disdain— Now
they are more miserable, more hopeless,
more impatient of their misery. Above
all they have become more ~~aware~~
universally aware of the true sources
of their misery. It is possible that   4180
the period of conciliation is past,
& that after having played with

[LEAF 87, VERSO]
    confidence
the ~~expec~~ ~~hopes~~ *& cheated the*
expectations of the people, their
passions will be too little under
discipline to allow them to wait
the slow, gradual & certain operation
of such a Reform, as we can im
agine the constituted authorities   4190
to concede.

     Upon the issue of this question
depends the species of reform
which a philosophical mind should
regard with approbation. If Reform
shall be begun by the existing
Government, let us be contented
with ~~small & gradu~~ *a limited*
~~beginning~~, *with any whatsoever*

line 4143. *summary*: *y* somewhat indistinct at edge of page.

line 4144. *friend*: possibly miswritten *freind*.

line 4155. *with*: this word and several others are affected by water blotting in the left-hand margins of leaves 86, verso, through 87, verso.

line 4162. *delusively*: Rolleston reads *derisively*.

line 4162. *the payment*: holes in paper caused by heavy concentrations of corrosive ink.

line 4163. *this*: altered from *these*.

line 4173. *tempted & betrayed,*: Shelley is obviously thinking about the government's use of spies and *agents provocateurs* (like Castle and Oliver) to betray workingmen like Brandreth, Ludlam, and Turner. (See Shelley's *Address to the People on the Death of the Princess Charlotte*.)

line 4184. *&*: heavily blotted but apparently uncanceled.

line 4190. *constituted*: this word, like several others on this page, is affected by blotting from opposite page (leaf 88, recto).

SC 546

opening; *let the rotten boroughs
be disfranchised,* ~~the great unre
presented cities be~~ *and their*
[LEAF 88, RECTO]
*right transferred to the unrepre
sented cities & districts of the
Nation; it is no manner how
slow, gradual & cautious be the
change; we shall* ~~firmly b~~ *dem*
~~quietly, but with firmness &~~
and more & more with firmness

4210 *& moderation, never anticipating
but never deferring the moment
of successful opposition, so that*
          habituated
the people may become ~~capable~~
*of exercising the functions of
sovereingty, in proportion as
they acquire the posession of it.*
          could
If ~~this~~ *reform* ~~should~~ *begin*
4220 *from within the Houses of
Parliament, as constituted at*

present; ~~any (–)~~ *it appears
to me that what is called*
[LEAF 88, VERSO]
moderate reform, that is a ~~limited~~
*suffrage, whose qualification should
be, the possession of a certain
small property; & triennial parliaments
would be principles a system in
which for the sake of obtaining
without bloodshed or confusion,*   4230
ulterior ~~views of a more~~ *improve
ments of a more important char
acter, all reformers ought to
acquiesce. Not that such are
first principles,* ~~of~~ *or that they
would produce a system of per*
          or one approaching to
*fect social institution But no
thing is more idle than to reject
a limited benefit because we*   4240
          without great sacrifizes
cannot ⌃ *obtain an unlimited one.
We might thus reject a Represen*

line 4200. *rotten*: badly blotted from opposite page.

line 4203. *transfered* (sic).

line 4203. *unrepresented*: Rolleston reads *unenfranchised*.

line 4205. *manner* (sic): MWS, Rolleston, and Peck read *matter*.

line 4206. *cautious*: badly blotted.

line 4207. *demand*: second syllable on line 4209.

line 4216. *sovereingty*, (sic).

line 4223. *what*: badly blotted.

line 4225. *whose qualification*: these words like others are blotted from page 89, recto.

line 4227. *triennial parliaments*: some reformers—notably Major John Cartwright—were calling for the annual election of Parliament to make the members more responsive to public opinion. England had, theoretically, elected annual Parliaments from the fourth year of King Edward III (1330) until the sixteenth year of King Charles II (1676), when election of Parliament was made triennial. (There had been, of course, many abridgments of this right.) In 1715 (1 George I) it was enacted that Parliaments could be extended to seven years. Shelley's proposal, again a consciously moderate one, is to return to the practice officially confirmed by William and Mary after the Glorious Revolution of 1688.

line 4231. *ulterior*: Shelley means *further*, lying beyond the present (*OED* 1).

line 4241. *without . . . sacrifizes*: caret and interlineation in fine hand with sharpened quill.

line 4243. *thus*: *?us* written in fine quill above *us*.

SC 546

[LEAF 89, RECTO]

tative Republic, if it were attain
nable, ~~because~~ on the plea that
the imagination of man can concieve
of something more absolutely perfect.
Towards whatsoever we regard as
perfect, undoubtedly it is no less
4250   our duty than it is our nature
to press forward; this is the generous
enthusiasm, which accomplishes
not indeed the consummation after
which it aspires, but one which
approaches it in a degree far
nearer, than if the whole powers
had not been developed by a ~~delusion~~
~~wh~~ which is ~~not a delusive.~~—It
is in politics rather than in religion
4260   that faith is meritorious.–
        If the Houses of Parliament
obstinately & perpetually refuse
to ~~consider commence an inqui~~

[LEAF 89, VERSO]

to concede any reform to the
people, my vote is for universal
suffrage, and equal representation——
        My vote is— but⟨————⟩
        It is asked, how shall this be
accomplished, in defiance of & in
4270   opposition to the constituted authorities
of the Nation, they who possess
whether with or without its consent
the command of a standing army

& of a legion of spies & police officers
  hold   complicated
& all the strings of that mechanism
with which the hopes & fears of
men are moved like puppets? They
would disperse any assembly really
chosen by the people, they would   4280
shoot & hew down any multitude
without regard to sex or age
as the Jews did the Canaanites
which might be collected in its
defence; they would calumniate

[LEAF 90, RECTO]

imprison, starve, ruin & expatri
ate ~~all the chiefs of the patriotic~~
~~party~~ every person who wrote or
acted, or thought, or might be suspec
ted to think against them; misery   4290
& extermination would fill the
country from one end to another . . ?
        This question ~~must be answered~~ I
                                    ⌊would
answer by another.
        Will you endure to pay the half
of your earnings, ~~& consent to impose~~
~~upon yr posterity to everlasting gener~~
~~ations~~ to maintain in luxury &
idleness the confederation of your
tyrants as the reward of a successful   4300
conspiracy to defraud & oppress you?
Will you make your tame cowardice
and the branding record of it

line 4244. *attainnable*, (sic): Rolleston and Peck read *obtainable*.

line 4251. *this*: written through indecipherable letters.

line 4258. *delusive*.—: word nearly obliterated by smeared cancel line.

line 4258. *It . . . meretorious.*– (line 4260): on Shelley's rejection of "faith" as a religious virtue, see Donald H. Reiman, *Shelley's "The Triumph of Life": A Critical Study* (University of Illinois Press, 1965), pp. 16–17.

line 4261. *If*: badly blotted.

line 4267. *but* ⟨————⟩: two or three illegible penciled words, canceled in pencil.

line 4280. *people,*: the comma is almost obliterated by a blot from the facing page.

line 4302. *cowardice*: MWS reads *coward*.

SC 546   the everlasting inheritance of your
degraded posterity? Not only this
[LEAF 90, VERSO]
~~What remedy~~

    ~~What resource is left to us but to
endure but~~ will you render by your
torpid endurance this condition of
4310   things as permanent as the system
of caste in India, ~~where the~~ by which
these same horrible injustice, is per
-petuated under another form?

    Assuredly no Englishman by
whom these propositions are understood
will answer in the affirmative;
        opposite
and the other side of the alternative
remains.—

4320   When the ~~minority in a nation
through successful fraud, have
entrenched themselves within the advan
tage of successful fraud~~ in any nation
          arrive at a conviction
the majority ~~are awake led to the
believ~~ that it is their duty & their

[LEAF 91, RECTO]
interest, to divest the minority of
a power employed to their disadvan
tage; and the minority are sufficiently
         as
4330   unprincipled mistaken ∧to believe
that their superiority is tenable,
a struggle must ensue.

    If the majority are enlightened,
        uniform
united, & impelled by a ~~powerful~~
enthusiasm, & ~~animated~~ & animated by
a ~~clear~~ distinct & powerful apprehension
        & full confidence in their
of there object,— the struggle is merely   4340
undoubted power
nominal.   The minority percieve the
approaches of the developement of an
irresistible force, by the influence of
    public
the opinion of their weakness, on those
political forms of which no govern
-ment, but an absolute despotism
is devoid. They divest themselves of
their usurped distinctions ~~& the~~   4350
~~sacrifize of individual happiness
to the general good is so slight~~

[LEAF 91, VERSO]
that ⟨   ⟩ the public tranquillity
is not disturbed by the revolution.——

    ~~But a case may unhappily occur
in which the majority, rendered abject
by the slavery~~

    But these conditions may only
be imperfectly fulfilled by the state
of a people grossly oppressed & im   4360
-potent to cast off the load. Thier
    have
enthusiasm may been subdued by
the killing weight of toil & suffering

line 4305. *degraded*: badly blotted and possibly canceled.
line 4311. *caste*: possibly *casts*; MWS reads *Casts*; Peck reads *castes*.
line 4312. *perpetuated*: MWS, Rolleston, and Peck all read *perpetrated*.
line 4321. *have*: *h* written through *&*.
line 4324. *arrive at*: MWS reads *come to*.
line 4327. The crossings of the *t*'s in *to*, *the*, and *minority* are badly blotted.
line 4338. *apprehension*: Peck reads *appreciation*.
line 4339. *full*: Rolleston reads *feel*.
line 4340. *there* (sic).
line 4340. *struggle*: MWS reads *contest*.

Shelley, *A Philosophical View of Reform*   November 1819–?1820

SC 546

panic-stricken
they may be ~~decieved~~ & disunited
                  & the demagogues influence
by their oppressors, the ~~success~~ of
fraud may have been sufficient to
4370   union of
weaken the ₍ₐ₎classes which compose
                suggesting
them by jealousies; & the position
of the conspirators, although it
is to be forced ~~at the first vigorous~~
                          by repeated
assaults ~~may have an appearance~~

[LEAF 92, RECTO]

~~of being tenable~~ be tenable until that
~~assault is made.~~ the seige can be
4380 vigorously urged. —— *It may happen*
~~that the least of two evils Such~~
The true patriot will endeavour
to ~~unite~~ enlighten & to unite the
nation   it
& animate ~~them~~ with enthusiasm
& confidence. ~~But it is dangerous~~
~~to delay, & even if the occasion be~~
~~After all union~~ For this purpose he
                              ⌊will
be indefatigable in promulgating political
4390 truth. He will endeavour to rally round
one standard the divided friends of
                              ⌊liberty,

& make them forget ~~their differences in~~
              subordinate
the₍ₐ₎objects ~~in w~~ with regard to which
they differ, by appealing to that
                              ⌊respecting
which they are all agreed. He will
                    confederations
promote such open ~~combinations~~
among men of principle & spirit as
may tend to make their ~~ef~~ intentions   4400
& their efforts converge to a com
mon centre. He will discourage

[LEAF 92, VERSO]

                164
all secret associations which have a
                                    will
tendency by making ~~the~~ national ~~act in~~
develop itself in   premature
a partial & ~~unsympathising~~ manner to
cause   ~~ineffectual~~
~~promote~~ tumult & confusion. ~~he will~~   4410
He will urge the ~~necessity of boldly~~
~~& in de calling together num proposed~~
necessity of ~~frequent &~~ exciting the
people frequently to exercise their
right of assembling, in such limited
numbers as that all present may
~~par~~ be actual parties to the
          Lastly If circumstances had collected a more
proceedings of the day. If the troops

line 4368. *their:* whole word badly blotted.

line 4379. *seige* (sic).

line 4383. *the:* altered from *them* with a sharpened quill, which Shelley also used for *nation, it,* and the cancel line in line 4385.

line 4388. *After all union:* Shelley began anew here with a sharpened quill.

line 4401. *their efforts:* beneath these words is an ink smear from the cancellation in the first line of leaf 91, verso.

line 4402. *He will . . . confusion.* (line 4410): Godwin had argued against all associations because they tended to lead and manipulate, rather than educate and motivate the people. Shelley distinguishes between open and secret associations, as he had earlier in his *Proposals for an Association.*

line 4406. *national:* altered from *nation* when *will* replaced ~~act~~. MWS and Rolleston read *nation's.*

line 4410. *confusion.:* period altered from semicolon.

line 4414. *frequently: fr* written through *to.*

line 4419. *troops:* may have been added after Shelley canceled ~~send their~~ in line 4421.

SC 546

considerable number at at Manchester
tyrants ~~send their~~ command ~~their guards~~
                   on the memorable 16th of August
to fire upon them or cut them down
unless they disperse, he will exhort
                        risque
them ~~to~~ peacably to ~~defy~~ the danger
                                   without resistance
& to, & to ~~wait~~ expect ~~unarmed,~~ the
          onset
4430   ~~charge~~ of the cavalry, & wait with
                               fire
folded arms the event of the ~~discharge~~
of the artillery & ~~the charge of~~
                          receive with unshrinking
bosoms the
[TWO UNNUMBERED STUBS]

[LEAF 93, RECTO]
          charging
bayonets of ~~the~~ battalions ~~of~~ ⟨———⟩
Men ~~have been persuaded to~~ are every
day persuaded to incur greater perils
4440   for a less manifest advantage. And
             active
this, not because resistance is ~~in~~ not
                   when all other means shall have failed
~~case~~ justifiable, but because in this
~~particular case the benefits~~ instance a
temperance & courage would produce
greater advantages than the most decisive
victory. In the first place; ~~soldiers are~~
                             are
4450   men the soldiers ~~would be~~ men &
                                 ⌊English-
men, & it is not to be believed that

they would ~~unre~~ massacre an unresisting
              drawn up in unarmed array before them
multitude of their countrymen ~~which~~
& bearing in their looks the
~~regarded them with steady resolution, &~~
              & deliberate resolution
a calm ~~determination rather~~ to perish
rather than abandon the assertion of their
rights— In the confusion of flight the   4460
ideas of the soldier become confused, &
     massacres
he ~~cuts down~~ those who fly from him
by the instinct of his trade—~~In~~

[LEAF 93, VERSO]
~~the struggle of conflict & resistance~~
              ideas are governed
he ~~is impelled by the same law as those~~
of the
dogs ~~who chases a flock o sheep to the~~
~~corner, & when they~~ In the struggle of   4470
conflict & resistance ~~all those passions~~
~~of~~ he is irritated by a sense of his own
danger, he is flattered by an apprehension
of his ~~own courage~~ magnanimity in
incurring it, he considers the blood of his
countrymen at once the price of his
valour, the pledge of his security. ~~The~~
~~worst passions of our nature are~~
                              ⌊awakened
in ~~him &~~ he   He applauds himself
by reflecting that these base & dis-   4480
                              ⌊honourable
motives will gain him credit among his

line 4420. *at at:* apparently miswritten for *as at.*

line 4426. *peacably* (sic).

line 4428. *& to, & to* (sic).

line 4432. *folded arms:* Rolleston completes the thought with the words *the points of dispute* (lines 4846–4847) and omits all intervening material.

line 4435. *bosoms the:* indistinctly written in gutter of notebook. MWS reads *courage the.*

line 4441. *active:* MWS reads *actual.*

line 4443. *when all other means:* written over ink smear, which possibly resulted from Shelley's smearing wet ink to erase an earlier phrase.

line 4467. *he:* written over illegible letters.

SC 546

comrades & his officers who are animated
as if they were ~~something~~ the same
by the same, ~~his ideas are governed~~
should
~~by the~~ But if he observes neither
resistance nor flight ~~he is~~ he would
be ~~would~~ astonished ~~probably be reduced~~
to ~~a complete impotence of mind, &~~

[LEAF 94, RECTO]

4490   *167*

suddenly ~~thrown back upon a recollection~~
reduced to impotence & indecision
of ~~the true nature of the me~~ action
~~which he was on the point of com-~~
were
~~-mitting.~~ Thus far, his ideas ~~a~~ governed
by the same law as those of a dog
who ~~having~~ chased a flock of sheep to
the corner of a field, & ~~retires or~~ keeps
4500   aloof when they make the ~~accustomed~~
firm
parade of resistance.— But the soldier
is a man & an Englishman. This

unexpected reception would probably
⌊throw
him back upon a recollection of
the true nature of the measures of
which he was made the instrument
& the enemy might be converted into
the ally
true
The patriot will   publish   4510
He ~~would~~ be foremost to ~~write &~~
~~speak~~ the ~~most~~ boldest truths
in the most fearless manner, &
~~to excite the others~~ yet without

[LEAF 94, VERSO]

the slightest tincture of personal
⌊malignity
He ~~would en~~ would encourage all others
to the same efforts & assist them with
to the utmost of his power with the
~~pee~~ resources both of his intellect &   4520
fortune. He would call upon them to
despise imprisomnent & persecution

line 4484. *same,*: comma altered from period.

line 4490. *167*: in pencil.

line 4497. *a dog . . . resistance.*— (line 4502): a homely simile deriving from Shelley's childhood experience on his father's Sussex estate appears amid the abstract language of eighteenth-century political theory.

line 4500. *the*: altered from *their*.

line 4510. *true*: possible reading.

line 4515. *yet without . . . personal malignity* (line 4516): Shelley is the one controversial writer of the period who never in his published writings attacked his personal enemies. (The allusion to Malthus at line 2833 above is the kind of reference which Shelley would certainly have deleted before publishing this treatise.) Byron, Hazlitt, and Hunt dealt as freely with the personal foibles of their political and literary adversaries as did Gifford, Croker, Jeffrey, Southey, Lockhart, and John Wilson. The level of ideality or abstraction to which Shelley mythologized his message allowed him to reach over the individual sinner to the class of sin, as can be seen even in his angry allusion to the unnamed "base and unprincipled calumniator" in the Preface to *Adonais* and in his direct satires *Peter Bell the Third* and *Œdipus Tyrannus; or, Swellfoot the Tyrant.*

line 4518. *with to* (sic).

line 4519. *the*: second *the* written through *his*.

line 4522. *despise*: MWS reads *suffer*.

line 4522. *imprisomnent* (sic).

SC 546

& *lose no opportunity of bringing the*
⟨—⟩
~~*power of*~~ *public opinions &* ~~*the exertions*~~
            power
~~*of barefaced power claims*~~ *of the*
tyrants into circumstances of perpe-
-tual contest & opposition ——

4530
        ~~*In spite of all the acti*~~
        All might however be ineffectual
        so   an
to produce ~~*a*~~ *uniform impulse*
of the national will, as to preclude
a farther struggle – ~~*The very*~~
~~*necessity of reform has perhaps*~~
~~*reduced the public spirit of that*~~

[LEAF 95, RECTO]
~~*numerous class whose are ne who*~~
~~*are neutral & indifferent in*~~ *The*

4540
strongest argument perhaps for the
necessity of Reform is the inoper-
ative & unconscious abjectness to
                    considerable
which the purposes of a ~~*great*~~ *mass*
of the people are reduced. They
neither know nor care, –   They
~~*are resem*~~ *are sinking into a resem*
-blance with the Hindoos & the
Chinese, who were once men ~~*like*~~

4550
~~*themselves*~~ *as they are. Unless the*
cause which renders them passive
subjects instead of active citizens
be removed, they will sink with
accelerated gradations into ~~*the*~~ *a*
that barbaric & unnatural civilization which
~~*condition of despotic servitude*~~

destroys all the differences among men
It is in vain to exhort us to
wait until all men shall desire
~~*Liberty*~~ *Freedom whose real*   4560

[LEAF 95, VERSO]
        17c
interest will consist in its establishment
It is in vain to hope to enlighten
them whilst their tyrants ~~*employ*~~
employ the utmost artifices of
~~*their*~~ *all their complicated engine to*
perpetuate the infection of ~~*fana*~~
                error &
~~*ticism*~~ *every species of fanaticism*
& error from generation to generation   4570
~~*All that*~~ *The advocates of Reform*
ought indeed ~~*to exh*~~ *leave no effort*
unexerted, & ~~*the large class of*~~
~~*these neutral*~~ *they ought to be*
indefatigable in ~~*asserting*~~ *exciting*
all men to examine, – ~~*But it*~~
~~*is impossible*~~

        But if they wait until those
~~*torpid class of*~~ *neutral politicians*
        whose opinions represent the actions of this   4580
class
are persuaded that ⟨   ⟩ effectual
reform is necessary, the occasion

[LEAF 96, RECTO]
will have past, or will never arrive
& the people will have exhausted their
strength   & will have sunk
~~*energy*~~ *in ineffectual expectation-*
    into   incurable supineness

line 4553. *will*: *w* written through *s*.

line 4558. *exhort*: MWS reads *expect*.

line 4573. *unexerted,*: MWS reads *untried*.

line 4578. *those*: altered from *the*.

line 4582. ⟨*some*⟩: possible reading; MWS reads *some*; Peck reads *so soon as*.

line 4586. *& will . . . supineness* (line 4588): interlineations added later in sharpened quill.

line 4587. *expectation–*: MWS reads *exhortations*.

Shelley, A Philosophical View of Reform   November 1819–?1820

SC 546

was principally the
It ~~was by a fo~~ similar quietism
~~& perhaps by a train of arguments~~
that the ~~great~~ *populous & extensive*
nations of Asia have fallen into
their existing decrepitude; and that
the anarchy insecurity ignorance
& barbarism, the ~~ultim~~ *symptoms of*
the confirmed disease of monarchy
have reduced   in
~~cover nations of men of the most~~
4600 ~~fortunate climates~~ *& of the most*
delicate physical & intellectual
under
organization, & ~~within~~ *the most*
fortunate climates of the globe to
a blank in the history of man.

~~We have~~ *The manufacturers to*
a man are persuaded of the
[LEAF 96, VERSO]
immense
necessity of reform. An ~~great~~ *majority*
4610 *of the inhabitants of London*

$$\begin{array}{r} 160 \quad I \\ 3 \\ \hline 480 \quad I \end{array}$$

The ~~motive which has prompted some~~
~~political reasoners to incline to the~~
~~opinion that no has been a consi~~
~~-deration of the horrors of tumult~~
~~bloodshed anarchy & b~~
The f reasoners who ~~incline to~~
the opinion that, ~~a m~~ *it is*   4620
the innovators
not sufficient that ~~th reformers~~
should produce a majority in the
nation, ~~we ought to~~ *but that*
we ought to expect such an
unanimity as would preclude
any thing amounting to a serious

[LEAF 97, RECTO]
dispute, are prompted to this
view of the question by the dread
of anarchy & massacre. ~~Doubt~~   4630
~~-less these excesses are the most~~
~~to be dep~~ *if Infinite & inestim*
able calamities belong to oppression;
but the most fatal of them all
is that mine of ~~ex~~ *unexploded*
~~calamity~~   *has*
~~mischief by which~~ *it practised*
beneath the foundation of society
with   "pernicious to one touch"
and ~~in~~ *which* ~~it threatnes~~ *to involve*   4640
the ruin of the entire building

line 4606. *manufacturers*: the term meant factory workers in Shelley's day.

line 4609. *An*: changed from *A*.

line 4620. *the*: altered from *this*.

line 4623. *should*: written over illegible word.

line 4635. *mine . . . to one touch"* (line 4639): Shelley here uses *mine* to mean a tunnel or underground gallery in which an explosive charge has been placed (*OED* 3) and *practised* (line 4637) in the rare *OED* sense 8, meaning "effected" or "completed," and concludes with a quotation (almost exact) from Milton's *Paradise Lost*, VI.520, the passage in which the Devil's invention of cannon is described.

line 4640. *which*: altered from *whose*.

line 4640. *threatnes* (sic).

line 4641. *entire*: MWS reads *whole*; that Dowden follows MWS in this reading (which is clearly an error) suggests that Dowden took some of his text from MWS rather than from this holograph.

SC 546　*together with it's own.　　　But delay*
merely renders ~~the inevitable~~
~~crisis more tremendous~~ these
　　　　mischief
~~crisis~~ more tremendous, not the
　　　　　　the utmost
　　　　For ~~what~~ may now be the crisis if the
less inevitable. ~~In proportion to~~

4650　*social disease, is rendered thus periodical, chronic*
　　　& incurable.
The savage brutality of the populace
is proportioned to the arbitrary
character of the government, &

[LEAF 97, VERSO]
　　tumults &
~~sanguinary~~ insurrections soon,
as in Constantinople, become ~~the~~
consistent with the permanence
of the ~~governm evil~~ causing evil,

4660　*~~to which they of which they might,~~*
　　　　　critical
have been the determination.

　　The ~~shape~~―――――in England first
　　　~~forms~~ public opinion$_\wedge$ought to
excited to action, & the durability
of those forms within which the

oppressors intrench themselves brought
　　perpetually　　No law or institution can
to the test of its operation. For
last if this opinion be ~~decively pronounce~~ disti⟨　⟩ 4670
this purpose govermnent ought
pronounced defied
to be ~~dared~~ in cases of question
　　against
it.　　　　　　　　　　political
able result to prosecute for$_\wedge$libel.
　　　~~doubtful~~
　　All questions relating to ~~the~~
　　　　　　to
~~pay tithes~~ & the jurisdiction 4680
of magistrates & courts of law
respecting which any doubt

[LEAF 98, RECTO]
could be raised ought to be agitated
with ~~per~~ indefatigable pertinacity.
Some two or three of the popular
leaders have shewn the best spirit
in this regard; they only want
system & co-operation. ~~If possible~~
the tax gatherer ought to be compelled
　　　practicable
in every$_\wedge$instance to distrain, whilst 4690

line 4644. *these*: altered (with a sharper quill) from *the*.

line 4648. *For . . . & incurable.* (line 4651): this inserted sentence and *calamity* (line 4636), "*pernicious . . . touch*" (line 4639), and *mischief* (line 4645), were all written later with a sharpened quill.

line 4652. *The*: changed from *the*.

line 4654. *character*: MWS reads *nature*.

line 4661. *critical*: inserted later with sharpened quill.

line 4664. *to excited* (sic): the editor must insert *be*.

line 4668. *No law . . . pronounced against it.* (line 4675): sentence added later.

line 4670. *decively* (sic): for *decisively*.

line 4670. *disti⟨　⟩*: word crowded and blotted at right margin; MWS and Peck give *distinctly*.

line 4685. *Some two . . . in this regard;* (line 4687): Shelley surely has in mind William Hone and Richard Carlile, in whose trials he had been recently interested.

line 4687. *regard;*: written through *respect*; Shelley's alteration eliminates the echo of *respecting* in line 4682. MWS and Peck read *respect*.

line 4691. *distrain,*: "To constrain or force (a person) by the seizure and detention of a chattel or thing, to perform some obligation" (*OED*).

line 4691. *whilst*: *w* written through *&*.

Shelley, *A Philosophical View of Reform*   *November 1819–?1820*

SC 546

the right to impose taxes, as
was the case in the beginning of
the resistance to the tyranny of
    is
Charles the 1ˢᵗ, formally contested
~~even before the~~ by an ~~increas~~
overwhelming multitude of
defendants before the ~~legal~~ courts

4700   Confound the subtlety of lawyers
of common law. ~~This simult~~
   with the subtlety of the law All of the
~~By simultaneous~~ The ~~Public~~
    nation
~~opinion~~ would thus be excited to
develope itself, & to declare

[LEAF 98, VERSO]
     176
whether it acquiesced in the ~~mis~~
existing forms of government.— The

4710 manner in which all questions of
     might
this nature ~~would~~ be decided would
~~shew make evident the~~ develope the
occasions, & afford a prognostic
as to the success, of more decisive

measures. Simultaneously with this
active & vigilant system of opposition
       solemnly
means ought be taken of ₍ₐ₎conveying
the ~~sense~~ sense of large bodies, &   4720
various denominations of the people
in a manner the most explicit
to the existing depositaries of power.
~~The system of~~ petitions, but
couched in the actual language
of the petitioners, and emanating
from distinct ~~bodies of the~~
      assemblies
~~people~~ men, ought to load the
tables of the house of commons.   4730

[LEAF 99, RECTO]
    The poets, philosophers
The ~~Literary men~~ artists &
    remonstrate its the
ought to ~~come forward,~~ & the
    entitled
memorials ~~called~~ their petitions
    diverse of
might shew the ~~various~~ convictions
they entertain of the inevtable connection

line 4692. *the right . . . formally contested* (line 4696): the resistance to King Charles I came to a head in 1637 when John Hampden came to trial for his refusal to pay the "ship-money" tax levied by Charles on the inland counties as a means of raising revenue without consent of Parliament. On March 2, 1817, Mary Shelley wrote to Leigh Hunt: "Shelley & Peacock have started a question . . . and . . . as they seem determined to act on it I wish them to have the *best advise*. As a prelude to this you must be reminded that Hamden was of Bucks and our two worthies want to be his successors for which reason they intend to refuse to pay the taxes as illegally imposed—" (Mary Shelley, *Letters*, I, 18–19). It is not clear, either from Mary's account or from the present passage, whether Shelley thought that all taxes were illegally imposed because the House of Commons as constituted did not truly represent the English people or whether he resisted certain excise taxes, imposed during the war as emergency measures, that had not been rescinded after peace had come.

line 4700. *Confound . . . law* (line 4702): written later with sharpened quill.

line 4702. *All*: possible reading.

line 4706. *develope*: last syllable written through illegible letters.

line 4716. *this*: altered from *these*.

line 4724. *petitions,*: altered from *petitioning*.

line 4731. *The . . . philosophers*: badly written and blotted in gutter.

line 4733. *remonstrate*: possibly *demonstrate*.

line 4733. *its the*: Shelley may have begun *their* without canceling *its*.

line 4739. *inevtable* (sic): possible reading.

SC 546

national prosperity   Freedom
between ~~liberty~~ & the cultivation
of the imagination, & the cultiva
                            & the profound
tion of scientific truth.– ~~These memorials~~
developement of moral & metaphysical
~~might be worthy of the age & of the~~
enquiry
~~cause~~ Suppose these memorials to
be severally
4750   ~~were~~ written by Godwin & Hazlitt &
                Bentham & Hunt
~~Lord Byron;~~   they
would be worthy of the age & of the
the ⟨——⟩ of radiant & irresistible
cause & ~~would strike~~ like the meri
-dian Sun would ~~strike blind~~ strike
all but the eagles who dared to
gaze upon its beam, with blindness
& confusion. ~~Instead of n Let them~~
4760   ~~devote but~~ Let but a fortnight's
~~talen employment of that talent~~
~~which is now buried~~

[LEAF 99, VERSO]
appeals
These ~~memorials~~ of solemn & em-
-phatic argument from those who
have already a predestined existence
among posterity, would appall the
enemies of mankind by thier echoes
from every corner of the world in
which the majestic literature of   4770
England is cultivated; it would be
like a voice from beyond the dead
of those who will live in the memories of men, when they must be
forgotten; it would be Eternity
warning Time.
     ~~It is not to be~~ Let us hope
that at this ~~period of~~ stage of the
progress of Reform, the oppressors
would feel their impotence, &   4780
reluctantly & imperfectly con
cede some limited portion of

line 4740. *Freedom*: written later with sharpened quill.

line 4741. *between*: written through indecipherable word.

line 4742. *the cultiva*: *the* written through sketch of a cloud.

line 4744. *~~memorials~~*: *~~orials~~* curves down right margin.

line 4745. *metaphysical*: probable reading.

line 4750. *Godwin . . . Hunt* (line 4751): Shelley's list is interesting chiefly for his cancellation of Byron's name and for his inclusion of Hazlitt's. Shelley must have had high regard for Hazlitt's powers as a writer and a controversialist. Perhaps he also admired Hazlitt as a thinker, though it is certain that they differed on many issues. Mary Shelley's Journal records that at Hunt's on February 9, 1817, there was "a discussion untill 3 in the morning with Hazlitt concerning monarchy & republicanism." Charles Cowden Clarke in his *Recollections of Writers* (p. 26) recalls "a very warm argument in favour of the Monarchy upheld by Leigh Hunt and Coulson, and in favour of Republicanism by Shelley and Hazlitt." Walter Coulson was a protégé of Jeremy Bentham, as Shelley was — in his political thinking — a follower of Godwin, and Shelley's list in lines 4750–4751 may simply have been an attempt to name eloquent spokesmen for four reformist viewpoints. Note the absence of William Cobbett, whom he feared at this time as an incendiary influence upon ignorant people. (See, for example, Shelley, *Letters*, II, 53, 75, 94.)

line 4750. *&. . .&*: each ampersand written through *or*.

line 4754. *radiant . . . meridian Sun* (line 4756): the sense seems to require that this phrase be set off by commas or dashes to modify *cause*.

line 4776. *Time.*: *T* altered from *t*.

Shelley, A Philosophical View of Reform   November 1819–?1820

SC 546 [LEAF 100, RECTO]
the Rights of the people; & disgorge
some morsels of their undigested
prey. In this case, the people
ought to be exhorted by every thing
ultimately dear to them to pause
~~to~~ until by the exercise of those
                  have regained
4790 rights which they ~~have~~——they
become fitted to demand more. It
is better that what we ~~demand should~~
gain what we demand by a process
of negotiation which would occupy
twenty years, than that ~~a sudden~~
~~extinction~~ by communicating a sudden
shock to the interest of those who
are the depositaries or dependants of
power we should incur the ~~chance~~
4800 ~~that they~~ calamity which their
revenge might inflict upon us
by ~~sounding the~~ giving the signal
of civil war.—— ~~If Yet the~~
       If, after all they
[LEAF 100, VERSO]
       180
~~are obstinately bent upon involving~~

~~the destruction of the Nation in their~~
~~own,~~ consider the chance ~~fame~~
~~life, credit & the infamy, death,~~
personal ruin, & the infamy of   4810
figuring on the page of history as
the promoters of civil war preferable
to resigning ~~an~~ any portion how
small soever of their usurped authority
we are to recollect that ~~not~~
~~only as men but as Englishmen~~
~~we possess~~ we possess a right
~~as men, which~~ beyond remonstance.
~~We are entitled by~~ It has been ~~ac~~
acknowledged by the most approved   4820
writers on the English constitution
(which is in this instance merely declaratory of the
    that we posess a right of
⟨——⟩ superior decisions of eternal justice.)
resistance. ~~It is familiarly known~~
~~that~~ The claim of the ~~reigning~~ family
~~of t now reig~~ is founded upon

[LEAF 101, RECTO]
a memorable exertion of this
solemnly recorded right.
      The last resort of resistance is   4830
undoubtedly insurrection.— ~~But before~~

line 4783. *Rights*: R altered from r.

line 4791. *become*: c written through ?f.

line 4802. *signal*: possible reading; may be *signs*.

line 4803. *of*: o written through indecipherable letter.

line 4808. *chance*: apparently Shelley left this word an adjective ("random") modifying *personal ruin*, (line 4810).

line 4818. *remonstance.* (sic).

line 4820. *approved*: probable reading.

line 4822. *is*: written through ?has.

line 4824. *eternal*: MWS reads *co-eternal*.

line 4826. *The claim . . . right.* (line 4829): the reference is to the Parliamentary Act of Settlement of 1701, which denied the English throne to Roman Catholic heirs and thus brought in the House of Hanover, instead of the direct Stuart heir from Charles I through primogeniture — James, the "Old Pretender" (son of James II). This act and its enforcement in 1714 established that the king was, in fact, subject to acts of Parliament in all regards.

line 4826. *The*: T altered from t.

Shelley, A Philosophical View of Reform   November 1819–?1820

SC 546

~~we proceed Insurrection is, in certain~~
~~emergencies, the duty of the merely~~
~~the performance is not only an~~
~~inalienable right, but our~~ and ~~is a~~
~~duty from which no personal conse~~
~~quences temporary consequences can~~
~~dispense us.~~ The right of insurrection
is derived from the employment of
4840   ~~arm standing~~ armed force to counter
act the will of the nation. Let the
government disband the standing
    purpose
army, and the ~~objects~~ of resistance
~~by~~ would be sufficiently fulfilled
by the incessant agitation of the
points of *legal* dispute before the
courts of common law, & by an
unwarlike display of the

[LEAF 101, VERSO]
4850   irresistible numbers & union of the
people. ~~The courts of common law~~
~~distinct from the system of precedents~~
~~which is not inseperable from their~~
~~practise, are unlike those which~~
     a
~~are founded in written law,~~
     ⌊*jurisprudence,*

~~Before we proceed to recommend~~
~~a system of measures which~~
  ~~There are many~~
Before we enter into a consideration   4860
of the measures which ~~might plunge~~
~~those men who could~~ might terminate
in civil war, let us for a moment
consider the nature & the ~~end of~~
consequences of war. This is the alter
native which the unprincipled ~~op~~
cunning of the tyrants ~~has~~ presented
 & from which we must not ⟨ ⟩ bred
to us, ~~And there is~~ There is ~~something~~
secret sympathy between ~~Massacre~~   4870
& ~~Absolute Power.~~ Destruction &

[LEAF 102, RECTO]
Power, between Monarchy & War; &
~~it is to be feared~~ the long experience
~~of the world teaches us~~ of the history
of all recorded time teaches us with
what success they have played into each
others hands. ~~What has been the~~
~~consequence of all the wars~~ The moment
~~that the si~~ In France the Revolution
~~was already accomplished, when the~~   4880
~~signal for Massacre was given~~ The
War is a kind of superstition; the

line 4835. ~~and~~: altered from *ind.*

line 4851. ~~The courts . . . jurisprudence,~~ (line 4856): Shelley obviously distrusted the laws enacted under the kings and by the Parliaments he accuses of having subverted English liberties and rights. The Court of Chancery, which in Shakespeare's day (see commentaries on *The Merchant of Venice*) was seen as a moderating influence on the absolutism and primitive inflexibility of common law, had by Shelley's day become a tool of the establishment to bend the law to its will.

line 4853. ~~inseperable~~ (sic).

line 4854. ~~those~~: a comma may follow this word.

line 4865. *This*: written through *It.*

line 4868. *from*: written through *within.*

line 4868. ⟨ ⟩: MWS and Peck read *shrink*, Rolleston reads *shun*; the word is too small and indistinct to read; there is no riser at the end of the word for the *k* of *shrink*, which is the logical choice contextually.

line 4869. *us,*: possible reading; comma originally period.

line 4874. *the history*: *the* altered from *this.*

Shelley, *A Philosophical View of Reform*   November 1819–?1820

SC 546

pageantry
~~parade & the circumstance~~ of arms
& badges corrupts the imagination
of men. How far more appropriate
would be the symbols of an inconso
        muffled drums, & melancholy music, & arms
lable ~~sorrow~~, when men mourn at
        grief
4890
                reversed & the livery of sorrow
funerals for what do they mourn
rather than of blood.
in comparison with the calamities
which they hasten with ~~every~~

                all

circumstance of festivity to suffer
& to inflict. ~~If we can picture~~

[LEAF 102, VERSO]
        Visit in   the scene
4900 ~~to our~~ imagination ~~but the outlines~~
of ~~the the a~~ field of battle, ~~the~~ or
                        collect int
a city taken by assault, ~~if we~~
~~bring~~ into one group the groans &
the distortions of the ~~dying~~ innum
erable dying, the inconsolable grief
& horror of their surviving friends,
the hellish exultation, & unna
tural drunkenness of destruction
4910 of the conquerors, ~~the ruin frequently~~
~~of the ruin of all monumen~~ the
~~country the country~~ the burning
of the harvests, & the obliteration
of the traces of cultivation.——To this,

in civil war, is ~~united~~ to be added
the sudden disruption of the bonds
of social life, & "father against son

~~Lastly the danger lest some~~
        If there had never been war
[LEAF 103, RECTO]
there could never have been tyranny   4920
in the world. tyrants take advan
-tage of the mechanical organization
of armies to establish & ~~p~~ defend
        encroachments
their ~~power~~.——It is thus that the
        ~~The~~ The ~~heaps of dead & unsightly~~
~~heaps of corpses~~ mighty advantages
of the French Revolution have been
almost compensated by a succession
of tyrants, ~~f~~ (dema (for demagogues   4930
oligarchies usurpers & legitimate Kings
are merely ~~disgus~~ varieties of the same
class,) from Robespierre to Louis 18.
        War, ~~unfits carried~~ waged from
whatever motive extinguishes the
sentiment of reason & justice in the
mind. The motive is forgotten, or only
adverted to in a mechanical & habitual
manner. . A sentiment of confidence
in brute force & in a contempt   4940
[LEAF 103, VERSO]
        186
of death & danger is considered as

line 4883. *pageantry*: MWS reads *pageant*.

line 4888. *muffled drums, . . . blood.* (line 4893): the three-line interlineation was added later with a sharpened quill.

line 4891. *reversed*: may be preceded by a (superfluous) ampersand.

line 4895. *~~every~~*: canceled, then reinstated with underline.

line 4898. *~~can~~*: *n* may be formed from original *ll*.

line 4918. *~~danger~~*: probable reading.

line 4922. *organization*: altered from *organized*.

line 4924. *encroachments*: written with sharper quill and in darker ink that Shelley began using on leaf 104, recto.

SC 546

the highest ~~virtue~~, when in truth ~~they~~
are ~~no~~ merely ~~means &~~ however indis
pensible to ~~it~~ they are merely the
means & the instruments, highly
capable of being perverted to destroy
4950 the cause they were assumed to
promote. ~~The It~~ is as a foppery the
most intolerable to an amiable &
philosophical mind.— It is ~~like faith~~
like what some reasoners have observed
of religious faith; no fallacious
& indirect motive to action can subsist
in the mind without weakening the
effect of those which are genuine &
~~sati~~ true. The person who think
4960 it virtuous to believe, will think
~~that~~ a less degree of virtue attaches
to good actions than if he had

[LEAF 104, RECTO]

                    as
considered it indifferent. The person
who has been accustomed to subdue
men by force, will be less inclined to
the trouble of convincing or persuading
them.
        These brief considerations suffice

to shew that the true friend of man   4970
kind & of his country would hesitate
before he recommended measures
which ~~would~~ tend to bring down so
                    heavy
~~mighty~~ a calamity as war—
        But I imagine however that before
the English Nation shall arrive at
that point of moral & political
degradation now occupied by the
Chinese, it will be necessary to   4980
appeal to an exertion of physical
strength. ~~If the m It is necessary
because it~~ If the madness of
parties admits no other mode of

[LEAF 104, VERSO]
determining the question at issue,

[LEAF 105, RECTO, BLANK]

[LEAF 105, VERSO]

When the people ~~h~~ shall have obtained
by whatever means the victory
                    oppressors
over their ~~tyrants~~, & when persons
appointed by them shall have   4990
taken their seats in the Represen
tative assembly of the nation, &
assumed the controul of ~~the~~ public

line 4943. *liberty*: possible reading; word heavily canceled.

line 4946. *the* (sic): for *them*.

line 4947. *merely*: MWS reads *only*.

line 4951. *as*: altered from *is*.

line 4955. *fallacious*: written through *false*.

line 4959. *think*: MWS, Rolleston, and Peck read *thinks*. There is less evidence of an *s* at the end of this word than in *think* immediately below in line 4960. Presumably Shelley intended the subjunctive, and the editor can solve the problem by inserting [may] after *who*.

line 4974. *heavy*: written later in darker ink.

line 4975. *as war—*: written in darker ink over the very faint light brown ink that Shelley used from leaf 90, verso, to this point. The remaining portion of this text is written in the blacker ink that begins here (see facsimile, page 1009).

line 4985. *issue,*: the remainder of this page, the next page, and the top quarter of leaf 105, verso, are blank.

line 4993. *controul*: contemporary alternative spelling.

SC 546

affairs according to constitutional
rules, ~~nothing remains~~ there
will remain the great task of
accomodating all that ~~cannot~~
~~be~~ be preserved of antient forms
with the improvements of the

5000   *knowledge of a more enlightened*
age in legislation, jurisprud

[LEAF 106, RECTO]
ence, government ~~finance~~ &
religious & academical insti
tution. The settlement of the
national debt, is on the principles
           circumstance
before elucidated, merely ~~an affair~~
of form, & however necessary &
important is ~~after a subj~~ an

5010   *affair of mere arithmetical &*
proportions readily ~~settled~~ (deter
mined; nor can I see how those
who, being deprived of their unjust
advantages will probably inwardly
murmur, can oppose one word of
open expostulation to a measure
of such irrefragrable justice.——
There is one thing, which certain
vulgar agitators ~~te~~ endeavour

5020   *~~to teach the~~ to flatter the*

most uneducated part of the
people by assiduously propo

[LEAF 106, VERSO]
sing, which they ought not to
do, nor to require; & that is Retri
bution.

     Men having been injured, desire
to injure in return. This is falsely
called an universal law of human
nature; it is a law from which
many are exempt, & all in pro-   5030
-portion to their virtue & cultiva
tion.– The savage is more revengeful
than the civilized man, the the
ignorant & uneducated than the
person of a refined & cultivated
~~mind~~ intellect, the generous &

[UNNUMBERED STUB]

[LEAF 107, RECTO, TO LEAF 108, RECTO,
BLANK]

[LEAF 108, VERSO, SC 547]

[LEAF 109, RECTO]
05000,000,000

     To consider inequal of property
       as an incentive to <u>*industry*</u>
   150   5040
         industry what 5000,0⟨ ⟩

line 4997. *accomodating* (sic).

line 4998. *antient*: contemporary alternative spelling.

line 4999. *of the*: *the* written through **a**.

line 5006. *circumstance*: Rolleston reads *arrangement*.

line 5017. *irrefragrable* (sic): Peck reads *inescapable*.

line 5018. *certain...Retribution*. (line 5025): here Shelley certainly means to include William Cobbett, among other demagogues.

line 5026. *having*: ink showing through from recto causes *ing* to appear canceled.

line 5033. *than*: altered from *that*.

line 5033. *the the* (sic).

line 5037. The numerals in lines 5037–5041 are written in pencil on leaf 109, recto. Four-fifths of leaf 109 have been torn away.

Shelley, Note on Ode to the West Wind   *?November–*
December 1819

SC 546   [LEAF 109, VERSO, PENCIL SKETCH OF   [LEAF 138, VERSO]
          TREE]   *On the punishment of*
          [LEAF 110, RECTO]   *Death*
5042   2ᵈ   *We would disband the standing*   ────────────
          Army   150   [LEAF 139, RECTO, SKETCH OF TREE]
          [LEAF 110, VERSO, TO LEAF 132, VERSO,   [LEAF 139, VERSO, TO LEAF 140, RECTO,
          BLANK; UNNUMBERED STUBS BETWEEN   SC 549 AND PENCIL CALCULATIONS, ALL
          LEAVES 111 AND 112 (1), 112 AND 113   *REVERSO*]
          (1), 114 AND 115 (2), 124 AND 125 (1);   [LEAF 140, VERSO TO LEAF 141, VERSO,
          LEAF 119, HALF TORN OFF]   BLANK]
          [LEAF 133, RECTO, PENCIL SKETCH OF   [LEAF 142, RECTO]
          SAILBOAT AND TREE-LINED BANK]   ~~*Nor can*~~
          [LEAF 133, VERSO, TO LEAF 138, RECTO,   ~~*And*~~ *It has been*   5047
          BLANK]   [LEAF 142, VERSO, BLANK]

line 5042. Lines 5042–5043 are written in pencil. Between *2ᵈ* and *We* is a drawing of a tree. To the right of, and below *150*, is a sketch of a flat-bottom boat.
line 5044. Title written *reverso*.

The leaves following leaf 142, containing Shelley's essay, "On Life," have been removed and are now in The Pierpont Morgan Library. The inside back cover is filled with sketches of faces and calculations in ink and pencil and the back vellum cover is filled with sketches of trees and calculations in ink.

SC 547   P. B. SHELLEY, NOTE ON *ODE TO THE WEST WIND*, ?NOVEMBER–
          DECEMBER 1819

HOLOGRAPH MANUSCRIPT, 1 page, written on leaf 108, verso of SC 546, which also contains SC 549.
Addition: pencil sketch of boat, outlined in ink, drawn in lower right corner of page.
For further details, see SC 546, Bibliographical Description.

~~*The three first st*~~
        This poem was concieved & chiefly written in a wood which skirts the
    Arno near Florence, & on a day when that tempestuous wind, ~~*of*~~ *whose*
    temperature is at once mild & animating, was collecting the vapours which
5   *pour down the autumnal rains. They began, as I foresaw at sunset with a*
    violent tempest of hail & rain, attended with that magnificent thunder &

Shelley, Note on Ode to the West Wind ?*November–December* 1819

SC 547 *lightning peculiar to the cisalpine regions.— The phenomena alluded to at*
the conclusion of the third stanza, are ~~frequently~~ well known to naturalists.
The vegetation at the bottom of the sea, of rivers & lakes, sympathises ~~like that~~

10 *are*
with that of the land, in the change of seasons, & consequently influenced
~~approach~~ of the winds which announce it— at least   in poetry

line 2. *concieved* (sic).
    written: *w* written through *in*.
line 6. *magnificent*: *c* possibly an *s*.
line 11. *influenced*: written through illegible word.
line 12. *of . . . announce*: occupies almost all of the penultimate line of the manuscript page and

is written through indecipherable penciled words.
line 12. *least   in*: the space between these two words is occupied by part of Shelley's sketch of a boat which was drawn before he drafted this note. Shelley has outlined the boat in ink to mark it off more clearly from his writing.

THE DATE conventionally given for the composition of Shelley's "Ode to the West Wind" is October 25. But, as Neville Rogers points out in a wide-ranging and stimulating discussion of the poem's growth, although the date "Oct. 25" heads the fair copy of the first three stanzas (which Rogers designates Stage Four of the poem's composition), the first verse fragment related to the genesis of the "Ode" begins, "'Twas the 20th of October."[1]

The idea and basic imagery of the poem had been in Shelley's repertory since at least 1817, when he developed them in *Laon and Cythna*, IX.xxi–xxv.[2] But the evidence of the various draft notebooks fixes the date for inspiration and much — if not all — of the composition of "Ode to the West Wind" itself late in October 1819.

Dating the draft of the note to the "Ode" (SC 547) is somewhat more difficult. In the notebook only three blank pages (besides the stub of a leaf torn out of the notebook) intervene between the end of the consecutive draft of *A Philosophical View of Reform* (see SC 546) and the drafted note. But a few fragments apparently related to the *Philosophical View* follow, and there is no way to be certain that Shelley did not draft the note near the end of a nearly blank notebook and only later fill the bulk of pages with his *Philosophical View of Reform*.

1. See Neville Rogers, *Shelley at Work* (2nd edition, Oxford University Press, 1967), pp. 222, 226.
2. See SC 393.

The Carl H. Pforzheimer Library

Shelley, Note on Ode to the West Wind   *?November–*
December 1819

SC 547   It is clear that Shelley used the Pforzheimer notebook while he was composing regularly in the notebooks denominated Bodleian Ms. Shelley adds. e. 12 and Huntington Ms. 2176 (volume I of Shelley, *Note Books*). The scraps from Act IV of *Prometheus Unbound* appearing in SC 549 were, for example, composed at the same time Shelley was working out the antiphonal songs of the Spirit of the Earth and the Spirit of the Moon (IV.319–502) that are, for the most part, drafted in Bodleian Ms. Shelley adds. e. 12 and Huntington Ms. 2176.[3] To establish the relative dates of the note to the "Ode" (SC 547) and the *Prometheus Unbound* first drafts (SC 549), one might suppose that it was necessary only to establish that in Bodleian Ms. Shelley adds. e. 12, the drafts for *Prometheus Unbound*, IV.319 ff. precede the fair copy of the first three stanzas of "Ode to the West Wind." But, in fact, Shelley's notebook entries are always more difficult to order and date than they initially seem to be. Though parts of the draft for *Prometheus*, IV.319 ff. appear on the pages preceding the "Ode," other, interrelated portions of the fourth act appear much later in the same notebook, and it could be argued that Shelley was, in these nonadjacent drafts, working around the portion of the "Ode" which had earlier been copied in the notebook.

The evidence of the manuscripts being inconclusive and there being no reference to "Ode to the West Wind" in Shelley's or Mary's letters or Mary's or Claire's journals, we must fall back on internal evidence in the note's text. Here we observe that the canceled beginning of the note (line 1) must refer to the first three stanzas, as drafted in Bodleian Ms. Shelley adds. e. 12 — Rogers' "Stage Four" — which are dated October 25. Thus the note, though written after the completion of the five-stanza poem, was written soon enough after October 25 for Shelley to have the stages of the poem's composition uppermost in his mind. Given only this slender thread on which to hang a date, I cannot venture beyond saying that the note was certainly written after October 25 and almost certainly before the end of 1819.

One logical question might be: Could not the last two stanzas and

---

3. The holograph fair copy of *The Mask of Anarchy* now in T. J. Wise's collection in the British Museum was also employed for trial drafts for this section of Act IV. See Lawrence John Zillman, *The Complete Known Drafts of Shelley's "Prometheus Unbound"* (Ann Arbor, Mich.: University Microfilms, 1967), pp. 44, 75–98.

SC 547   the note itself have been drafted in the evening of October 25, when Shelley had returned from the Cascine with the first three stanzas in hand? This seems very improbable, not only because a more likely sequence would have been for Shelley to write the "beautifully penned fair copy of stanzas I–III"[4] from the pencil rough draft in Huntington Ms. 2176,[5] but also because on the evening of October 25 there occurred an argument with Charles Clairmont of enough importance to be recorded in Mary's Journal and to be, apparently, the subject of a comment in one of Shelley's notebooks: "I am no proficient in the knowledge of the human heart if there is not something in the scene of tonight deeper than what seems."[6] Charles Clairmont stayed with the Shelleys from September 4, through their move from Leghorn to Florence, until November 10, when he left for Vienna via Trieste.[7] We might learn more about this incident, as well as Charles Clairmont's general relations with the Shelleys during this period, if we could locate a letter from Charles to the Shelleys dated December 3, 1819, which, together with other items of Shelley interest, was sold in the Roderick Terry sale.[8]

4. Rogers, *Shelley at Work*, p. 226. Though the second and third stanzas are in simple fair copy, the latter half of the first stanza has been substantially revised.

5. See Shelley, *Note Books*, I, 163–170.

6. Bodleian Ms. Shelley adds. e. 15, p. 2. The comment is dated "Oct. 25, 1819."

7. On November 17, 1819, Shelley writes to Henry Reveley that Charles will send "an account of the Trieste Steam Boat" (Shelley, *Letters*, II, 158).

8. The American Art Association, November 7–8, 1934, lot 297.

SC 548   P. B. SHELLEY, *PROMETHEUS UNBOUND* FRAGMENT, II.iii.82–89, ?NOVEMBER–DECEMBER 1819

HOLOGRAPH MANUSCRIPT, ⅓ page. Page 1 of 3 consecutive single sheets (5.5 x 3.5 inches), containing also SC 532 and SC 536.
For further details, see SC 532, Bibliographical Description.

~~Like a diamond which shines~~
~~In the~~ A lamp which
~~Like~~ a diamond which shines
In the darkness of mines
5   *A spell is muffled, but for thee alone*
Down Down

The Carl H. Pforzheimer Library

Shelley, Prometheus Fragment   *?November–December* **1819**

SC 548 Portions of each line are partially obscured by Shelley's sketches of trees which seem to have been drawn before the text was written.

line 2. Lines 2–5 are written through three pencil lines, of which only a few words are legible:

> *The* ⟨   ⟩ ⟨   ⟩ ⟨   ⟩
> ⟨   ⟩ ⟨   ⟩ *has been ?long* ⟨   ⟩
> *in* ⟨   ⟩

line 2. *A*: written through an indecipherable letter.

line 5. *for*: possible reading; the word is written through a heavily canceled word and obscured by Shelley's sketches.

line 6. This line appears on the same level as line 1 of SC 532.

Through accidents of Shelley's method of composition and the distribution of his manuscripts, rough drafts for *Prometheus Unbound* are now found in four libraries; most of the drafts are in the Bodleian Library, Oxford, but there are fragments in the Henry E. Huntington Library (in two of the so-called Bixby-Huntington notebooks), the British Museum, and The Carl H. Pforzheimer Library, which has two unrelated snippets. SC 548 is written, as the Bibliographical Description indicates, on the first of three consecutive leaves torn from one of the Huntington notebooks (HM 2177), where they were originally between what are now numbered leaves 6 and 7 of that notebook.

Lawrence John Zillman, in *The Complete Known Drafts of Shelley's "Prometheus Unbound,"* states that "there can be no certainty as to the order" of the stanzas in the "Song of Spirits" (*Prometheus Unbound,* II.iii.53–98) "since they were put in where space permitted, regardless of lines irrelevant to *Prometheus Unbound* which might be on the same page."[1] But Zillman fails to draw the logical inference from this fact, which is that this lyric was written later than *The Mask of Anarchy,* the rough draft of which occupies a series of consecutive leaves of HM 2177, dividing the draft of the "Song of Spirits." Inasmuch as *The Mask of Anarchy* could not have been begun before September 1819, the passages of *Prometheus* II.iii that are thus drafted around it and around Shelley's draft of the Dedication of *The Cenci* to Leigh Hunt (see SC 532 and Commentary) must postdate September 1819. As Neville Rogers observes, the "Down, down" lyric is thematically compatible with *The Mask of Anarchy.*[2]

1. Ann Arbor, Mich.: University Microfilms, 1967, p. 34, fn. 11.

2. Rogers, *Shelley at Work* (2nd edition, Oxford University Press, 1967), p. 216. Robert A. Hartley ("Images of Change in *The Revolt of Islam,*" unpublished doctoral dissertation, Columbia Uni-

Shelley, Prometheus Fragment   **?November–December 1819**

SC 548   This late draft thus shows (as does sc 554) that Shelley did not complete and polish the first three acts of *Prometheus Unbound* early in 1819 and then leave them unaltered, but that he actually made at least one substantial later addition to Act II while he was working on Act IV in Florence between October and December 1819. Perhaps Shelley intended the "Song of Spirits" that urges Asia and Panthea to descend into the Abysm for their rendezvous with Demogorgon as a counterpiece to some of the soaring lyrics of Act IV. In any case, the lyric was drafted late in 1819 and was probably among the "lyrical insertions" to which Shelley refers in sc 554. Were a discriminating critic to make a complete analysis of the drafts of *Prometheus Unbound* in relation to drafts of other poems of known date, he might well contribute valuable new information about Shelley's creative method and a better understanding of the related functions of various parts of Shelley's lyrical drama.

versity, 1971, pp. 87–89, 104–106) has, quite independently, shown that there is a close thematic and symbolic relationship between the last stanza of the "Down, down" lyric (*Prometheus Unbound*, II.iii.90–98) and a passage near the end of Act IV of Shelley's drama (*Prometheus Unbound*, IV.562–569).

SC 549   P. B. SHELLEY, *PROMETHEUS UNBOUND* FRAGMENT, IV.319–322, 376–377, 397–399, ?NOVEMBER–DECEMBER, 1819

HOLOGRAPH MANUSCRIPT, ¾ page, written *reverso* on leaves 140, recto, and 139, verso, of sc 546, which also contains sc 547.
For further details, see sc 546, Bibliographical Description.

O   *&*   *&*
The joy the triumph, the delight & madness
     Boundless &   *gladness*
Glory & life & transport not to be contained
       Joy If
       Ha ha tis life, tis

And like a wind bursting its rocky prison
     With earthquake & with lightning—it has risen

5

The Carl H. Pforzheimer Library

Shelley, Prometheus Fragment   *?November–December* **1819**

SC 549

11

> *The unquiet Republic of the spheres*
> *Of ever wandering planets, whom*
> *The great Sun rules as with a tyrants gaze*

line 4. *contained*: written directly beneath the rest of the line because of lack of space; *prison* (line 7) and *it has risen* (line 8) are positioned similarly.

line 5. *Joy*: probable reading; both words on this line are intertwined with words in line 6 and Shelley may have intended to cancel them.

THE THREE disconnected short passages from Act IV in sc 549, written *reverso* on two facing pages in the back of the notebook containing *A Philosophical View of Reform* (sc 546), present something of a puzzle. In each case they are early versions of lines that Shelley revised frequently in the rough drafts.[1] Zillman has identified three draft versions of IV.319–322, four versions of IV.376–377, and no less than five separate drafts of IV.397–399. According to Zillman's analysis, the Pforzheimer notebook contains the first draft of IV.319–322 and IV.397–399, and the second draft of IV.376–377.[2] As a matter of fact, Shelley's practice in other poetic manuscripts is to waver so often between two variant readings, canceling and later reinstating the first reading, that one cannot always be guided by simply the genetic development of images and rhymes; that is, Shelley's first version is not *always* the one farthest away from the final reading he retained for the published texts. But if, in the absence of contradictory evidence, one employs the test of genetic development, then the Pforzheimer notebook's fragments must be judged the earliest drafts of all three passages.

To examine the four variants of IV.376–377 (and I follow Zillman's transcriptions of the versions in the Huntington and Bodleian notebooks), Shelley began the image with lines 7–8 of sc 549 in the Pforzheimer notebook. Then, apparently turning back to Huntington Ms. 2176 in which he had drafted the preceding lines,[3] Shelley first wrote: "And like a whirlwind bursting its craggy prison." Next (after canceling the metrically superfluous "And" and reducing "whirlwind" to the

1. See Lawrence John Zillman, *The Complete Known Drafts of Shelley's "Prometheus Unbound"* (Ann Arbor, Mich.: University Microfilms, 1967), pp. 75, 84–85, 88; and Zillman, *Shelley's "Prometheus Unbound": The Text and the Drafts* (Yale University Press, 1968), pp. 212–213, 216–219.

2. Zillman, *Complete Known Drafts*, pp. 75, 88, 84.

3. HM 2176 is the one Forman discusses in the first volume of Shelley, *Note Books*.

P. B. Shelley, *Prometheus Unbound, IV.319–322, 376–377, 397–399, ?November–December 1819* (SC 549, which occupies leaves 140, recto, and 139, verso, of SC 546)

SC 549 monosyllabic "storm"), he shifted away from the metaphor of the wind's home as *rocky* or *craggy prison* to the more obvious image of a *cloudy prison*. In the next line he first replaced *lightning* with *whirlwind* and then tested the replacement of *earthquake* with *lightning* or *thunder*.[4]

In the third draft (on an adjacent page of Huntington Ms. 2176), both lines of the couplet have been corrected to their final form:

> Which
> Like a storm bursting its cloudy prison
> With thunder & with whirlwind, it has arisen

The final word was changed from *risen* to *arisen* when *it* was canceled. The fourth "draft" of these lines (Bodleian Ms. Shelley adds. e. 12, page 54) is simply a clean transcription of the third draft, together with the prior and subsequent lines.[5]

Having demonstrated (by analyzing the only passage under dispute) that all three fragments of *Prometheus Unbound*, Act IV, found in the Pforzheimer notebook are first drafts, insofar as the order can be judged by the criterion of genetic development, I would like to be able to argue convincingly why Shelley used just two of many blank pages in the Pforzheimer notebook to jot down the first attempts at these particular fragments. But nothing occurs to me except to note that all three fragments are found in the Spirit of Earth's part of the long antiphonal exchange with the Spirit of the Moon. This lyrical section (IV.319–502) forms a distinct division of the fourth act, following a long passage of blank-verse dialogue between Panthea and Ione. When Shelley began to draft the earliest part of the answer from the Spirit of the Moon (IV.325 ff.), he quickly shifted from the Huntington notebook to the *Mask of Anarchy* manuscript now in the British Museum to work out the draft of the first lyric stanza.[6] His apparent need to rewrite his ideas several times and to develop gradually his patterns of versification and imagery may have forced him to go to scraps of paper outside the main manuscript to sketch his ideas until he had mastered the lyric form of the passage. He may have used other scraps of paper, since lost, to

---

4. HM 2176, f. 18ʳ; Zillman, *Complete Known Drafts*, p. 83.

5. Zillman, *Complete Known Drafts*, p. 85.

6. Zillman, *Complete Known Drafts*, pp. 75–77.

SC 549   draft other lines and images that now first appear in the Huntington notebook.

To comprehend the genesis of Shelley's *Prometheus Unbound* and the poems published with it in 1820 from their inception through the various drafts and fair copies to the printed volume both requires and deserves the sustained attention of a sensitive critic thoroughly versed in the study of Shelley's notebooks and in the principles of textual criticism and bibliographical analysis. Lawrence John Zillman's three volumes on *Prometheus Unbound* itself could provide helpful groundwork for such a study.

SC 550   LEIGH HUNT, *ANGLING*, NOVEMBER 15 OR 16, 1819

HOLOGRAPH MANUSCRIPT, 6½ pages. 6 single sheets, 8ᵛᵒ (7.6 x 4.8 inches).
Laid paper. Watermarks: 1. (pages 1, 5, 6): [fleur-de-lis (quadrant to half)]|;
2. (pages 2, 3, 4)*:* FINE|.
Notation, page 1, upper right corner: *Leigh Hunt's| writing|.*
Additions: 1. Finger and thumb prints in printers' ink; 2. Leaves of manuscript hinged onto blank leaves 9.5 x 6.8 inches, which were bound by Riviere in red Levant morocco.

PROVENANCE: Sotheby, July 24, 1922, lot 797.

Angling.

　The ~~Angler~~ anglers are a race of men who puzzle us. We do not mean,
*　　　　　　　　　　　laudable*
5　*for their patience, which is ~~commendable~~; nor ~~for even~~ for their the infinite*
non-success of some of them, which is desirable. Neither do we agree with
the ~~jok~~ good joke attributed to Swift, that ~~an~~ angling is always to be con-
sidered as " a stick & ~~str~~ a string, with ~~f~~ a fly at one end & a fool at the
other." Nay, if he had books with him & a pleasant day, we can even account
10　*for the joyousness of that prince of all ~~pun~~ punters, who*

　　　　　　　　　　　　　　　　T.O.

*　　　　　　　　　　　one*
having been seen ~~stand~~ in the same identical spot for morning & evening, &

[1075]

SC 550

success
asked both times whether he had had any ~~sort~~, said "*No; but in the course of the day, he had had "a glorious nibble.*"

Angling.

But the Anglers boast of
20 ~~The Anglers t are a race of men who puzzle us. They boast of being extremely harmless; yet they pass their time in putting animals to the tortu~~

fellow-creatures
the innocence of their pastime; yet it puts ~~fishes~~ to the torture. They pique
themselves on their meditative faculties; & yet their only excuse is a want of

It is this that puzzles us.
25 thought.₍₎Old ~~Isaak~~ Isaac Walton, their patriarch, speaking of his inquisi-
tional abstractions on the banks of a river, says,

> Here we may
> Think & pray,
> Before death
30 > Stops our breath—
> Other joys
> Are but toys,
> And to be lamented.

So saying, he "stops the breath" of a trout by plucking him up into an
35 element too thin to respire, with a hook & a tortured worm in his jaws.

> Other joys
> ⟨—⟩
> Are but toys.

skait,
40 If you ride, walk, or ~~run~~, or play at cricket, or at rackets, or ~~make yourself~~
~~& your friends chearful~~ enjoy a ball or a concert, it is "to be lamented."
To put pleasure into the faces of half a dozen agreeable women, is a toy
unworthy of the manliness of a worm-sticker. But to put a hook into the
gills of a carp,–there you attain the end of a reasonable being;– there you
plant
45 shew yourself truly a lord of the creation. To ~~have~~ your feet occasionally in
the mud, is also a pleasing step. So is cutting your ancles with weeds &
stones.

> Other joys
50 > Are but toys.

[1076]

SC 550   *The book of Isaac Walton upon angling is undoubtedly a delightful*
                    It smells of the country air, & of lavender in cottage windows.
   performence in some respects. But ˄Its' pictures of much scenery, its' sim-
plicity, its' snatches of old songs, are all good & refreshing; & his pro-
55 *digious relish of a dressed fish would not be grudged him, if he had killed*
it a little more decently. He really seems to have a respect for a piece of
salmon;   to approach it, like the grace, with his hat off. But what are we
to think of a man who in the midst of his tortures of other animals is always
valuing himself on his wonderful harmlessness; & who actually follows up
60 *one of his most complacent passages of this kind with an injunction to impale*
a certain worm twice upon the hook, because it is lively & might get off?
All that can be said of such an extraordinary inconsistency is, that having
been bred up in an opinion of the innocence of his amusement, & possessing
                              (as far as he had any), he must have
65 *a healthy power of exercising voluntary thoughts, ~~he could really blind himself~~*

                                                          so as to
~~to the cruelty~~ he dozed over ~~that side~~ the opposite side of the question, & become
                                                    ˄
almost, perhaps quite insensible to it. And angling does indeed seem the
next thing to dreaming. It dispenses with loco-motion, reconciles contradic-
70 *tions, & renders the very countenance null & void. A friend of ours, who is*
      an
a ~~great~~ admirer of Walton, was struck, ~~but~~ just as we ~~are~~ were, with the
likeness of the old angler's face to a fish. It is hard, angular, & of no expres-
sion. It seems to have been "subdued to what it worked in;" to have become
75 *native to the watery element. One might have said to Walton, "Oh flesh, how*
art thou fishified!" He looks like a pike, dressed in broadcloth instead of
butter.

line 11. *T.O.*: written at the bottom right corner of the first sheet, recto, directing the printer to "turn over"; the text continues on the lower third of the verso side, the only leaf of the six with writing on the verso.

line 17. *Angling.*: to the right of this word there is a large 2̄, which was emended from *1* after Hunt drafted lines 1–16 on a separate sheet which he inserted at the beginning of his essay. Each of the remaining four sheets has a large numeral, similarly altered (from *2* to *3, 3* to *4,* etc.) in the upper right corner.

line 20. *tortu*: probable reading; neither *t* was crossed.

line 22. *pique*: probable reading.

line 30. *Stops*: probable reading.

line 39. *skait,*: obsolete spelling recorded in *OED.*

line 41. *chearful*: spelling recorded in contemporary dictionaries.

line 47. *pleasing*: *a* written through indecipherable letter.

   ancles: alternate spelling (*OED*).

The Carl H. Pforzheimer Library

Hunt, Angling   *November 15 or 16, 1819*

SC 550   line 53. *performance* (sic).
line 59. *on*: may be *in* with the *i* left undotted.
line 62. *is, that*: comma placed first after *is*, then canceled and inserted after *that*, then canceled again and reinserted after *is*.

line 69. *reconciles*: *o* inserted between *c* and *n*.
line 72. *but*: probable reading.
line 76. *broadcloth*: originally followed by a comma.

THIS MANUSCRIPT contains the first half of Leigh Hunt's essay on "Angling," which appeared in the *Indicator* for Wednesday, November 17, 1819. Since Hunt confessed to Shelley on December 2 that he "was obliged to write for...Wednesday's paper on Monday & Tuesday,"[1] we can date the composition of this piece as Monday or Tuesday, November 15 or 16, 1819.

Evidently sc 550 was sent to the printer and type set directly from it, the first and only draft. That sc 550 was the first draft appears not only from the many cancellations but also from the fact that Hunt originally began the essay on what is now the second leaf of the manuscript (line 17) and later inserted lines 1–16 and revised the original beginning to form a smooth transition. He thus saved his harsh remarks for later in the essay. That the manuscript went to the printer appears from both a collation of the uncanceled text with the printed version in the *Indicator* and from such marks as the "2" at the top of the first leaf, which signified to the printer that "Angling" was to be the second article in the issue of the *Indicator* in which it appeared. The light traces of printers' ink also testify that the manuscript visited a composing room.

sc 550 thus provides an opportunity to see how Hunt went about his weekly task of writing. Apart from the use of the editorial "we," Hunt's style is very much like that in his personal letters, except that in his press copy he revises his phrasing more often.[2] The central conception of "Angling" is, in this case, a humanitarian appeal that Charles Lamb would have found surprising but that Shelley and Byron would

---

1. sc 552, lines 24–25.

2. Hunt's two quotations from Shakespeare (lines 74, 75–76), from Sonnet 111 and *Romeo and Juliet*, II.iv.40, respectively, are more integral to his thought than are the allusions and puns in his next letter to Shelley (sc 552).

[1078]

Hunt, Angling   *November 15 or 16, 1819*

SC 550   heartily approve.[3] Leigh Hunt was something of a *bon vivant*, but though he undoubtedly took as much delight in eating roast suckling pig as Lamb did, he could not have described the process of roasting with equal delight. Hunt would have tried to ignore the prior history of his tasty meal. He disliked facing the hard realities from which the newly urbanized civilization of nineteenth-century London conveniently shielded him. (Note the revulsion he feels for mud, weeds, and stones.) Lamb and Shelley both looked squarely at the origins of "animal food" and came to some opposite conclusions about what their personal behavior ought to be. Shelley tried to maintain a vegetarian diet in the most carnivorous society in Europe; Hunt continued to enjoy his meal, while averting his eyes from the kitchen and the butcher shop.

Hunt's criticism of anglers[4] — particularly of Izaak Walton — also lacks some sense of history. When Walton and other sportsmen of the seventeenth century spoke of the harmlessness of their pastime, they were not comparing it with riding, walking, skating, playing at cricket or rackets, dancing, or listening to music (lines 39–41). Walton specifically compares angling with hunting with hounds and with falcons, and in the speech in which Piscator speaks of anglers as harmless, he says that "most Anglers are, quiet men, and followers of peace; men that were so simply-wise, as not to sell their consciences to buy riches,"[5] contrasting angling with the quest for military glory, commercial wealth, or political or ecclesiastical power. Walton and his followers were forerunners of the eighteenth-century writers who went on to distinguish "greatness" from goodness. When Swift (lines 7–9), Fielding, Shelley, Hunt, or Byron turned his moral indignation against the folly or cruelty of men who spent their entire lives engaged in field sports, he was confronting a moral problem that came into view only after the evils of

3. According to Benjamin Robert Haydon, "Shelley said he could not bear the inhumanity of Wordsworth in talking of the beauty of the shining trout as they lay after being caught [*The Excursion*, VIII, 558–569], that he had such a horror of torturing animals it was impossible to express it" (Haydon, *Diary*, II, 89). Byron records his revulsion toward angling (and Izaak Walton) in *Don Juan*, XIII.cvi.5–8 and note (Byron, *Poetry*, VI, 513–514).

4. The British term "angling" places emphasis on the sport; the American term "fishing," on the catch. The pertinence of each term would probably depend on how hungry one was — whether one was merely angling for sport or fishing for sustenance.

5. *The Complete Angler of Izaak Walton and Charles Cotton* (London, 1823), p. 6.

SC 550   more "serious" human endeavors were widely recognized, thanks to the efforts of humane men like Walton.

For his own time or ours, Hunt's message to fishermen has greater merit. In an age that recognizes greater kinship among all sentient creatures than did the seventeenth century and that has evolved as one of its higher ideals a reverence for life, there is certainly no harm in reminding men that the fisherman's pleasure is the fish's agony. Leigh Hunt and journalists of his type have probably aided popular awareness of some of the profounder problems of modern ethics by oversimplifying them.

SC 551   P. B. SHELLEY TO LEIGH HUNT, NOVEMBER [16], 1819

AL signed *PBS.*, 3 pages. Double sheet, 4to (10 x 8.4 inches).
Wove paper. Watermarks: 1. (lower right corner of first leaf)*:* [cipher] *GCC*|;
2. (lower right corner of second leaf)*:* [six-pointed star]|.
Seal (trace): wax, red.
Postal fees: 1. 14; 2. 5/9.
Postmarks: 1. FIRENZE|; 2. M[ILANO]; 3. (Foreign Post Office stamp, London)*:*
FPO| DE·2| 1819|.
Additions: 1. (page 3)*:* large seal tear affecting text; 2. (page 3)*:* two small tears on folds; 3. manuscript hinged onto recessed page, which was bound together with calligraphic transcription and commentary, by Sangorski and Sutcliffe in tan morocco, elaborately tooled and gilt.

PROVENANCE: Leigh Hunt; Thornton Leigh Hunt; Walter T. Spencer. *De Ricci 445* (pp. 152–153).

My dear friend

Two letters both bearing date Oct. 20 arrive on the same day. . one is always glad of twins.

5   *We hear of a box arrived at Genoa with books & clothes; it must be yours. Meanwhile the babe is wrapped in flannel petticoats, & we get on with him as we can. He is small but healthy & pretty. Mary is recovering rapidly. Marianne I hope is quite recovered.*

I ~~have sent you three~~ You do not tell me whether you have recieved my lines on the Manchester affair. They ~~were~~ are of the exoteric species, & are

SC 551 *meant not for the Indicator, but the Examiner. I would send for the former*
if you like some letters on ~~the art~~ such subjects of art as suggest themselves in
Italy. Perhaps I will, at a venture, send you a specimen of what I mean next
post. I inclose you in this a piece for the Examiner; or let it share the fate,
whatever that fate may be, of the ~~Mas⟨-⟩~~ Masque of Anarchy.

15   *I am sorry to hear that you have employed yourself in translating*
Aminta, though I doubt not it will be a just & beautiful translation. You
ought to write ~~Amita~~ Amintas. You ought to exercise your fancy in the per-
petual creation of new forms of gentleness & beauty. You are formed to be a
living fountain & not a canal however clear. When I read your "Nymphs"
20 *which is a poem original & intense, concieved with the clearest sense of ideal*
beauty & executed with the fullest & most flowing lyrical power, & yet de-
fined with the most intelligible outline of thought & language, I envy Tasso
his translator because it deprives us of a poet.– I speak rather of the Nymphs
than of the Story of Rimini; because the former is in my judgement more
25 *intensely & perfectly a poem, in the sense in which Tasso speaks of Poetry*
"Non c'è creatore fuorché Iddio ed il Poeta"; the latter affects the passions &
subdues the understanding more completely, but the former appeals ~~the~~ to
the Imagination who is the master of them both, their God, & the Spirit by
which they live & are.—— With respect to translation— even I will not

              seduced
30 *be ~~tempted~~ by it although the greek plays & some of the ideal dramas of*
Calderon (with which I have lately, & with inexpressible wonder & delight
become acquainted) are perpetually tempting me to throw over their perfect
& glowing forms the grey veil of my own words.— And you know me too
35 *well to suspect that I refrain from the belief that what I would substitute*
for ~~them~~ them, would deserve the regret which yours would deserve if sup-
pressed. I have confidence in my moral sense alone, but that is a kind of
originality. I have only translated the Cyclops of Euripides when I could
absolutely do nothing else,– & the Symposium of Plato, which is the delight
40 *& astonishment of all who read it.– I mean the original or so much of the*
original as is seen in my translation not the translation itself.

I do not wish it to be mentioned publickly that I am coming in the
spring; for reasons which you can readily guess.

[1081]

The Carl H. Pforzheimer Library

SC 551   *I think I have an accession of strength since my residence in Italy,
though the disease itself in the side, whatever it may be, is not subdued. Some
day we shall all return from Italy. I fear that in England things will be
carried violently by the rulers, & that they will not have learned to yield in
time to the spirit of the age. ~~But~~ The great thing to do is to hold the balance
between popular impatience & tyrannical obstinacy; to inculcate with fervour*
50   *both the right of resistance, & the duty of forbearance.*

    *You know my principles incite me to take all the good I can get in
politics, forever aspiring to something more. I am one of those whom nothing
will fully satisfy, but < >o am ready to be partially satisfied by all that is
< > We shall see – ⟨——————⟩ < >y a thousand*
55   *thanks from me for wri< > < >t, in that pretty neat hand your kind
& powerful defence . . . Ask her what she would like best from Italian
land? ~~I~~ We mean to bring you all something & Mary & I have been wondring
what it shall be. Do you each of you choose . . .*

                                    know how ought to published–
60   *The " Julian & Maddalo" I do not ~~wish to be printed now~~. What do
you think best to do with it— Do as you like— The Prometheus I wish
to be printed & to come out immediately. I think you will be pleased with the
spirit in which it is written*

                             Adieu my dear friend
65   *Yours affectionately Ever PBS.*

[Address, page 4]
Leigh Hunt Esqʳ
    Examiner Office
      19. Catharine Sᵗ
          Strand
70   *Angleterre.*

             London

line 7. *Marianne*: Shelley dipped his pen before writing *anne* and two drops of ink fell between this word and *I*.

line 8. *I*: there is a short vertical mark before this word.
    three: probable reading.
    recieved (sic).

line 14. *Mas⟨ ⟩*: the last letter, having a riser and descender, may be a long *s*. Perhaps Shelley then spelled *Masque* as he did so that Hunt would not confuse *Mask* with *Mass*, as *he* had almost done.

line 19. *clear*.: may be *clean*.

line 20. *concieved* (sic).

Shelley to Hunt   *November [16], 1819*

SC 551   line 26. *creatore*: final *e* of *creatore* written through *i*.

    fuorché: may have been intended to be two words.

line 27. *appeals*: written through a word smeared out while ink was still wet.

line 28. *Spirit*: may be *spirit*.

line 35. *refrain*: *n* written through *d*.

line 42. *publickly*: contemporary spelling.

line 48. *The*: *T* affected by fold tear, but legible.

line 53. *but*: *b* possibly *B*.

    <*wh*>*o*: tops of letters visible above extensive seal tear; text from Hunt, *Lord Byron and Some of His Contemporaries*, p. 242.

line 54. <*practicable*>: seal tear; text from Hunt, *Lord Byron*, p. 242.

    ⟨————⟩: canceled word illegible.

    <*Give Bess*>*y*: seal tear; text from Hunt, *Lord Byron*, p. 242.

line 55. *wri*<*ting*>: covered by seal.

    <*ou*>*t*: text from Hunt, *Lord Byron*, p. 242.

line 57. *wondring*: *d* inserted over what may have been *e*.

line 59. *to published*– (sic).

line 60. *now.*: probable reading.

THERE WAS an end to Hunt's burst of creative energy that had enabled him to write for the *Examiner*, finish his drama on the Cid, edit the *Literary Pocket-Book*, and launch the *Indicator*, while carrying on what was for him an unusually voluminous correspondence with the Shelleys. His letters became less and less frequent. And because Hunt had turned over to Marianne Hunt the chief responsibility for sending Mary Shelley the layette requested long before the birth of Percy Florence Shelley (lines 4–6), the baby clothes did not arrive until long after they were needed.[1]

The Shelleys, meanwhile, had been sending Hunt a steady stream of letters and packets. On September 23, Shelley had mailed the manuscript of *The Mask of Anarchy* for publication in the *Examiner* (lines 13–14).[2] On September 24 Mary Shelley wrote to Leigh Hunt, and on September 27 Shelley wrote again after returning from a house-hunting visit to Florence.[3] Shelley next wrote on November 2, enclosing his poem *Peter Bell the Third*[4] and thanking Hunt for the personal defense of him in the *Examiner* against the slanders in the *Quarterly Review*.[5] On November 6, Shelley sent Hunt his long, thoughtful letter on the trial of

1. See sc 535 and Commentary.

2. Mary Shelley, *Journal*.

3. Mary Shelley, *Letters*, I, 80–82; Shelley, *Letters*, II, 121–123.

4. Shelley, *Letters*, II, 134–136.

5. See sc 543 and Commentary. Sometime Shelley also sent Hunt a copy of his Dedication of *The Cenci*. See sc 532, sc 552, and Commentaries.

SC 551   the bookseller Richard Carlile (1790–1843), addressed to the Editor of the *Examiner*.[6] On Saturday, November 13, the day after the birth of his son, Shelley wrote Hunt a letter announcing that event and mentioning that financial complications might force him to visit London in the spring. In a postscript he complained that he had received no letter from Hunt "for a *month*."[7] The next delivery of mail from England was not until Tuesday[8]; therefore, sc 551 cannot have been written before then. Since Shelley's letter of November 13 and sc 551 both reached London the same day, they cannot have been mailed more than one post apart. The November 13 letter which was postmarked "Milano" presumably went in the Tuesday mail via Milan; sc 551, which has an obscured postmark beginning with "M," could have gone either via "Milano" (Tuesday) or "Mantova" (Saturday), but not "Torino"

6. Shelley, *Letters*, II, 136–148; composed November 3–6 (Mary Shelley, *Journal*). In 1817, after William Hone had stopped selling the three parodies for which he was later charged with blasphemous libel, Carlile took up their sale (and wrote similar ones), imprinting each title page as follows: "Printed and Published by R. Carlile, ... 183, Fleet Street: and sold by all those who are not afraid of incurring the displeasure of his Majesty's Ministers, their Spies or Informers, or public plunderers of any denomination." Sentenced in November 1819 to three years in prison for publishing Paine's works, Carlile actually served six full years. In the sixth year he wrote King George IV the following letter (manuscript in The Carl H. Pforzheimer Library):

Dorchester Gaol Decr 13
1824

Sir,

    Having entered upon a sixth year of imprisonment, because I cannot be a conscientious Christian and will not be a hypocritical one, I have the pleasure to inform you, that in meditating upon the properties of matter, I have discovered, that intelligence is a result of animated animal matter, and that no animal nor any other matter can be a result of intelligence. The inference of this discovery is, that all religion has a bad foundation, and all the expence and distraction attending it may be well saved.

I am, Sir,
your prisoner
Richd Carlile

To the King

7. Shelley, *Letters*, II, 150–151. The Shelleys had received sc 535 on September 22 and sc 539 on October 12.

8. Letters sent from Florence to England were carried on Tuesdays by the Milan courier, who left Florence for Milan at 1 p.m., on Thursdays by the Turin courier, who left at five in the morning, and on Saturdays by the Tuscan courier, who went to Mantua at 1 p.m. (*L'Indispensabile Almanacco ... per L'Anno 1819*, Florence: Pagani, 1818, p. 249.) Letters arrived in Florence from England via the Tuscan courier from Mantua on Tuesday mornings, via the Turin courier on Wednesday during the day (Thursday mornings in the winter) and via the Milan courier on Saturdays.

Shelley to Hunt   *November [16], 1819*

SC 551 (Thursday). This second letter, then, must have gone with the November 13 letter in the Tuesday mail and had to be written between the time Shelley picked up Hunt's letters on Tuesday morning and the departure of the Milan courier at 1 p.m. the same day — November 16.[9] Mary Shelley next wrote to Marianne Hunt on November 24 (the letter reaching London on December 15).[10] When Hunt received Shelley's two letters on December 2, he wrote promptly and with apologies (see sc 552, Commentary) but failed to send the letter for several weeks. Shelley was becoming somewhat upset by the time he next wrote on December 23 (sc 555). Not until Bessy Kent sent a letter explaining the Hunts' current problems in a letter dated January 6, 1820, did the Shelleys learn the causes of Hunt's neglect.[11]

Shelley's major concerns in sc 551 are literary. He asks about *The Mask of Anarchy* and encloses another poem either "for the Examiner" or to share the fate of *The Mask of Anarchy*. Forman, followed by Jones, identified this poem as "Love's Philosophy." Hunt's comments in sc 552 (and the appearance of "Love's Philosophy" in the *Indicator* for December 22, 1819 [I, 88]) establish almost beyond question that the anacreontic[12] was enclosed in this letter. But I find it difficult to believe that "Love's Philosophy" is the poem to which Shelley is referring here, for it is not the kind of poem he would have thought of as a companion piece to *The Mask of Anarchy*. Rather, there are several political poems, like *The Mask* "of the exoteric species," that would better fit Shelley's remarks and to which Hunt also alludes in sc 552.[13] It seems clear (from the postal fee as well as this reference) that Shelley enclosed "Love's Philosophy" in addition to the political poem he originally planned to enclose.

9. Shelley's use of "arrive" in the present tense suggests that he is writing in immediate response to Hunt's letters.

10. Mary Shelley, *Letters*, I, 83–86.

11. Mary Shelley, *Letters*, I, 95–98; Shelley, *Letters*, II, 179–182.

12. Traceable, according to James Henry Dixon, *Notes and Queries*, 4th Series, I (January 25, 1868), 80, to a French song beginning "Les vents baisent les nuages" (Shelley, *Poetical Works* [Forman], IV, 24–25).

13. Hunt speaks of Shelley's "political songs & pamphlets" (sc 552, line 38). The pamphlets could include the letter on Richard Carlile, *The Mask of Anarchy*, *Peter Bell the Third*, and the "songs" must have included "Song to the Men of England," and similar poems.

The Carl H. Pforzheimer Library

SC 551   Shelley's inclusion of "Love's Philosophy" in this letter is ironic insofar as the inspiration for that poem is a French paraphrase of Anacreon, because a long paragraph of the letter is devoted to Shelley's thoughts on the evils of translation. He suggests that Hunt is wasting his time in translating Tasso's *Aminta* rather than writing original poems like "The Nymphs." It is likely that Shelley found Hunt's translations in *Foliage* (about half the volume) exceptionally bad and untrue to their originals — thus doing more harm than good.[14]

In passing, Shelley mentions his own translations. That of *The Symposium* (lines 39–40) is well known and the time that he did it is well documented.[15] But little has been established about his translation of *The Cyclops* of Euripides (line 38) except that Mary Shelley eventually published it in *Posthumous Poems*. The draft of the *Cyclops* translation appears in a notebook that was part of Lady Jane Shelley's original gift to the Bodleian in 1893 (Bodleian Ms. Shelley e. 4).[16] This notebook, containing the watermark "W Turner & Son," is definitely English, and from its contents one can establish that Shelley used it both at Marlow in 1817 and in Italy. Full discussion of the notebook's contents and their dating belongs in a study of the Bodleian rather than the Pforzheimer manuscripts. Suffice it to say that *The Cyclops* was the last piece drafted in the notebook, for Shelley drafted the later portions of the translation in blank spaces of scattered pages which contained other writings. One of the poems that Shelley evidently wrote prior to translating *The Cyclops* was the fragmentary "Passage of the Apennines" (beginning, "Listen, listen, Mary mine") on folio 41ᵛ *reverso*. This poem was composed May 4, 1818.[17] The earliest possible date for *The Cyclops*, then, would be the period at Leghorn, from May 9 to June 10, 1818,

---

14. Most readers were of the opinion of the reviewer for the *Eclectic Review* (usually friendly to Hunt), who said: "They [the translations] will not give satisfaction to those who are acquainted with the originals; they will not interest those who are not. They are disfigured by Mr. Hunt's usual faults of style, with here and there a touch of more than ordinary vulgarity . . ." (*Eclectic Review*, 2nd Series, X, November 1818, 493).

15. See sc 488, Commentary.

16. Information about this notebook can be found in C. D. Locock's *Examination of the Shelley Manuscripts in the Bodleian Library* (Oxford University Press, 1903) and A. H. Koszul's *Shelley's Prose in the Bodleian Manuscripts* (London, 1910).

17. Mary Shelley's Journal gives the dates of crossing the Apennines (May 4–6) and she dates the poem in *Posthumous Poems*.

Shelley and his Circle : Manuscripts

SC 551   during which time Shelley was reading Euripides.[18] Dr. Timothy Webb of the University of Leeds, who is completing an edition and a study of Shelley's translations, has sent me a thoughtful letter in which he argues that *The Cyclops* was probably written during the latter half of 1819, perhaps in July and August of that year. If Dr. Webb's tentative dating is correct — and, though he intends to investigate the matter further before publishing his evidence, his reasoning seems to me convincing — the dating of *The Cyclops* need not conflict with my suggestion in SC 554, Commentary, of a later date for *Prince Athanase* than is usually assigned to it.

Shelley's remarks to Hunt about translation reveal several aspects of his maturing literary theory. In preferring Hunt's "The Nymphs" to *The Story of Rimini*, Shelley was reasserting the judgment implied in his earlier letters to Hunt that Hunt's theory of poetic diction, which advocated the use of coinages or slang terms of the day, was not likely to produce great poetry.[19] In his August 15 letter Shelley had used the term "vulgar" to describe the "cant terms" of both the *beau monde* and the Cockneys. His reason there was that both high and low slang were "equally expressive of bare conceptions" — that, in other words, such terms were merely one-dimensional, without imaginative overtones or the possibility of growth. "The Nymphs" was an original mythopoeic creation, with vitality to inspire new mythic creations. The *Aminta* of Tasso was a pastoral drama in a form so artificial, stylized, and conventional — so filled with the cant of courtiers — that Shelley might well have doubted whether it could bear translation from the context of *cinquecento* court-society, in which the genre flourished, into the smoke and commercial bustle of London in the midst of the Industrial Revolution. In any case, it was not a form to come to grips with the revolutionary intellectual upheavals of the day — not nearly so well adapted (Shelley demonstrates in his *Œdipus Tyrannus; or, Swellfoot the Tyrant*) as Aristophanic comedy or even the satyr play like *The Cyclops*.[20]

Shelley's prejudice against translation could have arisen from analy-

---

18. See Mary Shelley, Journal.

19. SC 469 and SC 531 and Commentaries.

20. Shelley's debts to Aristophanes are obvious in *Swellfoot*, but Shelley's translation of *The Cyclops* also contributed to his handling of the seriocomic tone of that poem and to his use of the Chorus.

SC 551   sis of the connotative, evocative aspects of language and their importance for great literature. Not only are the individual rhythms and sounds of a particular language lost in translation, but the translator into English must pick and choose one basic meaning from among the possible meanings of a word or phrase in its original language and then choose an English word or phrase that also has many shades and overtones of meaning, thus inevitably bringing to the context associations that are relevant in English but irrelevant to the passage in the original language. In quoting Tasso's own description of a poet — "None is a creator except God and the Poet"[21] — and in distinguishing between the "understanding" and the "Imagination" as he does in the following lines, Shelley looks forward to important ideas developed in his *Defence of Poetry*.

Shelley's remarks on the English political crisis following Peterloo (lines 46–50) reflect the serious concern that caused him to devote much energy and attention to political writings toward the end of 1819. Gone were whatever dreams he had enjoyed of reforming the world in a few frenetic years. Yet he was so sincerely dedicated to the beliefs he had earlier espoused that he would not willingly sacrifice the great principles of love and reason, forgiveness and understanding, simply to see change come more quickly. He advocated only those means — "the right of resistance, & the duty of forbearance" — that would truly help to eradicate basic social evils (without simply replacing one set of tyrants or oligarchs with another). It is significant to see him reaffirming these basic principles not only in such pronouncements intended for the public as *The Mask of Anarchy* and *A Philosophical View of Reform*, but also in this private letter to his closest friend.

21. Line 26. Shelley also quoted the sentence (which he found in Marcantonio Serassi's *Vita di Torquato Tasso*) to Peacock in SC 491.

SC 552   LEIGH HUNT TO P. B. SHELLEY, DECEMBER 2, 1819

AL signed *L H*, 3½ pages. Two single sheets, 4to (first sheet, 9.1 x 7.5 inches; second sheet, 9.6 x 7.7 inches).
Wove paper.
Seal: wax, red: [angel with olive branch, following serpent].
Postal fees: 1. [?Fr] 36; 2. 3/10 [repeated].
Postmarks: 1. (receiving house stamp, London): CRAWFORD STREET|; 2. (Foreign Post Office stamp, London): F 19| 94|; 3. (transit stamp): ANGLETERRE|; 4. CHAM-

Shelley and his Circle : Manuscripts

Hunt to Shelley   *December 2, 1819*

SC 552   BERY|; 5. CORRISP^{ZA} [ESTERA DA GENOVA]| [encircling fleur-de-lis]|; 6. 8| GENNAIO|.
Notation, page 4, in same pink ink as second postal fee: [?*Crawford*]|.
Addition, first sheet: the verso of this sheet has been badly stained by ink,
apparently when an ink bottle was tipped over. The ink (contemporary with
Hunt and perhaps the same used to write the letter or used by Shelley in answering it) is very corrosive and parts of the paper are disintegrating.

PROVENANCE: Colonel Charles Shelley Leigh Hunt; Mrs. Beryl Dodgson
(Sotheby, April 8, 1935, lot 205).

8. York Build^{gs} New Road
2^d Dec. 1819

My dear Shelley, dear friend,

What shall I say to you for my long silence? You have
5   *been loading me with letters & with honours, & yet I have been looking all*
the while like the most ungrateful person upon earth. I say looking, for I
have not really been so; nor indeed do I suppose, after all, that you thought
me any thing of the sort. Perhaps it was in the confidence of knowing other-
wise, that I have reposed; if repose it may be called, which repose has been
10 *none, distinguishable in conscience, pen, or limb. But I believe there are*
times when at the very moment one's friend shews himself the most trusting
in us, one does the least on that very account, out of a certain fullness &
insolence of security. Hav< > you ever felt it to be so on these occasions? I
hope you have:– but you will understand & feel what I mean, if there be any
15 *truth in it. I can nevertheless assure you, my dear friend, that I have been*
intending, & vowing, & remorsing, every day, to write to you, & nothing
would have hindered me from doing every week, but some unpleasant matters
of business {the conclusion of my late struggles to settle my difficulties, all
about which, & how I am mastering them,–for ever I hope – I will tell you
20 *when we meet.– What a word that is! Mind, – now you have put that word*
into my head, it will not get out again till we do meet}. These matters of
business, by a singular & regularly recurring fatality, took me away from
my pen every week on the very days I had devoted to the next weeks Indicator.
The consequence was that I was obliged to write for my Wednesday's paper
25 *on Monday & Tuesday, & then I regularly repented of not writing to you;*
as regularly vowed to do it this day & the other ; & as regularly behaved

[1089]

SC 552   *like a — —   I'll leave you to supply the word, for I know it will be as kind a*
one as possible. And yet in the mean time comes your Dedication, & all
your kind letters with all your other enclosures. How shall I thank you for

30   *that true & cordial honour,— true, I mean, to the height of the sentiment of*
friendship, whatever it may be with regard to the qualities which your flatter-
ing hand has set on a level with that height. I scarcely know what I am saying
in the extremity of pleasure which this testimony of your <   >d & of
your sense of my intentions has given me; but my very <   > as if

35   *you had bound, not only my head, but my very <   > & body with laurels.*
Language is a poor thing sometimes, is it not? even when it may seem, to
unyearning hearts, excessive.—   I will write more speedily, & tell you about
your political songs & pamphlets, which we must publish without Ollier, as
he gets more timid & pale every day;— I hope I shall not have to add time

40   *serving; but they say he is getting intimate with strange people. What a*
delicious love-song is that you enclosed! I would put it into the Indicator
by & by; — at present this boldness of benevolence must go into the more
+*(See Final Final Postscript.)*
established Examiner.ₐAs to the Indicators, I make up my mind that you

45   *& Marina will like them, as they tell me I am at my best in this work,*
which succeeds beyond all expectation. There are some articles I am sure
you will like. I send you as many as the post-office will let me get into one
letter; & to say the truth you would have had them before, but I was so poor
I could not afford the out-post money, But I shall do very well.

50   *Evᵣmo. trᵤ yʳˢ*
                                                        L H

I intended to say so much about Marina's new work, that I have left myself
no room for it. I can only say therefore at present, that we are delighted to
hear of it, as an earnest of fresh comfort to both of you. Kiss my new friend

55   *for me twenty times, & it's mother (Boccaccione volente) twenty more; at*
least if she is volent also.

You may judge by what I tell you at the close of this page, what a struggle
I have had. It has indeed been a tremendous one: but my industry, added

Hunt to Shelley   *December 2, 1819*

SC 552 *to your former & never-forgotten kindness, will carry me through it all. I*
am now in fact emerging, & pay for every thing as I go to a farthing.
Final Postscript. – I have been compelled, after all (Pluto nolente) not to
send even as many as 3 Indicators; & this too, after much additional waiting.
Imagine, my dear friends, what this waiting has cost me, especially after
Marina's.. reproaches. It has really made me very uneasy. But I hope
65 *now to be richer every day, & will write as before at all events; besides sending*
what Indicators I can. See below.

Final Final Postscript. I have altered my mind upon reading your
delightful song, Shelley, for the ninth or tenth time & shall put it, incon-
tinently, into the Indicator. Many, many thanks to Marina for her letter,
70 *which Marianne as well as myself will answer.*

[Address, page 4]
                        Italie
P. B. Shelley Esqʳᵉ
                Ferma in Posta,
Florence,   Firenze,
75   *Italy.   Italia.*

line 13. *Hav<e>*: paper affected by ink corro-sion.

line 15. *that I . . the mean* (line 28): occupies the second page of the manuscript and is covered with spilled ink, which affects the legibility of the text.

line 17. *every*: probable reading.

line 24. *was that*: possibly followed by a comma.

line 26. *vowed*: probable reading.

line 27. *be*: possibly underscored, but line may be an accidental ink mark.

   a one: probable reading.

line 33. *<regar>d*: beginning of extensive seal tear.

line 34. ~~*my very*~~: probable reading; may be *any way*.

       <   >: seal tear.

line 35. <   >: seal tear.

line 43. *Postcript.* (sic): see also line 67.

line 52. *I intended . . . also.* (line 56): written at the top of page 1, above and to the left of the first two lines.

line 57. *You may . . . farthing.* (line 60): written on three cramped lines at the top of page 3 of the manuscript, which extends from *time comes* (line 28) to *L H* (line 51).

line 61. The last two postscripts are written on page 4 of the manuscript.

THE COURSE of the Shelley-Hunt correspondence during the last three months of 1819 has already been outlined in sc 551, Commentary. In this letter, Hunt answers Shelley's two letters that arrived in London on December 2. Beginning as a prompt, spontaneous reply, it is viva-

The Carl H. Pforzheimer Library

SC 552   cious and playful in Hunt's best manner. The fourth sentence contains a wild literary echo and the first postscript exhibits an outrageous pun.[1] Hunt's literary echoes and puns in this letter are nonfunctional, reverberating no significant overtones to Hunt's statements. They exemplify humor rather than wit, but fancy rather than imagination.

Hunt's excuses for having neglected to write sound genuine. Reading to gather material for, as well as writing, the *Indicator* would obviously take time away from his private correspondence, and business negotiations, which Hunt detested, would drain his energy quicker than that of most men. Hunt's pleasure at Shelley's public avowal of friendship in the Dedication swallows up his shame for not having written.

Hunt's financial problems, in turn, swallowed up his intention to mail this letter promptly. By the time of his "*Final* Postscript" (lines 61–66), Hunt was alluding to "reproaches" in Mary Shelley's letter of November 24, which reached London on December 15.[2] His letter of December 2 finally reached Florence on January 8, 1820.[3] The double postal charge on the letter indicates that Hunt did enclose at least some *Indicators*, but without Shelley's January 12, 1820, reply to Hunt, we have no record of the Shelleys' early reactions to Hunt's new periodical.[4]

Hunt is laconic on the question of great interest to us and of much concern to Shelley — the fate of the political poems and papers Shelley had recently sent to England.[5] Hunt indicates that Charles Ollier is not the man to publish them — that, indeed, he *will not* publish them because "he gets more timid & pale every day." But Hunt does not tell

1. Lines 9–10 ("I have reposed . . . conscience, pen, or limb") echo Milton's *Paradise Lost*, II, 666–668, where the description of Death begins: "The other shape,/ If shape it might be call'd that shape had none/ Distinguishable in member, joynt, or limb. . . ." (Shelley echoes the same passage, to much different effect, in *The Triumph of Life*, lines 91–93. See Reiman, *Shelley's "The Triumph of Life": A Critical Study*, University of Illinois Press, 1965, pp. 29–30.) In line 55, Hunt introduces the pun on Boccaccio's name ("Boccaccione volente" [your "big old" mouth willing]) as he elsewhere tells that he has no money for postage in terms of the god of wealth's *un*willingness ("Pluto nolente," line 61).

2. See Mary Shelley, *Letters*, I, 83–86.

3. See final postmark in Bibliographical Description; Mary Shelley mentions its arrival in her Journal entry for that date. According to Mary, Shelley answered Hunt on January 12, 1820, but that letter has not survived.

4. According to a note by Trelawny in Edward Williams' manuscript Indian hunting journal (Bodleian Ms. Shelley adds. e. 21), Shelley liked the *Indicator* better than he did either Hunt's poetry or his translations.

5. See sc 551, Commentary, fn. 13.

Shelley and his Circle : Manuscripts

SC 552   of the pressures in England caused by the growing polarization in British politics and the enactment by Parliament of a series of repressive measures in the wake of Peterloo and other riots. These laws, known collectively as the "Six Acts," were debated and passed the Commons during November and December 1819. Their open intent was to weaken the agitation for reform and to prevent the radicals from attempting armed rebellion. The first act limited the rights of citizens to bear arms and engage in military drills; the second authorized local magistrates to seize unauthorized weapons; the third attempted to speed up the trials of those charged with misdemeanors. These first three acts contained nothing strictly tyrannical, though the radicals and liberal Whigs in Parliament protested them vehemently. The fourth act curtailed the right of assembly to protest government actions or social conditions; the fifth strengthened laws against "Blasphemous and Seditious Libels," and the sixth act extended taxes to cover more periodicals and strengthened laws against circulation of "blasphemous and seditious" publications. These last two acts, of course, increased the power of the government over the opposition press and gave it power to jail or fine those publishers and booksellers who overstepped certain limits.[6]

Charles Ollier, who had been fearful of the laws against such libels in 1817,[7] was not likely to have braved the even more stringent laws in 1819–1820. But Hunt does not explain the legal situation in England to Shelley — the kinds of laws then being debated by Parliament. His remark about Ollier "getting intimate with strange people" suggests a personal resentment beyond any discrepancy in political courage between Hunt and Charles Ollier and almost certainly reflects Ollier's growing ties with *Blackwood's Edinburgh Magazine*. Even while *Blackwood's* continued its vicious attacks on Hunt, Keats, Hazlitt, and Haydon under the title "the Cockney School of Poetry," it was praising not only Shelley but also Charles Ollier, both as publisher and as author of *Altham and His Wife*.[8] Though Hunt does not explain the cause of his

6. See A. Aspinall and E. Anthony Smith, eds., *English Historical Documents, 1783–1832* (London, 1959), pp. 335–341.

7. See sc 435 and Commentary.

8. In 1821 Ollier contributed at least two articles to *Blackwood's*, in one of which he discussed Shelley's *Epipsychidion*. For the relevant reviews and comments on them, see *The Romantics Reviewed*, ed. Donald H. Reiman (New York: Garland Publishing, Inc., 1972).

SC 552 resentment, Shelley, after reading this letter, became somewhat more upset by Ollier's neglect of him than he might otherwise have been.

Hunt is explicit and enthusiastic about Shelley's facile anacreontic lyric "Love's Philosophy" (lines 41, 67–69), which he finally published in the *Indicator* for December 22, 1819 (see SC 551, Commentary). His relative neglect of Shelley's more serious political writings, coupled with excitement about his love lyrics, marks Leigh Hunt as a precursor — and probably one of the chief shapers — of the popular Victorian attitude toward Shelley.

Mary Shelley's "*new work*" (line 52) was, of course, Percy Florence Shelley.

SC 553 P. B. SHELLEY TO MARIA AND JOHN GISBORNE, DECEMBER 14, 1819

AL signed *PBS*., 1 page. Double sheet, 4to (9 x 7.3 inches).
Laid paper. Watermark: ALMASSO [letters written on banner held aloft by cherub]; countermark: [cipher] *TP*|.
Seal: wafer, orange.
Postmarks: 1. FIRENZE; 2. 15 DECEMBRE|.
Docket, page 4: *Shelley*—| *rcd. 15. Dec.*| *Ans*|.
Addition: adhering strip of paper from album mounting.

PROVENANCE: Maggs, December 1948.

My dear Friends
        It is worth a line written from the Stationers shop near the post office, to tell you that I this moment hear that the rest of my money is safe. You will recieve it in a few days.

5   *Most Affectionately yours*
                                              PBS.

[Address, page 4]
John Gisborne Esqr
        Livorno

line 3. *my money* ... *PBS*. (line 6): since the   line 4. *recieve* (sic).
final four lines of the manuscript are blotted,
Shelley must have written and folded the letter
hastily.

Shelley to Gisbornes   ***December 14, 1819***

SC 553   THE PRESENT note was date-stamped in Leghorn and docketed by
John Gisborne as having been received on December 15. The year
1819 is quickly established by the FIRENZE postmark and by the contents of the letter. Since Shelley's letter written at Florence on December 23 reached the Gisbornes on December 24, we can confidently date
this note December 14, 1819.[1]

As we have seen in the survey of Shelley's financial transactions in
1818–1819 (SC 545, Commentary), Shelley had heard from Brooks, Son &
Dixon and from Horace Smith, and on December 7 he had sent Henry
Reveley an order for the £100 that Smith had lent him. At that point
Shelley was still concerned about £200 — half of which had been trans-
mitted in the form of four £25 "circular notes" from Herries & Co. and
the other half of which Shelley eventually located at Torlonia's bank in
Rome. On the same day that Shelley wrote SC 553, Mary sent Maria
Gisborne a long, undated letter that began, "You see — my dear Friend
— by the receipt of your crowns that we have recovered £100 of our
money — there is still £100 in jeopardy. . . ."[2] If the £100 that reached
Shelley on December 14 was the long-awaited sum in Herries' notes,
Shelley could have gone directly to the bank, converted the £100 or
part of it into a bank order for the equivalent amount in Italian currency, and given it to Mary to enclose in her letter. But it is difficult to
determine whether or not he did so, or whether Mary's allusion to "the
receipt of your crowns" refers to the money Shelley sent Henry on
December 7.

Maria Gisborne's long reply to Mary's letter, dated by Jones *circa*
December 20, 1819,[3] should probably be dated December 16, 1819. There
Maria Gisborne responds to individual points in Mary's letter that
reached her on December 15, and she differentiates between Henry
Reveley's activities on "Tuesday" and those of "yesterday" (page 58).
The first two sentences of her letter suggest that Henry's steamboat
building had been suspended until he received the £100 Shelley mailed
on December 7 and that Henry had spent the week from the arrival of

1. Shelley, *Letters*, II, 165–166. On December 14, a Tuesday, the courier left Florence at 5 p.m.
with the mail for Pisa, Leghorn, etc. (*L'Indispensabile Almanacco . . . per L'Anno 1819*, Florence,
1818, p. 249.)
2. Mary Shelley, *Letters*, I, 88–89.
3. Gisborne, *Journals and Letters*, pp. 57–62.

SC 553 that money on Wednesday, December 8, until December 15 hiring blacksmiths, buying coal, and beginning production again. Her allusions to how hard Henry had been working would be, then, an oblique apology for Henry's failure to acknowledge the receipt of that money. If Mary in her letter sent on December 14 enclosed another sum, Maria Gisborne does not specifically acknowledge it.

It is probable, then, that Mary's letter which went out of Florence on December 14 was written earlier than Shelley's and that Shelley sent no further money for the steamboat until December 23, when he mailed the Gisbornes "a mandate, for 396 francesconi, which is what Mr. Torlonia incorrectly designates an hundred pounds."[4]

Unfortunately, Shelley was to learn once again to his sorrow that foolish old Polonius was a wise man when commenting on borrowers and lenders. In the autumn of 1820 the Shelleys became estranged from the Gisbornes and Henry Reveley because of the then-abandoned steamboat project and Shelley's wasted money.[5]

4. Shelley, *Letters*, II, 165.

5. Shelley's later remonstrances with Henry Reveley will be discussed in the next volumes of *Shelley and his Circle.* See also White, *Shelley*, II, 229–230, and Shelley, *Letters*, II, *passim.*

SC 554 P. B. SHELLEY TO CHARLES OLLIER, DECEMBER 23, 1819

AL signed *P B Shelley*, 2 pages. Double sheet, 4to (9.8 x 8.6 inches).
Wove paper. Watermark: [   ]NCI|.
Postal fees: 1. 12; 2. 5/9.
Postmarks: 1. FIRE[NZE]|; 2. (Foreign Post Office stamp, London): FPO| JA·8| 1820|.
Notation, page 3:

$$\begin{array}{rl} 1,151.556 & 2 \\ \underline{4} & 2 \\ 4.606.224 & 2 \\ \underline{3.2} & \\ 1,406,224, & \end{array}$$

Additions: 1. Spindle hole through near-center of double sheet; 2. (page 2, lower left): ink sketch of building, probably a church; 3. upper right section of double sheet (*ca.* 5 x 4 inches) burned away; 4. (page 4, at fold): traces of yellow paper from album mounting.

PROVENANCE: Goodspeed, 1931; George L. Howe (Ritter-Hopson Galleries, May 24–25, 1932, lot 303); Audrey Wurdemann (Mrs. Joseph) Auslander; John Fleming, February 1954.

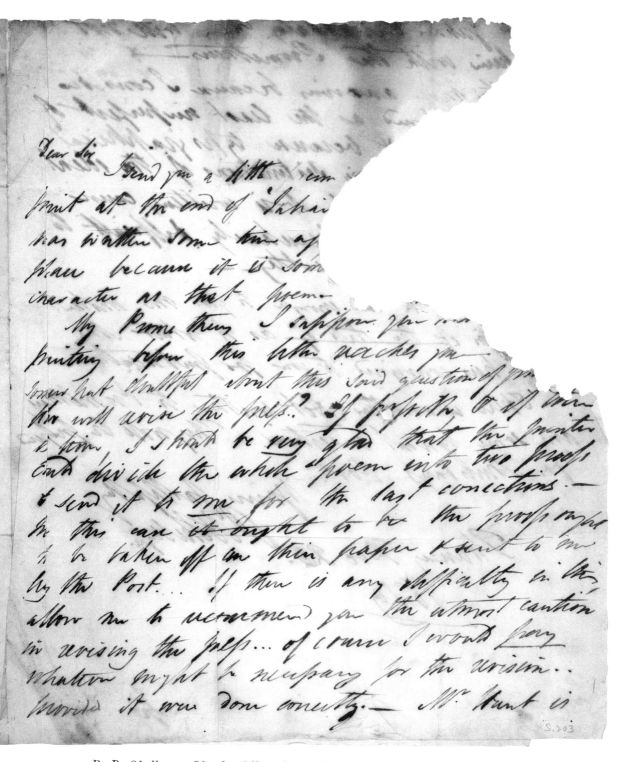

Dear Sir	I send you a little poem to
print at the end of 'Julian'. It
was written some time ago — I send it to you in this
place because it is somewhat of the same
character as that poem.

My Prometheus I suppose you were
printing before this letter reaches you —
somewhat doubtful about this said question of you
this will arise the press. If possible to all mere
a time, I should be very glad that the Printer
could divide the whole poem into two proofs
& send it to me for the last corrections. —
In this case it ought to be the proof ought
to be taken off on thin paper & sent to me
by the Post. If there is any difficulty in this
allow me to recommend you the utmost caution
in revising the press... of course I would pay
whatever might be necessary for the revision...
provided it were done correctly. — Mr Hunt is

S.203

P. B. Shelley to Charles Ollier, December 23, 1819 (SC 554), page 1

[1097]

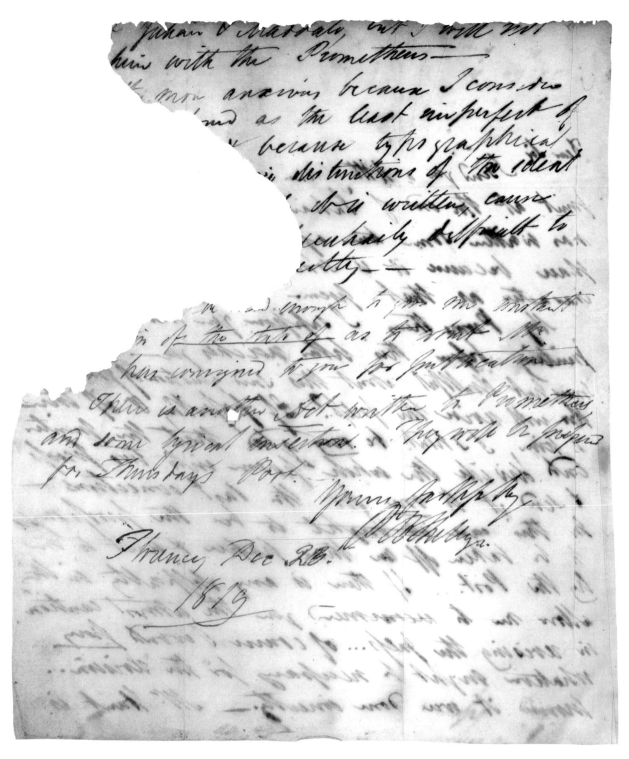

P. B. Shelley to Charles Ollier, December 23, 1819 (SC 554), page 2

Shelley to Ollier   *December 23, 1819*

SC 554 *Dear Sir*

> *I send you a little poem* < > *print at the end*
> *of 'Julian* < > *was written some time af*<
> < > *place because it is som*< > *char-*
5 *acter as that poem–* < >

> *My Prometheus I suppose you* < > *printing before this*
> *letter reaches you——* < > *somewhat doubtful about this said question*
> *of* < > *Who will revise the press.? If possible, & if there is time, I*
> *should be very glad that the printer could divide the whole poem into two proofs*
10 *& send it to _me_ for the last corrections.— In this case* ~~it ought to be~~ *the*
> *proofs ought to be taken off on thin paper & sent to me by the Post. . . If*
> *there is any difficulty in this, allow me to recommend you the utmost caution*
> *in revising the press . . . of course I would _pay_ whatever might be necessary*
> *for the revision. . provided it were done correctly.— M*r *Hunt is* < >
15 *Julian & Maddalo, but I will not* < > *him with the Prometheus——*
> < > *the more anxious because I consider* < >*bound*
> *as the least imperfect of* < > *& because typographical*
> < > *distinctions of the ideal* < >
> *it is written, cause* < >*eculiarly difficult to* <
20 >*ectly– —* < > *enough to give me constant*
> < >*n* ~~of the state of~~ *as to what M*r < > *has consigned to*
> *you for publication——*

> *There is another _Act_ written to Prometheus, and some lyrical insertions.*
> *They will be prepared for Thursday's Post.—*

25   *Yours faithfully*
                                   P B Shelley

> *Florence, Dec. 23.*
> *1819*

[Address, page 4]
*Mess*rs *Ollier— Booksellers*
30   ~~*Welbeck*~~ *Vere Street*
                    London
     Angleterre

The Carl H. Pforzheimer Library

SC 554   Reconstruction of portions of the text affected by the burn (see Bibliographical Description) appears in square brackets. If more than one conjecture is given, the brackets are separated by semicolons.

line 2. *poem* [*which you may*]; [*which I desire you to*]; [*which you may wish to*].

line 3. '*Julian* [*and Maddalo.' It*]; [*and Maddalo.' Although it*].

　　　　time af[*terward but I assign it to that*]; [*terward I wish it in this*].

line 4. *som*[*ewhat of the same general*]; [*ething of the same ideal*].

line 6. *you* [*will be*]; [*will have begun*]; [*had begun*].

line 7. *you*——[*I am*]; [*I feel*].

　　　　question of [*yours.*]; [*proofreading.*]; [*proofs.*]; [*printing.*].

line 8. *press.?* (sic).

　　　　possible,: *o* damaged by spindle hole.

line 11. *on*: written through indecipherable letters.

line 14. [*revising*]; [*to revise*] *Julian & Maddalo*.

line 15. [*trouble*]; [*burden*] *him*.

line 16. [*I am*] *the more anxious.*
　　　　[*Prometheus Un*]*bound as.*

line 17. [*my compositions*]; [*my poems*] *& because.*

line 18. [*errors would, considering minute*]; [*errors might, considering minute*] *distinctions.*
　　　　[*& figurative style in which*]; [*& metaphysical style in which*]; [*& allegorical style in which*]; [*& philosophical style in which*] *it is written* (line 19).

line 19. [*one to find it p*]*eculiarly difficult.*
　　　　[*read & interpret corr*]*ectly* (line 20).

line 20. [*Please be good*]; [*Please be kind*] *enough.*

line 21. [*informatio*]*n.*
　　　　[*Hunt*] *has.*

line 27. *23.*: *3* written through zero (*o*).

line 29. *Booksellers*: some letters partially obliterated when manuscript was damaged.

line 30. *Welbeck*: *k* not completed.

IN SEPTEMBER 1931 Seymour de Ricci wrote to the late Carl H. Pforzheimer from Boston describing this letter, then for sale at Goodspeed's, and pronouncing it "certainly genuine." At that date, with plenty of undamaged Shelley manuscripts on the market, Mr. Pforzheimer was not interested in purchasing this one, and it did not come to The Carl H. Pforzheimer Library until 1954. Though the text of the letter is badly affected by burning, somewhat reducing its value to scholars as well as to collectors, the surviving (hitherto unpublished) text provides important information about Shelley's plans for the publication of *Julian and Maddalo* and *Prometheus Unbound*. Shelley's remark in late December that he is sending another "little poem" to be published with *Julian and Maddalo* fills out the story of Shelley's plans for publishing that poem. And, significantly, sc 554 adds information about another interesting, though fragmentary poem by Shelley — *Prince Athanase.*

That the first part of *Prince Athanase* was the "little poem" Shelley enclosed in this letter seems clear from Shelley's next reference to the publication of *Julian and Maddalo*. On May 14, 1820, he wrote to Ollier: "If you print Julian & Maddalo, I wish it to be printed in some unosten-

SC 554   tatious form, accompanied with the fragment of Athanase, & exactly in the manner in which I sent it. —"[1]

"Prince Athanase: A Fragment" was first published by Mary Shelley in *Posthumous Poems of Percy Bysshe Shelley*.[2] Later in that volume, Mary printed additional portions of *Prince Athanase* apparently garnered from Shelley's rough drafts. The first fragment concluded with an "Author's Note" explaining why the poem was published in its fragmentary form. This portion of *Prince Athanase* was, therefore, prepared for the press by Shelley, and Shelley's references to his "little poem" in the present letter and to "Athanase" in his letter of May 14, 1820, are to this first section.

Though the first printed version of *Prince Athanase* concludes with the date "December, 1817," that date cannot be considered reliable.[3] If Shelley considered *Prince Athanase* closely related to *Julian and Maddalo*, he may have been eager to disguise the occasion of its inspiration and composition for the same reason he apparently misrepresented the date of composition of *Julian and Maddalo* (see SC 531, Commentary).

C. D. Locock, in his study of the Bodleian manuscript notebook containing the drafts of *Prince Athanase* inferred "from MS. evidence . . . that Shelley must have made another copy" of the first fragment of *Prince Athanase*, and from ink changes in that draft he inferred that portions of it had been written in Italy. He concludes: "Part I is dated by Mrs. Shelley 'December, 1817,' but a considerably later date must probably be assigned to its final elaboration, as also to the remaining fragments dated by Mrs. Shelley 'Marlow, 1817.'"[4]

Shelley's final press copy did, in fact, survive into the twentieth century. In Maggs Brothers' catalogue #373 (December 1918), item

1. Quoted from the original manuscript in The Carl H. Pforzheimer Library (see also Shelley, *Letters*, II, 196).

2. London, 1824, pp. 103–110.

3. It is dated thus in *Posthumous Poems*. Without examining the manuscript Shelley sent to Ollier, it is impossible to tell what Shelley wrote in 1819 and what Mary added in 1824.

4. *An Examination of the Shelley Manuscripts in the Bodleian Library* (Oxford, 1903), pp. 50–52. I would qualify Locock's statement, however, by saying that the end of the translation of Euripides' *The Cyclops* seems to have been written in the notebook later than the draft of *Prince Athanase*. Shelley *may* have completed his version of *The Cyclops* about the time he mentioned it to Hunt (see SC 551). See also *Shelley and his Circle*, II, 896, fn. 13.

SC 554   2565 was described as Shelley's "original autograph manuscript" of
Prince Athanase, which from the description appears to have been the
manuscript enclosed in sc 554.[5] This manuscript, as is evident both from
Maggs's quotation of the headnote[6] and first two tercets and from the
facsimile reproduction of lines 55–69 in Plate VII of the catalogue, was
a fair copy carefully prepared for the press in Shelley's usual manner,
with all necessary punctuation supplied.

 "Prince Athanase: A Fragment," which was published in the first
section of *Posthumous Poems*, was, then, prepared for the press in 1819,
and according to Shelley himself, has some affinity with *Julian and
Maddalo*. The harmony between the two poems is obviously not stylistic.
Shelley's note refers to "the ideal character of Athanase," and he is
using "ideal" in the sense in which he spoke in the Preface to *Prometheus Unbound* of "idealisms of moral excellence." "Idealisms" are
the opposite of realistic characters. In his August 15 letter enclosing
Julian and Maddalo, Shelley distinguished between the characters of
Julian and Maddalo themselves and the third character ("also in some
degree a painting from nature, but with respect to time & place, ideal"),
and between "common life" and "that which is ideal."[7] The style of
Prince Athanase is, in all respects, closer to the "idealism" of *Prometheus Unbound* than to the "*sermo pedestris* way of treating human
nature" in *Julian and Maddalo*.[8]

 What, then, *are* the affinities of *Prince Athanase* and *Julian and
Maddalo*? The character of Athanase himself, as drawn in the fragment
Shelley sent to Ollier, resembles that of the unfortunate madman of
Julian and Maddalo. Like him, Athanase has been bowed down by sor-

---

5. Though the manuscript is described as "comprising 41 verses on 9 pp., sm. 4to.," the "41 verses"
probably is an unorthodox way of indicating forty-one tercets or stanzas — the number in the first
fragment as published in *Posthumous Poems*. The small quarto pages could well have been made up
from refolding a full-size quarto letter sheet into eight small quarto (actually octavo) pages. This
size would have been compatible with the surviving manuscripts of *Julian and Maddalo* (in The
Pierpont Morgan Library) and *Peter Bell the Third* (Bodleian) sent to Ollier in the fall. The present
location of this manuscript is unknown to us.

6. The manuscript gives the final word as "diffidence" rather than "difference" — surely a correction that should be adopted in future editions.

7. sc 531, lines 26–27.

8. Shelley to Ollier, May 14, 1820 (Shelley, *Letters*, II, 196); original manuscript in The Carl H.
Pforzheimer Library.

SC 554 row and afflicted unjustly. Like him, Athanase is long-suffering and patient, loving his enemies and refusing to retaliate. As *Julian and Maddalo* closes with Julian, the narrator, refusing to tell "the cold world" the secret of the maniac and the lady, so *Prince Athanase* concludes with the cause of the protagonist's grief remaining untold.

The portrait of Athanase in the fragment bears a marked resemblance to Shelley's other idealized poetic self-portraits, especially to that of Lionel in *Rosalind and Helen* (lines 610 ff.). It conforms, in most respects, to the *beau idéal* of self that emerges from Shelley's letters — those to Byron, for example. The links between *Prince Athanase* and *Julian and Maddalo* strengthen the position of those critics who see in the madman another of Shelley's idealized self-portraits. But even if the portraits of the maniac in *Julian and Maddalo* and Prince Athanase arose from the same crisis in Shelley's relations with Mary in 1819 — or if "Prince Athanase: A Fragment" was drafted in 1817 but polished and revised in 1819 because Shelley then found the fragment thematically related to *Julian and Maddalo*, the two portraits produce quite different effects. The portrait of the madman in *Julian and Maddalo* is integral and subordinate to larger thematic concerns.[9] It is distanced from Shelley the man partly by the character of Julian, who is another self-portrait, far more recognizable to Shelley's friends, no doubt, because it pictured the external gentleman. Prince Athanase, on the contrary, is by any standard of judgment a sentimental characterization. Shelley hardly disguises his feelings of being misunderstood and persecuted and his frustration at not being able or willing to retort directly to those who were responsible, and in the very act of portraying his selfless patience, he terminates it.

According to the theory of poetry set forth in Shelley's *Defence of Poetry*, *Julian and Maddalo* is a better poem than *Prince Athanase* because, though more closely tied to local customs and manners, it is wider in its appeal through its sympathetic portrayal of four quite different types of human beings — the madman, Julian, Maddalo, and Maddalo's daughter. It embodies in a more universal form the problem of the wounded sensitive idealist because it approaches him from the

9. See Donald H. Reiman, *Percy Bysshe Shelley* (New York, 1969), pp. 69–73, and sc 531, Commentary.

The Carl H. Pforzheimer Library

SC 554 outside and dramatizes the significance of his situation and its effect upon those who do not at first understand or sympathize with his problem. Thus, it communicates more effectively to all classes of readers the fate of a particular type of individual, thereby broadening their sympathies through "love," "a going out of our own nature, and an identification of ourselves with the beautiful which exists in thought, action, or person, not our own."[10]

Shelley's chief topic in this letter is the printing and correction of *Prometheus Unbound*. His stated assumption that the first three acts were already in press was doubtless a hint to Ollier to begin the printing as soon as possible. Shelley, as we have seen, originally sent the manuscript of *Prometheus* to England with John Gisborne in September 1819. But Gisborne brought the manuscript back to Italy with him, and Shelley then had it sent to Ollier with the printed copies of *The Cenci*.[11] We learn from a later letter that the ship carrying the printed volumes of *The Cenci* and the manuscript of *Prometheus* sailed from Leghorn in mid-December,[12] but on December 23, Shelley must have assumed that the Gisbornes had shipped them in mid-October, when he first requested them to do so.

The delay in printing *Prometheus Unbound* enabled Shelley to write a fourth act for the poem. He had told Ollier on December 15: "You will receive the additions, which Mrs. S. is now transcribing, in a few days,"[13] but in SC 554 he first reveals to Ollier that these "additions" consisted of "another *Act*" and "some lyrical insertions," one of which was certainly the "Down, down" lyric of Act II, Scene iii.[14] Shelley sent these additions to the Gisbornes to transmit to Ollier with a letter to them written the same day as the present letter to Ollier.[15]

Now that he had completed *Prometheus Unbound*, Shelley was concerned about having it carefully proofread. His letters discussing *Prometheus Unbound* provide additional evidence that he took all possible

10. *A Defence of Poetry*, Shelley, *Complete Works*, VII, 118.

11. See SC 543, Commentary.

12. Shelley to Ollier, March 6, 1820, Shelley, *Letters*, II, 174.

13. Shelley, *Letters*, II, 163–164.

14. See SC 548 and Commentary.

15. Shelley, *Letters* II, 165–166. That the manuscript of Act IV accompanied Shelley's letter of December 23 to the Gisbornes is clear from John Gisborne's endorsement of the letter.

SC 554   pains to insure that his poem was published exactly as he had prepared it for the press and that if any changes of words or significant punctuation were introduced, they be changes he himself had chosen. Shelley's one experience of publishing from abroad — *Rosalind and Helen* — had not been particularly happy in this regard, for on September 6, 1819, as soon as he had seen the volume, he wrote to Ollier: "In the *Rosalind & Helen* I see there are some few errors, which are so much the worse because they are errors in the sense. — If there should be any *danger* of a 2ᵈ Edition I will correct them."[16]

From the present letter, it is clear that two solutions of the problem had occurred to Shelley: First (lines 8–10), he proposes that the proofs be mailed to him so that he can correct them himself; or, failing that, he suggests that Ollier hire someone at Shelley's expense to revise the press (lines 12–14). In this context, "revising the press" means, of course, to correct typographical errors by checking proofs against "copy" (the author's manuscript).[17] From this second alternative, it seems clear that Shelley had been at some pains to prepare his manuscript for the press in a form that could be followed by the printer *ad verbum* and possibly even *ad litteram*. Undoubtedly there were errors in the copy sent to Ollier, and there were probably — as in the case of the *Laon and Cythna* manuscript — words that the typesetters could not read accurately. But Shelley was, it appears, more willing to risk errors attributable to his manuscript (as he had in the case of *Laon and Cythna*) than to sanction the introduction of random changes by compositors — particularly when such changes might affect the rhythms of his lyrics.

Shelley next raised the question of correcting the proofs in a letter to Ollier on March 13, 1820. There he suggested that Ollier send (instead of first proofs printed on thin paper, as he suggests here) "*revised* sheets."[18] This method would give the book two stages of correction, the first a thorough proofreading against copy by someone in London, and the

16. Shelley, *Letters*, II, 117.

17. Because Lawrence John Zillman apparently failed to understand the meaning of similar phrases in other letters by Shelley, he bases his text of *Prometheus Unbound* on a mistaken notion of Shelley's intentions; see *Shelley's "Prometheus Unbound": The Text and the Drafts* (Yale University Press, 1968), pp. 11–12 fn., and Donald H. Reiman's review in *Journal of English and Germanic Philology*, LXVIII (July 1969), 539–543.

18. Shelley, *Letters*, II, 178.

sc 554   second, Shelley's own final corrections of the revise. The second stage would have enabled Shelley to catch the errors attributable to his manuscript, as well as anything else missed by the first proofreader.

It is easy to see why, from the publisher's and printer's point of view, Shelley's plan was unacceptable. Quite apart from the postal charges and delay involved, it would have seemed unwise to let an author as willful as Shelley correct his poem without his manuscript at hand. For he would be likely to introduce numerous stylistic changes from the manuscript version that would raise printing costs. So Ollier and the printer saved their mite, and then one of them or Peacock disposed of Shelley's manuscript. And posterity has not, and may never have, a text of *Prometheus Unbound* that accurately conforms to Shelley's intention.[19]

19. Posterity may have lost some of Shelley's errata to *Prometheus Unbound* through an error recorded in the catalogue of Harry B. Smith's *Sentimental Library* (Privately Printed, 1914), p. 187, where a copy of the first edition of the *Prometheus Unbound* volume is described as follows: "The glory of this copy has departed. When it came into the possession of the present owner it was soiled and in poor condition, but it contained manuscript notes by Mary Shelley. In an evil hour it was sent to be bound, and in the process of cleaning the manuscript notes were neatly removed."

sc 555   P. B. SHELLEY TO LEIGH HUNT, DECEMBER 23, 1819

AL signed *P B Shelley*, 2½ pages. Double sheet, 4to (10 x 8.4 inches).
Wove paper. Watermarks: 1. (upper right-hand corner of first leaf): [six-pointed star]|; 2. (upper right-hand corner of second leaf): [cipher] *GCC*|.
Seal: wafer.
Postal fees: 1. 8; 2. 3/10.
Postmarks: 1. FIRENZE|; 2. (Foreign Post Office stamp, London): FPO| JA·8| 1820|.
Addition: Pasted-on strip (.4 inches) once used to tip letter into an album.

PROVENANCE: Pearson, Catalogues 10 [?1892] and 11 [?1893]; Charles W. Frederickson (Bangs, May 24, 1897, lot 2352); Sotheby, July 29, 1898; Franklin; Pearson, Catalogue 81 [?1899]; Sotheby, December 3, 1900, lot 1248; Maggs; P. J. Dobell, September 1922.

SC 555   *Florence, Dec 23–1819*

My dear Hunt.

  *Why don't you write to us? I was preparing to send you some
thing for your "Indicator," but I have been a drone instead of a bee in this*

5 *business, thinking that perhaps, as you did not acknowledge any of my late
inclosures, it would not be welcome to you— whatever I might send*

  *We have just recieved all your Examiners ~~for~~ up to October 27ᵗʰ—— I
admire & approve most highly of those on religion; there is one very long
one, that especially pleases me . . . Added days & years & hours add to my*

10 *dissapprobation of this odious superstitition; & to my gratitude to any who*
      you
like ͜ break forever its ever-gathering bubble . . .

  *What a state England is in! But you will never write politics. I dont
wonder; but I wish then that you would write a paper in the Examiner on*

15 *the actual state of the country; & what under all the circumstances of the
conflicting passions & interests of men, we are to expect;—— Not what we
ought to expect or what if so & so were to happen we might expect; but what
as things are there is reason to believe will come; & send it me for my information. Every word a man has to say is valuable to the public now, & thus*

20 *you will at once gratify your friend, nay instruct & either exhilarate him
or force him to be resigned & awaken the minds of the people——*

  *I have no spirits to write, what I do not know whether you will care
much about— I know well, that if I were in great misery poverty des &ᶜ you
would think of nothing else but how to amuse & relieve me.— You omit*

25 *me if I am prosperous. You are like Jesus who ~~came~~ said he came only
to heal the sick, when they reproached him for feasting with publicans &
sinners.——*

  *I could laugh if I found a joke in order to put you in good humour
with me after my scolding – in good humour enough to write to us I suppose*

30 *we shall soon have to fight in England— Affectionate love to & from all——
This ought not only to be the Vale of a letter, but a superscription over the
gate of Life———*

         Your sincere friend
         P B Shelley

The Carl H. Pforzheimer Library

Shelley to Hunt   *December 23, 1819*

SC 555   *I send you a* Sonnet*. . . ~~not that you~~ I ~~dont~~ not expect you to publish
it—— but you may shew it to whom you please*

[Address, page 4]
          (*Private*)
Leigh Hunt Esqr
              Examiner Office
40   *19 Catharine Street*
                  London
Angleterre—

line 6. *send*: punctuation has been omitted.

line 7. *recieved* (sic).

line 10. *dissapprobation* (sic).
          superstitition; (sic).

line 16. *are*: *a* written through an indecipherable letter.

line 18. *it me*: probable reading.

line 20. *&*: possibly canceled.

line 25. *said*: *s* written through an indecipherable letter.

line 26. *for*: *f* written through an indecipherable letter.

line 28. *found*: *u* is peculiarly formed and resembles *a*.
          order: partially obscured by ink smear.

line 29. *to us*: the two words are separated with a slash; there is no terminal punctuation.

line 32. *gate*: the *t* is uncrossed.

line 35. *not*: probable reading.

line 36. *please*: again the terminal period is lacking.

line 40. *Catharine* (sic).

SHELLEY did not, apparently, celebrate Christmas, but like all mankind, pagan, Christian, or skeptic, by late December he had begun to settle into a winter feeling of isolation that cried out for friendly gatherings, or at least for news from old friends. At Marlow on December 25, 1817, Shelley had written a letter to William Thomas Baxter that turned Baxter's coolness into an open breach.[1] At Florence in 1819, December gloom and cold also combined with loneliness and concern for the course of English politics to bring out the sense of neglect that Shelley had once exhibited at the slightest rebuff but over which he had more recently exercised considerable control.

Shelley is not particularly hard on Hunt. He writes to him as to a wayward child, scolding him both for not writing letters to the Shelleys and for not writing more on politics in the *Examiner*, while at the same

1. See SC 440 and Commentary.

[1108]

SC 555   time praising the articles on religion in that paper.[2] Shelley expresses strongly his continuing disapprobation of the "odious superstition" of organized religion (his censure extends farther than simply to Christianity in its various forms). Shelley's initial antagonism was grounded on objections to specific theological dogmas and political orientations that were characteristic of the churches of his day, but that are rejected by many twentieth-century Christians and Christian denominations. He was also a man of his time in identifying himself (on certain occasions at least) as a Deist,[3] a term that had intellectual respectability in its favor. Shelley had been hardened in his rejection of conventional doctrines and institutions by facing repeated ostracism from polite society; those who undergo similar ostracism in any age for expressing unpopular ideas tend to react in much the same way.

The chief literary aspect of the present letter is a negative one. Shelley tells in the first paragraph that he has *not* written for the *Indicator* because he has not heard from Hunt.[4] The sonnet that Shelley enclosed in the letter (line 35) was undoubtedly "England in 1819," which begins: "An old, mad, blind, despised, and dying king."[5] The tone of that poem harmonizes well with that of this letter, burdened with discouragement but doggedly, dutifully hopeful at the conclusion.

The year 1819 was Shelley's *annus mirabilis*. It saw the bursting forth of his genius in *Prometheus Unbound* and *The Cenci*, two of his most ambitious and successful completed poems. In addition, he completed "Lines written among the Euganean Hills" and *Julian and Maddalo*, wrote *The Mask of Anarchy* and *Peter Bell the Third*, besides numerous

---

2. Though over a dozen articles on religion appeared in the *Examiner* over various signatures between the beginning of 1819 and the end of October 1819, only four are followed by Leigh Hunt's standard mark of the pointing hand (☞): "Catholic Emancipation," May 2, pp. 273–274; "Lamented Irreligion of the Reformers," August 8, pp. 497–498; "Deaths of Voltaire, Luther, Calvin, &c.," September 12, pp. 585–587; and "Clerical Magistrates," October 10, pp. 641–642. Of these, the second seems most likely to have appealed to Shelley.

3. In his long letter to the Editor of the *Examiner* on the trial and sentencing of Richard Carlile, Shelley calls himself a deist (Shelley, *Letters*, II, 140). There is no doubt that Shelley believed in a supreme being and little question that he saw the supreme being as impersonal and nonanthropomorphic. But Shelley had, of course, earlier written a skeptical dialogue entitled *A Refutation of Deism* (1814), which seems to refute both Christianity and deism.

4. Shelley uses the "drone"/ "bee" metaphor (line 4) because the "indicator" was a bird that located honey (see sc 540 and Commentary).

5. Shelley, *Poetical Works* (OSA), pp. 574–575.

SC 555   shorter poems that included "Ode to the West Wind." He began to draft his *Philosophical View of Reform* and probably wrote the essay "On Life." But the year was also one of great personal disappointment. Most shocking to him were the death of his son William and what seems to have been the resultant estrangement between him and Mary Shelley.[6] Late in 1819 or early in 1820, he learned that three individuals to whom he had given great financial assistance — Godwin, Hunt, and Henry Reveley — were no better off than when he had undertaken to help them at great sacrifice to himself and his family. By the end of 1819, Shelley felt that he was permanently exiled from his homeland and his closest friends, unappreciated as a poet, neglected by his publisher, and vilified by men like Southey and Godwin whom he had once revered. In the political realm he feared civil war in England (line 30). The wonder was not that Shelley felt discouraged and slightly irritable by December of that year, but rather that in the two-and-a-half years of life that remained to him, without any appreciable change of fortune, he yet had spirits enough to write some of the best and most hopeful poetry in the English language. Detailed study of those years lies before us in subsequent volumes of *Shelley and his Circle*.

6. See sc 531 and Commentary.

Appendix

BYRON MANUSCRIPTS, 1807–1815

SC 556 LORD BYRON, *TO E. N. LONG*, APRIL 19, 1807

> MANUSCRIPT signed *Byron*, with a date, revisions, and Note in his hand, 8 pages.
> Two double sheets, 4ᵗᵒ (8.9 x 7.2 inches).
> Wove paper. Watermarks: (first double sheet): ?IL.|; (second double sheet):
> 1806|.
> Addition: both double sheets folded as if for mailing and worn along center folds.
> PROVENANCE: Mervyn L. Poston; Sotheby, May 21, 1968, lot 368.

To E– N– Long

Dear Long! in this sequester'd scene,
While all around in Slumber lie,
The joyous days which ours have been
Come rolling fresh on fancy's eye;
Thus, if amidst the gathering Storm
While clouds the darken'd noon deform,
Yon heaven assumes a varied glow,
I hail the Skies celestial Bow,
Which spreads the sign of future peace,
And bid's the war of tempests cease. ———

Ah! Though the present brings but pain,
I think those days may come again,
Or if in melancholy mood,
Some lurking envious Fear obtrude,
To check my bosom's fondest thought,
And interrupt the golden dream,
I crush the fiend with malice fraught,
And still indulge my wonted theme,
Although we neer again can trace,
In Granta's vale, the Pedants lore,
Nor through the groves of Ida chase
Our raptured visions as before,
Though Youth has flown on rosy pinion
And Manhood claims his stern dominion

5

10

15

20

25

[1113]

Byron, "To E. N. Long"   *April 19, 1807*

SC 556   *Age will not every hope destroy,*
                 But Yield some hours of sober Joy.————

                 Yes, I will hope that Time's broad wing,
                 Will shed around some dews of Spring,
30   *But if his Scythe must sweep the Flowers,*
                 Which bloom among the Fairy bowers,
                 Where glowing Youth delights to dwell,
                 And hearts with early rapture swell,
                 If frowning age with cold controul
35   *Confines the current of the Soul,*
                 Congeals the tear of Pity's eye
                 Or checks the sympathetic sigh,
                 Or hears unmoved Misfortune's groan,
                 And bids me feel for self alone;
40   *Oh! may my bosom never learn,*
                 To soothe its young romantic flow,
                 Still, still, despise the Censor stern,
                 But neer forget anothers woe.
                 Yes, as you knew me in the days
45   *Oer which my fancy yet delays,*
                 Still may my breast to Boyhood cleave
                 With every early passion heave,
                                unawed &
                 Still may I rove untutor'd, wild,
                                 ^
50   *But never cease to seem a child.——*

                 Though now on airy visions borne,
                 To you my Soul is still the same,
                                'twas mine
                 Since we have met, I learn'd to mourn
                                 ^
55   *And all my former Joys are tame,*
                 But hence ye hours! of sable hue
                 Your frowns are gone, my sorrows oer,

SC 556

By Every bliss my childhood knew,
    I'll think upon your shade no more;
60 *Thus when the Whirlwinds rage is past,*
    ^{roar}
    And Caves their sullen ~~tean~~ enclose,
We heed no more the Wintry blast,
    When lull'd by Zephyr to repose.———

65 *Full often has my Infant Muse,*
    Attuned to Love her languid Lyre,
But now without a theme to chuse,
    The Strains in stolen sighs expire,
My Youthful Nymphs, Thank heaven! are flown,
70   *E– is a Wife, and C– a mother,*
And Carolina sighs alone,
    And Mary's given to another,
And Cora's eye which roll'd on me,
    Can now no more my love recall,
75 *In truth, Dear Long, 'twas time to flee,*
    For Cora's Eye will shine on all.—
And though the Sun with genial rays,
His beams to all alike displays,
And every Lady's eye's a Sun,
80 *These last should be confined to one,*
    ^{soul's Meridian}
The ~~glances really~~ dont become her,
Whose Sun displays a general Summer.
Thus faint is every former flame
85 *And passions self is now a name,*
As when the ebbing flames are low,
    The aid which once improved their light,
And bade them burn with fiercer glow,
    Now quenches all their sparks in night.
90 *Thus has it been with passion's fires,*
    As Many a Boy and Girl remembers,

Byron, "To E. N. Long"   *April 19, 1807*

SC 556

While all the force of Love expires,
    Extinguish'd with the dying Embers.——

But now, Dear Long, 'tis Midnights noon,
95 *And Clouds obscure the watery Moon*
Whose beauties I shall not rehearse,
Described in every Stripling's verse,
For why should I the Path go oer,
Which every Bard has trod before,
100 *And what much worse than this I find,*
Have left their deepen'd tracks behind.
Yet eer yon silver Lamp of Night,
    Has thrice perform'd her stated round,
Has thrice retraced her path of Light,
105   *And chased away the gloom profound,*
I trust, that we, my gentle friend,
Shall see her rolling Orbit wend,
Above the dear-loved, peaceful Seat
Which once contain'd our Youth's retreat.
110 *And then with those our childhood knew,*
We'll mingle with the festive crew,
And many a Tale of former day
Shall wing the laughing hours away,
And many a present Joy shall pour,
115 *Its pleasure with increasing Shower,*
Nor cease till Luna's waning Horn
Scarce glimmers through the Mist of Morn.———
                    Byron
              April 19ᵗʰ 1807.

120 + *Note.*

        E— is a west Indian married to a Creole, C— is Mʳˢ Musters
Chaworth, a former flame; Caroline is her mother in Law; Mary is a
Mʳˢ Cobourne, & Cora, a Notts Girl, her real name is Julia Leacroft, there
                            addressed
125 *is a poem ʌto her, under the name of Lesbia.——*

Byron, "To E. N. Long" April 19, 1807

SC 556 The manuscript is in two hands using two different inks (both black); the basic text of the poem is a fair copy by an amanuensis, possibly Elizabeth Pigot. The revisions, the signature, and the prose note are in Byron's hand; the ink bears evidence that he also added some of the terminal punctuation.

line 5. *eye;*: followed by a slanting stroke in blue ink which is accidental and not contemporary.

line 6. *Thus,*: *us* written through an erasure.

line 15. *lurking*: written through an erasure beginning with *d*, probably the *daring* of the Newstead-Texas manuscript.

 Fear: *F* written through erasure of *f*.

 obtrude,: *ob* written through erasure, probably revising *intrude* of the Newstead-Texas manuscript.

line 27. *sober*: underscored by amanuensis.

line 34. *controul*: contemporary variant spelling.

line 48. The underlining, canceling line, caret, and inserted words of lines 48–50 are by Byron.

line 54. The cancellation and revision were made by Byron.

line 60. *past,*: *p* written through an erasure.

line 62. *tean*: evidently a misspelling of *teen*, meaning anger, grief; the cancel line and insertion of line 61 are in Byron's hand.

line 69. *heaven!*: the exclamation point was inserted by Byron.

line 76. The underscores in lines 76–83 were drawn by Byron.

line 82. The cancel line and insertion of line 81 were added by Byron.

line 90. *passion's*: apostrophe inserted by Byron.

line 92. The two underscores were drawn by Byron.

line 97. *Stripling's*: apostrophe inserted by Byron.

line 100. Single and double underscores in lines 100–101 were drawn by Byron.

line 101. *tracks*: *t* crossed by Byron, perhaps to affirm lower case.

line 104. *Has thrice retraced*: written through erasure (yet the earlier Newstead-Texas manuscript has the same reading; so there may have been merely a scribal mistake here).

line 106. The three underscores were drawn by Byron.

line 109. *Youth's*: apostrophe added by Byron.

line 118. Lines 118–125 are in Byron's hand.

THIS MANUSCRIPT is of textual interest as being intermediate between the early draft in the Newstead-Texas manuscript and the version printed in *Hours of Idleness*, though more improvements were made after it than in it. Revisions of some substance in lines 15, 62 (perhaps), 82, and 85 were retained in *Hours*. But the trial revision in line 48 (*unawed* for *untutor'd* — possibly suggested by Coleridge's "Unawed I sang, amid a slavish band" in *France: An Ode*, a poem Byron was fond of) — as well as the lavish underscoring for emphasis — was not.

Of rather greater interest is the prose Note with its identifications of persons alluded to in this and other poems of the Southwell period.[1]

1. sc 556 was described by Dr. M. L. Poston in an article in the *Times Literary Supplement*, August 7, 1943, p. 384, which pointed out that the Note (lines 120–125) would be useful to a friend of Byron's like Long, who was not familiar with Southwell society. See also Captain Anthony Hammond's letter to the editor in the *Times Literary Supplement*, October 9, 1943, on the question of Byron's identification of "Caroline" with Mrs. Musters. For a study of the Southwell period, see Willis W. Pratt, *Byron at Southwell* (Austin, Texas: University of Texas Byron Monographs, No. 1, 1948).

The Carl H. Pforzheimer Library

SC 556   We knew that "*Cora*" stood for Julia Leacroft, "a *Notts* Girl," or rather we knew that the poem "To Lesbia" was first called "To Julia." We can easily believe that, in this poem, "C—," now a mother, is "Mrs. Musters *Chaworth*," that is, Mary Chaworth, whose name John Musters took when he married her so that she became Mrs. Chaworth; she had a daughter referred to as a two-year-old in November 1808.[2] But that her mother-in-law, that is, John Musters' mother — or a stepmother of Mary's (for the usage would equally apply) — is to be found as "Caroline" ("Carolina" in the poem) among Byron's "youthful nymphs" is something beyond credence, surely a Byronic put-on. Carolina, however, may not be intended to be the same as the "Caroline" of Byron's other lyrics, and if she is Mrs. Musters, the fact that she "sighs alone" may allude, not to what the context seems to require (that her desire is no longer reciprocated by the poet), but to: (1) the break-up of her reputed romance with the Prince Regent, or (2) to the loss of John, her son, in marriage, or (3) the loss of both son and lover. In any event, the earlier poems that address erotic sentiments "To Caroline" (not "Carolina") can scarcely be to the same woman.

As for the Mary who "is a Mrs *Cobourne*," this nicely fits Byron's "first love" Mary Duff, who did marry "a Mr. Co^e" as Byron rather cryptically indicated in his journal of November 26, 1813.[3] This leaves "E—," described as "a west Indian married to a *Creole*": "E- is a Wife."

Byron met Edward Noel Long at Harrow and the two remained friends during their Cambridge years. Long joined the Guards, but was drowned early in 1809 when the ship that was bearing his regiment to Lisbon collided with another.[4]

2. Marchand, *Byron*, I, 159. On Mary Chaworth and the poem to Mary, see G. Wilson Knight, *Lord Byron's Marriage* (London, 1957), pp. 24–28, 121, 126.

3. Byron, *Letters and Journals*, II, 347.

4. For the effect of Long's death upon Byron and an account of their friendship, see Marchand, *Byron*, I, 66, 104–128, 170–171.

SC 557   LORD BYRON TO JOHN "GENTLEMAN" JACKSON, MARCH 27, 1808

AL signed *Byron*, 1½ pages. Double sheet, 4to (8.8 x 7.4 inches).
Wove paper. Watermark: GATER| 1805|.
Seal: wax, red: [coronet]| *B*|.

Byron to Jackson   **March 27, 1808**

SC 557   Addition: the manuscript has been crudely mended with heavy laid paper (watermark: Britannia in crowned oval), which is pasted over the seal tear and another, horizontal tear on the first leaf of the double sheet and over most of the second leaf.

PROVENANCE: Maggs, July 20, 1970.

March 27ᵗʰ 1808 ———

Dear Jack,

      *I shall take your advice, and remain in town till the fights are over, but my V*alet *must proceed to Cambridge for my Plate &c* ———

5   *I will take the same twice over on Belcher's Battle, but Cropley's will surely be the principal combat, I heard nothing on the subject before the delivery of your note, how the Devil should I? confined to the house with my Dis-order. —— If Sir H. Smith's expedition takes place after Wednesday, I shall be happy to avail myself of his polite invitation, I am afraid I must*

10   *not stir before. —— At all events make my acknowledgements to the Baronet; —— <*   *> give my Compts to your* li*ttle woman, and believe me, dear Jack,*

Yours very truly

Byron

15   *Mʳ J Jackson*

[Address, page 4]

Mʳ J. Jackson

    4 Grosvenor Street

       Pimlico

line 11. A sentence or clause occupying most of one manuscript line has been torn out.

line 11. *give*: covered over by paper patching the tear referred to above; legible when manuscript is held up to a strong light.

JOHN ("GENTLEMAN") JACKSON (1769–1845), British boxing champion from 1795 to 1803, on retiring from the ring had opened rooms at 13 Old Bond Street, where a club had begun to form of pugilists and fanciers of the sport, including such "men of birth and distinction" as Jackson's pupil Byron and an active organizer, Sir [George] Henry Smyth (1784–1852), sixth baronet (1802) of Berechurch Hall, Essex. They

The Carl H. Pforzheimer Library

Byron to Jackson   *March 27, 1808*

SC 557   raised funds to put on matches and set prizes, developed orderly procedures, and sought to improve the public acceptance of the sport.
Within six years from the year of the present letter, Jackson would be
entrusted by government with the managing of a boxing carnival for the
London visit of allied monarchs and, in May 1814, Sir Henry Smyth
would chair the formal inauguration of the Pugilistic Club at a banquet
in the Thatched House Tavern.

    In August 1807 Bill Cropley (fl. 1807–1810) had defeated Tom Hazel
after a match between Dan Dogherty and Tom Belcher (1783–1854, not
to be confused with the champion James "Jem" Belcher, 1781–1811).
Spring matches were now being organized. Byron has just been informed
of elaborate plans for matches that would defy the official prohibition
of public boxing, and he intends to join in the excitement. He is apparently sending his valet to his Cambridge rooms for some silver plate
that he intends to gamble on the fights. Matches between Cropley
and the Jewish boxer "Dutch Sam" Elias (1775–1816) and between
Dan Dogherty and Tom Belcher were being scheduled for April 5, and
Sir Henry Smyth was apparently planning a boxing tour afterward.

    On the day of the announced fight, Bow Street officers took Dutch
Sam and Cropley into custody as they approached the ring, and the
Belcher-Dogherty match was put off to April 14, when it took place at
Epsom Downs (about eighteen miles south of London), Belcher winning
in thirty-three rounds. The Cropley fight was rescheduled for May 10
at Woburn (midway between Oxford and Cambridge). As the day approached, hundreds of spectators converged on Woburn and the Dun-
stable volunteers were out "in awful military array."[1] At the last minute the fight was moved to Markyate, Sir John Sebright's park in
Hertfordshire; Dutch Sam, one of the most colorful as well as most successful prize fighters of the period,[2] defeated Cropley in twenty-five
minutes.

---

1. *Pancratia, or a History of Pugilism* (London: W. Oxberry, 1812), p. 309. See also *Pugilistica* by
Henry Downes Miles (3 vols., London, 1866); Bohun Lynch, *The Prize Ring* (London, 1925).

2. According to *The Fancy* (see fn. 5, below), Dutch Sam, though he "despised the care and kindness
of his training companion, drank *gin* to excess, besides other enervating habits, as late hours and
paphian sacrifices; yet did he conquer his antagonists" (I, 345). He lost only one fight in his career —
on December 8, 1814, to Bill Nosworthy, who, though he floored Sam thirty-two times in the fight's
thirty-eight rounds, died shortly afterward as a result of Sam's punishing body punches. Dutch Sam

[1120]

Shelley and his Circle : Manuscripts

SC 557   On his return from Greece, Byron resumed his lessons with Jackson and an interest in the club's progress. "Jackson has been here," reads his journal of late November 1813, "the boxing world much as usual; — but the club increases."[3] *The Prize Ring* by Bohun Lynch reproduces with identifications the four panels of a montage screen of pictures and clippings of boxing personalities and events made for Byron about 1814.[4] The montage includes a print by A. Forbes Sieveking, Esq., F.S.A., of Byron sparring with Jackson and portraits of famous boxers from the first champion, James Figg in 1750, to Tom Cribb, the champion from 1808 to 1822, including Molineaux, the black contender.

The growth of boxing's respectability in British society was concurrent with its entry into *belles lettres*. In 1812, in the same year as the anonymous *Pancratia* was published, there appeared a similar but more significant work — *Boxiana; or, Sketches of Ancient and Modern Pugilism,* "By One of the Fancy." In 1818 Pierce Egan (1772–1849), a journalist who had long covered London sporting events, began an expanded form of this monthly serial publication under the title *Boxiana; or Sketches of Modern Pugilism*, containing copperplate illustrations, a series which continued to 1824.[5] The lore of the sport had gained enough popularity by 1819 to enable Thomas Moore to use boxing celebrities and slang as the medium for his political satire on the Holy Alliance in *Tom Crib's Memorial to Congress*,[6] and the following year John Hamilton Reynolds evoked the milieu largely for purposes of literary parody in *The Fancy: A Selection from the Poetical Remains of the Late Peter Corcoran.*[7] Most pertinent of all, Byron in the eleventh canto of *Don Juan* (1823) wrote a stanza in boxing slang and in the note alluded to his old mentor:

was a protégé of Dan Mendoza, the great Jewish teacher of boxing and first autobiographer in the profession. See Daniel Mendoza, *Memoirs of the Life of D. Mendoza. To which are added, observations on the art of pugilism; . . . A new edition* (London, 1816).

3. Byron, *Letters and Journals*, II, 336.

4. The original screen is in the collection of John Murray.

5. John Badcock was the presumed editor of a rival fortnightly serial entitled *The Fancy; or, True Sportsman's Guide: Being Authentic Memoirs of the Lives, Actions, Prowess, and Battles of the Leading Pugilists* (London: McGowan, 1821–?1826).

6. "By One of the Fancy" (London: Longman's, 1819).

7. London: Taylor and Hessey, 1820.

SC 557 If there be any gemman so ignorant as to require a traduction, I refer him to my old friend and corporeal pastor and master, John Jackson, Esq., Professor of Pugilism; who, I trust, still retains the strength and symmetry of his model of a form, together with his good humour, and athletic as well as mental accomplishments.[8]

8. Byron, *Poetry*, VI, 432–433 and fn.

SC 558 LORD BYRON TO JOHN HANSON, JUNE 21, 1809

AL signed *Byron*, 1 page. Double sheet, 4to (8.9 x 7.3 inches).
Wove paper. Watermark: [Prince of Wales feathers]| M J L| 1806|. Impressed stamp: LONDON| [crown]| SUPERFINE|.
Seal: wax, red.
Postmarks: 1. (mileage stamp)*:* FALMOUTH| [275]|; 2. (morning duty franking stamp, London)*:* FREE| 23 JU 23| 1809|.
Docket: *21st June 1809| Lord Byron|.*
Notation, page 4: [penciled account of Byron's life through date of this letter].

PROVENANCE: Maggs, September 9, 1967.

Wynn's Hotel.   Falmouth
— June 21st 1809.

Dear Sir,

As it is probable the Packet will not sail for some days, let
5 *my Letters of Credit be sent if possible either to the Post office or to this Inn:*
Believe me

yrs &^{c}
Byron

J. Hanson. Esqr

[Address, page 4]
10 *Falmouth June Twenty one*
1809
J. Hanson Esqr
6. Chancery Lane
Temple Bar
15 *Byron   London*

line 2. *21st*: written through *10th*.

Byron to [   ]   **June 20, 1810**

SC 558   To BEGIN his Continental travels, Byron left London on June 19 to take the Malta packet boat (mail-carrying boat) from Falmouth. But it had sailed the day before; so his next choice was the Lisbon packet, expected to sail the 26th; it actually sailed July 2, still some time before the next ship for Malta. The present letter adds the name of Byron's hotel to the information given by Marchand.[1]

1. *Byron*, I, 180–185.

SC 559   LORD BYRON TO DOCTOR [   ], JUNE 20, 1810

AL signed *Byron*, 1 page. Single sheet (4.1 x 7.3 inches).
Wove paper.
Addition, verso: traces of gray paper adhering to each corner, indicating that the manuscript was once pasted in an album.
PROVENANCE: Charles Hamilton, September 22, 1966, lot 39.

Dear Doctor,

    They tell me the wind is too high for our expedition to Seraglio point, & I cannot think of putting your precious life in peril, but I hope to have the pleasure another day & beg you to believe me

                                   yrs very sincerely
                                       Byron

5

June 20th 1810

WHEN BYRON'S frigate the *Salsette* reached Constantinople on May 13, it anchored near the Seraglio point. A few days later he wrote to his mother that the "walls of the Seraglio are like the walls of Newstead gardens, only higher," and he preferred riding by the walls of the city on the land side.[1] By May 31 he was participating in excursions in Ambassador Robert Adair's cutter.[2] The present letter shows him organizing an excursion himself, but the unnamed doctor has not been identified.

1. Marchand, *Byron*, I, 240, 243.
2. Marchand, *Byron*, I, 245.

SC 560 LORD BYRON, *ON PARTING*, ?MARCH 1811

HOLOGRAPH MANUSCRIPT, 1½ pages. Single sheet, 4ᵗᵒ (9 x 7.3 inches). Wove paper. Watermark: Iᴏʜɴ Hᴀʏᴇs| 18[ ]|.
Additions: 1. manuscript folded as if for mailing; 2. right margin of manuscript pasted onto heavy album leaf, along with an engraving showing the monument to Lord Byron, Bucknall Church, Nottinghamshire.

PROVENANCE: Sotheby, November 27, 1970, lot 441.

XI.

On ~~Parting~~ Parting.

The kiss, dear maid, thy lip has left
Shall never part from mine,
5 *Till happier hours restore the gift,*
Untainted back to thine.

2

Thy parting glance, which fondly beams,
An equal love may see:
10 *The tear that from thine eyelid streams*
Can weep no change in me.

3

I ask no pledge to make me blest
In gazing when alone;
15 *Nor one memorial for a breast*
Whose thoughts are all thine own.

4

Nor need I write;— to tell the tale
My pen were doubly weak:
20 *Oh! what can idle words avail,*
Unless the heart could speak?

5

By day or night, in weal or woe,
That heart, no longer free,
25 *Must bear the love it cannot show,*
And silent ache for thee. —

———

[1124]

Shelley and his Circle : Manuscripts

Byron, "On Parting"   *?March* **1811**

SC 560

line 1. Numeral possibly added in a different hand.

line 2. *Parting*: *P* changed from *p* before entire word was rewritten.

line 3. *lip*: *p* written through *f*.

line 19. *doubly*: *b* has been mended.

      weak:: followed by a scribble which may have been made in jest or may have been in-

tended as a deletion mark for a comma which was replaced by a colon.

line 21. *heart*: an underscore (for italics) has been canceled.

line 23. *weal or woe,*: *a* of *weal* and *o* of *woe* written over thickly.

line 26. The mark below the final stanza may be a deleted dash.

THE NUMERAL "XI" at the top of this manuscript is one indication that sc 560 served as printer's copy for the poem's first printing. It marks the poem's position as eleventh in a group of fourteen lyrics that followed the two cantos of *Childe Harold's Pilgrimage. A Romaunt.* in the first edition of that poem.[1] Collation of sc 560 with the first two editions confirms this identification, for the only substantive variant ("eyelids" for "eyelid" in line 10) was an illogical typographical error committed in the first edition and corrected in the second. The accidental variants — all minor changes in punctuation except the introduction of a numeral "1" over the first stanza to conform with what follows — can be assigned either to the compositor or to corrections in proof. sc 560 must, in any case, have been written later than the Murray manuscript described by E. H. Coleridge, which shows major substantive variants from the published text in four lines.[2]

The arrangement of the fourteen lyrics in the first edition produces a kind of narrative continuity and probably does not represent their order of composition. In the seventh lyric, "Maid of Athens, ere we part," the poet speaks of "that lip I long to taste." Leslie Marchand infers that Byron's relations with Theresa Macri had been, thus far, "if not Platonic, at least in the realm of longing rather than of possession"[3] and that "On Parting" was begun, at least, at the time of Byron's first leaving Athens in March 1810. The poet's confidence that her tears "Can weep no change in me" leaves open the possibility of change in her. A year later there was a second and final parting, the record of which is meager and enigmatic.

1. *Childe Harold's Pilgrimage. A Romaunt.* (4to, London: John Murray; Edinburgh: William Blackwood; Dublin: John Cumming, 1812). "On Parting" appears on pp. 190–191. In the second edition (8vo, same publishers, same date), "On Parting" is the eleventh of twenty lyrics and appears on pp. 230–231.

2. Byron, *Poetry*, III, 23–24.

3. Marchand, *Byron*, I, 232.

The Carl H. Pforzheimer Library

SC 561   LORD BYRON TO LOUIS FAUVEL, MARCH 10, 1811

> MANUSCRIPT signed and dated by Byron, ¾ page. Single sheet, folio (12 x 9 inches).
> Laid paper. Watermark: [illegible]].
> Notations, page 2: 1. series of calculations in ink; 2. miscellaneous scribblings in pencil.
> Addition: manuscript is pasted down onto a leaf of a large album.
> PROVENANCE: Sotheby, February 2, 1963, lot 490.

Aspice—quos Scoto Pallas concedit honores,
   Subter—stat nomen, Facta superque Vide!

Scote miser! quamvis nocuisti Palladis aedɩ,
   Infandum facinus vindicat ipsa Venus.
5   *Pygmalion statuam pro sponsa arsisse refertur*
   Tu statuam rapias Scote! — sed Uxor abest.

                           Byron.
                      March 10ᵗʰ
                         1811

10   Eις τον ευγενεστατον κυριον
    τον κονσολον Φαυυελ
    μετα προσκυνηματα
    του μπαιρων· ———

Behold what honors Pallas yields the Scot.
Below, his name; above behold his deeds!

Wretched Scot! though you have despoiled the temple of Pallas,
Venus herself avenges your unspeakable villainy.
Pygmalion is said to have desired a statue for his bride;
You rape a statue, Scot! but your wife is gone.

                           Byron.
                      March 10ᵗʰ
                         1811

Byron to Fauvel   *March 10, 1811*

SC 561   To the most noble lord the consul Fauvel
              with the compliments of Byron

line 3. *quamvis*: *s* has been written through another lighter *s*.

line 5. *refertur*: *tur* written above the line running into the edge of the page.

line 7. Lines 7–9 in Byron's hand.

line 10. Lines 10ff. probably in Byron's hand.

line 13. τοῦ: ου written as ligature.

    μπαιρων: Byron transliterates his name
by using μπ instead of β, following the modern Greek practice, as in words like μπαλλόνι
(balloon) and μπαλέτο (ballet).

THE FIRST of the Latin couplets, roughly a translation of lines 107–
108 of the printed text of *The Curse of Minerva* — "For Elgin's
fame thus grateful Pallas pleads,/ Below, his name — above, behold his
deeds!" — was written by Byron on one of the manuscripts at this
point.[1] The other four lines[2] condense the sarcastic insinuations of the
subsequent lines in *The Curse* and Byron's footnote on them. The footnote tells us that Lord Elgin's name and his wife's "are carved con-
spicuously on the Parthenon" below "the torn remnants of the basso-
relievos." The verses (lines 117-122) argue that "Venus half avenged
Minerva's shame" since one of the carved names shows what Elgin
"lost" — an allusion meaningful for those who knew that Elgin's marriage had been dissolved by Act of Parliament in 1808.[3]

A week before the date of completion of his manuscript poem,
March 17, we see Byron bestowing this Latin version of a passage that
could have been libelous in forthright English — consider the pun in
rapias — upon his intimate friend the French consul, Louis Fauvel, in
memory perhaps of many sarcastic or gossiping conversations. Byron's
note on the second canto of *Childe Harold* is in praise of "M. Fauvel, the

1. Byron, *Poetry*, I, 462 n. 2. E. H. Coleridge, the editor, states that the only manuscript of the
Curse that he saw was "in the possession of the Earl of Stanhope," but there is at least one other
surviving manuscript. The Berg Collection, New York Public Library, has a holograph manuscript
dated by Byron at Athens which may possibly be the manuscript which Coleridge "believed to
have perished in a fire in 1879" (Byron, *Poetry*, I, 457). It lacks the Latin lines Coleridge said appeared in the Stanhope Ms. The Carl H. Pforzheimer Library has recently acquired what appears
to be a proof copy of the earliest printing of *The Curse of Minerva*, which Byron intended to publish
in 1811 along with the fifth edition of *English Bards and Scotch Reviewers* and *Hints from Horace*.

2. Quoted in Byron, *Poetry*, I, 462 n. 2, from a holograph.

3. In a preceding note E. H. Coleridge supplies this information and quotes a later exploitation of
Byron's Pygmalion comparison by James and Horace Smith in "The Parthenon" in *Horace in
London* (London and Edinburgh, 1813).

SC 561   French Consul, who has passed thirty years principally at Athens" and of his "talents as an artist, and manners as a gentleman."[4] Presumably Fauvel, an archaeologist as well as artist and diplomat and a member of Byron's Greek circle from his first settling in Athens in 1809, shared — perhaps he originally stimulated — Byron's "increasing indignation [at] what he considered the depredations and robbery that Lord Elgin was perpetrating in Greece."[5]

4. Byron, *Poetry*, II, 190.
5. Marchand, *Byron*, I, 224.

SC 562   LORD BYRON TO FRANCIS HODGSON, NOVEMBER 4, 1811

AL signed *Byron*, 1 page. Single sheet, 4to (8.9 x 7.2 inches).
Wove paper.
Docket, page 2: *Novr 4th 1811*|.
Addition: right margin has been mended and the manuscript pasted on leaf of drab backing, which has an illustration on the reverse side of Byron holding the mask of tragedy to his face.

PROVENANCE: Paul Richards, June 20, 1967.

> 8. St James's Street
> Novr 4th 1811
>
> *Dear Hodgson,*
>
> *Dine with me on Saturday next & meet Rogers, Campbell, &*
> 5 *Moore whom I have just left, & who spoke highly of you & yours. — Do*
> *pray contrive to meet me at Dorant's on that day as I think they are men*
> *you would not dislike to know.*
>
> *yrs ever*
> *Byron*

AFTER HIS RETURN from Greece in July 1811, Byron's first stride outside the private circle of old friends from Harrow and Cambridge was to a delightful, tension-relieving dinner at the house of Samuel Rogers on Monday, November 4. Byron had met none of the company, but he and Thomas Moore, an intimate friend of Rogers, needed to be released from an exchange of opened and unopened letters tending to make an affair of

Shelley and his Circle : Manuscripts

SC 562   honor of the satiric thrusts at Moore in *English Bards and Scotch Re-*
viewers, and upon meeting they were quickly persuaded to become fast
friends. A fourth poet, Thomas Campbell, joined the party, and Byron
found himself suddenly on intimate terms with men he considered the
"first" literary men of the land.[1] We see from the present letter, written
when he returned to his rooms at 8 St. James's Street, that Byron means
to introduce his scapegrace schoolmate Francis Hodgson to this exhil-
arating company. They have agreed to dine again on Saturday. Hodgson
is to meet Byron first at Dorant's Hotel. Perhaps they are to dine there,
more probably at the Alfred, Byron's club.

On Saturday, November 9, Byron wrote to Hobhouse that he had
"lately been leading a most *poetical* life with Messrs. Rogers, Moore, and
Campbell," that "Rogers and Moore are very pleasing, and not priggish,
as poetical persons are apt to be," and that he had "also seen a good deal
of Ward, the eloquent, who meets me to day with Rogers, Moore and our
Hodgson to dinner."[2] Campbell, whom he also liked, was to have dined
with them "but is laid up at Sydenham, however, I shall see him next
week."[3] John William Ward, whom Byron had met in Lisbon in July
1809 and seems recently to have encountered at the Alfred, would take
his place.

The experiment was hardly a success. Byron's ensuing letters to
Hodgson are cordial enough,[4] but writing to Hobhouse on November 16
he explained that Hodgson was embarrassingly "drunk and Sensibili-
tous," from his involvement in an absurd and vulgar conflict with another friend and an officer of dragoons "all about a bitch not worth a
Bank-token."[5] The published letters of December show Byron making
a quick visit to Hodgson and William Harness in Cambridge, planning
to bring Moore and Hobhouse together, calling with Moore on Campbell,
and dining with Rogers to "go to Coleridge's Lecture" — Coleridge

1. See Byron, *Letters and Journals*, II, 59–69; Marchand, *Byron*, I, 302–305.

2. Byron, *Correspondence*, I, 58.

3. Byron, *Correspondence*, I, 58.

4. See Byron to Hodgson, November 17 and December 4, 1811, Byron, *Letters and Journals*, II,
70–73.

5. Marchand, *Byron*, I, 305–306, quotes the unpublished part of Byron's letter of November 16,
1811 (Byron, *Correspondence*, I, 59).

SC 562 having attacked Campbell's "Pleasures of Hope" and "all other pleasures whatsoever" — and protesting, "Why, Hodgson! I fear you have
left off wine and me at the same time. . . ."[6]

6. Byron to Hobhouse, December 3 and December 15, 1811, Byron, *Correspondence*, I, 64, 66;
Byron to William Harness, December 8, and to Hodgson, December 8 and December 12, 1811,
Byron, *Letters and Journals*, II, 78, 83, 88.

SC 563 LORD BYRON TO SAMUEL ROGERS, MARCH 27, 1813

AL signed *B*, 1½ pages. Single sheet, 8ᵛᵒ (7.3 x 4.5 inches).
Wove paper.

PROVENANCE: Winifred Myers, July 13, 1967.

Dear Rogers

*I send you some of my obscurities — one of which I should
like to give to Moore & the other to Mʳ R. P. Th – I dare not write his
name at length.— The others to any of your fair or bearded acquaintance*
5 *you think proper.— If you think the picture you saw at Murrays worth your
acceptance it is yours. & you can put a glove or a masque on it if you like.*

ever yrs

B

Mʰ 27ᵗʰ 1813.-

line 3. *to Mʳ*: written in the left margin after   line 9. *27ᵗʰ*: *2* written through *1*.
the other words on the line were penned.

BYRON is sending to Samuel Rogers his "obscurities," that is, copies
of a recently but privately printed poem, either *The Giaour* in its
earliest version or *Waltz*. "He doubted the advisability of publishing
either poem under his own name," notes Marchand, "but he had given
copies to various friends."[1] The Turkish tale had been printed for John
Murray, but the "malicious publication on Waltzing" — so he described it to Murray — was eventually issued by Sherwood, Neely, and
Jones.[2] Both were printed before Byron left London March 28.[3]

The picture "you saw at Murrays" is probably the one Byron men-

1. Marchand, *Byron*, I, 387; Marchand does not allude to sc 563.

2. Byron, *Letters and Journals*, II, 202 and n. 2. On the roles of Murray and Sherwood, Neely, and
Jones in the proofs of *Waltz*, see sc 514, Appendix, fn. 10.

3. Marchand, *Byron*, I, 386.

SC 563   tions in his letter to Murray dated March 29 (a mistake for 27?): "the portrait (which you saw to-day) of the friend who is mentioned in the text at the close of Canto 1st [of *Childe Harold*], and in the notes,"[4] where the friend is identified as John Wingfield of the Guards who died of a fever, causing "unavailing woe" to burst from Childe Harold's heart (stanza 91).[5] I take it that Byron and Rogers had stopped in at Murray's together and examined the painted portrait which Byron was urging as an illustration for Murray's edition of the first two cantos and which Byron must have brought with him, wrapped up. Returning to his rooms, Byron then wrote the "March 29th" letter to Murray to overcome doubts of justification of its use in the book, and the present letter to Rogers from which the latter's delight in the portrait may be inferred. Did it seem too fair or adolescent for a Guard? A glove or masque might help. One has a feeling that Rogers had been made fully cognizant of Byron's bisexuality; note the phrase, "your fair or bearded aquaintance." The identity of "Mr R. P. Th –" has not been discovered.

4. Byron, *Letters and Journals*, II, 200. The date must be mistaken. The letter indicates that Byron was in London (at Murray's or with Murray) "to-day"; he left town the 28th.
5. See Byron, *Poetry*, II, 82–83, 94–95.

SC 564   LORD BYRON TO JOHN MURRAY, JUNE 19, 1813

AL signed '$\underline{B}$', 1 page. Single sheet, 8vo (7.3 x 4.6 inches).
Wove paper. Watermark: [   ]AINS| [18]10|.
Addition, page 2: traces of tape in each corner, indicating that the manuscript was pasted to an album leaf.

PROVENANCE: Paul Richards, June 26, 1966.

Dear Sir –

 You will perceive by the ₄*first lines of the enclosed of what part of the text it is a continuation– the 4th line is also also altered from the published*
5 *copy— the rest are all new & will be printed accordingly*

             yrs ever

               '$\underline{B}$'

June 19th—1813 —

line 4. *4th*: written through *2nd*.   line 4. *also also* (sic).

SC 564   THIS LETTER must have been accompanied by a sheet of alterations and additions for the second edition of *The Giaour*, which was published (approximately) June 24, 1813.[1] From E. H. Coleridge's convenient table of additions to the text of *The Giaour* and a copy of the first edition, it can be determined that the lines referred to began with what is now line 995 and probably continued through line 1023. Of the new passages inserted in the second edition, only this one required the alteration of a line in the first edition to introduce it.

1. See Byron, *Poetry*, III, 78 ff.

SC 565   LORD BYRON, HOLOGRAPH EMENDATION OF *THE BRIDE OF ABYDOS*, DECEMBER 2, 1813

HOLOGRAPH EMENDATION, 1 page. Single sheet, 4to (8.9 x 7.2 inches).
Wove paper. Watermark: B| 1812|.
Docket, page 2: *Lord Byron*|.
Notation, lower right corner, page 1, in contemporary hand: *Lord Byron*|.
Addition: left margin discolored by traces of paste which indicate that the manuscript was once mounted in an album.

PROVENANCE: Michael Lewis, October 3, 1968.

> *Page 45 (I believe but having no*
> *copy am not certain)*
> *after line*
> " *And tints tomorrow with prophetic ray*
> 5   ~~*Insert or*~~ *read* —
> " *Sweet as his native song to Exile's ears*
> " *Shall sound each tone thy long-loved voice endears.*
>
> ————
>
> *Insert this in it's proper place – as also the*
> *other insertions & alterations before sent*
> 10   *on the first opportunity*
>   *B*

line 1. *45*: written through *47*.
    (*I believe . . . certain*): written in a bolder hand than the rest of manuscript; the sentence was probably added later.

line 8. *it's* (sic).
line 11. *B*: Byron made his initial with elaborate flourishes.

Byron, *Bride of Abydos* Emendation   *December 2, 1813*

SC 565   Byron's *The Bride of Abydos* was published December 2, 1813, according to his journal entry of December 5,[1] and was rushed through seven editions before the revisions and additions to the text fully caught up with its printed form. "I wish I could write so fast," lamented Thomas Moore to his music publisher, James Power, on December 4.[2] "He *could not* write anything bad," Moore continued, loyally, to another correspondent when he had read the poem, "but it would have been much finer if he had taken more time about it."[3]

E. H. Coleridge gives a fairly full account of the piecemeal additions to the original fair copy of the poem set in type by November 11, additions which included seventy lines in stanza 20 of Canto II and forced the printer to make ten or twelve revises before publication, and he corrects the sequence of Byron's hasty notes bearing "insertions & alterations" to his publisher, John Murray, between November 13 and December 3, not 2.[4] His reconstruction implies a publication date of December 3 for the first edition. The present document increases the available evidence but leaves both that date and the sequence of revisions still partly conjectural.

In the second edition (issued perhaps within a day or so) there are four lines of poetry after "And tints to-morrow with prophetic ray!" (line 883) but before the two lines (888–889) given in the present note. When Byron had ceased revising them, lines 880–889 read:

> "Or since that hope denied in worlds of strife
> Be thou the rainbow to the storms of life!
> The evening beam that smiles the clouds away,
> And tints to-morrow with prophetic ray!
> Blest — as the Muezzin's strain from Mecca's wall
> To pilgrims pure and prostrate at his call;
> Soft — as the melody of youthful days,
> That steals the trembling tear of speechless praise;
> Dear — as his native song to Exile's ears,
> Shall sound each tone thy long-loved voice endears."

1. Byron, *Letters and Journals*, II, 361.   2. Moore, *Letters*, I, 287.

3. Moore to Mary Dalby, an old friend in Ireland, December 1813, *Letters*, I, 289.

4. Byron, *Poetry*, III, 151–153, 211–213, and 195–196, n. 6. Coleridge silently corrects the date, December 3, 1813, of the undated note numbered 349 among items of November 13 in Byron, *Letters and Journals*, II, 282, because the reading "*prophetic* ray" given in it is inserted in a revise dated December 3, 1813; but see below.

SC 565   The words "Sweet as" were replaced by "Dear—as" in the printed version of line 888. And the present note, taken literally to refer to a proof of page 45 in which lines 888–889 are to follow immediately "after line [883]," must have been sent to Murray before a manuscript fragment consisting of these two lines (verbatim) preceded by lines 886–887. Since the latter fragment is dated December 2, we must suppose the present document to belong to that date if not earlier.[5]

The difficulty is that even the December 2 material failed to get into the first edition, whereas the epithet "prophetic" in line 883, though "inserted in a revise dated December 3, 1813,"[6] did get in. Possibly that revise was misdated by the printer and Byron's publication date of December 2 is correct. But possibly Byron, not the printer, is wrong, and there was still time to incorporate a single-word correction on proof dated December 3 though not time enough to insert an addition of two or more couplets dated December 2 by Byron but perhaps not received that day by Thomas Davison, the printer.

5. The fragment is given in Byron, *Poetry*, III, 196, n. 1; its date stated in Byron, *Poetry*, III, 211.
6. See above, fn. 4; cf. Byron, *Poetry*, III, 195–196, n. 6. It is of course possible that the epithet got lost when the printer made a revise for the second edition and it had to be reinserted.

SC 566   LORD BYRON TO JOHN H. MERIVALE, JANUARY 1814

AL unsigned, 2 pages. Single sheet, 8ᵛᵒ (7.3 x 4.3 inches), tipped in first edition of J. H. Merivale, *Orlando in Roncesvalles.**
Wove paper. Watermark: [?GA]TER| [18]11|.
Notation, top of page 1: *Scrap of a note from| Lord Byron——Jan. 1814|.*

PROVENANCE: The Bookman, October 19, 1970.

* ORLANDO| IN| RONCESVALLES,| A POEM,| IN FIVE CANTOS.| [rule]| BY| J. H. MERIVALE, Esq.| [rule] ALERE FLAMMAM.| [printer's device]| LONDON:| PRINTED FOR JOHN MURRAY, 50, ALBEMARLE STREET,| BY RICHARD AND ARTHUR TAYLOR, SHOE-LANE.| [rule]| 1814.| Extra illustrated copy, illuminated in colors and gold by Edward Vernon Utterson, and bound in contemporary full red morocco stamped and tooled in gold. Fly-leaf contains inscriptions in three different hands and inks: 1. *LAM| Jan. 9 . .1846|;* 2. *Illuminated by Mʳ Utterson|;* 3. *Philip Merivale|.*

SC 566   *My dear Merivale*

*I have redde Roncesvaux with very great pleasure and
(if I were so disposed) see very little room for Criticism – there is a choice
of two lines in one of ye. last C^{os} I think "Live & protect, better because
5 "Oh who? implies a doubt of Roland's power or inclination.— I would
allow it — but that point you yourself must determine on – I mean the doubt
as to where to place a part of the poem –whether between the actions or no—
only if you wish to have all the success you deserve—never listen to frien< >
and as I am not the least troublesome of the number—leas< > of all to
10 me.— I hope you will be out soon   Marc< > Sir– March is the month–
the teeming time for the trade & they must be considered.— You have written
a very noble poem & nothing but the detestable taste of the day can do you
harm —but I think you will beat it—your measure is uncommonly well
chosen & wielded. —*

line 4. *protect,*: Byron omitted the end quotes here and after *who?* in line 5.

line 6. *it*: probable reading; the word is peculiarly formed.

line 8. *frien<ds>*: this word, along with <*least*>

(line 9) and *Marc<h>* (line 10), was the final word on a line of the second page of the manuscript; bracketed portions were obscured when the manuscript was tipped in to the bound volume (see Bibliographical Description).

JOHN HERMAN MERIVALE (1779–1844) was a friend of Byron's tutor, Henry Drury, and his Cambridge companion Francis Hodgson. In 1805 Merivale married Drury's sister. The next year he collaborated with Robert Bland in *Collections from the Greek Anthology*. His *ottava rima Orlando in Roncesvalles, A Poem, in Five Cantos* was evidently in the press; it was published by John Murray before September 1814,[1] with a dedication to Thomas Johnes of Hafod.

1. The work was not published until late summer, apparently. Byron on September 2 (Byron, *Letters and Journals*, III, 127) wrote to Murray expressing pleasure at news in a recent letter (late August) to the effect that Merivale's poem was in line for "good entreatment" by certain "Journals." The earliest reviews known to William S. Ward, who has made an exhaustive search for such things in journals of the period, are those in the September issues of the *British Critic* and the *Eclectic Review*. These would not have been out until the end of September, a reason for Murray's only mentioning them to Byron and not including them in the August journals or clippings he had just sent him.

[1135]

sc 566   Merivale had apparently submitted a manuscript copy for Byron's criticism. Perhaps Murray had suggested this; possibly Byron had originally recommended his friend's work, sight unseen, to Murray. An entry in Godwin's diary of about the right date, August 4, 1813, records Godwin's meeting Merivale with Byron — at John Murray's.

Byron's specific textual suggestion (lines 3–7) seems to refer to Canto V, where the published text of the last line of the ninth octave stanza reads: "Live thou! and guard my sister Aldabelle." Merivale had apparently debated whether to express this, the whole of Oliver's dying request to Orlando (Roland), as a question ("Oh who will guard my sister . . . ?") or as an imperative ("Live and protect my sister . . ."). What Byron may not have known until the poem was published (when a note informs us all) was that the line is a paraphrase of two lines from Luigi Pulci's *Morgante Maggiore*.[2] Merivale's poem is, in fact, founded on the last four cantos of Pulci's *Morgante*, which he describes and discusses in his Preface. Thus Byron was exposed to the serious side of Pulci in 1814, while he was engaged in his own Byro-heroic romances, encountering the "ludicrous" side of the Italian master in 1817 through the mediation of John Hookham Frere's burlesque of heroic romance.[3] Though critics often forget, Byron first employed *ottava rima* in "Epistle to Augusta."[4]

The copy of *Roncesvalles* in which sc 566 is tipped and bound was owned (according to a binding-leaf inscription) by Philip Merivale, doubtless a relative of the author's, and "Illuminated by Mʳ Utterson," who, according to the Preface, drew the designs that illustrate ordinary copies of the poem.

2. In Merivale's note the lines read: "E bisognò intender, che Alda la bella/ Raccomandar volea, la sua sorella."

3. See Byron, *Letters and Journals*, IV, 172–173 and fn.

4. Byron, *Poetry*, IV, 57–62. Cf. Keats's use of the stanza in "Isabella."

SC 567 LORD BYRON TO THOMAS CLAUGHTON, SEPTEMBER 4, 1814

AL signed *Byron*, 4 pages. Double sheet, 4ᵗᵒ (9 x 7.3 inches). Wove paper. Watermark: T EDMONDS| 1810|.

PROVENANCE: Sotheby, October 29, 1968, lot 463.

SC 567   *Newstead Abbey. –*
                                          Sept. 4th 1814

    Dear Sir

          Whenever your business or leisure prompts you to visit this place
5 *you can take your choice of it's apartments   I will take care that they are*
 ready for your reception. — The key of the cellar will be left with Murray so
 that I hope you will not find it more uncomfortable than heretofore. ——
 I cannot yet fix any day for my departure– but probably it will take place
 within the ensuing ten days – but if you are disposed to come here before that
10 *period I trust you will not doubt that you will be very welcome. I have to*
 thank you for your answer on the subject of Mr Kirkby's lands– and shall
 come to some agreement with him on the subject. — Upon the subject of New-
 stead I will be explicit with you— it is my intention to sell the estate— and
 I would certainly rather renew the sale with yourself on the same terms—
15 *than part with it to any other — even should chance or circumstances offer*
 a more advantageous purchase — upon this point you can determine for your-
 self — you have the preference. — In the mean time I have not interfered
 with the new tenants— nor disturbed or removed any of the furniture—
 perhaps it may be as well even to leave the things which you directed to be
20 *sent to Haydock (spoons &^{c}) till you arrive and may choose to order their*
 removal in person — as the plate may hardly be safe in a parcel— but if
 required they shall be forwarded now. — — — I hope you are now satis-
 fied that "the channel of Negotiation is left open" nor would it ever have
 been closed on my part— but for the necessity that existed of some decision
25 *one way or the other for the time being; but I am by no means insensible to*
 the handsome part you have acted in not seeking fresh litigation for the
 purpose of delay; ~~and~~ *$_\wedge$the whole of your recent conduct, and have only to*   *nor to*
 regret the untoward circumstances which produced the temporary (or final)
30 *relinquishment of your purchase.—*
       Believe me very truly yrs
              Byron

The Carl H. Pforzheimer Library

Byron to Claughton   **September 4, 1814**

SC 567   *P.S.*

35   *I believe there is a Gun of yours here— I have long given up sporting
— but you will find plenty of game (by all accounts) and if you like to
bring f^r any friend with you there will be room & birds enough for both.—
The gun (if here) shall be taken care & not used except by yourself. ——*

line 5. *it's* (sic).

line 11. *your*: *y* written through *m*.

line 18. *the furniture*: *the* written through *you*.

line 25. *insensible*: written through indecipherable word.

line 37. *used*: written through indecipherable word.

A COMPENDIOUS way to indicate the juncture at which this letter
finds the negotiations between Byron and Thomas Claughton over
the purchase of Newstead Abbey will be to quote from the index to
Marchand's *Byron*. "Claughton . . . offered £140,000 for Newstead
[August 15, 1812]; repented of bargain [soon]; paid £5,000 of deposit
[November 5, 1812]; . . . witholding payments [while Byron's creditors
swarmed, January 1813]; ready to pay £15,000 [July 1813]; . . . delayed
payment [April 1814]; Byron tried to force conclusion on [July 19, 1814];
sacrificed £25,000 to Byron [August 1814]; . . . Newstead forfeited by
[October 1814]; still interested in Newstead [December 1814]; his forfeit
spent [by February 1815]."[1] The immediate situation is elaborated in
Byron's letters of September 11 to John Hanson, his agent,[2] and September
13 to his friend Hobhouse.[3]

Byron is being most courteous and considerate in the present letter,
even offering the services of Joe Murray to open the wine cellar (line 6)
should Claughton wish to visit Newstead. But the decision he had
reached is stated firmly in the letter to Hobhouse. "Claughton has re-
linquished his purchase, and twenty-five thousand pounds out of twenty-
eight ditto, paid on account, and I am Abbot again—it is all signed,
sealed, and *re*-delivered. . . . he wishes to *renew*—but I will first see an'
[whether] the monies be palpable and tangible, before I re-contract with
him or others—though if he could complete, I should have no objections,
on the old terms."[4]

1. I take the liberty of replacing (without elision marks) Marchand's page numbers with dates
found on the pages referred to and of transposing two entries into chronological order.

2. Byron, *Letters and Journals*, III, 133–134.

3. Byron, *Correspondence*, I, 266.   4. Byron, *Correspondence*, I, 266.

Byron to ?Lewis   **?Spring–Summer 1815**

SC 568   LORD BYRON TO ?[MATTHEW G.] LEWIS, ?SPRING–SUMMER 1815

AL signed *Biron*, 1 page. Single sheet, 8ᵛᵒ (7.3 x 4.5 inches).
Wove paper.
Notation, written on album leaf, beneath manuscript, in red ink: *The above note to Mʳ| Lewis is curious, showing| Lord Byron's caprice even| as to his Name.| The Lady M. is Lady Melbourne.|*
Addition: manuscript has been pasted on white album leaf which contains another manuscript as well as two clippings, one of which is dated 1868.
PROVENANCE: Sotheby, May 2, 1966, lot 245.

My dear Lˢ –

I will call about 6— we have both *an offer of places from Lʸ Mᵉ in Lᵈ Egremonts' box– but I think we shall have more of the audience – (always more amusing than the performers on a first night–) in ~~your box~~*
5   *the seats you have taken. — We can go to which you please –*

ever yrs

Biron

IN AN UNPOSTED letter similar to sc 292 of June 6, 1815 (III), Byron is discussing plans for an evening at the theater with M. G. Lewis (probably). Given the mutual availability of Byron and Lewis in London from November 1813 until Lewis' departure for Jamaica in November 1815, it is difficult to date sc 568 with precision. However, in sc 292 it was established that Byron and Lewis were neighbors in June 1815 and it seems likely that sc 568 may have been written in the spring or summer of 1815.

In November 1813, Byron had written, "I have taken Lord Salisbury's box at Covent Garden for the season; and now I must go and prepare to join Lady Holland and party, in theirs, at Drury Lane."[1] However, it appears that a little more than a year later, Byron himself had "the alternate weeks of a private box at Drury-lane Theatre" which he offered to Lady Melbourne and to Hobhouse in January 1815 (while he was away from London getting married), and to Hunt in May–June 1815.[2]

1. Byron, *Letters and Journals*, II, 334.
2. Byron, *Letters and Journals*, III, 199; Byron, *Correspondence*, I, 293, 294.

Byron to ?Lewis   *?Spring–Summer* **1815**

SC 568   In SC 568 Lady Melbourne has places to offer — possibly at Covent Garden — in the theater box of Lord Egremont, long her particular friend and allegedly the father of her son William Lamb, Caroline's husband.[3] "Was not you at the play on Thursday?" wrote Byron mockingly on April 22, 1815. "I thought you were visible, but obscurely, in Ld E.'s box."[4] Byron seems usually to have taken greater interest in the audience than in the performers.[5]

3. Marchand, *Byron*, I, 342. That she offered places in it we only learn from the present letter.

4. Byron, *Correspondence*, I, 306.

5. On Byron's use of the spelling "Biron" (line 7) in connection with Allegra, see SC 506, Commentary.

Reference Sources, Abridged Title List

Index of Names

REFERENCE SOURCES, ABRIDGED
TITLE LIST

Abinger Manuscripts

The manuscripts and letters of William Godwin, Mary Wollstonecraft, and others in the possession of Lord Abinger (Pforzheimer Microfilm).

Alcock and Holland

R. C. Alcock and F. C. Holland. *The Postmarks of Great Britain and Ireland, Being a Survey of British Postmarks from 1660 to 1940*. Cheltenham, England [1940].

Allibone

S. Austin Allibone. *A Critical Dictionary of English Literature and British and American Authors*, 3 vols. London, 1884; Supplement, 2 vols., Philadelphia, 1891.

Alumni Cantabrigienses

Alumni Cantabrigienses, ed. John Venn and J. A. Venn, 10 vols. Cambridge University Press, 1922–1947.

Alumni Oxonienses

Alumni Oxonienses, ed. Joseph Foster, 4 vols. Oxford, 1888–1891.

Annual Register

The Annual Register, or a View of the History, Politics, and Literature. London [various dates].

Archibald Constable

Thomas Constable. *Archibald Constable and His Literary Correspondents*, 3 vols. Edinburgh, 1873.

The Ashley Library

The Ashley Library, A Catalogue of Printed Books, Manuscripts and Autograph Letters Collected by Thomas James Wise, 11 vols. London, Privately Printed, 1922–1936.

Bailey's Dictionary

A New Universal Etymological English Dictionary, originally compiled by N. Bailey, revised by Joseph Nicol Scott. London, 1772.

Bate, *Keats*

Walter Jackson Bate. *John Keats*. Harvard University Press, 1963.

Beavan, *James and Horace Smith*

Arthur H. Beavan. *James and Horace Smith*. London, 1899.

The Carl H. Pforzheimer Library

Reference Sources

Blunden, *John Taylor*	Edmund Blunden. *Keats's Publisher: A Memoir of John Taylor (1781–1864)*. London, 1936.
Blunden, *Leigh Hunt*	Edmund Blunden. *Leigh Hunt, A Biography*. London, 1930.
Blunden, *Shelley*	Edmund Blunden. *Shelley, A Life Story*. New York, 1947.
Boas, *Harriet Shelley*	Louise Schutz Boas. *Harriet Shelley, Five Long Years*. Oxford University Press, 1962.
Boase	Frederic Boase. *Modern English Biography*. Truro, England, 1892–1921.
British Army List	*A List of the Officers of the Army and Royal Marines on Full and Half-Pay*. War Office [London, various dates].
Brown, *Letters*	*The Letters of Charles Armitage Brown*, ed. Jack Stillinger. Harvard University Press, 1966.
Brown, *Godwin*	Ford K. Brown. *The Life of William Godwin*. London, Toronto, and New York, 1926.
Burke's Landed Gentry	*Genealogical and Heraldic History of the Landed Gentry*, ed. John Burke, Bernard Burke, *et al.* London [various dates].
Burke's Peerage	*Genealogical and Heraldic History of the Peerage, Baronetage and Knightage*, ed. John Burke, Bernard Burke, *et al.* London [various dates].
Byron, *Correspondence*	*Lord Byron's Correspondence*, ed. John Murray, 2 vols. London, 1922.
Byron, *Letters and Journals*	*The Works of Lord Byron, Letters and Journals*, ed. Rowland E. Prothero, 6 vols. London and New York, 1898–1901.
Byron, *Poetry*	*The Works of Lord Byron, Poetry*, ed. Ernest Hartley Coleridge, 7 vols. London and New York, 1898–1904.
Cameron, *The Young Shelley*	Kenneth Neill Cameron. *The Young Shelley, Genesis of a Radical*. New York, 1950.
Cary's *Roads*	*Cary's New Itinerary or an Accurate Delineation of the Great Roads, Both Direct and Cross throughout England and Wales*. London [various dates].

Shelley and his Circle : Manuscripts

CBEL	*Cambridge Bibliography of English Literature*, 4 vols. Cambridge University Press, 1940; Supplement, 1957.
Claire Clairmont, *Journals*	*The Journals of Claire Clairmont, 1814–1827*, ed. Marion Kingston Stocking with the assistance of David Mackenzie Stocking. Harvard University Press, 1968.
Clarke, *Recollections of Writers*	Charles and Mary Cowden Clarke. *Recollections of Writers*. London, 1878.
Coleridge, *Letters*	*Collected Letters of Samuel Taylor Coleridge*, ed. Earl Leslie Griggs, 6 vols. Oxford, 1956–1971.
Complete Peerage	*The Complete Peerage*, ed. George E. Cokayne and Vicary Gibbs. London, 1910.
DAB	*Dictionary of American Biography*, ed. Allen Johnson and Dumas Malone. New York, 1928.
De Ricci	Seymour de Ricci. *A Bibliography of Shelley's Letters, Published and Unpublished.* [Bois-Colombes, France], Privately Printed, 1927.
DNB	*Dictionary of National Biography*, ed. Leslie Stephen and Sidney Lee. New York, 1908–1909.
Dowden, *Shelley*	Edward Dowden. *The Life of Percy Bysshe Shelley*. London, 1886.
Feltham, *Picture of London*	*The Picture of London, for 1802; Being a Correct Guide to All the Curiosities, Amusements, Exhibitions, Public Establishments, and Remarkable Objects in and near London* . . . . London [1802].
Forman, *Shelley Library*	H. Buxton Forman. *The Shelley Library, An Essay in Bibliography*. London, 1886.
Gisborne, *Journals and Letters*	*Maria Gisborne & Edward E. Williams, Shelley's Friends, Their Journals and Letters*, ed. Frederick L. Jones. University of Oklahoma Press, 1951.
Godwin, Journal	The manuscript journal of William Godwin (from 1788 to 1836) in the possession of Lord Abinger (Pforzheimer Microfilm).

The Carl H. Pforzheimer Library

Reference Sources

Godwin, *Memoirs*	William Godwin. *Memoirs of the Author of a Vindication of the Rights of Woman*. London, 1798. (The first edition is used unless otherwise noted.)
Godwin, *Political Justice* (Priestley ed.)	William Godwin. *Enquiry Concerning Political Justice and Its Influence on Morals and Happiness*, ed. F. E. L. Priestley, 3 vols. University of Toronto Press, 1946.
Grabo, *The Magic Plant*	Carl Grabo. *The Magic Plant, the Growth of Shelley's Thought*. University of North Carolina Press, 1936.
Grove, *Dictionary*	*Grove's Dictionary of Music and Musicians*, ed. H. C. Colles, 6 vols. London, 1948.
Grylls, *Clairmont*	R. Glynn Grylls. *Claire Clairmont, Mother of Byron's Allegra*. London, 1939.
Grylls, *Mary Shelley*	R. Glynn Grylls. *Mary Shelley, A Biography*. Oxford University Press, 1938.
Halkett and Laing	Samuel Halkett and John Laing. *Dictionary of Anonymous and Pseudonymous English Literature*, 9 vols. Edinburgh and London, 1926–1962.
Harben, *Dictionary of London*	Henry A. Harben. *A Dictionary of London, Being Notes Topographical and Historical Relating to the Streets and Principal Buildings in the City of London*. London, 1918.
Haydon, *Autobiography*	*Life of Benjamin Robert Haydon, Historical Painter, from His Autobiography and Journals*, ed. Tom Taylor, 3 vols. London, 1853.
Haydon, *Diary*	*The Diary of Benjamin Robert Haydon*, ed. Willard Bissell Pope, 5 vols. Harvard University Press, 1960–1963.
Hazlitt, *Complete Works*	*The Complete Works of William Hazlitt*, ed. P. P. Howe, 20 vols. London, 1930–1934.
Hazlitt, *Memoirs*	W. Carew Hazlitt. *Memoirs of William Hazlitt*, 2 vols. London, 1867.
Hogg, *Shelley*	Thomas Jefferson Hogg. *The Life of Percy Bysshe Shelley*, in *The Life of Percy Bysshe Shelley . . .*, ed. Humbert Wolfe, 2 vols. London, Toronto, and New York, 1933.

Reference Sources

Hogg, T. J., *The Life of Percy Bysshe Shelley* — Thomas Jefferson Hogg. *The Life of Percy Bysshe Shelley*, 2 vols. London, 1858 (first edition, used for Collations).

Horwood, *Plan of London* — R. Horwood. *Plan of the Cities of London and Westminster the Borough of Southwark, and Parts Adjoining Shewing Every House*. London, 1792–1799.

Howe, *Hazlitt* — P. P. Howe. *The Life of William Hazlitt*. London, 1947.

Hughes, *Nascent Mind* — A. M. D. Hughes. *The Nascent Mind of Shelley*. Oxford University Press, 1947.

Hunt, *Autobiography* — *The Autobiography of Leigh Hunt*, ed. Roger Ingpen, 2 vols. Westminster, 1903.

Hunt, *Correspondence* — *The Correspondence of Leigh Hunt*, ed. [Thornton Hunt], 2 vols. London, 1862.

Hunt, *First Editions* — *My Leigh Hunt Library, the First Editions*, ed. Luther A. Brewer. Cedar Rapids, Iowa, Privately Printed, 1932.

Hunt, *Letters* — *My Leigh Hunt Library, the Holograph Letters*, ed. Luther A. Brewer. University of Iowa Press, 1938.

Hunt, *Lord Byron and Some of His Contemporaries* — Leigh Hunt. *Lord Byron and Some of His Contemporaries*. London, 1828.

Hunt, *Poetical Works* — *The Poetical Works of Leigh Hunt*, ed. H. S. Milford. Oxford University Press, 1923.

Ingpen, *Shelley in England* — Roger Ingpen. *Shelley in England: New Facts and Letters from the Shelley-Whitton Papers*. London, 1917.

Johnstone's Guide — Johnstone's *London Commercial Guide*, August 1817.

Keats Circle — *The Keats Circle*, ed. Hyder Edward Rollins (2nd edition), 2 vols. Harvard University Press, 1965.

Keats, *Letters* — *The Letters of John Keats 1814–1821*, ed. Hyder Edward Rollins, 2 vols. Harvard University Press, 1958.

Koszul, *Jeunesse* — André Koszul. *La Jeunesse de Shelley*. Paris, 1910.

The Carl H. Pforzheimer Library

Reference Sources

Lamb, *Letters*

The Letters of Charles Lamb to Which Are Added Those of His Sister Mary Lamb, ed. E. V. Lucas, 3 vols. London, 1935.

Lamb, *Works*

The Works of Charles and Mary Lamb, ed. E. V. Lucas, 7 vols. London, 1903–1905.

Landré, *Hunt*

Louis Landré. *Leigh Hunt*, 2 vols. Paris, 1935–1936.

Letters about Shelley

Letters about Shelley Interchanged by Three Friends — Edward Dowden, Richard Garnett and Wm. Michael Rossetti, ed. R. S. Garnett. London, 1917.

Lovell, *Medwin*

Ernest J. Lovell, Jr. *Captain Medwin, Friend of Byron and Shelley*. Austin, University of Texas Press, 1962.

Lowndes

William Thomas Lowndes. *The Bibliographer's Manual of English Literature*, 6 vols. London, 1865.

MacCarthy, *Shelley*

Denis Florence MacCarthy. *Shelley's Early Life*. London, 1872.

McAleer, *The Sensitive Plant*

Edward C. McAleer. *The Sensitive Plant, A Life of Lady Mount Cashell*. University of North Carolina Press, 1958.

Marchand, *Byron*

Leslie A. Marchand. *Byron, A Biography*, 3 vols. New York, 1957.

Marshall, *Mary Shelley*

Mrs. Julian Marshall. *The Life and Letters of Mary Wollstonecraft Shelley*, 2 vols. London, 1889.

Mary Shelley, Journal

The manuscript journal of Mary Shelley in the possession of Lord Abinger (Pforzheimer Microfilm).

Mary Shelley, *Letters*

The Letters of Mary Shelley, ed. Frederick L. Jones, 2 vols. University of Oklahoma Press, 1944.

Mary Shelley's Journal

Mary Shelley's Journal, ed. Frederick L. Jones. University of Oklahoma Press, 1947.

Medwin, *Byron*

Medwin's Conversations of Lord Byron, ed. Ernest J. Lovell, Jr. Princeton University Press, 1966.

Medwin, *Shelley*

Thomas Medwin. *The Life of Percy Bysshe Shelley*, ed. H. Buxton Forman. Oxford University Press, 1913.

Shelley and his Circle : Manuscripts

Reference Sources

Moore, *Letters*

The Letters of Thomas Moore, ed. Wilfred S. Dowden, 2 vols. Oxford University Press, 1964.

Moore, *Memoirs*

Memoirs, Journal, and Correspondence of Thomas Moore, ed. Lord John Russell, 8 vols. London and Boston, 1853–1856.

Moorman, *Wordsworth*

Mary Moorman. *William Wordsworth, A Biography*, 2 vols. Oxford University Press, 1957, 1965.

New Shelley Letters

New Shelley Letters, ed. W. S. Scott. Yale University Press, 1949.

Nitchie, *Mary Shelley*

Elizabeth Nitchie. *Mary Shelley, Author of "Frankenstein."* Rutgers University Press, 1953.

Notopoulos, *Platonism*

James A. Notopoulos. *The Platonism of Shelley*. Duke University Press, 1949.

OED

The Compact Edition of the Oxford English Dictionary. Oxford University Press, 1971.

Paterson's *Roads*

[Daniel] Paterson. *A New and Accurate Description of All the Direct and Principal Cross Roads in England and Wales and Part of Scotland*. London [various dates].

Paul, *Godwin*

C. Kegan Paul. *William Godwin: His Friends and Contemporaries*, 2 vols. London, 1876.

Peacock, *Complete Novels*

The Novels of Thomas Love Peacock, ed. David Garnett, 2 vols. London, 1963.

Peacock, *Memoirs*

"Memoirs of Percy Bysshe Shelley," *The Works of Thomas Love Peacock*, Vol. VIII, ed. H. F. B. Brett-Smith and C. E. Jones (Halliford Edition). London, 1934.

Peacock, *Works*

The Works of Thomas Love Peacock, ed. H. F. B. Brett-Smith and C. E. Jones (Halliford Edition), 10 vols. London, 1924–1934.

Peacock, *Works* (1875)

The Works of Thomas Love Peacock, ed. Henry Cole. London, 1875.

Peck, *Shelley*

Walter Edwin Peck. *Shelley, His Life and Work*, 2 vols. Boston and New York, 1927.

Pigot's *Directory*

Pigot's London and Provincial Directory for 1822–23; 1823–24. London, 1824.

The Carl H. Pforzheimer Library

Reference Sources

Pigot's Metropolitan Directory	*Pigot and Co.'s Metropolitan New Alphabetical Directory, for 1828;9, Commencing with the Regulations, Rates of Postage, and Receiving Houses of the General Post Office* . . . [*including an*] *Alphabetical Directory for Middlesex, &c.* . . . . London, 1829.
PMLA	*Publications of the Modern Language Association.*
Polidori, *Diary*	*The Diary of Dr. John William Polidori, 1816,* ed. William Michael Rossetti. London, 1911.
Pollin, *Godwin*	Burton Ralph Pollin. *Education and Enlightenment in the Works of William Godwin.* New York, 1962.
Robinson, *British Post Office*	Howard Robinson. *The British Post Office, A History.* Princeton University Press, 1948.
Robinson, *Diary*	*Diary, Reminiscences, and Correspondence of Henry Crabb Robinson,* ed. Thomas Sadler, 3 vols. London, 1869.
Robinson, *London Theatre*	*The London Theatre, 1811–1866: Selections from the Diary of Henry Crabb Robinson,* ed. Eluned Brown. London, 1966.
Robinson, *On Books*	Henry Crabb Robinson. *On Books and Their Writers,* ed. Edith J. Morley, 3 vols. London, 1938.
Royal Kalendar	*The Royal Kalendar: and Court and City Register, for England, Scotland, Ireland, and America.* London, published annually at various dates.
Scott, *Hogg*	Winifred Scott. *Jefferson Hogg.* London, 1951.
Shelley and Mary	*Shelley and Mary,* 3 vols. Privately Printed [London, 1882].
Shelley, *Complete Works*	*The Complete Works of Percy Bysshe Shelley,* ed. Roger Ingpen and Walter E. Peck (Julian Edition), 10 vols. London and New York, 1926–1930.
Shelley, *The Esdaile Notebook*	*The Esdaile Notebook: A Volume of Early Poems by Percy Bysshe Shelley,* ed. Kenneth Neill Cameron. New York, 1964.

Shelley and his Circle : Manuscripts

Reference Sources

Shelley, *Essays, Letters*	*Essays, Letters from Abroad, Translations and Fragments by Percy Bysshe Shelley*, ed. Mary Shelley, 2 vols. London, 1840.
Shelley, *Letters*	*The Letters of Percy Bysshe Shelley*, ed. Frederick L. Jones, 2 vols. Oxford University Press, 1964.
Shelley-Leigh Hunt	*Shelley-Leigh Hunt: How Friendship Made History and Extended the Bounds of Human Freedom and Thought*, ed. R. Brimley Johnson. London, 1928.
Shelley, *Note Books*	*Note Books of Percy Bysshe Shelley*, ed. H. Buxton Forman, 3 vols. Privately Printed [1911].
Shelley, *Poetical Works* (1839)	*The Poetical Works of Percy Bysshe Shelley*, ed. Mary Shelley, 4 vols. London, 1839.
Shelley, *Poetical Works* (Forman)	*The Poetical Works of Percy Bysshe Shelley*, ed. Harry Buxton Forman, 4 vols. London, 1876–1877.
Shelley, *Poetical Works* (OSA)	*The Complete Poetical Works of Percy Bysshe Shelley*, ed. Thomas Hutchinson. Oxford University Press, 1960 (Oxford Standard Authors Edition).
Shelley's Prose Works	*The Prose Works of Percy Bysshe Shelley*, ed. Harry Buxton Forman, 4 vols. London, 1880.
Smiles, *John Murray*	Samuel Smiles. *A Publisher and His Friends, Memoir and Correspondence of the Late John Murray*, 2 vols. London, 1891.
Southey, *Life and Correspondence*	*The Life and Correspondence of Robert Southey*, ed. Rev. Charles Cuthbert Southey, 6 vols. London, 1849–1850.
Southey, *New Letters*	*New Letters of Robert Southey*, ed. Kenneth Curry, 2 vols. Columbia University Press, 1965.
Ticknor, *Life, Letters, and Journal*	*Life, Letters, and Journal of George Ticknor*, ed. George S. Hillard, 2 vols. London, 1876.
Timperley	C. H. Timperley. *A Dictionary of Printers and Printing*. London, 1839 (including *The Printers' Manual*, 1838).
TLS	*Times Literary Supplement* (London).

The Carl H. Pforzheimer Library

Reference Sources

Trelawny, *Adventures*	Edward John Trelawny. *Adventures of a Younger Son*, ed. Edward Garnett. London, 1890.
Trelawny, *Letters*	*Letters of Edward John Trelawny*, ed. H. Buxton Forman. Oxford University Press, 1910.
Trelawny, *Recollections*	*Trelawny's Recollections of the Last Days of Shelley and Byron*, with an Introduction by Edward Dowden. London, 1931.
Trelawny, *Records*	Edward John Trelawny. *Records of Shelley, Byron, and the Author*, 2 vols. London, 1878.
Van Doren, *Peacock*	Carl Van Doren. *The Life of Thomas Love Peacock*. London, 1911.
Ward, *Keats*	Aileen Ward. *John Keats, The Making of a Poet*. New York, 1963.
Ward, *Men of the Reign*	*Men of the Reign. A Biographical Dictionary of Eminent Persons of British and Colonial Birth*, ed. Thomas Humphrey Ward. London, 1885 (facsimile reprint, Graz, Austria, 1968).
Wardle, *Wollstonecraft*	Ralph M. Wardle. *Mary Wollstonecraft, A Critical Biography*. University of Kansas Press, 1951.
Wheatley, *London*	Henry B. Wheatley. *London Past and Present, Its History, Associations, and Traditions*, 3 vols. London and New York, 1891.
White, *Shelley*	Newman Ivey White. *Shelley*, 2 vols. New York, 1940.
White, *Unextinguished Hearth*	Newman Ivey White. *The Unextinguished Hearth, Shelley and His Contemporary Critics*. Duke University Press, 1938.
Williams, *Journals and Letters*	*Maria Gisborne & Edward E. Williams, Shelley's Friends, Their Journals and Letters*, ed. Frederick L. Jones. University of Oklahoma Press, 1951.
Wise, *Shelley Library*	Thomas James Wise. *A Shelley Library, a Catalogue of Printed Books, Manuscripts and Autograph Letters by Percy Bysshe Shelley, Harriet Shelley and Mary Wollstonecraft Shelley*. London, Privately Printed, 1924.

INDEX OF NAMES

Boldface type is used to designate authors whose manuscripts are in The Carl H. Pforzheimer Library and are transcribed in the present volumes. The following abbreviations are used: TJH — Thomas Jefferson Hogg; TLP — Thomas Love Peacock; PBS — Percy Bysshe Shelley; MWS — Mary Wollstonecraft Shelley; EJT — Edward John Trelawny.

"A.B.," VI:664–665, 667–668, 939
Abbas, Shah, VI:988
Abbey, Eleanor Jones (Mrs. Richard), V:433
Abbey, Richard, V:434
Abbey Church Yard, Bath. *See* Bath
'Abd al-'Aziz, VI:988
Abderites, VI:764, 766, 769
'Abdullah, VI:988
Abdy, Lady, V:44
Abercrombie, John, V:131
Abinger, James Richard Scarlett, 8th Baron, V:344n; VI:599, 903
Academy, V:515
Adair, Robert, VI:1123
Adam, Charles, V:57
Adam, Sir Frederick, V:57
Adams, Dr., of Cork, V:495
Adams, George, V:478, 484
Adams, J. and G., V:484n
Addison, Mrs., V:74, 95, 311
Addison, Caroline Julia. *See* Trelawny, Caroline Julia Addison
Addison family, V:322
Adelaide of Saxe-Meiningen, V:499
Aderman, Ralph M., V:232n, 234n
Aemilia, Via, Italy, VI:598
Aeschylus, V:239, 304; VI:628
Afghanistan, VI:988
Aglietti, Dr. Francesco, VI:692, 693–694, 707
Aimèe, VI:543n, 546n. *See also* Romieux
Aire, France, VI:527
Aix-la-Chapelle, France, Peace of, VI:1003
Akbar, VI:713

Akbar, H.M.S., V:41n
Alacrity, H.M.S., V:56
Alaric, VI:563
Alba. *See* Biron, Allegra
Albania, V:16, 196
Albion House, Marlow: advertisements for, V:146n, 148n, 293n, 363–364; Claire Clairmont's life at, V:460–461; Hunts at, V:215, 227–228, 231, 292–293; sale, V:480, 481; Shelleys at, V:122, 145, 148, 200, 251, 255, 327, 491, 501; VI:521, 618; Tylecote and, V:516n. *See also* Marlow
Albrizzi, Isabella Teotochi, V:199
Album Wreath of Music and Literature for 1834, V:181, 182
Alcyone, myth of, V:236, 238
Alderson, Amelia. *See* Opie, Amelia Alderson
Aldis, Mr. and Mrs. Charles, VI:541
Alexander, Mr., VI:648
Alexander, William, V:297
Alexander the Great, V:237, 238; VI:527n, 1004
Alexanders & Collett, V:371
Alexandria, Egypt, VI:989
Alfieri, Vittorio, V:162, 163, 268, 269; VI:690, 691n, 766, 847, 849
Alfred (club), VI:1129
Allegra. *See* Biron, Allegra
Allen, Ralph, VI:571
Allman, T. and J., V:439n; VI:916n
Allsopp, Mr., V:322, 324–325
Allston, Washington, V:232, 234, 235
Alnwick, Northumberland, V:471
Alpha Cottage, St. John's Wood, London, V:226, 231

Index of Names

Alpha Road, St. John's Wood, London, V:231n

Alps, VI:553

Alsager, Thomas Massa, V:263, 316; VI:541, 554, 612, 791, 796; biography, V:264–266

Altarnun, Cornwall, V:39

Amboise, Georges d', VI:822

Ambrogetti, Giuseppe, VI:521

American Revolution, VI:1003, 1028

Amestris, VI:626, 630

Amiens, Peace of, VI:1003

Amphitrite, VI:553, 560

Anacreon, VI:1086

Analectic Magazine, VI:747

Ancona, Italy, V:60

Angeli, Helen Rossetti, V:60n, 188

Angoulême, Duc and Duchesse d', VI:529n

Angoulême party, VI:525, 529n

Angrisani, Carlo, VI:521

Anguisola, Giovanni, VI:547

Annual Register, VI:937, 982

Anthologia Palatina, V:213

Anti-Jacobin, V:494n

Apennines, Italy, V:454, 463; VI:1086n

Apocrypha, "Wisdom of Solomon," V:212

Apuleius, V:215, 330, 332

Aquila Nera, L', Leghorn, Italy, V:455; VI:599

Arabia, VI:988–989

Argos, Greece, V:54

Ariosto, Ludovico, *Orlando Furioso*, V:229, 314, 318; VI:610, 615, 616, 744

Aristophanes, V:299, 304; VI:922, 1087n; *The Clouds*, VI:627, 918–919, 921

Aristotle, V:299; *Poetics*, V:285, 307

Armstrong, Margaret, V:324

Arno (river), V:455; VI:598, 1066

Arnold, Matthew, *Thyrsis*, V:191

Arrian, *Historia Indica*, V:237, 238–239, 345

Artois, Compte d' (later Charles X), VI:529n

Ascham, John, VI:860n

Ashe, Thomas, V:285, 289

Asia, VI:1004, 1048

Athenaeum, V:61, 182n

Athens, Greece, V:54,56, 252; VI:1028

Auber, Peter, VI:710, 711, 719n

"Auburn, Miss." *See* Biron, Allegra

Augusta of Hesse-Casell, V:499

Aulnoy, Marie Catherine Le Jumel, Baronne d', V:284n

Australia, V:64, 260

Austria, VI:1038

"A.Z.," VI:665n

B

abylon, VI:632

Back Church Lane, Whitechapel, London, V:449

Bacon, Francis, VI:792, 946, 967, 970, 971, 973

Bagnères de Bigorre, France, V:35, 359

Bagni di Lucca, Italy, V:506; VI:547, 557, 558, 586, 591n, 598n, 615, 626, 639, 656, 658, 665, 675, 676, 680, 685, 783, 939; PBS's life at, VI:658–659, 676, 768; MWS's trip from, VI:679–680

Bagot, Richard, VI:547

Bahar, India, VI:718n

Baiae, Bay of, VI:764

Bailey, Benjamin, V:405, 407, 410, 411n, 435, 444; VI:809

Baker, Mr., V:193, 194

Baker, Carlos, VI:861

Baker Street, London, VI:606

Balbi, Signor, VI:599n

Baldi, Bernardino, VI:906, 909, 910

Baldwin, Robert, V:221; VI:743

Baldwin, Cradock and Joy, V:221, 393; VI:743

Ballygiblin Castle, Cork, Ireland, VI:897n

Baltimore, Md., V:357

Bandler, Samuel Wyllis, V:482

Barberino, Italy, V:454, 455; VI:598

Barbié du Bocage, J. D., *Recueil de Cartes Géographiques . . .*, V:464

Barclay, Rf, Co., V:493

Baring, Mr. and Mrs., V:59

Barlow, Sir George, VI:716

Barnes, Thomas, V:264

Barrie, James, VI:720n

Barry, Charles F., VI:942n

Barthelémy, Jean Jacques, VI:979; *Voyage du jeune Anacharsis . . .*, V:451, 464; VI:627, 628n

Barton, Bernard, V:369, 370–371; *Verses on the Death of Percy Bysshe Shelley*, V:370

Basinghall Street, London, V:449

Bassano. *See* da Ponte

Bassano del Grappa, Italy, VI:909n

Batavian Republic, VI:966n

Bate, Walter Jackson, VI:800

Bath, Somerset, V:283, 380; VI:571n; Shelleys at, V:8, 16, 18, 27, 32, 33, 80n, 87, 88, 89,

Index of Names

114, 402, 403; Trelawnys at, V:45, 71, 72, 80n, 94, 279, 280, 282; Whites at, V:71, 72, 95, 103, 139, 277, 280, 281, 282, 312, 313, 319, 323, 324; VI:582

Bawtry, Yorkshire, V:471

Baxter, Christina (Christy), V:334–335, 336, 338, 377, 389, 390, 391; letter to, from MWS (quoted), V:341–342

Baxter, Cowley, V:342, 377

Baxter, Elizabeth, V:342, 377

Baxter, Mary Ann, V:377n

Baxter, Robert, V:334, 340, 342, 377

Baxter, Thomas, V:368, 377

Baxter, William Thomas, V:32, 33, 36n, 146, 205, 218n, 472n; VI:520; and sc 440, V:372, 377; and Shelleys, V:293, 301–302, 327, 334, 335–336, 339–341, 346–347, 367–368, 371–372, 378–379, 381–385, 387, 388–389, 391, 506; VI:659, 1108; Booths live with, V:377; VI:705; correspondence, listed, V:337–339
  Letters to, from:
    MWS, V:332–333
    PBS, V:345–346, 371–372, 381–385
  Other letters by, to (quoted):
    Isabel Booth, V:339–341
    PBS, V:379–381
  Other letter to, from (quoted):
    MWS, V:507

Bayle, Pierre, VI:970

Beaconsfield, Buckinghamshire, V:299, 302, 377n

Beauchamp, Eliza Westbrook. *See* Westbrook, Eliza

Beaufort Buildings, Strand, London, V:125

Becks and English, V:200n

Bedford, Duke of, VI:822, 825

Bedford Row, London, V:440

Beethoven, Ludwig van, Mass in D, V:266

Begbrooke, Oxfordshire, VI:571

Beilby (Bilby), Mr., question of, VI:599–600

Belcher, James "Jem," VI:1120

Belcher, Tom, VI:1119, 1120

Belgium, VI:966n

Bell, John, VI:652, 768, 784, 873n

Bell and Bradfute, VI:835

Bell and Crown Inn, Holborn, London, V:438n

Bell Savage, Ludgate Hill, London, V:280, 283

Belle Assemblée, La, V:511; VI:597n

Bengal, VI:713–721 *passim,* 738

Bensley and Son, V:119, 222

Bentham, Jeremy, V:63, 316, 317; VI:946, 947, 953, 973, 1046, 1060; *Introduction to the Principles and Morals of Legislation,* VI:974

Bentinck, William Charles Augustus, V:44

Bentinck, William Henry, VI:716

Bentley, Richard, V:60, 127–128

Berechurch Hall, Essex, VI:1119

Berg Collection, The. *See* New York Public Library

Berkeley, George, VI:850, 946, 971

Bertini, Francesco, VI:658n

Berwick-on-Tweed, Northumberland, V:471

Bestermann, Theodore, VI:522n, 924

Bethune, France, VI:527

Bevan, Joseph Vallence, V:233; and Godwin, VI:745–746, 747; letter to, from Godwin, VI:745

Bible, quoted, VI:703, 705, 1002

Billing, John, V:303

Bion, "Lament for Adonis," V:191; "Lament for," V:190–193

Birmingham, Warwick, VI:937, 999

Biron (Byron), Allegra (Alba), V:115, 192, 451–452, 454, 460, 491, 492; VI:606, 678; birth, V:82, 83–84; Booth on, V:391; Byron on, V:199, 292, 364–365; VI:748, 750, 751; in Este, VI:689, 690, 692, 694; in Venice, VI:675–676, 679; sent to Byron, V:462, 513; VI:577–578, 598; PBS on, V:196, 197, 241–242, 243, 244, 290, 291, 361–362, 363; VI:542, 543, 546, 564–566, 568–569, 574, 575

Bisham Abbey, Marlow, V:476; VI:684

Bisham Wood, V:147

Bishop's Castle, Shropshire, VI:999

Bishopsgate, Berkshire, V:28, 35; VI:652, 802, 804

Black, John (1783–1855), VI:527n

Black, John, of Colyton, *Life of Torquato Tasso . . .,* VI:591

Black Dwarf, The, V:163, 245

Black Swan Inn, York, VI:802, 804

Blackstone, Sir William, V:162

Blackwood, William, VI:743n

Blackwood's Edinburgh Magazine, V:162, 360n, 472, 503; VI:742n, 743, 931n, 1093

Blaetterman, Mr., V:234

Blagden, Isa, V:67

Index of Names

Blainey, Ann, V:126n

Blake, William, V:60, 68, 439n; VI:614n, 643

Bland, Robert, VI:1135

Blessington, Marguerite, Countess of, V:66

Bloomsbury Square, London, V:441

Blunden, Edmund, V:126n, 406n; VI:830

Boas, Louise Schutz, V:86n

Boccaccio, Giovanni, VI:610, 611, 616

Boccella, Jane, Marchesa, V:61

Bodleian Library, Oxford: PBS's copies of *Literary Pocket-Book*, VI:742n; PBS's manuscripts, V:144–145, 148–150, 152, 171–172, 180, 184, 186–187, 188, 206, 211–212, 420n; VI:547n, 630, 640, 658n, 678, 786, 864, 898, 1068, 1069n, 1070, 1072, 1086, 1102n; MWS's transcript of *Philosophical View of Reform*, VI:955, 956; Shelley-Rolls bequest, VI:638; Williams' notebook, VI:832

Boehm, Edgar, V:68

Boiardo, Matteo Maria, VI:610, 616, 744; *Orlando Innamorato*, V:229, 318

Boileau-Despréaux, Nicolas, V:411n, VI:979

Boinville, Alfred, VI:797

Boinville, Harriet Collins, V:32, 36n; VI:797

Boinville family, V:98; VI:572, 764, 769

Boler, M., V:328

Bolingbroke, Henry St. John, Viscount, VI:973

Bolivar, Simon, V:195

Bolivar (boat), V:49, 50

Bologna, Italy, V:454; VI:598, 674, 679, 708, 763, 812, 816

Bolt Court, Fleet Street, London, V:222

Bombay, India, V:41, 477; VI:713, 722, 723

Bonaparte, Jerome, V:499

Bonaparte, Napoleon. *See* Napoleon I

Bond, William H., VI:799

Bond Street, London, V:497

Booth, Catherine, V:335n, 337, 342

Booth, Charles, V:377

Booth, David, V:146; and Godwin, VI: 704–705, 903; and Shelleys, V:301, 302, 327, 334, 336, 337, 346, 379, 383, 384, 385, 387, 506–508; VI:659; correspondence, listed, V:338–339; described, V:386–387

Letter to, from:
    Godwin, VI:703–704
Other letters by, to (quoted):
    Isabel Booth, V:390–392
    PBS, V:388–389

Other letter to, from (quoted):
    Isabel Booth, V:341
    lives with Baxter, V:377; VI:705; on Albion House, V:200; works, V: 386, 387; VI:704–705

Booth, Edwin, V:357

Booth, Isabel (Isabella) Baxter, V:200, 377, 491; and MWS, V:301, 333, 334–337, 339–341, 342, 347, 382, 384, 385, 386n; and PBS, V:385; VI:659; correspondence, listed, V:337–339

Letter to, from:
    MWS, V:505–506
Other letter by, to (quoted):
    David Booth, V:341
Other letters to, from (quoted):
    W. T. Baxter, V:339–341, 379
    David Booth, V:390–392

Booth, Isabel (daughter of Isabel Baxter Booth), V:337, 505

Booth, Margaret Baxter, V:334

Boschini, G. B., V:344n

Boscombe Manor, V:67, 69

Boswell, James, the younger, VI:771

Boulogne, France, V:72

Bourdillon, Pierre, V:21n

Bourg, France, VI:832

Bouverie Street, Fleet Street, London, V:139

Bowles, William Lisle, V:411n

Boxiana, VI:1121

Boyer, Jean Pierre, VI:990

Bracknell, Berkshire, V:343

Bradford, Yorkshire, VI:999

Brandreth, Jeremiah, VI:1049

Branston, Virginia, VI:798

Brawne, Fanny, V:414

Brenta (river), VI:679

Brereton, Catherine Trelawny (later de Cadignan), V:62, 311

Brereton, Charles Trelawny, V:39, 40, 61, 91, 94, 279, 283

Brereton, Charlotte Trelawny (later Trevanion), V:62, 311

Brereton, Harry Trelawny, V:39n, 61, 91, 279, 283

Brereton, Maria Hawkins Trelawny, V:57, 61–63, 72, 79, 81, 95, 311

Brereton, Mira Trelawny (later d'Estampes), V:62, 311

Breslau, Poland, VI:982

Index of Names

Brewer, Luther, VI:742n

Brewster, Sir David, VI:767n

Brewster, W., V:510, 511

Brezé, Seneschal of, VI:822

Brighton, Sussex, VI:817

Bristol, Gloucestershire, V:72, 156; College Street, V:43

British Critic, VI:1135n

British Institution, VI:614

British Museum: Claire Clairmont's journal at, V:460, 461; PBS's manuscripts at, V:152, 172; VI:893n, 1070, 1074; Williams' journal at, VI:832; Wise collection, VI:1068n

British Stage and Literary Cabinet, VI:682

Brittany, V:439

Broadhurst, Mr., V:282

Brooke, Stopford A., VI:956

Brookfield, Jane Octavia, V:46

Brooks, George, V:121n

Brooks, Son and Dixon, V:19n, 121–122, 338, 481, 516; VI:653, 654, 655, 666n, 782n, 928, 939, 940–944, 1095

  Autograph checks to, from:

    PBS, V:120–121, 302, 326–327, 367, 448–449, 466–467, 488–490, 496, 508–510, 513–515; VI:653, 668

    Thomas Hume, VI:695

  Letters to, from:

    PBS, VI:800–801, 937–939

Brougham, Henry, V:156; VI:759

Broughton, Lord. *See* Hobhouse, John Cam

Broughton, James: and Godwin, VI:681–682, 684, 771, 772; biography, VI:682; letter to, from Godwin, VI:681

Brown, Charles A., V:59, 60, 260, 413, 434, 444; VI:518, 799, 809

Browne, Hamilton, V:54

Browne, Sir Thomas, VI:698, 699n

Browning, Elizabeth Barrett, V:60; VI:914

Browning, Robert, V:60, 67–68, 399

Brunswick Square, London, V:327

Brydges, Sir Samuel Egerton, V:494

Buchy Head, VI:817

Buckinghamshire, George Robert Hobart, Earl of, VI:717

Budbrooke, Warwick, V:297

Budge Row, London, V:450

Buenos Aires, Argentina, V:322, 324

Bull and Mouth, Aldergate, London, V:471

Buller, Charles, V:64, 67

Bullock, William, V:281, 283

Bulwer-Lytton, Edward George Earle, V:66; *Pelham*, V:127

Bunch, Mother, V:281, 283, 321, 324. *See also* Tolson, Mrs.

Bungay, Suffolk, VI:958

Burdett, Sir Francis, VI:563

Burgate House, V:97, 98; VI:569

Burges, Sir James Bland, V:494

Burghersh, Priscilla Anne, Lady, V:59

Burke, Edmund, V:477

Burley, John, V:43n, 95n

Burley, Maria Julia Trelawny. *See* Trelawny, Maria Julia

Burlington House, V:252

Burney, Charles, Jr., V:360

Burney, Charles Parr, V:355, 360

Burney, Fanny, V:71; VI:541, 571

Burney, Martin, V:316; VI:541

Burney, William, V:42

Burns, Robert, "Jolly Beggars," V:390

Burr, Aaron, V:357n, 359

Burton (Haliburton), James, V:327

Butler, Pierce, V:64

Buxton, John, *Byron and Shelley*, V:133

Byron, Allegra. *See* Biron, Allegra

Byron, Anne Isabella (Annabella Milbanke), Lady, VI:749, 758–761; letter by, to Reverend Richard Wallis, VI:757–758

Byron, Augusta Ada (daughter of Byron), VI:750

Byron, George Anson, VI:749

"Byron, Major George Gordon," V:9

Byron, George Gordon Byron, 6th Baron:

  and "Angling" theme, VI:1078–79

  and Allegra Biron, V:82–84, 199, 229, 241–244, 292, 364–365, 513; VI:576–578, 675, 679, 690, 694, 748, 750–751

  and Claire Clairmont, V:19, 130, 197, 227, 229, 242–243, 466; VI:562–563, 567, 568, 576–577, 678

  and Teresa Guiccioli, VI:811–816

  and Earl of Guilford, V:271

  and F. Hodgson, VI:1128–30

  and Hunt, V:50, 291, 294–295, 401; VI:575, 678, 701–703, 916

and J. H. Merivale, VI:1134–36
and J. W. Polidori, V:268–271; VI:778n, 780
and *Quarterly Review*, VI:933
and Schiller, V:309n
and PBS, V:15–17, 19–21, 51–52, 82–83, 85–86, 104–105, 107–108, 109, 113, 114, 115, 195–200, 239, 241–248, 290–296, 361–364, 366–367, 425; VI:542–543, 546, 548, 563–569, 574–576, 578–579, 859, 861, 862n; in Venice, VI:586, 591, 592n, 673–676, 679–680, 689–690, 694, 706–708, 764, 767, 768, 864
and Trelawny, V:37, 42, 47–48, 52–55, 67, 195; VI:671–672
Booth on, V:392
boxing, VI:1119, 1121
death, V:55; VI:760, 914
health, V:248
incest theme, V:162, 163
letter style, V:437
Letters by, to:
  Thomas Claughton, VI:1136–38
  Doctor [   ], VI:1123
  Louis Fauvel, VI:1126–28
  Teresa Guiccioli, VI:811–814
  John Hanson, VI:1122
  Francis Hodgson, VI:1128
  John "Gentleman" Jackson, VI:1118–19
  ? [Matthew G.] Lewis, VI:1139
  John H. Merivale, VI:1134–35
  John Murray, address leaf, V:494–496; VI:1131–32
  Samuel Rogers, VI:1130
Letters to, from:
  PBS, V:15–18, 82–83, 195–197, 241–243, 290–292, 361–363; VI:542–543, 563–567, 574–576, 689–690, 706
love affairs, VI:566, 567n, 568
Manuscripts, miscellaneous:
  Codicil to will, VI:747–749
  Emendations of *The Bride of Abydos*, VI:1132
  "On Parting," VI:1124–25
  "To E. N. Long," VI:1113–18
on *Christabel*, V:21
on Elgin Marbles, VI:1126–28
on Keats, V:419
political sympathies, VI:946
portraits, V:123, 130–133; VI:1130–31

sale of Newstead Abbey, VI:1137–38
theater plans, VI:1139–40
travels, V:18–19, 84, 199, 230, 256; VI:1122–23
wills, VI:749
mentioned, V:49, 56, 68, 118, 146n, 154, 252, 257, 315, 359, 401, 405, 417, 420, 424n, 448, 452, 459, 460, 462, 463; VI:555, 614, 628, 691n, 768, 769, 791, 794, 922, 927, 970n, 1055n, 1060, 1103

WORKS
  Beppo, V:248; VI:575, 578
  The Bride of Abydos, V:162, 246; VI:671; emendations in, VI:1132–34
  Childe Harold's Pilgrimage: Cantos I, II, V:248, 366; VI:1125, 1127, 1131; Canto III, V:86, 198, 242, 245, 246, 247, 291, 366; Canto IV, V:291, 362, 366, 393, 394; VI:592, 597, 662, 674, 863
  The Corsair, V:246; VI:671
  The Curse of Minerva, V:248; and sc 561, VI:1127
  "Darkness," V:198n
  "The Destruction of Sennacherib," V:248
  "Il Diavalo Inamorato," V:309n
  Don Juan, V:248, 295; VI:1121–22
  English Bards and Scotch Reviewers, V:248, 367n; VI:651, 1127n, 1129
  "Epistle to Augusta," VI:1136
  The Giaour, V:248; VI:671, 1130, 1132
  Hebrew Melodies, V:247–248
  Hints from Horace, VI:1127n
  Hours of Idleness, VI:1117
  The Lament of Tasso, V:268, 270, 290, 294–295, 421; VI:591, 863
  Lara, V:242, 245, 246, 247
  "Maid of Athens, ere we part," VI:1125
  Manfred, V:162, 198, 241, 242, 245, 246, 290–291, 294–295
  Monody on the Death of Sheridan, VI:701
  Parisina, V:162, 246; VI:671
  The Prisoner of Chillon, V:198n, 242, 245, 246, 247
  "Prometheus," VI:844
  "The Prophecy of Dante," VI:993n
  "She Walks in Beauty," V:248
  "Sonnet on Chillon," V:198
  "To Lesbia" ("To Julia"), VI:1118
  The Vision of Judgment, V:248
  Waltz, V:156; VI:778n, 1130

Index of Names

Cà Zen, VI:815
Cadell, Robert, VI:775
Cadell, Mrs. Robert, VI:775n
Cadell, W. A., VI:548
Cadell & Davies, VI:743
Cadignan, Charles Duplaix de, V:62
Cadiz, Spain, VI:984
Caerhays, Cornwall, V:62
Calais, France, VI:517, 524, 527, 553, 966
Calderon de la Barca, Pedro, V:504n; VI:986, 1081; *El magico prodigioso*, V:47
Caligula, V:452, 465
Camberwell, Surrey, V:450
Cambrai, France, VI:527; cathedral, VI:588
Cambridge, Adolphus, Duke of, V:499
Cambridge, VI:1129; University, V:152, 468n; VI:922, 1128
Cambridge Apostles, V:399
Camden Town, London, VI:907
Cameron, Kenneth Neill, V:3, 423n, 480n; VI:931
Campbell, Mr. (American), V:64
Campbell, Mr. (friend of EJT), V:75, 318, 320
Campbell, Thomas, V:382, 385; VI:595, 700, 1129; "Lochiel's Warning," VI:993; "Pleasures of Hope," VI:1130
Camporese, Violante, V:461; VI:583
Canada, Augusta White in, V:75–76, 96, 314, 325
Candaux, Jean-Daniel, V:21n
Caninius Rufus, VI:755, 756
Canning, George, V:494n; VI:573, 719–720, 771
Cannon Street, London, V:377n
Canova, Antonio, V:227, 231, 252, 414
Canterbury, Kent, V:5
Capuccini, I, Este, VI:679, 691, 694
Capurro, Niccolò, V:421–422
Carlevariis, Luca, VI:554
Carlile, Richard, VI:854n, 901, 952, 1058, 1084, 1085n, 1109n; letter by, VI:1084n
Carlyle, Thomas, V:260
Caroline, Queen of England, V:156
Carpenter, Mr., V:303
Carr, Sir John, V:494; VI:756
Cartwright, John, VI:1050
Cary, Henry, VI:631n
Cary, Henry Francis, V:342, 343–344; VI:631n
Casa Bertini, VI:658n
Casa (Villa) Magni, V:49, 79; sketch, V:181–182

Cascine, the, VI:1069
Castle, John, V:244; VI:1049
Castle Eden, Seaham, Durham, VI:758
Castle Street, London, V:234
Castlereagh, Robert Stewart, Viscount, V:266n
Castro, Guillen de, V:117–118, 119, 120
Catherine, VI:924
Catherine Street, London, VI:885
Catlin, M. R., promissory note to, from Godwin, V:223–224
Catlins & Co., V:223
Cato, VI:552
Caxton, Bedford, V:471
Cefn Ila, Usk, Monmouthshire, V:66, 67, 77
Celebrated Fairy Tales of Mother Bunch . . ., The, V:283n
Cenci, Beatrice, VI:873, 897, 1020
Cenci family, manuscript history, V:455, 464; VI:873, 874, 897–898
Cervantes, Miguel de, VI:986; *El Ingenioso Hidalgo Don Quixote de la Mancha*, V:504; VI:684, 687
Ceylon, V:269
Chalmers, George, VI:770, 771, 772n
Châlons-sur-Marne, France, VI:527–528, 832
Chambery, France, VI:543, 546
Chamonix (Chamouni), France, V:230, 315
Champagny, Philippe de, VI:822
Champion, V:435, 438, 472n; article on PBS, V:167n; Keats writes for, V:428, 434; VI:806
Chancery, Court of, V:5, 6; VI:1028, 1062. *See also* Westbrook vs. Shelley
Chapeau Rouge, Le, Dijon, VI:528
Chapman, George, *Homer*, V:265
Chappe, telegraph, V:320
Charles I, King of England, VI:711, 967, 1059, 1061
Charles II, King of England, VI:967, 981, 998, 1050
Charles IV, King of Spain, VI:984
Charlotte, V:277, 278, 279, 311, 322, 325
Charlotte, Princess: death, V:125n, 324, 499; medals for, V:434, 442
Charlotte Sophia, Queen of England, V:324n
Charters, Thomas, V:497; VI:944; judgment against PBS, V:1–4, 483
Chatterton, Thomas, V:423
Chaucer, Geoffrey, VI:911, 965
Chaumont, France, VI:528

Chaworth, Mary Musters, VI:1115, 1116, 1118
Chelsfield, Kent, VI:650
Cheltenham, Gloucestershire, V:266, 276
Cheltnam, Charles Smith, V:262
Cheltnam, Jacintha Shelley Leigh Hunt, V:262
"Chequers," VI:602n, 686
Chertsey, Surrey, VI:602
Chester Street, Grosvenor Place, London, VI:573
Chiappa, G. B., VI:658n
Chigi Palace, Rome, VI:610
China, VI:986, 1004
Chipping Norton, Oxfordshire, V:5
Christian II, King of Denmark, VI:983
Christie, Alexander Henry, V:201, 204, 216, 217
Christophe, Henri, VI:990
Christ's Hospital, London, VI:558n, 807n, 922
Cibber, Colley, *The Refusal*, V:282
Cicero, VI:910, 919; "Pro C. Rabirio," V:308, 309
Cid, The. *See* Corneille; Hunt
Clairmont, Charles, V:334, 335, 355; and PBS, V:29, 32, 35–36, 121, 359; VI:944, 1069

Clairmont, Claire (Clara Mary Jane):
  and Allegra, V:82, 83, 84, 115, 192n, 196, 241–242, 362, 364, 451–452, 454, 460, 462; VI:543, 546, 577, 578, 675–676, 694
  and Byron, V:19, 130, 197, 227, 229, 242, 243, 291, 466; VI:562–563, 567, 568, 576–577, 678
  and Hobhouse's visit to Hunt, VI:556, 562
  and PBS, V:32, 33, 35, 88, 107–108, 114–115, 165, 337; PBS on Allegra, Byron, and, VI:564–566, 568, 574–575
  and Trelawny, V:47, 48, 56, 58, 60, 63, 65, 66, 70, 462
  Booth on, V:385, 391, 392
  in Bath, V:87, 89, 401
  in London, V:292, 327, 328, 336, 479, 491, 492
  Journal, V:479, 491, 497; VI:527, 546, 587, 591, 873, 915n, 953
  learns German, V:463; VI:527n
  Letters to, from:
    PBS, V:31–33, 86–87; VI:692–693
  life at Albion House, V:451, 460–461
  Manuscript: Journal, text, V:450–458; discussed, V:459–463
  music, V:263, 267, 460–461; VI:519, 522

portrait, VI:891n
  pregnancy, V:16, 19, 100
  reading, V:464–466; VI:591
  MWS on, V:342
  "Silly thoughtless Teresa!" VI:577
  travels, V:452–455, 461–463; VI:526, 527–529, 546, 598, 666, 673–674, 676, 678–679, 690, 693, 694, 708
  mentioned, V:45n, 143, 257, 261, 298, 333, 340, 355, 359, 365n, 380, 410, 416, 420, 484, 500, 507n; VI:537n, 555, 562, 579, 586n, 599, 609, 611, 615, 658, 689, 739, 750, 780, 793, 897, 915n, 1068

Clare Court, London, V:450
Clarence, William Henry, Duke of, V:499
Clarendon, Edward Hyde, Earl of, *The History of the Rebellion*, VI:951–952, 953
Clark, David Lee, VI:641, 642
Clark, James, V:414
Clark, William, V:43
Clarke, Miss, V:224
Clarke, Charles Cowden, V:125, 265, 272; VI:617, 741n, 744, 745, 805n, 1060; and Hunt and Coulson, V:316–317; and Keats, V:401, 403, 413n; VI:808–809
Clarke, Edith Nicholls, VI:720
Clarke, John, V:438
Clarke, Mary Victoria Novello, VI:744, 809n
Claughton, Thomas, VI:749; letter to, from Byron, VI:1136–38
Clawson, John L., V:9, 15
Clay & Sons, Richard, VI:958
Clayton & Kingsland, V:358n
Cleasby, East Gilling, Yorkshire, VI:922
Clement's Inn, Strand, London, V:479; VI:682
Cleobulus, V:289n
Clough, Arthur, VI:914
Cobbett, William, V:163, 245, 379; VI:951, 1019, 1060, 1065; *Paper Against Gold*, VI:1014; *Twopenny Trash*, VI:915
Cobbett's Weekly Political Register, V:250, 253–254, 255, 333, 368; VI:783, 900, 923, 925
Cobourne, Mary Duff, VI:1115, 1116, 1118
Cogni, Margarita, V:130n
Cohen. *See* Palgrave, Francis
Colburn, Henry, V:60, 127; and Godwin and Polidori's *Vampyre*, VI: 777, 778, 780–781; letter to, from Godwin (quoted), VI:780

Colburn and Bentley, V:127

Coleman, Thomas, V:43–45, 72, 74, 80, 81, 94, 102

Coleman Street, London, VI:655n

Coleridge, E. H., VI:1125, 1127n, 1132, 1133

Coleridge, H. N., VI:915n

Coleridge, John Taylor, VI:617; review of *Laon and Cythna* and *Revolt of Islam*, V:448; VI:931–932, 933

Coleridge, Samuel Taylor, V:399, 407, 411n, 448, 450; VI:558n, 682, 691, 849, 931, 971, 992, 1015, 1129; lecture on Donne, Dante, and Milton, V:344; VI:915n; *Christabel*, VI:781; *Christabel; Kubla Khan, a Vision; The Pains of Sleep*, reviews, V:17, 20, 21; *France: An Ode*, VI:1117

College Hill, London, V:368, 377

Collier, John Payne, VI:684; Godwin's challenge to, VI:770–772; letter to, from Godwin, VI:769–770

Collins, E., VI:541

Colman, George (the elder), *The Comedies of Terence*, V:451, 465

Cologne, Germany, VI:588

Colonna, Palazzo, VI:873, 874n

Colossus, H.M.S., V:41n, 42

Como, Lake, Italy, VI:543, 546–548, 549, 552, 565, 566, 567, 575, 576, 584

Companion, VI:617, 843, 844

Condorcet, Antoine de Caritat, Marquis de, VI:946

Consentia (Cosenza), Italy, VI:553, 563

Consistory (Ecclesiastical) Court, V:45

Constable, Archibald, V:22, 23–24, 25–26, 30, 33, 34–35, 158, 357, 366, 494, 498; VI:740, 770, 772, 775–777, 811; letters to, from Godwin, VI:774–775, 809–811

Constable, Charlotte Neale, V:26

Constable & Co.: and *Mandeville*, VI:772–773; letter to, from Godwin, VI:773–774; memorandum to, from Godwin, V:22–23

Constance, Peace of, VI:964

Constantinople, VI:988, 989, 1058, 1123

Contemporary, The, V:69

Cooper, Mary Fairlie, V:357

Cooper, Mr. and Mrs. Thomas, V:355

Cooper, Thomas A., V:355–361; letter to, from Godwin, V:354–355

Corfu, V:57, 269

Corgan, Michael, V:5

Corgan, Paget, and Matthews, V:5

Cork, Ireland, V:495

Corinth, Greece, V:54

Corneille, Pierre, V:118; VI:611, 825, 979

Cornelia, H.M.S., V:41n

Cornelius Nepos, VI:629n

Cornwall, V:39, 59, 77, 320

"Cornwall, Barry" (pseud.). *See* Procter, Bryan Waller

Cornwall Road, London, V:261

Cornwallis, Charles Cornwallis, 1st Marquis, VI:714, 718n, 721

Cornwallis, H.M.S., V:41n

Corry, H., VI:781

"Coterie, A.," *The Philosopher's Jest Book*, V:155, 156n

Cottage Crescent, Bath. *See* Bath

Coulson ("Colson"), Walter, V:100, 233, 314, 410, 474, 476, 477; VI:608, 612, 613, 615, 616, 720, 740, 791, 796, 847, 917, 923, 936, 1060; biography, V:287–288, 316–318

Coutts, John & Co., VI:941n

Coutts, Thomas & Co., V:127; and PBS's finances, VI:938–943 *passim*

Covent Garden, London, V:491, 515; VI:555, 803

Covent Garden Theatre, London, V:252, 253, 279, 356, 428, 434, 464; VI:744, 840, 843, 857, 896, 929, 1139

Covert, Colonel, V:75

Coward's Academy, Hoxton, V:355

Cowper, William, VI:1002; *The Task*, VI:671n

Cox, (?) George, VI:817, 830, 831

Crabbe, George, *The Borough*, VI:1019

Craig Leith, VI:775

Crashaw, Richard, VI:589, 914n

Creevey, Thomas, V:499n

Cribb, Tom, VI:1121

Crichton, James, VI:720n

Cripps, Charles, V:435

Croce di Malta, La, Leghorn, Italy, VI:599

Croce d'Oro, La, Leghorn, Italy, VI:599n

Croesus, VI:620, 623, 631

Croker, John Wilson, VI:932, 1055; review of *Endymion*, VI:742

Croker, Thomas Crofton, V:495; VI:931n

Croly (Crowley), George (?), V:232, 234–235, 236

Cromwell, Oliver, VI:602, 686, 998

Cromwell, Richard, VI:998

Index of Names

Cropley, Bill, VI:1119, 1120

Crosse, Michael, V:40

Crown and Anchor Tavern, VI:539, 540, 542, 835n

Curran, Amelia: and Godwin, V:512; VI:540–541; illness, VI:838; in Italy, V:500; letters to, from Godwin, V:497; (?) VI:539; portraits of Shelleys, V:500; VI:891n

Curran, J. B., V:498

Curran, John Philpot, V:358, 386, 497, 498, 500n; VI:540, 608, 615, 797

Curran, S. and R., V:498

Curran, William Henry, V:498, 499n; VI:792, 796–797

Curtis, John, V:450n

Curtis, Thomas, the stationer, V:218, 224, 449, 450; VI:836

Curtis, T. and G., V:450n

Cyrus the Great, VI:631

Daily Telegraph, V:260

d'Alembert, Jean le Rond, VI:519, 522

Dante Alighieri, V:60, 163; VI:566, 610, 616, 687n, 740, 744, 915n, 983; and PBS, V:212, 342, 343–344, 397, 461; VI:587, 647, 691

da Ponte, Francesco Bassano, VI:909n

da Ponte, Giovanni Battista Bassano, VI:909n

da Ponte, Girolamo Bassano, VI:909n

da Ponte, Jacopo Bassano, VI:906, 909n, 910

da Ponte, Leandro Bassano, VI:909n

Darius I, VI:623, 631, 632, 1004

Darius, III, VI:1004

Darlington, Durham, V:471

Darlington Cottage, V:277, 278

D'Arvilles, V:97, 98, 501, 505

Darwin, Charles, Origin of Species, V:68

Davenant, Sir William, V:455, 463; VI:698

Davide, Giovanni, V:461; VI:583

Davis, Mr., VI:775

Davison, Alexander, William Noel, Templer Middleton, and Wedgwood, V:126–127

Davison, Thomas, V:24, 224; VI:1134

"Davus," VI:593, 597n

de Beer, Sir Gavin, V:21n

De Gibler. See "Byron, Major"

De la Rue & Co., V:181

de Ricci, Seymour: on SC 374, V:9, 15; on PBS autographs, V:121–122; on PBS's letters to Ollier, V:129; SC 554, VI:1100

Deioces, VI:620

"Demogorgon," V:284, 287–288, 502, 503

Denham, V:43

Denman, Thomas, V:156

Denmark, VI:983

Dennet, Misses, V:434

Descartes, René, VI:970

d'Estampes, Viscount, V:62

Devonshire, V:410, 437

D'Holbach, Paul Henri, Baron ("Mirabaud"), V:21n

Dickens, Charles, Great Expectations, VI:807n

Didot, Firmin, types of, V:420, 421n

Dieppe, France, VI:817, 821, 831

Dignam, Thomas, V:478, 479

Dijon, France, VI:528, 831

Dilke, Charles Wentworth, V:434, 444; VI:809

Dilke, Mrs. Charles Wentworth, V:434

Dillon, Lord, VI:934n

Diodorus, VI:629

Diogenes Laertius, Life of Plato, V:212, 213; VI:552

Dionysius of Halicarnassus, V:255

Diphilus, VI:689n

Disraeli, Benjamin, V:68

Dodgson, Beryl, V:261

Dogherty, Dan, VI:1120

Dole, France, VI:831

Domenichino (Domenico Zampieri), VI:828

Don Juan (boat), V:49, 50, 51, 181n; VI:829

Doncaster, Yorkshire, V:471

Donne, John, V:344; Hunt on, VI:911–912, 914–915

Dorant's Hotel, London, VI:1129

D'Orsay, Alfred, Comte, V:66

Dorset Street, London, V:377

Douai, France, VI:524–525, 527

Dover, Kent, V:516; VI:653

Dover Street, London, V:223

Dowden, Edward, V:116n, 275, 458, 459, 460, 480, 504; VI:585, 900n; and Philosophical View of Reform, VI:956, 957, 958

Downing Street, London, V:203

Drake, Nathan, Shakespeare and His Times VI:555, 562

Draper, Augusta White. See White, Augusta

Draper, Kathleen, V:76

Draper, Molly, V:76

Draper, William Henry, V:65, 75, 76, 77, 325

Dresden, Germany, VI:982

Drummond, Sir William, VI:911, 946; *Academical Questions*, VI:573
Drury, Henry, VI:1135
Drury, Michael, VI:836
Drury Lane Theatre, V:252, 253, 279, 357, 410n, 428, 433; VI:840, 842, 843, 881, 885, 1139
Dryden, John, VI:542
Dublin, Ireland, VI:579, 650
DuBois, Edward: and TLP, VI:592–595, 596–597, 754–756; biography, VI:595–596; letters by, to TLP, VI:592–595, 754–755 works, VI:595, 756
Du Cane, Peter, V:5
du Chaillu, Paul Belloni, V:46
Dumas, Alexandre, V:61
Dunbar, E. Lothian, Scotland, V:471
Dundas, Henry, 1st Viscount Melville, VI:715, 716
Dundee, Scotland, V:334, 335
Durham, Durham, V:285, 471
Dusautoy, John Abbott, VI:751, 754

Ealing Grove, Middlesex, VI:760
Easingwold, Yorkshire, V:471
East India Chambers, V:201, 204, 217, 218
East India Company, V:355, 477; VI:682; Indian land taxation settlement, VI:712–719, 738; Lamb at, VI:558; TLP at, V:492; VI:522, 552, 663, 688, 709–712, 719–721, 722, 723, 737, 792, 803, 895, 921, 925
Eclectic Review, VI:1086n, 1135n
Edinburgh, Scotland, V:24, 356, 471, 472, 473, 487n; VI:835
Edinburgh Magazine, VI:747, 770, 772
Edinburgh Review, V:26n; VI:700, 759; on *Christabel*, V:17, 20, 21; and Hunt, V:119; on *Hyperion*, V:416n; on innovative poets, V:448; on *Mandeville*, V:218; on *Manfred*, V:290–291, 294
Edward III, King of England, VI:1050
Egan, Pierce, VI:1121
Egremont, Lord, VI:1140
Egypt, VI:624, 632, 988, 989, 1028
Egyptian Hall, Piccadilly, London, V:283
Eldon, John Scott, Earl of, V:87, 197, 297; orders, VI:647–649
Elgin, Thomas Bruce, 7th Earl of, marbles, V:249, 252; VI:1127, 1128

Elias, "Dutch Sam," VI:1120
Elise. *See* Foggi, Elise [   ]
Elizabeth, Princess, V:497, 499–500
Elizabeth I, Queen of England, V:39; VI:712, 967
Ellenborough, Edward Law, 1st Baron, V:164
Ellerker, Edward, VI:829n
Elliston, Robert William, V:120; VI:843, 881, 885
"Elphin Knight" (pseud.). *See* PBS: WORKS
Elston, Mr., V:203, 204, 217
Enfield, Middlesex, V:438
Engels, Friedrich, VI:999
England, Bank of, VI:1003, 1004
Epaminondas, VI:629
Epicharis, VI:985
Epictetus, V:239
Epsom Downs, VI:1120
Erdman, David V., VI:946
Erostratus (Herostratus, Eratostratus), VI:525, 527n
Esdaile, Ianthe Shelley (daughter of PBS), V:86n; guardianship, V:6, 85, 98n, 197, 297, 481n; VI:648–649, 650, 652, 695, 978; in PBS's will, V:107, 114, 115, 116
Este, Italy, VI:674, 675, 679, 680, 689–691, 694, 708, 763, 765, 783, 851, 858, 859, 862n, 863, 864, 1024
Eton, VI:829, 931, 933n
Euphrates (river), VI:688
Euripides, V:163, 304; VI:584, 764, 766, 803, 804n, 805, 921; PBS's translation of *The Cyclops*, VI:1081, 1086–87, 1101n
Europe, hotel de l', Dieppe, VI:818
Europe, hotel de l', Lyon, VI:528
Eustace, John Chetwode, V:249; *Tour through Italy*, V:253n
Evans, V:201, 218
Evans, J. H., V:113, 116, 117
Evvenus (river), V:55
Examiner, V:125, 332n, 340; VI:540n, 556, 806, 848, 854, 920, 923, 925, 937n, 1107, 1108; and Hobhouse, VI:563; and H. L. Hunt, VI:795, 808, 888; and *Mask of Anarchy*, VI:1081, 1083; articles on religion, VI:1109n; Hazlitt's *Letter to William Gifford, Esq.* in, VI:617, 743, 797; Leigh Hunt and, VI:881, 884, 912, 916; on *Christabel*, V:20; on *Mandeville*, V:25, 434; on Moore, VI:701–702; on Murray, V:222; on Peter-

loo, VI:892, 896; on riots in Dundee, V:335; on PBS, V:411, 448; VI:841, 932; on Spain, VI:984; on James Williams, V:164; sent to PBS, VI:603, 604, 783; PBS to, on R. Carlile, VI:901, 952, 1084; PBS's poems in, V:160, 162, 401, 402

Exeter, Devon, V:428, 438n; VI:807

"Extract of a Letter from Geneva," VI:779

Ezzelino da Romano, VI:983

Fabricius, V:552

Fairley, Mr., VI:775

Fairlie, James, V:357

Falconet, M. and Mme., VI:768

Falmouth, Cornwall, V:438n; VI:1123

Fano, Italy, VI:708

Farquhar, Sir Walter, V:487

Faulder, Robert, V:449

Faulder, Thomas, V:449

Faulder, William, & Co., V:449

Fauvel, Louis, VI:1127, 1128; manuscript to, from Byron, VI:1126–27

Featherstone Buildings, High Holborn, London, V:433, 438

Fellenberg, Emanuel de, VI:759, 760, 761n

Feltham, John, *Guide*, VI:571

Fénelon, François de Salignac de la Mothe-, VI:527, 979

Fenton, Thomas, V:55, 56

Ferdinand VII, King of Spain, VI:984

Ferrara, Italy, V:465; VI:708, 763, 863

Ferrybridge, Yorkshire, V:471

Fialon, V:97, 98

Field, Barron, V:266; VI:558, 560n

Field (or Fielde), Francis, V:438

Field, Francis John, VI:558n

Field Place, Horsham, Sussex, V:33, 477n

Fielding, Henry, V:295, 434; VI:571n, 838, 911, 914, 1079

Figg, James, VI:1121

Finch, Robert, V:420; VI:707

Fireside Magazine, VI:597n

Firminger, Walter Kelly, ed., *The Fifth Report . . .*, VI:717n, 733, 734, 738

Fitzgerald, Mrs. Thomas, V:504n

Fladgate, Francis, V:435, 443n; VI:807

Flaminia, Via, VI:708

Fleet Market, London, V:493

Fleet Prison, London, V:450

Fleet Street, London, V:221, 222; VI:834, 924n

Fletcher, William, V:53, 55; VI:748

Fleur-de-Luce Court, Fleet Street, London, VI:915n

Florence, Italy, V:67, 199, 416; VI:553, 585n, 656, 666, 673, 674, 679, 680, 685, 690n, 764, 766, 784, 860, 890n, 914, 934n, 938, 941, 944, 964, 1066, 1069, 1071, 1083, 1084n, 1092, 1095, 1096, 1108

Florida, H.M.S., V:55

Fodor-Mainvielle, Joséphine, V:501, 504; VI:521, 846

Foggi, Elise [ ], V:89, 267, 327, 491; VI:563, 575, 678, 706; relatives, VI:543, 546n; with Allegra en route to and at Venice, V:462; VI:569, 577–578, 580, 598, 666, 674, 675, 676

Foggi, Paolo, VI:546n, 674, 676, 680

Foote, Maria (later Countess of Harrington), V:282

Foote, Samuel, V:282

Foote, Samuel T. (?), V:279, 282

Ford, Miss. *See* Smith, Mrs. Horace

Ford, Mrs., V:326, 328

Ford, J., V:328n

Fordingbridge, Hampshire, V:288

Fore Street, London, V:479, 484

Forman, Harry Buxton, V:399; and *Julian and Maddalo*, VI:857, 860n; and "Lament for Bion," V:191, 192; and *Laon and Cythna*, V:153n, 154, 155, 159, 166, 188; library, V:15, 459, 464; on "Love's Philosophy," VI:1085; on *Mask of Anarchy*, VI:893n, 894; on "Mighty Eagle," V:206, 211; on "On Love," VI:641, 642; sale, VI:832; Westbrook vs. Shelley documents, VI:647, 649; *Note Books of Percy Bysshe Shelley*, VI:871

Forman, Maurice Buxton, V:440

Forrester, James, V:56–57

Fortnightly Review, VI:956

Foulis, Robert and Andrew, V:318n

Fowler, Henry, *Modern English Usage*, V:386

Fox, William, V:365n

France: Mary Jane Godwin and, V:204, 358; PBS on, VI:966, 972, 979–981, 990, 1038, 1062; PBS on the French, VI:583. *See also specific places*

Francis I, Emperor of Austria, VI:982

Francis, John, V:182

Index of Names

Franklin, Mr., V:218

Franklin, Benjamin, VI:904

Fraser's Magazine, VI:521, 658n

Frazer Smith, Mr., V:95

Frazer Smith, Caroline Trelawny. *See* Trelawny, Caroline Julia Addison

Frederica Caterina of Wurtemberg, V:499

Frederick, Prince of Hesse-Homburg, V:497, 499, 500

Frederick II, Holy Roman Emperor, VI:983

Frederick II, King of Prussia, VI:924

Frederick VI, King of Denmark, VI:982

Frederick Augustus of Saxony, VI:982

Frederick Barbarossa, VI:964

Frederick William III, King of Prussia, VI:982

Frederickson sale, V:15

Free Mason's Tavern, London, V:232

Freeling, Sir Francis, VI:603

Freeman, Arthur, VI:771n

Freinsheim, Johann (Freinshemius), V:239n

French Revolution, V:239, 269, 477; VI:826, 895, 901, 948, 978, 980, 981, 989, 993, 999, 1028, 1062, 1063

Frend, William, VI:758

Frere, Henry Bartle Edward, VI:722–723, 742

Frere, John Hookham, VI:1136

Frontenac, Canada, V:75

Fry, William, V:358n

Fualdès, Antoine Bernardin, V:465

Fulham, Middlesex, Elysium Row, VI:562

Furnivall, F. J., V:515

Fuseli, Henry, VI:586

Fusina, Italy, VI:675, 679, 693

Gale and Fenner, V:450

Gamba, Pietro, V:53

Garcia, Manuel, VI:521

Garden Court, Temple, London, VI:924, 937

Garnett, David, VI:521n

Garnett, Edward, V:440n

Garnett, Richard, V:116n, 126n, 275, 439n; VI:832, 871

Garrick Club, V:443n

Garrison, William Lloyd, V:499n

Gattie, John Byng, V:317

Gattie family, V:409

Gattie(s), Maria. *See* Ollier, Maria Gattie

Gatton, Surrey, VI:999

Gavita, Vincenzo, VI:639

Geneva, Switzerland, V:19, 21n, 46, 100, 200, 327; VI:526, 546, 568, 831, 832

Geneva, Lake, Switzerland, V:315, 366, 460

Genoa, Italy, V:261; VI:1080

Gentleman's Magazine, VI:682

George I, King of England, VI:1003

George III, King of England, V:248, 499, 500; VI:946

George IV, King of England (earlier, Prince Regent), V:85n, 157, 487; VI:946, 1118

George Yard, Lombard Street, London, VI:603

Georgia, Russia, VI:988

Georgia Journal, VI:747

Germany, V:358; PBS on, VI:965n, 966, 981–982

Gerrard Street, London, V:298

Ghibelline party, VI:964, 983

Ghouras, V:56

Gibbon, Edward, V:247; VI:910

Gifford, William, V:17, 294, 417, 419; VI:612, 1055; and Hunt, VI:740, 742–743, 791, 797, 932

Gilbert, Allan H., V:216n, 465

Gilley, W. B., V:358

Giotto (di Bondone), V:60

Gisborne, John, V:115, 211n, 412, 413, 414, 415, 417, 419, 420, 455, 513; VI:580, 597, 599, 600, 628, 642n, 783, 873, 897n, 930–931, 943, 952, 953, 954, 1104; letter to (with Maria Gisborne), from PBS, VI:1094–95

Gisborne, Maria James Reveley, V:455; VI:690n; and Godwin, V:498, 512–513; VI:858; and Keats and PBS, V:412, 413, 414, 415, 417, 419, 420; and Shelleys, V:513; VI:579, 580, 678, 680, 768, 783; and PBS's manuscripts, VI:930–931; correspondence with Shelleys, V:48, 508n; VI:562, 597–600, 676, 691, 767, 782n, 784, 892, 929n, 952, 954, 1094–95; loan from PBS, VI:941, 942, 943, 1095–96

    Letters to, from:

      Godwin, V:511–512

      MWS, VI:597–598

      (with John Gisborne), PBS, VI:1094–95

Gittings, Robert, V:441, 443n, 444

Giustiniani-Lolin, Palazzo, VI:693, 707

Glasgow, Scotland, VI:937, 1043

Gliddon, Alistasia, V:475; VI:791, 796

Gliddon, Arthur, VI:791, 796

Index of Names

Gliddon, Charles, V:260

Gliddon, John, VI:796

Gliddon, John (son of preceding), V:260; VI:796

Gliddon, Mary Florimel Hunt, V:226, 260; VI:555, 609, 796

Globe, V:288

Glorious Revolution of 1688, VI:967, 981, 1050

Gloucester Place, London, VI:606

Gloucestershire, V:5

Goddard, Charles, VI:573

Godoy, Manuel de, VI:984

Godwin, Hull, V:33

Godwin, Joseph, V:224

Godwin, Mary Jane, V:29, 157, 203n, 204, 205, 355, 360, 377, 410, 498; VI:540, 747; and *Mandeville*, V:358; and Lady Mount Cashell, VI:579; and PBS, V:31, 32, 33–34, 35, 391–392; vacations, VI:902–903

Godwin, Mary Wollstonecraft. *See* Wollstonecraft, Mary

Godwin, T. H., I. W., or J. W., V:514, 515–516

Godwin, William:

  and Thomas Alsager, V:264, 265

  and William Baxter, V:334–337, 340, 377–378

  and Joseph Bevan, V:233; VI:745–747

  and David Booth, V:334, 336, 346, 377, 386; VI:703–705

  and James Broughton, VI:681–684

  and Claire Clairmont, V:391, 392

  and Archibald Constable, V:22–26, 30, 34–35, 158, 357, 366, 494, 498; VI:774–777, 809–811

  and Thomas Cooper, V:354–361

  and Amelia Curran, V:498–499, 512

  and J. P. Curran, V:498

  and East India Chambers, V:201–204, 217, 218

  and Maria Gisborne, V:512–513; VI:858

  and Hazlitt, VI:834–836; *Lectures*, VI:539–542

  and Leigh Hunt, VI:555, 562, 792, 795, 796

  and Keats, V:410

  and T. N. Longman, V:493–494

  and Lady Mount Cashell, V:512; VI:579

  and James Ogilvie, V:231–236

  and Polidori's *Vampyre*, VI:777–781

  and sc 374, V:8, 15n

and MWS, V:31, 33, 196, 198, 204, 205, 389, 391–392; after William's death, VI:848–849, 857–858

and PBS, V:24, 28–30, 31–36, 85, 88, 101, 196, 200–205, 211n, 215, 224, 228, 239, 296–297, 303, 315, 316, 317, 327, 328, 329n, 350–351, 363, 390, 418, 449, 478–482, 486, 491n, 507, 512–513, 516; VI:653–655, 852, 854, 857–858, 862, 939, 940, 1110

dinner parties, V:235–236

finances, 1817–1818, V:203–204, 218–219, 224–225, 449–450

Juvenile Library, VI:902–903

letter style, V:436, 437; VI:616

Letters by, to:

  [   ], V:235

  J. V. Bevan, VI:745

  David Booth, VI:703–704

  James Broughton, VI:681

  John Payne Collier, VI:769–770

  Archibald Constable, VI:774–775, 809–811

  Constable & Co., VI:773–774

  Thomas A. Cooper, V:354–355

  Amelia Curran, V:497; (?) VI:539

  Maria Gisborne, V:511–512

  R. W. Hayward, V:216

  T. N. Longman, V:493

  J. Ogilvie, V:231–232

  John Richardson, VI:902

  PBS, V:200–202, 296–297

  John Taylor, V:217–218

  John Taylor (publisher), VI:833–834

Letter to, from:

  PBS, V:6–7 (forgery)

Manuscripts, miscellaneous:

  Autograph Memorandum with Constable & Co., V:22–23

  Document from Hayward to, VI:772–773

notes in Herodotus, VI:625, 626, 627n

on family, V:355, 359–360

on letters sent by parcel, V:394, 468

on printers, V:158–159

Other letters by, to (quoted):

  Henry Colburn, VI:780

  William Sherwood, VI:778, 779

portrait, V:130n

Promissory notes by, to:

  M. R. Catlin, V:223

  John Over, V:492–493

Index of Names

mentioned, V:59, 100, 118, 127, 157, 165n, 215, 293, 371n, 405n, 443, 469, 472, 474, 477, 483n, 503; VI:586, 598n, 608, 617n, 639, 877n, 946, 947, 971, 973, 1034, 1044, 1053, 1060

WORKS

Caleb Williams, V:25, 127n, 358n; VI:848
Cloudesley, V:127n
Cursory Strictures . . . VI:901n
Deloraine, V:127n
Essay on Sepulchres, V:157
Fleetwood, V:127n
History of the Commonwealth of England, V:127n
Letter of Advice . . . V:233; VI:746–747
Life of Geoffrey Chaucer, VI:684
Lives of Edward and John Philips, V:494; VI:684
Mandeville, V:22–26, 30, 34–35, 158–159, 218, 333, 351, 357–359, 362, 366, 380, 390, 434, 444, 494, 498; VI:579, 599, 772–777, 809–811
Memoirs of the Author of a Vindication of the Rights of Woman, VI:541n
Of Population . . . *Being an Answer,* V:25, 26, 211n, 360, 494; VI:655, 704, 775, 776, 903, 1025
Political Justice, VI:527, 595, 949n, 974, 1041, 1043
St. Leon, V:127n; VI:595, 756

Godwin, William, Jr., V:355, 359–360, 472, 479
Goethe, Johann, V:455; *Faust,* VI:691; "Harzreise im Winter," V:463
Golby, James, V:5
Gooch, Dr. Robert, V:485, 487
Gore House, V:66
Goring, Augusta. *See* Trelawny, Augusta Goring
Goring, Harry Dent, V:66, 77
Gosse, Edmund, V:440n; VI:743n, 956
Goujon, Jean, VI:822
Gow, A. S. F., V:191
Grampound, Cornwall, VI:999
Grande Bretagne, Hotel, Venice, VI:707
Grantham, Lincolnshire, V:471
Gray, Thomas, VI:911
Grays Inn Square, London, V:27
Great Marlborough Street, London, V:231n

Great Marlow. *See* Marlow
Great Russell Street, London, V:8, 491, 496, 507, 508, 515, 519
Greece: Byron in, 53–55; VI:914, 1128; PBS on ancient, VI:988, 991, 1048; Trelawny in, V:52–58
Greenwich, Kent, V:355, 360
Gregson, John, V:483n, 484
Grenville, William Wyndham Grenville, Baron, VI:573
Griffith, Benjamin W., Jr., V:142n
Groenvelt, Mr., V:494n
Grotius, Hugo (Huig van Groot), *De veritate religionis Christianæ,* VI:919, 922
Grove, Harriet, V:142n
Gryffydh, Jane. *See* Peacock, Jane Gryffydh
Guarini, Giambattista, V:457, 465
Guelph party, VI:964
Guiccioli, Count Alessandro, VI:812, 814, 815, 816
Guiccioli, Teresa, V:53, 365n; VI:814–816; letter to, from Byron, VI:811–814
Guilford, Francis North, 4th Earl of, V:269
Guilford, Frederick North, 5th Earl of, V:268, 269–270, 271

Habeas Corpus Suspension Act, V:163, 198n, 244, 245
Haber, Louis I., sale, V:15
Hackney, Middlesex, VI:541, 705
Haileybury, Hertfordshire, V:477
Haiti, VI:990
Hall, Basil, *Account of a Voyage* . . . , VI:579
Hallam, Arthur, V:441n
Hallam, Henry, V:441n
Hamilton, Samuel, V:218n
Hammond, Anthony, VI:1117n
Hammond, George, V:494
Hamond, Elton, V:494n
Hampden, John, VI:998, 1035, 1059
Hampshire, V:98; VI:751
Hampstead, Middlesex, V:88, 256, 402, 403, 405, 408, 410; VI:661, 700, 793, 907
Hampton, Middlesex, VI:602
Hanger Hill, VI:760, 761n
Hanson, Charles, VI:751
Hanson, John, V:19n; VI:567, 568n, 749n, 751, 1138; letter to, from Byron, VI:1122
Hanson, Newton, VI:748, 749

Index of Names

Hanwell, Middlesex, VI:652

Harbottle, Mrs., V:327

Harcourt, J. J., VI:721

Hare, Julius Charles, V:124

Harlow, George Henry, V:123, 130, 235, 236

Harness, William, VI:1129

Harrington, James, VI:946, 971

Harris, Robert, V:434

Harris, Thomas, VI:843, 929

Harrison, Charles, V:491

Harrison, George, V:488, 490, 491

Harrow, Middlesex, VI:573, 582, 791, 1118, 1128

Hart, Horne, Wetherell and Montague, V:273

Hartley, David, VI:946, 971

Hartley, Robert A., VI:1070–71n

Harvard University, Houghton Library, VI:799

Harvey, William, V:303

Haslam, William, V:422n, 434, 444

Hastings, Sussex, VI:760

Hawkins, Sir Christopher, V:39, 57, 59, 61

Hawkins, John, V:40, 42, 61, 95n

Hawkins, Maria. *See* Brereton, Maria Hawkins Trelawny

Haydock, Lancashire, VI:1137

Haydon, Benjamin Robert, V:231n, 252, 404, 405, 407, 408n, 410, 422n–423n, 435; VI:579, 809, 1079n, 1093; "Immortal Dinner," V:433, 441–442; VI:1079n

Hayley, William, *Life of Milton*, VI:792, 796

Haymarket, London, V:503n

Hayward, Richard William, V:303n, 469n; and Godwin, V:201, 203, 204, 217, 479; VI:776, 811; and PBS, V:113, 114, 116, 117, 121; (?) legal opinion from, to Godwin, VI:772–773; letter to, from Godwin, V:216

Hazel, Tom, VI:1120

Hazlitt, William, V:100, 233, 235, 236, 264, 316–317, 438, 474; VI:558n, 611, 682, 702, 796, 847, 894n, 1055, 1093; and *Christabel* review, V:20; and Godwin, VI:834–836; and *Posthumous Poems* review, V:448; attack on Southey, V:222n; on Italian women, VI:587; PBS and, VI:1060; *Characters of Shakespear's Plays*, V:124; VI:617, 835; *Lectures chiefly on the Dramatic Literature of the Age of Elizabeth*, V:265; VI:835, 836; *Lectures on the English Comic Writers*, V:265; VI:835; *Lectures on the English Poets*, V:265, 411n; VI:539–542, 835–836;

Letter to William Gifford, Esq., VI:612, 617, 743, 791, 797; *Political Essays*, VI:835; *A View of the English Stage*, VI:835n

Hazlitt, William (son), V:316

Heath, James (artist), V:421

Hecate, H.M.S., V:41n

Hegesistratus, VI:626, 632

Henley-upon-Thames, V:377n

Henry V, King of England, V:39

Hentsch family, Geneva bankers, V:15, 18, 19, 21, 84, 200

Hercules (boat), V:54

Hermes, VI:917, 921

Herodotus, V:299; VI:1004; and PBS, VI:626–633, 659; PBS's and Godwin's notes in, VI:618–626; PBS's notes in Bodleian manuscript, VI:638, 639

Herries & Co. (Herries, Farquhar, Halliday, Chapman, & Halliday), VI:941, 942, 943, 1095

Hertfordshire, V:439

Hervey (Harvey?), E., V:457, 466, 467

Hessey, James Augustus, VI:809; and Godwin and Hazlitt, VI:834–835; and Hunt, V:220; VI:517–518, 531, 538; letter by, to John Taylor, VI:517

High Holborn, London, V:345

High Street, Bloomsbury, London, V:345

High Wycombe, Buckinghamshire, V:302, 377n

Higham, John, VI:648

Highgate, Middlesex, VI:907

Hill, Lady Anne, V:41–42, 95n

Hill, Thomas, V:205; VI:541, 595, 596

Hitchener, Elizabeth, V:142, 337

Hobbes, Thomas, VI:970

Hobhouse, John Cam (Lord Broughton), V:18, 19, 199, 494, 495; VI:567, 568, 576, 751, 1129, 1138, 1139; visit to Hunt, VI:556, 562–563; *Historical Illustrations of the Fourth Canto*, VI:592; *Notes and Illustrations to the Fourth Canto of "Childe Harold's Pilgrimage,"* VI:563, 592

Hodgson, Francis, VI:1129, 1130, 1135; letter to, from Byron, VI:1128

Hodgson, John, VI:718n, 733, 738

Hodgson's (auction house), V:122; VI:695

Hofwyl school, VI:759, 760, 761n

Hogan, Frank, VI:661n

Hogg, John, V:253n

Index of Names

Hogg, John Ewer Jefferson, V:475n
Hogg, Richard J. Jefferson, V:475n

Hogg, Thomas Jefferson:

and Walter Coulson, V:317–318
and Leigh Hunt, V:307, 473–476, 503, 504;
VI: 561, 600–601, 606, 696–700, 791, 792,
796, 836–837, 839, 935–937
and Dr. Lambe, VI:585n
and the Newtons, V:96–98, 500–505; VI:585n
and TLP, V:215, 248–251, 254–256, 284–289,
304, 306, 307, 308, 309, 408; VI:518–521,
548–552, 572, 601–602, 661, 684–688, 720,
761–763, 802–805, 916–925
and MWS, V:58, 100, 215, 330–331; VI:805
and PBS, V:99–101, 108, 114, 115, 192, 212,
214–216, 236–241, 249, 287, 304–310, 330–
332, 418, 469–470, 471, 472, 473, 477, 505;
VI:582–586, 763–769; and *Philosophical
View of Reform*, VI:955; provenance of
letters, V:275n
letter style, V:308–309, 436, 437; VI:699,
920–921
Letters by, to:
J. F. Newton, V:500–503
TLP, V:248–250, 284–286; VI:801–803,
916–920
PBS, V:304–308
Letters to, from:
J. F. Newton, V:96–97; VI:569–570
Hunt, V:473–474; VI:600–601, 696–699,
836–837, 935–936
TLP, V:254–255, 299–300; VI:518–520,
548–550, 601–602, 684–686, 761–762,
922–923
PBS, V:99–100, 214 (fragment), 236–237,
330–331, 469–470; VI:582–585, 763–
765
love affairs, VI:804–805
on Richard Carlile, VI:901n, 952
on William Cobbett, V:250, 253–254
on London activities, V:249, 251–253, 503
view of travel, VI:590
walking, V:251; VI:921, 922, 924
mentioned, V:67, 165n, 198, 233, 294, 316,
409, 410, 441, 451, 461, 462, 468, 492;
VI:546, 612, 663, 719n, 740, 847, 885,
897n, 932, 1030

WORKS
Life of Shelley, V:97, 98, 99, 100, 101, 475;
VI:805
Memoirs of Prince Alexy Haimatoff, V:28;
VI:767
Two Hundred and Nine Days, VI:590,805

Holborn Hill, London, V:449
Holbrice, R., V:223
Holcroft, Thomas, V:356, 357
Holland, Elizabeth Vassall Fox, Lady, VI:1139
Holland, Henry Richard Vassall Fox, 3rd
Baron, V:118–120, 230, 477; VI:702; letter
to, from Leigh Hunt, V:117–118; *Life of
Guillen de Castro*, V:120; VI:611, 616; *Some
Account . . . of Lope Felix de Vega Carpio*,
V:119
Holland House, Kensington, V:118; VI:701
Holy Alliance, VI:1038
Homer, V:299, 306, 318n, 397, 452; Hogg and,
V:306; VI:918; TLP and, VI:629n, 685,
687; PBS and, V:236–237, 238, 239–240,
241, 250, 397, 471; VI:611, 615, 621, 632,
790
Homerton, Middlesex, V:377; VI:661, 705
"L'homme Gris et le Physiognomiste," VI:529
Hone, William, V:99n, 156, 163, 164, 352n,
434, 444; VI:541, 835, 1058, 1084n
Hook, Theodore, VI:595
Hookham, Edward T., VI:551n
Hookham, Thomas, Jr., V:28, 89, 123, 125,
166n, 315, 316, 317; VI:551n, 592, 596,
627, 755, 756
Hope, Thomas, V:270
Hoppner, Isabelle (Mrs. Richard Belgrave),
VI:673, 674, 676, 678, 692, 694, 768
Hoppner, John, VI:676
Hoppner, Richard Belgrave, VI:546n, 673,
674, 678, 679, 768; and Allegra, VI:675–
676; and the Shelleys, VI:692, 694, 706–
707, 708
Horace, V:212; VI:628n; *Satires*, VI:550, 552
Horne, Richard Hengist, V:439; *Ballad Ro-
mances*, V:128
Horner, Francis, V:270; VI:651
Horsemonger Lane Gaol, V:125, 265
Horsham, Sussex, VI:945n
Howard, H. L. (pseud.). *See* Wells, Charles
Jeremiah
Howe, P. P., V:20

Howe, Samuel Gridley, V:57

Hughes, E., V:181, 182n

Hume, Caroline (Mrs. Thomas), V:298; VI:648, 649, 651–652, 695

Hume, David, VI:628n, 641, 651n, 946, 970, 971, 988; *Enquiry concerning . . . Morals*, VI:974

Hume, Gustavus, VI:650n

Hume, Dr. John Robert, VI:651n

Hume, Joseph, M.P., VI:651n, 771

Hume, Joseph, V:224

Hume, Dr. Thomas, V:298; VI:940; biography, VI:650–651; check by, to Brooks, Son & Dixon, VI:695; guardianship of PBS's children, VI:648, 649, 650, 695

Hummums Tavern, London, V:491

Hundred Years' War, VI:966

Hunt, Arrabella (or Arabella), V:262

Hunt, Charles Shelley Leigh, V:261, 275

Hunt, Emily (Mrs. Percy B. Hunt), V:260

Hunt, Henry Leigh, VI:796, 805n, 892; and *Examiner*, VI:791, 795, 888; and Reynolds, VI:806, 808; and PBS, V:226, 230; VI:791, 795

Hunt, Henry "Orator," VI:893

Hunt, Holman, V:68

Hunt, Jacintha Shelley Leigh. *See* Cheltnam, Jacintha

Hunt, James Henry Leigh. *See* Hunt, Leigh

Hunt, (James) Henry Sylvan Leigh, V:261; VI:850, 914

Hunt, John, V:116, 226, 228, 258, 263, 422n, 444; VI:560, 743; and Leigh Hunt, V:229, 230; retirement, VI:791, 795, 888

Hunt, Mrs. John, V:228, 257

Hunt, John Horatio Leigh (Hunt's son), V:226, 260; VI:555

Hunt, Julia Trelawney Leigh, V:261–262

Hunt, Katharine Gliddon, V:258, 260; VI:796

Hunt, Leigh:

  and Byron, V:50, 291, 294, 295, 401; VI:575, 678, 701, 702, 703, 916; Byron's portrait, V:123, 130

  and Walter Coulson, V:314, 317, 318

  and William Gifford, VI:740, 742–743, 791, 797, 932

  and Godwin, VI:555, 562, 792, 795, 796

  and TJH, V:307, 473–476, 503, 504; VI:561, 600–601, 606, 696–700, 791, 792, 796, 836–837, 839, 935–937

  and Lord Holland, V:117–120; VI:611, 616

  and Keats, V:119, 263, 264, 266, 399, 401–415 *passim*; VI:740, 742, 806, 808, 809, 849, 916

  and Thomas Moore, VI:698, 700–703

  and Charles Ollier, V:120n, 125–126, 127, 129, 222; VI:884, 887, 1090, 1093–94

  and TLP, VI:555, 561, 596, 796, 846–847, 849

  and J. H. Reynolds, VI:806–808

  and MWS, V:226–227, 231, 264; VI:524–525, 845–850, 891–892, 908–910

  and PBS, V:32, 34, 50, 52, 83, 88, 89, 119, 215, 227, 231, 242, 273–274, 292, 299, 314–317, 327, 344, 350, 351, 393, 394, 399, 401–403, 405n, 418, 491; VI:519, 523–524, 529, 769, 806, 1060, 1107–10; and *Adonais*, V:425–426; and *The Cenci*, VI:865–872, 898, 927, 1070, 1083n, 1090; and *Julian and Madaalo*, VI:851, 859, 860, 862, 1099; and *Laon and Cythna — The Revolt of Islam*, V:143, 146–147, 148, 160, 161–162, 170, 181, 182, 188–189, 239, 424n; VI:798; and death of William Shelley, VI:837–838, 839–842; correspondence, discussed, V:315; VI:557–558, 560–563, 609, 614–618, 794, 848, 882–883, 888–891, 909–910, 1083–85, 1091–92; provenance, V:261, 275; defense of PBS, VI:926, 932–933, 1083; inability to meet in Italy, VI:791, 794–795; layette parcel, VI:877–878, 891, 911, 913, 914, 927, 928, 1083; piano, VI:522; PBS's manuscripts, VI:885, 893, 952, 1083, 1085, 1094; *see also under* finances, *below*.

  character, taste, and style, V:228, 229, 257, 437, 474; VI:558–561, 795–798, 844, 908–909, 916, 1078–81

  children, listed, V:258–262

  drama on the Cid, V:120; VI:560, 611, 616–617, 740, 744, 790, 793, 798, 840, 842–844, 852, 854, 881, 1083

  finances, V:256, 485–488; VI:795, 849, 880–881, 883–884, 909–910, 935–937, 1090–91, 1092; and publishers, V:219–222; VI:517–518, 531–539; and PBS, V:88, 202, 205, 228–229, 244, 262–267, 272, 303, 402, 475, 482; VI:531–539, 561, 790, 940, 1110

  imprisonment, V:88–89, 125–126, 487; VI:906

Index of Names

Letters by, to:

  Lord Holland, V:117–118

  TJH, V:473–474; VI:600–601, 696–699, 836–837, 935–936

  Sir William Knighton, V:485–486

  J. H. Reynolds, VI:805–806

  MWS, VI:790–794, 845–848, 904–908

  MWS and PBS, VI:553–557, 739–741, 879–882, 886–888, 910–913

  MWS and PBS (with Marianne Hunt), VI:605–614

  PBS, V:271–272, 314; VI:839–842, 1088–91

  John Taylor, V:219–220

Letters to, from:

  PBS, V:262–264; VI: 850–854, 1080–83, 1106–08

  (and Marianne Hunt), PBS and MWS, V:225–227; VI:523–526

  John Taylor, VI:530–537

Manuscript: "Angling," VI:1075–78

nicknames, V:229, 301

on Donne, VI:911–912, 914–915

on DuBois, VI:595

on Greek writers, VI:790–791

on Italy and Italian writers, VI:610–611

on Michelangelo and Raphael, VI:886–887, 890

on Robert Owen, V:272, 274–275

on poets dying abroad, VI:911, 914

on Spanish politics, VI:984

portrait, VI:606, 608–609, 614, 871, 872, 877, 886

residences, V:227–228, 231, 297; VI: 606, 612, 614–615, 697–698, 881, 884–885, 906–907, 909

translation of "Lament for Bion," V:192

mentioned, V:36, 87, 100, 116, 165n, 198, 211, 215, 233, 235, 236, 237, 241, 282, 302, 329n, 331n, 340, 352n, 419, 433, 434, 444, 463, 467, 508; VI:583, 586, 590, 661, 663, 691, 708, 765, 805, 874, 920, 922, 923, 953, 954, 1055, 1059, 1139

WORKS

  Amyntas (trans. of Tasso's *Aminta*), VI:591n, 616n, 884n, 912, 913, 916, 1081, 1086

  "Angling," VI:1075–80

  Autobiography, V:118, 120, 405, 487; VI:616–617, 703, 884n, 894n, 909n

  Bacchus in Tuscany, VI:616n

  "Coffee Houses and Smoking," VI:796

  Companion, VI:617

  Correspondence, V:275

  "Deaths of Little Children," VI:837, 838

  Descent of Liberty, V:265n

  "Evergreens," V:155, 156n

  "The False Lion & the Real Puppy," VI:702n

  Feast of the Poets, The, VI:700

  Foliage, V:124, 156n, 192, 265n, 394; VI:523, 529n, 579, 617, 662, 707, 708, 742, 743, 797, 872, 884, 931, 1086

  "Godiva," VI:617

  "Hero and Leander," V:221

  Hero and Leander, and Bacchus and Ariadne, V:124, 155, 156n; VI:790, 798, 840

  Indicator, VI:560, 796, 838, 898, 912–913, 915–916, 935, 937, 1078, 1081, 1083, 1085, 1089, 1090, 1091, 1092, 1094, 1107

  "Letters of Harry Brown," V:220, 221n; VI:796

  Literary Pocket-Book, The, VI:617, 739, 741–742, 791, 841, 905, 906, 909, 1083

  Lord Byron and Some of His Contemporaries, V:119, 188; VI: 702, 853, 860

  "Nymphs, The," V:154, 156n, 406n; VI:523, 529–530, 553, 660, 662, 883n, 1081, 1086, 1087

  "Occasional," No. XV, VI:561n

  "On the Nile," V:192, 410

  Poetical Works, V:124; VI:703

  Sir Ralph Esher, V:127n

  Stories from the Italian Poets, VI:616n, 740, 744

  Story of Rimini, The, A Poem, V:119–120, 124, 161–163, 220, 222; VI:517, 531–533, 537, 538, 539, 700, 1081, 1087

  Town, The, VI:884n

  Ultra-Crepidarius, VI:702, 743

Hunt, Leigh (Hunt's nephew), V:230n

Hunt, Marianne:

character, V:257–258, 262; VI:558

dream, VI:740, 742

errands for Shelleys, V:226, 257, 258, 263; VI:877, 887, 891–892, 911, 1083

H. L. Hunt and, VI:795
in London, V:228
Letters by, to:
  MWS, V:256–257
  PBS and MWS (with Leigh Hunt),
    VI:605–614
Letters to, from:
  PBS and MWS (with Leigh Hunt),
    V:225–227; VI:523–526
new houses, V:228; VI:606, 614
on Byron's portrait, V:130
pregnancies and childbirth, V:258, 434, 444;
    VI:847, 850, 881, 907, 910, 1080
school, VI:553, 560
sculptures, V:231
MWS's January 13, 1817, letter to, V:83–84n
PBS to, on Keats, V:414, 415
mentioned, V:50, 299, 485; VI:519, 554, 561,
    603, 604, 792, 793, 794, 805, 839, 853, 905,
    907, 1085, 1091

Hunt, Marriott, V:230n
Hunt, Mary (Hunt's sister), VI:837
Hunt, Mary Florimel. *See* Gliddon, Mary
    Florimel Hunt
Hunt, Percy Bysshe Shelley Leigh, V:248,
    260–261, 444; VI:555, 606, 882
Hunt, Robert, VI:795, 806, 807
Hunt, Rosalind ("Dina") Williams, V:261
Hunt, Stephen Shewell, VI:795
Hunt, Swinburne, V:226, 260; VI:884
Hunt, Thornton, V:188, 227, 228, 257, 258,
    260, 266, 275; VI:555, 606, 608, 612, 614,
    615, 796, 883n, 888, 890
Hunt, Vincent Leigh, V:261
Hunter, Dr., V:158
Hunter, Mr., V:236
Hunter, Rowland, V:124
Huntingdon, Huntingdon, V:471
Huntington Library: Godwin letters at, VI:777;
    PBS manuscripts at, V:211; VI:630, 857,
    871, 893, 1068, 1069, 1070, 1072, 1074
Husley, Mr., VI:903
Hutchinson, Sara, V:442
Hydra, Greece, V:54

Ibn Saud, VI:989
Ibrahim Pasha, VI:989
Icarus, VI:553, 560

Imlay, Fanny, V:21n, 325; VI:797n; and
    Christina Baxter, V:334–335; death, V:8–9,
    28, 30, 86, 100, 355, 359, 391; on Godwin's
    finances, V:29, 30
Indapore, India, VI:722
India, V:477; VI: 624, 632, 688, 710, 712–722,
    723, 724, 727–737 *passim*, 987–988, 1004,
    1052
India Act of 1784, VI:75n
Indicator. See Hunt: WORKS
Ingpen, Edward T., V:122
Ingpen, Roger, V:30, 122, 214, 396; VI:652
Inner Temple, London, V:558n; VI:682, 803
Iowa, University of, Luther A. Brewer collec-
    tion, VI:649n
Ireland, V:35, 492; VI: 747, 950, 1046
Irving, Washington, V:232n, 233, 234
Italy: Claire Clairmont on, V:454; Hazlitt on
    women of, VI:587; Hunt on, VI:610, 616,
    793; J. F. Newton on, VI:570, 572–573;
    TLP on, VI:605, 685; MWS on, VI:560n,
    590, 909, 916; PBS on, VI:583, 586–587,
    764–765, 767, 769, 964. *See also specific
    places*
Itinerario Italiano, VI:547n, 548

Jackson, John "Gentleman," VI:1119–20,
    1121, 1122; letter to, from Byron, VI:1118–
    19
James I, King of England, VI:967
James II, King of England, V:39; VI:967, 981,
    1061
James, "The Old Pretender," VI:1061
James Street, Adelphi, London, V:29n
Jarvis, Charles, translation of Cervantes,
    V:504; VI:684, 687
Jefferson, Thomas, VI:951
Jeffrey, Francis, V:20, 21, 294, 416n; VI:529n,
    651, 700, 1055
Jenkinson, Robert Banks (later Lord Liver-
    pool), VI:573
Jersey, Isle of, V:283
Jesus Christ, V:246; VI:963, 968, 969, 971, 983,
    987, 1043, 1044, 1107
Joan of Arc, VI:824, 825
Johnes, Thomas, VI:1135
Johnson, Mrs. Jane Cleveland. *See* Williams,
    Jane Cleveland Johnson

Index of Names

Johnson, Samuel, and family, V:90, 102, 103, 276, 279, 282–283, 311, 319, 320, 322; VI:581; and EJT's daughter, V:95, 139–140
Johnston, James, V:20, 124n
Johnston, Margaret, VI:757
Jones, *Greek Grammar*, V:397
Jones, Frederick L., V:215, 479–480; VI:599, 679n, 691, 832, 1085, 1095
Jones, Howard Mumford, VI:703
Jonson, Ben, VI:686n
Jordan, Mr., V:236
Joyce, Herbert, V:394n
Jungfrau, Switzerland, V:230
Jura, France, VI:524, 526, 832
Juvenal, *Satires*, V:249, 253n, 367
Juvenile Library, V:157, 236, 357; VI:902, 903

Karbala, Iraq, VI:988
Kean, Edmund, V:279, 282, 356n; VI:596, 840, 842–843
Keats, Fanny, V:433, 434, 442
Keats, George, V:351n, 405, 412, 440, 443n; VI:742, 797, 807; letter to (with Tom Keats), from John Keats, V:428–436
Keats, Georgiana, V:440, 443n; VI:742, 797, 807

Keats, John:

and Hunt, V:119, 263, 264, 266, 399, 401–415, 433, 434; VI:740, 742, 806–809, 849, 916
and *Quarterly Review*, V:416–417; VI:742, 743, 931, 932
and Reynolds, V:428; VI:806, 807–808
and PBS, V:317, 344, 399, 403–419; VI:876, 878–879; and *Adonais*, V:419–427
and C. J. Wells, V:428, 433, 434, 440
death, V:415, 418–419; VI:914
friends, V:444; VI:808–809
Haydon's dinner, V:433, 441
illness, V:412–415
letter style, V:436–437, 442–443
Letter by, to:
   George and Tom Keats, V:428–436
mailing of sc 444, V:437–438
Manuscript: Fragment from "Isabella," VI:798
on Hazlitt's attack on Southey, V:222n
mentioned, V:60, 129, 154, 265, 492; VI:518, 542n, 596, 601, 608, 615, 701, 744, 797, 801, 842, 894n, 921, 1093

WORKS
   Endymion, V:144–145, 344, 405n, 406–407, 411, 413n, 415, 416–417, 424n, 426; VI:591n, 742, 743, 876, 878
   "The Eve of St. Agnes," V:416
   "Fancy," V:416
   "Great spirits now on earth . . . ," V:409n
   "Happy is England!" V:409n
   "The Human Seasons," VI:742
   "Hyperion, a Fragment," V:409, 415, 416–418, 419, 426–427
   "I stood tip-toe," V:406n, 426
   "Isabella," V:416, 426; VI:616, 1136n; fragment from, VI:798–800
   "Keen, fitful gusts . . . ," V:409n
   "La Belle Dame sans Merci," VI:662
   "Lamia," V:416; VI:662
   Lamia, Isabella, The Eve of St. Agnes, and Other Poems, V:415, 416
   "Lines on the Mermaid Tavern," V:416
   "Ode ('Bards of Passion and of Mirth')," V:416
   "Ode on a Grecian Urn," VI:646
   "Ode to a Nightingale," V:426
   "On the Grasshopper and Cricket," V:409n
   "On the Nile," V:192, 410
   Poems (1817), V:124, 351n, 409, 415
   "Robin Hood," V:416
   "Sleep and Poetry," V:227, 411n, 416
   Sonnet on Chapman's Homer, V:402, 409n
   "To a Friend who sent me some Roses," V:440
   "To Ailsa Rock," VI:742
   "To Autumn," V:426
   "To My Brothers," V:409n
   "Written on a Blank Space at the End of Chaucer's Tale of 'The Floure and the Lefe,'" V:408–409

Keats, Tom, V:410n, 428, 435, 437, 438, 440, 492; letter to (with George Keats), from John Keats, V:428–436
Keepsake for 1829, The, VI:639–641
Kemble, Charles, VI:541
Kemble, Fanny (later Butler), V:64–65, 67, 76; *Record of a Girlhood*, V:65
Kemble, John Philip, V:356, 357
Kendall, John, V:273, 297
Kendall, Wilfrid, V:297n
Kennedy, John, V:477n

Index of Names

Kenney, James, V:205

Kenney, Louisa (formerly Mrs. Thomas Holcroft), V:205

Kensal Green Cemetery, V:260

Kensington, London, VI:792

Kent, Edward, Duke of, V:499

Kent, Elizabeth (Bessy), V:220, 226, 228, 404, 434, 444; VI:517, 518, 525, 537, 554, 561, 606, 612, 613, 614, 615, 793, 841, 853, 881, 885, 907, 911, 932n, 1085

Kent, Thomas, VI:606, 615

Kentish Town, London, VI:907, 909

Kern, Jerome, sale, V:338, 344n

Kernott, (?) Henry, V:201, 203

Keswick, Cumberland, V:142; VI:850

Keynes, Geoffrey, VI:835

Kilburn, London, VI:793

King Street, London, VI:796

Kingdom (Kingdon), Mr., V:29

King's Bench, Court of, V:3, 45, 95n, 483

King's Royal Irish Hussars, Eighth Dragoons, VI:830

King's Theatre or Opera House, V:503

Kingston, John, V:433, 441, 442, 443

Kinnaird, Charles, 8th Baron, VI:816

Kinnaird, Douglas, V:20, 199, 364; VI:562n, 563, 568, 750, 751, 816

Kirkby, Mr., VI:1137

Kirkby Mallory, Leicestershire, VI:758

Kirkman, Joseph, V:267; VI:522

Kirkup, Seymour, V:59, 60

Knight, G. Wilson, VI:767n, 862n

Knighton, Sir William, V:303, 486–488; VI:910n; letter to, from Hunt, V:485–486

Knightsbridge Terrace, Kensington Road, London, VI:562

Koszul, André H., V:192

La Fère, France, VI:527

La Marie, H.M.S., V:41n, 49

La Scala (town), Italy, V:454; VI:598

Labarre, E. J., V:488

Lacarte, Augustin, V:21n

Lackington, George, V:28n, 396

Lackington, James, V:28n, 396, 445, 472, 473

Lackington, Hughes & Co. (Lackington, Allen & Co.; Lackington, Hughes, Harding, Mavor & Jones), VI:537n; account sheet, V:397–398; and *Frankenstein*, V:31, 298–299, 394,

395, 396; and PBS, V:27–28, 121, 343; letters to, from PBS, V:26–27, 298, 395

Lads of Kilkenny, V:234n

Lake Country, VI:850; Lake poets, VI:616

Lamb, Caroline, VI:1140

Lamb, Charles, V:129, 233, 316, 438, 491n, 498; VI:542, 612, 744, 771n, 791, 796, 841, 876; and Alsager, V:264, 265; and "Angling," VI:1078, 1079; and Hunt, VI:555, 558, 561, 847; and Lloyd, VI:849, 850; at East India Company, VI:682, 723; at Haydon's dinner, V:433, 441–442, 443; on Coleridge's poems, V:21n; on *Mandeville*, V:25n; "Oxford in the Vacation," V:287; *Rosamund Gray*, VI:844, 878, 888; "The Two Races of Men," V:205; *Works*, V:124, 411; VI:554, 558, 844, 878

Lamb, Mary, V:233, 491n; VI:542, 555, 561, 584, 771n, 791, 796; illness, VI:608, 612, 615

Lamb, William, VI:1140

Lambe, Mary, VI:584, 585

Lambe, Dr. William, V:412; VI:585

Lambert, Mrs., V:392, 394

Landor, Walter Savage, V:59–60, 66, 159, 293n; VI:585, 914

Landseer, John, V:433, 441

Lanfranchi Palace, V:50

Lang, Andrew, VI:700

Langres, France, VI:528

Lansdowne, Henry Petty, 3rd Marquis of, VI:702

Laon, France, VI:527; cathedral, VI:588

Law, Hon. Edward, Hon. H., or Ewan, V:1, 3n

Law, Thomas, VI:718n

Lawrence, James Henry, *The Empire of the Nairs*, VI:549, 550–551, 631

Lawrence, William, V:143, 293; VI:551, 652

Le Sage, Alain René, VI:979

Leacroft, Julia, VI:1116, 1118

Leadenhall Street, London, V:201, 217; VI:709, 711, 713, 719, 720, 803, 917, 921. *See also* East India Company

Leader, Temple, V:64, 66, 67

Leader, the, V:188

Lear, Edward, V:68

Lectures on the History of Literature . . ., VI:921

Leech, John, V:68

Leeds, Yorkshire, VI:937, 999

Index of Names

Leghorn (Livorno), Italy, V:50, 67, 394, 413n, 414, 455, 463, 513; VI:557, 563, 579, 580, 591, 598–599, 604, 628, 654, 658n, 690n, 764, 766, 768, 782, 848, 873, 874, 877, 880, 882, 897, 900n, 911, 914, 923, 930n, 931, 942, 951, 1069, 1086, 1104; mail rate, VI:877n

Legnano, Italy, VI:964

Leicester's, Earl of, Hospital, V:297n

Leigh, Augusta, V:199; VI:749

Leigh, Chandos, V:127n, 128

Leigh, Henry James, V:104, 115–116

Leigh, James Henry, V:116

Leoni, Michele, *Lamento del Tasso di Lord Byron*, V:270n

Leonidas, VI:625

Leopold of Saxe-Coburg-Saalfeld (husband of Princess Charlotte), V:499

Lerici, Italy, V:51

Lewes, Agnes Jervis, V:260

Lewes, George Henry, V:188, 260

Lewi, Angela, V:130n

Lewis, Matthew G. ("Monk"), V:130n, 230, 472n; letter to (?), from Byron, VI:1139

Liberal, V:50; VI:702

Library of Congress, VI:893n

Lincoln, Lincolnshire, V:75, 318, 320

Lincoln's Inn Fields, London, V:483n

Lind, Dr. James, VI:652

Lisbon, Portugal, VI:911, 914, 1129

Lisson Grove North, Paddington, London, V:228, 231, 297, 307, 410, 491; VI:614

Literary Examiner, V:360n

Literary Gazette, V:61; VI:597n

Literary Panorama, VI: 597n

Literary Pocket-Book. See Hunt, Leigh: WORKS

Little Britain, London, VI:807

Little Distaff Lane, London, V:479

Little Marlow, Buckinghamshire, VI:569. *See also* Marlow

Little St. Thomas Apostle Street, London, V:372, 377, 472n

Liverpool, Lancashire, V:323; VI:903–904

Livy, VI:628n, 629, 633

Lloyd, Charles, VI:691, 847, 881, 885; biography, VI:849–850

Lloyd, James Martin, VI:945n

Locke, Mr. (dyer), VI:608

Locke, John, VI:946, 970, 973, 988

Lockhart, John Gibson, V:162–163; VI:931n, 1055

Locock, C. D., V:211; VI:1101

Lombard League, VI:964

Lombardy, Italy, V:269; VI:528, 983

London, University of, University College Library, V:386n

London Coffee-house, London, VI:902, 903, 904

London Exchange Banking Company, VI:941n

London Magazine, V:423n; VI:537

Long, Edward Noel, VI:1113–18

Long Acre, Drury Lane, London, V:496

Longacre Street, Covent Garden, London, VI:581

Longden. *See* Longdill

Longdill, Pynson Wilmot, VI:695; and PBS, finances, V:27, 28, 30, 31, 121, 228; and Westbrook vs. Shelley, V:273, 297; VI:650, 652

Longman, Thomas Norton, V:494; letter to, from Godwin, V:493

Longman and Co. (Longman, Hurst, Rees, Orme, & Brown), V:154, 494; VI:691

Lonsdale, Prudentia Hogg, V:275n, 475n; VI:804n

Lons-le-Saunier, France, VI:831

Loreto, Italy, VI:915n

Louis XVIII, King of France, VI:525, 529n; VI:982, 1063

Louis Napoleon, VI:966

L'Ouverture, Toussaint, VI:990

Love, Harriet, VI:803, 805

"Lowless" (or "Lawless"), V:434, 444

Lucan, V:269; VI:666

Lucas, E. V., VI:558

Lucca, Duchy of, Italy, VI:558, 658n, 666, 674, 680, 793, 990. *See also* Bagni di Lucca

Lucian, V:330, 332; *Erotes*, V:249, 253n

Lucretius, V:237, 238

Ludgate Hill, London, V:450; VI:904

Ludgate Street, London, V:156n

Ludlam, Isaac, VI:1049

Lukin, Allen & Beech, V:496, 497

Lushington, Stephen, V:156

Lycophron, VI:623

Lycurgus, VI:918, 921

Lydia, VI: 620, 631

Lynch, Bohun, *The Prize Ring*, VI:1121

Lyon, France, VI:523, 525, 528, 529, 543, 553, 568, 588

Index of Names

"Maberly the Army Taylor," V:379

Mabledon, Kent, V:327

Mabledon Place, London, V:317, 327, 328, 336, 344, 410

MacFarlane, Charles, VI:768

Mackintosh, Sir James, V:476, 477

Maclean, Catherine, VI:539

McLeod, Donald, VI:829

McLeod, John, *Narrative of a Voyage . . .*, VI:578–579

McMillan, Buchanan, V:157, 159–160, 188–189, 224, 446n; VI:836

Mâcon, France, VI:528, 832

Macready, William Charles, V:282n

Macri, Theresa, VI:1125

Maddox, Robert, V:516n

Madocks, Robert, V:364, 516n

Madras, India, VI:713, 715–717, 721, 722

Maggs Brothers, VI:1101, 1102

Magna Graecia, VI:563

Maida Place, Paddington, London, V:127

Maidenhead, Berkshire, V:377n

Malabar, India, VI:551n, 631

Malibran, Garcia, VI:521

Malone, Edmund, VI:771

Malta, VI:1123

Malthus, Thomas, V:25, 26, 211n, 477; VI:704–705, 1022, 1023–24, 1055. *See also* Godwin, *Of Population*

Man, Isle of, VI:903, 904

Manchester, Lancashire, VI:999; "Peterloo Massacre," VI:854, 892, 893, 895, 900, 925, 937, 951, 1080, 1088, 1093

Mandeville; or The Last Words of a Maniac . . ., V:25n

Manners, George, VI:585n

Manso, Giovanni Battista, *La Vita di Torquato Tasso*, V:465; VI:591

Manson, Mme. Marie Françoise Clarisse, *Mémoires*, V:452, 465

Mantua, Italy, VI:1084

Marathon, Battle of, VI:624, 632

Marchand, Leslie A., V:130, 365n; VI:1123, 1125, 1130, 1138

Marchmont Street, London, V:327

Marcus Aurelius Antoninus, *Meditations*, VI:905, 910

Maremma, Italy, V:47, 52

Maria Louisa of Parma, VI:984

Markham, Osborn, V:1, 3n

Markyate, Hertfordshire, VI:1120

Marlow, Buckinghamshire, V:288, 380, 472, 476; Baxter visits, V:335, 336, 340; Coulson visits, V:316, 317; Godwin visits, V:203, 392, 479; Hogg visits, V:215, 474, 475; Hunts at, V:227–228, 231, 292, 405; Ollier visits, V:165, 369–370; TLP at, V:166n, 215, 250–251, 254, 300, 302, 340; VI:520, 550, 555, 561, 604, 659, 687, 710, 804; postage and postmarks from, V:8, 243n, 377, 396; Shelleys at, V:24, 88, 89, 114, 122, 143, 145, 146–147, 165, 193, 200, 203, 213, 267, 272, 286, 292–293, 297, 327, 328, 333, 336, 363, 390, 391, 392, 402, 413n, 447, 460–461, 470–471, 506, 507n; VI:700, 786, 883, 910n, 1086; Shelleys move from, V:491, 501, 505; VI:618; PBS's philanthropies at, V:347, 368, 470–471; VI:1028

"Marlow, The Hermit of" (pseud.). *See* PBS: WORKS

Marlowe, Christopher: and *The True Tragedie of Richard, Duke of Yorke*, VI:770, 771, 772n; *The Massacre at Paris*, VI:682; *Tamburlaine*, VI:681, 682

Marne (river and valley), VI:527

Marseilles, France, VI:942

Marshal, James, V:203, 355, 360, 479; VI:579

Martin's Lane, London, V:408n

Marx, Karl, VI:999; Marxism, VI:1034

Mary II, Queen of England, VI:967, 997, 1050

Masi, Glauco, VI:900n

Masi, Tommaso, VI:900n

Masistes, VI:630

"Mason, Mr." *See* Tighe, George W.

"Mason, Mrs." *See* Mount Cashell, Margaret, Countess of

Masterman, Peters, Mildred, Masterman, & Co., V:223–224

Mastoxithi, V:199

Mathews, Mr., V:402n

Mathews, Charles, VI:595

Matthews, Elkin, V:181

Matthews, G(eoffrey) M., VI:591n, 639n; and *Julian and Maddalo*, VI:858, 861, 862, 865

Maturin, Charles, V:230; *Bertram*, V:279, 282

Maudslay, Henry, V:360n

Mavrocordatos, Prince Alexander, V:52, 54, 56

Index of Names

Mawe, Thomas, *Every Man his own Gardener . . .* , V:123, 133

Maxwell, Lt.-Col. Charles or Christopher, V:205

Maxwell, J., V:358n

Mayer, Samuel Ralph Townshend, V:188

Mayne, Ethel, *Life and Letters of Anne Isabella, Lady Noel Byron*, VI:758

Mecca, VI:988

Mecklenburg Square, London, V:265

Medici family, VI:964

Medina, Saudi Arabia, VI:988

Medwin, Thomas, V:124, 125n; and Keats and PBS, V:405–406, 414, 418; and "On Love," VI:640–641, 642n; and Trelawny, V:47, 48; VI:672; *The Angler in Wales*, V:127n; *Conversations of Lord Byron*, V:62, 127n; *Life of . . . Shelley*, VI:649

Melbourne, Lady Elizabeth, VI:1139, 1140

Mendelssohn, Moses, VI:989

Mendoza, Daniel, VI:1121n

Merionethshire, Wales, VI:661

Merivale, John H., *Orlando in Roncesvalles*, VI:1135–36; letter to, from Byron VI:1134–35

Merivale, Philip, VI:1136

Merryweather, Francis, VI:569, 577

Metastasio, Pietro, VI:740

Metaxata, Greece, V:54

Michelangelo Buonarotti, VI:554, 886, 890

Middle Temple, London, V:99; VI: 932

Milan, Italy, V:454, 462; VI: 528, 529, 546, 553, 690, 964n, 1084; ballet, VI:764; Byron at, V:16, 17, 18, 21n; VI:690; cathedral of, V:452, 461; VI:583, 587–589; La Scala, VI:589–590; London post, V:18; PBS at, V:461; VI:548, 549, 551, 556, 557, 564, 575, 580, 582–584, 598, 604, 658n, 768

Milanie, Mlle., V:461, 501, 503, 504

Milbanke, Judith, VI:758n

Military Register and Weekly Gazette, VI:667–668

Military Review, V:61

Mill, James, VI:719n, 721, 924; *History of British India*, VI:923, 924

Mill, John Stuart, VI:925n, 947, 948n, 951

Millais, John, V:68, 69

Millais, Euphemia Chalmers Gray Ruskin, Lady, V:69

Miller, Joaquin, VI:671–672

Milman, Archibald, VI:933n

Milman, Henry Hart, V:424n; VI:933

Milton, John, V:269, 344, 409, 423; VI:792, 911, 1002, 1021, 1035; *Lycidas*, V:191; *Paradise Lost*, V:145; VI:628, 985–986, 1057; *Paradise Regained*, VI:983

Mira, Italy, VI:679

"Mirabaud." *See* D'Holbach

Mirabaud, Jacques, V:15, 21

Mirabaud & Cie, Messrs., V:21n

Mirabeau, Honoré Gabriel Riquetti, VI:884

Mirror of Literature, Amusement, and Instruction, The, VI:640

Mirror of Parliament, V:360n

Missolonghi, Greece, V:54, 55

Mitchell, Thomas, VI:921–922

Mocenigo, Palazzo, VI:675, 707

Modena, Italy, V:454; VI:598

Mohammed (Mehemet) Ali Pasha, VI:988, 989

Mohammed ibn Sa'ud, VI:988

Moira, Francis Rawdon-Hastings, 2nd Earl, VI:717

Molesworth, Sir William, V:64, 67

Molière (Jean Baptiste Poquelin), VI:979

Molineaux, Tom, VI:1121

Moloch, VI:986

Mombelli, Signor, V:452, 461

Momus, VI:685

Money, W. T., VI:676n

Monk, General, VI:998

Monkhouse, Thomas, V:433, 441, 442n

Monselice, Italy, VI:693

Mont aux Malades, Rouen, VI:825

Mont Blanc, France, V:315; VI:524, 526

Montagu, Anna Dorothea Benson Skepper, VI:541

Montagu, Basil, V:317; VI:541

Montaigne, Michel Eyquem, V:393, 394; VI:970, 973, 979

Montalègre, Switzerland, V:365n

Monte di Tremezzo, Italy, VI:548

Montesquieu, Charles Louis de Secondat, Baron de la Brède et de, VI:946, 971, 972, 973, 979

Monthly Magazine, VI:597n

Monthly Review, V:269; VI:597n

Monti, Vincenzo, VI:690, 691n

Moore, Anastasia Jane Codd (T. Moore's mother), VI:700, 701

Moore, Barbara, V:353

Index of Names

Moore, Doris Langley, V:130n

Moore, Margaret King. *See* Mount Cashell, Margaret, Countess of

Moore, Thomas, V:19n, 125n, 199, 230, 248, 366; VI:541, 698, 838, 908, 922; and Byron, VI:1128–29, 1133; and *Christabel*, V:20, 21; and Thomas Hume, VI:650–651, 695; and Leigh Hunt, VI:698, 700–703; and *Laon and Cythna*, V:350, 352, 353; and St. Columbanus, V:8n; as "Thomas Brown, the Younger," V:221n; in *Adonais*, V:424, 425; *Anacreontics*, V:425n; *Fudge Family in Paris*, V:425n; VI:706, 707; "Here's the Bower," V:461; VI:521n; *Irish Melodies*, V:425n; VI:701n; *Lalla Rookh*, V:154, 422, 425n; *Letters and Journals of Lord Byron . . .*, VI:702–703; "The Living Dog and the Dead Lion," VI:702; *Odes of Anacreon*, VI:651; *Tom Crib's Memorial to Congress*, VI:1121

Morel, Jeanne, V:35, 359n

Morgan, Pierpont, Library, V:166; VI:86on, 956n, 1102n

Morning Chronicle, V:17, 25, 316, 360n, 408; VI:665n, 854, 900, 901n; advertisement for Albion House, V:146n, 148n; Westbrook vs. Shelley in, V:272–273

Morning Post, The, V:219

Mortimer Street, Cavendish Square, London, V:433, 438, 442

Mortimer Terrace, Kentish Town, London, VI:885, 909n

Moscheles, Ignaz, V:266

Moschus, V:191, 192

Moscow, V:58; VI:982

Mothe-Fénelon. *See* Fénelon

Mount Athos monastery, V:53

Mount Cashell, Margaret King Moore, Countess of, V:153n, 159, 293n, 462, 512; VI:579–580

Mount Parnassus, Greece, V:55, 67

Moxon and Co., VI:898

Moylan, Denis Creagh, V:499n

Mozart, Wolfgang Amadeus: *Don Giovanni*, V:253, 503, 504; VI:805n; *Marriage of Figaro*, V:504

Muhammed ibn 'Abd al-Wahhab, VI:988

Muley Ismael (Moulay Ismail), Emperor of Morocco, VI:983

Mulready, William, V:235

Munro, Thomas, VI:716, 717, 718n

Murray, Joe, VI:1137, 1138

Murray, John, V:119; VI:558, 579n, 742n, 1135; and Byron, V:17, 19, 20, 130, 199, 294, 419; VI:575, 578, 694, 778n, 1130–31, 1133; and *Christabel*, V:21; and Hunt, V:222; and Moore, VI:702; and PBS, VI:931n; letters to, from Byron, V:494–496 (address leaf); VI:1131–32

Murray, Sir John, V:130

Murray, Jr., John, V:495

Murray, John G., V:130

Musters, Caroline (?), VI:1116, 1118

Musters, John, VI:1118

Nairs, VI:549, 551, 631

Naldi, VI:521

Napier, Charles, V:54

Naples, Italy, V:293; VI:553, 605, 610, 873; Keats at, V:413, 414, 415, 418; San Carlo opera house, VI:764, 767–768; PBS at, VI:558, 708, 763–765, 767, 768–769, 782, 783, 784, 794, 940; Royal Museum, VI:890n

Napoleon I, V:39, 247; VI:525, 587, 676, 980, 982, 984, 988, 989

Napoli di Romania, V:54, 56

Nash, Andrew John, V:483n

Nash, George Augustus, V:483n

Nash, John, V:360n

National Library of Scotland, V:152, 341

Naval Academy, Gosport, V:42

Nearchus, *Periplus*, V:237

Nelson, Horatio, Lord, VI:1028

Nero, VI:983, 985

Netherlands, VI:754, 966

New Bond Street, London, V:449

New Hummums Hotel, London, V:328, 490, 491–492, 515

New Lanark, Scotland, V:274

New Monthly Magazine, VI:778, 779, 780, 781, 796

New Shoreham, Sussex, VI:945n, 999

New South Wales, Australia, VI:560n

New York, N.Y., V:357

New York Public Library, The Berg Collection, V:337; VI:1127n

New Zealand, V:64

Newark, Nottinghamshire, V:471

Newburgh, Fife, Scotland, V:335n, 336, 341, 342, 389, 390; VI:704

Newcastle-upon-Tyne, Northumberland, V:471

Newgate Street, London, V:156

Newman Street, London, VI:894n

Newstead Abbey, V:130, 241, 291, 293; VI:568n, 614, 749, 1137–38

Newton, Augustus, V:97, 98–99; VI:571

Newton, Cornelia Collins, V:98

Newton, John Frank, V:412n; VI:585; and TJH, V:98, 500–505; and TLP, VI:572; and PBS, VI:764, 769; as "Demogorgon," V:288; biography, VI:571, 573; letters by, to TJH, V:96–97; VI:569–570; letter to, from TJH, V:500–503; on Italy, VI:570, 572–573; works, VI:571, 573

Niagara, N.Y., V:65, 67, 76

Nicholson, Peter, V:360n

Nitchie, Elizabeth, V:182n

Nonnus, V:397; *Dionysiaca*, V:343, 344–345; VI:685, 687–688

Norfolk, Charles Howard, 11th Duke of, V:142; VI:542, 546, 945n

Norfolk, Bernard Edward Howard, 12th Duke of, VI:945n

Normandy, France, VI:818–819

North. *See* Guilford

Northcote, James, *Conversations*, V:235

Norton, Caroline, V:66

Norton, George, V:66n

Norton-upon-Tees, Durham, V:308; VI:699, 937

Norway, VI:983

Nosworthy, Bill, VI:1120

Notopoulos, James: on "On Love," VI:641–642; on PBS and Plato, VI:639n, 786; on PBS's Greek translations, V:212

Novello, Clara Anastasia, VI:744

Novello, Joseph Alfred, VI:744

Novello, Mary Sabilla, VI:791, 796, 798n, 847

Novello, Vincent, V:267, 405, 409; VI:522, 740, 791, 796, 808, 809, 847; biography, VI:744

Novello & Co., VI:744

O'Briens (Obryans), the, V:102, 103, 277

Odysseus (Greek chieftain), V:54, 55, 56, 60

Ogden, Henry, V:234n

Ogden, Peter, V:232, 234

Ogilvie, James, V:232–236; VI:745; letter to, from Godwin, V:231–232; *Philosophical Essays*, V:232

Old Bond Street, London, V:222

Old Sarum, Wiltshire, VI:999

Oliver, Mr., VI:823, 825

Oliver the spy (W. J. Richards), V:244; VI:1049

Ollier, C. and J., V:120, 124–125, 127, 154–155, 222, 439n

Ollier, Charles:
and *Frankenstein*, V:263, 267, 393
and Hunt, V:120n, 125–126, 127, 129, 154, 155, 222; VI:884, 887, 906, 910, 1093
and Keats, V:411, 412, 418; VI:808, 809
and Lamb's *Works*, VI:554, 558
and PBS, V:123–125, 128, 155, 157, 160–167 *passim*, 239, 342–343, 347–353, 369–370, 392–394, 421, 422, 444–447, 467–468, 476–477; VI:659, 664–668, 781–784, 851, 862, 874–879, 885, 926–929, 932, 934, 939, 940, 1094, 1096–1100, 1104–06; errands and packages, VI:603, 604, 606, 608–609, 614, 739, 782, 783, 840, 853, 871, 874–878, 890, 899n; letters, V:129; political poems, VI:1090, 1092, 1093
biography, V:126–129
Letters to, from:
TLP, VI:603–604
PBS, V:123–124, 342–343, 347–350, 369, 392–393, 444–445, 446–447, 467–468, 476; VI:664–665, 781–782, 874–876, 926–928, 1096–1100
seal, V:352
mentioned, V:274, 315, 366, 409, 420, 448, 468, 472, 473, 516; VI:537, 740, 741, 838, 893, 901, 953, 954, 1102

WORKS
Altham and His Wife . . ., V:128, 155, 156n, 370n, 393, 394, 411, 467; VI:591n, 876, 878, 1093
Fallacy of Ghosts, Dreams, and Omens, V:128
Ferrers . . ., V:128
Inesilla, V:128; VI:876, 879

Ollier, Charles (son of C. Ollier), V:129

Ollier, Edmund, V:125n–126n, 129, 352n

Ollier, James, V:126, 127; VI:927, 928

Ollier, Maria Gattie, V:125, 126

Ollier's Miscellany, VI:786

Olschki, Leonard, VI:569n

O'Neill, Eliza (Mrs. W. Wrixon-Becher), VI:897, 929

Index of Names

"Onwhyn," VI:915
Opie, Amelia Alderson, *Adeline Mowbray . . . ,*
   V:251n
Opie, John, V:249, 251
Orange Street, London, V:313
O'Regan, William, VI:615
Orger, George, V:253
Orger (Orber), Mary Ann Ivers, V:249, 253
Origo, Iris, VI:676
Otanes, VI:623, 632
Otello (ballet). *See* Viganò, Salvatore
Othman (Osman) al-Bardisi, VI:989
Othman Bey, VI:989
Over, John, promissory note to, from Godwin,
   V:492–493
Ovid, VI:563, 662
Owen, Robert, V:272, 274–275
Oxford, Oxfordshire, VI:602
Oxford University, V:99, 141, 297n, 469;
   VI:573, 588, 786, 931n, 933n, 945; Press,
   V:397
Oxford University and City Herald, V:212, 460

Padua, Italy, VI:673, 678, 679, 693, 694, 706,
   708, 983
Paine, Thomas, VI:951, 952; *Age of Reason,*
   VI:901; *Rights of Man,* V:156
Paisley, Scotland, VI:937
Palacio, Jean de, V:466
Palgrave, Francis, V:494n
Pall Mall, London, V:126
Pallerini, Antonia (Maria), V:452, 462
Palsgrave Place, V:204n, 216, 217
Pancratia, or a History of Pugilism, VI:1121
Pangbourne, Berkshire, VI:519
Paris, France, V:61–62, 269, 479, 483, 484, 501;
   VI:562, 831; Notre Dame, VI:588; Peace
   of, VI:1003
Park Theatre, N.Y., V:360
Parliament, V:17, 45, 477; VI:604n, 702, 711,
   946, 1019; anti-slave trade acts, VI:990;
   elections, VI:563, 686, 945; repressive
   legislation, V:85n, 197, 198, 244; VI:1093;
   PBS on, VI:997–1001, 1038–39, 1042,
   1044–45, 1048–51, 1059, 1062
Parma, Italy, V:454; VI:598
Parmentier, A. A., V:366n
Parr, Samuel, VI:585n
Parry-Jones, Corbet, VI:944

Partridge, Eric, V:443n
Paternoster Row, London, V:154, 156, 479
Paul, Charles Kegan, VI:541n
Paulding, James Kirke, V:234n
Pausanias, V:255; VI:629
Payne, John Howard, V:232, 233, 235, 236;
   Brutus, VI:843
Peachey family, V:433
Peacock, Jane Gryffydh, VI:660–661, 710, 849
Peacock, Sarah Love, V:115, 121, 286, 492;
   VI:687, 710, 803, 805

Peacock, Thomas Love:

  and William Baxter, V:336, 340
  and Walter Coulson, V:317–318
  and Edward DuBois, VI:592–597, 754–756
  and East India Co., V:492; VI:522, 551–552,
    663, 688, 709–712, 719–721, 723–738, 792,
    803, 895, 921, 925
  and TJH, V:215, 250–251, 254–256, 284–289,
    299–300, 304, 307, 308, 309, 408; VI:518–
    520, 521, 548–550, 572, 601–602, 661, 684–
    688, 720, 761–763, 802–805, 916–920,
    922–925
  and Hunt, VI:555, 561, 596, 795n, 796, 846–
    847, 849
  and MWS, V:331; VI:849
  and PBS, V:104, 105, 107–108, 109, 114–115,
    122, 143, 147, 148n, 161, 165, 166, 192,
    212, 251, 293, 310n, 330, 344, 418, 516;
    VI:549, 552, 596, 695, 769, 938, 940, 942;
    and PBS's departure, V:461; VI:518–519,
    520, 521, 522; and death of William Shelley,
    VI:837; and *The Cenci,* VI:897–899, 929,.
    930; and *Prometheus Unbound,* VI:929–
    930; as executor, V:4, 113, 115, 484;
    correspondence, V:315, 463; VI:546, 547,
    548, 583, 586, 587, 601, 606, 627, 628,
    656–658, 680, 686, 708, 763, 765–766, 784,
    787n, 797, 851, 852, 859, 890, 892, 893, 900,
    925, 1024; errands and packages, V:511;
    VI:556, 575, 603–605, 783, 840, 891
  classicism, V:300–301
  diary, VI:686–687, 688
  letter style, V:436, 437
  Letters by, to:
    TJH, V:254–255, 299–300; VI:518–520,
      548–550, 601–602, 684–686, 761–762,
      922–923
    Ollier, VI:603–604

Letters to, from:
    DuBois, VI:592–595, 754–755
    TJH, V:248–250, 284–286; VI:801–803,
        916–920
    PBS, VI:656–658, 895–896
Manuscript: "Ryotwar and Zemindarry
    Settlements," VI:724–738
"nympholepsy," VI:657, 660–663
pedestrianism, V:302; VI:917
portrayals: of Byron, V:245; of Hogg,V:251
reading, V:345, 504–505; VI:551, 552
residences, V:8, 250–251, 402, 492; VI:659,
    687, 710, 803, 854
mentioned, V:67, 117, 198, 236, 237, 316n,
    333, 341, 408, 409, 410, 416, 463, 464, 465,
    471, 474, 475, 503, 504, 516; VI:524, 529n,
    555, 590, 606, 617n, 666, 676, 791, 798n,
    874, 885, 928, 929, 1059, 1106

WORKS
Crochet Castle, V:127n, 345
Four Ages of Poetry, V:345, 417; VI:597,
    629n–630n, 663, 688, 786
Gryll Grange, VI:521, 688–689
Headlong Hall, VI:709, 723
Maid Marian, V:127n; VI:688, 709, 710,
    762, 924
Melincourt, V:225n, 251, 365; VI:521n, 572,
    597, 686, 709
Memoirs of Shelley, V:288; VI:804
Misfortunes of Elphin, V:345
Nightmare Abbey, V:127n, 245, 309; VI:549,
    551–552, 570, 572, 596, 597, 657, 660,
    663, 686, 709, 754–756
Rhododaphne, V:288n, 309, 330, 332, 501,
    503; VI:570, 592, 596, 597, 661, 663
"Ryotwar and Zemindarry Settlements,"
    VI:714, 717, 718–719, 722–723, 724–
    738, 756

Peasants' War, VI:965n
Peck, Walter E.; and *Philosophical View of
    Reform*, VI:957–958, 960; and sc 399,
    V:214; on PBS's checks, V:122, 347, 467,
    481, 515
Pelham Crescent, London, V:67, 77
Pellegrini, Pellegrino, VI:588
Pencarrow, Cornwall, V:64
Penney, V. R., V:503n
Perelli, Gaspare, VI:815

Periander, VI:623
Persia, VI:988, 1004
Persian Gulf, VI:988
Pertinax, VI:1004
Pervigilium Veneris, VI:924n
Pestalozzi, Henry, VI:759, 760
"Peterloo Massacre." *See* Manchester
Petrarch, VI:572–573, 610, 616, 647
Petronius, V:330, 332
Pforzheimer, Carl H., VI:957, 1100
Pforzheimer, Carl H., Jr., V:130
"Phalanstery," V:260
Philadelphia, Pa., V:357, 358
Phillips, Charles, VI:615
Philosophical Society of London, VI:915n
Phocion, VI:629
Physick, John, V:94n
Piacenza, Italy, V:454; VI:598
Piazza di Spagna, Rome, V:415
Piccadilly, London, V:314, 443n
Pickering, Basil Montagu, V:69
Piedmontaise, H.M.S., V:41n
Pierce, Anna Maria. *See* Polidori, Anna Maria
    Pierce
Pindar, V:299, 300
"Pindar, Peter" (pseud.). *See* Wolcot, Dr.
    John
Pinner, Middlesex, VI:582, 670
Pisa, Italy, V:47, 51, 244, 269–270, 290, 293,
    412, 413, 414, 422, 454, 455, 463; VI:548,
    557, 562, 575, 579, 580, 583, 591, 598,
    672, 860
Pitt, William, VI:715n
Plataea, Battle of, VI:632
Plato:
    and Hunt, VI:696–697, 699
    and "Mighty Eagle," V:212, 213
    Phaedrus, VI:663
    Republic, VI:951; and TJH, VI:918, 921;
        PBS's translation of Book VI, VI:784–789
    PBS's editions, V:212, 344n; VI:549, 552,
        628, 706, 707
    PBS's interest in, V:407; VI:647, 786–787,
        789, 946
    Symposium, V:255, 407; VI:549, 552; and
        "On Love," VI:639, 641–642; PBS's trans-
        lation of, VI:627, 629, 641, 656–657, 658–
        659, 1081, 1086
    mentioned, V:452, 465; VI:519
Pliniana, Villa, VI:543, 547–548, 565

Pliny the younger, VI:547, 629, 755, 756
Plutarch, V:249, 253n, 285; VI:519, 627, 629, 633, 662, 1004
Plymouth, Devon, V:438n
Pocock, Isaac, V:252–253
Polidori, Agostino, V:268
Polidori, Anna Maria Pierce, V:269
Polidori, Francesca Maria. *See* Rossetti, Francesca Maria Polidori
Polidori, Gaetano, V:268–271, 293n; translation from Byron, V:268; works, V:269, 270–271
Polidori, John William, V:268, 269–270, 293; *Vampyre*, and Godwin, VI:777–781
Polidori, Luigi, V:293n
Political Register. See Cobbett's Weekly Political Register
Pollin, Burton R., V:232; VI:640n
Polyphemus, VI:793, 796
Pomposa, Italy, VI:815
Pool House, Menheniot, V:39
Poole, John, V:235, 236
Poona, India, VI:722
Poor Laws, VI:1019, 1025
Pope, Alexander, V:411n; VI:542, 600, 601, 755, 756, 947, 973, 1002
Pope, Robert, V:288; VI:652, 804
Popkin, Parr, V:1, 2, 3, 4n
Porcupine, The, V:253
Porphyrius, V:255, 285, 289
Port Folio, VI:747
Portland Island, Dorset, VI:570, 571n
Portman (Portram) Square, London, VI:606
Portugal, VI:988
Poston, M. L., VI:1117n
Power, James, VI:701, 1133
Powis, Edward Clive, 2nd Earl of, VI:999
Pratt, P., V:239n
Preston, Jean F., VI:872n
Prévost, Antoine François Prévost d'Exiles, l'abbé, VI:979, 1024
Prexaspes, VI:623, 632
Price, Richard, VI:904
Priestley, Richard or G., V:343, 345
Priestly, Joseph, VI:904
Procter, Bryan Waller ("Barry Cornwall"), V:124, 141n, 415, 425n; VI:742, 791, 796
Procter, Nicholas Waller, V:141n
Propertius Sextus, VI:662
Prout, Mrs., V:43, 44, 45, 93, 94

"Prull (Pruel), Mother." *See* White, Mrs. Mary
Puccinotti, Francesco, VI:838
Pugilistic Club, VI:1120
Puissant, H.M.S., V:41n, 42
Pulci, Luigi, VI:616, 744; *Morgante Maggiore,* VI:1136
Portsea, Hampshire, V:164, 165
Pulham, James, VI:682
Putney Hill, London, V:66
Puttick and Simpson, V:129
Pym, John, VI:998

Quarterly Review, VI:706, 923; and Keats, V:416–417, 419; VI:740, 742; attack on *Laon and Cythna — Revolt of Islam,* V:146, 165, 417, 448; VI:743, 878, 922, 930, 931–934; attacks on PBS, Hunt, and Hazlitt, VI:611, 617, 707–708, 740, 742–743, 797, 872, 926, 1083; TJH on, VI:918–919, 921–922; on *Frankenstein,* VI:617, 707, 740
Queen Anne Street East, London, V:441n
Queen Mab: Containing a Select Collection of Only the Best, Most Instructive, and Entertaining Tales of the Fairies . . . , V:284
Queen Square, Bloomsbury, London, V:266
Queen's Bench, Court of, V:483
Quimper, Brittany, V:439
Quincy, Anna, V:64–65
Quincy, Josiah, V:64
Quintus Curtius Rufus, V:237, 239n

Rabelais, François, VI:685, 979
Racine, Jean, VI:979
Ramsay, George, V:24
Raphael, VI:553, 554, 610, 616, 886–887, 890
Ravenna, Italy, VI:707, 814, 815, 816
Raymond, Mr., V:340
Raymond Buildings, Grays Inn, London, V:116
Read, Caroline, VI:688n
Reading School, V:468n
Reddell (Redhall, Redall), George Smith, V:434–435, 443
Redding, Cyrus, V:198n–199n; VI:558, 560
Rees, Owen, V:494
Reform Bill of 1832, VI:945n, 999
Reformation, VI:965, 966n
Reid, Dr. John, VI:541
Reid, Thomas, VI:641

Index of Names

Rendell, Kenneth W., Inc., sale, V:122n
Reni, Guido, VI:873n–874n
Resistance, H.M.S., V:41n
Restoration, VI:967
Reveley, Henry, V:508n; VI:599, 1069n; kaleidoscope, VI:764, 766–767; steamboat, VI:688, 930, 941, 942, 943, 1095–96, 1110
Reveley, Maria. *See* Gisborne, Maria
Reynell, C. H., V:155; VI:86on
Reynolds, Charlotte and Jane, V:428
Reynolds, Eliza Powell Drewe, VI:807
Reynolds, John Hamilton, V:403, 405, 407, 410n, 411n, 428, 444; biography, VI 806–807; letter to, from Hunt, VI:805–806; works, VI:806
Rhampsinitus, VI:621, 630
Rheims, France, VI:527; cathedral, VI:588
Rhone (river), VI:524, 526
Ricardo, David, VI:1004
Ricci, Angelo Maria, VI:900n
Rice, James, V:433, 435, 444; VI:807, 809
Richard I, King of England, VI:822
Richards, Charles, V:408n
Richardson, Dr., VI:903n
Richardson, James or John, VI:903, 904; letter to (?), from Godwin, VI:902
Richardson, R. and H., VI:603
Richardson, William, V:478, 479, 480
Richman, N., V:328
Richmond Bridge, VI:923, 924
Ridgway, James (Ridgeway), V:156
Riot Act, VI:936, 937
Ritchie, Anne Thackeray, V:67
Ritchie (Richer), Joseph, V:433, 441
Robert, Prince, VI:822
Roberts, Daniel, V:49, 51, 52, 56, 182n
Robertson, Henry, VI:740, 744, 745
Robespierre, Maximilien François Marie Isidore de, VI:1063
Robinson, H., V:57
Robinson, Henry Crabb, V:25n, 164, 264, 316, 358, 386, 469, 498, 507; VI:541n, 558, 771n, 850, 904, 915n
Robinson, Howard, VI:665n
Robinson's Magazine, VI:747
Rochfort, Harriette Wilson. *See* Wilson, Harriette
Rochfort, Henry, V:62
Rodd, Thomas, V:125n
Rogers, Henry, V:229

Rogers, Neville, V:426n; VI:1067, 1068, 1070
Rogers, Samuel, V:228, 229, 241, 244; VI:691n, 700, 701, 1129, 1130, 1131; letter to, from Byron, VI:1130
Roget, Peter Mark, *Thesaurus*, V:386
Roland, M., VI:818
Rolleston, Maud (Mrs. T. W.), VI:956, 957
Rolleston, T. W., VI:956–957, 958, 960
Rollins, Hyder E.: on Bath Vellum, V:488; on Thomas Harris, VI:843n; on sc 444, V:440, 442–443
Romagna, Italy, VI:812
Romano, Giulio, VI:553–554, 610, 616
Romani, Felice, V:461
Rome, Italy, VI:553, 573, 605, 610, 914, 940; Byron in, V:84, 199, 200, 241; A. Curran in, V:500; Keats at, V:413, 414, 415, 418, 419, 420; PBS in, VI:586, 708, 763, 764, 766, 781, 782, 784, 794, 837, 838, 859, 861, 873, 941, 942; PBS on classical, VI:991, 1004; PBS's grave, V:52, 399; William Shelley's grave, V:50; Teatro Argentina, VI:521n
Romieux, M. and Mme., VI:543n, 546n. *See also* Aimée
Romilly, Sir Samuel, VI:563
Rooke, Rev. Mr., VI:831
Rose, Polly, V:365
Rosenbach, A. S. W., sale, V:15
Rosenbach Museum, V:265n, 267n
Roskilly, Dr., VI:768
Rosser, Henry Blanch, V:507; VI:541
Rossetti, Dante Gabriel, V:60, 399, 439, 440; *Sir Hugh the Heron*, V:269
Rossetti, Francesca Maria Polidori, V:269
Rossetti, Gabriele, V:269
Rossetti, William Michael, V:188, 211, 268, 399; and Trelawny, V:60, 68, 69, 70; on "On Love," VI:641, 642; on PBS's seal, V:22n
Rossini, Gioacchino Antonio, *Il Barbiere di Siviglia*, VI:521, 549, 550
Rouen, France, VI:821–828, 831; cathedral, VI:822–823
Rousseau, Jean Jacques, V:393; VI:789, 946, 973, 979, 988, 1044; *Confessions*, VI:568; "Discours sur les Sciences et les Arts . . . ," V:394
Rownhams, V:344n
Royal Academy, VI:614

Index of Names

Royal Fort Boarding School, Bristol, V:40
Royal William, H.M.S., V:41n
Royston, Hertfordshire, V:471
Ruskin, John, VI:589
Russell Street, London, VI:793
Russia, V:459; VI:981, 982, 988, 1038
Rydal Mount, Westmorland, V:266
Ryland, Mr., V:394

St. Aubyn, Sir John, V:46–47
St. Christopher's (St. Kitts), B.W.I., VI:573
St. Columbanus, V:6, 8
St. Croix, Marianne de, VI:661
St. Croix, Sarah de, VI:661
St. Croix, William de, VI:661
Saint Dizier, France, VI:528
St. Gallen, VI:832
St. James Street, London, VI:941n, 1129
St. James's Place, London, V:244
St. Mary's Church, Paddington, London, V:42–43
St. Michael's Mount, Cornwall, V:46, 59
St. Mildred's Church, Bread Street, London, V:31, 80, 377n
Saint Omer, France, VI:524, 527
St. Ouen, Rouen, VI:826
St. Peter's, VI:588
Saint-Pierre, Charles Irénée Castel, Abbé de, VI:979
Salamis, V:54
Salisbury, James Cecil, 7th Earl and 1st Marquess of, VI:1139
Salisbury, Robert Cecil, 1st Earl of, VI:792
Salisbury Square, London, V:377n
Salona, Dalmatia, V:55
Salsette, H.M.S., VI:1123
San Giuliano, Baths of, Italy, VI:580
San Nicolò, Forte di, VI:694n
San Terenzo, Italy, V:181
Sardinia, Kingdom of, VI:528
Sartoris, Adelaide, V:67
Sa'ud, VI:988
Saudi Arabia, VI:989
Savoy, VI:543
Sawrey, Solomon, V:428, 440–441
Scapula, John (Joannes), V:285, 287, 299, 300, 306, 309, 330, 332, 473
Scheffer, Johann, VI:593–597

Schiller, Johann Christoph Friedrich von, V:162, 163; *Der Geisterseher*, V:309n
Schiller, Justin G., V:283n
Schlegel, August Wilhelm von, *Über dramatische Kunst und Litteratur*, VI:527, 528
Schulz, Herbert C., VI:872n
Scott, John, V:423n, 472n; VI:806
Scott, Sir Walter, V:397, 405, 434; VI:700; and *Frankenstein*, V:471–473, 503; letter to, from MWS (quoted), V:472–473
Scott, Walter Sidney, V:475n
Scott, William Bell, V:188
Scythia, VI:622, 630
"S.E." (Elston?), V:203
Seaham, Durham, VI:758
Sebright, Sir John, VI:1120
Seditious Meetings Act, V:198n
Serassi, Pietro Antonio, *La Vita di Torquato Tasso*, V:452, 465; VI:591, 663
Sesostris, VI:622
Settlement, Act of (1701), VI:1061
Severn, Joseph, V:408n; and Keats, V:403, 413n, 414, 415, 420, 422n, 428, 433, 434, 444; and Keats's "Isabella," VI:798–799
Seville, Spain, cathedral, VI:588
Seyer, Samuel, V:40, 41
Sgricci, Tommaso, V:18
Shadwell, Lancelot, V:98n
Shadwell, Thomas, *The Libertine*, V:253
Shakespeare, William, VI:520n, 521n, 610, 691, 797n, 851, 857, 967, 1002, 1035, 1039, 1062; and Thomas Cooper, V:356; and Keats, V:423n, 443; and EJT, V:42, 48, 102, 103, 134, 140, 194, 276–277, 278, 279, 282, 311, 313, 319, 320; VI:669, 671; and *The True Tragedie of Richard Duke of Yorke*, VI:770, 771, 772n
Sharif Husain ibn 'Ali, VI:989
Sheffield, Yorkshire, VI:999
Shelley, Sir Bysshe, V:5, 27, 30n; VI:542n, 945n, 1017
Shelley, Charles, V:116; VI:585n; guardianship, V:6, 85, 98n, 197, 297; VI:648–649, 650, 652, 695, 978; in PBS's will, V:104, 105, 114, 115
Shelley, Clara Everina, V:333; VI:606; birth, V:151n, 257, 291, 292n, 299, 301, 304; death, V:9n, 50; VI:647, 675, 692, 751, 858, 859, 861, 863; health, VI:678, 680, 689, 690, 693, 694

Index of Names

Shelley, Elena Adelaide, VI:578, 676n, 782

Shelley, Elizabeth, V:337; VI:805

Shelley, Frances, Lady, VI:801

Shelley, Harriet Westbrook, V:34, 98, 141, 142, 205, 251n, 273, 337, 471; VI:585n, 805; and PBS's will, V:114, 115; death, V:33, 35, 50, 82, 85, 89, 100, 302, 391, 404, 481n

Shelley, Hellen, V:337

Shelley, Ianthe. *See* Esdaile, Ianthe Shelley

Shelley, Lady Jane Gibson St. John, V:22, 67, 70, 475; VI:871, 893, 933; and Shelley letters, V:129, 275; and Shelley manuscripts, VI:956, 1086; *Shelley Memorials*, V:129

Shelley, Mary Wollstonecraft Godwin:

additions to letters, V:343, 384; VI:575–576, 765

and Baxters, V:332–342 *passim*, 367, 371, 378, 379, 380, 381, 384, 385, 387–388, 389, 391, 507

and David Booth, V:384, 387, 390, 392, 508

and Isabel Booth, V:334–335, 339, 347, 382, 385, 386n, 387, 389, 505–508

and Claire Clairmont, V:87–88, 342

and Thomas Cooper, V:360–361

and Walter Coulson, V:317, 318

and T. C. Croker, V:495n

and Gisbornes, V:512, 513; VI:579–580, 597–600, 676, 678, 767, 783, 784, 892, 930–931, 943, 1095–96

and Godwin, V:31, 33, 196, 198, 204, 205, 389, 391–392; VI:848–849, 857–858

and TJH, V:58, 100, 215, 330–331; VI:805

and Hunts, V:226–227, 231, 264, 292–293, 402; VI:524–525, 557–558, 605–606, 608–612, 615, 794, 795, 844, 904–910, 914, 936–937, 1091; and death of William Shelley, VI:838–842, 845–849

and Keats, V:404–405, 408, 409, 410, 413, 419

and Payne and Irving, V:233

and preface to Polidori's *Vampyre*, VI:778–781

and PBS: after children's deaths, VI:644, 646–647, 858, 861–865, 1110; and "A.B." affair, VI:666; and *Julian and Maddalo*, VI:859–861; and *Laon and Cythna — Revolt of Islam*, V:143–144, 146, 147–148, 151, 161, 165, 182; VI:798; and *Mask of Anarchy*, VI:893–894; and PBS's last days

and death, V:49–52; and PBS's trip to Venice, VI:676, 678–679; and PBS's will, V:110, 114n, 115; correspondence, V:315, 403, 505; finances, V:303–304, 482, 484; marriage, V:31, 33–35, 80, 89, 196, 355, 359; on PBS's health, V:470; on PBS's poetry, V:424; VI:660; on PBS's reading, VI:591, 627–628

and EJT, V:37, 43n, 47–48, 52–53, 59, 60, 63, 70

birth of Clara Shelley, V:151n, 291, 301

birth of Percy Florence Shelley, V:50; VI:864, 953, 1080, 1090, 1094

copies: *The Cenci*, VI:899; Cenci history, V:464; VI:897–898; letters of 1816, V:315–316; *Peter Bell the Third*, VI:952; sc 494, VI:672–675, 678

death of Clara, V:50; VI:692, 863

death of William, V:50; VI:838, 839, 842; depression, VI:845, 848–849, 852, 854, 857, 863–864, 874, 892, 910

errands, V:257, 258, 267, 511; VI:603–605, 877, 887, 891–892, 911, 914, 1083

health, V:461; VI:526, 527, 543, 678, 680

in London, V:327, 491

letter style, V:437

Letters by, to:

W. T. Baxter, V:332–333, 338

Isabel Booth, V:505–506

Maria Gisborne, VI:597–598

Leigh and Marianne Hunt (with PBS), V:225–227; VI:523–526

postscript to sc 441, V:384

letters in hand of, V:467–468, 469–470, 476

letters of introduction, V:512; VI:579–580

Letters to, from:

Leigh Hunt, VI:790–794, 845–848, 904–908; (with PBS), VI:553–557, 739–741, 879–882, 886–888, 910–913

Leigh and Marianne Hunt, VI:605–614

Marianne Hunt, V:256–257

PBS (in her hand), VI:672–675

on Charles Clairmont, VI:1069

on La Scala, Milan, VI:589–590

on *Otello*, VI:590

on William Shelley, VI:873

on Horace Smith, VI:562

on taxes, VI:1059

other letter by, to (quoted), Christina Baxter, V:341–342

publishers, V:127n, 394

reading, V:464; VI:690–691, 707, 708, 766

remains at Marlow, V:315, 504

seal, V:22n

transcripts: fragments of poems, V:181, (illus.), V:175; "On Love," VI:633–635, 639–642; *Philosophical View of Reform*, VI:955–956, 957, 958, 961; sc 399, V:214–215; translation of *Symposium*, VI:656

travel, V:463, 500; VI:524–525, 526–529, 543, 546, 547, 598, 708; at Bagni di Lucca, VI:615, 658, 665, 676; in Naples, VI:558, 768, 769n; in Rome, VI:784, 794; in Venice, VI:558, 692, 693–694, 706–707, 863; on Douai, VI:524–525, 527; on Italy, VI:560n, 590, 909, 916; plans, V:363, 364; trip to and at Este, VI:674, 679–680, 689, 690–691, 694

mentioned, V:7, 8, 15n, 21n, 24, 30n, 36, 85, 133, 141, 187, 192, 197, 228, 230, 239, 251, 252, 261, 262, 263, 272, 292n, 310n, 355, 358, 401, 450, 460, 461, 483n; VI:586, 655, 703, 782n, 871, 898, 915n, 1060, 1068, 1082, 1086, 1091, 1101

WORKS

Fortunes of Perkin Warbeck, The, V:127n

Frankenstein, V:31, 127n, 151n, 267, 366, 393–394, 395, 446, 451, 481, 502, 503; VI:556, 575, 579, 599, 617, 661n, 707, 740, 780, 781, 806, 808, 848; accounts, V:396–398, 445; proofs, 298–299, 316

History of a Six Weeks' Tour (with PBS), V:125, 151n, 155, 156, 315–316, 390; VI:588, 765, 1014

Last Man, The, V:127n

Lodore, V:127n

"Note on the Cenci," VI:898, 899, 929

"Note on the *Revolt of Islam*," V:147–148, 470

"Notes on Poems Written in 1818," VI:660

Rambles in Germany and Italy, VI:693n

Shelley, Percy Bysshe:

(*This entry is limited to topics personally concerned with Shelley, his letters, manuscripts, and works. For his relations with other people, residences, etc., see under specific entries.*)

and "Angling" theme, VI:1078, 1079

and "damsels in distress," V:336–337

and fine and performing arts, V:461, 501, 503–504; VI:583, 589–590, 764, 767–768, 890

anonymity, VI:862, 934n, 1014

Baxter-Booth correspondence, listed, V:338–339

books and reading, V:25, 47, 191–192, 212, 215, 236–240, 256, 293n, 304–307, 309, 332, 343–345, 358, 394, 464–466, 470, 471, 473, 477; VI:551, 552, 584, 590–592, 615, 626–633, 639, 647, 662, 687n, 690n, 691, 766, 786–787, 789, 863, 951, 953

chariot, V:496–497

death and burial, V:50–52, 70; VI:829

eagle image, V:212–214

effect on of *Quarterly Review* review of *Laon and Cythna*, VI:933–934

1819, VI:1109–10

finances, V:1–4, 27–30, 31, 35, 36, 120–123, 145, 201–205, 224, 267, 302–304, 316, 317, 328–330, 396–398, 447, 449, 466–467, 478–484, 486, 488, 490–492, 510, 514, 515–516; VI:653–655, 664–668, 695, 800–801, 884, 928–929, 938–944, 1095–96

forged letters, V:6–9, 15, 479–480

health and diet, V:34, 143, 226, 230–231, 242, 245, 293, 316, 332n, 333, 350, 363, 365–366, 461, 468, 470, 477; VI:553, 574, 605, 680, 690, 768, 1082

Hoppner scandal, VI:578, 666, 782n

in London, V:8n, 88, 228, 292, 297, 300, 315–316, 327, 469n, 479, 491–492, 496, 501, 503–504, 507, 515

influence of, VI:804

leaves England, V:510, 516; VI:518–519, 520–521, 523

letter style, V:436–437

Letters by, to:

William Baxter, V:345–346, 371–372, 381–385

Brooks, Son and Dixon, VI:800–801, 937–939; autograph checks, V:120–121, 302, 326–327, 367, 448–449, 466–467, 488–490, 496, 508–510, 513–515; VI:653, 668

Byron, V:15–18, 82–83, 195–197, 241–243, 290–292, 361–363; VI:542–543, 563–567, 574–576, 689–690, 706

Claire Clairmont, V:31–33, 86–87; VI:692–693

Index of Names

Gisbornes, VI:1094

"Godwin" (forgery), V:6–7

TJH, V:99–100, 214 (fragment), 236–237, 330–331, 469–470; VI:582–585, 763–765

Leigh Hunt, V:262–264; VI:850–854, 1080–83, 1106–08

Leigh and Marianne Hunt (with MWS), V:225–227; VI:523–526

Lackington, Hughes and Co., V:26–27, 298, 395

Charles Ollier, V:123–124, 342–343, 347–350, 369, 392–393, 444–445, 446–447, 467–468, 476; VI:664–665, 781–782, 874–876, 926–928, 1096–1100

TLP, VI:656–658, 895–896

MWS (her transcript), VI:672–675

William Willats, V:478

Letters to, from:

Godwin, V:200–202, 296–297

Hunt, V:271–272, 314; VI:839–842, 1088–91; (with MWS), VI:553–557, 739–741, 879–882, 886–888, 910–913

Leigh and Marianne Hunt, (with MWS), VI:605–614

TJH, V:304–308

Manuscripts, miscellaneous:

The Cenci, Dedication to Leigh Hunt, VI:865–871

Herodotus, Notes in copy of (with Godwin), VI:618–626

"Lament for Bion," translation of, V:190–191

Laon and Cythna fragments, V:170–172, 182–187

Mask of Anarchy, draft stanzas, VI:892–893

"Mighty Eagle" fragment, V:205–206

Note on "Ode to the West Wind," VI:1066–67

"On Love," VI:633–638

Philosophical View of Reform, VI:961–1066

Plato's *Republic,* fragment from translation of, VI:784–786

Prometheus Unbound fragments, VI:1069–70, 1071–72

will, copy of, V:103–114

nicknames, Italianized names, epithets, V:229, 251, 287, 289n, 505; VI:553, 560

notebook habits, V:144–145, 211–212; VI:638–639, 786–787, 1067–68, 1069, 1072, 1074–75

Other letters to, from (quoted):

William Baxter, V:379–381

David Booth, V:388–389

philosophy, ideas, comments: friendship and personal relationships, V:36, 240–241, 388; historians as poets, VI:629; life and mind, V:198–199; love, VI:633–635, 641–647; poetry, poets, poetic language, V:246–247, 248, 291, 295–296, 406–407, 424; VI:647, 789, 851–852, 927, 1087, 1103–04; politics and political events, V:16–17, 19, 197, 198, 244–245; VI:854, 893, 896, 900–901, 945–951, 962–1066, 1088, 1107; political poems and papers, VI:1085, 1092; principles, V:84, 142; religion, V:246; VI:1109; supernatural, VI:663; translations, V:310, 332; VI:1081, 1086–88; virtue, V:246; wealth, V:310

physicians, VI:652

plans for Italy, V:231, 242, 245, 290, 293, 303–304, 340, 363–364, 501–502

portraits, V:500; VI:891n; (illus., silhouette), VI:889

promissory note, to Horace Smith, V:328–330

provenance, V:121–122, 129, 188–189, 261, 275

publishers and printers, V:124–125, 154–167, 221, 223, 347–353, 369–370, 393, 445–446; VI:517–518, 531–539, 781, 783, 876, 878, 926–931, 1099, 1100–01, 1104–06; and *Frankenstein,* V:298–299, 393, 395–398, 471–473, 503

seals, V:21–22; (illus.), VI:752

self-portraits in poems, VI:1102–03

Clara Shelley's birth, V:291, 299, 301, 304, 308; death, V:129; VI:692, 694, 859, 861

William Shelley's death, V:129; VI:837–838, 839, 842, 858, 861–862, 863–865, 874

travels, V:462–463; VI:523, 524–525, 526–529, 543, 557, 572, 575, 580, 583, 598–599, 656, 666, 672, 676, 680, 685, 690, 693–694, 706–707, 708, 763–764, 765, 784, 923, 1069; 1816 trip to Switzerland, V:315, 327, 460; VI:526, 546, 804; maps of travels, VI:544–545, 677, 855; on Bagni di Lucca, VI:658–659; on gondolas, VI:673; on Italy and Italians, VI:583, 586–587, 764–765, 767, 769; on Rome, VI:764; on Milan, V:461–462; VI:583, 587, 588–589; on Villa Pliniana, VI:547–548

Index of Names

Westbrook vs. Shelley, V:6, 84–85, 96, 98,
  145, 195, 197, 272–274, 297–298, 390–391;
  VI:648–650
wills, V:103–117

WORKS

An Address, to the Irish People, VI:948,
  949n
*An Address to the People on the Death of the
  Princess Charlotte* (by "The Hermit of
  Marlow"), V:125, 146n, 244, 324; VI:1049
Adonais, V:125, 145, 191, 270n, 371n, 388;
  VI:589n, 646, 647, 660, 691, 838, 883, 933,
  934, 1055; and Keats, V:399, 417–418,
  422–427; composition and publication,
  V:419–422
Alastor, V:125, 141, 146n, 167n, 191, 221,
  295, 341, 370n, 393, 406–407, 445;
  VI:642, 644, 804, 931n, 1017
"The Banquet of Plato," VI:629n, 639n,
  642. *See also* Translations, below
The Cenci, V:125, 422n, 424, 464; VI:546n,
  589n, 680, 857, 878, 933, 1109; composi-
  tion and publication of, VI:628, 895–900,
  926, 929, 930, 931, 1104; dedication,
  VI:557, 865–874, 1070, 1083n, 1090
"Chameleons feed on light and air,"
  VI:992
"Charles the First," V:214
"The Cloud," VI:530
Contraception, fragment on, VI:956, 961
Declaration of Rights, VI:948
A Defence of Poetry, V:191, 239–240, 247,
  310, 388, 424, 426n; VI:590, 629, 642,
  645, 647, 663, 786, 787, 789, 947, 991,
  992–993, 1088, 1103
"A Discourse of the Manners of the
  Ancient Greeks Relative to the Subject
  of Love," VI:628–629, 638, 639, 642
"England in 1819," VI:1109
Epipsychidion, V:125, 211, 212, 295, 388,
  422; VI:646, 647, 862, 934n, 1093n
The Esdaile Notebook, "The Voyage,"
  VI:882
Essay on Christianity, V:192, 246; VI:786
Essays, Letters from Abroad, VI:640, 658n,
  678, 860, 900n, 955
"Fiordispina," V:211
"Fragment of the Elegy on the Death of
  Bion," V:86

"Fragment: Zephyrus the Awakener,"
  VI:872
"Ginevra," V:211
Hellas, V:52, 125, 213–214, 388; VI:589n,
  630, 934n
History of a Six Weeks' Tour (with MWS),
  V:125, 151n, 155, 156, 315–316, 390;
  VI:588, 765, 1014
Hubert Cauvin, V:142n
"Hymn to Intellectual Beauty" (by
  "Elphin Knight"), V:401, 402, 406,
  411n, 506; VI:530
"Lament for Bion," V:190–193
Julian and Maddalo, V:199; VI:568, 616,
  639, 690, 851–852, 857, 891, 1082, 1099,
  1100, 1109; and *Prince Athanase*,
  VI:1101, 1102–1104; compositions and
  dating, VI:858–865; identity of characters, VI:859, 861, 863, 1103
Laon and Cythna, V:125n, 240, 246, 256,
  293n, 316, 336, 390; VI:630, 701, 798, 1067;
  composition and publication, V:141–166,
  239, 264, 267, 291, 292, 295, 297, 309n,
  347–353, 446n; VI:537, 836; draft loca-
  tions, V:168–169; provenance, V:172,
  181, 188–189; review, V:146, 165, 448;
  VI:878, 922, 930, 931–934; suppression
  and revision, V:158, 164–166, 363, 369,
  370–371, 448; stanzas, V:170–189. See
  also *The Revolt of Islam*, below
Letter to Lord Ellenborough, VI:854
"Letter to Maria Gisborne," VI:616, 699n,
  934n
"Lines written among the Euganean
  Hills," V:506; VI:560n, 589n, 639, 645,
  680, 769n, 783, 784n, 859, 1109; review,
  VI:881, 885
"Love's Philosophy," VI:1085, 1086, 1094
"Marianne's Dream," VI:740, 742
The Mask of Anarchy, V:211; VI:854, 871,
  872, 896, 901, 934n, 951, 1068n, 1070,
  1074, 1081, 1083, 1085, 1088, 1109;
  draft stanza, VI:892–895
"Methought I was a billow in the crowd,"
  V:181; (illus.), V:175
"Mighty Eagle," V:205–214
"Mont Blanc," V:125, 143n; VI:530, 589n,
  947, 1014
"The Necessity of Atheism," V:340
"Ode to Liberty," V:213; VI:934n

"Ode to Naples," VI:667–668

"Ode to the West Wind," V:189; VI:901, 1110; Note on, VI:1066–69

"An Ode, written October, 1819, before the Spaniards Had Recovered their Liberty," VI:952

Œdipus Tyrannus; or, Swellfoot the Tyrant, V:20, 124n, 211; VI:667–668, 934n, 1024, 1055, 1087

"On a Future State," VI:639n, 643

"On Keats," V:181; (illus.), V:175

"On Life," VI:956, 961, 971, 1110

"On Love," VI:633–647

"On the Nile," V:192, 410

"One word is too often profaned," VI:646

"Ozymandias," V:506

"The pale, the cold, and the moony smile," V:370n

"Pan, Echo and the Satyr," V:191

"Passage of the Apennines," VI:1086

Peter Bell the Third, V:424, 511; VI:707, 808, 901, 934n, 952, 1055, 1083, 1085n, 1102n, 1109

A Philosophical View of Reform, V:146n, 310, 388; VI:896, 901, 949, 950, 1067, 1072, 1088, 1110; discussed, VI:951–961; text, VI:961–1066

Poetical Works (1839), V:147; VI:526, 660, 860, 929n

Poetical Works (1840), VI:693n

Poetical Works (Forman), V:166

Posthumous Poems, V:191, 448; VI:646, 678, 859, 1086, 1101, 1102

Prince Athanase, VI:1087, 1100–04

"Prince Athanase; A Fragment," VI:1100–01, 1102

Prometheus Unbound, V:125, 146n, 148, 211, 294, 408, 424; VI:530, 589n, 628, 639, 660, 662, 680, 690, 691, 784n, 844, 851, 854, 871, 872, 878, 883n, 901, 933, 934, 950, 952, 1024, 1068, 1082, 1102, 1109; fragments, VI:1069–75; printing and correcting, VI:1104–06; sending, VI:926, 929–931

Proposals for an Association . . . , VI:948, 1023, 1053

A Proposal for Putting Reform to the Vote throughout the Kingdom (by "The Hermit of Marlow"), V:124, 125, 274

Queen Mab, V:46, 141n–142n, 196, 197, 231n, 245, 273, 284, 291, 336, 341, 390, 406, 408; VI:573, 589n, 910, 934n

A Refutation of Deism, VI:1109n

The Revolt of Islam, V:36, 125, 240, 295, 405n, 406, 424, 446, 467, 468, 477; VI:560n, 579, 589n, 642, 644, 661n, 740, 1023–24; advertising and review copies, V:393, 445–448, 476; and "Mighty Eagle," V:212–213; collation (sc 391, sc 392, sc 393), V:171–172, 184, 186–187; composition and publication, V:142, 144, 147–148, 150n, 153n, 158, 159, 166, 362, 363, 369–370; review, V:417, 447–448; VI:743, 934. See also *Laon and Cythna,* above

Rosalind and Helen, V:125, 146n, 315, 411, 424, 482; VI:547, 589n, 642, 656, 659–660, 666, 667, 783, 854, 859, 862, 864, 878, 885, 899n, 1103, 1105; Booth character in, V:506–507; Hunt on, VI:841, 844

"The Sensitive Plant," VI:645, 934n

"Song to the Men of England," VI:1085n

"Stanzas written in Dejection, near Naples," VI:639, 645

"To Constantia," V:460, 461

"To Stella — translated from Plato," V:181; (illus.), V:175

Translations: from Goethe, "Harzreise im Winter," V:463; *Cyclops* of Euripides, VI:1081, 1086–87, 1101n; Greek poems, V:191; "Lament for Bion," V:190–193; Plato's *Republic,* VI:784–789; Plato's *Symposium,* VI:627, 629, 641, 656–659, 1081, 1086

The Triumph of Life, V:148; VI:646, 660, 789, 882, 890, 934

"The Witch of Atlas," V:213, 424n; VI:530, 934n

"The Woodman and the Nightingale" (fragment), V:426n

Zastrozzi, V:371n

Shelley, Sir Percy Florence, V:22n, 50, 261, 413, 475, 483n; VI:744, 838, 914, 1080, 1083; and Hunt's letters to PBS, V:275; birth, VI:784n, 850, 864, 944, 953, 1084, 1094; letter to Isabel Booth, V:508

Shelley, Sir Timothy, V:29, 33, 104, 115, 297n, 483, 484, 512; VI:546, 678; and Parliament,

VI:945, 999; and PBS, V:27, 28, 29, 30, 31, 121, 142; and Westbrook vs. Shelley, VI:648, 649, 650

Shelley, William, V:32, 34n, 52, 89, 333; VI:606, 612, 675, 689, 694; death, V:9n, 50; VI:557, 647, 751, 766, 784, 837, 839, 842, 858, 861, 862, 863–864, 865, 941, 1110; illness and health, VI:706, 784, 873, 874; in PBS's will, V:106, 114, 115; portrait, VI:838n, 891n; PBS on, V:214, 216, 242, 243, 245, 291, 362

Shelley Family Settlements, V:30

Shelley-Rolls, John, bequest, VI:638

Shelley Society, The, VI:893n

Sherborn Lane, London, VI:603

Sheridan, Richard Brinsley, VI:843n

Sherwood, William, V:156; Godwin's letters to (quoted), VI:777–779

Sherwood, Gilbert, and Piper, V:156n

Sherwood, Neely and Jones, V:154, 156, 349; VI:777, 778, 1130

Shields, Amelia (Milly), V:267, 405n, 491, 492; VI:569, 577, 578, 676

Shorter, Alfred H., VI:751

Sicily, VI:563, 793

Siddons, Sarah, V:64, 356

Sidmouth, Henry Addington, 1st Viscount, V:475

Sidney, Algernon, VI:946, 971, 973

Sidney, Sir Philip, VI:696, 699n

Sieveking, A. Forbes, VI:1121

Silvestrini, Fanny, VI:815

Simplon Pass, Switzerland, V:230

Simpson, Mr., V:277, 279

Sind, VI:722

Siri and Wilhelin (Willelin; Wilhelm), V:243, 363; VI:543, 566

Sismondi, J. C. L. Simonde de, *Histoire des Républiques Italiennes du moyen âge,* VI:964n, 983

Sistine Chapel, VI:890

Skinas, Dr., V:199

Skinner Street (Godwin's residence), V:8, 32, 101, 314, 315, 328, 334, 342; VI:655, 747, 775n, 902, 904; Godwin's lawsuit, VI:655, 777

Sloperton Cottage, Devizes, Wiltshire, V:353

Smith, Adam, VI:1043

Smith, Eliza (daughter of Horace Smith), VI:562

Smith, Mrs. Emily, V:260

Smith, Harry B., V:459

Smith, Horace, V:317, 418, 442, 469n, 494; VI:529n, 585, 701, 754, 809, 910n, 929, 1127n; and Edward DuBois, VI:592, 595; and Hunt, V:229, 263, 267, 486; VI:916; and PBS, V:302, 303–304, 328–330, 482, 516; VI:562, 596, 654, 667–668, 939, 942, 943, 944, 1095; marriage, VI:556, 562; on Keats and PBS, V:403–404, 419; portrait, V:130n; promissory note to, from PBS, V:328–329; *Amarynthus the Nympholept,* VI:662; "Graybeard's Gossip . . . ," VI:667

Smith, Mrs. Horace (née Ford), VI:562

Smith, Horatio Shakespeare, VI:562n

Smith, James, V:130n; VI:595, 1127n

Smith, Robert M., V:84n

Smith, J., and Son, V:223

Smollett, Tobias, V:434; VI:911, 914

Smyth, Sir [George] Henry, VI:1119, 1120

Society for the Diffusion of Useful Knowledge, V:386n

Socrates, V:452; VI:787–789, 797n, 919, 921

Soho Square, London, V:40, 42, 139

Solon, VI:620

Somers Town, London, V:327n

Sompting, Sussex, V:68, 69, 77

Sophocles, V:163, 304

Sosicles of Corinth, VI:624, 632

South America: EJT on, V:195, 311, 313–314, 324, 325; PBS on, VI:986

South Carolina, V:232; University of, VI:745

South Street, Grosvenor Square, London, VI:744

Southampton, Hampshire, V:91, 279

Southend, Essex, VI:902

Southey, Robert, V:142, 405, 423n; VI:700, 1015, 1055; and PBS, VI:708, 743, 850, 926–927, 931–932, 933, 934, 1110; Hunt and, VI:791, 796, 797; letter-writing, VI:908n; on summer, 1817, V:293n; views in *Letter to William Smith,* V:222n, 245; VI:951n; *Wat Tyler,* V:99n, 156

Southwark, London, V:195

Spain, VI:573, 954, 982–986

Sparta, VI:624, 632

Spectator, V:61, 129, 260, 393, 394

Spence, Robert, VI:799

Spencer, Lord Henry, VI:573

Spencer, W. T., V:122

Index of Names

Spenser, Edmund, VI:610, 628, 1002; *Astrophel*, V:191; *The Faerie Queene*, V:293n
Spezia, Gulf of, VI:548
Spinoza, Baruch, VI:966, 970, 973
Spoleto, Italy, VI:708
Springall, John, V:113, 116, 117
Squibs, William, V:435
Stacey, Sophia, VI:969n, 944
Stäel, Anne Louise Germaine de, V:230; VI:953; *Corinne* . . . , VI:766
Stamford, Lincolnshire, V:471
Stamford Street, London, VI:895
Stanhope, Lady Hester, V:56
Stanhope, Leicester, V:54, 55
Stanley, Mr., V:279, 282
Staplehurst, Kent, V:321, 323, 325
Star, London, V:337, 338, 339–341, 380
Statius, VI:563; *Thebais*, VI:684–685, 687
Steel, Mrs. Almera, V:260
Steffen, Truman Guy, VI:898n
Stella d'Oro inn, Padua, Italy, VI:693
Stendhal (Henri Marie Beyle), VI: 767–768
Stephens, Alexander, VI:615
Stephens, Catherine (Stevens; later Countess of Essex), V:249, 252–253, 433, 441
Sterne, Lawrence, VI:635
Stewart, Dugald, VI:644
Steyning, Sussex, VI:945n
Stillinger, Jack, *Letters of Charles Armitage Brown*, V:258
Stith, Mrs., V:66
Stockdale, John Joseph, V:156
Stodart, Robert, VI:835n
Stodart and Steuart, VI:835
Stoddard, R. H., V:9, 15n
Stoke-upon-Trent, Staffordshire, VI:999
Stothard, Thomas, V:155, 156n
Stower, Caleb, V:188n
Strabo, V:255
Strachey, Edward, VI:721, 925n
Strand, the, London, VI:540, 835, 924n
Stuart, Isobel, V:339, 380, 385
Suffolk Street East, London, V:265
Suffolk Street Gallery, London, VI:614
Sun, The, V:219; VI:541
Superb, H.M.S., V:41n; VI:829, 830n
Surrey, Henry Howard, Earl of, VI:911
Surrey Gaol, London, V:89
Surrey Institution, V:265, 411n; VI:539, 542, 835

Sussex, Augustus Frederick, Duke of, V:497, 499n
Swansea, Glamorgan, V:86, 359
Swartwout, Samuel, V:354, 357
Sweden, VI:982, 983
Swedenborg, Emmanuel, VI:790, 798n
Swift, Jonathan, V:355, 360; VI:973, 1075, 1079
Swinburne, Algernon Charles, V:38, 68, 439, 440; VI:884
Swinburne, Sir John, VI:872, 881, 884
Switzerland, V:46–47, 198, 229, 248, 401, 460; VI:526; 672, 760, 804, 966
Sydenham, Kent, VI:595
Sykes, Paul, V:130n
Symonds, H. D., V:156
Syria, VI:988

Taaffe, John, *Comment on Dante*, V:420
Tacitus, VI:629
Tadcaster, Yorkshire, V:471
Talfourd, Thomas Noon, V:468n; VI:542, 558, 850n
Talleyrand, Charles Maurice de, Bishop of Autun, V:253n
Talma, François Joseph, V:236
Tansillo, Luigi, VI:906, 909, 910
Tanyrallt, Carnarvonshire, VI:561n, 627
Tasso, Bernardo, V:270n
Tasso, Torquato, V:270n; VI:657, 663, 744, 1088; Hunt's translation of *Aminta*, VI:591n, 616n, 884n, 912, 913, 916, 1081, 1086, 1087; PBS and, V:465–466; VI:584, 590–592, 639, 657, 861, 863, 864, 865
Tatchell, Molly, *Leigh Hunt* . . . , V:258, 261
Taunton, Somerset, V:115, 116
Taunton Courier, V:221n
Tavistock Street, London, VI:796
Taylor, John (of the *Sun*), V:219; VI:541; (?) letter to, from Godwin, V:217–218
Taylor, John (publisher), V:407; VI:547; and Godwin and Hazlitt, VI:833–836; and Hunt and PBS, V:220–223; VI:517–518, 531–539; and Keats, V:414; VI:809; letter by, to Hunt, VI:530–537; letters to, from Godwin, VI:833–834; from Hessey, VI:517; from Hunt, V:219–220
Taylor, John "of Norwich," V:29, 218, 219
Taylor, Robert H., V:84n

Index of Names

Taylor and Hessey, V:119, 124, 154, 344, 402, 408n; and Godwin and Hazlitt, VI:833–835; and Hunt and PBS, V:220–223; VI:517–518, 531, 537, 701

Téméraire, H.M.S., V:41n

Temple Bar, London, VI:924

Tennyson, Alfred, Lord, V:399, 441n; VI:797n

Terence, Colman edition, V:451, 464

Terni, cataract of, Italy, VI:764

Terrot, William, V:309n

Terry, Roderick, sale, VI:1069

Texas, University of, Stark Library, V:152, 468n

Texas Christian University, Lewis Collection, V:153, 188; VI:799

Thackeray, William, VI:719n

Thackeray, William Makepeace (first), VI:719n

Thackeray, William Makepeace, V:46, 67, 443n; VI:719n

Thames (river), VI:601, 688

Thatched House Tavern, VI:1120

Thelwall, John, V:472n

Theobalds Park, Hertfordshire, VI:924n

Theocritus, V:191, 192, 299, 393, 394; VI:700, 952

Thermopylae, battle of, VI:625, 632

Thirsk, Yorkshire, V:471

Thomas, Moses, V:358

Thomirey, France, VI:528n

Thomson, James, *The Seasons*, V:280, 282

Thorey, France, VI:528

Thornhill, Mr., VI:603

Thornton, Mr., V:218

Thracians, VI:631

Thucydides, VI:627, 629

Ticknor, George, V:358n

Tieck, Johann Ludwig, V:358n

Tighe, George W., V:153n, 159; VI:579

Tilson & Preston, VI:655

Timaeus of Locri, *De anima mundi . . .* , VI:552

Times, The, V:265; advertisement for Albion House, V:146n, 148n

Timoleon, VI:629

Timperley, C. H., V:158

Titus, Arch of, VI:786, 787n

Toland, Mr., VI:792

Tolson (?), Sarah, V:277, 281, 283; VI:581, 582

Tolson, Mrs. (Mother), V:193, 194, 277, 283, 321, 323, 324; VI:581, 582

Tomkyns, Mr., VI:891n

Tompkins, J. M., P. R., or P. W., V:120, 122–123

Took's (Tooke's) Court, London, V:116, 117, 216, 217, 469

Topping, Mme., V:204

Torlonia, Giovanni-Raimondo, Duke of Bracciano, VI:801, 1096

Torlonia, Mme., Duchess of Bracciano, VI:801

Torlonia, V:414; VI:800, 801, 940, 941, 943, 1095

Toronto (York), Canada, V:75

Tour-du-Pin, France, VI:543

Tournus (?), VI:528n

Traveller, V:288

Tre Donzelle, Le, Pisa, V:454

Tre Mori hotel, Bologna, VI:674, 679n

Trelawne, V:39–40, 59, 77

"Trelawny, Mrs.," puzzle of, V:81

Trelawny, Augusta Goring, V:66, 67, 77

Trelawny, Caroline Julia Addison, V:42–45, 59, 71, 72, 74, 80, 81, 94, 95, 276, 277, 279, 311, 313

Trelawny, Edgar, V:66, 77

Trelawny, Edward (EJT's cousin), V:95n

Trelawny, Edward John:

 and Byron, V:37, 42, 47, 48, 52–54, 55, 195; VI:671–672

 and Fanny Kemble, V:64–65, 76

 and MWS, V:22n, 37, 43n, 47–48, 52–53, 59, 60, 63, 70

 and PBS, V:37, 42, 46–52, 70

 and Augusta White, V:45, 65, 66–67, 71–72, 74–75, 77–78, 91, 92, 95, 102–103, 193–194, 282, 311, 313, 322, 324, 325; VI:582, 669–671; correspondence discussed, V:71, 76, 78. *See also* Letters by, to, *below.*

 and Capt. White's death, V:78, 101–102, 324

 and Mrs. White, V:72, 74, 102, 103

 and Edward Williams, V:47, 48; VI:672, 830, 1092n

 character, V:37–38, 78–79

 early life, V:39–42

 family, V:60–63, 91, 139–140, 279, 283, 311

 friends, V:59–60, 67–68

 handwriting and spelling, V:79, 81, 95–96

 later years, V:58–70

 Letters by, *to* Augusta White, V:79–80, 89–93, 101–103, 133–134, 139, 193–194,

Index of Names

275–277, 278–281, 310–313, 318–323; VI:580–581, 669–670

marriages and divorces, V:42–45, 55, 56–57, 58, 66, 67, 71, 72, 74, 77, 79–80, 94, 276, 277, 313

portrait, V:278, 281, 283

religion, V:324

seal, V:325–326

South American plans, V:195, 311, 313–314, 324, 325

travels, V:41–42, 52–58, 59, 62, 64–66

mentioned, V:127, 261, 462

WORKS

Adventures of a Younger Son, V:37, 39n, 40, 41, 42, 60, 61, 64, 127n, 324–325; VI:671

Records, V:37, 47, 49, 55, 69, 181n

Recollections, V:37, 47, 49, 55, 67, 69, 181n

Trelawny, Eliza, V:45, 59, 71, 79, 95; christening, V:71, 134, 139–140; death, V:60, 76

Trelawny, Jonathan, V:39

Trelawny, Rt. Rev. Jonathan, V:39

Trelawny, Laetitia (later Mrs. Charles Call), V:69, 78

Trelawny, Maria Julia, V:43, 95

Trelawny, Tersitza, V:55, 56–57

Trelawny, Zellâ, V:57, 58, 59, 60–61, 77

Trelawny. *See also* Brereton

Tremezzina, Italy, VI:548

Trevanion, John Charles, V:62

Treves, Peregrine, VI:665n

Treviso, Italy, VI:815

Trewithen, Cornwall, V:39, 41, 59

Trieste, VI:1069

Trinity College, Dublin, VI:650

Triphook, R., V:120, 124, 155, 220, 222; VI:534, 537

Tripolitza, Greece, V:54

Troyes, France, VI:831; cathedral, VI:588

Turin, Italy, VI:589, 768, 1084

Turkey, VI:988, 989

Turnbull, Mr., V:204, 216, 217

Turner, Mr. and Mrs., V:102, 103, 134, 139, 322; VI:581

Turner, Cornelia Boinville, VI:797

Turner, Dawson, V:23n

Turner, Thomas, V:234; VI:792, 797

Turner, William, VI:1049

Tuscany, Italy, V:269, 414

Twickenham, Middlesex, VI:602

Twomey, Paul B. G., VI:659n

Tylecote, Mr., V:516n

Tyler, John, V:357

Tyler, Robert, V:357

Ulysses. *See* Odysseus

Union Bank of London, V:121, 122

United States: Cobbett in, V:163, 245; Cooper in, V:357; Declaration of Independence, VI:1036; TJH on, V:285–286, 289; PBS on, VI:974–978; EJT in, V:64–66

Unterwalden, Switzerland, VI:759

Upsala, Sweden, VI:597

Utrecht, Union of, VI:966

Utterson, Edward Vernon, VI:1135, 1136

Vaccà, Andrea Berlinghieri, V:269–270, 293; VI:652

Vaga (boat), V:238; VI:684, 685, 687, 688

Vale of Health, Hampstead, V:227, 402, 403, 405, 474

Vallerini, Fernando, V:421n; VI:900n

Valpy, Abraham John, V:467, 468–469

Valpy, Edward, V:468n

Valpy, Edward John Western, V:468n

Valpy, Francis Edward Jackson, V:468n

Valpy, Richard, V:468n

Valpy, Richard, merchant, V:469n

Vansittart, Colonel George, V:476

Vansittart, Nicholas, V:474, 475–476

Van Winkle, C. S., V:358n

Vega Carpio, Lope Felix de, *Some Account of the Life and Writings of . . .*, V:117, 119; VI:611

Venice, Italy, VI:554, 689, 859; Allegra's trip to, and residence at, V:462, 513; VI:577–578, 598, 675, 748; Byron in, V:18, 19, 21, 195, 199, 230, 241, 248, 256, 462, 495, 513; VI:543, 566, 567, 568, 576, 674, 676, 690, 751, 764, 815, 816; mail to, V:200, 243n; Rialto, VI:706–707; Clara Shelley's death at, V:301; VI:692; PBS at, VI:558, 586, 591, 592n, 628, 672, 673–675, 692, 693–694, 706–707, 763, 764, 863; PBS on, VI:560; PBS's trip to, VI:666, 676, 679, 680

Verona, Italy, V:18; VI:983

[1193]

Index of Names

Verplanck, Gulian C., V:233; VI:745
Versailles, France, VI:831
Vesuvius, Italy, VI:764
Viareggio, Italy, V:51, 261
Vicenza, Italy, VI:983
Vienna, Austria, V:58; VI:1069
Victoria of Saxe-Coburg-Saalfeld, V:499
Viets, Henry R., VI:778n, 781
View Cottage, Bath, V:321
Viganò, Salvatore, *Otello, ossia Il Moro di Venezia*, V:452, 462; VI:583, 590
Villa Diodati, V:19, 367n; VI:781, 844
Villa Lanzi, VI:547
Villa Valsovana, VI:874
Vincigliati, castle of, Italy, V:67
Virgil, V:249; VI:563; *Aenid*, V:253n; tenth *Eclogue*, V:191
Virginia, V:232
Virginia Water, VI:519, 602, 685, 686, 802
Vitry-le-François, France, VI:528
Vivian, Charles, V:50
Viviani, Maria-Teresa Anna Vincenzia Torella, V:337
Volney, Constantin François Chasse-Bœuf, Comte de, VI:946
Voltaire, Jean François Marie Arouet de, V:247; VI:519, 522, 923, 924, 946, 979

Wade, Thomas, V:439
Wahhabi movement, VI:988–989
Wales, V:66–67, 77, 439
Walford House, V:116
Walker, William, V:121, 122
Wall, Mr., V:203, 204
Waller, Mr., V:141
Wallis, the Misses, VI:757, 758
Wallis, Dr. John, VI:652
Wallis, Richard, letter to, from Lady Byron, VI:757–758
Walton, Isaak, VI:1076, 1077, 1079–80
Ward, Messrs., VI:943
Ward, Aileen, V:440, 441
Ward, H. B., VI:943
Ward, John William, VI:1129
Ward, T. H., *Men of the Reign*, V:265
Ward, William S., VI:1135n
Ware, Hertfordshire, V:471
Wark, Robert R., V:130n; VI:872n
Warner Street, London, V:403

Warren, John, VI:835n
Warwick, Warwickshire, V:297; VI:585n
Warwick Street, London, V:233
Waterloo, VI:1003
Waterloo House, London, V:77
Watson, Miss, V:503n
Webb, Timothy, VI:1087
Webb & Co., VI:942, 943
Weigl, Joseph, *Il rivale di sè stesso*, V:452, 461
Wedgwood, Josiah, V:218, 360n
Welbeck Street, Cavendish Square, London, V:127, 222
Wellesley, Francis, V:130
Wellesley, Richard, 2nd Earl of Mornington, VI:715, 716
Wellington, Arthur Wellesley, 1st Duke of, VI:715, 1028
Wells, Charles Jeremiah, V:428, 433, 434; VI:806n, 807, 894n; biography, V:438–440; works, V:439, 440
Wells, Mrs. Charles Jeremiah, V:435
Wells, Gabriel, V:122
West, Benjamin, V:236; "Death on the Pale Horse," VI:894n
West, Mrs. Benjamin, VI:894n
West Indies, VI:990
Westboook, Eliza, V:82, 83, 86, 116; VI:648, 650
Westbrook, John, V:116; VI:648, 650, 695
Westbrook vs. Shelley, V:6, 34, 82, 84–85, 87, 96, 98, 242, 272–274, 297–298, 390–391; VI:674, 978; chancellor's orders, V:197; VI:647–650
Westminster Abbey, VI:583, 588
Westmorland, VI:686, 709
Weymouth, Dorset, V:288; VI:570, 571
Wheatley, Miss, VI:903n
Whitall, W. Van R., sale, V:9n, 15
Whitcombe, W. G., V:56
White, Augusta (later Draper):
    and Johnsons, V:95, 276, 311, 322
    and EJT, V:45, 65, 66–67, 71–72, 74–75, 77–78, 91, 92, 95, 102–103, 193–194, 282, 311, 313–314, 322, 324, 325; VI:582, 669–671; correspondence discussed, V:71, 76, 78. See also Letters to, from, *below*.
    background, V:71
    character, V:75, 76, 325
    emigrates to Canada, V:65, 75–76, 96

Index of Names

family, V:79, 90, 92–93, 102, 133–134, 193, 194, 276, 279, 311, 313, 321, 323–324; and father's death, V:101–102, 139
in London, VI:580–582
Letters to, from EJT, V:79–80, 89–93, 101–103, 133–134, 139, 193–194, 275–277, 278–281, 310–313, 318–323; VI:580–581, 669–670
White, Ben, V:92, 134, 139, 193, 194, 279, 282, 313
White, Capt. George, V:71, 79, 80, 90, 92–93, 319, 320; and Caroline Trelawny, V:74, 81; suicide, V:72, 78, 101–102, 103, 139, 324
White, "Jog" [?Georgiana], V:92, 103, 134, 139, 193, 194, 276, 277–278, 311, 313, 321, 323–324, 325
White, Mary, V:134, 139, 194, 312, 313
White, Mrs. Mary ("Mother Prull, Pruel"), V:71, 134, 139, 194; VI:580, 581; and EJT, V:72, 74, 90, 92, 102, 103, 276, 277, 278, 311, 312, 313, 319, 320; and Augusta White, V:321, 322, 324
White (?), Mary Ann, VI:670, 671
White, Newman Ivey, VI:591n; and "A.B.," VI:667–668; on PBS and MWS, VI:863, 864
White Hart Court, London, V:224
Whitehaven, Cumberland, V:297n
Whitehead, Alfred North, VI:788
Whitman, Walt, V:129
Whitton, Richard, V:30
Whitton, William, V:5, 29, 117, 483n
Wieland, Christoph Martin: *Aristippe et quelques-uns de ses contemporaines*, V:452, 454, 455, 466; VI:584, 586; *Die Abderiten*, VI:766
Wigmore Street, London, V:392, 394
Wignell, Mr., V:356
Wildman, Edmund, VI:614n
Wildman, John R., VI:606, 608, 614
Wildman, Thomas, V:293n; VI:614
Wiley, C., and Co., V:358
Willats, William: and PBS's finances, V:3–4, 304, 478–484; VI:940; letter to, from PBS, V:478
William the Conqueror, VI:828
William III, King of England, VI:967n, 981, 997–998, 1001, 1003, 1050
William IV, King of England, V:330

Williams, **Edward Ellerker**, V:261, 275; and Jane Johnson, V:47, 48, 49, 50, 51; VI:830–831; and EJT, V:47, 48; VI:672, 830, 1092n; biography, VI:829–830; death and burial, V:50–51; drawing for *Adonais*, V:421; *manuscript:* "Private Journal," V:816–829; discussed, VI:831–832; naval journal, VI:829, 832; provenance of manuscripts, VI:832–833; *The Promise*, VI:832, 833
Williams, Edward Medwin, VI:831
Williams, Helen Maria, V:358n
Williams, James, of Portsea, V:164–165, 351
Williams, Jane Cleveland Johnson, V:67, 261, 310n, 329n; VI:909n; and Edward Williams, V:47n, 48, 49, 50, 51; VI:830–831; as Mrs. TJH, V:58; VI:805
Williams, Jane Dale, VI:829
Williams, John, VI:829
Williams, Rosalind. *See* Hunt, Rosalind Williams
Wilmington, Del., V:253n
Wilson, Harriette, V:62
Wilson, John, VI:1055
Wilson, Sir Robert Thomas, V:46, 193, 195
Windsor Great Park, Berkshire, VI:804
Wingfield, John, VI:1131
Wise, T. J., V:125n, 155, 459; VI:1068n
Woburn, Bedfordshire, VI:1120
Wolcot, Dr. John ("Peter Pindar"), V:251n, 433
Wollstonecraft, Mary, V:358n; VI:551, 579
Wolverhampton, Staffordshire, VI:999
Woodbridge, Suffolk, V:371
Wooler, Thomas Jonathan, V:163, 245
Woolwich, London, V:91
Woolwich, H.M.S., V:41n
Wooster, Ohio, VI:957
Wordsworth, Dora, V:442
Wordsworth, Dorothy, V:491n
Wordsworth, Mary Hutchinson, V:266, 433, 441n
Wordsworth, William, V:264, 266, 371n, 401, 407, 411n, 433, 438, 441, 442, 448; VI:558n, 616, 686, 691, 709, 838, 916, 971, 1079n; PBS on poetry of, V:382, 385, 444; VI:927; "I Wandered Lonely as a Cloud," VI:520n; *Lyrical Ballads*, V:409; *Peter Bell*, VI:808, 934n

Index of Names

Worrall, Lettice Esdaile, V:86n
Worthing, Sussex, V:77
Wrangham, Francis, V:371n
Wren, Sir Christopher, VI:924n
Wright, Gabrielle, V:49
Wright, J. S., V:316n
Wright & Co., Messrs., V:302n
Wrixon-Becher, W., VI:897n
Wye (river), V:300, 302

Xenophon, VI:627
Xerxes, VI:630

York, Canada. *See* Toronto
York, Yorkshire, V:471; VI:802, 803–805, 849;
    Minster, VI:583, 588
York Buildings, New Road, London, VI:606,
    612, 614–615, 699, 854, 885
York Street, London, V:492; VI:720, 803, 854

Zalmoxis, VI:622, 631
Zante, Greece, V:57
Zillman, Lawrence John, VI:930n, 1070, 1072,
    1075, 1105n
Zopyrus, VI:622, 632
Zotti, R., V:344n